SEPARATE REALITIES

W.W. WORLEY

ISBN 978-1-950818-44-0 (paperback)

Copyright © 2020 by W.W. Worley

All rights reserved. No part of this publication may be reproduced, distributed, or transmitted in any form or by any means, including photocopying, recording, or other electronic or mechanical methods without the prior written permission of the publisher. For permission requests, solicit the publisher via the address below.

Rushmore Press LLC
1 800 460 9188
www.rushmorepress.com

Scripture quotations marked KJV are from the Holy Bible, King James Version (Authorized Version). First published in 1611. Quoted from the KJV Classic Reference Bible, Copyright © 1983 by Zondervan Corporation.

Scripture quotations marked NIV are taken from the Holy Bible, New International Version®. Copyright © 1973, 1978, 1984 by International Bible Society. Used by permission of Zondervan. All rights reserved. [Biblica]

Printed in the United States of America

Thank God.
Only By His Grace
Can Our Feeble
Efforts Succeed.
He Continues To Create
Reality,
All Reality,
Always.
To God Give The Glory.

DEDICATION

For Red and Louise, for their love and laughter,
which is what life is all about. They never have given up.
And for Sam, my long, lost friend.

Acknowledgements

No writing which intends or pretends to be an accurate historical novel can be attempted without research. In this endeavor, I must express my appreciation of the many contributions of my steadfast and true brother Bill and my loyal and loving sister Barbara. Without them, my hopes would have surely died. Because of them, the history within these pages is as accurate as those who have written history portrayed it. Any deviation from history texts is fully my own failing.

Thank you sister and brother for your love, encouragement and support. Better friends hath no man.

INTRODUCTION

> "It is a damn poor mind that can think of
> only one way to spell a word."
> ---Andrew Jackson

IN MANY WRITING primers it is promulgated that dialogue should not be phonetically spelled to reveal character. I wholeheartedly disagree. Those intellectuals who issue this commandment may by themselves speak as dictionaries dictate or as their grammar teachers urged, but we lesser mortals absorb our own environments and suffer no shame in speaking the speech that surrounds us.

Individual patterns of speech distinguish personality, is locative and reflects character. A thriving language proliferates through slang, regionalism, acronyms, expanding occupational terminology, through the mixture and blending of races, nationalities and languages and myriad other methods and nutrients. Meaning is shaded by locution, flavored with humor and a multitude of moods are communicated by accent and heart-born tone. Much is lost in purely grammatical recording of conversation; character is distorted by clinical, homogeneous rendering. Language, 'living' language, is art, not science.

I could extend this apology, but the reality of how each of us differ in our speech,--the truth, needs no defense. Those conditioned intellectual critics who disagree need to think, and speak, for themselves.

The historically famous characters residing in this story were in the places they are placed in the tale at the times indicated. I hope you will find interest in some of the less famous historical characters in their cameos.

The conditions of the Texas prison written of herein are derived from the state congressional record. Larceny and corruption in government has always been pervasive in Texas, just as it is throughout civilization. Though this is a work of fiction, the facts presented are undeniable.

I apologize for any language, viewpoint or description of violence which may offend, reality isn't always pleasing.

You can contact the author at:
W.W. Worley
320695 Ramsey
1100 F M 655
Rosharon, Texas 77583

Chapter One

"Thou tellest my wanderings: put thou my tears
into thy bottle: are they not in thy book?"
David, Psalm 56:8 (KJV)

"When I consider the short duration of my life, swallowed up
in the eternity before and after, the little I fill, and even can see,
engulfed in the infinite immensity of space of which I am ignorant,
and which knows me not, I am frightened, and am astonished
at being here rather than there, why now rather than then?
Blaise Pascal (1623-62)

"He has gone to join the majority."
Petronius Arbiter

SAM WAS DOZING on the porch. He had not slept all night. The mid-morning sun warmed his back and the spring air was rich with the fragrance of new growth. The quiet was interrupted only by the bickering of a committee of sparrows from the edge of the woods. Sam had suffered through the night, heart-broken, worried, and confused.

His tired, burning eyes slowly blinked open and focused on the empty road that wound down from the hill a quarter mile away. Lifting his weary head against the hand that hung from the rocking chair, he glanced at the man seated there above him and moaned. The ancient chair swung and groaned as the breeze gently moved it. Thought was absent. Sam's brain was silent, receptive to instinct and some strong sense sent a flutter of hope to his young heart. He struggled to his feet as an unconscious yearning whine escaped his open mouth. The next instant he jumped from the porch and was running, flying, stretching out in long leaps for the figure striding down the hill toward him.

The large silhouette carrying a pack stopped, shed its shouldered load and hollered, "Sam!" Ezekial caught the dog as he leaped into his arms and hugged him close as they fell beside the road. Sam licked Ezekial's face and barked joyously as they rolled on the green Carolina grass.

"Sam! I missed you buddy. I'm glad to see you too."

"You're skinny boy. And almost full grown. I missed you buddy. Where's Gramps? Has he seen me?" Zeke asked as he peered down at the weathered farmhouse.

Sam whined and lowered his head, then looked mournfully up into Zeke's eyes. He trotted toward the farm house, then looked back to ensure that Zeke would follow.

"What is it Sam?"

Ezekial gazed at the farm down in the small valley, then picked up his pack and began walking toward it. Sam trotted ahead, stopped and whined, then trotted ahead again looking back. Zeke began walking faster, then trotting with Sam. He dropped his baggage and broke into a run, yelling "Gramps!"

Before he reached the porch he could see the dear old body slumped in the rocking chair. The great head was bowed as if in thought, the cleft chin on his chest. He walked slowly, reverently to the body of his ancestor, his last living kin. He knelt beside the ancient rocker and lifted his grandfather's head. He held the wrinkled, noble face gently, peering into the open, glazed blue eyes of his precious Gramps.

Dead. He's dead, Zeke thought.

"Gramps! Oh Gramps."

He hugged the big cold body to himself and rocked back and forth on his knees. Sam cried with him. Ezekial reached out and pulled Sam into the hug. The three who had shared life and laughter would share together no more. The remaining two cried and cried over the one who had died.

As he cried, Zeke imagined his Gramps comforting him, consoling him as he did when his brothers had died. He heard the sure, deep voice telling him to 'cry now and to get the crying done.' Crying was good for the soul, to a point, but, as with all things, crying time must end. A man must be a man and put sorrow and self-pity aside. He must be strong and make his departed kin proud. Would he want to have traded places with his old Gramps and have Gramps suffer this sorrow? No, he was young and brave. He must bear the pain of parting and carry on, remembering all the good that God had allowed them to share and just keep smiling through the sadness.

After half an hour, somewhat encouraged, Zeke stood. He pulled a bandana from his back pocket, wiped his face, blew his nose. He left his beloved grandfather propped in the old rocker and walked down the steps toward the barn. He stopped, turned and looked back at the body moving slowly back and forth in the breeze. He visualized his last kin who loved him sitting there, dying, waiting for him, waiting just to see him once more before darkness came. It tore his heart apart that he hadn't been there for him. Oh! How he had loved him! If he had loved him rightly he would have been there holding his hand as he left this world. What would he do without him? He had no one now.

He had looked forward all these months to this homecoming, to a happy reunion with his Gramps. His mother had passed away giving birth to his baby sister. His sister had lived only three days. His father had died when he was just a sprout, just after his sixth birthday. His Gramps had been both mother and father to him. His brothers had been killed in the War of Northern Aggression, one at Bull's Run and one at Vicksburg. He'd joined the Confederate Army and followed his brothers in sixty-four, just short of his fifteenth birthday. He'd been big already, just over six feet and bit chubby, well-fed on beef, beans and Gramp's crops of corn. He'd grown taller through the many months and miles of tramping through the south from one skirmish to another, but though his shoulders were wide, he looked gaunt. There was little food in the southern army in the final months, and little of everything else. His size told others he was a man, a big man, but in his tender heart he was a lost and lonely boy.

Gramps had asked him, pleaded with him not to go. He had told him that he was too young, that his brothers had served and paid the family's dues, that he was all the family that he had left. He reasoned with him that he would be fighting for an unjust cause, for rich men's purposes, for causes that were morally wrong, but Ezekial didn't understand. Gramps feared that he would suffer and die under Yankee guns, but Zeke had to prove he wasn't a coward, that he was a man, that he honored his brothers' memory. He never even thought that Gramps might die. He'd been young and ignorant and selfish. He'd given his time and strength to those who had wasted it in a hopeless and prideful cause while his loving Gramps' time had slipped away.

Staring up at the grand face carved by character, thoughts came to mind of days gone by and simple joys they had shared. The hunting and fishing, the stories told on the porch under starlight while the crickets sang in the summer nights. The games of checkers in the flickering firelight through the days of cold and rain. Tales of his grandfathers' youth and carefree days of laughter and love around the kitchen table. Through Gramp's well-loved stories, Ezekial came to know his grandmother, his mother and his father. All he knew and loved had died with his Gramps. The best of them all was gone.

Zeke walked back up the steps and across the porch. He watched the red and white hair on Gramp's great head move with the whims of the breeze. Then he bent and kissed the crest of his head and choked out the words, "I love you Gramps."

He found two skinny mules and the big destrier in the stall. He divided what hay and corn there was between the animals and watered them. He opened his pack and fed the chickens with the quarter loaf of stale bread that remained to him. The pigpen was broken, the pigs were gone. The two milk cows they'd had when he'd left for war were gone too. Maybe they'd all ran away, maybe Gramps had sold them all. Or maybe the Yanks had taken them.

SEPARATE REALITIES

Tears flooded his face and his jaw muscles clinched as he carried the pick and shovel from the barn. Sam followed his every step. He stood beside the plot of his grandmother's grave and began to dig. All his family were gone now, some buried here, some in fields far away. His hope was that they were all together now, somewhere over that river Jordan Gramps had told him about, somewhere beyond the sorrow.

The earth was black and loamy and the sweet smell of the soil spurred more dear memories of plowing and planting with Gramps and his brothers. How many years did Gramps dig a living out of this gracious ground to feed them all? What life would spring now from planting the planter? Death bringing life. A full circle. What a crazy thought!

When the hole was deep enough he threw the pick and shovel up out of the grave and stood still and silent in the place where Gramps would lie. No. Gramps was no longer inside that stately, regal form. He'd truly passed on. Where he'd gone, Zeke didn't know. He only knew what he'd been told, what he'd been taught, and he took what comfort he could from that. Still, the body was a symbol of all he had been, all he'd lived and suffered and loved and savored. He would bury his remains with all the dignity, respect and love he felt. He took a deep breath, letting his senses taste the rich earth that would embrace the vehicle that had contained his Gramps. And he cried. Sam lay on the edge of the grave and licked his tears and whined.

Inside the barn, covered by a tarp, Ezekial found the casket he was going to build. It was mostly complete, lacking only a lid for the sturdily constructed box. As the smell of the pine came to his senses, he felt the tears start to come again and with great effort he fought them back.

Gramps knew his time had come and did not want to be a burden to those who buried him. At last he must have lost his great strength, leaving the lid unfinished. With trembling hands Ezekial measured, sawed and planed, fashioning a top for the casket that Gramps would have approved of.

An hour before sunset, Zeke laid the tools and boards aside and walked back to the porch. He found Sam there lying beside Gramps's body, guarding it, and obviously mourning. He propped open the front door, then lifted the great, yet light corpse and carried it inside. He laid the body on the oaken kitchen table gently, then removed the everyday work clothes Gramps had last dressed in. Lighting a lantern, he went into his bedroom and found Gramp's Sunday-go-to-meeting clothes in the wardrobe. He struggled to get him properly dressed for his funeral, then stood back and assayed his effort. He found a comb and did what he could with his wild hair. Funny, he thought, his hair seemed to have become redder than it was when Zeke had left. Why not whiter?

Ezekial found himself standing over Gramps, talking to him, though he knew he wasn't there. Still, he felt he must say his goodbye. He thanked him for loving him and showing his love everyday by working and providing for him and sacrificing for him and teaching him all about life. He told him how much he loved him, how much he would always miss him, how much he'd cherish the memories, how alone he felt without him in the world. He cried, and cried, and cried.

Sam interrupted his self-pity by scratching at Zeke's leg with a cry of empathy. Ezekial knelt and hugged him.

"I'll wager you're hungry boy. Let's see what we can find."

There wasn't any meat in the house, but he found a bit of beef in the smoke house and fed Sam a bit while he nibbled a bite or two. He carried the heirloom rocker inside and sat it beside the kitchen table. He looked in the pantry for the whiskey he knew was there and found half a bottle. He'd never drank more than a sip of whiskey, and hated it then, but tonight it would be his comfort. He sat and drank, thought of bygone days and cried. He stared at Gramps and spoke to the now broken carriage that had contained him for four score and more years, and drank some more until his eyes grew heavy. Finally he rose, dug in his pocket for his poke and removed two big copper pennies. He closed those sky blue eyes for the final time, weighed them shut with the pennies and cried. He sat, drank, cried, and finally found merciful sleep.

After washing his face, drinking deeply from the well, and feeding the animals, Ezekial's morning headache diminished. He made a fire in the stove and put some beans he'd found in the pantry on to cook over the coals. The silent corpse on the kitchen table attracted his attention despite his efforts not to think about it. For a time, he stood, stared and thought. Abruptly, he strode out the door and walked quickly to the grave he had dug yesterday. He suddenly felt an urge to get this sorrow finished and behind him. His inspection of the grave ensured the walls had not caved in. Ezekial had become proficient at grave digging by burying his share of slain soldiers.

Sam trotted along beside him to the barn where he finished fashioning the casket's lid. Then he turned his hand and his mind to a grave marker. He made it like the others in the small family cemetery, a simple wooden cross. On this cross, he painstakingly carved:

BARTHOLOMEW ROBERTSON
1782 – 1865
A GOOD MAN

After hitching the stir-crazy mules to the old but sturdy wagon, he loaded up the casket, the marker and the shovel and drove the wagon to the porch on the farmhouse. Tenderly he lifted the only parent he remembered and placed him in the coffin. Seeing him confined in the pine box caused the tears to begin to fall again. He arranged his hands across his chest and his attention became focused on those big strong hands. The fingers weren't long but the nails were longer than he ever remembered them being. The skin still stretched taut over the muscles, there was no wrinkling on his hands. These hands had been too busy burying and planting and raising and building, and all they'd done was done in love. Crouching beside the casket he kissed the heavy old hands, kissed the creased cold forehead and bathed the dead white skin with his hot tears.

He took the last letter he had written Gramps, which he had found in the rocking chair where he had died, and slid it into his Sunday suit. In that letter he had told Gramps that he would be coming home soon. He suspected that the letter had beat him home only by a few days. He had hurried home but he'd been afoot. Gramps had faithful Sam.

He turned the wagon and, with Sam at his side on the seat, drove slowly up the hill to the grave he had prepared. He thought of the words he had written in his last letter to Gramps. He thought that those final words had been both true and false. He had written that he would be seeing Gramps, hopefully soon.

Gramps, hopefully soon. Well, he knew that although what was in the box in back of the wagon was revered, it wasn't Gramps. Gramps was gone. His hope was that Gramps was in the everlasting home in the heavens that Gramps and the preachers had taught him about. He hoped it was true in a very real sense, not like Santa Claus, the Tooth Fairy, and the Booger Man. Gramps had told him much that he discovered as he matured was not true in a real sense. It turned out that Gramps was Santa and the Tooth Fairy and the Booger Man was only a tool to make him mind. He hoped heaven was real and not just a comforting myth.

Gramps said he 'believed.' Ezekial knew that he only 'hoped.' He wished he had the seeming certainty Gramps had, but he simply did not. God forgive him, but he just did not know. He surely 'hoped' he would be reunited with Gramps and his family in the everlasting home he had been taught about. God knew he did.

With deliberate solemnity he slid the coffin from the wagon bed into the earthen bed. Lowering himself into the hole Zeke straightened the body, kissed his kin a final time while teardrops fell. He placed the lid on the coffin and nailed it shut, tears fogging his vision. He lifted himself from the grave and walked to the wagon where he removed the family Bible from under the wagon seat. He walked back and stood with Sam before the grave and opened the old book. It opened to a place where a paper had been folded and placed between the pages. Unfolding the sheet, he read enough to see that it was a letter to him, a letter that was, of course, never mailed. He refolded the letter and slipped it into a pocket to read later.

Before Ezekial could restrain him, young Sam leaped down upon the coffin, whining and scratching at the lid.

"Sam! Sam, no! C'mon Sam."

Ezekial had to hop down into the grave and lift the confused and crying dog up and out.

"He's gone Sam, Gramps is gone. He's not in that box, not in that body, he's...he's gone Sam."

A stream of tears drenched Ezekial's face as he held the dog. With an effort he fought the tears back, looking up into the sky, searching for strength. He held Sam and spoke softly to him as Sam licked his salty tears. After a while they calmed one another.

He stood still and silent before the hole, staring down at the pine coffin until the tears slowed and stopped. The wind was soft against his face, there was a stillness in the air, a seeming pause in time. He looked up into the clear sky at the warming white sun. Taking a deep breath, he spoke.

"Lord, I don't know if I'm doin' this the way it's s'posed to be done. I'm jes' doin' the best I can. There's no one here but me an' Sam, we're the only ones left that loved 'im. Guess it's fittin' we should be the only ones to say goodbye.

"Gramps taught me how to read with this Good Book. He taught me how to live. He taught me that You give us life and You take it away. That we are dust and to dust we all return. But, I know that ain't all we are Lord. Gramps taught me about the spirit that lives forever.

"God, I don't know the words that should be said here over Gramps' grave, so if I leave anything out please forgive me. And don't hold it against Gramps.

"I sure was looking forward to seeing my Gramps when I came home. Guess I'll jes' have to keep on looking forward to it. I'm hoping and praying You've taken him home with You. And that You'll take me home with You and my family whenever my time comes. I hope he's there with my family now.

"He was a good man Lord. A decent, hard working and lovin' man. But, You already know about that. I was happy to share the time I had with him. Thank You. And please thank him for me for giving me all he could. And for his love. And tell him I miss him."

Words failed to come anymore as tears drowned them out. He picked up the shovel and managed to choke out "Goodbye Gramps." As he cried and Sam whined he filled the grave with the heavy earth.

As he finished and tamped the mounded dirt, he felt Sam nudge him and heard his mournful whimper. He looked down into his deep brown eyes and saw his sorrow. He keeled down and hugged him. Eventually he drew a breath deep into his big chest and raising his young swollen face to the sky he whispered, "Thank You for leaving Sam here to keep me company." He held Sam close and cried. And cried.

Ezekial fed and watered the mules and the big horse. There wasn't any feed for the scraggly chickens, but they were already chasing grasshoppers through the new grass. He gathered a bucket of eggs and scrambled Sam and himself a mess of eggs. Hungry as they were, the eggs tasted delicious.

Life had been hard on Gramps lately, that was evident, but still he had managed to plow and plant a good sized truck garden and a field of oats that were just now ankle high.

Ezekial wondered if Gramps knew this crop would be his last, then the letter he had found in the old family Bible came to mind. He took the single page from his pocket and stuck it back in the pages of the Bible on a shelf. He didn't feel up to reading it yet. He'd wait a few days until some time, and hopefully some pain, had passed.

Ezekial sighted down the last rows that Gramps had plowed and planted and smiled. As they had ever been, the rows were straight and uniform and the sprouts were vigorous. His life had reached out beyond the grave to continue not only in his grandson, but in other seed that he had sown.

He hitched the skinny mules to the wagon. He thought it would do them good to stretch their legs. It was ten miles to town and he thought the distance not too far to exercise them. Tying the last horse on the farm, the big destrier to the tailgate, he struck out. The animals seemed to enjoy the walk and in less than two hours Sam was sitting on the sidewalk watching Ezekial speak with the proprietor of the general mercantile. There were not a lot of items stocking the shelves, but there was more than there had been through the war and the owner told him that more supplies were beginning to come in daily.

SEPARATE REALITIES

The proprietor was generous and gentle in his understanding that Ezekial's sorrowful wounds were still too fresh to speak long about Gramps' passing, and he allowed Ezekial to put the horse up for collateral for some food and merchandise. He and the store employee loaded the wagon bed with potatoes and beans, sugar and flour, a little ammunition for hunting, seed, feed for the mules and chickens, salt, coffee, pork and a quarter side of beef. Sam smelled the meat and licked his chops.

"You jes' wait 'till we get home, Sambo and we'll have ourselves a feast," Ezekial chided as he playfully shoved Sam's head away from the cloth-covered meat.

He stepped up to the wagon in one long stride, released the brake and allowed the mules to ramble down to the blacksmith's shop. Greeting Old Smokey who had been the only blacksmith and liveryman all Ezekial's life, they each caught up with one another's losses of the past year before getting down to business. He gave Smokey the last of his Union money to replace three shoes on the pair of mules before heading home. Once the wagon was a mile out of town he allowed the tears to come.

The people in town had all asked about Gramps and he had briefly told them the story of his homecoming. They had offered their condolences and sincere pronouncements of what a fine man his grandfather had been and what a great loss it was not only for him but for the community. An especially grievous loss especially at this time when wisdom and leadership was so sorely needed. As the tears fell from Ezekial face, Sam wailed. He hugged Sam to his side and talked to him as he had since he was a pup.

"Good ol' Sam. It's jes' you and me now boy. The good Lord brought me home jes' in time to bury Gramps an' take care of you and these mules. I wish I had more time with Gramps, with all the family, but who can understand God's plans? I s'pose it would have been harder on me if I had to watch him die those last few days. But you were there for him. I know he took comfort in you being there with him. He knew by my letter that I'd survived the war and was on my way home. He was jes' a-sittin' and waitin' for me. Bless you for watchin' over him 'til I got home."

Sam kept his eyes on Zeke's face, ears perked up, listening as if he understood every word. When Ezekial finished speaking Sam whined and barked. Zeke laughed and hugged him with his free arm shaking his head. They laughed and they cried. Together.

During the next days Ezekial made repairs on the house and barn and began doing some plowing, switching out the mules periodically so one wouldn't get overly fatigued considering their health. After a couple of weeks he could see some meat sticking to their ribs and they started kicking and getting ornery. For the first few days Sam took every step with Ezekial, seemingly afraid he would leave again without him. After a while though, he would lay on the turn-row under a tree and watch Zeke and a mule plod back and forth, turning the earth. Ezekial stopped plowing when he knew it was getting too late to plant, cotton and corn were all he planted.

Providence blessed his efforts with a day-long gentle rain to water-in his planting. He added a few rows to Gramps's vegetable patch, adding okra, peas, carrots, watermelon and sweet potatoes.

He worked his hands at something from sun-up to sundown, but his heart wasn't in it. There was no one to share the old life with, except Sam, and the two mules named Smiley and Jolly. Nights he would sit watching the coals in the cook fire fade or watch the stars appear in the evening sky. His thoughts continually regressed to the life of yesterdays gone by. He knew he should look forward, that he should plan a life. Here, everywhere he looked, he was reminded of the past. And the lonely empty present. He began to think of selling out, packing a few things in the wagon and heading west, leaving the past in the past.

He had soldiered with a Latin Texan named Samuel Chavez who had invited him to come to Texas, who had told him romantic tales of beautiful land that never ended, wild Indians, Mexican bandits and beautiful women. He missed Samuel. He missed the way he could make him laugh, make life interesting and new, each day filled with fresh promise.

But, he had no money. All he had in the world was the old farm and there were no legitimate buyers, only Yankee carpetbaggers trying to buy the whole South for a song. No, he wouldn't sell this farm to just anyone for just anything. Gramps and the whole family had put too much into it for it not to be respected and appreciated. There was nothing to do except continue on as he had and see how life developed.

Mr. Dunlap, a neighbor, had stopped by a few times on his way to town to see how he was doing. It was comforting to just see and talk to another person. It also made him feel uncomfortable because he had grown accustomed to being alone. He came by yesterday and had invited him to church on Sunday. All the members were bringing food and there would be dinner on the grounds. Ezekial explained that he no longer had decent clothes that fit, only these old work clothes of his Gramps' which were too small. Mr. Dunlap had chuckled and told him that there were only two or three suits in the entire congregation. In the end, Ezekial had agreed to attend.

Now, on Sunday morning, as he drove the mules toward town, his natural shyness caused him to wish that he had refused the invitation. He had washed his pants and shirt as best he could and run around the farm in his long-johns until they dried this morning. There were no shoes on the farm that fit him so he was barefooted as usual. He had not had a pair of shoes in about a year. Through last winter he had wrapped strips of torn blankets around his feet and they were so calloused that he busted the dirt clods by stomping or kicking them while he plowed. He had bathed, in a fashion, standing by the horse trough with a bucket in the barn, so he was passably clean. He'd also wrestled Sam through a bath, but it hadn't been easy, and Sam's resentment still kept him aloof as he rode on the wagon seat beside Ezekial. Using the horse comb to push the soap through Sam's fur he must have dislodged hundreds of fleas and after a few minutes Sam seemed to begin to like it. His back leg kicked and trembled in response to the brush massage, making Ezekial laugh. Sam didn't seem to appreciate or even notice the removal of the population of parasites from his flesh. He was acting as if his dignity had been bruised.

Ezekial had combed his own long hair as best he could and he had shaved the few hairs off his chin and lip. He had done his best considering his big face would not fit the cracked little mirror.

Before he even got through the door of the church he had shook the hands of a dozen men, women and children and he remembered some from when he had gone to church with Gramps. As he sat quietly in a pew toward the back he noticed several ladies in big hats peeking back at him disapprovingly. Under the condemnation of their eyes he felt like a heathen outcast sitting in a shirt with sleeves ending halfway down his arms and pants ending just below his knees. His toes curled on his bare feet and he began to sweat. Embarrassment changed into irritation. He thought it unchristian like of them to look down on him because of his poverty. He grit his teeth and stared back at the accusing harpies.

Mr. Dunlap came over, leaned down and whispered, "You should leave your dog outside, if you would please."

His cheeks burning bright, he turned to Sam who was sitting on the bench beside him and said, "Sam, I'm sorry buddy, but you'll have to wait outside."

Sam chuffed and looked at Ezekial accusingly at being so disparaged, then hopped down and, head held high, strode out of the building. At the side of the church Sam found a bench sitting below a window and he jumped up, put his nose against the window and looked forlornly at Zeke.

Directly the song service began and the singing was loud with an accompanying old piano. Ezekial knew some of the words to the first hymn and began to sing, haltingly along. Presently he noticed one of the old matrons in the big hats glancing back toward the side window where Sam sat on the bench. Sam, head thrown back was howling away with the music.

Zeke tried to get Sam's attention and motioned for him to hush, but Sam had his head pointed to the sky and was singing his own song of praise. A couple of the old ladies were looking like they had bit into a lemon and whispering to their neighbors, peeking back at Sam and Zeke. All the children and the rest of the congregation were smiling and enjoying Sam's robust efforts. Zeke didn't think the song would ever end and gave thanks to God when the final note sounded.

A wizened little pastor limped up to lean on the podium and said, "You may be seated." He looked over the congregation with a wide grin and Ezekial felt the pressure of the dark gaze lock onto him like a heavy shroud.

"It is good to hear 'all of God's creatures' raising a joyful noise to the Lord on this fine Sunday morning. Amen?"

There was a resounding, echoing "Amen" from the pews along with relieved laughter. Ezekial noticed even the meanest looking old battleaxe crack a smile.

After a few announcements by the pastor of community births and deaths, approaching weddings and upcoming church events, deacon's meetings, Sunday school teacher's meetings, young people's meeting and a quilting bee, the song leader led them in a few more hymns. Now everyone seemed to accept and enjoy Sam's enthusiastic participation.

Following a reading from the Good Book the sermon was a long lecture that Ezekial knew was meant for his correction. Though his big butt was numb from the oak bench, he knew he must not move or take his eyes from the fiery gaze of his accuser. Ezekial was certain that everyone knew that the preacher's words were meant specifically for him. He was filled with guilt and remorse for his sin- filled life. Images of dead and wounded suffering soldiers came to mind and he regretted firing the ball that so hurt and killed. Finally(sweet release), an altar call was given. Ezekial was the first one on his knees at the altar, feeling no shame, indeed giving no thought to his dirty and calloused bare feet as he confessed his wickedness to heaven. The small pastor knelt beside him and made petition to heaven for this repentant, prodigal son.

"…..and Lord, only You can see into this young man's heart, only You can forgive his sins, whatever they may be. We know that Jesus cleansed us from all our sins on that old rugged cross and if we believe in our hearts that He died for us and rose from the grave, then our sins are washed white as snow by the blessed blood of Jesus."

The prayer was momentarily interrupted by a bumping between them and they both opened their eyes to see Sam licking the tears from Ezekial's big face and joining in the crying. The preacher smiled and included the devoted dog in his embrace.

"And we thank You Lord for the example of this beloved beast whose perfect praise and love is made evident in his instinctual nature. Bless these friends Father and comfort them in the loss of Grandfather Robertson. Give them faith and blessed assurance that he is there with You. Guide them now that they have lost their earthly father. Keep your gentle, loving hand on their tender heart. In Jesus name we ask, Amen."

Now that Ezekial had once again been welcomed into the fold, he had to answer a few dozen questions about Gramps and the farm and shake hands all over the church yard. He and Sam eventually found a place out of the way and he sat on an old box in the shade. He was just beginning to catch his breath and relax when a group of ladies accompanied by a dour old deacon surrounded him.

The prettiest female Ezekial had ever laid eyes on put her light, delicate hand on his big arm causing him to flinch involuntarily. In a voice that sounded like a song this angel spoke.

"Brother Ezekial, I'm Cynthia. All of us here realize that all your folks have gone home to God and you have no one now to help you. The Lord has led us to clothe those who are naked and you are not far removed from the state. Please stand so that we can measure you so we can make you clothes."

Ezekial was mesmerized by the sight, sound and closeness of this heavenly creature, lost in the endless blue of her eyes, and was mortified that his tattered clothing had been the theme of discussion by the ladies of the church. The blonde and blue-eyed beauty touched his hand and he quickly stood but his mouth wouldn't seem to work. He was entranced and incapacitated, charmed and conquered by this celestial being and as the flock of church ladies had him raising his arms, spreading his legs, turning around and squatting down so they could measure him, his eyes remained fixed on the amazing apparition named Cynthia.

Using a string and a yardstick they measured him twice in every direction. "Measure twice, cut once," a voice explained to him. He grew quiet dizzy from the turning and the attention. Finally, they had him stand beside the wall of the church where Cynthia stood on a box and made a mark on the wall at the top of his head. They measured the distance from the ground to the mark.

"Do you know how tall you are Brother Zeke?"

"No Ma'am."

"You are just over six feet seven inches and still growing I'm sure."

"Is that right?" Ezekial managed to say.

"That's sure right. And how old are you Ezekial?"

"I'm about sixteen, or will be next month."

"My goodness! Did you finish school Zeke?"

"Never went. My Gramps taught me to read and write and cipher."

"You never read history or literature or studied music or geography or science?"

"No ma'am."

The older ladies t'sked at this admission.

"Well, Mr. Ezekial Robertson, you must begin to attend the classes I teach at the church here from Monday to Friday."

"Yes ma'am, I would like that. But, I have a farm to work, animals to feed and crops to care for. I'm 'fraid I don't have time."

"Perhaps you could attend half of each day?"

"I live too far away."

"Then one day a week. Surely you could manage that."

"Well,….."

"No argument. I'll arrange with Mr. Dunlap to feed your animals. You'll spend the night here at the church attend classes tomorrow, and return next Sunday prepared to do so again. You need further education in this day and age. Most of the students are younger than you, but you'll soon catch up with them in knowledge. Don't you want to be educated?"

"Well….."

"It's settled then. We'll bring quilts and blankets and a pillow and you'll be quiet comfortable here until tomorrow. We'll get Old Smokey to take care of your mules and I'll bring you something to eat tomorrow. You'll be fine."

"Yes Ma'am."

Ezekial looked at Sam and shrugged. "Ladies, you have this boy's measurements. I hope we can gather enough cloth! And I'll leave it to your own experience as how much bigger to cut his clothes to give him room to grow. Now Ezekial, put your foot up here and let Brother Benjamin measure it."

Ezekial put first one foot and then the other on a piece of canvas Brother Benjamin spread out on the box while he traced around his feet with chalk. They explained that Brother Benjamin was a saddle maker but he was a cobbler too when need be. Zeke stuttered that he couldn't pay, but they all protested that he wouldn't owe them anything, that he should just thank the Lord.

"Well," Zeke muttered, "Thank the Lord."

They were amused and captivated by his natural, boyish charm and the ladies kept on bringing him plates of chicken and ham and potatoes and corn and cobbler and pie and cake. Cynthia was gracious and thoughtful enough to bring Sam a big plate of ham.

By the time church services began again Ezekial was stuffed with good food and he fought to stay awake through the seemingly endless sermon. By the end he was nodding so hard that he almost fell out of the pew a couple of times. Sam took refuge under the wagon seat through it all, sleeping comfortably and deep.

Since the Dunlap's lived just down the road from Zeke, Mr. Dunlap drove into the Robertson farm and made sure all was well at the place before he continued on home. Before the Dunlap's had left Ezekial had confessed that there were no animals left on the farm to feed except chickens, what animals there were made the trip to town with him.

The parsonage was just down the hill from the church and Ezekial and Sam sat on the porch and chatted with the Pastor, Brother Denton, until after sunset when Cynthia drove up in a buggy bringing him blankets, a quilt and a pillow. She gave him a lift back to the church and being so close to her on the ride made Ezekial nervous. He did not understand his feelings. Why did just the sight of her affect him so?

As he picked up the folded bedroll and stepped down from the buggy her sweet warm breath touched his face as she bade him goodnight. He mumbled something in reply, she smiled and drove away into the night. He thought he never wanted her to leave him again.

Chapter Two

"The nature of the one Reality must be known by one's own clear spiritual perception; it cannot be learned by a pandit(learned man). Similarly, the form of the moon can only be known through one's own eyes. How can it be known through others?"
--Shankara, Viveka Chudamani

"You have made us for Yourself, and our hearts are restless till they find their rest in You."
-- St. Augustine

ON THE WAY home that first Monday afternoon Ezekial thought of how the good Lord had blessed him for just cleaning up and going to the church. He had been forgiven his many sins, had eaten more delicious food than he'd had for longer than a year and had met the most beautiful creature God had ever made.

During the day at school, after the children had grown somewhat accustomed to a giant being there among them, he also had become more comfortable in Cynthia's presence. He still wasn't completely comfortable, but he had come to realize that she wasn't an angel, not really. Still, she was so entrancingly exquisite that Ezekial found it difficult to focus his eyes or his mind on anything else when she was near.

It seemed to him that she had spent an inordinate amount of the day seated at his side in one of the pews explaining fractions or the difference between a noun and a pronoun. Not that he objected, he would remain forever ignorant if it would keep her near to him.

With her close to him, he couldn't concentrate and she must think him thick-headed as a mule. Was it possible that she liked him? Why would she? No, it was only because she knew he was so dumb and she was so kind and gracious.

All week Ezekial worked hard and long, getting another few acres planted in corn and cotton. The farm was beginning to look good, well tended. He thought Gramps would approve. The days were depressing when he wasn't busy at work because everything reminded him of Gramps or his brothers. Loss and loneliness strangled him here. He longed for Sunday to come. His days and nights were pain filled, tears came often, he felt so alone.

Saturday morning he decided to go fishing, just get away from chores for a day. He could take some fish to the preacher, Brother Denton, and give some to Cynthia if she liked them. Also, he could wash his clothes in the river, lay naked in the sun while they dried. He thought he may as well go whole hog and take a bath himself.

He knew just where the fat worms were and he dug some up before the dew had burned off the grass. He couldn't thread worms on his hooks quick enough, as soon as they sank below the surface the fish were biting. He had a stringer full in an hour, good sized ones too, most black crappie.

As he was gathering up his poles and gear Sam froze and quietly growled, looking up river. Zeke followed Sam's line of sight and saw a good sized white-tailed buck drinking from the river maybe fifty yards away. He eased his gear to the ground and picked up his rifle, easing down on his knees beside a tree. Using the tree for a rest he made a good shot just above the shoulder. The deer made a reflexive jump away from the river, then fell, legs kicking for a few seconds. Only then did Sam bark.

Ezekial felt no thrill in the killing. Gramps had taught him that some must die so others might live. It was God's curious design, but it was how life was and questioning it only brought more confusion. He gave thanks first to God, then to the deer, then to Sam.

"Good boy Sam, you'll eat good tonight."

After cleaning and dressing the deer, he carried the carcass home, hanging it in the smoke house to be butchered later. He returned to the river and again washed himself, then carried his clean clothes and the fishing gear and stringer of fish home. He put the fish in a tub in the spring house to keep them wet and cool until he got around to gutting and cleaning them. He butchered the big deer and fed Sam some of the raw red meat. He put some venison aside for later in the week and made two packages to take to church the following day for Brother Denton and for Cynthia's family.

While cleaning the fish, Ezekial thought of the many happy times he and his brothers, his Dad and Gramps had spent on the river. In that dark water he had learned to swim and learned to fish and he could not remember a time when he couldn't swim and fish. As just a tyke he had run a trot line with his family and none of it had ever seemed like work. Even now, cleaning and preparing fillets wasn't work, it was enjoyable, something he did well without thought or effort. But the memories hurt. The comradery was no longer there. No one was here at home for him anymore. Only Sam.

After wrapping the big mess of fish in clean cloth, he hitched up the mules to the wagon and drove the three miles to the Dunlap farm. Mrs. Dunlap invited him to stay for dinner while she cooked up the fish, so he stayed and ate with them. Fish and cornbread slathered with butter, black-eyed peas, potatoes and corn. Ezekial ate two plates full and thought he would do this again soon. It definitely beat his cooking. He was stuffed, but he still found room for two slices of apple pie and two glasses of cool milk.

After Mrs. Dunlap and her daughter, Trinity finished cleaning up the kitchen they joined Ezekial, Mr. Dunlap and the son-in-law on the long shady porch. After a time of small talk, Mr. Dunlap asked what Ezekial's plans were. Zeke told them about his Gramp's planting and his own.

"So your intentions are to stay and farm the place?" Mr. Dunlap asked.

"Well, yes sir. I'm hoping to be able to get by and feed myself by hunting and the truck garden 'til I can get that cotton picked and corn pulled. Hopefully I'll be able to sell it."

"I hope you will too Zeke. No telling what the market will be this year. You remember we're here if you need some help or if you get hungry. And everyone of the members of the church are there to help you if you need it, so don't be mule-headed and full of pride and not come to us.

"The reason I asked about your plans for the place Zeke, is because my son-in-law and daughter are looking for a place of their own. I think he's wanting to stand on his own hind legs and my daughter wants her own nest to feather."

The Dunlaps all smiled at one another, indicating this subject was well-trodden ground.

"If you was of a mind to sell your farm, well, John here probably has the cash to buy it outright. He sold his inheritance in Virginia so they could settle close to us to raise a family, and your place would be just about perfect for all of us. Far enough away to keep me and Momma out of their personal business, but close enough for easy visiting."

Well, yes sir, I'll keep it in mind."

Once back at the farm Ezekial unhitched the mules, gave them corn and water rubbed them down and laid down in the dry hay with Sam. He thought about what Mr. Dunlap had offered, and it was painful to be here without Gramps and his brothers, but he didn't think he could sell this place, his home. Where would he go? He thought about his soldier friend from Texas, little Samuel, and his invitation to come there. Soon the full belly, the warmth and the softness of the hay pulled both he and Sam into sleep. While he napped he dreamed about Texas. About beautiful senoritas and wild Indians, about fast horses and mean cows. And then he dreamed about Cynthia. He didn't want to wake up.

That evening he was brushing cockleburs out of Sam's coat and again noticed his hind leg kicking and trembling in the ecstasy of the sensation. It made Zeke laugh. The more he brushed, the more Sam's leg kicked and shook in utter enjoyment and the more Zeke laughed. Soon he was rolling in laughter and Sam, laughing with him in his own peculiar way, barking while grinning on one side of his face with one eye winking and blinking. The dog had exhibited this reaction to human laughter, even as a pup he had grinned winked and blinked, and barked. Zeke laughed until he lost his breath and cried. When he had regained control he hugged Sam to his chest and buffed his head.

"Oh Sam. Sam, Sam, Sam…. You're my buddy. You'll always be my best buddy."

They went into the house, laid down and slept, side by side.

Seeing Cynthia made Ezekial nervous, but it wasn't a nervous he wanted to avoid, he enjoyed this excitement. It was different from the agitation he had experienced before and during battle. This was an arousal that allowed him to feel life more fully, to experience an energizing elevation in the limits of sensation. His sight brought him more color and more light, his ears seemed to hear music in every sound and her fragrance and her touch were harbingers of heaven.

Sam looked through the church window at Ezekial and followed his gaze to the golden tresses falling down Cynthia's neck and back and the one-sided grin and blinking eye appeared on his happy face. He joined in the song service with spirit. Ezekial turned to Sam and motioned with his hand to hold it down. Sam just chuffed, grinned on one side of his face, and howled a bit lower in volume.

After church Ezekial loaded half the meat in Cynthia's folks' wagon. They were very appreciative. The pastor, Brother Denton, was pleased with his portion also. Mrs. Denton had prepared a roast with gravy and potatoes with fat, fluffy rolls that just melted in Ezekial's mouth. She thoughtfully prepared Sam a plate of gravy and beef bits that he woofed down greedily.

There was only one service at church that day and to relieve Brother and Mrs. Denton from having to entertain him, he and Sam went on a hike. Strolling over the bridge and down the path along the river they were blessed to view a beautiful white egret as it rose majestically from the dark shaded shallows into a cerulean sky. The beauty of form and the effortless grace of function was breath-taking and cut an indelible memory in his mind. The moment of perfection brought Cynthia to his mind.

When opportunity presented, Ezekial studied her various parts, the pleasing line of her neck, the perfectly formed ears, the dizzying height and depths of her eyes and the seductive sweep of lashes, the slim, strong hands, the long, lithe limbs, expressive, shining mouth, every separate part and portion was perfect and the whole was infinitely more than the gathering of the divisions. To Ezekial's eye and mind, there were no imperfections.

He weighed his feelings and had come to believe this wasn't love he felt. It was more than love. It was adoration, and probably sinful. Certainly she didn't feel the same way, he realized that. She loved him in a Christian manner, as a brother, a friend, a child. For that he was grateful, but not fulfilled. Was his sin greed? Lust? Was it even sin?

All week he yearned for Sunday to come so his eyes could drink in the sight of her, he would never be filled. Every day he went over and over his studies so he might please her with his learning and he surprised himself with his commitment and diligence. Already he had learned much. Her attention was so precious to him, her glance, her smile, just a word was held so dear and relived through the week, his ears resounding with the music of her words. He actually saw a halo or nimbus surrounding her blonde crown at times. Was it all in his mind? Or his heart?

He had thought of speaking to Brother Denton about it, but he believed that he wouldn't understand. His best counselor was Sam who listened without comment or condemnation. Sometimes Sam's silent smile came to be the best advice: just enjoy the moment.

Atop a hill just outside town Ezekial sat and admired the view and let his thought wander where they would. What would he be doing a year from now? Ten years? What did he want to do? To be? Where would he spend his life? Would he live and die on the land his Gramps had carved out and left him? If so, who would he leave it to? Looking down and across the green land, he listened for answers in the wind. He lay and looked up at the slow floating clouds, no answers were written there. He humbly asked God for guidance.

He was waiting on the steps of the church house when Cynthia rode up in the buggy next morning.

"Good morning Ezekial. It's good to see you here early and anxious to learn."

"Mornin Miss Cynthia. Here, let me take care of the horse and buggy."

"Why thank you Ezekial. I'll go in and prepare for the children."

After turning the healthy horse into the pasture to graze, Ezekial entered the church house turned school house. He approached Cynthia as she stacked books on a table down front.

"Miss Cynthia, could I ask you somethin'?"

"Of course Ezekial, what is it?"

"Do you think I could learn to be someone important, like a doctor or lawyer or maybe a railroad engineer?"

"Ezekial, you have the intelligence to become whatever you want. But you must want it enough to go through the hardships of training and learning. Let me say though that you are already important, you are well loved by all of us here who know you. Why do you ask? Have you thought of some vocation you would like to pursue?"

"Well Miss Cinthy, seems to me that people sorta' group up an' spend their lives with other people like them. I mean, important folks and rich folks seem to end up together an' not so important folks and not so rich folks, they end up together too. I heard a church lady say that such and such a fella' married 'beneath' him, an' that gal was jes' ' a gold digger.' Seems ever'one is 'spected to stay with their own kind. But, Miss Cinthy, the people who interest me are all smarter, more educated, richer, and, well, jes' more beautiful an' powerful people than me or my family has been. Seems most ever'one is jes' more'n me, one way or another an I jes' don't never want nobody to be 'shamed of being 'round me. That make sense?"

"Yes Ezekial it does make sense. People tend to want to be around people who have similar interests and values. But, I think they are all important and the work of all honest men make them noble. What would the lawyer eat if not for the farmer? Where would the doctor live if not for the carpenter? The person who would be ashamed to be a friend of an honest laborer, in my opinion, is a person of shallow wisdom and of counterfeit character. Ezekial, the great people of this world, the ones who are revered and remembered are those who most selflessly serve others. Think about your grandfather. He gave his all everyday for those he loved. And when he died he gave all he had worked for all his life to you. Do you think he was a less admirable man than a lawyer or doctor?"

"No, Miss Cinthy. He was a good man. But he was a simple man, the rich and powerful men would have little to do with him. They wouldn't want their daughters to wed a poor, simple farmer."

"The world is built on the shoulders of the poor and honest hard-working men and women. They are the 'salt of the earth' the Good Book says, not the rulers and the rich, the poor believers who suffer and serve and love one another through it all."

Here Cynthia chuckled and a blush tinted her tender cheeks. "I'm sorry Ezekial, I didn't mean to preach. What brought all this on anyway?"

This was Ezekial's turn to blush. "Well, I don't know. I guess I'd just want people not to be 'shamed to have me around. I mean, I don't even have a pair of shoes an' it's only by the charity of the church that I have any prospect of getting decent clothes."

"Ezekial, the children are arriving, but we'll talk more of this later. Let me just say that it is evident that you are honest and industrious and those are qualities that will carry you far, but it is good that you are seeking direction now, because planning is very important too. We'll speak of this again, but now it's time for school."

Ezekial absorbed all Cynthia taught through that day and everyday he attended class. She seemed an unending storehouse of knowledge to him. Until earlier that same year she had been taught by an English tutor who had died of old age at their plantation as well as by her gentle mother of English birth. Because of those who had taught her, Cynthia's speech was different from those in the area. It was musical, poetic, charming, Ezekial loved to listen to her, whatever she was saying. Her words were a melody.

They didn't again discuss Ezekial's observation of the social strata and what he should or could do with his life. He spoke of these things with Brother Denton and was advised to pray about it and follow the Lord's direction. Ezekial had been directed to follow what the Lord moved him to do all his life by Christians and the Lord had not yet spoke a word to him. He didn't know if it was the Lord or not who gave him a gut feeling or instinctual guidance. What did the Lord's voice sound like? Often he heard, (in memory or in spirit he could not tell), wise words of Gramps advising him as he had when

Gramps was with him, and though these words were wise, they did not derive from God. Did they? Ezekial prayed that he would learn to recognize God's voice. Other people often said the Lord spoke to them. Were they lying? Mistaken?

All he thought he could do was to continue on, struggling down the path that presented itself to him the best he could. He was learning everyday in all he did but felt he should be headed in another direction, he wanted to accomplish more than bountiful crops from year to year. He felt life should be more than that.

Life on the farm was passable, but Ezekial was young and was itching for excitement. The war, despite the horrors and hardships, had caused him to feel alive. It had made him think, make meaningful choices. The danger was delicious, addicting. He knew more about himself now, had stretched his limits. He knew what he felt was usually right, as opposed to what was simply logical or expedient.

Gramps, his Poppa too, had told him it was wrong to own slaves, to believe one person could own another and think that it was morally right. Many argued that it was the way it had always been, but that did not make it right. He had never felt that he was fighting for slavery when he had sworn into the Confederate Army. He had felt he was fighting for freedom, for his family, his honor, his home. He realized now, with temporal distance and perspective, that rich men and politicians had manipulated him and thousands of others to take up arms in the mistaken belief that it was an honorable cause they had joined and defended. The wealthy had used the brave manhood of the South in an endeavor to preserve the status quo. The luxurious lifestyle of the large plantation owners depended on the many black hands to tend the crops and pick the cotton. Emancipation meant they would have to pay those thousands of black employees. In actuality it would not have cost them much more to pay workers a wage and let them provide their own housing, food, clothing, health care, etc. They were ill-prepared for such change, and believed the only way they could continue the life handed down to them by their fathers and to hold on to their land, prestige and power was to preserve slavery.

Plantation owners were a tiny minority in number but held a sinful glut of southern wealth and power. Their education also allowed them to lord over the unschooled masses of the proletariat. And so, through inciting speeches, published and printed free-bills of propaganda, they influenced the proud poor to take to arms and protect them from the abolitionists. The hardscrabble farmers and small shopkeepers sent their sons to war to defend 'states rights', southern homes and 'honor' and the only life they had ever known. The true sacrifice of their beloved sons was on the altar of the preservation of power and wealth in the hands of the few. This truth dawned on the survivors only after the deaths of so many dear, brave sons. The great Civil War was another catastrophe caused by a few evil, greedy men.

Within the first weeks of service Ezekial, as so many others, had realized the facts had been misrepresented and this was no honorable war. The knowledge that he had become a puppet of political and economic factions caused him to want to separate himself from this wicked farce. He would then be labeled a deserter,...a coward. As he witnessed his comrades die so bravely, knowing they were outgunned, outnumbered and fighting an unwinnable war, as they charged well defended Yankee battlements with no powder or ball but only fixed bayonets and were literally blown to pieces by thousands of guns and cannons, he followed them, often led them across the bloody battlefields because they inspired in him a courage he did not understand, because his brothers had given their very lives in the same hopeless cause, because there was hate and revenge and violence that this war had bred and born in the hot blood that impelled him to murder other innocents. The war was insane, and inevitable. There were no winners.

When Ezekial allowed himself to revisit in memory some of the engagements and battles, he was always astounded that he was still whole. Only by the grace of God had no bullet or ball found the meat of his massive frame. Others, in droves, fell in bleeding bits beside him as he mauled and murdered those young boys in blue before him. How many had fallen beside him? How many had fallen before him? What were their names? Who would remember them or honor their terrible, lonely dying, in pain and in pieces in the smoke and the roaring and screaming? Who would miss them? How many tears had fell? Why would God allow it?

Sometimes at night he would awake in a sweat, trembling and growling like a wild animal, dreaming of those hellish days. And, Sam, faithful Sam would be right there nuzzling him and comforting him. What a great gift of God was Sam, a never failing friend.

Ezekial and Cynthia developed a friendship that was restrained by the social expectations of the age, by their genders and by the roles of teacher and student. Ezekial was inspired by her knowledge and began to keep the lamp lit late in the night reading books she lent him. Brother Denton lent him books also, religious books, which seemed to raise more questions in his mind than they answered.

One glorious morning in early June Sam trotted to his seat outside the window of the church as Ezekial took his place inside. Ezekial had been pleasantly surprised that Sam's understanding and manners had improved so rapidly. The improvement did not extend to his singing however, which was as loud and discordant as ever.

After the services, the ladies pushed several sets of clothing into his hands and made him go into the church office to try them on. He was to model each of the three sets of clothes, two sets for everyday and a fine set for Sundays. The ladies chirped their complements to one another on their tailoring skills as well as their wisdom in constructing each item a little large to allow for shrinkage when washing and because this oversized boy was still a boy for all his size and still growing. Exiting the church office after dressing in each set of pants and shirts, the godly gaggle were there to cluck and peck and pull at the material as he was ordered to turn and bend and hold out his arms. He was made even more ill at ease by their gushing compliments of how handsome he looked. He knew his face was red as a tomato, and that realization made it even redder.

Ezekial was most impressed with the brogans the saddle-maker gave him. They were made a bit big also, but the buckskin laces allowed him to tighten them against his feet. He hadn't had shoes on his feet for many months and the last ones he'd had, in fact, all the shoes he had worn in his life, were made by Gramps. Gramps did the best he could, but it did not matter which foot you put into which shoe, the fit was about the same. But these shoes fit like a glove. One for the right foot, one for the left. Fancy.

Mrs. Denton had knitted him a pair of socks and, seeing they were about the right size, promised him some more. With the clothes on, stiff and new, and the socks and shoes on his feet, he felt more important somehow. He stood up a little straighter, held his head a bit higher.

Embarrassed by all the attention and by his inability to repay them for their generous time, work and money, it was all he could do to stammer his appreciation to the ladies fussing over him. When he was at last allowed to walk outside the church and join the men, Sam approached him warily, stepping around him in a half circle, looking and sniffing, growling and whining.

"Sam, it's just me with some new clothes on," Ezekial explained as he held out his hand and kneeled. The men who had watched chuckled as Sam slowly approached, allowed Ezekial to pet him and barked as if scolding him for his mischief. Sam continued to sniff the clothing, looked up at Ezekial and turn his head inquisitively studying this changed creature that he had been familiar with.

Ezekial's close neighbor, Mr. Dunlap drew him aside and, after small talk about the new clothes, the sermon and the weather, asked if he had given any further thought to selling the farm.

"Yessir, I've shore thought about it. And if I decide to sell it, I'd like it to be to someone like yer fam'ly, someone who'll keep it up and runnin' like Gramps did. Truth is, it's a lonely ol' place there by myself an' I just don't know if I can settle down there. I'm givin' thought to goin' to school to study law or medicine. You know, jes' try to be something better, someone other folks could be proud to be 'sociated with."

"Well, you'd need money to study law or medicine. This might be an opportunity."

"Yes sir. I'd have to give it some thought."

"I understand that. Let us know soon as you can though, because these kids are anxious to get a place of their own."

"I will Mr. Dunlap. I'll let you all know soon's I can."

At lunch next day, as he and Cynthia finished up their dinner, he mentioned Mr. Dunlap's offer and his thoughts of attending classes and studying law or medicine.

"Ezekial, to be frank, before you pursue law or medicine, you will need to continue your basic education for awhile longer, perhaps another year or two. Certainly you are intelligent enough to learn to practice law or medicine."

"Well, I suppose I could go 'head and sell the farm, move to town and rent a place, let you teach me 'til I'm ready to go on to a college somewhere."

"Ezekial, I'm sorry my friend, but that won't be possible. You see, my fiancée and I are to be married next Saturday. We haven't told anyone other than our families because we don't want a big crowd or fuss at our wedding. He'll return Thursday or Friday, we'll be quietly wed on Saturday here in the church, then we'll leave together for a short honeymoon somewhere, we haven't decided where yet, then we'll return to the home he has prepared for us in Baltimore where his business is located."

Ezekial was speechless. He just stared at her, shocked.

"I don't know who will take my place here as teacher. There are many qualified people in the area. I don't expect classes to be suspended for long. You can continue here until you are better prepared for higher education."

Ezekial's mind was numb. Mouth agape, he just continued to stare.

"Ezekial? Are you all right? I'm sorry I haven't warned you, but the wedding was moved forward lately because of the success of my fiancée's building company. You'll be fine. Let's go back to class. Come along students, let's get back inside."

The afternoon passed in a haze. Slowly the reality of losing her began to penetrate his denial. With her, it seemed he was losing his hope, his inspiration, his ambition. Life would return to the depressing desolation and dull oppression that had encompassed him before Cynthia. He noticed that his stare made her uncomfortable through the short afternoon. There seemed to be so little bliss in life and he was determined to enjoy what remained to him. To let it burn into his memory while it presented itself. Soon joy would leave him and emptiness was sure to follow. To light the dark days ahead he instinctively savored the sight of her. He would often relive and relish these happy days, the shining, glorious days spent in the glow of her. The clean, feminine scent in the brisk, morning air, the music of her voice, the gentle grace of her movement, her fresh, enthralling beauty. All this he would ever treasure in the storehouse of his memory.

Ezekial knew that he understood little of love, did not realize that young love is not to be understood but simply enjoyed. He could not but love her, could not save himself from the broken heart. This first love would live in him for all his days, each golden moment cherished.

"That will be all for today class, I will see you all bright and early in the morning."

These words jarred him from his trance and he picked up his books and rushed from the church house. As always, he caught her horse first and hitched up the buggy, then tied the buggy before the church. As he finished fighting his mules into their harnesses she came out closing the door behind her.

"Thank you Ezekial."

"Yes ma'am, you're welcome."

Cynthia walked to a spot before Ezekial and looked up into his face. "Ezekial, we have grown close, we've become a special kind of friends in these past months. I know you think of me as someone special, but I'm really quite ordinary.

"You see, I was born into a genteel family, a family of some wealth. What I am, the way I look, my education, my values and perceptions have been mostly determined by my birth. I am a follower. I have been expected to behave a certain way and I have tried not to disappoint."

"You however have an opportunity to excel. You have ambition and the intelligence and physical attributes to achieve beyond what you were born to. Your parents, your grandfather, all your family would want you to continue your striving to attain status. They would all be so proud of you. You are the last of your family, the only, and I'm sure the best chance to create a legacy and enhance a sense of pride in your family name.

"I envy you Ezekial. I've been proud to be your friend. I hope we'll be friends always and that we'll meet again from time to time. Please don't let me down, but more importantly, do not let your family down. Become a good man, a solid foundation of a strong family. You owe it to your forbearers, to your progeny, and to yourself."

She walked to the buggy and placed her books and basket on the floorboard, then turned again to him. "I know you care for me. Please don't hate me because I love another. You will find a woman to love later, a better woman than me, one who will grow with you and help you grow. Stay busy becoming the man you are meant to be and the woman you love will be drawn to you."

"So long my friend."

"Goodbye Miss Cinthy."

Ezekial was surprised he could speak, his emotions were so overwhelming just then.

Cynthia stood on her toes, reached up and pulled his big face down to hers and gently, so tenderly, kissed his lips. Quickly she turned, boarded the buggy and took the reins in hand. She smiled in her magical way, turned the horse and hurried away.

Ezekial touched his lips which still seemed to tingle from her touch. He stood in silence and watched her disappear in the distance. Sam's soft whimper drew his attention from the empty road and he turned his eyes on the dog.

"I've lost another one Sam. I hope you stick with me."

Sam barked and smiled on one side of his face, the one eye fluttering open and shut.

Ezekial chuckled and tears burned his eyes as he picked Sam up and put him on the wagon seat. He looked at the church house once more, then down the long deserted road. Stepping up on the wagon he spoke to the waiting mules and headed home.

After tending to the mules and the other chores that needed attention, Ezekial began to wander around the farm letting this latest development penetrate all his denials. She was gone, he must accept it. It hurt him. He felt less confident in himself. She had become an inspiration, the delight of his meager life. What would he do now?

"It'll be alright in the mornin'."

The almost audible remembrance of Gramps's words startled him. Those were the words his grandfather had always offered to encourage him when he was a boy and some event in life had injured him. It seemed a part of Gramps was still there with him, hurting in empathy, trying to comfort him. Gramps would put an arm around his shoulders and tell him to keep his chin up and "keep grinnin' through the pain." Ezekial smiled at the memories.

And, standing, looking over the healthy green crop of oats Gramps had planted, his final crop, he realized that he too was Gramps' last seed. He felt determination and resolve rise up in his chest, a decision that neither the crop of oats that Gramps had planted nor the grandson he had seeded and nourished and raised would suffer neglect. He took a deep breath and filled his chest with a fixed intention that, for Gramps, he would suffer through this and whatever else life brought, and become the man he knew Gramps would want him to be.

These thoughts of Gramps brought the unread letter to mind. The letter was in the family Bible in the house. He felt that now was the time to read it.

"C'mon Sam, let's get some supper and see what Gramps wrote to me in his last letter."

They headed into the empty house at sunset.

Chapter Three

All that is gold does not glitter, Not all those who wander are lost: The old that is strong does not wither, Deep roots are not reached by the frost.
--J.R.R. Tolkien

Human law is law only by virtue of its accordance with right reason, and by this means it is clear that it flows from eternal law. In so far as it deviates from right reason it is called an unjust law; and in such a case, it is no law at all, but rather an assertion of violence.
--St. Thomas Aquinas, Summa Theologica

Authority is never without hate.
--Euripides

We think caged birds sing, when indeed they cry.
--John Webster

THE SEVEN PRISONERS unloaded clumsily from the barred prison wagon. Some fell to the muddy ground, their joints stiff from the torturous days in shackles and chains. On flatbed railway cars and rumbling prison wagons they had traveled through freezing, foggy nights and days over hundreds of miles to get here. The long, wet journey from the jail in Fort Worth to Huntsville, going from county seat to county seat picking up prisoners was over. Two nights they had slept on cold jailhouse floors and the respite from wind and weather had been welcome. All the prisoners were thin. Beside the corpulent guards they appeared skeletal. Their raw skin bled from the constant, maddening weight of the iron clasps and chains on ankles and wrists. Their bodies stank of stale sweat and worse. Their heads pounded from exposure to the freezing February sleet and shivers seemed to steal their breath. The endless miles of misery were behind them and they were relieved that they had finally arrived at the Walls prison. Their hopes were minimal: food, warmth, rest.

The last two weakened prisoners fell headlong into the frozen mire pulled by the long chain that bound them all together. A tobacco chewing, grossly obese guard kicked the last convict to splash into the mud and yelled, "Git yer sorry ass up ol' thang! An' git in line. C'mon! Git in line. I ain't wasting my time with you pieces of shit!"

The wagon that had met them at the rail yard was pulled away by the double team of mules, back to the sally port next to the high guard tower they passed through to enter this Texas prison. The heavy double gates opened once again allowing the mules to leave as a shotgun toting guard in the tower looked on from under the tower roof, out of the drizzling rain. While the fat prison guard berated the chained convicts, two other guards unlocked and removed their chains.

"All you scummy punks lissen good, cuz I ain't say'n none o' this twict. My name is Sergeant Snyder. Not Sarge. Not Mister. Sergeant Snyder. They is rules on this here farm. Whatever I say, is a rule. If you don' folla' the rules, yer rusty ass will be whupped an' thrown in the hole where yu'll be starved down 'til ya decide t' folla' the rules."

A sunken cheeked prisoner said, "Sir, I have a question. When do we...."

His question was never asked as the fat guard slapped him with a gloved backhand across his face, bloodying his nose. He kicked him in his groin, folding him up on his knees in the mud. Then he punched the kneeling prisoner, laying him flat out in the frozen slush. He looked around at the other prisoners and a smile slowly stretched across his porcine face revealing brown, decayed remnants of teeth.

"Rule numba one: keep yer real stooped moufs shut."

Turning to two of the guards standing by, he ordered, "Take this punk ta tha hole."

As the guards drug the unconscious man away, the big, greasy sergeant took a couple of steps and kicked the helpless convict hard in the ribs. He chewed the cud of tobacco in his cheek, spit, then pulled his long, double-breasted raincoat close around his neck.

"Anybody else wanna ass a question? Good. I guess I answered his question purty good," he smiled.

"Now all of you low-down whores' sons know that Abe Lincoln freed the nigger slaves. Well, when yer sorry asses broke the law you volunteered to become slaves of the state of Texas. Yer ass will work every day, 'cept Sunday, yule work while the sun shines an' you won't lollygag. Rest up taday cuz t'morra' yule be out in tha fields workin.

"Right now though, yer nasty asses are goin' ta tha baffhouse an' wash. We'll douse ya'll down fer bugs an' then we'll git ya some clean close an' brogans. Take care of dem close an' shoes cuz ya might not neva' git no mo. Now, ya'll stay in a line an' foller that boss down ta tha baffhouse."

Jack was dog-tired and bone weary after the seemingly endless trip from Fort Worth jail. His arms and legs were raw and bleeding from the cuffs and shackles, the thin cotton jail clothes did nothing to prevent the cold air from his weak, shivering body and his patience was being tested to the snapping point by this ignorant, sadistic fool. Even though he was to be in prison for the next twenty five years he was glad to be here and out of that bouncing, freezing wagon and off that flatbed railway car. He didn't know how much of this jawing he could stand from this self-righteous reprobate. He had never been able to ignore insults for long. He just wanted to be left alone, to lay down somewhere warm. But the pig-faced, loudmouthed hack would not quit.

"C'mon ladies, get yer bitch asses outa' that water and get dressed."

"How 'bout a towel Sergeant Snyder?" one black man ventured.

"Nigger, you did'n have no towel in the free world an' yer black ass won' have no towel in here. Jes' get dem close on and get lined up so I kin lock yer sorry asses up. C'mon, c'mon."

As Jack buttoned up the oversized striped shirt he mumbled to himself about the peckerwood guard's raucous voice.

"Whad you say dipshit?" the sergeant yelled at Jack, putting his putrid breath in Jack's face. In character, unfortunately, Jack was unable to keep his thoughts to himself.

"I know you couldn't hear me Fatso, 'cause you were too busy running that watermelon head. What I said was, I wish you'd shut that rotten-tooth, foul-smelling, trash-can mouth before you ruin my appetite."

The corpulent face turned reddish purple, spluttered and spat, then turned and motioned to the accompanying guards who took positions on either side of Jack and held his weakened arms to his sides. Jack tried to pull away but before he could free an arm the fat man put his three hundred pounds of pork into a fist that exploded in Jack's solar plexus, doubling him over and paralyzing him. As he gasped like a perch on the bank, the sergeant hit him with an uppercut that busted his lip and loosened his teeth. Somehow, without Jack noticing, the guards had handcuffed him behind his back. He realized he was in real trouble now, helpless. The two flunkies held him up while the big hog threw ham-sized fists into his ribs and face. Jack could hear a rushing, like a high wind and could see only blinding, blinking lights as he felt his body being dragged, beaten and thrown. Then he felt nothing at all.

When his conscious mind began to swim back to reality he instantaneously tried to roll over to take pressure off his damaged ribs, but managed only to swing like a pendulum. The swinging further disoriented his waking mind, his head ached like a rot-gut whiskey drunk. Opening the only one of his swollen eyes he could just a slit, he took half a minute trying to focus and the other half trying to convince himself that what he saw was real.

It was ridiculous. He would have felt foolish if he didn't feel so much pain. His throbbing thumbs were tied tightly to a pipe about eight feet off the ground, his toes not quiet reaching the floor. He groaned from the electric pain in his head, his ribs, his hands. His mind could not comprehend the situation. Where was he? He could not even remember who he was. How,.... Why did this circumstance occur?

Through a narrow slice of vision appeared a grotesque face up close to his that smelled of something dead and rotten. Instinct caused his head to jerk away from the offensive odor and his entire body swung round causing extreme vertigo and nausea. The malodorous apparition placed its paws on Jack's shoulders and pulled down, causing an exquisite explosion of pain to shoot from his thumbs up his arms to his brain. The noxious sensation brought his somnolent mind to a horrifying waking state.

"Mownin' Mista' Badass. Jew sleep good? Ready ta start scule ag'in? Ya know, it takes some boys longer to learn rule number one than it does others. But, I figger yule learn purty fast, with this lesson I'm gonna give you this mownin!"

Sergeant Synder stepped back and drove his big fist into Jack's vulnerable kidneys.

"Ahhh!" Jack heard someone scream from far away. He didn't realize that it was his scream. He didn't feel he had the breath to scream.

After some eternal second Jack was making an effort to think of something more pleasant than the unbearable pain pulsating from his thumbs and radiated down his arms to trigger other endless shocks of punishment in his shoulders, his ribs, his back, his temple, his eyes. Every breath, every beat of his heart was a lash of suffering. He tried to remember how long he had been here hanging from this hateful pipe. It seemed he'd been hanging here for weeks, hanging like dead flesh in meat locker. He had been a punching bag for several cowardly, sadistic guards who had beaten him until he twitched unconsciously. His body, urged him to scream, to cry, to beg. But he bit his tongue until the blood choked him and ran over his chin and chest and down into his britches. He would hang here forever. Until his thumbs fell off. Until he was allowed to die.

He couldn't recall what terrible sin had merited such treatment. He faintly remembered something to do with his smart-alec mouth, but surely it was more than that. He couldn't bring to mind the murder he must have committed.

An oily, obese and foul-smelling visage floated into his consciousness, but he couldn't bring an infraction to mind that would require such torturous punishment. He wanted to ask what his terrible transgression had been; instead he focused his wavering concentration on being silent and still. Every tiny movement added fresh rushing waves of drowning pain. It was easier to endure the steady unrelenting suffering of remaining motionless. Try as he might, he could not stop the trembling, chilling sweats and fear of increasing weakness and the certainty of approaching death. The trembling ceased. His breath grew shallower. A hot, deep darkness washed over him.

His spirit floated in a burning, dizzying darkness, an otherworldly womb akin to coma where time and space were not. It was the abode of fear and pain and helplessness and he felt the light of life diminishing, flickering, failing.

The eruption of acute physical suffering shocked him back into the prisoner's world. He moaned involuntarily and fleetingly surfaced into light and consciousness when the meat and bone that contained him hit the floor. Though he was mostly unaware, he had been thrown into a nine by five foot cell by two brutish guards. The cell door crashed closed, the big brass key locking the steel tumblers.

Ezekial lay on the metal lower bunk wondering if he were awake or dreaming. He stared and blinked at the near naked and bloody apparition spread across the tiny floor like a macabre rug.

Slowly it dawned on his waking mind that the man on the floor was the one the guards had hung in the pipe chase all weekend. The face was swollen grotesquely, one ear looked like a pearlescent, large seashell. Blood covered his face and chest and the pants were caked with black blood. His thumbs were black and blue and bulged until the skin had broken in ragged tears exposing white tendons and pink muscle. His ribs were sprouting impossible knots that were deepest blue and violet, green, yellow and red. In the poor light that penetrated into the tiny cell through the iron bars Ezekial saw no indication that the man was alive. Was he breathing? Had they placed a corpse in his cell to frame him with another murder charge?

Ezekial had been living in this cell alone for more years than he cared to remember. No one wanted to be locked in a cell with the huge and insane killer. Why had they thrown this severely beaten, possibly dead man in the cell with him now? Ezekial knew it was not only paranoia that made him wary, in this separate world the words 'usual' and 'normal' held connotations unimagined in the outer world of freedom. The body on the cold floor jerked and began to tremble. The movement gave Ezekial some hope.

Big Zeke stood and unrolled the thin cotton mattress on the iron shelf that served as an upper bunk. Gently, he lifted the suffering soul and laid him on his back on the mat. He placed the man's terribly swollen hands on his chest and covered him with the only thin blanket. Silently, Ezekial surveyed the damage to this stranger, and appraised the sudden situation. There was little he could do just then to help the man. He would let him sleep awhile.

Turning and lowering his huge old frame, he sat on the lower bunk. His hand made the motion of petting a dog beside him. He muttered, "We got company Sam."

Hours later, as the sun penetrated the prison gloom and golden stripes fell across the floor of the dismal man cage, Jack woke, aching all over. He groaned aloud and wondered where he was. His curiosity was dissolved by immobilizing pain. A welcome thought came to him that it might be wise to sink down into the abyss and leave the pain in life. He began to move his hands and experienced excruciating, electrifying pain which paralyzed him and rendered him unconscious again.

Within an hour of his arrival to his office on the Monday morning, Assistant Superintendent Peterson had been fully informed by his inmate bookkeeper of all that had transpired within the prison since he had left last Thursday morning. The report of Sergeant Snyder's excessive and unauthorized punishment of the newly arrived prisoner took precedence over other business. Snyder was a loose cannon and his repeated sadistic treatment of convicts must cease.

There were other situations he must deal with, he had been told of an escape in the planning and possible serious trouble between factions over gambling debts. No one really knew how Peterson found out so much of prison events. He had snitches snitching on snitches. For example, he knew his bookkeeper was financing and supplying a wine-brewing operation, but he would allow it to continue as long as it caused little trouble. The inmates needed some periodic relief and diversion, and he couldn't condemn a man who enjoyed a drink once in awhile, he had a nip himself most evenings. Still, there were a few secrets within the Walls he wasn't aware of, but very few.

Peterson strode to the cell block where Big Zeke was housed and motioned for the dozing turnkey to follow him. He walked purposely up the wooden stairs and down the catwalk to cell thirty three. He peered in at the body lying on the upper bunk, noting the injuries to the man that were apparent. His gaze moved from the severely wounded man to rest on Big Zeke.

"It wuden me who done that Pete."

"I know it wasn't you Zeke. If it had been you the man would surely be dead. Open this door," he ordered the turnkey.

The superintendent stepped into the small space and Ezekial raised up and stood.

"What's your new celly's name Zeke?"

"Well, he ain't felt like doing much talking Pete."

Peterson threw the blanket off the prone figure and was rewarded with the brutal visage of the prisoners hands and ribs. His jaw muscles flexed as he gritted his teeth and his eyes narrowed. His face went from pale to fiery and a vein throbbed in his neck. His words were clear and concise.

Ezekial, you will lift this man and carry him to the infirmary."

Yes sir. Shore will."

"Gently Zeke. Let's not do him further damage."

Ezekial easily carried the bloody weight following the lanky, suited official down the stairs and across the muddy prison yard to the infirmary. Placing the beaten prisoner in the doctor's care, the superintendent asked to be called when the examination and treatment had been completed. Returning to his office he instructed the shift captain to send Sergeant Snyder to him "forthwith." He sipped a steaming cup of coffee his bookkeeper brought to him and fumed.

"Superintendent Peterson, you wanna see me?" Sergeant Snyder choked out from the door.

"Come in Snyder. Close the door."

Peterson sat and stared at Snyder for half a minute, then rose and walked around his desk to stand before him, inspecting him from head to toe. The silence stretched to a full minute as the superintendent stared at the sergeants face.

"Superin....," Snyder started.

"Shut up! Shut your ignorant mouth!" Peterson screamed in Synder's face. After taking a moment and a breath the superintendent asked, "Do you have any idea about how the new prisoner, Jack Williams, has sustained such serious injuries?"

Snyder swallowed and tried to get saliva into his dry mouth, then ventured, "Well superintendent, truth is, he was housed with that big ol' crazy killer Ezekial Robin..."

"Snyder! Don't insult my intelligence. You have one more opportunity to explain to me how this prisoner was so critically injured on your watch."

The sergeant's jowls trembled and greasy sweat covered his pocked face. "Ah,...well,...I mean,...you wasn't here last Friday afternoon when the chain wagon brung those new prizners in heah an' this sorry-ass prizner 'salted me in the baffhouse. So, I thought I'd go 'head and larn him a lesson like you would sir."

"Snyder, I mete out punishment only to the most recalcitrant inmates as a last resort after a thorough investigation and I sentence corporal punishment very rarely. You are not authorized to punish prisoners and have never been. As I've told you before, you are to put problem prisoners in solitary confinement and let me decide if and what punishment will be given. It is obvious that you and your minions have beaten and tortured this prisoner severely, and done so without authorization or just cause. If this prisoner had assaulted you there would be some evidence, some resultant wound on your fat face, which I would relish, but the fact is you were not assaulted and you are not only a liar, but a bad liar and a sadistic bully."

The superintendent let his eyes study the disgraceful specimen before him in silence and took several deep breaths to calm himself.

The sergeant fidgeted and drew himself up to speak but Peterson held up his hand.

"Snyder, I told you to shut your foul mouth. I'll do the talking here and you'd be wise to listen well. There is no excuse nor explanation which might justify the bestial beating and torture to which you have subjected this prisoner. I do not for a moment believe this prisoner attacked you, but if he did it was almost certainly in self-defense. I say again, and listen well, you do not have the authority to dispense any punishment in this prison. Do you understand That? Do you!?"

"Yessir, I..."

"And certainly you cannot lawfully brutalize and torture inmates at your whim."

"Sir, I..."

"Shut your damned mouth! The next time anything like this occurs you will find yourself not only out of a job but you'll be a prisoner yourself as I will personally charge you with any assault you are involved in from this day forward."

The red-faced superintendent took a deep breath, stepped away from the sweat-dripping guard, and removed his coat, hanging it on the rack on the wall. He walked back around his desk to the high backed chair and sat silently. Shaking his head he spoke again. "I am aware that such practices of inhumane thrashings and inflictions of various devilishly conceived punishment have been routinely administered by gangs of guard here for many years, but those days are over. Not on my watch. The Holy Bible teaches that mercy should triumph over justice and so I will have it. And so you will benefit, this one and final time Snyder. But, make no mistake, my mercy, unlike the Lord's, has it limits, and I will make you regret it for a long, long time should anything like this ever happen again.

"Now, you will leave these Walls immediately. You will return promptly for work tomorrow morning without those stripes on your sleeve or you will not return at all. You will start afresh on your seniority, you will be a probationary guard at the bottom of the pecking order here. If it were not nigh impossible to find men to work in these conditions, long hours and low wages I would fire you and several others. And I 'will' fire you Snyder, at the slightest provocation, don't think I won't. Now get out of my office. And take a bath before you return."

The assistant superintendent had been working on a composition regarding procedures of charging prisoners with rule violations and treatment of prisoners generally. The rules for prisoners were vague and not clearly defined. Some of the rules were ludicrous. A guard had put a prisoner in solitary a week ago charging him with 'reckless eyeballing.' When Peterson ask him to explain the charge the guard explained that the convict was looking him in the eye and not looking at the ground like he was supposed to. Peterson advised the guard to get used to it because not only was he dismissing the ridiculous disciplinary infraction but henceforth encouraging convicts to look all men in the eye.

Peterson knew that his efforts to change prison protocol would have to be unyielding and strong enough to overcome decades of harsh treatment of prisoners and malignant malfeasance as well as corruption. It may take more than a generation to make a difference, but it must begin somewhere. The daily struggle to re-train and discipline the mostly ignorant and hard-assed hacks who had ruled this prison with an iron fist was a lonely and thankless task. But, he was a hard-ass too, and it takes steel to shape steel.

Not that he believed prisoners should be coddled either, they should be treated fairly, humanely. They could only learn respect by experiencing respect. The men here were mostly redeemable. They were sent here, separated from family and freedom 'as' punishment, not 'for' punishment. Many had known little social training and knew only survival skills. Most had no occupational education either, except as thieves. And he knew being a thief was hard work. Not the man who occasionally stole something, but the thief who stole to live had to work hard mentally and physically to manage to get by day after day. The successful thief had to get away every day, he could never stumble or he'd be in jail. Some adept thieves stole daily for years without getting caught. If he could show them a way to focus that intelligence and determination into a legal enterprise it would be such a boon to them and to society as a whole.

A convict who worked with the doctor knocked on his door and advised him that the doctor had completed his treatment of the injured man.

"Tell the doctor I'll be there directly."

The assistant superintendent put the papers he was working on away in his desk and stood, straightening his coat and tie. Peterson knew he would have to make a report of this incident to the superintendent who may or may not make the report available to the prison committee of the state legislature. The ongoing 1909 investigation of this committee had already revealed the brutality common in the prison system. One of the general observations of the committee was that the rules and regulations adopted for the discipline of Texas prisoners had "been totally ignored." The committee found prisoners "in a great many instances" whose bodies had been badly scarred by prison officials using whips made by whatever means "their fancy or brutal inclinations might dictate." Peterson knew that in the great majority of cases these whippings were not recorded and that many prisoners died as a result of these cruel, inhumane beatings.

There had been testimony at the legislative committee's hearings that a prisoner who was working in the fields had asked a guard for permission to relieve himself. The guard gave permission and as the prisoner began to lower his pants the guard shot him in the back and killed him.

A Mexican prisoner named Antonio and an Irishman named Mike Dunn died a few hours after severe whippings. The morning following, the guard forced another prisoner to do a dance on one of the coffins before they were hurriedly buried. No inquests were ordered in these murders and the cause of death was recorded as "sunstroke."

There was testimony of prisoners dying after being dragged through the fields by guards mounted on horseback. Dogs were sicced on prisoners who were shackled and handcuffed. Many were beaten to death with fists and clubs. There were unnumbered deaths from malnutrition and prisoners simply being worked to death.

Jake Hodges, chaplain of the Walls Prison, testified to the investigation committee that a young man named Oscar Peterson who was mentally retarded was so terrified of living on the farm that he cut off two of his fingers in a planning saw in one of the shops. As soon as the wounds healed he was whipped to unconsciousness. Hodges identified the man who had brutally whipped the Peterson boy as Captain R. H. Coleman, then the assistant superintendent of the Walls. When confronted with this testimony, Coleman admitted whipping the retarded young man and testified that he had done so with the approval of Superintendent J.A. Herring. The boy had been whipped for violation of the rules in avoiding work. Because Coleman had requested and received permission to whip Peterson, his action was ruled fully justified by established prison procedures.

This retarded boy was Assistant Superintendent Peterson's nephew and the incident was the impetus that caused him to hand over his several businesses to managers and contrive to be appointed assistant supervisor at the Walls through his cronies in the legislature. He had unseated the sadistic Coleman and began his battle for the humane treatment of prisoners.

Chaplain Hodges had also testified that a fifty-four year old prisoner named Foster had been shipped to the Walls to recover from torture he had suffered at the Whatley-Herring prison farm. Guards had whipped him because he could not keep up with the work due to his age. They stripped him, whipped him, threw sand on him and whipped him again. Then they made him climb a tree covered with ants which bit him all over his body.

There were months of evidence of horrible torture and brutality from other state employees, guards as well as courageous prisoners who testified despite justified fear of the probable retaliation of their keepers. As they expected, no quarter was given inmates who had cooperated in the investigation, they were all sent directly back to the torturous prison farms and camps they came from.

None of the prison personnel were ever punished for their actions and Governor Campbell took absolutely no action on the evidence of ongoing torture and brutality found by the investigative committee.

Peterson had volunteered to come into this hellish system. Single-handedly he fought against the tide of generations of this savage and pitiless world. He was beginning to find confederates and the bestial behavior of some of the guards was beginning to change. Even the inmate guards often employed by the prison staff were showing signs of relenting from their violence and these "building tenders" and "turnkeys" were often much more dangerous to their fellow prisoners than were the state employees.

The typical living conditions of prisoners were disgusting. On the Imperial prison farm near Sugarland the prisoners were fed a biscuit or two before dawn which were near raw dough and molded and sometimes a half inch of coffee if they were lucky and could fight others to get it. At first light they were made to run two or three miles to the work site and then forced to labor at a breakneck pace "until the stars were shining down." Lunch was eaten on the turn-rows in the fields. The men were given a tiny piece of meat, cold and hard cornbread and, as a treat, cold black-eyed peas. Supper was the same. Often the smaller and weaker prisoners were "hogged" for their meager rations by bigger and stronger inmates. Prisoners being stabbed and killed in their sleep was commonplace. Some days there was no meat, just cornbread.

Baths were allowed once a week in groups of eight or ten on Saturday nights in a big tank dug in the ground. There was never any change of underwear or socks given. A change of outer clothes was sometimes given, but most prisoners did not exchange their clothes because the clothes they were given were usually worse and dirtier than those they had. Most prisoners were ridden with louse.

The building which housed prisoners on Imperial farm allowed twenty square feet of living space per prisoner. The building emitted "a very strong, offensive odor." The investigating committee further described the bedding as having never been changed, it stayed deplorably filthy. The exhausted prisoners often could not clean the mud from their clothes after a long days labor before falling into bed. Lice and bedbugs infested the bedding and cockroaches ran everywhere.

The legislative investigatory committee described the Eastham women prison farm in Houston county owned by Mrs. Delha Eastham, as follows: "The work force was divided into two camps, one predominantly black one exclusively white. White women worked inside, black women toiled in the fields. All the guards were men and this led to "grossly improper conduct." Testimony was given that women were forced to work in the fields despite any and all sickness or infirmity. Menstrual cycles did not excuse them from heavy labor. When punished for any imagined infraction they were stripped of all clothing, tied hand and foot and whipped "on the naked meat" in front of other guards. Guards came at night and used them for their pleasure.

One black woman was in prison for eight years when she gave birth to a child. The father was a guard named Jerry Bowden, the son of the man in charge of the camp. The witness would never identify the father while incarcerated because she knew she would be killed.

The women suffered beastly work, abusive language, physical abuse of every imaginable type and pregnant women had delivered their babies in the fields where they worked.

All this testimony was confirmed by the state investigatory committee.

Nothing was done to correct any of these conditions.

Peterson kept a transcript of these hearings in a file cabinet in his office and re-read portions of it from time to time when he felt his resolve and energy flagging. His was a thankless effort for the most part, but he felt it was his God-given calling, his mission. It was a daily grind, an endless task, he thought as he leaned into the cold driving wind crossing the prison yard to the infirmary. He prayed, "One day at a time, my Strength and my Redeemer, step by step, little by little."

Peterson looked up at the infirmary window from which the crazy Indian killer Santanta had jumped to his death many years before. The bloodstains were still in the rock over a quarter century later. How long had his corpse laid there? His thoughts ran through wild men and rapists and murderers by the dozens like J.W. Hardin who had killed around two dozen white men. He didn't count

Mexicans nor Negroes. Such as these he must somehow do more than simply warehouse, guard and manage.

It was an insane asylum as much as a prison, where little asylum was afforded. And many of the more seriously deranged were among the keepers, not the kept.

The legislative hearings had made a portion of the populace to call for reform and that had allowed Peterson to wedge his way into the appointment of assistant superintendent. He knew his head was on the chopping block. Should he succeed in reorganizing the prison into a humane, efficient divisions of the judicial branch, the superintendent and the governor would reap the glory. Should he fail, the axe would fall on his head alone.

"Morning Doctor Lewis."

"Yes. Another fine morning minding the wounded. Thanks to your guards."

"I've not been allowed to hire a single guard Doctor, so they are not 'my' guards. And, the one responsible for this latest torture has been demoted as well as duly warned he will be fired if any other such brutality occurs."

"Why won't you fire him now?"

"You realize the prison is far understaffed now and no new hires are authorized. And, due to the nepotism of the employees here, I may turn the majority of the guards against me. I must try to reform the guards before I can begin to reform the inmates."

"Hmmm. Sergeant Snyder I presume?"

"Yes. Again. His final chance. And it's 'Officer' Snyder after today."

"And who will be promoted to his position?"

"I am considering Officer Roach."

"A good man. Not too hard, not too soft. Sensible, pragmatic."

"Yes, and willing to help change things."

"In any case, the prisoner is resting. I've tried to reposition his broken ribs and secure them with tight wrappings. Facial bones have been fractured also. Not a lot I can do there. I've stitched several cuts and iced the major knots and swellings. I've treated his severely injured thumbs but they will likely never be normal again. Not a lot I can do about his swollen scrotum, and his kidneys are likely damaged. There is probable brain bruising. He will need bed rest and pain medication for at least several days."

"So he will need to remain hospitalized awhile?"

"Yes Mister Peterson, in normal circumstances. But, there just isn't room here now. I have neither the staff nor the beds, too much other disease that needs be isolated, tuberculosis, hepatitis, and other infectious maladies. He would be further endangered here."

"I suppose I can put him back in the cell with Ezekial Robertson. I believe he will care for him."

"Superintendent, you are aware Ezekial is insane?"

"Of course he is insane Doctor. Who within these Walls is not? But, he is gentle and goodhearted and his size and reputation will deter the cowardly Snyder and his cronies from attempting further retaliation against this prisoner."

The doctor sighed and turned away as the assistant superintendent left the ward. He walked to the table that the beaten prisoner laid on and looked down on him. Without doubt, he'd had a rough welcome. Moving to the large medicine cabinet he unlocked it and took out one of the large bottles of laudanum. He poured a dose into a spoon and drank it down. Then took another dose. Employing a small funnel he filled a small bottle with the thick, brown liquid. He replaced the large bottle in the medicine cabinet and locked it. Then he slid the chain with his keys on it back around his neck.

Putting his hand gingerly on Jack's shoulder, he shook him until he groaned and woke.

"Mister Williams, I've sewn your cuts and disinfected them, iced your swellings, leveraged your thumbs and ribs back into their proximate natural positions and bandaged your wounds. Some of you will heal, in time, most of you. Your hands may never completely heal. Although it will cause you pain, the more you use your hands, the more they will return to normal. Try to avoid picking up heavy weight for awhile. Your urine will be bloody, you may have headaches, but hopefully these symptoms will pass in a week or two.

"I will write you a medical lay-in so you won't have to work in the fields for awhile. I'm putting this bottle in your shirt pocket. Take half a spoon every four hours, no more than that. I suspect you are well acquainted with laudanum. Did you take opiates before your incarceration?"

"Yes, some." Jack managed in a hoarse whisper.

"Um hmmmm. Judging from your tolerance, more than some I would guess. When this bottle is empty come to the infirmary or send your cell partner Ezekial Robertson, and I will fill it. When I deem that your wounds are bearable, I will still fill the bottle, but you will have to pay. Cold, hard cash. I'll help you with your addiction should you choose to continue it here in prison, but as you know, laudanum is not cheap. And, I must supplement the state's allocation with my own funds. There is a relatively new drug available now, said to be less addictive which I've ordered. It is called heroin. But, it is no less expensive. So, I hope you have access to money Mister Williams, otherwise you will be suffering withdrawal pains in two, three weeks."

Ezekial came in and with an inmate orderly's help placed Jack on a stretcher and carried him to the cell. Ezekial lifted him easily and gently onto the upper bunk. Jack was mostly unconscious, floating in a drugged oblivion, and the thin prison mat felt soft as a cloud as he drifted into dreams of other, sweeter times.

A few hours later Jack awoke in the dark, aching all over. An irrepressible groan escaped him. He wondered where he was but his curiosity did not overcome his fear of unavoidable pain sitting up to investigate would cause. Every breath was torturous. He thought it may be better to die than to suffer so. The unceasing pain enveloped him. Vaguely the weight of the small bottle in his shirt pocket surfaced into his consciousness. As his hand reacted to the thought and moved toward his pocket he was shocked by a flash of pain that took his breath, dulled his vision and caused his ears to ring. He must have cried out aloud, for a foggy form appeared over him, a big, out-of-focus face. He felt the bottle being removed from his pocket; soon after heard a voice, "Open up." He opened his stiff, split lips and gratefully accepted the spoon of foul tasting liquid. A blanket which covered him was adjusted and the face dissolved in darkness.

An unknown time later Jack realized he was awake again, awareness slowly dawning. After initial confusion passed, he gingerly slid his hand over his shirt pocket. A fearful panic further cleared from his lethargy when he realized the merciful elixir was gone. The chains which attached the iron upper bunk to the wall rattled as Jack slowly moved to peer over the side and down at a man sitting on the lower bunk. The man was hunched over to accommodate his big body in the space between the upper and lower bunks. He sat scratching at the air beside him. Jack estimated the man to be closer to seven feet tall than six and weighed much over three hundred pounds. Jack was in awe. But, he was also in pain. He certainly could not chance angering this monster, he had sustained as much damage as he could stand for now. The man was muttering something, something barely audible, Jack strained to hear.

"Won't be any trouble to have him here fer awhile Sam, he sleeps most the time. And Pete said somebody might wanna' hurt him some more, so we have to look out fer 'im. You be sure an' let me know if somebody like ol' sorry Snyder comes slippin' 'round."

Jack drew his head back from looking over the edge of the bunk when he realized the man was talking about him. But who in the hell was he talking to? The chains rattled again as Jack settled back on the bunk and the reactive movement caused a wincing stab of pain and an involuntary intake of breath.

The big head arose over him, not floating in a fog as before but intensely distinct and terrifying. It spoke.

"Well, 'mornin'. I'm Ezekial. They tole me you's Jack Williams. They th'owed yew in here last night after they cut you down. I guess ol' Snyder thought it'd be more punishment for ya' ta live with me. Heh-heh. Ya' see, they believe I'm crazy. But don't you worry son, me an' Sam 'll look out fer ya'."

He reached down and came up holding food.

"You'll have trouble holding things 'til yer hands heal up some. They hung me up by my thumbs and whupped me a long time ago, so I know how you feel. This ain't nothin' but a big ol' cat-head biscuit with a slice of hog meat in it, but I expect yer near starved. I'll hold it fer ya. Take a bit."

It hurt Jack's loose teeth to bite it off and to chew but the simple fare tasted delicious. Jack wolfed it down.

"Want somethin' to drank? Ain't nothin' but water."

Jack drank too fast and choked up a bit.

"Let that settle on yer stomach an' I'll feed ya some more. The doctor left you some med'cine fer the pain. You 'bout ready fer some?"

"Yes."

"He said no more'n half a' spoon."

The big man measured the amount carefully into a tablespoon and administered it. Jack shuddered at the taste, but welcomed it. He'd had a love-hate relationship with opium for years and his tolerance was still high despite being separated from it for months in jail. Still, in his weakened and injured condition a half-spoon undiluted dose overwhelmed him and dissolved all his pain.

"Thanks. I suppose I pissed off that fat sergeant really bad somehow. I don't quite recall what I did."

"Don't have to do much to give Snyder an excuse. But scuttlebutt I heard over at the infirmary has it that this assistant superintendent don't cotton to all the meanness that he deals out an' ever'body's lookin' fer him to put a stop to all tha' whuppin's."

"I hope so. I don't know how much more of that shit I can take."

"Well. You jes' lay up an' heal fer a few days That ol' doctor gave you a work lay-in 'til you get better. I'll feed ya. Ol' Pete's scared somebody might try'n hurt you ag'in, so he's havin' our food brought here. I'll feed ya 'til you kin hold a knife and spoon. I won't let Sam eat all yer food." Ezekial chuckled.

Jack looked down and around and asked, "Sam?"

"Yep. Sam's m' dog. Ever' since he got shot and killed people can't see 'im and think I'm crazy. Tha's awright. They don' mess with me. Know whut I mean?"

"Uh. Yea. I wish I could see your dog Ezekial. What kind of dog is he?"

"Aw, he's jes a plain ol' dog. Mongrel, guess you could say. Smart though. An' stubborn as a mule," Ezekial laughed. He shook his hand in the air beside his knee like he was rubbing a dog's head. "I love ol' Sam. We been together fer a long time. He's m' best friend. Listen, if you need to gidown and use the slop bucket er sumpin, don't try ta gi' down by yerself. I'll he'p ya down easy. I'd rather he'p ya down than have you fall on me. Likely it'd hurt you more'n me. Heh heh. I'd use tha top bunk but I'm 'fraid it'd bust outa' the wall. I' ma heavy load. Case you ain't noticed."

They smiled at each other.

Jack estimated Ezekial to be in his early fifties, when actually he was ten years older. He was still solidly built and capable of lifting him easily as he already had demonstrated, evidenced by his present location on this metal shelf they called a bunk five feet from the floor of the cell.

"Well, help me down if you would Zeke, I'd better take a leak before I have an accident."

Ezekial slipped his plate-sized palm under Jack's shoulders, the other under his legs and lifted his two hundred pounds easily to the floor. Jack stood before the metal pail and fumbled at his fly with his swollen thumbs. Observing his struggle, Ezekial reached over as if to help.

"Let me..."

"No! I'll manage," Jack spluttered.

When Jack completed his business, he turned to Ezekial who was sitting on his bunk.

"Maybe it'd be easier if I just put that mattress on the floor."

"Naw, 'at's where Sam sleeps. I don't mind heppin' you up there."

He lifted Jack effortlessly into the upper bunk.

"Uh, you say Sam sleeps on the floor?"

"Yep. Only cell partner I've had fer years now. I 'magine they thought they'd put you in here to scare you or punish you, but, seem's like I's put here to he'p you. Ya' see, all these prizners think I'm crazy."

"Because of Sam?"

"'Cause they can't see Sam, nor hear him. But I can see and hear, can't I Sambo?" Ezekial patted the air beside his knee and smiled.

Uh-oh, Jack thought, this big, old boy is bent bad, can't be straightened out.

"I gotta' admit, I don't see no dog either Ezekial."

"I'd be su'prised if ya did Jack? But that's awright. It don't bother me an' Sam none. Now, you jes get yerself a nap. You don' need to move 'round much 'til those ribs mend a bit."

In less than a minute Jack was sleeping.

Later Jack was awakened by the clatter of metal trays being passed through the 'bean hole' in the cell door and a shadow fell over his slitted swollen eyes.

"You 'wake Jack? Here, sit up. Chili beans and cornbread."

Ezekial helped Jack sit up on the bunk, his back to the wall, his legs crossed. He placed the tray of food on his legs and Jack had to wait for the vertigo to pass and the nausea to subside before he could focus on the food.

He watched Ezekial scratch the air beside his knee and heard him say, "Yes, you can smell mine Sam, I wouldn't forget you." Jack watched Ezekial facial expressions as he held the other tray of food close to the floor and patted the air. He really believed there is a dog here Jack told himself. I've got to be real careful around this old man, he may be dangerous.

Ezekial filled a metal cup with water from the bucket in the corner of the cell and handed it to Jack, then filled another cup and placed it on the floor. "You thirsty Sam?"

Looking up, Ezekial saw Jack's look of incredulity and laughed.

"You don't have to be afraid o' me Jack. I kin see it on yer face. I won't hurt you an' won't let nobody else hurt you."

Jack looked at the big honest face and had to return the smile. He said. "Zeke, you gotta admit the idea of you feedin' and waterin' an invisible dog is a bit scary."

"Yep, I kin see how it might be. But maybe you'll get used to it. Truth is, Sam don' really eat, but somehow he kin still sorta' taste through his smell. He kin still hear, taste, smell, feel and see somehow, and without a body or ears or mouth or nose or eyes. I can't explain it. He jes' don' like ta be left out at chow time.

"I ain't never had no cell partner over a night or so. They all think I'm insane an' get scared and jes' flat out refuse ta live with me. I hope you won' feel that way. It's kind of nice to have someone to talk to 'sides Sam. Heck, after all these years, we know all each other's stories."

Jack had to laugh. He certainly never met anyone like this.

"How long you been here Ezekial?"

"Well, how long's it been since seventy-three?"

"You been here since eighteen seventy-three? Damn Zeke that's thirty-six years!"

"I reckon."

"No wonder you're crazy!"

They both chuckled.

"Hot damn Ezekial. Who'd you kill?"

"The man who killed Sam. His daddy was a big wheel in the state railroad commission. I been told the fam'ly wants me locked up forever. An' I had a run in with a guard here an' I accidentally broke him."

"Broke him? Didja' kill him too?"

"Not on purpose."

"Aw Zeke, you been locked up longer than I been alive. Don't you ever think about escaping?"

"Naw. They'd catch me or kill me right quick. It's hard to hide when you're big as me."

"Damn Zeke, we gotta' do something about that. It's time you were free. You been punished enough. I'll help you write some letters. Something."

"Well." Ezekial hung his head.

"Damn."

After about a week of convalescing in the cell, Jack began ambling to the chow hall with Ezekial. He met and talked with several other prisoners. He was invited out to play dominoes in the evenings and soon became a regular at the moon table, making enough money to buy his laudanum. He rarely partook of a sufficient amount of the opiate to get high, but took moderate doses, just enough to keep the pain away.

Jack had begun taking laudanum on a lark, but later, when he was shot in the hip during an altercation in a bar, he became a regular user. The doctor there in prison knew the number of addicts, ordered sufficient quantities to provide for the market and made a healthy second income without much trouble. The addicts kept each other in line and treated him like a king. They protected the doctor, he was the primary source for their nepenthe.

Two weeks after Jack's torturous beating, a building tender, which was an inmate guard, came to the cell and told him that he had been assigned to number one hoe squad and that he should fall out for work at the work whistle at dawn the next morning. Before first light next day, Ezekial help him put his socks and shoes on because his ribs still would not allow him to bend that far. Ezekial tucked Jack's thin cotton pants into his brogans and laced them up tight so they wouldn't come untied and so the cold morning air wouldn't blow up his thin pants legs.

The inmates assigned to field work gathered in their respective squads and then formed two lines, pairing with another prisoner as they walked through the sally port and out the back gate of the prison. This formation allowed the major, captain, sergeant and squad guard to count the prisoners more efficiently as they filed out.

Jack noticed that the guard of his squad who was counting them out the gate had a handful of something small he was putting in his shirt pocket. The old squad boss buttoned his pocket over the small bulge. Jack turned to a younger man with spectacles walking beside him and asked him about it.

"That's old Two Gone. He can't count too good so he puts a pebble in his pocket for each prisoner in the work squad."

"How come you call him Two Gone?"

"Years ago, when he first started working here as a field boss he miscounted his squad. One evening when the major and him were counting prisoners back in the gate after work, he had one pebble left when the squad had been counted. He told the major, 'I think I got one gone major.' The major told him, 'You ignorant fool, you got two gone.!' He's been called Two Gone ever since."

"Has anyone else ever escaped from him?"

Nope. A few have tried and he's rode 'em down and shot 'em. Killed two who tried it together, and let the hounds chew on the others after he shot their legs."

"Mean ol' bastard, ain't he?"

"He can be. Don't get too far away from the rest of the squad 'cause he'll shoot ya' jes fer practice. He don't lose no wages if he shoots ya, but he will if you run and get away. An' that snuff-dippin' peckerwood ain't gonna lose no money."

The ten squads of about thirty men each walked at a fast pace for about three miles and stopped, lining up on a turn-row where a tool wagon and a water wagon pulled by long-legged mules were parked.

"Get you an aggie and get on down away from there. Just get one, this ain't no shopping spree. Just get one!"

Jack was handed a long handled, heavy-headed hoe and followed the squad down the turn-row.

Two Gone hollered, "Stop right there. Get you a row an' cut down ever thang on it. Flat weed it all. Don't leave nothin' standing."

Jack was jostled to one of the middle rows of cotton stubble and winter weeds and began beating the vegetation down with the dull hoe. All the squad bosses were hollering to keep the aggies busy,(an aggie was a hoe, a facetious abbreviation for agricultural instrument), to stay in a straight line, to keep their heads down and the mouths shut.

Ezekial had told Jack a bit of how these field squads worked. A man on the extreme left of the line of convicts was the lead-row and everyone else in the line faced him. It was his job to keep the squad in a line and he acted as the guard's foreman. The man beside the lead row was the push-lead and he set the pace for the squad as well as acted as the lead-row's confederate. At the other end of the line was a prisoner dubbed the tail-row and he was to stay abreast the lead-row. All the prisoners lined up between the lead-row and the tail-row were called the swing. That's where Jack worked, the swing. Behind the swing were three prisoners. One of these was the file boy who went from man to man down the line giving them his aggie to work with and taking theirs to sharpen. The other two prisoners behind the swing were called strikers and it was their job to help any worker whose row was harder to work or thicker with weeds so the man would not fall behind or get 'stuck-out' as they called it, causing the line of workers to be broken. If a prisoner habitually fell behind, couldn't or wouldn't keep up with the rest of the squad and keep the line straight, the lead and tail row, file boy and strikers would jump him and beat him so he would try a little harder or the squad boss would lock him up in solitary for a couple of weeks. If everybody worked together it wasn't so exhausting.

The low hanging, gray-blue clouds seemed to muffle the sound of the steel hitting the hardened soil and stalks. Jack was soaked in sweat in half an hour and the wet, cold air seemed to be more water than oxygen. His fragile strength was soon spent and without the help of the men around him as well as the strikers he would have fallen out of the line by mid-morning. Still, even with the help of fellow prisoners, the aggie jumped from his ungripping hands just before noon and when he bent to retrieve it, his knees gave way and he fell.

Two Gone began an oft-repeated diatribe. "Get yer sorry ass up and get back to work ol' thang. You ain't taking no holiday on me. Get up! It ain't dinner time nor quittin' time and you don't get no breaks, so get yer skinny white ass off the ground and down that row."

Jack tried to rise, but excruciating pain in his ribs paralyzed him. With the help of two other prisoners he managed to regain his feet, trembling and shivering.

"Go on, get back to work you lazy piece of shit. You lay down again on me I'll run this horse over you. Now move!"

With the help of those around him, Jack was just able to continue a semblance of work until the mid-day break. He collapsed after lining up and getting a chop of some boiled mystery meat and a stale chunk of bread. He ate only a single bite and gave the rest to those who had pulled his weight through the last hour. He drank from the metal cup and water bucket until another con warned him not to drink too much.

They called this meal eaten in the fields a 'John Henry' or a 'Johnny'. No one explained why. Jack had taken the small bottle back to the doctor the previous week and had it refilled. He had taken a small dose before work and now pulled the tiny bottle from his pocket in which he'd poured a healthy shot and slugged it down. In fifteen minutes the analgesic had taken effect and he was confident he could complete the day's work. He was bone weary, but at least no longer in pain. Laying back on the cold damp earth he was almost asleep when someone shook him.

"C'mon, let's go hit on it."

The squads lined up where they had left off. The air was fragrant with the rich earth and chopped plants, but Jack was many miles and years away. He envisioned his happy life with the woman he loved so dearly. Her mischievous smile, her long-legged walk, her insightful wit and her long, funny stories. Theirs had been a hard life, but now he was remembering only the happiness. All the pain of yesterday and today was comforted by the kind ministration to his mind and body by the medicinal magic.

"Hey Newboot! Come back here."

One of the strikers told him, "He's talking to you Williams."

Jack pointed to his chest questionably as he looked at the old guard on his horse.

"Yea, I'm talkin' to you. Drop that aggie and come 'ere."

As Jack approached Two Gone put his hand on his pistol and said, "Get that hat off."

When Jack got about ten feet from Two Gone, he backed his horse.

"That's close enough ol' thang. You ain't lookin too good convict, kinda pale. Been inside a cell too long, ain't cha'? Looks like yer ready to fall out on me. You get with Collie here, my striker, and you strike with him this afternoon. Jes stay on yer feet, an' if some of the brass rides over here, act busy. Collie, you show him what to do."

"Yessir boss."

Collie waived him over. Jack retrieved his aggie and joined the old convict behind the squad.

"We'll carry your row 'til we get out of this cut."

He and Jack, mostly he, flattened everything standing in the row, sidestepping and chopping.

"What you do man, is look for weeds the swing has missed and cut 'em at the ground or just stomp 'em so they lay down and look cut. Like that ol' son of a bitch said, just take it easy this afternoon. Takes a few days to get used to this shit."

Jack was surprised that the field boss had given him any slack. Two Gone had been hollering and screaming all morning, cussing the prisoners, telling them how lazy and sorry they were and how he was going to have these rows clean or he was going to whip somebody's ass. Not that the skinny old man could whip anyone in the squad, but every prisoner, with few exceptions, had been beat up by a gang of guards, some for what they called 'slow bucking' or not working hard enough to suit them. Many had been beaten or suffered whippings, thrown in a dark cell and subjected to several more beatings over a period of days through which they were fed just enough to keep them alive. Those torturous solitary cells were ice boxes in winter and the steel and stone was an oven through the Texas summer. They stripped you naked and you slept on the floor. All you had in the quiet, dark cell was a bucket for human waste and sometimes a water bucket. The silent suffering in the darkness fostered fear that the guards, or worse, the inmate guards, would come again to beat you and endlessly torture you. It drove some prisoners to insanity. And it filled many with a murderous rage and hate.

Jack became aware that Two Gone's screaming and cussing directly related to the proximity of the field major or captain. The closer they got the crazier Two Gone acted and the harder the squad worked. Everyone was more relaxed when they were away from the major and captain. Most of that first afternoon the snuff-dipping reprobate let his horse just stumble along behind them, allowing them to work at a slow, rambling pace. As they toiled, the steel hit the ground in a syncopated rhythm and a mesmerizing humming developed in Jack's ears. Feet shuffling through the brush and dirt, intermittent groans and some of suffering and hopelessness some tenor seemed to sing from a place very far away lulled Jack into a walking slumber where snatches of visions and recollection of life's best and worst moments drifted through his mind. His body ached pleasurably, muscles moving his meat and bone without thought. Thought was suspended, surrendered to the subconscious flow of dreams and memories of events that never happened in his life and of people he had never known. It was a strange and enjoyable suspension between sleep and waking, between reality and imagining, a pleasant confusion of this life with another.

The spell was broken as the file boy yelled, "Hat time!" Jack looked up to see the major sitting on his horse atop the turn-row in the distance waving his hat above his head as the cold, dim sun sank behind him.

"Let's go. It's hat-time. Work's done," Collie told him.

Somehow he made the march back to the Walls, leaning on his new friend at times. At the back gate Jack watched the other prisoners and followed their lead. They stripped naked and passed by the guards in a double line, being counted as they re-entered the prison. Their sweaty, muddy clothes and brogans they presented to the guards who pretended to search them for contraband. The guards averted their eyes mostly when the inmates went through the drill of showing the bottom of their feet, under their arms and between their buttocks. Hurrying to several troughs of water they quickly washed the worst parts, dressing without drying in the same dirty clothes, all the while suffering or ignoring the screaming obscenities of the guards urging them to finish.

Jack wasn't hungry but was funneled into the chow hall with the other members of his squad. He ate part of a cat-head and drank a cup of milk, giving Collie the rest of his food. Hurrying to the cellblock he stood impatiently in front of his cell on the catwalk waiting for the guard to come and lock him in. Ezekial sat on his bunk behind the bars eyeing him, asking how his first day went and other small talk. Jack grunted answers and silently cursed the lazy turnkey who took his sweet time ambling down to let him in the cell. Finally, the guard locked the door behind him and walked away. Jack toed his sweat-soaked brogans off and asked Ezekial, "Where's the bottle?"

Ezekial stood and took the bottle from his pocket. Jack snatched it from him and took a quick taste, grimaced, then took another sip. Gathering his strength, he climbed up onto the upper bunk.

"Want me to re-wrap yer ribs?" Ezekial asked.

"They took the wraps away from me when they stripped us down after work."

"Yea. They would. You hurtin' bad?"

But Jack was asleep. Exhausted. His hand clutched the small, corked bottle. Ezekial took it from his hand.

After breakfast next morning, Ezekial again wrapped Jack's sore ribs in strips of an old sheet he had torn. When the work whistle blew Jack patted the shirt pocket where he had placed the tiny bottle containing an opiate dose for mid-day. He had already partaken of a measure of the laudanum to get him through the long morning of hard work.

Prisoners were not paid for the tedious often back-breaking work, they were effectively slaves owned by the state. The prison system itself was self-sufficient, producing even more than it consumed and lining the pockets of numerous state officials, superintendents and legislators. Many state congressmen and senators had owned land worked by prisoners leased from the state and had grown wealthy by this legal slavery which they created. Many luxuries were obtained by state employees through the sweat of convicts and tradition and the practice of corruption was passed down from generation to generation. Privately owned slavery had been condemned as evil and outlawed, but the same abolitionists who had decried the institution of slavery and sent hundreds of thousands of innocent young men to their deaths to ensure its end continued to reap riches from the toil of slaves that they, the 'government' owned and managed. These sophistic politicians hid their greed behind specious and selfish argument using the public's disdain of criminals as justification to design punishment that would ultimately enrich themselves.

The next fortnight passed in much the same routine with Jack sleeping most of the time that he wasn't working. He was healing naturally and the work made possible by the efficient analgesic was increasing his strength and endurance. Ezekial wasn't required or allowed to work. He was viewed by prison administration to be too high a risk, too hard to control. He was assessed to be prone to violence because of his conviction and prison record, and also because of his size and fierce countenance, when, in fact, he was a gentle man. Ezekial did, however, detest bullies and had stepped in on numerous occasions to stop abuse and cruelties.

Ezekial was present in the small cell most of every day, but weather permitting, he did go out to the prison yard in the mornings or early afternoons when allowed. He enjoyed lifting his eyes to the sky there, viewing the only part of nature that could be seen from inside the Walls. He saw majesty, grace and freedom in the huge, floating clouds and a portion of the grand design of creation. Often he was blessed to see birds and rarely a rainbow presented itself and he felt a welling of thankfulness and blessing to view such rare wonders. He yearned to see a tree. The memories of the meadows in bloom with wildflowers seemed a million years ago. A million miles away.

Mostly other prisoners left him alone. If someone did speak to him he usually either ignored them or stared at them in such a manner as to discourage discourse. He had a particular place at which he sat, outside the hospital on a brick planter wall in which nothing grew. Sam had his place there beside him and if someone stood there Ezekial would tell them, "You're in Sam's place. Please move." The words were polite but weren't a request and the trespasser knew it. Ezekial would sit there talking to Sam, petting him, watching him. Other convicts would make jokes about him, out of his hearing.

Once in a blue moon the prison chaplain, the captain or the assistant superintendent would stop and speak with Ezekial and Sam. Ezekial treated them the same as he treated convicts, ignoring them politely. He knew they all believed him insane, but they were usually kind so Ezekial did not want to be rude and would stare at them silently, sometimes grunting one-syllable answers until they went away.

The Chaplain advised Ezekial that if he wanted people to believe him sane and safe enough to be released from prison someday, he needed to give up his childish fantasy of an invisible friend and pet. Ezekial advised the Chaplain that he didn't care if he got out of prison or not, that he was ready to go with Sam wherever they could go together. The Chaplain told Ezekial Sam wasn't real, that if he was real others could see him. Ezekial answered that he could say the same about God. The Chaplain gave up, telling Ezekial he would pray for him. Ezekial thanked him and promised he would pray for the Chaplain also.

Jack had made a friend who worked with him in the fields. They drank the wine they surreptitiously made, played poker and dominoes together and sometimes shared the laudanum he purchased from the doctor. This friend was named Edward Feltz, but everyone called him 'Hoss.' Ezekial wouldn't drink or take drugs, but he would allow Jack and Hoss to sit with him on the yard and share tales of their pasts. Sometimes they were joined by Collie, the striker in Jack's squad.

Hoss was a man blessed, or cursed, with an exceptional large penis, thus the nickname. Several times prison guards had stopped Edward and asked him what he was smuggling in his bulging pants. He would answer "That's all me Boss." The unconvinced guard would order him to lower his britches. When Hoss complied and the large organ sprang into view the guard would jerk his head away, cover his eyes and holler, "Put that thang up!" It's was highly entertaining for the informed convicts and knowing guards to watch this particular strip search. Never again would a guard thusly embarrassed and shocked ask to search the Hoss' person.

Because of this hesitancy of guards to search him Hoss was utilized to smuggle sugar and fruit from the kitchen for brewing wine. He also smuggled meat, potatoes and other edibles for snacks in the evenings and whatever else was needed to be moved past the hacks in the prison. Some officers would turn away and shake their heads when they saw the Hoss coming. A rookie guard once asked Hoss,

"Feltz, how come they call you Hoss? You ain't that big. Do you work with horses or something?" Hoss answered by exposing his physical anomaly. The young guard acted as if Hoss were invisible from that day forward.

One Sunday at suppertime Jack and Hoss had arranged to pick up five pounds of sugar in the chow hall to make three gallons of wine. Behind Jack and under the table, Hoss stuffed the cloth-wrapped bundle down his trousers, pulled it up tight against his crotch and tied it to his belt. Jack walked in front of Hoss leaving the chow hall past the scrutinizing eyes of their nemesis Snyder, and another guard. Ezekial and Sam were bringing up the rear as they followed the single file of prisoners back to the cellblock.

Looking back, Jack saw Snyder looking down at the floor, then hurrying down the line of walking convicts and looking down again at the floor. Snyder's eyes caught Jack's eyes and he began to chase them, yelling, "Stop right there Williams!"

Jack told Ezekial, "Block those guards Zeke!" then he increased his pace, "C'mon Hoss."

Ezekial turned around and stood looking back at the two running guards. The line of prisoners being pushed forward by the chasing, yelling guards, bunched up around the wide body of Ezekial in the narrow passage. Ezekial bent over and picked up Sam and said, "Are you talkin' to me bossman?" his hand cupped beside his ear. He really did look confused.

In the turmoil, Jack pointed out to Hoss the perfect trail of sugar the leaking package was pouring from his pants leg.

"Give it to me when I get in the cellblock," Jack told Hoss and he hurried ahead as Hoss began untying and freeing the diminished package. Jack stepped quickly by the turnkey at the door to the cellblock and back along the wall of bars to Hoss, who handed the leaking bundle through. Jack went to the desk sitting beside the barred cell block door and slipped the remaining sugar into the turnkey's lunchbox as he stood in the door trying to see what the uproar in the hall was about.

Jack hollered, "Ezekial! Come here!"

Ezekial then allowed the crowd of convicts and the two pursuing guards to push by him. Snyder kept his burning eyes on the winding trail of white, pushing prisoners aside. He followed the trail of sugar through the bars across the cellblock floor and to the desk. His broad, hyena smile transformed into a gaping frown as he stared at the turnkey's lunchbox. He jerked open the lunchbox, snatched the leaking remains of the sugar and held it up, glaring at the turnkey.

The dumb, hayseed turnkey stuttered, "Sh... Sh... shhugar!"

The laughter drowned out most of his denials, but Snyder was screaming, "Get in your cells! Rack up! Now! Real funny fellers. We'll see who gets the last laugh. I'm gonna get you wino sons of bitches! Rack up!"

The poor, dumb turnkey was forever after know as 'Ol'Sh-Sh-Shugar'

Chapter Four

In my beginning is my end.
T.S. Eliot

It is only rarely that one can see in a little boy the promise of a man, but one can almost always see in the little girl the threat of a woman.
Alexander Dumas

It is better to be the widow of a hero than the wife of a coward.
Delores Ibarruri

THE WELCOME SEPTEMBER night air pushed through the lace curtains and cooled the young girls as they lay under the rag quilt their grandmother had made. Whispers and yawns fought the drowsiness that drew them to their dreams.

"Sallie, when do you think we're leaving?"

"Soon as Momma gets everything ready Nellie, there's still a lot to do.

"Has she got to pack everything?"

"No silly, we can't take all our stuff. I mean all the stuff she has to do. She has to get the money from the man who's buying the farm and do a bunch of stuff with lawyers and bankers and papers. She has to decide what to take, what to sell and she had to buy a bunch of stuff for the trip."

"Like what?"

"I don't know. Like horses to replace the ones the armies took. And get the wagon fixed. Stuff like that."

"How far is it to Texas? How long will it take to get there?"

"It'll take a long time. It's about a zillion miles."

"A zillion miles?"

"Well, maybe not a zillion. But far, far away."

"Will we have friends in Texas?"

Yes, We'll have lots of friends in Texas. People won't hate us because Daddy was an officer in the Yankee army."

"Daddy was a ossifer? I thought he was a captain."

"Officer, not ossifer. An officer and a captain are the same thing."

"Will there be lots of girls there like us?"

"Yep. There'll be lots of girls. And boys."

"I don't care about boys."

"Well, maybe later on you will."

"Will we live on a farm there? Will there be a school?"

"Will you hush? Go to sleep. We've got to get up early and help Momma get ready to go to town in the morning."

"Okay Sallie. Goodnight. Sleep tight. Don't let the bed bugs bite."

"Goodnight Nellie, sleep tight, don't let the bed bugs bite."

They hugged softly and shifted on the feather mattress, curled like kittens.

In the parlor of the well built farmhouse sat the girls' mother on a couch, feet pulled up, reclining with a pencil and a piece of paper on a book. She made notes on a 'things to do' list. She wanted to not forget anything while she was in town tomorrow. The people shunned her because her husband had followed his conscience and had enlisted as an officer in the Union army. Many of the residents in and around this area of West Virginia had fought for or had relatives and friends who had fought for the South. Her family, even the innocent girls, were treated as traitors.

She had managed to sell the fine farm they had built for a good price and the banker had obviously spread the word, for all the merchants were now very friendly. She had thirty days to evacuate these premises that held such bittersweet memories and she wanted to get started for Texas before the cold, wet weather came. She could move north, but there were so many fleeing there, black and white, that she thought refugees there would come to be resented. Besides, her husband Phillip had convinced her that they should move to Texas after the hostilities, that they would ever be held in contempt here in the country they had loved so well. Together they had constructed a dream of a life on a ranch in Texas where land could be had for a song. The girls could grow up in a healthy atmosphere of hope and freedom and prosperity instead of the exclusion, hate and distrust each of them experienced here. Fate would have it that Phillip had been captured, wounded and made a prisoner of war. He had died in Andersonville before the war ended. She would not allow their dream to die, or her love.

Callie had traveled to Washington with her daughters and sought audiences with congressmen and senators, bureaucrats in the War Department and with any and everyone who might try to help her husband while he was a prisoner. There had been promises and rumors of prisoner exchanges which would free Phillip. Word had come with an exchanged Union soldier that her beloved husband had succumbed of his wounds and the hellish conditions at the Confederate prison in Andersonville.

Her heart broken, she did not allow this news to break her spirit. She determined to continue and fulfill their dreams. For Phillips memory and in his honor she would realize their dreams. And for their dear daughters. When she put the farm up for sale land speculators tried to take advantage of her but soon gave up in disgust. She was smart, and she was stubborn. After months of haggling with several potential buyers, she had been blessed to show the well-developed farm to a reasonable and honest man who had offered her a very generous price. She accepted the offer, despite her fear of the great journey that lay before her and her girls, she refused to be intimidated by the distance and hardships that separated her from the dreams she still held dear.

As she nodded over the notes that she had made, she awoke to the soft voice of her faithful, oldest daughter Sallie. "Momma, shouldn't you go to bed? Long day tomorrow."

"Yes, darling, I'll go to bed. Goodnight Sweety. Sleep tight."

"Don't let the bed bugs bite."

They exchanged sleepy smiles at the familiar conclusion of their days. Tender smiles remained as they drifted into slumber.

The air seemed so clear and clean next morn as Callie drove the single team to town. Atop the hills it seemed they could see until the globe dipped down out of sight. She felt sure in this glorious dawning that she had made the right decision, that their future was filled with promise. Even the birds seemed exuberantly happy and charged with the energy of faith and trust. The colorful leaves on the trees seemed to chuckle in the breeze and the daughters of her loins were vibrant and angelic in their beauty.

The foul-humored liveryman became agreeably optimistic that he could indeed provide her with a large freight wagon as well as the yoke and harness for a double team to go with it within a reasonable time. She also required two more teams of strong horses so she could give each team a rest every other day, as well as another team of horses for the smaller wagon. She wanted an extra wheel for each wagon, water barrels, axle grease and wanted to ensure all the horses were well shod. She was well aware that the sour-smelling liveryman had never agreed with her family's politics, she knew it was the money she had to spend that caused him to be so uncharacteristically pleasant. Still, she was grateful she had the funds in this post-war economy with the sale of the farm. Money caused even the hateful to be less so.

After completing her business with the cobbler and with the bank she went to the appointment with a man she might hire to help her with preparation for the move. He came recommended by the leather worker whom she had ordered tack and boots from for the trip. The cobbler had told her that he had hired the man for certain jobs at various times through the past several months, but did not need him nor could he afford him full time. He had found the man honest, conscientious, capable and stronger than his lean body suggested. He had prepared her for the man's subdued, placid manner and his appearance. Gaunt actually, and his face was long, dominated by a long thin nose. The wrinkles in his leathery cheeks were mostly hidden by the long, graying beard. A receding hairline made his face seem even longer. That face revealed little emotion, only heavily lidded eyes covering deep and dark orbs hinted at wisdom and hid a measure of mischief residing within him. His answers to her question were usually single syllables, polite enough and not appearing purposely secretive, yet not amenable to unreserved revelation of his history. Not that she would ascribe even a hint of deception about his quiet nature and character, he simply seemed contained and of a serene and thoughtful nature.

The cobbler had advised her of his missing right ear and when he had removed his floppy old hat when entering the restaurant she had been prepared for the scarf tied around his head covering the missing ear. She wondered if he wore the scarf to cover his shame or so not to offend others. Or perhaps it was necessary to protect the hole from infection. He wore a long sleeved shirt and heavy britches held up with suspenders. His shoes were old and stiff, the soles meticulously re-stitched to keep them attached to the uppers. Bare flesh was visible through holes in the thin old leather.

He did not stink. His clothes and person were obviously well washed. His hair was long as was his beard and neatly combed. His teeth were long and sound. His gaze was penetrating, attentive and not uncomfortable. It was a respectful, compassionate and candid look and it made her feel he was genuine and reliable.

He carried a knapsack over his shoulder, neither bowed nor proud, simply natural and unassuming. His hands were clean, fingers short and stout.

She decided she would hire him temporarily to help her prepare for the move to Texas and would evaluate him further. She wanted to be sure he was safe for her children before she sought to employ him to accompany them on the long journey. It would be best to have a man along in these unsettled times, when there were so many homeless and desperate souls in the South. And it would be necessary to have another adult drive the second wagon carrying their belongings. This traveling employment would be much more acceptable to someone who was not tied to home and family.

After the coffee, she called the girls inside the restaurant from the street where they had been enjoying the simple pastime of watching the people pass by. She ordered a mid-day meal for each of them, an especially substantial serving for her new employee.

She introduced the girls to Luther and watched in surprise as his stony face broke itself into a smile. It wasn't a tooth baring, deliriously happy smile, but a grin that moved his whiskers and made his furrowed eyes sparkle. It was a look of gentle favor and affection and it made her instinctively trust and like the man. The children plainly absorbed his kind and protective aura and made him their friend. They began to pester him with questions and she was a bit perturbed that the girls got more conversation out of him than she had. The soft, kind grin never left his face while the children were present. His attention from them was only distracted by the arrival of the steaming plate of steak, potatoes and hot biscuits to which he focused mind and body until the plate was clean. He wasn't ill-mannered in his obvious hunger, just a bit hasty. The children ate a few bites of their dinner then began peppering Luther with questions until she bade them cease. She noticed him peeking at their half-eaten plates and she told the girls to finish their meal. They complained it was too much food and they were full. She expressed how she hated to see food go to waste and asked Luther if he could finish eating their meal. Without shame, he grinned and complied, thanking them all.

She took him to the cobbler after eating and found a pair of boots that fit him. He loaded supplies at the mercantile into the wagon and drove the team home at her direction. Along the way she explained her plans to move to Texas and detailed all the work that must be done in preparation. Along with the land and buildings she had sold most of the implements, tools and furniture. Some valued furniture and a few trunks were to be packed, loaded on the wagon and transported along with them. She wanted him to repair and prepare the wagon she had now while another larger wagon she had purchased was being readied. She confided in him that she realized she was probably intent on keeping too much she couldn't part with.

There was a small room her husband had built in a corner of the barn and she installed him there when they arrived. After unloading what needed to be in the house, he drove the wagon to the barn and unloaded the rest of the supplies there. He unhooked, fed and watered the horses, then curried and combed them. He repaired a corral gate and was raking the floor of the barn when she had the girls call him for supper. She noticed him washing his hands and face from the bucket beside the well. He combed his hair and beard with a piece of comb he carried in a shirt pocket as she watched through the window. He stomped dust from his new boots before tapping on the door.

The girls ran to let him in, each taking a hand and pulling him to the place they had set for him at the table across from them. She smiled sorrowfully when she saw the girls had left their father's customary place at the head of the table bare and set Luther's place across from them. They had loved their Poppa so much, no one could ever take his place. She blinked back the tears. Much practice had made her adept in the continuing struggle against the sorrow, loneliness and loss.

"Did Old Hickory, the big white gelding give you any problems?"

"A little. He was hungry. Tried to taste me."

The girls giggled. Callie smiled.

"He's always hungry. He'll eat until he founders if he can get to oats or corn."

"I put the sacks in the storeroom where he can't get to them."

"Good. Let's say grace girls."

Everyone bowed their heads while she said a short prayer and immediately after amen the girls started passing food to Luther. He could barely get one platter or bowl passed to Callie before taking another being pushed toward him. Mashed potatoes, cream gravy, corn, okra, ham, beans and biscuits with butter. Luther slowed his eating only to briefly answer the girls incessant questions or grunt and appropriate response to one of their tales. Callie told the girls to let the man eat, then they could talk. Luther grinned in gratitude.

After cleaning his plate Sallie tried to pass him some more ham and biscuits. He held his hands out and shook his head, "No thank you Sallie, I ain't Old Hickory."

The girls giggled and began clearing the table without being told. Callie brought him a cup of coffee and led him out to the porch so he could smoke. He dug out a short, oft-smoked stogie that made Callie wrinkle her nose at the smell. She made a mental note to pay him so he could buy some fresh cigars next time they were in town.

After finishing washing the dishes and putting things in their places the girls joined the two adults on the porch. The full bellies, the long day and the cooling air of the gloaming served together to make them all slumberous. She asked the girls to get Luther clean bedding for the bunk in the barn, he thanked her and yawned as he stumbled to the barn in his new boots. Callie had been hoping for a bit of polite conversation before bedtime, but sighed, went inside and changed into her bedclothes. Maybe tomorrow she could learn something of Luther's history.

The mother and daughters went through their normal pattern of questions and answers, then each read a few verses from the huge, old family Bible. They had repeated their routine for hundreds of evenings. The girls had enhanced their reading skills this way and their sleep was comforted by the Word.

Luther spread the fresh linen and the clean blanket neatly over the narrow, homemade bunk and mattress. He sat down, removed the boots and smelled the new leather and smiled. Removing his clothes down to his long underwear, he fluffed up the feather pillow and stretched out. Before he slept he enjoyed a feeling of peace, a feeling of coming home. He was grateful. So grateful. It had been so long since he felt like he belonged, like someone cared. It felt like family. It felt so good.

The weeks leading up to the MacGillicuddy's exodus were busy and productive. Luther didn't work hastily enough to suit Callie, but worked at his own pace and did each job well. Callie purchased a double team with the big freight wagon as well as extra horses. The big wagon was outfitted with water barrels on the outer sides, extra wheels beneath and a double brake. The tailgate could be lowered to use as a counter top in preparation of meals or to repair harness, etc. A shotgun and a rifle were secured under the seat of both wagons.

The smaller wagon was fitted with planks that could be laid over the high sides to cover the boxes and supplies and on which a mattress was laid for the ladies to sleep on. Callie sewed curtains for front and back of the canvas cover. A chamber pot was taken along for those times when it might be expedient to avoid adjacent brush to relieve themselves.

After the first week Callie felt she could trust Luther and asked him if he would hire on to complete the move to Texas with them. He readily agreed, he had no other opportunities and he thoroughly enjoyed being around all the girls. It seemed that, after his inclusion in the move, he became more approachable and a bit more communicative. His quiet nature remained, but the single syllable replies came less frequently. The children grew quickly fond of him and their chirping and chattering left little opportunity for anyone's mutterings anyway.

Callie tried to keep the girl's attention focused on the trip and not let their thoughts linger on leaving the only home they had ever known and memories of the loving times they had shared there with their father. She was successful in this until the morning they left when both Sallie and Nellie grew quiet, shed tears and went to their mother to be held. She reminded them that their father had wanted them to move on and, that they were not leaving him, that he would always be with them, in love and spirit. And soon their tears were gone, replaced by the excitement and exuberance of youth.

As little Nellie rode beside her mother she softly asked "Momma, are you going to marry Luther?"

"No! Nellie! Whatever made you think that?"

"Well, he's going to Texas with us."

"As an employee. As a friend. We needed a man to drive the big wagon and to help with the heavy work."

"I just don't want a new daddy."

"Sweetheart, you will never have another daddy. Phillip MacGillicuddy will always be your daddy. So don't worry about that, baby."

"I'm glad Momma."

They all smiled at one another on the wagon seat and hugged. And they all felt so close and so sweet a love. Each of them began then to realize the possibilities of adventure before them down the long road they had just begun to travel.

Noah Lister rode the big red roan down the narrow, dusty street and exulted in the feeling of simply being in the saddle again. The new saddle squeaked with stiffness, but the polished, new leather atop the thick colorful blanket on the skittish, young stallion pleased him. He had adjusted the length of the right stirrup twice to fit his stiff leg and despite his efforts, his position still felt awkward. He realized that at some distance down the trail to Texas his wounded body and this new rigging and horse would adjust, adapt and become familiar.

Brandy had washed his butternut uniform and stitched the split leg and torn cuffs, but he didn't wear his Confederate clothes. He had decided to buy new clothes while he had the money and put the past in the past. Captain Lister of the Texas Cavalry, Confederate Army was finished. Captain Lister of the Texas Rangers was also finished. He was now simply Noah Lister, private citizen, returning home to Texas.

Except he had no home. He'd been homeless since he'd been orphaned as a boy. The rangers had been his home, his family, for many years, then the war came and he had joined the glorious, hopeless cause. He was returning to Texas because maybe he still had friends there. There might be some who remembered him, respected him. These southern states he had traversed these past years were foreign to him, like whole other countries. And these southern states had suffered, terribly. There remained a few remnants of natives who were trying to hold on and rebuild the life they knew before, but it was not to be. They resented the victors who seemed to be always in their business, they resented the recently freed whose unrestrained behavior taunted them and they even resented the poor and hungry beaten and tired former friends and Confederates like himself who, for various reasons, still hung around.

His reason for remaining past his welcome was obvious in his wounds. He had been wounded in his shoulder, chest and knee. The Yankee lead had not been removed in the hasty retreat and he had been left behind at the goodhearted prostitute's shack. If not for Brandy, he would have died in the meat wagon beside the other corpses during the retreat. She had dug the ball and the bullet from his shoulder and knee with only whiskey for anesthetic. The lead in his chest had passed out his back. He had coughed up blood for a fortnight, but now could breath deep without coughing. His only medicine had been whiskey and Brandy's human compassion.

At several stores in town he made purchases. He bought a couple of sets of new clothes, hat, boots, socks, underwear, handkerchiefs, a new repeating rifle and a holster for his Colt pistol. He visited a barber and got a bath, haircut and shave, leaving his wide gray mustache. His pain then directed him to the nearest saloon to medicate himself.

After an hour of drinking the pain of his wounds ceased. He paid for three bottles of the only available whiskey and strode out to the waiting roan. Riding to the livery barn he rented a little wagon and left his new horse there. At Brandy's shack he hustled the young hoyden out to the wagon. She giggled at his drunken and happy demeanor and was pleased at how much more healthy and handsome he looked with new clothes, a haircut and shave. He appeared much younger than his fifty years. He made her feel as young as she was.

He drove her to dress stores, shoe stores and other establishments where he bought her dresses and shoes and groceries and provisions. He bought her linens and towels and blankets and bonnets and shawls. He bought her coats and corsets and underwear, necklaces and earrings, powders and perfume. Over her protest, he filled the wagon with gifts for her. He parked the loaded wagon before a restaurant and gave a loitering black tyke two bits to watch the wagon and promised him more when he returned.

Noah had plans to get back to Texas and set himself up in some enterprise with the money he had relieved blue-coat prisoners of through the war. He had a sack of greenbacks and gold, he had taken many prisoners. The 'money' the Confederate government had printed and paid them would buy little but laughter. He was enjoying treating and rewarding the young woman who had saved his life, and he had enough money to spare.

The proprietor and waiter were not comfortable that he had escorted a town whore into their upstanding establishment. A few customers whispered behind their hands, but none ventured to speak any objection after viewing the demons dancing in the man's eye, the Colt hanging low on his hip and the swagger in his stride. Noah was feeling no pain, feeling alive again and eager for a challenge. Perhaps that is what motivated him to take Brandy on his arm into the most pretentious excuse for a high society restaurant in the second class city, maybe the old devil that had always pushed him to prove himself and to humble the hypocrites and shame the shams had once again entered him in the whiskey. And how he enjoyed it!

He held a chair while she seated herself then snapped a finger at the waiter.

"A bottle of your finest wine for the lady and your best whiskey for the Confederate hero and don't be slow about it."

He ordered the waiter to expound on the fancily printed menu that was partially in a language that surely was not English and when he faltered and began to stutter in reply to the interrogation, Noah called for the cook. The cook was most accommodating in his descriptions of the dishes they would prepare after accepting the sawbuck his new patron offered. Noah whispered to the cook that he feared the waiter might spit in their food and asked if the cook might be kind enough to serve each dish, to which request the chef readily agreed.

Noah's affected courtly manner and the vintage wine made Brandy giggle and some of the other diners smiled at his speech and antics. Others frowned, whispered behind their hands and hastily exited. It was the most fun she'd had in years, perhaps the most fun she'd ever had. At least she couldn't recall a happier time. Her memory was a mirror of misery which reflected only the still open wounds from a life of neglect, poverty and abuse. She'd never known her father and from her mother she had learned at an early age that she was a creature for others to use for their base desires and that she should accept whatever remuneration they may or may not proffer.

She estimated that she was twenty. She might be twenty three or seventeen or some age in between. Her mother had abandoned her before she attained puberty and she'd been taken from the cruel streets of New York by the strong arms of a traveling salesman who sold her from the North to the South. After around three years the bestial vendor of flesh was murdered in an argument with a drunken crew in Baltimore and she was 'free'. Knowing no life but that she had lived, she sold the trinkets from the salesman's wagon until highwaymen took the wagon from her and left her, raped and naked beside a lonely country road.

A passing farmer and his good wife covered her with a blanket, took her to their home, clothed and fed her and tended her wounds. The two of them preached to her that she had reaped what she sowed, that she had received the just deserts for her sin. The concept of sin was confusing to her. She was given an old blanket and allowed to sleep in the barn. Since they believed that idleness was the tool of the devil, she was worked from dawn to dusk, then listened to the old man read from the good book before being sent to the barn every night.

When the reprobate farmer woke her in the darkness with his calloused old claws on her young body, it scared her. If she had been awake and prepared for this she would probably have allowed him to have his way with her as so many other men had, but that particular night fear and hate and revulsion gave her strength and she reached for the pitchfork she'd used earlier and pushed the tines deep into his flesh. She took the old plow horse from his stable and mounted his bare back digging in her heels and hanging onto his mane as she rode away beneath the harvest moon.

At the end of the next day she had sold the old horse and bought food and a train ticket to "as far as the money will take me", and when she arrived there she got a 'job' in a saloon. She had survived through suffering the degradations and cravings of the crass. She took no pleasure in it and felt as much shame in milking her customers as a dairymaid would in relieving the cows of their swelling.

And then in the last days of the war the retreating, defeated scarecrows brought the bloody, dying man to her and laid him in her bed at her tiny shack on the edge of town. She screamed at them and fought with them, but they ignored her. The last soldier out the door told her the wounded man was slowing them down and would get them all killed. He'd probably die anyway, but would surely die in the bouncing bed of the wagon in their hell-bent retreat. He asked her to do what she could for him and then ran to join the others.

She had no idea how to help him. She went to the old saloon-keeper and he told her what to do, his ancient eyes were not up to the task. With rye whiskey, a lantern, a knife and spoon, and a needle and thread she did a rough but adequate job of it. She was surprised that he survived.

She stayed in the shack and nursed him, fed him and stared at him for hours, for days. And then one day he moaned and opened his eyes. His eyes were brown. She had wondered about that.

From that day, or perhaps even before, her affection for him had grown. Maternal instinct, a yearning for a father figure, pity and compassion, whatever else it was, it was love. And the more they talked as he lay almost helpless, the more her tender attachment grew. She helped him eat, tended his wounds, empathized with his pain and frustration, even helped him use the chamber pot despite his protests. She learned much from their long conversations and saw in his eyes, heard in his words and felt in her heart his gentle feelings for her. Soon, when he was able, on a sweet night she would always treasure she slipped out of her clothes and into the narrow bed with him.

He started to voice his objection but she shushed him with her delicate kisses. So slowly they shared their love and she was surprised by her hunger for him and by her pleasure. She finally understood the phrase 'making love'.

In the morning she laughed at his regret and embarrassment and exulted in her conquest. She knew he loved her and now understood what love was. He was uncomfortable in the differences in their ages, possibly thirty years. He felt he had allowed himself to take advantage of her. He wanted to treat her like a young woman, like a dear friend and not like a whore as other men had treated her. But through her bubbling excitement of first love, through the budding of her true womanhood and her persistence, her strong and true young love overcame his reservations. Still, he wanted the best for her and he knew he certainly wasn't best for her.

So, early in the morning after the shopping spree and dinner in the fancy restaurant, Noah gently left the bed they had shared and dressed. He glanced at her from time to time as he wrote a farewell letter. She was such a rare beauty. Her long dark hair fell in folds over her freckled shoulders and her full parted lips pouted even in her sleep. He hurriedly wrote the words he knew were falling far short of the emotions and thoughts that tore his heart because he knew that if she ever opened those heavily lashed deep brown eyes he would be lost.

He wrote "Brandy, I love you with all my heart, but I know I shouldn't love you like I do. You are young, your life is ahead of you, my life is behind me. Forget me. I've bought you the wagon and team. Take all your things, put them in your wagon and move to another place far away. Make yourself a new life. Don't sell your body to others anymore. Find a young man who loves you and will care for you. Have a wonderful life. Thanks for saving my life. Thanks for the memories. I must go before you wake. Please understand. Noah"

He folded a stack of greenbacks into the note and placed it on the small table. He looked at her lying there, so peacefully with the golden light of morning warming her. She was so very beautiful. So wonderful. But she deserved more than a busted down old drunk like him. Quietly he turned the doorknob, looked back once more at the angel who had saved him, blinked his burning eyes and walked out of her life.

He walked quickly to the livery and paid the man for the wagon and team, saddled the roan and loped him out of town, headed west. He rode steadily throughout the day, stopping only to rest and water the horse. He didn't eat, but drank one of the three bottles of whiskey he had purchased. After the sun set, he rode beneath the stars until the horse began to stumble. He found a grassy place under a tree and hobbled the stallion before he passed out with his boots and hat on, dead drunk.

Sam nudged Ezekial's leg with his head, diverting his attention from the letter. Sam was troubled by Ezekial's tears and he could smell Gramps on the paper and felt again the sense of loss. He stood placing his paws on Ezekial's thigh as he sat in the old rocker and licked away Ezekial's salty tears. With his big arm Ezekial hugged his faithful friend, looking far away to the horizon.

After a few readings he was able to absorb the words more dispassionately and objectively. Gramps had known his end was near. He had hoped he would see Ezekial come home before he died. Assuring his grandson of his faith that he would be waiting for him in a much better place after his passing, he urged Ezekial not to let sorrow rule him, but to build his own life, taking those things he may have learned from him and honoring him by applying them to his life.

Gramps went on to say that he had been tied to the land by the necessities of supporting a family. Not that he regretted his life, he had loved his family and enjoyed his life, but he wanted more for Ezekial. He wanted him to sell the farm, travel west, see the country, build his own life and not be tied to the past. He wrote that his family was gone, the little graveyard contained only bones and he should be free from chains binding him to relive his grandfather's life.

Gramps was sure he could get a good price because they had built a fine farm on God's rich earth. The brothers at the church had promised him they would help him get a fair price, some had made Gramps offers to buy the farm. But, he wanted Ezekial to make the decision when he felt comfortable with it. He remembered how travel and adventure had called to him in his own youth and he knew only sad memories, loneliness and yearnings to escape would haunt Ezekial if he remained. The farm had been Gramps' life, Ezekial should seek out his own.

Ezekial knew Gramps was right. He did feel the urge to wander, the longing to see what was over the next hill. And memories of happier days in the past did come to mind often and linger at every fence post they had set together, every tree and field, every foot of the house, yard and road. Every day and night bittersweet memories beset him. Every sight, sound, smell and touch recalled the dead. And now, the fresh wounding of his young and tender heart with the loss of Cynthia from his life, he had added cause to find another life in another place.

His thoughts began to wing over the places he could go. He could go anywhere, to Oregon, California, Wyoming, even Alaska. There was a soldier friend who had invited him to come to Texas, a small man of Mexican origin, Samuel Chavez. They had fought together, side by side trudged through eighteen hour marches, shared what little food they could scrape together and spoke of home through the dark days and cold nights. Through all the trials of war, the big and the little man had become fast friends. Ezekial thought of what it would be like to follow Gramps' counsel and journey to visit Samuel.

Sam stared up at Ezekial as he read the letter and studied his facial expressions as he stared out over the green and growing crops. He had watched him gaze at the paper as if there were something on it that Sam could not see or understand. In exasperation, Sam lifted his leg and pawed his friends large leg, gathering his attention, asking a question in his own way.

"Sam, you ready to do some traveling? Well, I believe you better get ready. We're gonna sell this ol' farm and go see the world! You ready buddy?" Ezekial laughed as Sam jumped up. Sam's one-sided grin and the wildly winking eye made him laugh all the more. Sam jumped straight up, spun and barked. He seemed ready to go forthwith. He didn't have to pack.

That evening the two friends walked over the farm together, absorbing the homely ambience of good black soil that fed the deep roots of the ever healthy plants. The strong trees, the waves of grass and flowers, the rustling of the crops, this was Gramps' legacy, this was the essence of the farm. For a long generation Gramps had nourished the family, the animals, the plants, the soil. He had been a true husbandman, faithful, loyal and true.

A life here with Sam would be good, but since experiencing Cynthia, his heart yearned for more. Sam was his constant companion but he longed for human companionship. He wanted someone to love. He needed a woman to care, someone to share life with. Perhaps it was a biological coming of age, maybe just natural emotional desire. He only knew he felt alone since Cynthia left. There was a wound in his heart that had not healed, an emptiness.

Throughout his days and nights thoughts came to mind of those he had lost. Mother, father, brothers, friends, Gramps, Cynthia, they had all left him. He grew ever closer to Sam. He was grateful that Sam remained.

The war, despite the horrors and hardships, had made him feel alive. He had seen new country, made new friends. Often the landscapes had become covered in corpses, some being his new friends, but in some ways it was a better life than this. There was an excitement, a thrill in living. Now life seemed drab, a tasteless existence.

The circumstances of war caused him to think for himself, make choices. He knew more of himself now, knew that what he 'felt' was right usually was even if it were not logical nor expedient. Gramps had told him it was wrong to own slaves or to believe one race or people had a God-given right to enslave another. Ezekial had never been around slavery in his childhood except when he saw Negroes in town or on the road so he had never given it much thought. His family, like the vast majority of white people in the South, owned no slaves but did their own work and supported their families by the sweat of their own brows.

The persuasive propagandists of the southern rich styled the struggle The War of Northern Aggression to mislead the proletariat and unread bourgeois into accepting the war as a defense of Southern property and honor. They promulgated deceitful half-truths like "states right" to cloak the more important issue of "human rights." They supported the pulpits that preached that the Holy Word of God ordained their right to enslave the descendants of Ham. Those men of God who taught otherwise were silenced. The soldiers of Dixie were duped into believing they fought for an honorable cause and that God was on their side, just as all soldiers have eternally been told.

Midweek he saddled a mule and went to discuss selling out to the Dunlap's. He showed Mr. Dunlap Gramps' letter and was told that Gramps had indeed discussed the sale with select members of the church. It was agreed that they would meet with those honest men after services on Sunday and discuss what might be done. Mr. Dunlap's son-in-law John Scott was happy to hear of Ezekial's decision, as everyone in the family seemed to be. They seemed more than happy actually, they seemed relieved.

On Sunday, Ezekial was somewhat distracted from Cynthia's absence by Sam. During the song service Sam was hamming it up outside of the window at the end of the pew where Ezekial sat. The dog was so absorbed by the music that he threw back his head and howled and even swayed in time with the rhythm. After each hymn he would smile his half smile and wink and blink the one eye as he panted and caught his breath. Ezekial had to choke back his laughter despite his intention to suffer in his sorrow of losing Cynthia.

The sermon was focused on the oath of Ruth of "whither thou goest, I will go..." and Ezekial imagined how wonderful it would be to have someone like that to love or to be loved by. And he never even thought to look to the window beside him where Sam sat patiently waiting for him, never realizing he was already blessed with such a love.

After the final amens, the Dunlap's and the elders gathered with Ezekial beneath the falling leaves in the churchyard. After discussion, it was agreed to meet at the Robertson farm the following Saturday to assess the worth of the place. The wives were consulted and persuaded to bring food to make a picnic. Ezekial looked forward to someone else's cooking.

He worked on the house, the barn, the fences and the fields all week, wanting the property to look as good as possible. Early Saturday morning he took a bath and put on the second set of new, clean work clothes. The families began arriving around ten o'clock, the women going right into the house. The men began gathering at the barn and when they had all arrived they began walking through it discussing their evaluations in lowered voices. They took the Dunlap's wagon as well as another and looked over the fields and fences, the water tank fed by the river, the corn crib and the smokehouse. Around one o'clock the women rang the dinner bell and the men gathered at the makeshift table beside the water well in the yard of the farmhouse.

Over plates of fried chicken and ham, potato salad and pinto beans, the women explained what must be done to the house to make it acceptable. Ezekial listened to plans of a nursery and perhaps another room later for other children. He thought of small children running around the farm and smiled, he knew John and Trinity Scott would make excellent parents and fine farmers. Gramps would be happy to have them here.

Trinity informed John of the paint and fabric needed to outfit the house. She was pleased with the house and excited with the prospect of making it theirs. It was old but well built and maintained. Trinity spoke as if it were her house already and John did not correct her, he liked what he'd seen also.

The banker, George Burnstein, began discussing sales of comparative properties in the county and after giving his opinions of the merits and short comings of the property, he gave an estimate of its worth. Other men gave their own appraisals and evaluations. Mr. Dunlap and John walked a ways apart and settled on an offer which was more than Mr. Burnstein had valued the property. Mr. Dunlap explained that they had tried to estimate a fair price for the standing crops.

A handshake sealed the deal and they agreed that transfer would be made at a date in October. Mr. Burnstein assured the parties he would provide sufficient cash by the time as Ezekial wanted half gold and half greenbacks. Trinity ran back into the house and began taking measurements for drapes and rugs with the help of other wives. The men were forced to cut and serve their own piece of pie and cobbler, which was a welcome hardship.

When the last wagon had left that afternoon, Ezekial turned to Sam on the porch and said, "Boy, we're going on a journey come October. We're going to Texas!" He did a little jig and Sam barked and danced around him. They felt the richness of youth and the joys of freedom and friendship. Life was sweet and full of promise.

The quiet of mid-morning and the late October sun glaring through the single window and through her closed eyelids caused her to awaken and roll away from the light. Her lethargic brain slowly registered she was alone in the bed and she squinted across the one-roomed shack to affirm he wasn't there. A dull headache caused a groan as she swung her feet onto the floor and she recalled the wine of the night before. A tiny smile moved her young lips as she remembered all else that had occurred last night.

Rising and stumbling to the wash stand she poured water into the bowl and washed her face and then her nude body. Drying with one of the new soft towels Noah had bought her, she breathed the clean, new smell. She noticed the folded paper bundle placed purposely on the table before her and a number of small denomination greenbacks fell out. It was a note signed by Noah. She studied the writing, then walked to the window and the light. She didn't read very well and Noah didn't write very well either, so her eyes traveled over the paper several times before she crumpled the note and fell back across the bed. She laid with her eyes tightly closed fighting the reality that he had left her. The cruel fact he was gone overcame her denial and permeated her reluctant consciousness.

Jumping to her feet, she spat out the words "That son of a bitch!" She quickly dressed haphazardly stomping into her boots as she tore out the door. She cornered one of the old mules in the small corral beside the shack and stuffed a bridle in his mouth and over his head and kicked her small heels into his ribs all the way to the livery. The liveryman stood in the door of the stables and watched the wild woman riding bareback on the frightened old mule head straight at him. She turned and reined the excited mule just before he would have jumped out of harm's way.

"What road did the old son of a bitch that paid you for the mules and wagon leave on?"

The liveryman quickly pointed down the road that led west.

"When did he leave?"

"About six this morning, just after sun up."

She turned the mule and kicked it into a trot heading back to the shack. By the time she rode the mule up to the corral she was talking to herself and fuming. Cursing the ungrateful old bastard, she began throwing clothes into trunks, boxing her meager belongings and food. In less than an hour she harnessed the stubborn Army mules, hitched them and backed the wagon to the shack. Throwing her possessions into the wagon's bed she continued to mumble angry thoughts. She placed the heavy old pistol close by under the seat. The liveryman heard her approach and witnessed her popping the reins over the mules backs, heading west.

"Woo-wee! I wouldn't want to be the man she's after! Or,… maybe I would." The liveryman smiled.

Perhaps ten miles down the road Brandy slowed the mules to a walk and began to think a bit more objectively. What if Noah was right in all he had written? When she was forty he would be about seventy, or dead. And she would be alone again. But what about the years between now and then, couldn't they have them? She loved him and it was easier to be ruled by love than logic. Should she pursue him? Could she force him to stay with her? Was it only their difference in age that caused him to leave? Did he love her? Yes, he did love her, she could see it in his eyes, feel it in his touch, hear it in his voice.

She stopped the wagon off the road beside a bridge and allowed the mules to drink. The silent stream reflected the gathering clouds, causing her to think of shelter. She knew the next town was still quite a ways and she could smell the coming rain. She felt a gathering chill in the breeze.

Regaining the road, she let the mules settle into a gait she felt they could sustain through the remaining day. She turned in the wagon seat and dug through a box of clothes for her coat and a hat. Soon, sporadic sprinkling rain hurried the mules as they plodded through the gathering gloom. The darkness had come when she approached lantern light in windows of a small community. She reined in the mules and set the brake before the first house she came to with a barn behind it. As she walked on the flat stone walkway to the covered porch a door opened framing an older lady in a housecoat.

"Ma'am, I like to rent a place in your barn tonight for my team, my wagon and me if you don't mind."

"Are you alone honey?"

"Yes ma'am."

"Girl, what are you doing out in this weather? Take off your shoes and step inside. Lordy, Lordy, it's too wet and cold to be going anywhere."

"Well, it was clear when I left home this morning."

"You've been on the road all day? Here take this towel Sweetie and stand here by the fire."

A stocky little man threw another log into the fireplace and stirred the coals.

"Well, truth is, my man run off and left me this morning and I was chasing him down. I suspect he's drunk."

"Sugar, if he run off and left you, is he worth chasing?"

"I don't know what I'll do when I catch him. I might just shoot him."

"I hope you won't do that. But right now, you need to get off those wet clothes and get warm. You got clothes out in the wagon?"

"Everything I own is in that wagon ma'am."

"Do you know where your night dress is?"

"Yes, everything I'll need is in the small orange trunk."

"Come on Roland, let's go out to the barn and take care of her team and get her some dry clothes. You stay right there by the fire missie."

"I'll come with you."

"No. There's no need for you to get back in that weather. Mind, you stay by the fire. We'll be right back."

She stood by the fire shivering turning one side then the other to the heat until the chill left her. She looked around her at the clean neat parlor and through a door to the dining room where the wooden tables and chairs were polished and the seats and back comfortably covered with photographs of family members she supposed, and wonderful prints in frames. Rugs covered the strong wooden floor and lace hung from the backs of the chairs and couches. She began to imagine how it must be to live in such a place and have such a life. A family, a home, comforts and love. When she heard the couple stomping the mud and water from their shoes she realized that they had been gone for quite awhile.

"Brrrr! It's plenty cool out there. Honey, Roland unharnessed your team, dried them off, curried them, fed and watered them. They're both asleep on their feet." she chuckled. "Some of your clothes were wet, as were some of your other things so we put them up to dry. There's a pot-bellied stove in the barn for the animals and its' warm enough to dry your things. Now come along with me and get out of those wet clothes, honey," she said as she led her down the hall to a bedroom.

"This is Rebecca's old bedroom. She's my youngest daughter. Just got married last summer. Last one to leave home. There's fresh linen on the bed. You'll sleep here tonight. I picked out some dry clothes for you to wear tomorrow. I hope they suit you. And here's your nightdress and housecoat. I didn't see any slippers, but here's some socks. Bring those wet clothes with you and we'll hang them in the kitchen to dry. I'll be warming you up some of the chicken and dumplings we had for supper sweetie."

She left Brandy and closed the door behind her. As she took off the wet clothes she appraised the room this lady's daughter had lived in. She felt uncomfortable in these surroundings: lace curtains, colored wallpaper, fancy lamps, a dresser with a big mirror, rugs and expensive looking bedcovers over a feather mattress on a brass bed softly shining. How wonderful it must be to live in such a place.

Returning to the lady of the house in the kitchen with a towel wrapped around her head and dressed in her housecoat covering her nightdress, she introduced herself.

"Ma'am, I am Brandy Womack."

"Well, howdy do. I'm Barbara and this is my husband Roland Schmidt. We plum forgot introducing ourselves didn't we?" The good wife chuckled merrily as she stirred the steaming dumplings in the pot.

"Mmm that smells delicious."

"I'm sure you're hungry chasing that scoundrel down all day. How long did it rain on you?"

"Off and on. Maybe two hours."

Barbara dipped out a generous portion of the meat and dumplings into a bowl and placed it on the table with a spoon and salt and pepper shakers.

Sit down and let that cool while I get your bread."

She took warmed over biscuits from a pan in the oven and placed them on a saucer before putting them before Brandy with a small bowl of butter and knife. Taking a glass from the cupboard and a cool pitcher of milk from the small ice box she poured sweet milk and handed the glass to Brandy.

"He's not really a scoundrel Mrs. Schmidt,..." Brandy began.

"Honey, call me Barbara."

"Yes. Barbara. He left me because he believes I am too young for him. He thinks I deserve a younger man."

"How old is he, sweetheart?"

"Well, he's over forty."

"My, my, Sugar! And you love this man?"

"Yes. Yes, I do."

"To be honest, I'm surprised you could be romantically attracted to a man so much older than you."

"So is he."

"Well, maybe you should give it some time honey, maybe meet some other men."

"Maybe you're right," Brandy sighed.

She finished every bite of the chicken and dumplings, biscuits and milk. They carried on a friendly conversation until her suppressed yawns told Barbara to put the tired girl to bed.

"We eat breakfast early sugar. I'll wake you."

"Yes, please do. I'd like to get on the road early."

The smell of the cool clean sheets and the softness of the deep mattress were a welcome and unexpected luxury. Her thoughts of tomorrow's chase quickly dissolved into deep slumber. And the warm soft bed felt so wonderful. When Barbara woke her, she wanted to sleep forever. Barbara lit a lamp and left her to dress before breakfast.

Brandy quickly made the bed, brushed her hair and folded her night clothes. She hurried to the delicious aromatic lure of bacon frying in the pan. The table was set with enough food for a feast it seemed to her. Barbara standing before the stove with eggs in her hand asked, "How do you like your eggs, sweetie?"

"Well, how do you like your eggs, Barbara?"

"I like mine over easy."

"Me too."

"Are you sure honey? It's no trouble."

"Yes ma'am, over easy, please."

Roland came in with a very cool rush of air blowing foggy breath.

"Chilly out there. But, sky's clear. Road's not too muddy."

"I'll wear my coat."

"And gloves, missie."

"Well, I don't have gloves."

"I have an extra pair. They'll fit well enough to keep out the cold."

"No. I couldn't. You've given enough."

"Oh please. It helps an old soul feel she's still of some use."

"You've done so much. And I said I'd pay. Here take this."

"You put that money in your pocket. It'll be a sad day when we Schmidt's take money from our guest."

"But,..."

"No buts, sweetheart. Eat your breakfast."

"Your wagon is ready for the road Brandy. Mules all hitched up. Those old Army mules don't have many miles left in them you know. I gave them a bait of oats and put a small sack of feed in the bed for the road.

"You are very kind, thank you so much Mr. Schmidt."

"Ha! I'm just old Roland, Brandy. And your very welcome. I put an old canvas cover over the bed. Mother re-folded all your dry clothes and re-packed them along with your other belongings."

"I don't know what to say. You two are the most wonderful people I've ever met. Thank you both."

"You're welcome. Eat girl, you'll need a good breakfast."

After eating she tried to stay in the kitchen and help clean up but Barbara would not allow it.

"You get in that wagon and get after that man and you decide what you need to do. You're a good girl Brandy, any man would be honored to have you as wife. Take care of yourself. If you're ever back this way you come and see us. And write us a letter anyway and let us know how you are. You promise."

"Yes, I promise. And I thank you both so much. I don't know what I would have done without you. Well, yes I do. I would have spent the night in the wet and cold. Thank you. You are so good."

"We were well repaid for our hospitality with the pleasure of your company. Your gloves are in the pocket of your coat. Now git, girl. Go catch that feller. Oh! There's a basket of food back in the bed too, enough for the day."

"Thank you. So much."

"God speed, Brandy," said Roland

"So long, sweetie. Write us, you hear?" said Barbara.

"Goodbye. Thank you," said Brandy as she shook the reins.

As she drove away she looked back and waved. She was surprised how emotional she felt, it was like she was leaving home although she had never had a home, not really. She didn't know there were people like that, there certainly weren't in the places she had been. They were like a fairy tale. She hoped she could do so much for some needy, weary soul someday. And to have a home filled with such nice things and more importantly, such love.

But now she was back in the heartless reality of the real world, the cold, the wet, the loneliness. She must travel long and fast if she was to catch Noah and these hard-used mules just didn't have it in them. Noah knew that. Maybe he thought she might chase him but knew these mules pulling a wagon wouldn't catch his young stallion. Well, he may be selling Brandy Womack short. He was still stiff and healing, so she didn't expect he would be traveling as fast as he reckoned. He may be consuming a fair amount of whiskey thinking it would dull his pain and speed his journey, but she believed the whiskey just might slow him down.

An hour before noon she pulled the wagon over beside the road and found the basket of food Barbara had packed for her. Bacon and cheese sandwiches, a jar of milk and a whole apple pie. She sat and ate a good portion, enjoying every bite. Before she pulled the wagon back onto the road she took out her purse and counted the money she had. It might be enough she figured.

Two hours later the mules stumbled down the main street of a fairly busy town. She found a place that sold horses and mules. The price she was quoted by the obese horse trader was more than she had and the man made a lewd suggestion of a trade for services rendered to cover the difference. A short time before she would not have been rankled at all and would have probably exercised her practiced art and wielded him out of even more money than he'd been thinking for the exchange. But now she was a woman in love, and today she raised her voice in outrage as she never had before and loudly upbraided the lecher for even suggesting she was such a woman.

"Aw shut up woman, I was only funnin'."

"There is nothing funny in treating me like a whore! You need to be horsewhipped! Why, if I was a man I would..."

"Excuse me ma'am, is this man bothering you?"

"He wanted me to 'make up the difference' between the price he wanted for these mules and the money I have by prostituting myself to him. If my father were here he would give him his pay alright! But he wouldn't enjoy it!"

"Mister, you need to apologize to this lady right now."

"Or what?"

"Or I'm going to beat a few pounds of fat off of your very corpulent ass. Now apologize!"

The very fat horse trader sized up the rather large and serious man who confronted him and glanced round at the gathering crowd. He turned to Brandy and tipped his hat.

"Well, I was just joking anyway. I apologize ma'am."

"The 'joking' was in very poor taste sir. I suggest you accept the money she has for the mules as a token of your sincere regret."

"She's a full twenty dollars short!"

"Well, you certainly want to leave her a little traveling money, don't you think that would be the gentlemanly thing to do? Sell her the mules for thirty dollars less than your asking price."

"I'd be losing money!"

"But you'd gain a measure of respect from me and all those here who have witnessed your despicable and disrespectful words. And, you would avoid an Alabama ass-whipping." The gentleman began removing his coat.

The small crowd that had gathered pushed closer, adding supporting comments.

"Besides, you would be acquiring these fine Army mules in trade I'm sure."

"Why, those ol' nags are wore out."

"Suit yourself sir," the young man said softly as he rolled up his cuffs. "I hope you have adequate funds to pay the doctor."

"Hold on! Just hold on a minute. Maybe I should do the Christian thing and help the lady out. I was thinking of selling the mules for twenty five dollars less than my asking price."

"Thirty."

"Damn it! Awright, awright. Thirty."

"And put the new mules in their harness. When you have accomplished that, come and get your money. The lady and I will be in the restaurant across the street."

"And keep your nasty paws away from my belongings," Brandy pulled the hog leg pistol out of her bag, "Or I'll come back and pay you more than the bargain struck."

The man offered her his arm and they walked away to a chorus of well wishers in the crowd.

"Thank you sir. I don't even know your name."

"Cecil. Cecil Richardson, at your service ma'am."

"And I am Brandy Womack. Mister Richardson, why did you get into my business and handle it so masterfully?"

"Well, you did say "if I were a man,..." he smiled.

"And I thank you for your kind assistance."

They carried on polite conversation while waiting for their food in the restaurant and she learned he was going home to Montgomery from Macon where he had gone on business.

"Is that on the way to Texas?"

"Well, yes Brandy. From here Montgomery is almost directly west. Maybe a little north, but yes, it's on the way to Texas. Why? Are you going all the way to Texas?"

"If I must." She explained her chase so he would not consider her an available lady. Her heart was set on Noah Lister and she would catch him and straighten his thinking out. His decision to leave her was probably made when he was drunk, that was another thing that he needed to change.

Cecil listened and retrained from any disagreeable comment. He had a wife and children in Montgomery and though Brandy was desirable in her own way, she wasn't a beauty like the woman he loved. And obviously Brandy was of the lower class, it was evident in her speech, mannerisms and dress. He did enjoy her company though. Her independence and determination were refreshing, and she was a feisty little specimen.

Brandy knew by the man's manner and dress that he was raised a gentleman in a wealthy family. He had not explained his business in Macon but she would bet that it entailed large amounts of money. She knew he was only traveling by horseback because there were no trains in the southern states. Otherwise he would certainly be traveling in a fine coach.

After the horse trader had delivered the harnessed young team and received his reduced payment and after eating a light meal, Brandy and Cecil headed out of town together, she driving the half wild strong young mules and he escorting her on a black thoroughbred, stepping lively.

In the early evening they found a blacksmith shop with a large, newly emancipated blacksmith who happily stabled and cared for their animals and directed them to the only local hotel for white folks in town. It seemed that the town was populated primarily by black folks. Brandy wondered if the whites had moved or if the war itself had decimated the white population. Before the war there were few blacks in the cities of the south, blacks typically resided in the rural areas then as they were mostly utilized as farm hands. Now there were thousands of loitering negroes in the towns and cities, unemployed, uneducated, untrained except as field workers and most refused to work for the low wages offered. Many were migrating northward where rumor had told them the government would provide for them and where there were high paying jobs. Brandy empathized with them. She had suffered her own poverty, hunger and humiliation.

Cecil paid for her room. She argued with him about it but he convinced her it was a small thing and, tired, but in good humor, she allowed it. She excused herself from eating with him and had a bite from Barbara's basket before going to bed. She thought about Cecil as she lay her stiff body down. He was good in his way, generous, protective, gentlemanly, but his comments about the crowds of homeless Negroes irritated her. He seemed to think it was their fault they were poor and hungry, no place to go. She saw the confused and angry faces of the young men, the near naked ebony children shivering in their thin mother's arms and her heart went out to them. She saw the disgust, the disdain in Cecil's face as he looked at the poor Negroes and did not like the man. How could he be so kind and good to her and so hateful toward these suffering innocents? Perhaps she would ask him.

After a small breakfast she paid for herself out of her remaining few dollars, Brandy hooked up her mules and went shopping. Cecil dogged her every step pestering her about needing to get on the road and she told him to go ahead, there were a few things she needed. Finding a second-hand store she bought a water barrel, a rain slicker and an axe. At the general store she purchased Lucifer matches and some ammunition for her pistol. At a small, run-down shack there was a second-hand store run by an old white haired Negro and despite Cecil's protest she bought an old U.S. Army hammock.

Brandy explained to Cecil during the short shopping mission that she had no money for hotel rooms or restaurant meals and she would accept no more of his charity. She told him that she appreciated all the kindness he had extended to her but she wasn't comfortable allowing him to pay her way. She still had the groceries Noah had bought and she was determined she would cook her meals beside the road where she would sleep under the wagon.

Cecil sighed and shook his head, then he also made some purchases. He bought two thick blankets and several sacks of food which he added to her store in the wagon. The morning was half gone before they left town.

Riding alongside the wagon, Cecil asked Brandy if she knew how to shoot the old pistol. She told him an old friend, (who was actually a regular customer), had taught her. It was a single action thumb-buster but she was a steady hand at close range.

While Cecil had gone shopping, she had asked around about an old traveler on a red roan stallion who may have passed this way. The blacksmith, the hotel clerk and the restaurant waiter did not recall such a one. She asked the right man when she asked the saloon keeper. He told her such a man had bought three bottles of whiskey the previous morning. So Noah was already more than a day ahead of her.

She stopped only twice that day to rest, feed and water the mules and continued into the darkness until she began to fall asleep on her seat. She hobbled and unharnessed the tired young animals, shared some apple pie with Cecil along with the remaining cheese Barbara had packed. She unfolded her hammock beneath the wagon, put the pistol beside her, covered herself with a blanket and bade Cecil wake her if he rose earlier than her.

She was woken by the popping of a knot or wet wood burning and Cecil was huddled under a blanket sitting on his saddle by the fire looking miserable. She hurriedly rose and washed her face with the cold water from the barrel and shivered as she walked away into the bushes. This early necessity of relieving herself reminded her how nice the outhouse behind her shack and at Barbara and Roland's had been, not to mention the chamber pots at the hotel. She assured herself that it would get easier and this rough traveling wouldn't last forever.

Back at the wagon she washed her hands again, then rushed to the fire where Cecil was pouring her coffee into a tin cup. She thanked him, then made the mistake of asking him how he slept.

He whined for ten minutes about the rock hard and ice cold Georgia earth and chastised her about her stubborn decision to boycott hotels thus condemning him to the misery of endless suffering through the nights ahead. Begging her to change her mind, to grant him reprieve from continued punishment and to please allow him to pay for their rooms in a hotel at least for one night so he could get some sleep and on and on until she at last relented.

"Alright! Hush! You big baby! If you'll stop crying and complaining, you can stay in a hotel tonight. But you have to help me make as many miles as we can today and get closer to Noah. Now help me get breakfast."

He mumbled thanks and assent and stood uselessly by as she gathered pan and bacon, eggs and flour and water for pan bread. The food cheered and warmed them. After eating she washed and picked the rocks out of pinto beans then covered them in water in the big cast iron pot adding bacon and tomatoes and onions and peppers and sat the pot on the coals as Cecil tended to the beast. At least he could deal with the animals. She wondered if he had ever prepared his own meal.

Within an hour the sun rose and revealed a thick cloud cover of gray-violet. A distant thunder rolled through the thick cool air that foretold rain. Each of them shrugged into their slickers. She put the heavy lid on the iron pot and lifted it by its bail and sat it in the well beneath the wagon seat beside her pistol. Cecil doused the fire and they started their day's travel. He rode in front a ways, scouting the road ahead. The lightening frightened the young, skittish mules, but she kept them on the road. The cloud grew darker and the sky opened above them pouring a blessing on the farmers along the road and a hindrance to the travelers upon it.

Brandy drove the mules successfully around the deepest mud holes, but the mules were soon struggling in their traces, nostrils flaring and muscles twitching in the effort to pull the wagon through the deepening muck and mire. After a three hour striving through the deluge Cecil motioned her off the road onto a raised rocky shelf beside a swollen, swirling stream and under a low, natural bower of vines laced through the drooping branches of ancient trees that lined the flooded channel.

"We aren't crossing this creek until the water goes down, at least the wagon can't. We'll have to wait out the storm. May as well eat and feed the animals."

"You can cross the stream Cecil. You may get soaked but your horse can swim across. I'll be alright. Go ahead."

"I'm cold enough without drenching myself in freezing dirty water. I'm not in that big a hurry. Besides which I would miss the pleasure of sharing that pot of beans. I'll build a fire if you'll finish cooking the beans."

"Could we float the wagon across?"

"That is crazy Brandy! Just have a little patience. He must be slowed by the storm also."

"Unless he's ahead of it."

"Please Brandy, cook the beans?"

"Alright."

After warming themselves by the fire and enjoying the hot red beans, Brandy walked in the continuing shower to the road and stared at the point it rose out of the creek bed on the other side of the rushing stream. The rain steadily drummed on and dripped from the thick arbor. She thought of Noah as far ahead and moving farther away from her. She knew that unless he stopped she would not catch up this side of Texas. Even then she would have to search every city and small town for word of his passing. Under the delaying rain it seemed she had set out on an impossible goal. She grew disheartened. Reality began to oppress her spirit.

She had just a couple of dollars and many hundred miles before her. She walked apart from Cecil and let the loneliness and the hurt overcome her. And she cried. She could not remember the last time she cried, surely she had cried as a child but she could not recall a single instance. Didn't he realize that he would never find anyone who loved him like she did? Her vision was blurred by the hot tears and cold rain, but in her mind's eye she could see him riding farther and farther away.

Ezekial repaired the picket fence around the family graveyard. He painted it as well as some of the markers, repainted some of the names, dates and words. He pulled weeds and smoothed the grounds. He knew John and Trinity would maintain it, but he wanted to remember this portion of the farm as pristine.

He helped Mr. Dunlap and John through two weeks of picking cotton and harvesting corn. The days of summer had passed while he hunted and fished often. Sam and he had feasted on deer, rabbit, duck, dove, quail and all kinds of fish, although Sam wasn't fond of fish. He had napped under the huge oaks and daydreamed of traveling west. John had paid him a part of the payment for the farm and Ezekial made lists for days of how it should be spent and not spent. Many items had been eventually crossed out as he realized there really was no need for them. On Saturdays he would drive the wagon to town and make the purchases he had decided were necessary. It was on one such shopping trip in late September that he met Micah and Beau.

He was loading a bolt of canvas when Beau, standing in the street behind the wagon called his name.

"Mista' Ezekial Robertson?"

"Yessir, That's how my momma blessed me."

"My name is Beau Johnson an' this is my frien', Micah Johnson. We is freed servants from 'Mista' Rubin Johnson's plantation a'ways east of here. We's lookin' to find work to he'p us down the road all the way to Texas where my wife be. Word is, you's headed that a'ways. Could you put us to work so's we could go 'long the way wit' you suh?"

"Well. Tell the truth, I haven't put any thought to goin' with anyone, 'cept Sam, my dog here."

Beau reached out his hand and let Sam smell it.

"How you Sam?"

Sam looked up at him, turned his head and grinned characteristically on one side of his face. His tail wagged in a friendly wave.

The men smiled and chuckled. Then the older man, Micah spoke.

"Suh, we ain't lookin' fer no wages 'specially, we jes' lookin' to travel with white folks so we don't get shot for thievin' nigga's. We'd work jes' fer food. You know Mista Rob'ason, lots of white folks don't cotton to no nigga's a' travelin' down the road on fine hosses like these. Truth be tole, we ain't got much money a' tall an' if we could jes' get meals fer our work, why, we'd be glad fer it."

"Where you say you all come from?"

"From Mista' Rubin Johnson's plantation over east a' here. An' we run into trouble right quick with some white folks chasin' after us a' thinkin' we stole some chickens an' musta' stole these hosses. So, we's thinkin' since you's goin' to Texas same as us, an' if we was to travel wit' a white man, why, we might make it to Texas 'fore we got hung or shot. Word is, a nigga' can get work chasin' cows in Texas an' I can't be beat ridin' a hoss. An' don't think we stole these hosses, me an' Micah got papers from Mista' Rubin Johnson sayin' these hosses is our'n."

"You all eat anything today?"

"No suh, not today, yestiddy neither."

"You all foller me an' Sam on home an' we'll eat sumpen an' talk some more, here? It's a 'ways, take near two hours."

"Yes suh."

"Sho' will."

Ezekial admired the fine young thoroughbreds the pair of freedmen rode and assayed the men themselves as they headed to the farm. Beau was a young man about twenty, small, and seemed even smaller mounted on the big beautiful black horse whose muscles were clearly defined with every stride. Micah was an older man, white headed, in his fifties or sixties Ezekial guessed. He rode a fine bred sorrel with an aristocratic air. Their saddles and bridles were old but well-repaired. They had little more baggage than bedrolls.

Arriving at the farm, Beau volunteered to unhitch the mules and take care of them and the horses. Ezekial showed him where the feed was. Micah volunteered to do the cooking, so Sam and Ezekial sat in the parlor looking at one another and feeling useless until Beau tapped on the door, hat in hand. Ezekial told him, "Come on in, make yourself at home. Have a seat."

"Well! I neva' was invited to a sit-down in a white man's house a' fore. Hear that Micah?"

Micah stepped to the door and raised his eyebrows as he wiped his hands on a towel.

"You neva' had no nigga's Mista Rob'son?"

"It's Ezekial, or Zeke. I'm not even full growed yet an' you're a white-haired gentleman. It's me who should be callin' you mister. An' no sir, my fam'ly always did our own work. Gramps taught me it was wrong to believe a man could own another man."

"Well, praise the Lord," said Micah.

"I'll be…," mouthed Beau.

"It ain't nothing to be proud of. Right's right an' wrong's wrong. But I did fight for the Confed'racy who would have preserved slavery if the South had won the war. I thought it was right to fight for my people, my home. Now, I expect I was confused about that, expect we all were."

A silence fell among them as their thoughts were drawn to bygone days. Micah broke the trance of memory as he said and smiled around long, strong teeth, "Zeke, if you ain't full growed yet, I'd like to witness your full maturity."

"Wu-wee! Ain't that the gospel! I ain't neva' seen nobody big as you Ezekial."

Ezekial grinned and said, "What I mean is, it'll be a few more years 'til I can vote."

"An' you know Ezekial, Masta Johnson tole us the black men would be able to vote purty soon. Ain't that sumpen?"

"Guess you'll both vote 'fore I do. That deer ready to eat yet Micah?"

"Oh! No suh. Lemme put it in the pan."

The stack of venison steaks and the small crop of potatoes on the table were quickly consumed and the two hungry Johnson's held their own with Ezekial in putting it away. Ezekial was pleased and gratified to see the hungry men eat.

After eating their fill, Micah asked Ezekial, "Are you a Christian, Ezekial?"

"Well. I try to be. I'm shamed you couldn't tell."

"Oh I could tell you's goodhearted, but I 'spect they's good in all religions."

"Why do you ask Micah?"

"Well, we always prayed 'fore meals at home. Today I jes' prayed inside."

"I suppose I've got out of the habit of prayin' here lately, there bein' only me an' Sam. Think it's too late to thank the Lord now?"

"No suh. Ain't never too late to come to the Lord in prayer."

"Would you pray for us Micah?"

"I'd be honored."

He stood and bowed his head and Beau and Ezekial did the same. When they were still Micah began.

"Merciful Father, we thank You for this day among days in which You have blessed us mightily. You led us by a sure path to this young Samson who surely will be a judge among your people, a man who has judged us as men and not as beasts, a man not ashamed to break bread with us. Lord, You said in Your word You would provide for all our needs and You have once again proved faithful to Your word. You have provided abundantly and we thank You. We praise You for Your gracious love. We pray You would bless this kind brother who has shared Your bounty with us. Protect us as we journey forth, together or separately, and keep us ever on the path that You have planned for us. Keep us mindful that we must love one another by humbly and joyfully serving one another in the manner in which You have enabled us. We present these petitions in the holy name of Your son, our savior, Jesus. Amen."

Both Beau and Ezekial added their own amens and they began to clean up. Sam had been given a plate of the deer meat, but agreeably dispensed with the small amount that remained. Working together, they had quickly cleaned and straightened the kitchen.

Ezekial brought out the box of cigars that had been Gramps' and gave them to Micah and Beau. He didn't smoke tobacco himself. As the black men had been raised on a tobacco producing plantation, they appreciated and enjoyed the cigars.

As the two guests smoked Ezekial asked, "Micah, I hope you'll not consider it ill-mannered of me to ask, but have you become educated through schooling?"

Micah and Beau chuckled.

"So, you noticed I spoke different when I prayed? Yes, I s'pose I can speak as well as most white men when it's called for, an' when I pray I offer my best.

"My old master, Mista' Rubin Johnson Senior, he hired a teacher who taught his children there on the plantation. He also taught my sista' an' me to read when we's little children. We were taught how to cook an' how to serve in the big house an' the master 'llowed us to read all the many books he had there in his library. His interests were in history an' geology so I've read quite a bit 'bout those subjects. My interest has always been God, so Mista' Johnson got some books fer' me 'bout religion. My sister was much brighter than me, and so pretty. One cold winter day, the Lord took her home to Him. The doctor said it was the poomonia, but I know it was God's will.

"But I enjoyed learnin', so I read mos' ever' night by candlelight. I studied the Bible too and Mister Johnson let the servants have Sunday church and sing. Usually I taught a Bible lesson to those less fortunate brothers who couldn't read."

"He sho' can preach good too," Beau interjected.

"Well sir, to answer yer question, it was illegal to teach a nigga' to read, so I could only talk to Mister Johnson and his missus like I'd learned. When other white folks was 'round I had to talk ignorant-like, so we could keep my learnin' secret. Over the years, I jes' got in the habit of only talking educated to the Johnson's and to the Lord."

"Is Mister Johnson still alive?"

"Jes' barely," Beau answered. "He knowed I's anxious to see my Ruby. He tole me where the man who bought my wife lived down in Texas. See, his son, Junior, he stole my wife jes' outa' meanness. I need to go find her, an' Micah an' me, we's like family, so we's goin' together. Micah an' me, we prays for Mister Johnson reg'lar. He a good man."

"Those horses fast?"

"They can out-run anythang, an' I can out-ride any mother's son on either one o' those hosses."

"I don't doubt that Beau. Not at all. Micah, you said you read history and religion and what was the other?"

"Geology. It's about rocks and the layers down in the earth. 'Bout minerals and metals an' how to look fer iron an' copper an' silver an' gold."

"Ha! You gonna' look fer gold in Texas Micah?"

"No suh, fust thang we gon' look fo' is Ruby. Tha's Beau's wife."

"She mo' precious than gold, Ezekial."

"I expect she is. An' that's fine, mighty fine. Have you read the whole Bible Micah?"

"Oh yes. Many times."

"Whew! That's considerable reading."

"I read the Word ever' day since I was a boy. I've found strength an' love an' patience an' direction an' faith an' hope an' wisdom an' so much more in those old pages. A man feeds his face ever'day. Shoulden' he feed his spirit as reg' lar?"

"Gramps' used to read it ever' day too, God rest his soul. Well. After that good cookin' I've gotten sleepy. Expect you all are too. Lemme show you where you can sleep."

Ezekial showed them Gramps old bed and told them about the big washtub in the barn if they cared to bathe or wash their clothes. He showed them where soap and rags and towels were. He also showed them the chifforobe where Gramps' and his brother's old clothes were and told them they were welcome to whatever they could wear. He assured them he would sleep.

Laying in bed and staring at the stars through the narrow window, he reviewed the developments and possibilities presented by the day. Gramps, then Micah came to mind and he prayed for wisdom and guidance. He slept, Sam at his side, and he dreamed. He dreamed of an easy road that wound up and over and round rippling hills of spruce and cedar, plains of undulating tall grasses dancing in the wind and of clear, promising skies that extended into forever.

Chapter Five

The Road goes ever on and on
Down from the door where it began.
Now far ahead the Road has gone,
And I must follow if I can.
Pursuing it with eager feet,
Until it joins some larger way
Where many paths and errands meet,
And whither then? I cannot say.
--J.R.R. Tolkien

We don't see things as they are, we see things as we are.
--Anais Nin

Man is made by his belief. As he believes, so he is.
--Bhaggavad Gita

For as he thinketh in his heart, so is he:
--Proverbs 23:7 (KJV)

THE COLD RAIN pelted Noah's hands and his horse and drummed on his hat. The downpour steadily pounded them through the afternoon until the wind blew them into the small Alabama town. He found a stable and a man opened the wide door of the barn and waved him in. The man invited him to stand by the pot-bellied stove and warm himself as he directed a boy to unsaddle and care for the tired, wet roan. Noah's slicker and clothes steamed as he accepted the tin cup of coffee gratefully. He learned there was no hotel in the town but the man would allow him to sleep in the stable. There was a small place a hundred yards farther on where he could buy a meal and whiskey, so he paid the stable man the amount required to lodge him and his horse and departed for the whiskey.

Stomping the mud from his boots and shaking the rain off his slicker under the narrow awning on the porch of the small establishment, Noah was greeted by a young girl who held open the door for him and bade him enter quickly. She shut the door behind him and bolted it, explaining that the wind would blow the door open unless it was bolted. The small establishment contained only three tables. Noah pulled back two straight back wooden chairs, placed his hat and slicker on one and sat in the other.

"Welcome stranger. You ready for some hot coffee?" asked an aproned bald man with a huge mustache.

"Yes sir. Half coffee and half whiskey would warm these old bones."

"Coming right up. Hungry?"

"Haven't eaten all day. About half starved."

"How does a beef steak and biscuits, fried taters and corn on the cob sound?"

"Like I died and went to heaven."

The fourteen or fifteen year old girl laughed and put a big pan on the stove which radiated heat through the small room.

"Did Clarence and Sonny take care of your horse?"

"Sure did. And they offered me a dry piece of ground to sleep on tonight."

"You know, I've been thinking of building two or three rooms onto my little building here renting out rooms. There's beginning to be enough traffic through here heading west to justify the investment. Don't know where all the people are going! Don't think all of them know where they're going either. Just getting out of Dixie."

"Well, I know where I'm going. Headed home to Texas. Not that I have a home or family there, but it's where I feel at home."

"A man needs a home, a place to drop anchor, rest and grow old."

"Well sir, I've been a rolling stone all my days and my feet get to itching if I roost too long in one place. Expect I'll die atop an old cayuse headed down some lonesome trail."

"You never know, some old gal may make you want to stay and enjoy the comforts of home someday. That's how my wife Willimay tamed me down to make a nest. By the way, I'm Wilburn and this is my daughter, Debra."

Noah shook both their hands as Debra placed the hot plate on the table before him.

"I'm Noah Lister. Pleased to meet you."

"Pleased to meet you Mister Lister," Debra curtsied quickly and prettily.

"We'll leave you alone awhile Mister Lister to enjoy your food."

"Could I have another cup of coffee and whiskey? Easy on the coffee," Noah smiled.

After consuming the steak, potatoes and corn, Noah sat, drank whiskey and gabbed with Wilburn for an hour until the warmth, the whiskey and the miles behind him coaxed him to the straw bed that awaited him at the stable. He purchased the last two bottles of whiskey Wilburn had in his store and ambled back to the livery. Entering the barn, he put another log in the pot-bellied stove and took the bottles and a blanket to the pile of straw. His snoring soon woke the horses and they huffed their complaints.

Before the sun next morning Clarence the stable master was surprised to find no trace of the traveler except an empty whiskey bottle in the straw.

Luther rose from the warmth of the bedroll beneath the big freight wagon and pulled on his boots. He slept in all his clothes except his boots, hat and coat. It was hard to recall a time when he'd had his own bed. Sleeping on the ground was no real hardship for him, but the cold seemed to seep all the way down to his old bones these days. Adjusting a thick cloth around his head and tying it on the back of his neck, he appraised the dark and the fog surrounding the wagons. He crawled out from beneath the wagon and put his coat and hat on. He slid out the bedroll and the rifle laying on the blankets and leaned the rifle against the big wheel. He rolled the bedroll and stowed it in its place in the wagon.

Picking up the rifle, he carried it with him into the brush. After relieving himself, he came back to the water barrel and dipped out enough into a pan to wash his hands and face. Shivering, he found a towel and dried his face, then found the pot and made the coffee. He added three short lengths of log to the fire and crouched close, relishing the heat.

While the coffee boiled, Luther let down the tailgate of the freight wagon, lit a lantern, and began slicing bacon. He felt a presence beside him and heard, "Morning Luther."

"Well. Morning, early bird."

There rubbing her fists in her eyes was Nellie. She had her coat over her night dress and her high top shoes, untied, on her feet. Her long, almost white hair, was wildly mussed and her big blue eyes, swollen with sleep, still smiled up at him. Something he had not felt in many years tugged at his heart and made his old face split and his eyes water.

"What's wrong Luther?"

"Aw, just got something in my eye I guess. You want to make the dough for pan bread?"

"Can I? But I can't reach up there."

Luther lifted a wooden box down from the wagon bed and placed it below the tailgate for Nellie to stand on. Then he got her the ingredients and a pan of water and she began mixing a batch of dough. He began frying the bacon and soon she was beside him with a bowl of dough.

"My arm's tired Luther. Is this mixed enough?"

"Why, it's just right. You must have been watching your mamma."

"Yes sir."

"Naw, don't call me sir. I'm your buddy. You don't talk to your friends like that."

"But you're a grown up man!"

"I can still be your friend."

"You can?"

"Why sure."

"Alright. Buddy." Nellie smiled.

When the bacon was all cooked and they both sampled a piece, he poured most of the bacon grease out of the pan into a grease jar, then poured some dough in the pan. It wasn't long before breakfast was ready. They folded pieces of the thin bread around the bacon and ate their fill. As Luther sat on a log beside the fire and washed the meal down with hot coffee, Nellie leaned on his side and asked, "What happened to your ear buddy?"

"Well, it's a long story, buddy."

"I can listen a long time."

"Ha! Let's see, I must have been about eighteen or twenty years old, just becoming a man when it happened. I was in the English army over in Africa and I was a scout. There's jungle over there and that means there's so many trees and vines you can't hardly see the sky sometimes. I was scouting out ahead of the troops looking for the enemy and I pushed back this big bush and there was this big daddy lion, big as a horse, and he roared and jumped out at me and knocked me to the ground. I looked up and all I could see was his huge mouth and big, sharp teeth. I barely had time to pull my bayonet before one of his razor sharp teeth had sliced off my ear. I stuck the lion with the bayonet in the ribs just deep enough to get him to get off of me and leave me alone. I didn't want to kill him. He roared and run off and I looked around, but I couldn't find my ear. I suppose that old Lion swallowed it."

"Did it bleed bad?"

"Terrible! But I wrapped a rag around it and it stopped. Funny thing. Now, when I take that rag off, I can hear that old daddy lion roar."

"Gollee Buddy! So that's why you have to keep it wrapped up?"

"Yup. If I don't, I can't hear nothing else but that roaring lion."

"You sure are brave Luther."

"I don't know about that. I was sure scared of that big old lion. But that's our secret now. You have to promise not to tell nobody. I only tell my real good buddies. Promise?"

"I promise. Buddy." Nellie beamed.

Later that morning, at a wide spot in the wagon track, Callie pulled her wagon over to the right and stopped, waving at Luther to pull up alongside.

"There's some rain blowing in from the northwest. Smell it?"

"Sure do."

"Let's hurry up and see if we can make it to the next town and find someplace dry to wait it out."

"Go ahead. I'll keep up."

"We should be within five miles or so by my estimation."

"Let's get 'em rolling."

The wind couldn't decide which way it wanted to blow but it was puffing cold air in every direction pushing the icy rain at a severe angle before they reached the town. They came to a big wagon yard and they drove up close to the doors of the big barn, set the brake and jumped off the wagons and ran through the rain and into the dark, fragrant building.

"Come on in folks. Come over here by the fire and get warm. I'm Bobby. You want me to get your animals and wagons out of the weather?"

"Yes could you?"

"Sure. Come on Coby. Hat on tight. Let's get them in here."

The not quite grown boy named Coby ran to the near wagon jumped into the seat, released the brake and turned the team into the barn as the bearded man held open the wide doors. When one wagon and team were in, Coby was immediately running for the other one and he expertly drove the big freight wagon in and parked it neatly, then hopped down and helped Bobby close the barn doors.

"Ma'am, that weather is going to be with us awhile, most likely all day and night. You'll be wanting to leave your wagons and animals here with us and get a room down the way at Miss Lawson's hotel."

"Yes, I suppose so."

"Coby, hitch up the buggy so you can get these folks to Miss Lawson's place. We'll dry and feed your animals and all your possessions will be safe right where they're at."

"Bobby, I'm Luther. You mind if I stay here the night and sleep in my bedroll?"

"You're welcome to stay here."

"Luther, let me get you a room at the hotel."

"No, thank you Callie. I'd be more comfortable here."

"Well, alright. Girls, help me get what we'll need. Put your night clothes and clothes for tomorrow in the little trunk," Callie and the girls climbed into the wagon as Callie continuing her instructions.

"Luther, are the ladies your kin?"

"No, Callie is my boss. And friend."

"Nothing in those wagons will be touched if you want to go to the hotel. You have my word."

"Oh I believe you Bobby, I believe you must be an honest man to have built such an enterprise as this. Truth is, I haven't done much sleeping indoors in recent years and an unfamiliar place filled with people makes me just feel jittery. I'm more at home with the animals."

"Well, you make yourself at home here Luther. How about a cup of Joe?"

"That'd be right welcome."

The boy Coby helped Callie and the girls into the covered buggy and loaded their necessaries. Bobby opened the big door for them and closed it behind them. Luther observed the man as he walked back from the door with a very pronounced limp. He was short and stout with a long, full gray beard. He was loud and authoritative and his laughter was infectious. After the women left the man cursed like a sailor, there was a certain artistry to his cursing.

Coby returned with the buggy and told Luther he was to meet Miss Callie and the girls at the restaurant two doors down from the Lawson Hotel in half an hour. Then the boy began cleaning the wagon wheels as Bobby unhitched the teams, dried and curry-combed each animal in each their separate stall. He fed and watered them, then returned to the stove and good naturedly cursed Coby for working so slow. Coby smiled and ignored his disparaging comments. When Luther put on his slicker to go to the restaurant, Bobby told Coby to take him in the buggy as the rain continued steadily in hard bursts. Coby dropped him at the restaurant door and promised to return if the rain continued in a bit over an hour. Luther did not have much and so offered the boy ten cents as a tip.

"Thanks Mister!"

"That'll have to do for the ride back too, since I'm just about busted."

"That's okay. I appreciate it." Coby grinned.

Luther thought here is a lad who will do well, he has a good work ethic and good attitude, plus he's friendly, good looking and a natural hustler. He wondered how much Callie had given him and whether he would mention the tip to Bobby.

Callie and her cotton-haired girls sat at a table near the window watching the wind slant the rain one way and then another. Nellie jumped up and pulled out a chair at the table close to her.

"Sit right here buddy."

"Why, thanks buddy."

Sallie said, "Can I be your buddy too Luther?"

"Well, what do you think Nellie? A man can't have too many buddies can he?"

"I don't know."

"Ain't your sister your buddy?"

"Sure she is."

"Well, can't she be my buddy too?"

"Hmmm. Maybe two buddies ain't too many."

"Aren't too many." Callie corrected.

"Good. Then we're all buddies."

"Is Momma a buddy too?"

"Sure she is. She's the main buddy."

The girls smiled and giggled. Then Nellie asked, "Since Sallie's a buddy now, will you tell her how you lost your ear?"

"Nellie! That's not polite."

"That's okay Callie. I guess since Sallie's a buddy now she'll have to be in on the secret. That is, if she promises not to tell anyone."

"I promise."

"Alright. But maybe it's not a tale to be told at the dinner table."

"Luther I ordered us some fried chicken, mashed potatoes and cornbread. Sound good?"

"Yes ma'am." Luther licked his lips and the girls grinned.

"It looks like we'll be here a couple of days waiting out the rain and wet. Are you sure you don't want a room?"

"No. Truly, I feel easier and sleep better on the ground."

"Well, if you change your mind,...Come to the restaurant again at six and then go with us to the hotel lobby to play some cards this evening."

"Don't know how."

"We'll teach you buddy," said Sallie.

Luther spent the afternoon working on a loose shoe on one of the mules and greasing the axles on the wagons with Cody's volunteered help. After enjoying a delicious supper the travelers retired to a round table and fat, overstuffed chairs in the lobby of the Lawson Hotel. Joann, the diminutive inn keeper, provided the playing cards and sweet tea for her only patrons. She was a chatty lady and knew quite a bit about the road west that would take them to Texas. Callie picked up much information from her that would benefit them down the road.

They played cards and taught Luther the rules for an hour until Nellie feel asleep in the big chair, the cards spread over her and the floor.

Sallie moved to wake her up and Callie grabbed her and said, "Let her sleep honey. I think we're all getting drowsy."

"Luther, before we go to sleep, you said you'd tell me how you lost your ear."

"Sallie..."

"No, it's okay. I'll tell you, but you got to promise not to tell anybody."

"I promise."

"Well, I was just a tyke, about your age, when I went to sea. I was on a sailing ship, a trading ship, and we sailed the seven seas buying and selling goods. China, India, Africa, England, France, Greece, Egypt, we traveled everywhere. We were sailing from Calcutta one stormy day when we were overtaken by two pirate ships. We fought 'em with cannon and rifle and then they managed to come longside and board us. A one-eyed, murderous scoundrel swung his cutlass at me, despite my being unarmed and little more than a child. I ducked fast, to save my head, and the razor sharp sword took my ear. My captain came to save me and ran the rascal through. The crew beat the pirates off even though we lost half our crew. I got in the habit of wearing a cloth over my ear hole to keep out the salt, the sea and the wind."

"That's not what you told me. Buddy." said the possum playing Nellie. "You told me a lion bit it off."

"Well. He did. He bit the 'rest' of it off. That was later on, when I was in the British army."

Callie smiled at the looks on the girls faces, their expression spoke volumes.

"Come along girls. It's bedtime." Callie winked at Luther.

"What?" Luther said innocently as Callie herded her brood to bed. "Goodnight buddies."

Ezekial found Micah and Beau on the front porch smoking cigars he'd given them.

"Morning."

"Morning," the two smokers answered.

"You two must have been up a while. You don't drink coffee?"

"Yes, we drink coffee," Beau answered.

"Why didn't you make some coffee? And breakfast?"

"Wouldn't be right to take freely of another man's food." Micah said.

"Well, I guess it's 'our' food now. And it's your job to cook it Micah. You're hired too Beau, at least 'til we get to Texas. I'll find work 'nough for both of you. I'm planning on heading for southwest Texas where a friend I soldiered with has a ranch with his family. I don't know if I'll put down roots there. I'll see how things are. I'm thinking there may be some highwaymen and maybe some wild Indians 'tween here and there and a couple of extra guns would be welcome."

"We ain't got no guns Zeke," said Beau.

"I'll get each of you a rifle in town 'fore we leave and there's a few guns here that I'll take. I'll also buy some other things you'll need. Figger I won't pay you 'til we get to Texas, but I'll pay for whatever we need to get us there. Then, when we get to Texas we'll decide what's fair and what we all want to do. What you think about that?"

"Sounds good to me."

"That's fair."

"Help me get ever'thing ready to go and I'll put some spending money in your pocket. You know, fer cigars or whatever. Will you help me?"

"Why sure. What else we gonna' do?"

"We 'ppreciate yer help Ezekial. We'll make you good hands."

"Well. How 'bout putting a hand to making some coffee and some breakfast for us?"

"Yes suh, boss," Micah smiled, "Beau, get some water and some firewood."

"On my way," Beau said as he grabbed the fur on Sam's neck and shook it. "And what's Sam gone do while we're all busy getting ready to go?"

"Same thing he's always done 'round here,...supervise," Ezekial answered. "He's good at that."

Sam gave half a grin, and winked.

When the coffee was ready Micah asked, "Got suga'?"

"Yep, right there in that big can in the cupboard. Gramps liked sugar in his coffee. I like mine jes' plain coffee," Ezekial answered. "Gramps liked cream in his coffee too, but cow's gone. No mind. Guess the Yankees took the cow or Gramps had to sell it with the horses while I was soldiering. Times were hard. Still are, but times will get better. I hope."

"Yes suh. Times are getting better already. First time me and Micah slept with a roof over our heads and a full belly in many days."

They sat at the heavy oak table and ate heartily. Simple fare, very appreciated, swiftly assimilated.

The three of them helped John and Mr. Dunlap pick through the cotton crop one time and helped them pull the ears of corn. They bagged some kernel corn to take on the road for the animals to supplement the oats Ezekial had purchased in town.

Also, while in town, Beau helped the blacksmith tend to the horse's and mule's hooves. Ezekial gave his new employees a bit of money for their help in harvesting the crop. Micah bought himself boots, clothes, blankets, tobacco and a pipe. Ezekial purchased a side of bacon, beans, flour, baking powder, sugar, coffee and other staples as well as three of the new repeater rifles and ammunition. He bought a Colt revolver and a holster for himself. He bought plenty of forty-four ammo. After an hour Beau joined them and bought a brightly colored and thickly padded saddle blanket and a new bridle for his horse. He looked at a fancy saddle but it was too expensive. He bought a leather coat with wool lining that matched the one Micah got. He also bought boots and leather gloves before he ran out of money. Ezekial smiled and bought him some cigars. The owner of the store was their best friend before they loaded the wagon. He wished them a safe trip.

Ezekial met John and Mr. Dunlap at the bank and finalized the transfer of the Robertson farm and received two bags of greenbacks and gold. He locked the bags into the iron box he had installed under the wagon seat. On the way out of town they stopped at the general store, paid the proprietor for his loan and picked up the big destrier from old Smokey at the blacksmith shop. Smokey shook his hand and told him he was sad to see him go, that so many were leaving, good folks from the good days before the war. He wished them luck and they left the town for the last time. As Ezekial passed the church, his big heart throbbed with the still fresh pain of the lost love, his first love. He wondered if she ever thought of him. Probably not, he admitted.

Friday was spent loading the wagon just right, making sure those items they would need daily were at hand and that no unnecessary things were loaded. At sunset, Ezekial visited the family graveyard and said his goodbyes once again. He knew those whose names were on the markers were not there, but, were surely in his heart. Inside the farmhouse, he wrote a note to John and Trinity asking them to please maintain the graves. He also asked them to take the enclosed money and pay the tithes from the sale of the property that he had forgotten to take to Brother Denton while he was in town. He asked them to thank everyone for their help and prayers. He folded the money into an envelope and placed it in the breadbox.

As they pulled out the gate, for the last time, Exekial's heart seemed to melt and he felt like calling it all off. He stopped the wagon, turned and gazed at the home place once more, the only home he had ever known. He would almost certainly, never see this place again in life. He sat there looking over the lay of the land, from the hill to the river and every foot of ground seemed to glow in the dawn and bring a golden memory. He said his goodbyes to this life, this land. He looked at the deep blue sky in the direction they would travel, then popped the reins and put the mules into a trot. Beau yelled, "Look out Texas, here we come!"

They made over thirty miles that first day and made camp before dark by a stream that crossed the road. They had eaten cold biscuits and bacon on the road and were building a healthy appetite by the time a fire was prepared and Micah had cooked a stew of venison, beans, onions and potatoes. They thoroughly enjoyed the simple fare which made them drowsy. Beau had hobbled the horses and mules in a place by the stream where they could crop the long grass or drink and had given each one a bucket of corn, except for Ezekial's mixed Percheron which required a second bucket. Ezekial had asked Micah to drive the wagon through the afternoon so he could ride the big destrier. Both the horse and Ezekial needed the exercise and soreness was settling into both of them. Conversation lulled as they spread their bedrolls and the dawn came too soon for Ezekial.

The first week went much the same. The good weather, their strength, health and eagerness contributed to the distance they accomplished. They met many other travelers on the road, many going their way and there were times when it seemed that they were part of a caravan. They were moving faster and without resting as others were and soon outdistanced those headed southwest. They camped with groups of travelers a few times and the company around the fire was always genial, despite the general poverty.

Micah was very hesitant about gathering around the fire after supper to hear the news and converse with the white travelers. He hung back in the shadows quietly listening and watching.

Conversely, Beau was not careful with his words or his demeanor. He was young and bold, too bold for some of the Southerners not yet accustomed to negroes who deluded themselves into believing they had been elevated to equal social status by proclamation or act of any congress of men. Beau was a quick-witted lad and was aware of the attitudes of those around him and for the most part was amendable to and unaffected by those who resented his confidence and sense of equivalence. There were exceptions however.

They had camped early as the sky had darkened ominously and the freshening aroma of approaching rain was undeniable. They had spread the large tent canvas from the top of the wagon hoops to a low spreading limb of a huge oak and tied the livestock under it at one end and built a fire and laid out their bedrolls at the other end. The camp was on a small knoll and would remain relatively dry through the coming rain. Before they'd finished eating their supper the rain began falling in a torrent. They ate in silence and pulled their coats tighter around them against the chilling wind. Beau found a place where the rainwater streamed off the makeshift canvas roof and was washing the plates by holding them under the small waterfall.

The drumming of the rain on the canvas and the wind rumbling through the trees disguised the mud-muffled sound of running hooves. With a whoop and a holler two men rode their horses at a run under the tarp and, hauling back on the reins, sat their lathered horses back on their haunches as they slid and kicked mud all over the camp. Beau was knocked back against a wagon wheel by the weight of the frightened horse.

"That's no way to treat those animals mister," Beau barked as he brushed some of the mud clods off his coat.

Obviously drunk, the men to whom Beau had addressed his comment reeled and tottered to regain his balance as he stood beside the exhausted horse. His eyes widened and focused as he spluttered, "Who are you talking to nigger?"

"I'm lookin' at you peckerwood, so I must be talkin' to you."

"Well, you won't be doing any more talkin' boy," the drunk said as he began to pull a long barreled pistol from beneath his coat. Before he could get the pistol cocked, the tin dishes had slammed into his throat and Beau had wrestled the gun away from him. The drunk had fallen on the ground and as he gathered himself to stand Beau cocked the hammer back on the big pistol and told him, "You just stay down there, 'boy!"

The other rider had laid his hands on the saddle gun on his horse when Micah warned, "Let that rifle lay mister," and cocked his rifle. Then he added, "Get over there on the ground with your partner."

The drunk responded, "Nigger, you know you ain't going to shoot a white man. The war is over and you may be free, but you'll hang in Georgia for shooting a white man," and he leaned to pull his saddle gun.

Micah put a bullet next to his boot, kicking up mud and causing both of the drunks horses to shy and run.

"Now look what you've done, Georgia cracker," Beau scolded, "those poor horses are back in the rain."

Micah handed Ezekial his rifle and told him, "Plug them in the leg if they move." He climbed up in the wagon and jumped back down in half a minute with a coil of rope.

"What you going to do with that rope?" the smaller drunk squealed.

"Why, I'm gonna hog tie you two drunken varmints so a body can sleep tonight."

"No you ain't," the bigger drunk started and began to rise when Ezekial brought the barrel of the rifle down across his hat a bit harder than he intended. He dropped like a bag of potatoes.

After hog-tying both of the drunks, Micah quickly tired of hearing the smaller drunk threaten and curse. He pulled the boots off him and threw them out into the rain. He jerked his socks off, stuffed one between his teeth and used the other to tie around his head and secure it between his teeth, effectively muzzling him. Then he turned to Ezekial and told him, "Give me a hand here." They pulled him out from under the sheltering tree and tarp and left him laying on his side in the puddle of rain.

"Think he might drown?" Ezekial asked.

"Naw, the Lord looks after drunks and fools," Micah answered.

Beau put on his slicker and rode out and caught the drunks' two mounts, brought them back under the tarp, rubbed all three horses down and dried them. He fed them oats and corn, watered them, then tended the drunks' horses' wounds made by the cruel spurs the drunks wore. He took the spurs off their boots and threw then as far into the brush as he could.

Exekial slept fitfully, waking every hour or so to check on the hog-tied drunks prodding them to make sure they were alive. Micah and Beau slept the sleep of the innocent, waking at the break of dawn refreshed.

After a hearty trail breakfast, they left the drunks in the middle of the road still tied hand and foot. Beau took the sock out of the little drunks' mouth, he spat and immediately began cursing and threatening. Sam looked at the bundled, screeching man and cocked his head. He walked over and smelled the drunk and shook his head away in disgust, blowing the odor from his nostrils. While the drunkard hollered and cussed, Sam smiled and his eye winked as he lazily lifted his hind leg and walking on three legs, relieved himself on the tied man from his crown all the way down. After a satisfying sprinkling he ran and jumped and scrambled up onto the wagon seat beside Ezekial.

The three travelers laughed as Micah said, "It's the 'hair' of the dog that's good for hangover Sam, not the 'pee' of the dog!"

"Let's put some miles behind us this morning friends, in case one of these is related to a sheriff hereabouts," Beau suggested. His wisdom was well heeded, they put many miles behind them that day and the next, plunging through the sprinkling rain.

On the third day after the encounter with the inebriated ruffians, the weather changed abruptly after dawn. The temperature dropped to below freezing and sleet began to cut through the air. Sam moved from his accustomed place on the seat of the wagon to the wagon bed, protected from the freezing rain by the canvas cover. He dug under a pile of clothes and blankets for warmth, sticking his head out only when the mules who had slogged and splashed through the frozen mire found the way blocked by another wagon broken down on the narrow road.

Ezekial set the brake and called, "Hello!"

Beau and Micah rode beside him and halted as he tied the reins and stepped down. Sam watched him disembark but did not follow down into the ankle deep frozen muck. One of the mules blew and shook the rain off his back causing a ringing of the chains and a head popped out of the drawn canvas above the tailgate of the disabled wagon. Ezekial was surprised to see the golden-white head of a pretty little girl. Then the head of a slightly older, but no less pretty girl appeared. A woman's head, obviously the mother, came in sight above the children.

"Howdy!" Ezekial loudly spoke over the screeching wind, "How are you?"

"Not well," the woman answered.

Just then a thin figure appeared beside the broken wheel with a double-barreled shotgun.

The woman noticed the man and said, "It's okay Luther. Maybe these men can help us."

"Got a broken wheel?"

"Naw," the thin old man with the shotgun said, "We're just letting one wheel rest...hell yea. The wheel fell off. Can't get a jack under the wagon to lift it so's I can get the wheel back on."

"Maybe I can help," Ezekial said and strode forward.

"We'll get down and lighten the load," the woman yelled over the biting wind.

"No need. Just have a seat inside."

"We'll get down and help. Let us tie these horses," Micah offered.

"No need in all of us getting muddy. Stay mounted."

Micah and Beau glanced at one another.

"I'm Ezekial."

"Luther."

"Well Luther, I'll lift the wagon. Can you get that wheel on by yerself?"

"Sure. But that wagon's mighty heavy mister. I don't think all of us could lift it."

"Just get that wheel ready Luther." Ezekial lumbered to the wagon and disappeared beneath it.

"You ready Luther?"

"Ready."

The wagon lifted to level immediately, and Luther, in shock just stood there.

"Slide that wheel on Luther. I can't hold it all day."

Hurriedly Luther slid the big wheel on and tapped in the cog.

"Alright mister, it's on there."

Mud to his knees, Ezekial came from beneath the wagon. The three heads again popped out from the inside of the wagon cover.

"Thank you sir."

"Thank you."

"Thank you Ezekial. I'm Callie. If we can find a place to stop I'd surely like to repay you men with a hot meal. If we can get a fire lit in this mess."

"That sounds wonderful Miss Callie. I expect we'll find a place down the road we can get under the trees and hang a tarp. Beau, if you would, ride ahead and see if you can find a place dry enough."

"Sho' will."

The woman smiled and said, "Fine, we'll see you down the road then."

Luther was staring open-mouthed up at Ezekial.

"Luther! Let's go."

Luther came out of his state of wonder and hurried ahead to the freight wagon up ahead.

"I think you mightily impressed Luther with your strength, sir."

"Well ma'am, I may impress you with my appetite."

She smiled and the three pretty heads ducked back behind the canvas.

A couple of miles down the soggy, frozen road Beau waved at Luther and all three wagons followed him up a rocky grade to a spot under trees halfway up a small hill where they parked the wagons in a semi-circle. Within fifteen minutes they had stretched and tied tarps for a roof and another tarp between wagons for a windbreak. A fallen tree furnished some reasonable dry wood and they built a roaring fire. When all the animals were dried, fed, watered and tied on a tether, they all gathered around the blazing fire absorbing the heat, waiting for it to die down for cooking.

The woman, who was a bit shy of five feet tall was dressed in heavy, lace-up boots, a long thick dress and even thicker leather coat. She wore a wide brim hat tied with a scarf under her chin. She stood with her gloved hands on her hips as she addressed the newly met men, her little ones bundled up before her.

"Gentlemen my name is Callie MacGillicuddy, and these are my daughters Sallie and Nellie. Sallie is the oldest and biggest but Nellie, my youngest, has the bigger mouth."

Nellie blushed and looked down at her small, booted feet. Sallie giggled.

Ezekial gave a shallow bow and tipped his hat.

"How do you do ladies. I'm Ezekial Robertson." With his big arm he indicated and said, "This is Micah Johnson and Beau Johnson. We are headed to Texas."

"We are headed to Texas also. San Antonio is our first destination. Oh, and this is my friend and employee Luther," she spoke as he joined the others at the fire.

"Howdy do," Luther nodded and placed a coffee pot on the edge of the flames.

"I'm headed to a ranch in south Texas where a friend lives. I may buy land there." Ezekial said.

"I'm in the market for ranch land myself. Want to raise beef cattle. I have a letter to a banker and land speculator there who may be of assistance."

They discussed their plans as they drank coffee and warmed themselves. Luther pounded two rods into the ground and placed a third rod through their eyeholes across the fire.

"Well, seems Luther is ready for me to cook. I'm afraid all we have to cook are vegetables, lots of taters and onions."

"Ma'am, we have three rabbits the dog Sam, cut out of the brush this morning before the rain started. If you would allow, I'll cut that meat up and we can add it to your vegetables. We have some flour too." Micah offered.

"Why, that's a fine idea Micah. Rabbit stew and dumplins is it? A fine warming meal for such a cold, wet evening."

The next while was busy for Micah and Callie, cutting things up and seasoning, while Ezekial introduced Sam to the girls. Luther and Beau discussed the weather, the road, and horses. The rain stopped and soon the smell of the steaming stew in the fresh autumn air was delicious of itself. They enjoyed the wait while the stew cooked talking about the stories they had heard and read about Texas, about the cheap land, the Indians, the heat and their hopes.

"I think this stew is about done, I just hope there's enough for you men to get full."

"Yes Ma'am, I believe there's plenty. Ladies first of course."

"Oh no. You all help yourselves."

Ezekial gestured to Micah, who handed Beau a plate and he ladled out a plateful, blew on it and sat down on his saddle. Micah served himself, then Ezekial made a plate for Sam, then for himself. The girls made their plates and Callie filled her plate.

"Why there's a plenty left here. You all will have to get a second helping."

"Ma'am, would you mind if Micah said grace over our food?"

"Yes, would you please?"

"Lord thank You for allowing us to be good Samaritans this evening and for the reward of the company of these fine ladies who have prepared this delicious repast for us in the midst of the storm. Keep us all safe in the shadow of Your wings, we ask in Jesus name. Amen."

Luther peeped out of the side of his eyes at this very dark ex-slave using such big words and high language. He was impressed, as was Callie.

There was a silence after the prayer in which the sounds of fork and spoon on plates filled the void.

After a second helping of the pot luck stew Ezekial said, "Ma'am, if you won't think me forward to say, since we're headed down the same road, headed to around the same place, would you consider traveling with us? We'd be handy then in case Luther wants to rest a while... and we can benefit from your cooking once in awhile. Not that Micah can't cook, but a woman's touch is sure appreciated once in awhile.

"That's a very thoughtful offer Ezekial. Land, I don't see why we couldn't travel together. Lord knows I've been concerned with just Luther and me to protect these girls down these lonely roads. We have rifles and shotguns and both of us would use them if push comes to shove; but blamed if it wouldn't be a comfort to travel with you men."

"If you don't mind me asking Callie, what happened to your husband?"

"The war," she felt that was explanation enough.

"Got all my family too, what was left of us. I've sold our place and headed west."

"Sold our place too. Didn't get what it was worth, but since my husband was an officer in the Union army, our neighbors made it hard on us. Treated us like we should be ashamed. Some of those people are still fighting the war."

"Where did you live?"

"Western Virginia. And you?"

"North Carolina. Near Raleigh."

The girls were petting Sam and he seemed to be enjoying their attention as he cleaned their plates. Micah took out his harmonica and began playing The Blue Tail Fly. After the first few notes the girls began to sing along, then Callie and Beau joined in. Ezekial clapped his hands and stamped his big feet. Luther did a little jig to everyone's delight.

After the song Callie told Luther, "I didn't know you could cut the rug like that Luther! Why didn't you sing along?"

"Can't carry a tune, don't have the ear for it," he winked, touching the side of his head.

The girls squealed for another song and Micah played Someone's in the Kitchen with Dinah. They enjoyed several old favorites until Micah pleaded for some air.

"That was more fun than we've had in months, wasn't it girls? But we'd better not wear Micah out, he may play for us again. And we all need to sleep. Tomorrow we'll make some miles. Goodnight gentlemen."

"Goodnight ladies"
"Goodnight."
"Goodnight everybody."

Micah was up early to prepare a breakfast of biscuits and gravy. And not a drop of the two pots of coffee was wasted through the shivering preparation. Beau and Ezekial led out. Beau on his thoroughbred and Ezekial on the big mongrel Percheron. Luther followed their lead, Callie and the girls next and Micah driving Ezekial's wagon with the unhitched animals tied behind. Beau slipped off the road at a shallow stream and caught up in an hour with two turkeys which Callie and the girls plucked as they sat by the tailgate.

Ezekial found a somewhat dry, shady place around noon and they rested the animals, feeding them each a feed bag of corn. Beau and Luther watered all the stock and checked shoes and harnesses.

"Beau, how long you known Ezekial?"
"Not long, few weeks."
"How'd you get hooked up with him?"
"Heard he was headed to Texas. We was headed that way too. We ast' him fer a job and bless his soul, he hi'ed us for the journey. Don't know how we could of got by wit'out him."
"He's sure a big one. Strong as an ox ain't he?"
"Heh-heh, sho' is. And young too, 'bout sixteen I think."
"Sixteen! Ain't even full growed yet! Lordy mercy! He'll be hard to feed in awhile."
"He already is."

They laughed together. Beau offered Luther a cigar and they smoked together, leaning back against tree trunks on their heels.

Micah cleaned and butchered the turkeys in preparation for supper while Callie re-heated the pot of beans and salt pork she had let simmer all the night before. Ezekial ate two big plates full of beans and was glad to be driving the last wagon in line that afternoon, so as not to be embarrassed by the fumes emanating from him with regularity and from the sound of gaseous explosion. Despite his efforts to release the recurring pressure silently, he was not always successful and one especially urgent relinquishment of methane sounded off something like a trombone. When hearing the girls in the wagon ahead giggle he loudly admonished the offending mules. He heard Callie hush the girls. He hoped the girls wouldn't look back, his face was red as an apple. Sam had much earlier evacuated his normal spot on the wagon seat for a place at the tailgate where he hung his head out into the fresh air, looking back at Ezekial with disdain.

The little caravan made it to Mississippi with no trouble. They enjoyed one another's company and began to like each other quite a lot. For various reasons all of them had been separated from others for awhile and the loners were making friends easily now with their traveling companions. They told one another stories of their pasts sometimes, and though they had led differing lives, their lives had meaningful similarities. All of them had lost a loved one in the past and each could empathize with the others. The group was beginning to feel like family.

At a mid-day rest Callie was resting on a blanket spread over dead yellow grass, day-dreaming of the house she'd like to have in Texas when her daughter's laughter drew her attention. She looked around for them but couldn't see them. Their laughter and whispers were near she knew and she twisted all around but could not see them. Her eyes fell on Ezekial who was smiling and looking up into the trees beside her. She followed his gaze and saw her "little ladies" twenty feet up into an oak watching a group of squirrels watching them.

"What in the world? Sallie and Nellie, you get yourselves down here right now!"

The girls quietly climbed down.

"You cannot climb trees with your dresses on young ladies. And never so high, as that. If you fell you would break your neck!"

"Yes ma'am."

"Yes ma'am."

"Now, load those dishes into the wagon and get ready to go."

Callie took a deep breath and looked relieved that the girls came back to the earth safely. She shook her head and told Ezekial, "I swear those girls act like boys sometimes, they are so wild! But, I suppose that's a blessing. It's likely they won't have much chance to be ladies in Texas. They'll have to learn to lend a hand."

"Well Callie, learning how to do for themselves won't make them less of a lady in my book. 'Fore we come along, you prob'bly chopped wood, hitched up and drove the horses and still managed to teach and raise your daughters. In Texas, if you don't have a man around, I'm sure you'll continue to do what needs be done. That don't make you any less a lady, it makes you more."

"Maybe you're right Ezekial. It's the times, the times are changing. In the war, with all the men gone, the women had to do for themselves. There are fewer men now and on the frontier there's just so much work to do. Everyone must lend a hand."

"My soldier friend from Texas told me of women who wear pants, boots and spurs out in the wilds doing the work of a man."

"Necessity's the mother of invention they say, we'll all do what we have to do I suppose."

"I suppose you'll be looking for a place nearby a large town and civilization so the girls will go to school and church and such."

"Yes, that would be nice, but I expect most of the places like that are taken. I'll listen to folks there and look around and do the best I can with the money I have. I've got to invest wisely and may have to live with a lot less than we were used to in Virginia. I can teach the girls myself, I taught the little school back home and did well at it 'til the war came and everybody began to hate us all because my husband joined the Union army. The children all learned, so did I. I learned how to teach, I was able to attend school at home 'til I was sixteen. Not that I'm any professor, but I know the lessons that are important to learn in life. People don't need to know much about Greeks and Romans so much as how to grow and market their crops and how they should treat their neighbors and what the men they elect should stand for. Children need to learn kindness, consideration, courage and love. Sure, they need to learn to cipher and read and write, and history and science and geography has its place, but it sure ain't first place."

"I believe you're right. I went to school once when I was oh, ten or eleven, 'til just after the war started. After my brothers went off to soldier, I was needed to help Gramps on the farm. I believe most of the lessons he taught me from experience in living and from his heart were better learned and more valuable than most of what was taught at school. I learned important lessons from just watching my Gramps. You know, he mostly lived his life by using what the Bible said as a kind of map. When we had trouble, that's where he would go to find his way."

"Amen. Many's the time I've searched the Scriptures and prayed the Lord to lead me through dark days. And I pray that these girls are learning well the good of life from watching me. It ain't easy being an example and feeling their young eyes on me. Sometimes I want to cry, but I can't. My tired body wants to rest and be lazy, but love just won't let me. Jesus taught we must be servants to those we love."

"You don't do everything for these girls though, I've seen your patience in letting them learn to do for themselves."

Callie chuckled. "Patience is right! And my patience is sorely tried by these...young 'uns. They're bright and they've learned if they dawdle long enough over a chore that Momma's patience may run out and she'll come and do the work for them. We don't none of us ever stop learning and I'm still being taught by these girls and by life."

Callie looked to the wagons and pointed. "Look at those girls lolly-gagging and listening to some wild tale that Luther has invented." She again chuckled and shook her head. "If his stories weren't so entertaining they'd be sinful. Let's go listen."

They crept quietly to a place behind the wagon where they could hear but wouldn't be noticed. Luther, his thumbs behind his suspenders, his shoulders held back, was pompously lecturing the girls about the intelligence of creatures.

"Yep, some varmints are highly intelligent. And it's the ones not generally held to be smart that are most clever. Now, take these horses. A man can teach them to pull a wagon or a plow or teach them to take a saddle and a man on their back. A horse can find his own way home and generally will head home if left alone because he's been fed there. If a horse is wild though he'll just eat grass or weeds or whatever vegetation is available. He'll get skinny in the winter. But an ant now, an ant will gather food and store it for the winter. And those squirrels you were watching they'll gather up pe-cans and acorns and other food that'll keep. Squirrels are usually plump and healthy 'cause they use that little brain God gave 'em. But, jes' like us, when they act 'for they think, they can get in lotsa trouble!

"I was a-watching a big fat squirrel one fine spring day as I was a-fishing down across the stream. He was across the creek and fussing with somethin' in the water. He was out in the middle of the stream on a log that'd fallen in the water and a-messing with something behind the log. I eased up and sneaked down the bank 'til I could see what he was doing. There was a piece of bark that'd fell off the log and there were a couple of fat pe-cans a-sitting on the piece of bark that was a'floating 'side the log. The squirrel was a-pawing at the water trying to make the piece of bark with the pe-cans a-sitting on it float closer to the log so he could reach them, but the bark and the pe-cans just kept drifting farther away. Pretty soon that big fat squirrel got fighting mad, a-screeching and a-hopping and he just dove in that stream and was a-swimming to get those pe-cans when an alligator come up out of that water and swallowed that big fat squirrel, hide, hair and all!"

"That alley-gator ate that big fat squirrel?" Nellie asked, her eyes big and round.

"Sure did. I went back to fishing and was a'thinking I mays well quit 'cause that 'gator prob'ly scared off all the fish. And then that old 'gator eased up out of the water, burped and grinned' an' put two more fat pe-cans on that piece of bark!"

Callie and Ezekial couldn't suppress their laughter as they walked around the wagon. When Sallie and Nellie saw their reaction to the story, they realized they'd been had.

"Aw Luther, you just told a big old windy," Sallie admonished.

"That's the truth or my eyes deceived me!" Luther protested.

"Let's load up girls, before lightning strikes," Callie urged.

Even Sam was grinning and winking.

CHAPTER SIX

"I don't like that man. I must get to know him better."
--Abraham Lincoln

"The Indians say you must never disagree with a man while you are facing him. Go around behind him and look the same way they do, when you are facing him. Look over his shoulder and get his viewpoint, then go back and face him and you will have a different idea."
--Will Rogers

Conscience is but a word that cowards use,
Devis'd at first to keep the strong in awe.
--Richard III v.3
--Wm. Shakespeare

Conscience, I say, not thine own, but of the other; for why is my liberty judged of another man's conscience?
--I Cor. 10:29 (KJV)

NOAH THOUGHT HE was in Alabama somewhere, but he couldn't be sure. He'd been sloppy drunk for days. He was able to keep his big roan heading west and stay in the saddle. He tried to remember the last time he had rested the horse or even got down. He knew he'd slept through the night. His legs were asleep, his butt was numb as was his head, but he stayed in the saddle until he found himself in a rather large town. He awoke once again to find his horse stopped at a water trough drinking deeply.

He dropped his reins and with repeated efforts lifted his right leg and fell out of the saddle. An old timer helped him to his feet and he leaned against the roan until the world stopped spinning. He pushed the old timer's arm off his shoulders and straightened. He adjusted his hat and dusted off his clothes surveyed his location and then asked the old fellow, "Where am I at?"

"You're in Birmingham, Mister. You alright?"

"Mmm. Maybe." He smelled his armpit and winced. "I need a bath. Hot meal. Whiskey. Is there a livery here?"

"This is the livery mister. Want me to take care of your horse?"

"Yep." Noah reached in his pocket for a coin, but it was empty. So was the other pocket. He dug into his saddlebags, found some coins and handed the liveryman one, throwing the bags over his shoulder.

"That's too much money mister. Let me get you some change."

"You can give it to me later. Could you direct me to a bath, a hotel, whiskey?"

"Yes sir. About two blocks up the road on the right, the Dixie Hostelry. You can get a room and a bath, a meal and whiskey. Can you walk that far?"

"Shirtainly. Just take good care of my horse for me. I'll be leaving at firs' light 'morrow," Noah slurred and then began a winding way down the muddy road.

He found the hotel, paid for a room and a bath and ordered a bottle of whiskey and a meal. He soaked in the hot water, smoked a cigar and let the whiskey clear his thinking. He fell asleep in the bath and awoke spluttering and coughing up bathwater. His cigar was drowned but, he hadn't spilled a drop out of the bottle of whiskey. He fought his way out of the deep tub and dripped across the frayed rug naked to the high bedstead and crawled across it. He was asleep almost immediately.

Brandy woke him just before the dawn. She was crying, calling his name and he awoke from the dream feeling the tugging on his heart. He blinked, shook his head and looked around the dark room for her. The dream seemed so real! He again wondered if he had done the right thing. He loved the young woman and knew that she loved him, yet she deserved a better man than he was. He was good for only one thing, fighting. He did not enjoy fighting in the U.S. Army through these past years but he did his job very well. He thoroughly enjoyed fighting and killing Comanches. He looked forward to getting back to Texas where the crop of Comanches would be ripe for the harvest. Given time, troops and opportunity, he would annihilate the snakes in the grass from the earth.

He poured a deep draught from the whiskey bottle down his neck, then dressed. After shaving around his mustache and goatee, he strapped his Colt on and poured out the coins from his saddlebags. Counting his money, he was satisfied he had enough to get to Austin and outfit himself after re-joining the Rangers.

It had been at least a couple of days since he had eaten. It seemed his stomach had drawn up and though the breakfast tasted good he couldn't stomach much. He bought three bottle of whiskey and a few cigars and was getting his change from the liveryman as the sun rose. As he rode out of town the image of Brandy and her tears went with him. The more he thought of her the more he drank and the faster he rode the roan.

Ezekial was dozing on the wagon seat when the mules stopped suddenly and the old wagon and its contents rattled and banged startling and waking him. He heard Micah's voice yelling to him. "Ezekial! Come around here."

He tied the reins onto the brake handle and stepped down, walking quickly around Callie's wagons. There was Beau on his horse looking down at a man laying in the road. Micah was standing beside his horse over the prone figure when Ezekial walked up.

"Is he breathing Ezekial?" Callie asked as she walked up.

Ezekial kneeled down and put his face close to the man. The alcohol burned his nose. Sam sniffed, wrinkled his face and pawed at his nose. He backed up a few steps and looked up at Ezekial questionably.

"Whew! Yea, he's breathing. I b'leve he's just real drunk. Smells like it. Give me a hand Micah. Let's carry him off the road over under that tree."

They picked him up gently and carried him to a spot beside the road. When they laid him down the man groaned, then started and sat up with a Colt revolver cocked and pointed so fast that it seemed to have just appeared in his hand.

"Easy mister! You was laying in the road. We just carried you out of harm's way," Ezekial said.

The man's blood-red eyes tried to focus on the figures surrounding him, squinting, then opening his eyes wide. His head wobbled atop his neck and he moaned.

"Awww,... head hurts," the drunk grabbed his head.

"Let me see." Callie said as she reached out to the man's head. "You have a knot on your head the size of a hen-egg. Did you fall off your horse?"

"Where is my horse?" the man asked, looked around and moaned at the movement. He lay back down.

Callie got a wet rag and washed the blood off the back of the man's head, then gave him a drink of water. He spewed it out and asked indigently, "What in hell was that?"

"It was water. I expect you need some," Callie answered.

"I expect not! Where's my whiskey?"

"We found no whiskey."

"I've been robbed! Sure as shooting." The man moaned and lay his head back on the ground and closed his eyes.

The group gathered a few feet away and were discussing what they should do when Beau galloped back down the road to them pulling a big red roan by his reins.

"Found this horse down the road a quarter mile."

The man sat up, groaned and said, "That's my horse. Are the saddlebags on him?"

"Nope. No saddlebags. Just this carpet bag."

"Damnation! Someone stole my money! Bring me that carpet bag boy."

Beau swung out of the saddle and lifted the carpetbag and untied it from the saddle horn. He carried it to the old man who sat up and took it eagerly from him. Jerking it open he removed a full bottle of whiskey.

"Thank heaven! They left me some medicine." He uncorked the bottle and poured a healthy swig down his throat.

"Medicine huh?" Callie asked, "More like poison."

The man grinned and scooted over the ground to lean against the trunk of the tree he was under.

"Nectar of the gods, my good lady. Nepenthe for life's pain and sorrows." the old drunk grinned. Beau had tied the horse to a nearby tree and had walked across the road. He returned carrying a saddle.

"There weren't no saddlebags with the saddle. This your saddle mister?"

"Yep, that's it. Not completely worn out, but well broke in. Seems like whoever hit me over the head did it when I was unsaddling my horse. The horse must have run off or they'd have taken him too. Left me my pistol too. Maybe they were drunk."

"You had all your money in your saddlebags?" Ezekial asked.

"Most of it. I have a few coins in my pockets."

"Have you eaten lately?"

"Uh. Must have been awhile."

"Hungry?"

"Yes ma'am. "A bit."

"We may as well make camp here don't you think Ezekial?" Somebody has to help this old reprobate."

"May as well. Only a couple hours of daylight left."

They made camp handily, everyone handling their assignment with practiced dispatch. Callie got her big fry pan out and fried beef and potatoes they'd purchased the previous day in a small community at a high price. Micah made the coffee, pan biscuits and gravy. Micah gave the drunk a cup and he sipped, made a face, then added a dollop of whiskey. Then sipped and smiled.

Callie brought him a tin plate full of delicious hot food and he sat it aside and stood shakily. "Why, I thank you," the stranger said. His skinny legs shook as he spread his arms and said to all, "Let me introduce myself. Ladies," here he bowed and stumbled, "Gentlemen. I'm Noah Lister, Captain, retired, of both the Confederate States and the Texas Rangers. I have lost all I own it seems, except my horse, saddle and pistol due to being a damned drunk, please excuse my language ladies." Here his old, weathered cheeks flushed, exhibiting his embarrassment and sincerity. "I am returning to Texas, the land of my youth to seek my fortune. I gratefully accept your kind hospitality. You are the instruments of the mercy and grace of Providence and, as such, He will bless you and I am indebted to you." Here he bowed with a flourish.

"Um huh," said Callie. "All that being said, you welcome. I'm Callie, this is Sallie, Nellie," she added gesturing to each child. "The man who served your coffee is Micah. The young man with, the horses is Beau and the young giant is Ezekial and that's Luther. We have all lost part of our families and our homes and are also traveling to Texas to establish homes and lives."

"I am duly d'sgraced," replied Noah, "that your first glimpse of me was so shameful, but everything you see of me from now will be an improvement." At this he put a hand to his head and sank to the ground. "My head wound is making me dizzy."

"Or the whiskey," Callie rejoined.

"The whiskey is a necessary elixir."

"Um huh."

Ezekial could tell that Callie didn't want her daughters to associate with this man. He wanted to extract what information he could from this Texas native so he sat down beside him on the ground to eat. He learned the area his friend Samuel had his ranch below the Nueces River was an area of bandits, rustlers and, in the west, lots of still wild Indians. He was told about the beautiful hill country in the middle of the state. He found out that Noah intended to secure a job with the Texas Rangers when he returned despite his age. Further inquiry was halted when Mr. Lister fell asleep, head on his saddle, one hand on his Colt, one hand on his whiskey.

Micah chuckled as he picked up the empty plate, "He's tired," he observed.

"He's drunk," Callie corrected.

Next morning, Sallie and Nellie finished cleaning up the breakfast utensils while everyone else was busy hitching up, packing up or saddling up. When everyone was ready to go Noah was still snoring. Callie had wrapped two biscuits and a hunk of bacon in an old cloth and laid them atop his saddle. They left his horse picketed and put a pile of oats and corn on the ground before him. They had tried to awaken him three times with no success, so they hit the road leaving him to sleep it off.

Early November in Mississippi was still warm and very humid. The trees still dressed in leaves and thick foliage grew right up to the edge of the narrow road, blocking most of the breeze. It was a sweaty, sticky journey for the humans, more so for the toiling beasts. Before noon they came upon a deep, muddy stream that ran beside the road and they stopped to rest and water the animals.

"How much farther to Texas?" Nellie asked everyone as she brushed away the hair stuck to the sweat on her face. No one really knew.

"Quite a few days yet baby," Callie answered.

"We've been making a good distance every day." Ezekial said.

"We'll still have a long way to go when we get to the edge of Texas from what I've heard," Micah pointed out.

"Where are you going Micah?" Sallie asked.

"Well, Beau here will be going to someplace called Gonzales, somewhere round San Antonio to find his wife who has his child somewhere 'round there. He got a letta' from her las' August at the old plantation. After that, well, we'll try to find a place we kin work and fit in and have some kinda' life. What about you all Callie?"

"We'll go to San Antonio first. I have a letter from my lawyer back in Virginny to a banker there. Maybe he can help me find a place to ranch. Land is supposed to be pretty cheap. I'll just have to see what's best when I get there. Ezekial, what do you have in mind to do?"

"San Antonio is on the way to where I'm going. I'll hang around there for awhile and see how things are. I want to see a friend of mine at his ranch a hunnerd miles north of a place named Laredo on the

Rio Grande and get his advice." Beau asked Luther where he planned to go.

"Well. I reckon that whenever body goes a different way, I'll see which way the wind blows me. Maybe I'll head to Californy or maybe I'll catch a boat to China. Can't say. Just have to see what opportunities come along."

"Luther. What would you do in China?" Callie asked.

"Well. I 'spect I'd eat rice and drink tea," Luther grinned.

"Um huh. Right now finish your coffee. We're wasting daylight."

Around the middle of the afternoon they passed through a messy little camp, just two tent-like hovels made of sticks and mud, canvas and rags. One of the rickety structures was open across the front that faced the road, a canvas spread like an awning propped above on sticks. Several shabbily dressed, dirty and bearded men sat around on stumps and boxes drinking from whiskey jugs. Some rude comments about niggers on high horses, about lonely women and kittens on parade as they passed. The ruffians quieted as Ezekial came up alongside them holding the big shotgun and staring hard at the half dozen men as he passed slowly by. Ezekial's blood was up, he wanted one of these bullies to say one more thing out of line. He couldn't abide incivility and discourtesy.

They made good mileage the rest of the day and made camp an hour before dark at another slow running, muddy river. After eating, Micah told Callie, "Zeke and Beau an' me are gonna' tie our horses close to us and double picket and hobble the other horses. That rough lookin' bunch we passed a ways back might be trailing us to rob us, and we need to be prepared. Sleep wit' your shotgun close by."

You're right Micah. We need to be prepared," Callie replied.

Ezekial woke sometime after midnight and listened to the night. The only sounds were the crickets and the frogs. He quietly rose and Sam stirred, then lay back down. He walked away from the camp to relieve himself. The misshapen moon was two days from being full and the slow black river was reflecting the cold, distant stars. All the horses stood still, resting peacefully. Dawn was maybe two hours away. He measured coffee into the pot and poured in the water, then added a chunk of wood to the fire and stirred the coals. After settling the pot down into the coals, he stretched his long frame down beside Sam. The comfort of Sam's warmth and the cool breeze coaxed him back down below the surface of consciousness.

Sallie's shrill scream shook the camp, then a gunshot. Callie woke to see a dark shape fall into the wagon, then another shot and another body fell over her from the near end of the wagon. She reached and pulled both her screaming daughters to her and grabbed for the shotgun. Then a fusillade of shots; Callie pushed the girls down and cocked her shotgun, peering out over the tailgate. A horse ran by and a body fell off it and through the coals. By the flare of firelight she saw Micah lying on the ground firing his rifle into the brush.

The shooting stopped. Everyone heard horses running away. Ezekial stepped to the wagon and called her, "Callie, you alright?"

She stepped down from the wagon with Ezekial's help saying, "I think so. Girls come out of there."

Sallie and Nellie jumped down. Sallie was trembling and her nightdress was torn from her shoulder. Nellie was staring wide-eyed at the blood on her sleeve. Callie quickly looked her over, asking, "That's not your blood is it?"

"No, it's one of those men who fell in the wagon."

"Light a lantern Luther," Callie directed as she kept the shotgun trained on the wagon.

Luther stepped up and held the lantern as Ezekial and Callie pointed shotguns inside. Ezekial lifted the closest still body out and let it fall to the ground, then walked to the other end of the wagon and threw the other body down.

Luther had examined each body and determined they were dead. Each one had a hole in their head. By the lanterns light they agreed that these were two of the drunken ruffians from the camp beside the road they had passed yesterday. There was a third dead outlaw lying by the fire. Ezekial pulled them outside the camp into a pile.

"They's two more dead un's out in the brush that was going fo' the hosses," Beau said as he walked into the lantern's glow. "I shot one and somebody else shot the other un."

Callie said, "Thank you Ezekial for shooting the two getting into the wagon," as she hugged her girls to her breast." "We were all asleep until Sallie screamed."

"Momma, he was touching me, he was tearing my dress."

"It's okay now baby."

"I got the one who rolled through the fire, but I didn't shoot the two trying to get in the wagon," Ezekial replied to Callie's thanks.

A voice behind them said, "I had to shoot those two varmints 'fore they got in the hen house."

Rifles and shotguns all swung toward Noah Lister, who held up his hands and said, "Easy," before leading his horse that had rags tied over its hooves into the light.

"I guess I'm late for supper and too early for breakfast." He took a final swig of whiskey and pitched the empty bottle out into the weeds. "Is there any coffee left?"

He walked to the coffeepot lying beside the fire, picked it up and shook it. "All gone."

Micah reached out his hand, "Here, let me have it. I b'lieve we could all use some coffee."

Callie said, "Mr. Lister, I suppose thanks are in order, you came along at just the right time."

"Oh, I been following these malefactors since they left their nasty little camp. I woke not long after y'all left. Thanks for the biscuits, by the way. I overheard the heathens loud-talking 'bout what they were going to do to the pilgrims with the wagons and the darkies with their prancing high horses. No offense meant. So, I waited until they finished their whiskey, refrained from drinking mine and tippy toed old Jughead here and trailed them right down the road to ya'll."

"You have our sincere thanks," said Callie.

"Sure do."

"Yes, thank you."

"You're all welcome. I been dealin' with outlaws for so long now that it seems like it's my job even when it's not."

Beau and Ezekial found the other two dead bandits out in the brush and drug them in and stacked them with the others. Noah carried a lantern out to the pile of bodies and searched them for valuables. He put watches, jewelry, guns and knives aside and put all the money in his pockets declaring, "I suspect this is my money they stole, what they didn't spend on whiskey."

Beau gathered three horses that were obviously the dead men's and Noah found his saddlebag on one of them. After breakfast, they packed the bodies on the horses and tied them to Ezekial's tailgate. Around eleven o'clock they drove into Jackson and stopped on the main road. A man came out of the building on which hung a shingle advertising a medical doctor.

Noah asked, "Are you the doctor?"

The gray haired man answered, "Yes sir, I am the doctor. But it appears these men are beyond my help."

"Yes sir, 'less you have a potion for resurrection. We were hoping you could direct us to the sheriff's office."

"I could, but there's no one there. All legal matters are now handled by the army of occupation. You will find the U.S. Army encamped around the court house. Someone there will likely escort you to the old Calander plantation which they have taken for their headquarters. You'll find many generals and colonels and majors and various and sundry factotums there to confound you in a miasma of tom-foolery."

"Sounds like we might save ourselves a right smart of trouble if we just dumped these bodies in the street."

"No. That would further complicate and delay your lives. Your actions are being noted by many eyes and the report of you has undoubtedly already reached the ears of our occupiers. No, you're in the soup already. May as well relax and patiently endure the cooking."

"Excuse me. I am Lieutenant Cates. I couldn't help but overhear your conversation. If you will follow me I will direct you to the major who is assigned to deal with such investigations."

"Investigations? Hell son, we don't require investigation. We only defended ourselves from attack, rape and plunder." "Patiently endure the soup," the doctor tipped his hat as he disconnected himself by walking away.

"Please follow me," the young lieutenant said as he mounted up.

Outside of town a mile or so the lieutenant led them through aisles of tents to the big plantation house. Directing them to wait, he went inside and returned with an officer who strode directly to the bodies. After a cursory examination, he gave the lieutenant orders, and then returned inside the large house.

The lieutenant supervised a squad of enlisted men who removed the dead from the horses and laid them in a neat row beside the lane. He then asked everyone to come inside. Once inside the commodious parlor they sat and waited for half an hour while several officers met inside a room upstairs. Two lieutenants and a captain eventually came to them and explained that they needed to get statements from each of them as to the occurrence that caused the deaths of the men outside.

After an hour the officers had written out each of their statements and had them sign them. They were instructed to return to their wagons but not to go anywhere. All the statements and officers went up the stairs as they went to their wagons.

They noticed a stocky man with a floppy hat inspecting the bodies laid out on the ground which were quite odorous by now. The man walked over to the group, removed his hat and spoke.

"Hello folks. I'm Judge Keyes. Well, I used to be the Judge hereabouts anyway." He motioned to the corpses, "Looks like the Quibedeaux brothers have robbed their last people. All four of them are laying there dead along with their cousin Pierre Monteux. I suppose they tried to rob you?"

"Among other crimes," Callie answered, glancing at Sallie.

"None of you were injured?"

"No sir."

"These fools must have been drunk."

"Yes sir, I believe they were."

"The powers that be have called me here to identify the bodies. Please be patient. The wheels of justice turn slow but grind fine."

He smiled and bowed as the young Lieutenant led him away.

"What did he mean by that?" Ezekial asked Noah.

"Hell if I know. Pardon my language," Noah glanced at Callie.

"He means we'll be here awhile. May as well get comfortable," Callie said.

Only about an hour later Judge Keyes, Lieutenant Cates and the stocky major returned and asked them to gather round. The big judge addressed them.

"There were rewards for each of these outlaws offered by the U.S. Government. By your statements it is clear that Mr. Lister shot Louis Quibeadeaux and Pierre Monteux. Mr. Lister, here are two bank drafts, payable at the bank established in Jackson in reward for your actions in bringing these men to justice."

"Also, Ezekial Robertson, Micah Johnson and Beau Johnson, here are bank drafts for your valiant efforts in defense of property, life and limb and for delivering these outlaws to their just reward." The major and lieutenant shook everyone's hand and thanked them on behalf of the United States of America. The major said they were free to go.

"Wu-wee! Is this here paper mean I is going to get money for killing that thief?" Beau asked.

"Sure does," answered Ezekial.

"If you'll follow me back into town I'll take you to the new bank, or what passes for a bank these days. It is a paymaster's office in actuality." the big Judge offered.

"Lead the way Judge Keyes," Noah said.

Noah received two hundred fifty dollars. Micah, Beau and Ezekial collected one hundred each. After discussion, they decided to give Luther and Callie a portion of their reward. Callie refused it, so they each gave a little to Luther and he ended up with eighty dollars himself.

There was no room available at the three hotels, the U.S. Army filled them all. Callie found a room at a boarding house for her and the girls and gave the owner money to buy and cook enough fried chicken, mashed potatoes and gravy for their little army. The men made camp on a grassy knoll on the edge of town then went shopping and bought some new clothes. All except Ezekial who could find nothing that fit. Noah volunteered to watch things for them while they were gone. He didn't want to tempt himself to buy more whiskey. He knew he needed to quit drinking for awhile, it had got out of hand. But he sure wished his headache would go away.

Ezekial and Luther stopped by the rooming house and helped Callie and the girls carry the big supper up to the wagons. Everyone was in good spirits except Noah and his mood improved with the chicken, potatoes and gravy.

Callie again thanked Noah for his protection and invited him to please accompany them for the rest of their journey, at least as far as Austin where he planned to re-enlist in the Rangers. Enticed by the good food and the subsequent relief from the pounding headache that had plagued him, he agreed. He enjoyed the company of all these folks and knew that if he continued alone he was likely to continue drinking and he didn't want that.

After shopping for supplies next day, the Texas bound travelers hit the road again. Noah taught the men about scouting and about standing guard on the dark and dangerous roads. There were many people on the road. There were freed slaves and homeless whites, the old and the young, a few who seemed rich and a multitude of the poor and hungry. There were many displaced and desperate souls in the south, so many just trying to survive. There was confusion, brutality, distress, disease, depression, despondency, and death. Many hands reached out to help others, surprisingly, and many persisted to outlast and overcome the daily adversities. They fed and helped as many as they were able yet Noah kept the thieves and predators at a distance, he was well experienced at spotting a bad penny.

They came upon a fair size camp of travelers when the road brought them to the Mississippi River. There were those trying to sell their possessions so they would have the money to pay the ferryman. One group was in the process of building a makeshift raft. And there was a line of those willing to pay the ferryman, but having to wait their turn. There were a handful just watching the slowly oozing mud they called the Mississippi River roll and slide south.

The adults had all dismounted and were standing around discussing and estimating how long a wait they were in for. Noah had rode ahead to see if he could expedite the lingering line. Sallie and Nellie were looking around wide-eyed at all the people and at the impossibly wide river when they saw a small boy about Nellie's size tied up by a wagon wheel. He was sniffling trying not to cry. They approached the boy and were intent on freeing him when a huge, vicious dog exploded out of the back of the wagon and ran toward them baring long yellow tusks. The girls froze, but screamed loudly and shrilly. The bristling mad dog sprang at them and then Sam was there, meeting him in the air. The two dogs tumbled and twisted through the air, rolled entwined through the brush then coiled, wound and writhed through the air again snarling, growling, snapping and biting and tearing at one another.

All the adults heard the girls terrified screams and ran to the sound. Beau and Ezekial got there first, being the youngest and fleetest. Beau stopped to access the pair of bleeding and battling beasts. Being outweighed two to one and not being bred to fight like the big bulldog, Sam had done all he could, he was pinned to the ground and long yellow teeth were being pushed deep into his neck by muscular, powerful jaws. Sam was bravely struggling, but he was done, defeated.

Ezekial slid his big fingers behind and through the gnashing and tearing teeth and his powerful arms strained with adrenaline, love and fear, and the dogs jaws were torn open, freeing a limp and severely wounded Sam. In his anger he threw the heavy, stunned animal thirty feet into the muddy river. The dog disappeared beneath the brown stream and did not reappear. But Ezekial didn't notice, he was on his knees holding Sam's trembling, bleeding body and saying, "Sam,…Sam,…Sam," and not even trying to hold back the tears.

Beau, Luther, Micah, Callie and the girls rushed to Ezekial and Sam. Sam went limp in Ezekial's arms and he collapsed over the inert body, crying, "Sam,…Sam," unmindful of the blood that covered his arms and hands and chest.

A man came around the wagon where the boy was tied cocking a big pistol. He was a big, bearded man and he bellowed, "Get away from him, all of you, get back! You big stupid son of a bitch, you, killed my dog and you're going to pay for..."

That's as far as he got with whatever he intended to say. His face exploded with blood when Noah came around the wagon and swung a club of firewood against his nose and mouth. The gun flew out of his hand, he staggered and Noah hit him again in the face. Teeth were shattered and blood sprayed! The man fell and made a feeble effort to rise and Noah hit him again so hard that his head bounced off the ground. Noah stood over him waiting for him to move, to twitch. He had the thick limb lifted, ready to chop down again, but the man lay very still.

There was a ringing silence in the air. The crowd that had gathered stood staring. The only sounds Noah's labored breath. Then Sam whined softly. Ezekial said, "Sam?"

A thin man of small stature touched Ezekial's arm. He spoke with an English accent.

"Sir, I am a doctor. Bring the dog to my wagon, let me help him. Come. Follow me."

Ezekial followed the little man gently cradling Sam.

"Why did the dogs fight?" Asked Callie.

"We walked over to that wagon to see why the boy was tied up and the big dog ran at us to bite us and Sam stopped him from getting us."

"Why is the boy tied up?" Callie asked, and the group walked over to the dirty little boy in ragged clothes and barefooted.

Luther knelt down and untied the wide-eyed boy. Callie knelt down beside him and asked, "Who tied you to this wheel?"

"It was the man that got beat up. The man with the mean dog," the boy pointed to the prone, unconscious man.

"Why did he tie you up?"

"I kept trying to run away. He tells everyone he's my Uncle and that I'm crazy and a liar. He tells me that he's taking me to west Texas or Mexico to sell me to the Mescaleros. I was trying to get away and fell out of the wagon."

"Where are your folks?"

"Momma was all I had left and she got sick and died. The owner of the house ran me out. That man fed me and I told him about my Momma and all hoping he would help me. He was always drinking and whipping me so I tried to get away and he tied me up."

The group turned to look at the unmoving man with the destroyed face laying on the ground. Well," Callie observed, "You'd better come with us for a ways, 'cross the river at least. Don't you think? What's your name?"

"My name is Charles Barker, but Momma called me Chas."

"Nice to meet you Chas," Callie replied, then she went on to introduce everyone. Do you have anything you want to take with you?"

"Yep, that man has Momma's wedding ring and Poppa's pocket watch in his pocket."

Noah stood over the unconscious kidnapper and went through his pockets. He found the ring, the watch and about $70.00 in gold and currency which he handed to Chas.

"Keep this money. You'll need it worse than he will. Is there anything else of yours in the wagon?"

"Yep, I'll get it. I know where he put my stuff."

It was only two or three minutes after Chas climbed into the wagon that he jumped down with a cotton bag half filled with things. Callie directed him to ride with Luther and they pulled the wagons around the still unconscious kidnapper's wagon and readied their wagons for the ferry ride. Ezekial and Micah made a thickly padded bed for Sam, then returned to the English doctor. The doctor had cut and shaved the areas where Sam's flesh had been bit and ripped and had stitched them closed. He told Ezekial that Sam's trachea had been injured and it may affect his ability to bark but shouldn't hamper his breathing or swallowing. He advised Ezekial to feed him soft foods and keep him rested and clean for two or three weeks and he should be okay. The stitches could be taken out gently in about a week or so.

Ezekial carried Sam back and laid him on the bed Micah had prepared at the front of the wagon. The girls were still weepy and wanting to touch and thank Sam. An hour later they were all on the other side of the wide muddy water. The ferryman told them they'd better make some distance down the road. He had already sent for the occupation troops who would want to investigate and delay them for a couple of days and likely keep the kid to place in an orphan's home and to testify against his kidnapper. He told them the man that Noah knocked out was almost surely a thief and when the army searched his wagon they would find evidence of his theft. He told them the man took a full wagonload of merchandise across the river two or three times a month and would return from Louisiana with an empty wagon. He would tell those who came to investigate everything but would leave the boy out and would ask the others not to mention the child, otherwise the army may telegraph ahead and make them return.

Ezekial paid the man for the ferrying and tried to give him a bit extra but he wouldn't take it. He just asked that they take good care of the boy. Just before arriving back on the Mississippi shore the ferryman removed a vital sideboard and floorboard on the ferry to disable it until it could be repaired, just in case the army's investigators wanted to pursue the boy. It would take him several hours to repair the damage if he worked really slow.

After being directed by a friendly farmer, they drove the wagons away from the main west bound road and took a southern road for twenty miles or so before they headed west again. Hopefully this would lose or delay any pursuit.

Ezekial taught the boy to drive the mules as they traveled and he learned quickly. He wasn't even in normal health, having been mistreated and fed irregularly while the prisoner of a kidnapper and soon tired of pulling the reins against the big mules. Ezekial coaxed him to get in the wagon-bed and rest awhile. The boy curled up beside Sam, being careful not to hurt him and was quickly asleep.

That night Callie and her girls made certain Chas ate his fill. The food seemed to render the boy somnolent once again. And perhaps he felt he could relax for the first time in weeks. Callie and her daughters all hugged him before they made him a bedroll beneath their wagon. He had found a new family, a new mother, new sisters and a bunch of uncles. What a difference a day had made. Ezekial cut and mashed some meat for Sam and heated it in a gravy. The dog ate some of it, but tired easily. The girls had to be pulled away from him.

Callie called everyone together around the fire.

"In a week or so, we'll be in Texas. It is my intent to go to San Antonio first to speak with a man who is a banker and who I am told is knowledgeable about land and prices in Texas. Land is cheap there right now and there's plenty of it. I want to buy enough land to raise both livestock and crops in a place which is suitable. It may be that I'll have to buy land on the edge of the frontier to get enough suitable acreage. I'll need help. I'll need people I can trust.

"Beau, it's my understanding that you intend to find your wife who was sent here during the war. I hope you're reunited with her. You'll need a job to build a life for you and your wife and I would like to invite you to come to my ranch to raise and train horses. We'll make sure there are suitable living quarters for you and your wife. I'd be grateful if you'd give it some thought.

"And Micah, I'll need a cook for the cowboys in the bunkhouse and a man to do odd jobs that I can trust. I would like you to be that man, and if you take the job I'll also provide room and board plus a decent wage.

"Luther, I know you to be a man of many talents and a loyal and stable hand. I'd like it very much if you would stay on and help me around the ranch.

"Noah as I said, I may have to purchase land on the edge of civilization and will certainly require defense against hostiles if that is the case. I'll need to retain an experienced soldier, a leader of men and a man who will help me hire men who are of good character to protect the lives of us all. You have demonstrated your ability with firearms and your willingness to protect my daughters...and myself,... from harm. This is a virtue which cannot be purchased or hired. You have also spoken of some knowledge of livestock, longhorn cattle in particular, and I want you to consider being foreman of the ranch and help me build it into a profitable enterprise."

"Callie, I..."

"I know you've planned to rejoin the Texas Rangers, but keep my offer in mind. Please.

"And Ezekial. You have told me of your plans to see your friend in south Texas before you purchase any property. You were raised on a farm and so was I. Between the two of us I believe we could build and be successful in a farm and ranch business. With your investment money joined with mine we could purchase a larger and better property. So, I am inviting you to be my partner in the business. What do you say?"

"Well Callie, this is a surprise. It's a good idea. Yer all good folks and we all work purty good together, don't we?" Ezekial was silent as he considered, then said, "Let me go see Samuel, my soldier friend, and I'll make a decision after that. Would that be alright?"

"That'll be fine. Give it some thought, all of you. Now come along girls, it's bedtime. We'll see you men in the morning."

Noah took the first watch, which he had persuaded the group to establish. Actually the night attack of the bandits were the most persuasive incentive. He poured an almost boiling syrup of strong coffee into the tin cup and sat the blackened pot back on the edge of the coals. Walking away from the camp he soon found himself atop a near hill where he could look down on the wagons and the animals.

Looking up at the uncountable stars he thought of the many countless nights he had spent beneath them standing watch as he was now. He thought he had probably slept more nights under the canopy of the stars than even most Indians, who at least had their teepees or huts. He'd had no home since he was a lad, he felt at home under God's ever-changing sky. If he accepted Callie's offer of a job he would likely be spending most nights under a roof in a bunkhouse. The years behind him had tested him, made him strong, a formidable man. For his age, he knew he was still a capable hand. And he had experience that these pilgrims sorely needed. Perhaps it was time to change his way. He wondered how it would feel to have a home.

The half a dozen hunters had followed the trail made by many thousands of hooves across the endless plain. In their thick leather and fur and on their stumbling mounts they continued their pursuit. The wind pelted and pestered them by constantly changing direction and velocity. The big wagon on which two of the unwashed men rode was stacked four feet high with thick, bloody carcasses of buffalo and was pulled by six squinting and unhappy mules directly into the wind. Four horses were tied to the tailgate and all the beasts hung their great heads and closed their clotted eyes to the dirty, shifting air.

Four other thickly clothed riders peeped intermittently beneath their caps and hats into the foggy distance trying to make some sense of the vision that presented itself, then faded and disappeared in the sandy, shadowed haze of the billowing wind. The horses and mules shied and pranced away from the path, only the reins held them. It seemed a spirit sat in the center of the trail fifty yards ahead, a horse with head bowed behind him. The wind brought snatches of a chanting dirge to the men's hooded ears. The song and the sight haunted and froze them. The horses shied.

"What in hell lies ahead?"

"From what I kin see it's a Injun. Maybe singing his death song."

"Well, may as well oblige him." Here he lifted his long rifle.

The blast of the gale suddenly stilled and in the silence they heard the mournful, melancholy melody fade away with the whistling wind. The vision had vanished.

"Where'd e go?"

"Sum bitch is gone."

The wind increased and its roar covered any sound of the approaching Comanches and horses. The sudden screaming startled them. Surprised and shocked, the panicked horses and mules jumped and reared and dislodged bloody hunks of meat that moments before were men. Scathing spirits slashed through shrieking air and fire flashed from gun barrels, lead cutting through the dusty coats of the hunters. Scarcely seconds were spent and they all lay dead and dying of the cold, windswept Staked Plain.

Some of the warriors called by their enemies 'the snakes you cannot see' caught the terrified team of mules racing away with the wagon of buffalo meat, a few rode after the now riderless horses of the slaughtered men. Two of the wraiths dismounted and ran to the wounded hunters, first ensuring they could reach no weapon and then scalping them alive, laughing with relish at their screams for mercy.

The taller of the two Comanches had a smile so wide that it bared all his teeth and the gaping rictus revealed the pleasure he enjoyed from the intense dying agonies of the helpless, mortally wounded man. Holding the bloody head with one arm, he poked his knife deep through the staring blue eyes. The paralyzed and perishing man jerked and trembled in death throes. Throwing back his head and laughing like a demon, he took the fifty caliber Sharps rifle the hunter's had, jerked the man's pants down and shoved the large barrel deep up into the choking, bleeding and blind hunter rectum, puncturing his guts and causing blood to gush out in thick steaming rivulets around the blue steel. Rolling him over, the crazed Comanche sliced and sawed off the man's privates and stuffed them down his throat, cutting off his final breaths.

Insane sounds of seeming childish glee escaped the cruel, quivering lips of the murderous savage, but his smile died with the maimed, mutilated man. His eyes jumped to the other warrior who was scalping the remaining dead heads. He took quick, long strides and struck the man in the temple with the steel handle of his knife rendering him unconscious. Snatching the slippery scalps from the other's waist cord, he carried them to his horse and put them down in a long leather bag. He searched each of the dead for what he considered of value.

The young brother warriors returned yelping like wolves and leading the meat hunter's horses. They were wild and exuberant with the decisive victory over the hated whites. Their leader who held the bag of scalps and valuables instructed them to take what they wanted from the fallen men. The dozen warriors took what weapons they wanted as well as coats, hats and boots leaving the dead naked men laying on the hard, cold dirt.

They cut the mules loose from the big wagon and drove them to the herd that the youngest ones had held while they murdered the hunters. The herd was made up of horses they had stolen in their deadly raid down into the Mexican settlements and back north along the edges of the outlying farms and ranches of the whites. They had cut a bloody swath from below the Rio Bravo, along the Nueces and Frio, the Conchos and the Colorado River, killing, torturing and burning such isolated frontier families as they came upon. In the stealthy surprise attacks that their war leader taught them, they had slaughtered over a score, slain and sadistically punished husbands, wives and children, grandparents and siblings. No scruple, no kindness restrained them. They found pleasure in the pain and death they caused, and they would return to their people proud and rich with spoils.

Some of the children they had taken as prisoners. Those who cried too loud they dispatched as they would swat a bothersome gnat, without thought or remorse. The children would be toys for their women to torture and might be sold to the Mescaleros as slaves or to the white whiskey traders. Sometimes, miraculously, a child might be ransomed in this way. Typically though, the children would be adopted into the tribe and would learn the ways of the wild.

Their self anointed leader, Roe in Rut, or Bloody Roe as the western Texicans called the despised murderer, rode apart from the others who drove their stolen herd and captives. He watched the big wagon filled with meat for the soldiers fort burn and surveyed the horrifying scene of corpses. He drank deep draughts from one of the bottles of rye whiskey he had found beneath the wagon seat. He let his eyes and thoughts absorb the sweet sight of the retaliatory strike. Of course these particular white people had made no war against his people, but all whites would pay for those who had killed his family.

It was still a two or three day journey to the place within the canyon where the tribe was encamped for the winter. This would be the last raid until spring. His tribe would rest until then, enjoying the spoils of the raids. They would tell tales of their bravery and of the stupid and cowardly whites and Mexicans. His thoughts drifted to the three women prisoners he had taken which were tied to the horses that were driven at a trot toward home. They were three very young women just past puberty, one yellow haired, one with red hair and a beautiful, Mexican girl. All had exceptionally long hair and their scalps would decorate his lance or shield when he tired of taking his pleasure with them. He would keep them most of the winter to warm his blanket.

Just a few years ago, when he was a child, he saw the fear his father and older brothers had of the Rangers. Those fears had passed with the recent years when no Rangers bothered them. There were stories of a war the whites fought against themselves, maybe that is where the Rangers had gone. There were rumors of a few remaining Rangers who herded the weak sister tribes north of the Red River. Maybe all the feared Rangers were dead. One thing was certain, the fear of them had passed away.

The grey-coated men had not pursued them for these past few years, but had only patrolled around the populous areas in the east. Now they were gone like the Rangers and were replaced in the forts by blue-coated men who were even poorer adversaries. Many of the blue-coats were black buffalo soldiers who only marched around on foot and then returned to the forts. His people ruled these lands now and made fools of any who came into Comancheria, usually dead fools.

Roe wished the Rangers would return so he could prove himself against them. He had searched for them since he had become a man three summers past, but they had never appeared to chase him after his murderous raids as they had chased his father and older brothers. The whites had grown weak, vulnerable, easily exploited. Only a foolish few still ventured into these lands the Comanche ruled. Just a few years ago the Rangers had attacked their camp and killed his mother and his father. Later, his brothers had fought the hated Rangers and also died. When the Rangers attacked the camp, Roe had hid in the prickly pear and it had protected him from the white devils. He had killed many whites to each of his family who had died and he vowed that whites would continue to pay with their lives as long as he cast a shadow. Stopping in the darkness and making camp, they quickly roasted meat from a crippled horse they had butchered earlier in the day. They tore at the half raw meat and grease and blood ran over their hands, chins and chest. They threw their scraps to the captives as they would to dogs and gave each of them a swallow of water. They remained tied with leather thongs, hand and foot.

A young buck knelt before the red-haired girl and cut the thongs binding her feet together. He pulled his loincloth aside and pushed the little girl onto her back, leaning over her. The girl clawed at his face and screeched, "Noooo!"

The scream alerted Roe who ran to the rapist and kicked him away. The stunned buck dropped his flint and bone knife beside the girl. Roe ordered him to quit trying to force these women who were his prisoners. He advised him to steal his own women if he wanted them instead of killing them. The foiled young buck, who was Roe's cousin Dark Cloud, frowned at such treatment, but silently assented. As a close relative, he expected to share in the spoils of Roe. Only fear kept him from fighting Roe. He would fight not for the women, but for the shame of being kicked like a dog. The seed of resentment and hate had been planted in his heart and would surely grow.

The red-haired girl spoke her thanks aloud, hoping that Roe was her protector, that he had saved her honor. Roe tied her feet back together tightly, then hit her with the heel of his hand in the face breaking her nose and knocking her onto her back. As he turned and walked away, she felt the flint knife under her back. Laughing as he walked to the fire, Roe imagined the scene three nights ahead when they arrived at the tribe's camp in the Canyon of the Big Stick. The red-haired one would learn quickly why the whites had named him Bloody Roe.

Roe cared little what the weak and pale called him. He was given his name by the Great Mystery who blessed him with the vision in his manhood quest. He had attained fifteen summers when he was sent apart by the elders and the shaman. On the third day of fasting under the sun, eating only the peyote buttons given him, the roe walked fearlessly to where he sat, motionless and amazed. Standing before him, the roe bent his neck, sniffed, then licked the salty sweat from his face and shoulders, anointing him with his spirit and his name. The deer's antlers were broken and bloody from battling for the does and for dominance of his territory. It was the season of rut, the season of battle. And so, this would ever be his habit, his life. In season after season he would fight for his land.

The boy anointed by the roe sat trembling. He wondered if what he saw and felt was real or only a dream or vision, so he mustered his courage and slowly reached out, touched the broken, bloody horns and tasted the thick, hot blood. Realization washed over him; vision and reality were the same. The rutting roe became his truth, his strong spirit and his name. He would celebrate his conquering spirit every season. The battle and the blood were his holy quest, his sacred spirit.

After Roe's anointing, his spirit urged him to move against the interlopers and punish any and all who dared, challenge his sovereignty. The older warriors had ignored his enthusiastic, martial spirit and had refused to follow an unproven man, a man little more than a boy, one to hold the horses in battle. Subsequently, Roe's untempered spirit drove him away from the doubters and the fearful. On the horse his brothers had left him to care for he rode out to prove his claim, alone. He employed the darkness of night to creep in and slaughter the sleeping frontier families. He cut the throats of the men first and they awoke only to die. When the strong were dead and there was no one who could oppose him, he terrorized and tortured the women and children, exulting in their screams and fear. In his murderous rage he was a rutting beast, unbound by morals, guilt or conscience and driven by the hedonistic megalomania of the evil spirit that inhabited him.

Weeks after he had left alone with a single horse he returned with a herd and captives. Two horses were loaded with pistols, rifles, knives, axes and other prizes. Immediately he was held in awe as a great warrior, when in fact he was only a cowardly murderer. He fought no battles except with unarmed women and children. He was a cruel, heartless predator unrestrained by any compassion or any thought of mercy.

All the men of the tribe, especially the young and ambitious, envied his riches and his fame. Many followed him eagerly when he again rode to punish the intruders. The Comanches seemed to have an innate ability for stealth and Roe taught them more. He also showed them trickery and a method of never attacking or fighting a foe fairly. Fair was not a concept that he had ever considered. If an enemy was prepared for battle Roe retreated, attacking only when the enemy slept or could be surprised. Roe's murderous mode of dispensing death to the unsuspecting and innocent was very efficient and evil. He would not face even the bumbling bluecoats in battle but would make wicked warfare only against the few, the weak, the isolated. He made those Comanches into creeping, cowardly creatures who murdered, mutilated and tortured those who had caused them no harm. And he made his followers rich.

The savages success was due to these effective tactics, attack the unsuspecting and frail, retreat before force. The Comanches' advantage also lay in their amazing talents in horsemanship and in their superior knowledge of the land. They could strike and disappear like demonic ghosts. The fear of Bloody Roe caused an exodus from the plains and only courageous and stalwart men dared to venture into the western lands.

Water was often scarce in west Texas and the bands would lead their pursuers into the deserts and disappear. Then they would attack in the night and vanish once again. These stratagems were methods which were successful, at least for awhile, against a numerically superior foe. The day was quickly approaching however, when these better armed and morally determined masses would decimate these savages whose inhuman deeds of deviltry infuriated the whites. But in this their day, the Comanche gave no quarter, nor asked any.

Roe had ridden into the east and south and viewed the cities which, to him, were unbelievably huge. The people looked like ants on a mound, and more were arriving from further east daily in wagons and ships, on horseback and on foot. It was evident that the many would eventually overcome the few. He realized that his days were numbered and he determined to employ any action which would delay the continuing migration westward. Fear was his greatest weapon. Fear would delay the timid, but the brave would not be hesitant. The more fear he could create, the longer his days would be on the land. He underestimated the strength and courage of the white race.

The red-haired girl waited until the moon had set and then moved slowly and carefully into a position to cut the leather thongs tying her ankles. The ties around her wrists she had cut hours before and the razor sharp flint had sliced her tender skin. Shivering both from the cold and from her fear, she struggled to be silent as she stiffly slipped away from the sleeping others. Guilt twisted her heart in her decision to leave the other captives, but she was intelligent enough to know it would be a miracle if she alone were able to escape. And she did not allow herself to even imagine the consequences if she were caught. Exhausted, she had fought sleep, realizing this may be her final chance to free herself. Her cold young bones popped as she crawled and the sound seemed as loud as gunshots in her terror, but she grimly and bravely continued.

One horse shied slightly as she approached the herd, but miraculously none neighed. The Comanche boy who guarded the herd sat sleeping, leaning against a tree. He looked asleep to her. She prayed he was asleep. If he was awake she had no chance. Trying to see her big chestnut horse in this darkness was impossible, all the black silhouettes looked the same. She quietly made the clicking sound in her cheek that she had always used to call her horse Betty and heard a snuffling response a distance away. Quickly and lightly she moved to the sound and found the big friendly mare coming to her. She hugged the lowered head and almost cried.

"Oh thank you Lord God! Thank you Betty! Come on. Let's go. Sssssh," she whispered.

She led the horse away, cringing as each heavy hoof hit the hardpan and rock. She walked beside the horse as long as she could make herself wait then mounted her and held her to a walk for another distance, finally allowing her to trot. In the dark night she was unsure of the direction Betty was taking her. She didn't care much about direction though, as long as it was away from the devils who had murdered her family and taken her away as all she loved had been burning.

There were no reins and she rode bare-back. She was accustomed to riding Betty around the farm without any rigging and could guide her fairly well with her knees, by shifting her weight and by her hands on Betty's neck. It was maybe three hours until dawn and she wanted to be as far away as possible by then, but she did not want to tire Betty out too quickly, she had many miles to go. And she had no idea where she was headed.

Pulling Betty's mane she stopped periodically to listen for any pursuit. Adrenaline was keeping her awake and alert for the present, but she knew she would not be able to remain conscious a lot longer. As the stars dissolved and the horizon to her left started to show a band of grey light she began to nod and in another breath, she slept. Betty just kept plodding on, balancing her friend on her back.

Awhile later she awoke with a start. Immediately she pulled Betty to a halt and listened. She heard nothing except honking geese very high in the cool cerulean sky. Looking down she noticed the tracks of many horses and considering the position of the sun, she realized she was on the path that the Comanches had taken in their retreat with their spoils and captives. Betty knew her way home. She lightly pushed her heels into the horses ribs and they set out again, following the trail, south and east.

After another while the girl got down, stretching her stiff legs and giving the horse a rest. She had not eaten in over four days and she was very thirsty. She silently thanked God that Betty was wise enough to head homeward. When the Comanches came for her would they follow the way they had previously traveled? Would they come for her? Of course they would. And they would follow the tracks Betty was still making. She then realized that she was not thinking as clearly or quickly as usual. The lack of sleep, exhaustion, hunger and the fear were taking their toll. She must hurry. The devils were surely coming for her. Using what strength remained to her she swung and pulled herself back on the tired horse. She touched her swollen broken nose gingerly and turned to look behind.

Dark Cloud awoke before dawn and gathered the thick buffalo robe closer around him against the cold. He listened to the quiet around him. Only the voices of a few early birds broke the perfect stillness of the morning. Opening his reluctant eyes, he peered into the sky. The solid black above him gave way to the darkest blue which flowed into the grey-violet of the cold dawn. Throwing back the robe he sat up and surveyed his surroundings. Stretching and yawning, he stood and began gathering his belongings. He placed his rifle, his bow and quiver and his spear on the buffalo robe. Something was missing. His knife was not in its sheath. He glanced around looking for it. Thinking of the last time he had used it, he walked to where the prisoners were gathered and discovered the red-haired one was not there.

Moving to the horse herd he caught one of his ponies. As he tied his rigging and belongings on the horse the boy who watched the herd approached him. He told Dark Cloud that one of the horses had wandered off and asked him to look for it. Dark Cloud advised him that a captive was also gone and that he would look for both the horse and the captive. As they spoke the light increased and Dark Cloud found the tracks where the small hard boots led the horse away and showed it to the boy. He swung up into his riggings and loped away following the tracks south and east.

The red-haired girl dozed and the big mare continued her plodding pace down the path leading to a place far away that she had known as home. The morning cold in the air had been warmed to a chill by the friendly sun and the comparative warmth had once again lulled her to sleep. She was awakened by an abrupt cessation of movement. Opening her eyes she saw that Betty had stopped hock deep in the waters of a narrow prairie stream.

Surprisingly, she had the presence of mind to unlace her boots, and tie them together and hang them over Betty's back before she dismounted into the welcome drink. The sweet water refreshed her and again she murmured her thanks to her mother's God. At the thought of her mother and the memory of how she had courageously tried to fight the murderous demons and the terrible horrible things they had done to her, she began to cry and the tears weakened her. She fell to her knees in the stream and she was soaked to her waist. Sorrow flowed over her threatening to overcome her, but then anger was born of the fear and she forced the tears to stop. She washed her face and stood. Nostrils flared, jaws clinched, she looked back up the trail and determined that she would not be caught. She would die first. She touched the knife of flint and bone tied in her apron string.

Wading across the stream she sat on the bank. She looked at the sky and estimated the time of day. It was sometime after noon, maybe two o'clock. She thought she may have traveled twelve hours. She also noticed a faint trail of smoke in the air to the south and smelled the stench of burning meat. As she had been held with the other captives and the stolen horse herd a distance away when the Comanches attacked the hunters she was unaware that the reek was the meat of animals still smoldering from the wagon that had been set afire. She thought that the smoke indicated civilization and she tried to get Betty back on the path, but she was hungry and stubbornly cropped the tall, green, grass beside the stream. Eventually the horse cooperated and they headed toward the distant smoke.

It was farther to the origin of the smoke than she had thought and she had to bring Betty back to a walk from a trot as the tired horse was stumbling and blowing. The stinking air grew thicker as she approached and the horse tried to pull away. She prayed it wasn't Indians who were ahead and she used her hand to shade her eyes as she peered across the endlessly flat plain. She saw a single figure moving in and out of the smoke and could make no sure decision whether she should approach or not. As she pulled Betty to a halt and the sound of her trudging, laborious hooves, quieted the alarming clatter of a charging horse behind made the decision for her. She drove her heels into Betty's ribs and headed her straight into the smoke.

As she neared the heavily smoldering carcasses the smoke shifted and she saw through the waves of heat a fur-robed figure aiming a rifle at her. Before she could turn the running horse away she saw the puff of smoke and heard the explosion of gunpowder. She tried to hold onto Betty's mane as the horse turned violently away, but she was slung off and through the air to tumble across the hard ground. She gathered herself and took inventory of her wounds. She was scratched and bruised but she could find no bullet wound. She wasn't hit. She wondered if Betty was. Over the strumming of her beating heart and Betty's stampeding, she heard English words yelled clearly, yet strangely, through the stinking air.

"Come to me! Come to me lassie! I shot the Comanche 'oo was chasin' ye. Come to me."

A man with a long flowing beard blown by the breeze and dressed in furs and leather waved her to him. Her hopes soared.

Hopes for refuge, for kindness. Warily, she walked to the bearded man as he coaxed her to him.

"Oh lassie! Wot 'as' appened to ye? The wretched savages have treated you roughly, sure, and stolen you away. Come 'ere young lady and let me see the damage done."

The red-haired girl called Betty to her with the clicking call, then surrendered herself to the bearded man's arms. He led her to a rocky seat and poured water from a canteen onto a scarf he pulled from his neck and gently washed the caked blood from her face and neck, then from the scratches on her arms. Despite his tender ministrations, pain made her flinch away from the slight pressure.

"Easy lass, wot 'as' appened to your nose? I'm not meanin' to 'oit ye. Your nose isn't terribly bad, ye'll be pretty again in just a few days. Ye may 'ave a lump, but it will only lend character to your beauty. Did the damned Comanches take ye from your 'ome?"

At the mention of home she could not restrain the tears. She told him of the rape and murder of her mother and the death and mutilation of her father, her younger brothers and her uncle. The man held her and let her talk and cry. He placed a smoky-smelling robe around her shoulders and tied it there against the cool breeze.

"There, there m' lil' lady, ye must be strong. I 'ave done all I can 'ere and we must be quick and get along back to the settlements before the red scoundrels catch up to us. Come along now. 'Ere ye go, ye ride this horse, 'e's fresher. We'll let your horse rest. I expect you've both 'ad a 'ard journey. Let's get along now."

The red-haired girl rode the fresher horse and looked behind her. Betty was tied behind and followed tiredly. The hide and hair attired man rode beside her and told her the Comanches had killed his six companions and he had buried what remained of them in a common grave. He had constructed a rugged cross to mark the spot where they were interred. He explained that he had been spared massacre because he had been following and scouting the buffalo herd which was many miles away. He had returned just this morning to find the horrible scene.

She greedily consumed the jerky he gave her. It was very salty and made a thirsty meal. She drank most of the water in the canteen.

Toward evening they stopped beside a river that flowed in the same direction they were traveling, southeast, and let the horses drink and graze for a short while. The red-haired girl was asleep soon after they stopped and the Irishman wanted to let the exhausted child sleep. But, he must ensure their safety, so they must press on. He woke her and put her on the horse. They followed the river. They ate the jerky and let the horses find their own way beneath the cold, dark sky.

Chapter Seven

"Make us glad according to the days wherein thou hast afflicted us, and the years wherein we have seen evil"
--Psalms 90:15 (KJV)

"...He hath sent me to bind up the brokenhearted, to proclaim liberty to the captives, and the opening of prison to them that are bound;"
--Isaiah 61:1 (KJV)

"The desire for safety stands against every great and noble enterprise."
--Tacitus 56AD

THE FORMER SERGEANT, Snyder, was driven to catch Jack breaking some prison rule so he could make him suffer with the harsh, corporal punishment that prison officials routinely meted out. He hated to see Jack smiling. He sought opportunity to erase that mocking smile with every means and employed informants who were always watching and trying to overhear anything that would allow Snyder to catch Jack doing anything wrong. Jack and Hoss took advantage of Snyder's myopic focus on Jack to slip things by him. The pair became adept at using these same prison stoolies to let Snyder's foolishness be revealed.

One lazy Sunday afternoon on the prison yard Hoss and Jack began acting like they were drinking home-brewed wine from a gallon bucket since they had spotted sorry old Figgers, one of Snyder's rats, watching them. They'd drink some of the water in the bucket surreptitiously, make a face or shake their head to demonstrate the harsh bite of the 'alcohol', spill water down their chests, hiccup, laugh and stagger. All the convicts on the yard were wise to the act, except Figgers, and were enjoying the show. Ezekial looked on and smiled. Hoss and Jack began to argue loudly and soon started a fake fight, which Ezekial seemed to struggle to stop. Out of the side of their eyes they watched Figgers take off to go inform Snyder of their inebriation. They laughed and lay back to rest from their exertions.

By the time Snyder arrived with two of his cronies, the thespian pair were laying in the dirt feigning unconsciousness. All activity on the yard ceased, all eyes watched the developing drama. Most everyone had been told beforehand to watch Figgers show his hand. The horseshoe pitchers, the domino and card players and all the other prisoners on the yard watched Snyder kick Jack's foot, then Hoss's leg and holler, "Get up! Get yer drunken asses up. You can sober up in a shitter cell."

Jack and Hoss gained their feet and the two big goon guards moved behind them grabbing their arms.

"What's the problem 'Mister' Snyder?" Jack asked with a smile.

"Yer the problem Williams, ya drunken bums. Where's the home-brew?"

"'Mister' Snyder! You must have been misinformed. We don't drink."

"Don't drink, my ass! Where's it at?" Snyder yelled. He went to the water bucket, sniffed and tasted, then threw the water out by the bail.

"Where's the wine Williams?"

"Why don't you ask ol' Figgers there Mister Snyder. Isn't he your liein' rat?"

"Lemme smell yer breath," Snyder growled, putting his porcine puss directly in front of Jack's face. "Blow!"

Jack blew a puff of breath in Snyder's face. Snyder frowned, then moved over to Hoss and repeated the order. He glanced over at Ezekial Robertson who was seated at his usual spot nearby and shook his head. Staring hard at Figgers, he strode directly to him and slapped him on the side of his head. He pushed Figgers who almost fell and said, "You come with me Figgers." There was menace in his voice.

The entire yard erupted in laughter as the guards and the snitch slunk away in shame. That night Figgers was honored with a blanket party and the socks filled with tin cans of beans and big rocks beat him to mush. The following morning Figgers skipped breakfast, he'd already eaten all his teeth.

Jack had very little money left and was earning his doses of laudanum by selling it to new arrivals, called 'newboots', who couldn't buy dope from the doctor. He doubled, sometimes tripled the prices to the newboots over what the doctor charged him. He was also hustling money gambling at cards, dominoes or pitching horseshoes at which he was very hard to beat. Thus his evening after work were usually busy earning his poison.

Hoss had managed to secure a job in the laundry and get out of the fields. He was making a few bucks taking care of prisoners' clothes. He could have made more money washing and ironing the guard's clothes, but he had a strong hate for his keepers. He would do mean, spiteful things to the guards clothes, like urinate in the wash water or spit big green hawkers on them after they'd been ironed. Hoss rarely bought any laudanum. He bought marijuana from the Mexicans sometimes. After rains he would buy a sack of mushrooms from the cowboys and brew black mushroom tea. He was usually waiting on a bucket of wine to ferment. It was all a way to beat the man. Most guards thought he was a model prisoner and ignored him. That was just how he wanted to be perceived, it allowed him opportunity to do his time the easy way.

Ezekial led a simpler life. He read his dog-eared Bible and talked to Sam. He slept when he got sleepy, he drank water when he was thirsty and he ate to keep the wrinkles out of his belly. Nothing seemed to bother him very much, he always seemed calm, peaceful, satisfied with life the way it was. There was usually a slight smile on his lips. Most everyone viewed him as crazy. And that was fine with him.

Ezekial was an enigma. He was as kind and tender with Sam and Jack as a mother would be, but he had murdered three men. Through the endless hours in the tiny cell Jack had eventually drawn the stories out of him. He had been sentenced to prison in eighteen seventy-three for beating a man to death in El Paso for shooting Sam. He had killed another prisoner who had bullied and raped a tiny old convict. When he had 'broke' (as Ezekial put it), a guard who was whipping him for some minor infraction of prison rules, they had charged him with murder in Walker County where the prison was and he had escaped hanging only because the jury was convinced he was insane. He accepted the probability that he would die in prison and seemed much happier and at peace than he had any right to be. Jack now enjoyed spending time with Ezekial as it seemed he shared his serenity and deep joy. Ezekial's great faith made him different from others, better, more honest, trustworthy, without fear.

Hoss was a different story. He'd been sentenced to fifteen years for a robbery and then a shootout with a posse. He had little fear also, his primary fear was of himself. At times he would get so mad he would lose control of himself. Those who witnessed him losing his temper once did not want to see it ever again and were careful thenceforth not to upset him. The posse had caught up with him and run him up onto a rocky hill outside Houston where they had shot and killed his horse. He had used up all his ammo and wounded two deputies and been wounded himself. He had almost served the whole fifteen year sentence and was anxious to leave Huntsville prison. His loyalty and friendship urged him to find a way to help Jack. As Hoss's time in prison began to get short, he spoke to Jack daily about helping him escape.

"Jack, you're going to be an old man when they finally let you out of here, don't you want to be free again while you're young enough to enjoy life?"

"Life ain't all it's cracked up to be Hoss. Most days here I can dull the pain with dope and who cares if I live or die? I don't."

"That's what I mean. If they kill you escaping, isn't it better than dying in this hole? You might find something or someone out there that will make you enjoy life, man. Ain't it worth a shot?"

"Aw hell Hoss, I don't know."
"And if they shot you escaping, your troubles would be over."
"Ha! Yea, they sure would."
"C'mon man. I'll help you. It'll be easier than you think."
"I'll give it some thought Hoss."

There was nothing for Jack out there he knew, nothing for him anywhere. Why make the effort to be free, he'd never be free of the sorrow, the regret, the guilt. He couldn't escape himself, except maybe in death and that was no guarantee. There might be one advantage to being out of prison though, he wouldn't have to hustle so hard for his medicine. He could buy a bunch at once and relax, well, relax as much as was possible being an escaped convict. It might be fun though. He could give the authorities hell for awhile, rob everything with a cash drawer. Ride wide and wild for awhile, until they killed him. Why not? He was slowly committing suicide here anyway. It might be a more enjoyable suicide out there riding wild and free.

Jack began to discuss the chances of escape with Hoss and the reality began to look more promising. Without Hoss on the outside to supply horses and clothes, money and hideouts, there would be little chance of success, but with his trustworthy support, chances were a lot greater he could be free for awhile. Hoss had been thinking about it for quite awhile and had concocted a feasible plan.

Jack and Hoss shared a half gallon of wine the night before Hoss was to be released. The home-brew gave them both a good buzz. Hoss gave Jack all of his meager prison property, cup, spoon, bowl, tobacco, two pair of mended socks, a pencil and some paper and a prison-made hat. Funny, Hoss thought, how attached to this almost worthless stuff he had become. When you have nothing, every little something means a lot.

"Write me back when I write you Jack and let me know how things are going here. I'll find a gal to be your 'sister' and come visit. I'll make sure that she's trustworthy so you can send me messages. It ain't that far from Houston and I'll bring her down here soon's you say."

"Awright Hoss. Just be sure you make an honest wage out there for awhile, I don't want to see you back in here."

"I'll work with my daddy and brother fixin' boats, it'll keep me out of trouble."

"Don't let one of those pretty Houston saloon girls put a ring in your nose either."

"You should know me better'n that Jack."

"Ummhuh. You don't watch out, those gals 'll take you fast, money, heart and soul."

The conversation dried up after awhile, both of them thinking thoughts of the hard times they'd shared and the good times they'd managed to have even in prison.

"You know Hoss, I'm gonna' miss you, you old sorry thang." Jack smiled and threw his arm around Hoss's shoulders.

"We had some good times through the hard times didn't we Pard?"

"Yep. Sure did."

The silence lengthened as they looked at one another and drank.

The next morning Jack was chopping weeds in a row of sprouting potatoes when the field boss on a horse behind him yelled, "Water time three hoe!"

Jack stumbled in his brogans back to where the water boy had placed the water bucket and got his cupful of tepid water. The old field boss, old Two Gone, slung his skinny legs over the pommel and bit off a chuck from a plug of tobacco.

"Well ol' Fast Jack, your ace boon coon is out on them streets somewhere this mawning. How long you recon ol' Hoss'll be out there 'fore he finds his way back home here to Huntsville?"

"I hope he'll behave himself. He got a good job, workin' reg'lar."

"Well, I don't wish him no bad luck, I ain't intending to burn his cornbread, but don't be su'prised if he don't make it out there. It seemed like Hoss is the kind who wants more from life quicker than life was willing to give it. A man who stays out of here has to have patience and be humble enough to be satisfied with what life gives."

"Guess your right boss, but I still got hopes for Hoss. He's a good man, all things considered."

"We'll see. We'll see. Now ya'll get your lazy, no 'count asses back on the busy end of those aggies and get your weeds out of 'my' taters. An' don't be long 'bout it. Get on down them rows!"

The endless days of sweat and work and misery blended into a meaningless existence of simply surviving for no reason or purpose. Every day was the same. Same slop for food, same backbreaking, endless work, same stupid conversations and same sights, smells and sorrows. Late one evening a guard came to the cell and threw a letter on Jack's bunk. It was a change in the same old every day. It was the first letter he had received in prison. It made Ezekial nervous.

"Who's it from Jack?" Ezekial said in amazement.

"It's got a girl's name 'Zeke, but I think it's from Hoss."

"Well, open it up!"

"It's already open. The guards already read it."

"Well?......you gonna read it?"

Jack smiled. Ezekial was more excited about the letter than even Jack was. Ezekial, in all his years in prison, had never received a letter.

Jack opened it up and took out a photograph and a folded sheet of paper.

"Well, lookee there," Ezekial said, amazed, "Who's that lady?" looking wide-eyed over Jack's shoulder.

Jack turned the photo so he could read the writing on it. He read, "With Love, Your Sister, Winnie Williams."

"Oh man! She's purty! I didn't know you had a sister Jack."

"Me neither. She is pretty isn't she? Let's see what she has to say." He unfolded the letter and the smell of roses permeated the tiny cell.

"Wu-wee! I forgot what women smelled like. Smells like a flour."

"Dear Brother Jack, I hope this letter finds you well. I have missed you. I have spoken with the prison superintendent on the telephone and he will allow me to come visit you on the Sunday before Christmas Day. I have much to tell you, but will save all the family news until I see you at the visit. I love you and look forward to seeing you. Your Sister, Winnie."

"Gollee. Jack she talked to the Superintendent! On the telly-phone!"

"Um-huh." Jack answered as he inspected the photograph.

"Jack, how come you didn't know you had a sister?"

"Sssssh!" Jack whispered, and then explained how the girl was a messenger from Hoss. He placed the photograph on a shelf where Ezekial could stare at it and say, "She's purty," every few minutes. So, Hoss was as dependable as ever. It was good Jack thought, to have a friend you could count on. He took the small bottle out of his pocket, took a healthy sip, then re-corked it. He rolled over on the narrow bunk and let his mind wander over future possibilities. Without Hoss, Jack knew he would have no future except what he now had. Yes, it was good to have such a friend as Hoss. He admitted to himself that he was not such a dependable friend, he was too selfish, too focused on self-pity and his own pains to think much of others. Hoss was an inspiration.

Major Frye called Jack to his office next morning. Being excused from work, given a 'lay-in', was a welcome respite from the fieldwork. The prisoners called Frye Cat-Man because he snuck around on cat's-feet trying to catch the convicts doing dope, drinking or gambling. And if he caught someone, he was a terror.

When Jack was called into his office Major Frye had his boots on his desk, leaned back in his chair, chewing-tobacco dripping down his chin. He glanced up as Jack stood in front of his desk, a crazed blue eye set in a yellow and red orb made a couple of rotations then moved to the bottle of whiskey in his hand. He poured four fingers in a short glass, then replaced the bottle in a drawer.

"Williams?"

"Yes sir."

"Yore sister telephoned the Superintendent yestiddy, er no, she telephoned last week sometime," he drawled as he glanced at a sheet of paper on his desk. "The Superintendent is going to let you visit her this Sunday morning. Can't say I agree with him, but he's the boss. You just doing too much time Williams. I suspect you'll try to escape first chance you get."

"No sir, I won't 'try' to escape," Jack said, and thought, "I 'will' escape."

"Why you nickel and dime, boot-scuffling, hope-to-die dope fiend," the Major growled, his voice rising and his crazy eye screwing around in his weathered old skull, "You'd run off bare-footed, howl at the moon, drink muddy water and we wouldn't see you 'til we caught you at the dope house sleeping in the dirt! Now get yore stinking ass outa' my office and stay outa' my face or I'll put a swoll-knot on yore forehead big enough to wear its own hat. Git!"

The insane and drunk Major was on his feet trembling with rage. Jack left with haste, thinking how crazy the old man must get if a prisoner did anything wrong. He was definitely dangerous. Half across the yard Jack heard a guard yelling at him, "Williams, come back here!" Reluctantly, Jack walked back to the Major's office.

The guard sent him back into the Major who was leaned back in his chair completely relaxed and at repose. He smiled at Jack as he entered and mildly stated, "Excuse me Mr. Williams, I forgot to tell you that the Superintendent wanted you to be ready at eight a.m. for your visit. You may go now. Have a happy day." And the toothless old lion smiled which made Jack more nervous and amazed.

The guard outside the door chuckled when he saw Jack's expression as he exited. Jack felt fright with the realization that his very life was in this mad man's hands.

When he returned to the cell Ezekial had placed the letter directly centered beneath the photo of Jack's 'sister' like a shrine and was still studying the photograph with his mouth open.

"Zeke, you're gonna go blind lookin' at that pitcher. How long's it been since you seen a woman?"

"Hmmm? Long time. Long, long time."

"Well, we need to talk about that."

When the turnkey let him into the cell and walked away Jack sat down on the end of Ezekial's bunk and watched him pet Sam.

"Looky here, Zeke, have you ever thought about leaving here?"

"Aw Jack, you know I got too much time. They'll never let me go."

"I'm talking about escaping Zeke."

"Naw, that'd never work. I couldn't get over that wall. And I couldn't outrun those hounds and horses."

"What if I showed you a way to get over that wall and get away from the hounds and horses? Would you go?"

"Where would I go? I'm too big to hide. And I wouldn't go without you and Sam."

"Well me and Sam would go with you. And we could hide you 'til you got far away. I'd find a place you'd be happy. You and Sam. Someplace where you could see other people besides guards and convicts. Someplace where you could see something besides steel and stone."

"Well, I'll sleep on it," Ezekial softly said as he stared into the photograph.

"What do you see in that picture Zeke? Don't you see freedom?"

"I suppose I do. In a way. I guess I see yesterday. What could have been. Maybe. That girl reminds me of another yeller-haired girl. Long, long time ago."

"Hmm. Well, 'night Zeke."

"Night Jack."

Ezekial stretched his big and old body out over the steel shelf he'd slept on forever and let his thoughts return to that yeller-haired gal who was so beautiful to him that, in his memory, she seemed to have a light about her, a halo, a luminous cloud about her that radiated a magnetism, a sort of mesmerism that charmed him then, and after all these years still enchanted him. 'Cynthia.' Whatever became of you? He wondered.

Jack was washed, shaved and brushed when the guard came to unlock him for the visit. As the turnkey relocked the cell door, Ezekial said in his deep, soft voice, "Jack."

"Yea Zeke?"

"If you'll have me, I'll try it. Got nothing to lose."

"Allright," Jack smiled, "Allright."

After watching Jack and the guard walk away down the rickety catwalk, Exekial took the sepia photograph from the shelf and sat down on his bunk. He held the photograph out to his side and quietly spoke.

"Sam, you 'member that girl? Well, not really this girl, but one a lot like her. She was young and new and had a shine about her. I don't guess life had ever touched her then with anything but sunshine and flours. Smart as a whip! I guess she knew jes' about ever'thang. You 'member? Heh-heh,… I bet she 'members you. Probably never met another dog who could sing the gospel."

Ezekial replaced the photo on the shelf, ensuring that it was properly centered among the various articles. He ruffled Sam's coat and laid back.

"I wonder what she's doing now? Prob'ly has yeller-haired gran'babies by now. Prob'ly has a man driving her carriage for her. Or heck, Sam, she prob'ly has an automobile to go to church in. Wonder if she still teaches school? Been a long, long time, hadn't it?"

She was sitting at a marble-top table when they let him in the visitors room with the polished brass bars. She smiled at him and stood when he approached. Primly dressed, her long blonde hair pinned up behind her, she caused Jack to think of a school marm. She acted her part perfectly, almost persuading Jack that this was a long lost sister.

"Brother Jack! It's been so long," she said as she hugged him. She smelled so wonderful and felt so soft against him that his head swam.

"You're so skinny! Don't they feed you here?"

Jack smiled. "Not much. My my. You've grown up little Sis. Can't pull your pig tails now." "Better not! Oh, I have so much to tell you," she gushed.

As they sat down across the table from one another the guards seemed to lose interest in their conversation and spread their attention to the few others who were visiting their relatives. But the guards were men after all and their eyes surreptitiously continued to return to the beautiful young woman.

Keeping her conversation low she delivered all of Hoss's messages, interrupting once in awhile to exclaim loudly enough for the guards to hear some familiar endearment or surprise at something Jack apparently told her. She advised him that Hoss was indeed ready anytime Jack was. He had horses, money, firearms, clothes, food and hideouts. He also had an automobile stashed away. She listened attentively to all the information he had to pass on to Hoss and took note especially of the new man who would accompany them. He'd need an especially big horse and big clothes because he was a big man. He'd be bringing his dog too, Hoss would know who it was.

The Superintendent came through the front gate of bars smiling and approached them. "Miss Williams, I expect you are having a nice reunion with your wayward brother."

"Oh. Yes sir. Thank you so much for letting me visit him on such short notice."

"You are very welcome young lady. And whenever you want to visit him again you can. I've written instructions to allow you to visit him any Sunday. If you should want to come another day, just telephone me and I'll arrange it."

"Thank you so much Superintendent. That's so kind."

"I've left instructions to allow you to stay until noon. When you finish please come to my office and allow me to feed you dinner at a restaurant nearby before you begin the trip back to Houston. Will you be riding the train?"

"Oh, no sir. I'll be driving my Hupmobile."

"Goodness! So you drive your own automobile?"

"Oh yes sir. And I'd be honored to have dinner with you sir."

"Fine. I'll leave you two to your visit. I'll see you at noon Miss Williams."

"Yes sir. Thank you sir."

When the Superintendent had left the visitor's room Jack blew air out, relieved.

"Whew!"

"Oh, he's easy. Nothing to worry about. I can wrap him around my finger. What do you want for dinner?"

"What do you mean?"

"I mean the Superintendent is going to buy your dinner."

"Yea. I'll be holding my breath."

"Don't do that. How about chicken?" "Ha! You're a bit too sure of yourself Miss Winnie, but if you get chicken you'd better have him send a lot because I have a very big cell partner who has a dog."

"Come on. Jack, they don't allow dogs in prison."

"Ask the Superintendent about Ezekial, he'll tell you about his dog."

"Alright. I will."

Winnie told him about Hoss and what he had been doing, about her own acting career which did not offer much opportunity in Houston and her plans to save enough money to travel to Denver or San Francisco, where people took theater seriously. Hoss was paying her well for this role of Winnie Williams and she promised to return next month to see when Jack would be ready. She would also be writing for Hoss and since Ezekial was so taken with the photograph she'd send another.

Three guards were there to open the door for her and she graciously thanked them as she passed out of the visitor's room. Jack chuckled in appreciation of her manipulative skills and looked forward to next month when he would see her again. She was very pretty and very bright with a confident and pleasing personality. Every success was surely in her future.

He carried the cheerfulness to the prison yard and went to Ezekial's spot to tell him all about the visit. Ezekial hung on to every word and asked about a hundred questions. Jack's spirits were higher than they had been for awhile. He even forgot he had a dose of laudanum awaiting him in the cell. Other convicts coming from the visitor's room came over to ask him about the beautiful lady who had come to visit him. He lied to everyone, telling them it was his sister and no, they could not write her.

A guard walked across the yard to the group around Jack and Ezekial.

"Williams and Robertson, you are to return to your cell. Now."

Ezekial and Jack exchanged glances.

"Now," the guard repeated sternly and the crowd around them melted away.

Side by side they walked in the direction of the cellblock, the guard following closely.

Jack whispered out of the side of his mouth, "Think they found the medicine?"

"Dunno," answered Ezekial.

The turnkey waited before the cell and held the door open for them. When they were inside he slammed and locked the door and without a word, walked away.

"What's going on, Jack?"

"Heck if I know," Jack answered. He dug into his cache and found his laudanum still there. "May as well get rid of the evidence," he said and threw the thick dark liquid down his throat. He poured some water from a bucket to his cup, then sank the small bottle into the cup, filling it halfway. Holding his thumb over the end he shook it, then drank the dregs.

The thick planks of the catwalk echoed the sound of approaching heavy boots and keys.

"You ready Zeke? They may be coming to whip our asses." Ezekial stood up in the door.

"Yep. I'm ready Jack."

The turnkey stuck the heavy brass key in the lock and ordered, "Step back Robertson."

Ezekial stood his ground. Jack told Ezekial to step back. Slowly, he complied.

Two other guards stepped forward. One handed Ezekial a wooden crate with a white cloth covering it and the other handed Jack a gallon pitcher of iced tea.

"Don't break the dishes," a guard said. "We'll be back for them after while."

The turnkey slammed the cell door and locked it. They walked quickly away.

Jack began to laugh as the delicious fragrance of southern fried chicken filled the small cell. He pulled the cloth off the top of the crate Ezekial still held and exposed a tray loaded with fried chicken, a bowl of mashed potatoes, a bowl of cream gravy, two china plates, silverware, napkins and crystal glasses. Jack looked up from the crate to Ezekial's astonished face and began laughing even more uproariously.

"What are you waiting for Zeke? Set that box down and let's eat."

Ezekial sat the box down on the floor and stared open-mouthed at Jack. "What?... Where?...How did?"

"Don't worry about it Zeke. Just eat. Compliments of my sweet sister."

There was almost too much chicken for the two of them and Jack thought about saving some for someone else for about five seconds. Ezekial was enjoying it too much and so was he. Ezekial was putting the bigger bones on the floor beside him, separating them from the small, sharp bones which he replaced into the box. Jack had witnessed this behavior before and knew Ezekial was letting Sam enjoy the memory of eating. Separating the small bones Sam once might have choked on was just an old habit. Ezekial would let bones or scraps of meat lie on the floor for awhile and then dispose of them. Sam understood about the cockroaches and ants or so Ezekial had explained. Jack thought that Sam must have been quite a dog.

In the days following Jack's visit, he was busy with arrangements for the coming escapade. Jack had a man in the leather shop construct Ezekial some shoes that did not resemble prison made brogans as there was no chance Hoss could guess at the size and provide footwear. The leather worker, when he saw the paper outlines of Ezekial's foot responded by saying, "Hell, have him kick a cow in the ass and just lace it up!" Ezekial asked about the cost of the shoes which was high, and then produced a roll of cash he had hidden and gave Jack the money to pay for them.

"Why didn't you ever tell me you had all that money?"

"'Cause you woulda' wanted some for dope Jack."

He was probably right, Jack knew, and was shamed by the self-admission. Jack also realized that he might need some of Ezekial's money to buy the barbiturate or other medicine necessary to make the plan work.

The shoes fit Ezekial well enough. They were even roughly stylish in their way. Ezekial smiled when he wore them. Jack decided to give Winnie rough measurements and have Hoss gather them some clothes and hats. He settled on a price with the hospital orderly for the proper barbiturates. He also recruited the one trusted trusty that would make the plan work.

The trusty was little Opie Jones, an ex-jockey who was jolly and witty and who conned the guards every day. He was so tiny and subservient that the officials had absolutely no fear of him and treated him like furniture. That was exactly what Opie wanted. They never suspected him of pinching small items that they 'lost', nor of having anything to do with the misplaced paperwork regarding disciplinary cases. Prisoners paid him handsomely to destroy necessary papers ordering punishment for prison rule infractions and for persuading a guard to accept a few dollars for bringing a sack of marijuana or a few pints of whiskey in the prison. He could get a prisoner's work duty changed or get him moved back inside the Walls from one of the terrible work camps where a prisoner was shackled always, worked twelve to sixteen hours a day and tied to a whipping post for anything that might irritate a camp sergeant. Opie made money in prison and rarely gambled, but saved his earnings.

Jack reckoned Opie was putting money back for an escape since there was no chance he would ever get out. Jack figured correctly. He approached Opie in just the right way, honestly laying the plan out for him. He knew he was taking a big chance, Opie could just rat him out or he could just refuse to participate. Either way the plan would fail. They needed Opie. Opie asked a hundred questions and strung him out for a few days, but eventually he agreed to join the escape. Together they worked out the smallest details. They knew that if the attempt failed it would be too many years before they might get another chance.

When Jack approached Ezekial for the money to pay for the barbiturates, Ezekial balked.

"I ain't buying you no dope Jack."

"No you ain't. I ain't asking you to. The dope is to put the hacks to sleep so we can get over the wall without being shot."

"Jack, I'm afraid you'll get doped up."

"Give the money to Opie, let him get the sleeping medicine and keep it till we need it."

"Well. I'll think about it."

"Ezekial, we've got to have that powder. Otherwise we ain't getting outa here."

"Well. I'll sleep on it."

Exasperated, Jack let it go.

Next evening on the prison yard Ezekial told Jack to go get Opie. When Opie arrived Ezekial got right to the point.

"Opie, I'm gonna give you this money fer the sleeping powders and you keep it till it's needed. Don't give Jack none of it. If I find out you have I'll break you."

"Sure Big Zeke, can't take a chance on Jack doing too much. You can count on me. I want out of here."

Ezekial handed him the money.

"You can't hear it but Sam's growling," Ezekial told Opie, "He don't like you." Ezekial stroked the air. "It's alright Sam. Sssssh."

"Thas' cause I'm skeered o' dawgs Zeke. Always have been."

"Well. Do things right Opie."

"I will Big Zeke."

Later that night when they were locked in the cell Jack informed Ezekial, "Well, Opie's got the medicine. We're ready to go."

"Aw Jack, I'm kinda hungry. You ain't talking 'bout goin 'fore breakfast are you?"

"Naw, it'll still be a few weeks Zeke," Jack grinned.

"Well. Okay then."

Jack laughed and put an arm around Ezekial's big shoulders and shook him.

It was almost two weeks before another letter from Winnie and Hoss came. Winnie composed the letter in such a way as to convey the necessary information but to cause no suspicion from whoever might censor it. She wrote that her brother had located and acquired a horse of sufficient size to convey that heavy weight of the freight he would soon be picking up. All was ready, even 'shipping point' for the merchandise.

Winnie promised to be down to visit on a date two weeks away, she had already got the permission of the "sweet Superintendant." She enclosed a photo of her standing by her Hupmobile and another of just her face in a portrait in which she seemed sad, her big eyes looking lonesome and lost. Ezekial added these photos to the Winnie niche on the shelf. He asked Jack a dozen questions about the automobile in the photograph most of which Jack could not answer. Ezekial instructed Jack to ask Winnie about this mysterious machine that seemed to be putting the horse out to pasture.

"Zeke, if I ask all those questions, it'll take up the whole time, we have for the visit. You sure are a curious ol' man."

"Well, I don't wanna' be ignorant my whole life. And I'm halfway skeered of being out there in that free world after all this time."

"You? Scared? Why, big as you are you shouldn't be scared of nothing."

"Well. I didn't use to be. But things are different out there now, people know mor'n I do."

"Like what Zeke?"

"Well. There's automobiles on the roads which I don't know nothin' 'bout. Tellyphones. Phonograph. 'lectric lights, all kinds contraptions."

"Aw Zeke, there's some electric lights in here."

"Yep. An' I'm skeered of 'em. They'll lectricute ya', if yer ignorant of 'em like I am. Or, that's what I've overheard."

"Aw Zeke, it don't take no time to learn all that stuff. You'll be driving an automobile and talking on a telephone quicker' n Mister Quick got ready."

"How quick did Mister Quick get ready?"

"Pretty quick."

They laughed together. Ezekial loved Sam. Sam was his best friend. But it was good to have a human friend too. Ezekial smiled at his friend Jack.

The days began to drag by for them. They were anxious for the freedom that the escape presented. Ezekial's apprehensions of the frightening aspects of freedom were being daily allayed by Jack's calming explanations and assurances. He had replaced the photographs of Winnie into the envelopes with her letters which were laid on the shelf. The wonder of the photographs and the memories and questions they had brought to mind were not as consuming now. He had returned to his old patterns of whispering his thoughts to Sam and to studying the worn Bible that Gramps had left him years ago. There were a few other books inside the prison and he had seen a few prisoners reading them. But the Bible was the only book he'd ever had in prison.

One of their last Sundays in prison together Jack had awoke from an afternoon nap and peeked over the side of the top bunk at Ezekial. Ezekial held open the old dog-eared pages of the Bible with one oversized hand and stroked Sam with the other as his eyes seemed to search the far distance for some mysterious notion. His vision seemed to penetrate the stone wall and his leathery brow wrinkled deeper as he sought an answer to the unanswerable. Ezekial's obvious state of meditation caused Jack to maintain his silence until he heard his big friend close the well-read tome.

"Hey Zeke, what' cha thinkin' about?"

"You woke up huh? Have a good nap?"

"Shore did. What' cha studyin' on?"

"I wuz jes' thinkin 'bout all the questions people must have had for centuries 'bout life,…. 'bout God,….'bout maybe why they can't be answered."

"That's pretty deep thinking Zeke, I wouldn't figger you thought 'bout stuff like that!"

"Well. All the years alone in this cell Jack, a man has to think about sumpin' or he'll go crazy."

Jack chuckled.

"Some would say, you didn't have far to go Zeke."

"Mmmhuh. More' n some' d say that, I' magine."

"What kind of questions you pondering Zeke?"

"Well. For instance. I's readin here in the good book 'bout a time the apostles brought a blind man to Jesus to heal. This man had been born blind. The apostles asked Jesus who had committed the sin that caused the man to be born blind, was it his parents or the blind man who'd sinned.

"Now, if the parents sinned and the punishment came on their son, I kin understan' why they ast that 'cus the Bible says that the sins of the fathers will be visited on the sons for generations. But why'd they ast Jesus if the man who'd been borned blind sinned? See whot I mean? How could his blindness be punishment for his sin if he'd been borned blind? Why, they musta' thought he coulda' lived 'fore he was borned. Know whut I mean?"

"Mmmhuh. An' did Jesus straighten em out?"

"No, he didn't. An' duden' it seem like he woulda tole them it was impossible fer a man to sin 'fore he was borned? Jesus,... he diden seem like he was surprised by the question."

Jack thought about the implications for a minute, then asked, "You think people live more'n one life?"

"Well. Maybe. Maybe we're all jes' livin' one life, a life that lasts forever."

Jack thought about that but it was too much to absorb in a moment.

"Bible talks 'bout man's life bein' like grass, how it lives fer a season, then dies. But the grass don't really die, only the part we can see. The part we can't see, the roots, their jes' sleepin' like, an' when the time's right an' the season changes, why that grass seems to come back to life. 'Cept it ain't never really died, only the visible part seemed to die. See whut I mean?"

"Umhuh."

"Well. These are the kinda' things I think 'bout. Sometimes."

Ezekial sat with his hand on Sam, looking far away through a stone wall mere inches from his face. Jack appraised this strange old man and let the silence lengthen.

There were many prisoners who were in undeclared competition to see who could make the most wine, the best-tasting wine, the most potent wine or make it under the guards noses. Every day a separate convict vintner produced another batch of wine. Regular runners moved the barter goods or the cash to the wine makers and smuggled the quarts of wine from cell to cell within the prison. Some inmates stayed drunk for years.

Jack seemed to be trying to continue his laudanum consumption for years. It had been many months since he had required the drug for physical pain. Ezekial was concerned Jack might do too much one day and die. There had been a few times when Jack did not seem to be breathing, when his lips and fingertips turned blue. Ezekial did not know how to help him, except to pray. And he did pray. Ezekial had grown fond of Jack through the months, but Jack did not seem to care about much of anything. Jack did not eat much and often threw up what little he did eat. He had lost weight alarmingly since his injuries. Ezekial had spoken to him about it and Jack had opened up to him about his feelings and history.

Jack told Ezekial about his woman, a woman he had known since they were children. She had traveled rough roads with him, a true and trusted friend. Their hearts and lives were melded into one, more than lovers, closer than best friends.

She had been diagnosed as having a form of consumption. There had appeared scabbed-over growths of brown, scaly tissue on her back and legs that would not heal. She had been in more pain than she would admit. There was no money for a doctor, a hospital. The doctor gave her laudanum for the pain and she seemed to be getting healthier and not so very depressed for awhile. Then Jack had been arrested for something he did not do. Not that he was innocent, he had stolen other things from time to time, but he was certainly and obviously guiltless of this particular infraction. Still, the prosecutor had no other defendant and the books must be balanced.

After he was jailed, she could not work and pay rent and there was no one to take her in. She found a little cabin and moved her meager belongings in. Her health and her hope quickly deteriorated. One cold winter's day she was found in the tiny cabin, dead, presumably from a lethal dose of the laudanum from the empty bottle nearby. So the deputy sheriff had told him.

Jack cried as he told Ezekial the story. His heart had never healed, he would not let it heal. He picked at the open wound with his anger, his guilt and his profound sorrow. Jack told Ezekial:

"Losing her broke me. The hurt reminds me of what was, what we had that was so beautiful, so wonderful, of what I've lived, and lost. Of love so sweet taken so heartlessly. The more it hurts, the deeper the ache, the closer the precious memories. So, I suffer the hurt gladly, I hold it close. It is all I have of her."

Jack was convinced that the law had killed her by arresting him. He had promised that he would be there for her, through thick and thin, to the end. The promise had been broken, he should have been there for her. The hopes and laughter in their simple and happy life together had died with her in that lonely and cold tiny cabin and that vision of her lying and dying alone on that narrow floor would haunt him ever. Hate, loss, guilt, loneliness, regret and despair dogged his every step.

Ezekial had seen pain and loss in Hoss's eyes too, there was a history of hurt hidden behind his hard stare. But, Hoss was not forthcoming with his past, he criticized those who, to his estimation, whined and cried. He detested the sissies who whimpered about their situation. He was a strong, tough man, unyielding in his beliefs. And it was killing him.

Ezekial knew how it hurt to lose someone you love. He had lost love to death and to life. The horror of finding his grandfather dead so many years ago. The feelings of being left behind, the regret of not loving them better, of not fully appreciating the gift of days they had shared, the inexpressible heartache, the tearing of the soul never to heal.

The death of Sam however had been a gift that very few others had ever received. It had given him faith above hope and love above faith and such joy and peace. God had truly blessed him. That which was most truly Sam had come back to him, enlightening him to the existence of continuing life. He knew that he would continue to be and would once again be with those who had left this realm of limited perception. Some would call what remained with him Sam's spirit, his soul, his essence. Ezekial called it Sam. It 'was' Sam.

Over time, the two of them had partially merged, blended, so that each of them experienced the others being. They saw through the others eyes, felt the others thoughts and emotions. There were moments when Ezekial was aware of what Sam smelled and this sense was a thousand times stronger than his own olfactory limitations. Not that he actually smelled the same smells, but the sense provoked images, visions that conveyed information his own perceptions alone could never have known. He also received trails of thought and fact derived from the sense of hearing he shared with Sam.

None of it seemed strange, he had accepted this rare grace of God. He was so grateful and comforted and though he couldn't understand it he was unbothered by his ignorance. Somehow he knew that certain knowledge was veiled from all that lived in this world for a purpose, for a good and loving purpose.

Ezekial yearned to share his experience and the gift of surety beyond faith that had been given him and tried to find words to comfort those who mourned. In the end however, words were only words and no one would accept the truth that had been revealed to him. Others scorned him, pitied him or feared him. They believed he was most certainly insane and found no solace in his vision of the continued being beyond death. If Sam had been human, perhaps some might approach belief but it was a sacrilege to suggest animals had spirits or souls. It wasn't a Christian teaching. It even seemed satanic to some.

Ezekial had tried to explain to Jack:

"You don't have to see ever' thang to know it's real and its meaning. You can't see a spoken word but you know its meaning by another sense. It's the same with Sam. I see him by another sense."

Jack had witnessed enough between Ezekial and the invisible Sam that, at times, for fleeting moments, he could truly believe the dog was there with them. Was Ezekial's insanity infectious? Or was denial the real insanity? But, Jack's human, logical mind could not contain, retain and sustain the illogical.

Sam did not actually occupy space yet Ezekial assigned and protected a small area for him. Jack usually thought Ezekial projected the image of Sam. A few times however, when Jack's mind was not actively engaged in thought but suspended in an unthinking consciousness there had seemed to be another presence there with them. Jack had witnessed and come to envy Ezekial's peace and assured certainty of Sam's existence and presence. Ezekial was never alone. Jack felt he was always alone, always, even when surrounded by others.

The quiet, painful moments of mind when loneliness washed over Jack came often. Memories would flow over him and flood him with loss. He fought to the surface of the deep and dark wash with drugs and alcohol but that chemically induced respite became more fleeting and soon the gloom and sorrow and loss, like an untamable tide rolled over him and submerged him in despair. Jack knew there was no salvation in drugs, still it was better to be numb for a few moments or even to be driven to madness by the mind-altering poisons than to endlessly bleed tears of lost love.

Jack saw that others suffered such loss and managed to struggle through and carry on. Why could he not find the way, the key, the strength, the mettle or the faith that would mend his tortured heart? Guilt and regret will heal if given time, but all that remained to him was remorse and bittersweet memory and he compulsively tore at the wound, not forgiving himself, hindering the healing.

He rarely yearned for his freedom, could not imagine that life would be easier outside prison walls. He was chained to the past and there was no one there anymore. Ambition and dreams had died. He wondered sometimes if there was oblivion in death. Another possibility in death would be reunion with the one he still loved. Subconsciously his fondest hope was in death, beyond these desolate, despondent days of distress.

This last hope of some continued existence beyond this life was what made Ezekial and Sam so intriguing. Jack watched him as he interacted with his friend, listened to the big man's limited explanations and studied him with fervent hope. No one besides himself thought Ezekial sane, but no one had spent time with him as Jack had. Men typically labeled those they feared or did not comprehend as insane, heretics, devils or charlatans. Jack judged Ezekial to be sane and certainly no faker. There was no evil in this gentle giant and Jack wanted what Ezekial had, the knowledge, the belief, the faith, peace and joy. This hope was his only motivation, the hope of heaven.

When Winnie came to visit again, Jack had a date in mind for the escape, but when he told her she said it was too soon. She and Hoss had agreed that she would be in a railroad car headed for San Francisco at least two days before the escape and she needed more time to erase all trace of her passage. She made him promise he would destroy the photos of her and the letters as well before they left the prison. Together they worked out another date which would work for all of those involved.

Jack gave her a short list of things he wanted Hoss to get and the rest of their visit was filled with tales of Hoss and his antics in Houston as well as stories of escapades within the Walls. No one would guess she came from a hardscrabble Georgia sharecropping family, she had no trace of such an accent and her mannerisms were of a high-class lady, educated and pampered. She was a beautiful enchantress and Jack had absolutely no interest in her beyond her usefulness as a messenger. He knew that he might never be capable of loving another woman. And that was okay with him.

When she was leaving Jack thought about thanking her for the chicken, but stopped himself. He didn't want to seem to be doing some calculated begging. Besides he'd be out soon and could get his own chicken. Of course, he had to narrate the entire visit for Ezekial and he asked of course, if any fried chicken was on the way. He hated to disappoint his friend, but reminded him they'd be free to get their own food fairly soon. As they discussed what they would order at the fine restaurant out there in the free world, a disgruntled turnkey unlocked the cell door and dropped a sweating metal bucket on the floor, slammed and locked the door and hurried away down the catwalk.

Jack and Ezekial looked at one another wonderingly. Lifting the lid off the bucket Jack smiled, then moved the bucket so Ezekial could see into it.

"Ice cream!" they both said simultaneously.

"Sam loves ice cream," Ezekial smiled and petted the air.

"Sam better hurry up!" Jack responded as he sank his spoon into the melting goodness.

"That Winnie is a wonder," Ezekial said, "She's shore got the gumption and gall."

"Yep. She does that."

Jack squatted and leaned against the wall of the infirmary out on the prison yard watching the small man approach him. Opie was in his sixties, wore wire-rimmed glasses and had no teeth. He had a perpetual wide-mouthed grin on his face and his light blue eyes still sparkled with life. He was always ready with a joke or a jibe and didn't mind if the joke was on him as long as there was laughter. He'd been in prison for over two decades and had been a trusty for ten. He had been fooled by shyster lawyers for many years into believing they could get him out on a writ of habeas corpus. He'd told Jack it was time he got out on a writ of habeas escapus! The guards all trusted Opie, as did the long- term convicts. Some of the new-boot prisoners thought he was a suck-ass snitch, but they didn't count. The old cons ran the prison and word was he be left alone.

Opie had a life sentence. Good lying lawyers had milked him of all his money and he had requested several governors to pardon him, but since his murderous record was notorious, it was not politically expedient to grant Mister Jones any relief. He had nothing to bribe anyone with and all his friends who might help him escape were either dead or lost to him. When Jack had approached him with the proposition to escape with them, he had given it careful consideration. He had to succeed the first time as it was sure to be the only time. He'd watched Jack over the past few years and had a good opinion of the man despite his use of laudanum. Hoss was also a stand-up fellow. Opie thought they'd do to ride the river with.

Opie slid down the wall onto his haunches and said simply, "Got a date?"

Jack named a day then asked, "You sure that medicine will do the trick?"

Opie assured him that the soporific he had purloined from the surgery room in the infirmary was more than adequate.

"We don't want to kill no guards now Opie. They'll be mad as homeless yellow-jackets anyway."

"I've read all about it and even tested it already twice on my unsuspecting cell partner. Heh-heh. I've got the dose measured perfectly. Don't worry bout that. Just be sure ever' thangs ready on the outside."

"It'll be ready."

"Ok. Later."

Opie stood and sidled up to a horseshoe pitching contest joking with the players like he always did. No one would ever suspect that Opie would be vanishing from inside these ugly old Walls real soon.

SEPARATE REALITIES

The following Friday afternoon Jack was sweating in the cell, kneeled down on the floor in front of Ezekial cutting the chain on each end of the shackles on his ankles. Ezekial held a small piece of broken mirror through the bars watching for anyone walking up the catwalk toward the cell.

"How long have these shackles been on you Zeke?"

"Long time. Since I broke that boss."

"What'd you break?"

"His back. His head."

"It'll take awhile to get used to having full use of your legs again. We'll use shoestrings to tie the chains back to the ankle cuffs for when the guard comes by to count. Later on, after we get away from Huntsville, we'll get the ankle cuffs off you."

Jack finished cutting through the link, bent and pried it off the cuff, then tied it back in place with string. He switched places with Ezekial, took the small broken piece of mirror from him and put it through the bars looking out for the guards as Ezekial began working the file over the links attached to the cuff around his ankles. Since Opie was a trusty, he had no shackles to cut. Hopefully, he would soon be dosing the guards coffee with the soporific and the adventure would begin.

Jack's periodic glance into the mirror to view the catwalk was double protection against a guard walking up on the cutting of the shackles. Jack had recruited a Mexican everyone called Monster who was housed on the ground tier into jiggering for them. If he heard Monster break out into singing La Cucaracha, he knew a guard was coming up the stairs toward them.

A turnkey would open Opie's cell about nine p. m. allowing him to go to the kitchen and help prepare coffee and sandwiches to distribute to all the night guards. There were only six guards working at the prison from six p. m. to six a. m., one in each of four towers on the four walls, one in the cell block and a rover who walked around checking on prisoners who worked at night and checked locks. After the coffee and food was prepared Opie would deliver some to the cell block turnkey, then to each of the guards in the perimeter pickets on the walls. The roving guard typically waited in the kitchen drinking coffee until the food was prepared then ate there. The guards in the towers lowered a bucket and the coffee in a small pot and sandwiches were passed up via a rope and pulley. Opie said that all the guards would be deep asleep twenty minutes after consuming the coffee and food.

When the guards were unconscious Opie would take the cellblock guard's keys and open Jack and Ezekial's cell. As they left, they'd give the keys to Monster, who would wait ten minutes, then start letting those others out of their cells who wanted to escape. By that time Jack, Ezekial and Opie would be over the wall and the two prisoners who worked nights in the kitchen would have taken the rover's keys and gained access to the first gate on the sally port at the back gate. Once there the kitchen workers would climb to the guard tower where the keys to the outer gate were kept, take them from the sleeping guard and throw open the last gate. There would be a chest of weapons in the back gate picket also which would be distributed to the escaping convicts.

Jack and Ezekial would follow Opie to the lower yard and scale the wall behind the bathhouse and laundry. This was the lowest tower and Hoss would be holding the horses just below.

Jack lay on his bunk listening for keys. The prison was quiet except for the usual snoring and the occasional moan. It was after midnight when without warning, he felt a shadow fall over him and heard a key scrape into the lock.

"They're all in dreamland Fast Jack, let's ride." As he put the big brass key in the lock Opie added, "I hope I didn't give them too much, I don't want the crackers to die, I want them to feel the shame of their failure."

Opie led the way down the catwalk followed by Jack, then Ezekial. On the first tier he stopped and handed the keys to Monster. Give us fifteen minutes amigo. Buena suerte." he said to the big prisoner in the dark cell.

The trio walked by the kitchen and were assured by the two cooks that the rover was still fast asleep. The turnkey in the cellblock had slid out of his chair and was in deep sleep on the stone floor, They hurried directly and quietly to the lower yard wall under the picket. The lantern up in the tower revealed nothing, the tower looked empty.

"You think the hack fell off the tower?" Jack asked.

"Naw, prob'ly just taking a nap," Opie smiled. "You'll need to get that crate and barrel over by the door of the bath house."

Jack went and began rolling the barrel over below the picket while Ezekial dragged the crate over. The movement was the only sound in the quiet of the night.

"Ssssh!" Opie ordered, "You lugs will wake the dead!"

They positioned the big heavy wooden crate under the picket and then placed the big barrel atop it.

"Okay Zeke, let's do this the first time, I don't want to fall," Jack said.

Ezekial climbed on the crate and then onto the barrel. Jack then climbed over the crate and up the barrel and over Ezekial to stand on his shoulders.

"Okay. Ezekial, lift me up. Slow and easy. Keep your balance. Ezekial put his hands to his shoulders and slipped them beneath Jack's brogans. He pushed up and back, focusing on his balance, easily lifting Jack's two hundred pounds. Jack's fingers grasped the edge of the tower, then said, "A little higher. Alright."

Jack grabbed the floor of the picket and swung himself up over the edge. He immediately saw the supine tower guard, mouth open and drooling in his sleep. He looked down and said to the two upturned faces, "He's knocked smooth out." He pushed his foot against the side of the guard who was softly snoring. He then picked up the rifle leaned against the wall and pitched the rope with the bucket attached down to Opie who was accustomed to catching it. Ezekial, again on the ground grasped Opie around the waist and pushed him up the rope by his butt and feet until he too was able to scurry up the rope and gain Jack's helping hand onto the picket floor. Jack lowered the rope and bucket again and watched Ezekial place something he couldn't see in the bucket.

"Lift 'im up Jack," Ezekial said, looking up.

"What?" Jack asked.

"Sam. Lift him up," Ezekial urged.

"Damn Zeke! Sam can't float over the wall by himself?"

"He ain't got wings Jack. He's a dog. Lift him up."

To appease Ezekial, Jack sighed his exasperation and hurriedly began turning the pulley. Surprisingly, the bucket seemed heavier than it should and he asked, "What you got in the bucket Zeke? It's heavy."

"Jus' Sam," Ezekial answered, "Take it easy."

Jack placed the bucket on the floor and it jiggled of its own accord as Jack observed it. He thought maybe he had taken too much laudanum.

"Don't forget me," Ezekial said and Jack lowered the rope again. He looked over to see Opie taking the guards pocket watch and money. Opie noticed Jack watching him and said defensively, "I'll need it worse than him."

The tower wobbled as Ezekial slowly lifted himself hand over hand up the rope and when he was securely on the floor, Jack took the lantern and swung it back and forth, the signal to Edward to bring the horses. There was no sound or movement on the dark street below for a couple of minutes and Jack began to wonder.

Hoss saw the silhouettes of the three figures in the tower from his spot in an alley a block away, and then he saw the swinging lantern. He eased the horses down the hard packed dirt road and Jack soon spied him and the horses through the gathering mist. Jack smiled.

Ezekial had cut the rope from the pulley and moved it to the banister rail on the freedom side of the tower. Jack smiled down at Hoss and slid down the rope. Hoss hugged him when he hit the ground.

"Mount up Fast Jack, let's ride."

"Gotta' wait for Zeke."

"He's got his horse here and clothes and provisions. Let him go his own way like the others."

"Nope. He goes with me."

"Aw, hell!"

Opie had slid down and shook hands with Hoss. Hoss pointed out the horse he had for him and told him clothes and provisions were in the roll behind the saddle.

"Take the guard's rifle Opie. Hoss has me a gun."

"Okay. I'm gone. Thank you boys. Thank you for a chance at a life. I mean it."

"Get going Opie. Luck to you."

"What are you doing Zeke? C'mon!"

"I'm comin'."

"What's the big 'um doin' Jack."

Jack answered, "Don't ask," as he tightened the cinch on his horse.

Ezekial had tied the bucket to the rope and lowered it slowly and gently. The bucket jumped and swung as it neared the ground. Jack and Hoss looked at one another, eyebrows raised then watched Ezekial lower himself down the rope. When he reached the ground he made the motions of picking something up and placing him in front of the saddle. The horse shied a bit, but Ezekial held him and mounted up.

"You an' Sam ready?"

"Yep."

"Let's get somewhere!" Hoss said and led out westward in a hurry.

Chapter Eight

"I am not sure that God particularly wants us to be happy, I think he wants us to love and be loved..... I suggest to you that it is because God loves us that He makes us the gift of suffering. Pain is God's megaphone to a deaf world. So, dear ones, I would exhort you to deny yourselves the luxury of self-pity. You are not the first human beings on earth to suffer, nor has your suffering been the most acute, by far."
—C. S. Lewis

"A man's life is what his thoughts make of it."
—Marcus Aurelius

"A man is what he thinks all day long."
---Ralph Waldo Emerson

"This is the day the Lord hath made; we will rejoice and be glad in it."
Psalm 118:24 (KJV)

THE SABINE RIVER was three days behind them and the road was much busier both ways. Noah was surprised there were so many travelers. All along the way there were men felling trees, the fellers planing the logs for barns and houses. And it seemed they passed through a new settlement every day where the fragrance of fresh-cut pine hung in the air. Noah was beginning to feel uncomfortable seeing all this civilization and population.

Noah had spent his life in Texas except for the recent war years. His parents were settlers on the frontier outside Bastrop who farmed the rich land there. The land was sparsely settled in the early eighteen thirties and game was plentiful. Noah had learned to hunt and fish at an early age. One often recalled the morning Noah left the farm at dawn to fish a couple of miles down the Colorado. He had already completed his morning chores and had promised to bring fish home for dinner. His mother had laughed and kissed him on the forehead. Sometimes his forehead still tingled from the love within that last kiss. His poppa had tousled his hair and told him to enjoy the day because tomorrow he'd have to help plant corn.

Noah still could envision the beauty of the early spring morn, the smells of new growth, the golden light gleaming in rays through the towering pecan trees growing along the river's shore. The joyous singing of the birds, the fresh zephyr and the constant flow and rhythm of the river.

In less than two hours his stringer was full of fish and he had headed home. As he came out of the trees along the river he saw and smelled the smoke, too much smoke. He began to run, throwing the fish and pole aside. He found his father in the freshly plowed field, almost naked, riddled with arrows, mutilated, scalped. He ran on to the house, which was almost completely burned and found his mother! She was lying beneath a clothesline on which hung a few articles of clothing. She was stripped, burned, mutilated, scalped, her skin black and smoking with an axe still wedged in her chest. The smell of his burning mother still came to him these forty years later and brought uncontrollable feelings of love and loss, and murderous hate.

He went to the well, filled a bucket of water and poured it over the smoldering remains of his recent young and pretty mother. Through years of battles with Indians, Mexicans and Yankees the smell of burning flesh would haunt him and torture his very soul.

He had been twelve when the massacre had occurred. When neighbors had arrived later that afternoon they had found him digging the second grave up the hill behind the still smoking embers of what had been a happy home. Tears had cut trails down his dirty cheeks and blisters on his hands were freely bleeding. He wouldn't allow the neighbors to help him bury his parents, only allowing them to place them in the graves. As he finished packing the earth he heard the others discussing the preparations to ride after the Indians who had driven all their livestock before them westward. He heard a man who was studying an arrow they had pulled from his poppa say, "Comanche. These were surely Comanche devils who have done this foul deed."

From that day he had burned with a hate for Comanches. Noah had fought to go along with the men who would chase the murderers. They had to lock him in a neighbor's smokehouse to prevent him and he had thrown himself against the door screaming, crying and ranting for revenge.

The Indians who had raided the Bastrop area settlements were never found. A few cows who had been too slow to keep up with the stolen horse herd were recovered and the corpses of two children were found along the trail. The tiny bodies of a boy of three and his seven year old sister were returned to their young mother who died of her wounds soon after.

Noah was an exuberant and spirited lad until that fateful day, afterwards he was quiet. He rarely spoke at all, only in monosyllable responses to questions and short sentences. He never smiled or laughed again, until later when he was introduced to alcohol. Alcohol became his salvation and his damnation. He became a man long before the usual years. Though the neighbors who had taken him in had doubts and were reluctant, they eventually allowed him to join the eight companies of mounted volunteers to serve for six months to protect the frontiers of Texas. The bill establishing this regiment was signed into law by President Lamar in the last days of eighteen thirty eight. Noah volunteered early in thirty nine. The good neighbors who had completed his raising offered to give him money along with the horse and gear they gave him, but he refused. The little money that they had he knew they would need. Texas money wasn't worth much more than Mexican money anyway. He wanted to give them his family's land, but they refused. They believed he would soon get his fill of the hardships and privations of a ranger company and would return to his land to farm. They were wrong. He never returned to his land to farm.

Noah's first action against Indians was under Colonel Edward Burleson fighting the Cherokees and Delawares who had refused to give up their land and move north to Indian Territory. They pursued the Cherokee up the Nuches River and caught them at a dense thicket and swamp. In an hour and a half over a hundred of the five hundred Cherokee lay dead or wounded. Chief Bowles had been killed. His successors in leadership were his son John and another warrior called The Egg.

The surviving Cherokee hid in the upper Trinity River Valley until December, then began to trail south toward Mexico. The trail was found by Colonel Burleson's scouts and the rangers attacked the retreating Cherokee on Christmas Day, eighteen thirty-nine, near the mouth of the San Saba River. Both John Bowles and The Egg were killed and twenty-seven women and children taken prisoners. Noah had stared long and hard at the women and children, thinking of his mother and her fate.

The next twenty years of Noah's life were filled with chases and gun battles, killing and hangings. With John Coffee Hays, Sam Walker and others he fought outlaws, Apache, Kiowa, Comanche, and both Mexican bandits and the Mexican Army which was seen as about the same thing. Noah was particularly relentless and merciless in his hate-filled efforts to exterminate the Comanche. He led many forays and chases against them and if one held to the maxim 'the only good Indian is a dead Indian,' he bestowed sainthood on many a Comanche.

On the Texas frontier from the Canadian to south of the Rio Bravo he had witnessed untold atrocities of 'the snake you cannot see'. Noses and lips burned off, breasts and tongues and organs hacked off, soles of feet skinned, eyes poked out, prisoners dragged through prickly pear cactus, staked and tied in red ant beds, and worse, much, he had seen. In Noah's estimation the Comanche were demons and he sent as many to their ancestors as he saw. He felt no remorse in disposing of them, no guilt, yet many times he would find himself weeping as he stood over dead Comanche, just as he did as a child when he had stood over his dead and desecrated parents.

Noah had chased the crazed Comanche who had raided down into Victoria and Linnville in eighteen forty and had recovered some of the women and children they had taken. He'd fought with famous Indian fighter 'Old Paint' Caldwell and at the Battle of Plum Creek. He had run Mexicans who had stirred up the Indians back into Mexico and chased Comancheros and Indian traders back into New Mexico and into Hell. When Texas became a state he helped whip the Mexican Army and he had fought the Yankees until the South had nothing left to fight with. Once he defined an enemy, he killed as many as he could. It was simpler for him that way.

Noah had not returned to the acreage he had inherited on that terrible day through all the years. Now, headed for Austin, he felt a desire to see it once again. He wanted to see if he could sign on with the rangers again, he was hoping that those who remembered his service would give him his own company. Beau wanted to go into Austin with him to visit the recently established Freedmen's Bureau to see if land might be available to him to homestead. Callie wanted to see if she might be qualified for government land also. She knew that the Homestead Act passed by the U. S. Government in eighteen sixty two did not apply to Texas as there was no federal land in Texas. Still, she thought that there may be some state offering of land for homestead.

As their train passed through East Texas they observed that the great majority of the men clearing and working the land, building fences and barns and bridges, were black men. Because of its geographical position Texas had emerged from the War of Northern Aggression relatively unscathed. Some of the Southern slaveholders had "refugeed" their chattel into Texas to prevent advancing Yankee armies from freeing them and to keep slaves from running to Yankee lines. This immigration of blacks as well as the resultant coming of their kin and friends after the war increased the labor pool significantly and expanded farming lands.

During these days of so-called Reconstruction, the black code specified that workers suspected of being truant from their jobs could be arrested and put to work on public projects without pay until they agreed to return to their former employer. Blacks could not marry interracially, hold public office, press charges, sue, or testify against white defendants. Thus, in many ways, emancipation was a more severe hardship than slavery. At least in slavery the blacks were fed, clothed and housed.

The Bureau of Refugees, Freedmen and Abandoned Lands was instituted in eighteen sixty five to extend aid and health care to blacks and eventually did provide some relief to basic conditions, but in the inception of this government program they lacked personnel to help blacks enter society as free persons. The age-old social decorum that demanded deference from blacks when addressing whites, or to yield to whites when encountering them on the streets, was abandoned by the freed blacks which caused trouble. Though teachers were difficult to persuade into schools, sixteen schools for blacks were started by the Freedmen's Bureau in Texas in eighteen sixty five.

As they passed the gangs of black men toiling in the fields Micah mused as to how much had changed yet remained the same. White men still owned the land and oversaw the work of black men. Lincoln proclaimed that they were free but that had not made it so. Yet, despite the ways things now appeared, Micah felt hope in his heart.

Micah had lived in slavery all his life and most of his life was spent. Initially, when he and Beau had left the old plantation, where he had spent his whole life, with little more than the clothes on their backs and the fine horses they had been gifted, he had felt old, afraid and lost. A life in captivity is all he had ever known. How was he to provide for himself? His life had been stable and now was unpredictable and uncomfortable. Uncertain thoughts filled his days, fear seemed to have overcome him.

The day came when hunger gnawed at his flesh and he felt his deepest despair. The breeze blew against his thin, tattered coat and he felt the bumps in his pocket of the Bible he'd been given so many years before. He took it out and ran his weathered old hand over the homemade leather cover he had so lovingly fashioned when the original cover wore out. He sat beneath a great oak tree and looked up through its mighty branches to the endless blue in the sky and whispered a prayer.

"Lord, I am free. I thank you for this freedom. But Lord, I am lost and afraid. I don't know where to go or what to do. Lead me Lord where you would have me go. Show me what you would have me do. I am old, and tired, and hungry, and weak. Lead me Lord and I will follow. Amen."

Later that same day they met Ezekial and he took them home and fed them and began to help them. Micah knew his prayer had been answered. And now, despite the evidence his eyes showed him, he knew that the Lord had not only heard his prayer, but had heard the cry of all his brothers and sisters who had lived in bondage. He was happy down in his heart because he knew that though the path was long and the obstacles were many, still there would come a day when the full glory of freedom would be found and felt. Now he was feeling younger, stronger, anxious to see what was over the next hill, confident that with the Lord's continuing grace he would be able to deal with what tomorrow might bring. His faith grew stronger each day.

Ezekial was a giant of a man in stature but he realized that his little experience had given him but little wisdom and he looked to Micah and Callie for guidance. Micah saw Ezekial watching Noah and knew he was evaluating him. He had likely met men like Noah Lister in the war and saw that they were brave, courageous men in battle, reckless with their lives and often filled with hate. Micah felt there was something inside Noah that he hated in others, maybe it was hate itself.

Noah had treated Micah well, as an equal, and Micah was glad Noah was with them to protect them from all those who would mean to harm them. He saw Noah was prideful and rather than avoid trouble, Noah welcomed it as a challenge, as if trouble were his stage. He would ride directly into trouble, consequences be damned, or so Micah felt. In that trait, Noah was not to be trusted.

The girls Sallie and Nellie were Micah's new-found joy. He felt something like he thought a grandfather must feel toward them and it made him ache in his chest to know that somewhere the daughters and sons he had produced had produced children and he longed to see them and know them. He admitted to himself that there was little chance that would ever happen. These precious girls who pestered him continually with questions, he held dear. They relied on his wisdom as they did their mother's wisdom. He was careful in how he answered them. They made him laugh and allowed him to feel a song in his old heart. They were so tender and fragile; pure, promising, an unwritten page.

Their mother was a good woman who gave her best for all those she loved. She couldn't help but be happy and feel blessed with children such as she had. There were times however when a great loneliness and yearning showed in her clear blue eyes. Micah believed it was the continuing pain of loss for the man she loved, the children's father, that brought the far-focusing of her eyes in quiet moments. Micah saw her try to keep the loneliness away with busywork until the yearning left her.

Beau was, Micah's 'boy'. Not his son, not really, but he felt that close to him. He knew Beau loved him in his youthful brash manner, but he kept the love at a distance, allowing friendship, no more. That was fine and acceptable to Micah, he understood the restrictions a young man kept on his emotions. He knew Beau's first priority, his primary goal, his dream was to find the woman he loved. He worried that time and distance may have altered the young woman's love for Beau. These times wrought many changes. He hoped and prayed that Beau wasn't headed for heartache down here in Texas.

As they all made the practiced moves to set up camp on the banks of the slow rolling Trinity and the day gave way to night, the sun surrendered rule of the sky to a huge ivory moon. In the cooling air, the silence was filled with welcome sound. The water washed against the bank in rhythm with the scratching of the last leaves in the fragrant breeze. A fish flopped midstream and a horse huffed and dug his hoof in the dirt. Sparrows rushed to their favorite roosts and the children's laughter was music to many ears, bringing joy and contentment to the tired travelers at end of day.

But Noah's thoughts returned for the millionth time to the morning that laughter left him. Once again he wondered where the

Comanche was that stripped his mother's body, violated her, burned her, and drove the axe into her young breast? Where were they who cut her and his father like devils would? Did they still breath the sweet air? He thought of the hundred battles and the bodies of dead demons he had executed. Were his parents murderers among them? Only if they all were killed could he be sure that justice was done.

The Civil War had been a distraction. He should never have wasted those years on those he didn't hate. He had been used, tricked into defending a social structure in which the wealthy continued their reign by the bondage of an innocent people. The soldiers of the South were told the war was about defending their land, their possessions, their families, that the North would impose their will on them and not allow them their freedom to choose their own way. Emancipation of the negro slaves could have been realized over time with discretion. The Yankees did not know how ill-prepared for freedom the negro was. And now, the starving and homeless black masses of humanity all along the roads were evidence of Yankee idealistic ignorance. Abe Lincoln was a fool.

Musing on these recent years, he regretted becoming involved in a war that wasn't his war. He found no joy in killing the ill-trained, ill-informed and innocent American lads who gave their lives so bravely. So many dead boys, so many mourning mothers. And for what? For this misery and poverty and hunger that permeated the South? This was freedom? This was their victory?

The past few days he had begun to enjoy being with and helping these good people on their way. They were naive, trusting babes, and he knew, if they didn't, that they needed him. He had given much thought to helping to establish and build a ranch and a life with these good folks he was getting to know and like. At such quiet times like this when peace and contentment threatened to overcome him he felt unbalanced and an urge to break away to search for Comanches to kill nearly overwhelmed him. He was afraid he might come to love these gentle people and he knew the pain that might come of that. He wished he could simply live and enjoy these times with these wide-eyed pilgrims and share their hopes and dreams.

Chas covered the buckets of water he had carried from the Trinity and wondered where the river had got its name. They had passed over many rivers and streams in the past weeks, the Sabine, the Neches and others, no one could tell him what these words meant. He felt a need to know. Noah had told him it was just a name to know it from another river, that the meaning was lost in the past. Chas felt an itch to know. Such knowledge should not be lost.

They had traveled over red earth to a settlement called San Augustine and Micah had told him that Augustine was a Catholic saint that lived long ago and far away. Chas had questioned him farther, but that was all he knew. Micah seemed to understand his curiosity more than the others and, even nourished it with daily teachings of the plants, the trees, and the animals they passed. Callie taught him practical things, as did Luther and Beau, and he gratefully absorbed these lessons too. Chas found that Noah knew a lot about Indians and he enjoyed listening to his lectures. During the days of travel, he jumped from wagon to wagon to horse as one teacher tired of his questions and he sought a change of subject. Now at end of day, he was tired, body and brain. He ate, nodded, then made his bed and used it.

Sallie admired the glorious moon that filled the parting of the canvas at the back of the wagon. Her gaze followed the glowing trail of soft moonlight as it bathed the face of her little sister and her mother. All three of them had blonde hair, her mother's more a true blonde than her daughter's. Sallie's had a golden tint approaching red and Nellie's hair was almost white. In the moonlight Nellie's locks, seemed to have a soft light of their own.

Sallie thought that her mother was the most beautiful woman that God had ever created and that Nellie was just as perfect. She didn't consider herself beautiful. The mirror showed her that her nose was a bit too long and straight and made her look snobbish or uppity, so she made every effort to compensate her snooty look by acting friendly and down to earth.

Nellie was curled up like a kitten in her mother's arms, as close as she could get. She had been a momma's girl from her start and fretted when separated from her for too long. Sallie loved her mother dearly, but she had been Daddy's girl and she thought she hurt more than even her mother because of his death. They had buried her father at a cemetery in Virginia and Mother had taken her and Nellie to see the place where his body lay as they left the farm and headed west. Sallie knew her Daddy wasn't there in the ground, he was in her heart. He wasn't dead; he would always live in her memories of golden days on the farm in Western Virginia. Even now, the tears flowed. She missed him so much.

At quiet times like these she could hear his deep voice full of tenderness telling her she had to be strong for her mother and help her with Nellie and with all the work and obstacles in starting a new life. She was twelve years old and Mother said she was on the verge of womanhood, whatever that meant. She didn't feel like she thought a woman should feel. At times like this she felt like a baby and so alone. She didn't like to be awake through the dark, lonely nights.

What she did like was riding one of the horses with Beau or Chas or riding in the wagon and talking to Micah or Ezekial. She didn't realize it to put it into words but they all felt like family; Beau and Ezekial were big brothers, Chas a little brother; Micah like a grandfather; Luther and Noah like crazy uncles. Noah, she supposed, was older than her father would have been, but he didn't seem to be a father. She felt protected and safer when he was around, he didn't seem to be afraid of anything. He was confident, unconcerned. She didn't feel he was stable. She felt he may disappear anytime. He was handsome in a rugged sort of way, he made her laugh in his dry, brash manner. But he seemed to hold everyone away at arm's length, like he was afraid he might have to love someone. She felt sorry for him, he seemed lonely, like she was sometimes.

She heard him putting wood on the fire, then heard him placing the coffeepot on the coals. She felt that he was thinking moody, gloomy thoughts like she was and she thought of getting out of the wagon and just go hug him, but she was too shy. So, she did what she had been taught to do, she prayed for him. She told God that she didn't know what made Noah sad, what kept him awake at night, but God knew and since He was going to be awake anyway, she asked

Him to comfort him. Putting her concerns in God's hands, sleep finally welcomed her.

The troop found a suitable ford at a gravel bar across the Trinity the next morning and Noah found a ford when they arrived at the Brazos. They crossed the Colorado by means of a small ferry which had to make four trips to get their train across. Noah took them to his own inheritance and there they made camp amongst misplaced pines, not far from the site of Noah's childhood home. The smell in the air brought visions of childhood days. The dark days of his parents murder did not come to mind, but the happy days when their laughter and love filled the piney air. Beau noticed the uncharacteristic and fleeting smile on Noah's face. He was totally unprepared for a smile on Noah's face at the sight of his family's massacre. It worried him.

Late in the evening, as the birds selected their roosts, Noah walked to the site of the burned house and sat on a stump his father had fashioned as a table all those years ago. Memories of happy times flooded his consciousness, and finally, it was the remembrances of good times that brought a tear. He was amazed at the tear. He laughed out loud as he cried. It felt like a cleansing, a release of long fermented poisons.

He walked to the river and bathed in the near dark. He felt a desire now, a need to seek some joy in what remained of life. Much of the hate he had harbored was gone. He kept smiling and shaking his head. He thought he should have returned to this place long ago. Now, instead of seeing the river he was experiencing the wonder of creation, instead of seeing the dark of night, he found himself admiring the endless array of stars that shone just for him.

Arriving in Austin about noon the next day, Callie invited everyone to go with her to a restaurant downtown. When she learned that Beau and Mich would not be allowed to eat with them but must go around to the back of the restaurant and eat outside the kitchen at a table there for 'servants', she gave the host a heated scolding. She was in high dudgeon. Luther found a Mexican restaurant which would allow Beau and Micah in, so the whole band filled the tables in the small room.

Callie, the girls, Chas, Luther, Ezekial, Beau and Micah had never ate Mexican food before, so Noah ordered for all of them. Enchiladas, tamales, Spanish rice and beans and asked the proprietor to go easy on the chilies. Everyone cleaned their plates and Callie paid the bill. The Mexican waiter was surprised that a woman should pay, it wasn't done in Texas when a male was present. It would have been more acceptable to give the money to pay the bill to one of the males, even Chas, than to disrespect the males in this way. All the Mexicans in the restaurant gaped at this audacious woman.

Callie and her daughters found a lawyer who directed them to a land speculator. She spent an hour drilling him with questions, then took the girls and went shopping for supplies which she had loaded in the wagons. Beau and Micah found a small bar and gambling shack frequented by blacks and gathered information there for awhile, then Micah went into a black Baptist church and spoke with a preacher and a deacon who were preparing for services that evening.

Noah, Ezekial and Luther went into a saloon which fronted on the wide, rutted Congress Street. Ezekial was relieved when Noah and Luther ordered only nickel beers and left the whiskey alone. Ezekial drank coffee. There were three men there who apprised them of much relating to the present circumstance in the state. A. J. Hamilton, a former Texas Congressman who had stood with the Union had been given a Presidential appointment as provisional Governor in July. Noah learned that an old friend, Tom Green had been killed at Blair's Landing in sixty-four and had attained the rank of Brigadier General. The men had told Noah that Tom Green's widow, five daughters and only son, Tom Jr. continued to live in Austin. He thought of seeing Mrs. Green and extending his condolences, but repented. It would likely just open old wounds. Beau and Micah returned to the wagons which were parked along Congress Street and found four black men accompanied by a blue-coat black sergeant going through the wagons, stacking some items on the boardwalk in a pile.

"'Scuse me Mista Sargen', these here wagons b' long to my friends, Mister Ezekial Robertson and Misses Callie."

"And who might you be nigger?"

"Seems to me that's like the pot calling the kettle black," Micah interjected.

"I am a sergeant in the United States Army and I will whip your black ass and lock it up if you don't get busy answering my questions."

Callie and the girls began walking quickly from half a block away.

"What are you doing with these things?" Micah asked.

"We are searching for stolen property and contraband and it seems there is a lot of each in these wagons. Now answer my question nigger or you'll wish you had."

Callie bustled up and screeched, "What do you think you're doing with my things!?"

"Lady, you quieten down or I'll be forced to arrest you for possession of stolen property and contraband."

"You will do no such thing,… let go of me!" Callie struggled as the sergeant grabbed her arms and pushed her down to the street, Sallie and Nellie attacked the sergeant and he swatted them to the ground also. And the next moment there was a loud crack and the sergeant flew through the air and landed on his back ten feet into the street. He lay perfectly still, eyes closed, legs at an awkward angle, teeth and blood dribbling down his chin. Ezekial took one long stride and stood over the prone soldier, fists clinched, waiting for a movement.

Noah grabbed one of the black hoodlums and slung him down from the wagon and the other three rushed him. Beau grabbed up the long barreled shotgun from the pile of stuff on the boardwalk and swung it like an axe against the back of one of the attackers, then lifted the barrel and fired a warning blast into the sky. The ruffians broke and ran. As the men helped the females up they were all quickly surrounded by blue-coats, rifles pointed at them.

"Stand down soldiers!" A young Captain entered the circle and removed his hat as he approached the ladies.

"Ma'am, are any of you injured?"

"I believe I'll survive. But, you had better get a doctor for my attacker there."

"Sergeant Washington seems to still be breathing, so chances are he'll live. Unfortunately. Corporal Roscoe, see to the Sergeant. Take him to the infirmary, then to the stockade. Madam, is that your property on the walk?"

"Yes, it is our property Captain."

"I think I know what happened here, it has happened before. Nevertheless, I will need to hear it from you. Madam?"

Callie told him. Beau and Micah told him. Then Ezekial, Luther and Noah told him. They were escorted to a house that had been seized for army headquarters, a house which had been the Texas Institute for the Blind. The young Captain assigned a small squad of soldiers to guard the wagons while each of the group suffered through questioning by other officers, then all had to give written statements.

Before they were allowed to leave, the commandant came out to have a word with them. He introduced himself as General George Armstrong Custer. Flamboyantly dressed from his silver-toed and spurred, shining knee-high boots to his cavalry hat with a long white plume flowing from the hat band, one gloved hand rested on an ornate polished sword and the other hand rested beneath a double row of brass buttons which shone on his breast. Long golden curls fell over golden epaulets and he smiled in a superior manner as he peered at these 'commoners.'

Bowing deeply, he addressed Callie, "Madam, I am sure my apologies to you for the indecent attack upon your person cannot sufficiently express my sincere regret that the proud widow of an American hero was subjected to such despicable treatment at the hands of a soldier of the United States Army whom your brave husband so proudly served. I offer my services in any manner to you Misses MacGillicuddy to compensate in the smallest way for the embarrassment, inconvenience, disrespect and injury which has so regretfully befallen you."

Callie answered him shortly. "Thank you sir. I believe the best thing you can do for us is to send us on our way."

"Yes ma'am, I certainly will. And I will have an honor guard escort you out of Austin on your way at your convenience."

Turning to a Colonel at his side he ordered "See to it Colonel."

SEPARATE REALITIES

The Colonel motioned to an accompanying lieutenant who hurried away.

"Before you do I would like to shake the hand of a well respected 'ex' adversary. Colonel, this man is the famous Texas Cavalry Captain Noah Lister, whose brave exploits and victories against United States forces were many and highly publicized. Captain, I am honored to meet you."

Noah dipped his head and answered politely, "A pleasure General."

"I must say that I pestered my superior officers repeatedly to be allowed to pursue you. You perplexed and defeated many of our officers and I desperately wanted to meet you in the field of battle so the honor of the United States Cavalry would be redeemed."

"General Custer, in all honesty, if we had met on an even field, evenly matched and armed, I would have spanked your skinny white ass so hard it would be striped as red and white as ol' Glory." Turning to Callie he offered his arm.

"Shall we go?"

With smiles on their faces, the traveling troop left the building.

Custer watched them go and replaced his feathered hat over his curls. Turning to the Colonel beside him who tried to hide his grin he observed, "Cocky son of a bitch isn't he?'

The Colonel looked the General up and down and answered, "Absolutely sir, a veritable peacock." Noah explained to Callie that, added to the incentive of leaving Austin forthwith because of the unrestrained freedmen and troops, there was disease sweeping through Custer's soldiers camped at Shoal Creek believed to be a cholera epidemic or yellow fever. Bodies of both Confederates and Federals were buried along Shoal Creek banks. Unreconstructed Confederates were still being held in 'bullpens' by Custer. Noah thought it typical that the officers quarters were so distant from the disease the soldier's were suffering in their tent city along the creeks banks.

Noah also explained that he had learned there was absolutely no prospect of any state ranger company being formed in the foreseeable future. U.S. Army brass still remembered the crazy courage and skilled fighting of the Texas Rangers during the Mexican War. Officials were justifiably concerned that any such reformed Texas Rangers would be at best uncontrollable and at worst, a costly rebellion. The U.S. Army was assigned all duties of peace keeping and protecting the citizens from the Indians and bandit attacks which had escalated during the war years. A state police force was being proposed which would employ some of the recently freed slaves. Noah was sure this would be a fine mess and he wanted no part in it. And he was right. In the next few years there were more criminals in the state police and the U.S. Army in Texas than there were in all the rest of the great state.

About six or seven miles out of Austin toward San Antonio de Bejar, they stopped to make camp. The young lieutenant of the cavalry escort that had accompanied them came to Noah and asked if he or his squad could be of further assistance. Noah chuckled and replied, "Lieutenant, were it up to me I'm sure I would find much to occupy these troops for most of the night. But, ask the lady. She's the boss."

Callie looked at Noah quizzically for a moment before telling the young officer he should return to Austin and thanked him and his men for their polite concern. She sent a polite and generous message of appreciation to Custer as well.

After supper the travelers sat enjoying coffee and conversation within the circle of wagons. Callie turned her head and studied Noah until he finally asked, "What's on your mind Callie?"

"You told the lieutenant that I was the boss. Does that mean you've accepted my offer of employment?"

"Callie, I've never worked for anyone else much except fer the gov'ment. I've been a ranger and army cavalryman but I don't have no 'sperience on a ranch. I know a little about cows, but not crops. It's seems to me, you comin' to Texas without a husband or kin, you and your daughters could use some protection from the rough elements here 'bouts. Bandits are still thick and pesky as flies here, the Indians ain't whupped yet and there seems to be quite an assortment of saddle tramps and owl hoots and Yankee scallywags. I haven't had a family all my grown life, an I was grown at a young age. This little group may come as close as I'll ever get to having a family. I've been drunk since before the war and I've dried up some since I've made your acquaintance. Don't get me wrong, I'll likely have a drink from time to time, I'm not built to be a teetotaler. But, if you can accept me on those terms, then, yes ma'am, I would be honored to work for you."

"Ezekial?" Callie asked.

"Noah, all I'd ask is you not let drinking get in the way of doing your job."

"Yes, I won't abide a man getting drunk very often around my children."

"Well. I'll be sure not to drink very often. And never around the girls."

Callie smiled. "Mister, you'd better stay sober."

"Yes ma'am." Noah grinned back.

Sallie ran over to him and hugged him. She said, "I'm glad you're not leaving us."

Following precedent, Nellie ran to hug him too. "I'm glad too."

"Me too," voted Chas.

Ezekial shook his hand. So did Callie.

He asked Beau and Micah once more if they would continue with Ezekial and work for them if Callie and Ezekial found a ranch to purchase together. Micah answered for them.

"I'll stick with Beau 'till he finds his wife, then we'd be proud to come to work with you and Ezekial."

"Luther?" Callie asked him.

"I'll stick with you."

Everyone smiled as the girls hugged Micah and Beau and Luther. The smiles remained until they slept. As the sun painted the eastern sky the pale yellow of morning light, the new founded company headed South to San Antonio. Cool air that was becoming increasingly cooler as the wind blew in puffs from the north hurrying their steps. Around noon Noah had found a friendly farmer who allowed them to water the beasts from his spring-fed tank. They enjoyed pleasant conversation with him in the shelter of a coppice of oaks.

A good distance was made that day and in the delicious fragrance of frying beef and potatoes cheered the weary souls gathered round and resting near the fire. The food warmed them and cheered them. The children begged Micah to play his harmonica so they could sing. For a while the chilly breeze carried the lively, sweet songs beneath the eyes of the witnessing stars.

Every minute and every mile seemed to draw the traveling troop closer together. There is an inherent closeness of blood that cannot be surpassed, but there is a special love among misfits, the broken and the lonely as they reach out for one another, that can become pleasurably melding also. Chas rode a horse with Ezekial and Noah, Beau and Micah rode together on one of Callie's wagon, Luther and Sallie took over Ezekial's wagon and Nellie rode with her mother and Sam. They changed up most days to keep things interesting. Sallie and Nellie even rode horses sometimes.

Today the mules seemed to feel the new hand at the reins and acted skittish. Luther uttered soothing sounds and syllables trying to settle them.

"What's wrong with the mules Luther?"

"Aw, they 's used to 'Zekial driving 'em and they don't like changes. A mule can't handle being stirred up."

"Why do they have those blinders on?"

"'Cause mules are naturally nosy. See those big, long ears a' twitchin' and turning all the way 'round tryin' to hear what we're saying?" Luther whispered.

"Can they understand us Luther?"

"Waal,… mules mostly just understand mules language," Luther whispered, "Like gee, or haw, or gidup, but these here mules are long-tooth mules and smarter 'n most."

"If they can understand us maybe we should say something good about them," Sallie whispered.

"Yer prob'ly right," Luther said out of the side of his mouth. "These here good-looking mules sure e strong and step lively don't they Callie?" he said loudly and winked at Sallie.

"They sure do. That's because they are so young. And they sure are strong and good-looking."

The mules ears were turned all the way backward seemingly to hear every word. And their heads came up and their pace increased. Luther smiled and Sallie giggled.

"These here mules surely do understand a little English don't they?" Luther whispered.

Sallie laughed. Callie heard the laughter and smiled. She could only imagine what nonsense Luther was telling her in the wagon behind her. Sallie was smart enough to realize much of what Luther said was to be taken as entertaining, but not necessarily gospel. Both her girls were smart like their daddy. She trusted them to do the right thing. They were loving and giving, not selfish. They were adventuresome like most children, and curious. Her girls were her life, she lived to hear the music of their laughter, to see the beauty of their smiles. She wanted a good a life for them and she had to grab the good things and good people along the way to help build that life. She believed all things happened for a reason, that people came into their life for a certain purpose. Some she understood and some she would never comprehend. Some she could help along the way as they helped her and she valued them and gave them love in the important ways. She had learned to respect Micah, she liked Beau and Ezekial and was still weighing what she should feel for Noah. Of course, she dearly loved Chas already; she loved them all in a Christian way. And she saw that they loved each other and felt a familial closeness.

Nellie's voice penetrated the volume of her thoughts, "What did you say honey?"

"Nothing Momma, I was talking to Sam."

"Do you think Sam can understand you?"

"Yes. Sometimes he can understand a lot, but sometimes I have to show him, then he understands."

"That's right. That's good sweetie. Sometimes all of us have to be shown before we really understand."

"I love Sam Momma. I hope Ezekial never goes away and takes Sam."

"We'll just have to love them a bunch so they don't want to leave."

Callie turned in her seat to look at her daughter and the sight of Sam and Nellie made her explode with laughter. Nellie had put a string of pearls around Sam's neck, a bonnet on his head and his front feet were stuck down into a pair of button up boots. He looked so patiently forlorn.

"Nellie MacGillicuddy! You get that stuff off of that poor dog!"

"But Momma, we're just playing."

"Sam doesn't like to play like that. He's a boy dog Nellie. Now, mind. Get those things off him and put them up where they belong."

Callie tried to look stern but couldn't manage.

"But doesn't he look cute Momma?"

Callie's suppressed laughter burst forth again.

"Yes. He does. But he doesn't like it. Put those things up."

The miserable dog seemed to show his gratitude by his characteristic one-sided grin and the one blinking eye. As soon as Nellie released him from the raiment, Sam jumped up onto the seat beside Callie and again grinned, then looked back into the wagon with an expression of trepidation. Laughing again, Callie grabbed Sam's neck and hugged him. She loved Sam too.

Chas, riding beside Ezekial on Micah's tall thoroughbred, asked, "What breed of horse is that Ezekial?"

"Percheron. Not very fast. Strong."

"It takes strong to carry you," Chas smiled.

"Yep." Ezekial smiled back.

"How'd you get so big Ezekial?"

"Jes' like this horse Chas, Daddy and Grandaddy was big."

"Wish I was big."

"It's not that great Chas. Ain't nothing fits. My granddaddy had this saddle special made. But usually most things don't fit. Clothes, chairs, trigger guards, outhouses,… heh, heh," they both laughed.

"An' can't get enough food on a fork, I noticed."

"Or on a plate."

"Or a long enough belt."

"That's why I wear suspenders," Ezekial laughed. "I'd better rest this horse and let Beau get back on his horse. I know he don't feel right on a wagon seat."

"I'll catch up to Noah."

"Keep an eye out for trouble."

"Yes sir."

The thoroughbred wanted to run and Chas let him have his head. Ezekial watched the boy lean over the horses neck and stand in the stirrups. He rode well. He was a well-rounded boy, polite and eager for life. There were times when he was somber, likely thinking of his lost parents, but usually he was happy and exuberant.

Noah heard the running horse long before it topped the long grade and knew which horse it was and who rode it. It was something he'd learned by paying attention. Those who learned, lived, in the bad old days and such skills stayed sharp. He would teach these green travelers all he knew and perhaps it may help one of them sometime. Like how to distinguish a real bird or animal sound from Indian signals and how to see an Indian by searching for shadows, reflections, motion and the ground. It was easy to find a Comanche camp, many times it was found under the buzzards circling. Comanches moved often to escape their refuse, the carcasses and their excrement.

Noah hopped down and picked up a small rock then rode his horse behind a curtain of blue spruce, letting Chas trot the thoroughbred by him. He threw the rock in a soft arc hitting Chas in the middle of his back. The rock hit the horses rump in falling and it crow hopped sideways to see what had touched his hindquarters.

Noah aimed his finger at Chas and mouthed, "Pow! Pow! You're dead."

"Aw Noah, I knew you were there."

"No, you didn't know anyone was around. I coulda' been an Indian or a bandito an' you woulda' been shot and killed, or worse. This ain't no playground Chas, this is Texas. People play for keeps out here. If you ain't careful, yer dead."

"I'm sorry Noah. I didn't aim to make you mad. I was just trying to catch up with you so's I could ride with you a while."

The old warrior felt cruel, like a bully, and he liked the boy. He didn't mean to come across so fierce and mean.

"Chas, I'm trying to teach you for your own good. I'm not mad. It's just that I know there's much to fear out here and I want you to be careful. I kinda' like you and want you to stay alive for awhile so we can be amigos." Noah smiled.

"I'll learn Noah. I'll listen and learn. But I ain't afraid of no bandito or Indian. 'Sides, this horse can outrun any horse around."

"Meybe. But that horse can't outrun no bullet, nor an arrow. And an Indian or outlaw you can see you can beat, but you need to be a-feared of those that you can't see."

"Yes sir."

Noah wanted to be gentle with the boy, but didn't know how to gently teach survival. He felt a kinship with Chas. He knew the hurt and loneliness Chas felt at times, he knew how it felt to lose your parents so young. No one could take his parents place he knew, but he wanted to be Chas' friend and he needed to be his teacher. Noah felt he wasn't doing very well at either job so far. There was much he still had to learn himself.

"You can figger Indians are around when all the bugs are quiet, like the cicadas, an' when the birds seem to all fly away from the area. Once you smell a Comanche, you'll remember the smell. Some folks say snakes nor Indians smell, well, meybe they can't smell 'em, but I can.

"When yer scoutin' like we are, try to gain the high ground so you can see farther and down into the low ground, but don't get so high that yer back-lit by the sky. Ride wide of tight corners and thick brush and try to put the wind in yer face when you can and always swivel yer neck and check yer back trail...."

Noah's drawling lecture went on and on and Chas did his best to pay attention. When there was a break in the teaching Chas asked, "How much farther to San Antonio?"

"We'll be there in the morning 'fore dinner."

"There's lots of people living along this road. You think there's Indians hereabouts?"

"Not usually. But there's lots more criminals son. They's cheatin gamblers and pickpockets and burglars and gun-hands and con-men and prostitutes."

"What's con-men and prostitutes?"

"Ah. Well, con-men is those who'd sell you something that ain't theirs to sell, or they'll trick you out of your money or property some way."

"And what's a prostitute?"

"Uh. Well son, that's a woman who'll trick you out of your money."

"Why don't they call her a con-woman then?"

"Well Chas,...some things you just got to learn on yer own, I guess. You'll know what a prostitute is in a few years."

"I want to know now. I don't want some woman in San Antonio tricking me out of my money."

"I don't think you have to worry about that son."

"Why not? I've got money. And I don't want to be tricked out of it. I've got plans for my money. I guess I'll have to ask Callie what a prostitute is."

"No! Don't do that."

"Well, why not? I'm sure she'll know."

"Yes she'll know. But, take my word for it, you don't want to open that can o' worms. It jest woulden' be a gentlemanly thing to do."

"Noah, you sure are talking funny-like. Are you scared of Callie?"

"Of course not. It's jes,...well, jes' don't say nothin' 'bout no prostitute to Callie or none of the girls. Tell you whut, I'll show you one sometimes and maybe you can figger it out."

"Well. Okay. If you say so."

Noah quickly changed the subject, talking about the money to be made gathering wild long horned cattle and driving a herd to market out in New Mexico or to Missouri or to Kansas. And he talked about branding and about Mexico and Mexicans and all the Germans who had built all the stone fences and houses and barns they were passing. He talked about things he'd never talked about before, just so prostitutes would be forgotten.

Micah asked Beau, "What if you can't find Ruby? Will you still go to work with Callie?"

"Oh, I'll find her. I won't ever give up. And I'll find her. She got my baby and she needs me to he'p her and love her and that baby."

"I've been praying about it."

"I have too. All the time."

Micah stopped the wagon when they drew up beside Ezekial standing in the shade of a cottonwood. He had stripped the big horse of the big saddle and bridle and put its' halter on.

"Tired of riding Zeke?" Beau asked

"Naw, but I think this horse is tired of carrying me."

"I'll saddle up then."

"'Preciate it."

"Ezekial, what'd you and Callie find out about free gov-ment land in Austin?"

"Found out there weren't none for Confederates 'cause the government is being run by Yankees and scallywags who want it all for themselves. And Callie decided she didn' want no free land when she found out the land was taken away from its owners 'cause they were Confederates and unreformed. What'd you and Beau find out?"

"They tole us that there may be some gov-ment land to give to freedmen later, but since there wasn't any federal land in Texas, it would be awhile 'fore the legislature got all the paperwork straight. The man tole us that the U.S. Army was gonna' take land from the rebels and give it to black folks. Well, jes' didn't seem right. An' it seems like it might cause a whole lot o' trouble. Me and Beau decided we'd jes' find Ruby and his baby and work for you and Callie 'til we could get our own place."

"We'll sure need you both. I'm happy to hear it."

Beau had saddled his beautiful horse and rode up to them. "I've got to go find Ruby and my baby first, like Micah said, then we'll make you a hand Ezekial."

"Good deal."

"See ya'll at supper," Beau said as he rode ahead.

After tying the Percheron to the tailgate, Ezekial climbed onto the wagon seat with Micah.

"Sure hope that Ruby's alright somewhere. Beau's heart woulden' never heal if something happened to her or that baby."

"Well Micah, we gotta pray."

"Ever' day Ezekial, ever' day."

That evening most everyone was gathered around the fire awaiting supper. The mid-day meal had been light, just biscuits and jelly and they were all anxious for the red beans, fried potatoes and pan bread.

Ezekial had been telling Callie about Beau and Micah's mission to find Beau's wife Ruby and their baby, that was their first priority above all else. Callie was ladling beans onto a plate and expounding on how wonderful it was that Beau loved Ruby so much and how deeply it affected her when Chas came running up, unaware of the conversation going on as he joined the group.

"When I think about how romantic it is that Beau would come so far to find his wife and child, well, I…, I…"

"What's for supper?" Chas asked as he slid to a stop beside Callie.

"…I've just got goose bumps," Callie finished her sentence.

"Well, give me a plate of those goose bumps please," Chas pleaded, "I'm starving."

Everyone got a giggle out of that, and red beans were thereafter often called goose bumps by this troop, into succeeding generations.

After the welcome supper of potatoes and goose bumps, Callie spoke of her plans in San Antonio.

"…and this banker in San Antonio is supposed to be an honest man, but it has been a number of years since my banker in Virginia has had dealing with this Mister Twohig, so we'll weigh his words and actions with care and make a mutual decision on his suggestions."

"Are you talkin' 'bout John Twohig?" Noah asked.

"Why yes Noah, his name is John. Do you know him?"

"Ever one knows John Twohig in Texas, he's a legend. Ya' see, back in '42 when the Mexican army marched on San Antone, Twohig had a large storage building there filled with all sorts of goods. All the Texicans were forced to evacuate the city, but before Twohig left, he poured a trail of gunpowder from his storage building and the explosives he had stored there to a safe distance away, an' lit it as they retreated an' about a hunerd Meskins ran in the building to loot it. The barrels of gunpowder, the dynamite and boxes of ammunition blew up 'bout three city blocks. An' a herd of Meskins."

"Later that same year, when the Mexican Adrian Wall captured San Antone, Twohig was wounded and taken prisoner. In Mexico he escaped from Perote Prison with some of the Mier prizners. He's a good man. Old as Genesis. And rich as Job now, I expect."

"So you know the man?"

"I met him 'round twenty years ago. Doubt he'd remember an ol' Injun fighter. But, he would recall some of my ranger captains."

"Can we trust him Noah?"

"Callie he's rich. And a banker. You do well to never trust either. But, if you deal with him with a healthy suspicion and don't let him sell you anything sight unseen, I suppose you can trust him as much as you can any money-changer. He didn't get rich by losing money or looking out for widows."

"Maybe you should join us in our dealings with him, don't you think so Ezekial?"

"Would you help us Noah?"

"Shore. It'd be my pleasure."

Noah knelt closer to the fire than the others. Everyone else had taken their coats and gloves out of the wagons, but Noah had neglected to purchase any warm clothes and it had not been cold enough yet for him to think to buy any. Now he was thinking of the warm clothes he'd buy in San Antonio.

"Mother." Sallie whispered, "Have we got an extra blanket for Mister Lister? He's cold."

"That's kind of you to notice Sallie. Yes, let's go find one for him."

"How far are we from San Antonio now Noah?" Ezekial asked.

"Oh twelve to fifteen miles I reckon. Should be there mid morning if we get an early start."

"That's good. I'm ready for a rest. And I'm wanting to try some more of that Mexican food."

"Yes son, I'm partial to Mexican cooking myself. And there's plenty of opportunity to sample it in ol' San Antone."

"Here Mister Lister," Sallie said as she handed him a folded blanket, "It's getting colder."

"Thank you Miss Sallie. I appreciate you thinking about me. I'm not used to that. Thank you very kindly."

Sallie blushed and muttered, "You're welcome."

"Goodnight everyone. Come along Sallie, let's get some sleep so we can get an early start."

"See you in the mornin'"

"Night."

Noah wrapped the clean smelling blanket around his shoulders and chuckled. Funny, he thought, how such a simple kindness had made him feel warmer. And significant. Of consequence. Cared for. He studied on it as he lay his head on his saddle outside the light of the fire. The cold winds moaned through the waving spruce and cedar and thin dark clouds curtained the moon with ragged tails. He tried to put a name on what he was feeling and the word that came to mind and comforted his sleep was 'home.' He felt at home. It was a place he hadn't been in a long, long time.

Ezekial and Callie paid for lodging for everyone while in San Antonio. Ezekial, Noah, Luther, Callie, Chas and the girls stayed in two rooms at the new Menger Hotel next to the Alamo. Micah and Beau stayed at a room attached to the livery where they had placed their possessions and animals. Callie inspected the rooms before she paid the liveryman. Surprisingly, it was a nice room, and clean. Beau wanted to stay close to the horses and they really needed someone to look after their things, so it worked out fine. Micah said it was as nice a place as he had ever stayed and baths were thrown in for free whereas at the hotel baths were an extra charge.

San Antonio was a bustling city, full of shops and busy people. The girls were in awe and with wide blue eyes they went shopping with their mother for rolls of cloth, needles and thread, ribbons and lace, fancy shoes, perfume and powder. They squealed with delight at every purchase. Chas was able to separate himself from shopping with them and do a little bit of shopping with Ezekial and Sam. Chas thought over every purchase and bargained for those few things he decided to buy. Those stores Sam wasn't allowed to enter caused him indignation. After all, these were not churches. The insult to his dignity was written on his furry face. Sam peered through the windows angrily or stared at the closed doors until Ezekial and Chas came back through them and each reunion was a celebration. Sam seemed to actually suffer through these separations.

Ezekial bought a ball for Sam to play with and he seemed somewhat mollified for the repeated abandonments. Ezekial visited a hat shop and though he found no hat that fit his head, he was able to order a planter's hat made. Chas was in need of a new hat but would not part with the money nor would he allow Ezekial to buy him one. He said the one he had, though old and tattered, was still serviceable and he was saving his money.

The clerk at the hotel would not allow Sam to stay in the room with Ezekial, Noah and Luther until Ezekial offered to pay extra. The clerk relented and allowed Sam to be snuck into the room only after Ezekial bathed him in a washtub behind the hotel. Sam enjoyed the warm bath and smiled his lop-sided grin through the brushing and drying, one back leg kicking involuntarily in blissful pleasure. Ezekial deposited the clean, soap-smelling mutt surreptitiously to the upstairs room, ordered him to be quiet, then shut him in and went to meet the others for supper.

They gathered at a Mexican restaurant that welcomed them all with smiles. It was a family staffed establishment with daughters as waitresses and sons as bus boys and dishwashers. Mommacita and Poppacita were the cooks and what wonderful cooks they were. The new refugees ate dishes such as avocados and burritos and red rice and beans,(goose bumps). Noah drank one shot of tequila and one glass of beer. Callie watched in silence, prepared to object if he overindulged, but he didn't. Surprisingly, it made her proud.

The conversation went from the efforts with and disposition of Sam to the maintenance and repair of the wagons which Luther and Micah had completed to the purchases each had made. Beau advised them all that he had learned through inquiries with the black and Mexican residents that a young black woman with a small child was working for a Mexican horse rancher in Gonzales, a small town south of San Antonio. He thought it might be his wife, Ruby, and his son, and he asked if it would be okay for him to ride out tomorrow and investigate. Callie and Ezekial urged him to feel free to go and assured him that the land search would keep them in San Antonio for a while, possibly for weeks.

Callie advised Noah and Ezekial of her plans to go to the bank in the morning and try to see John Twohig and tell him of her hopes he would help her find suitable land for a ranch. She said she would deposit the bank draft she had received for the Virginia farm with him.

"Callie, you asked me to help you deal with John Twohig. I hope you will allow me to do so," Noah replied. "If you want my help, just sleep late tomorrow morning and let me go see John Twohig as your employee. I'll tell him that you are recovering from the long journey from Virginia and I will ask if he would be so considerate as to come to the hotel after dinner tomorrow to speak with you about certain financial matters. As you said, your banker back home has written and told him to expect you. It's always best to meet an adversary on your own ground and terms and not on his. It's easier to defend than attack."

"Yes Noah, we'll do it your way. But, it seems to me we should try to make a friend of Mister Twohig and shouldn't view him as an enemy."

"Believe me, the money you plan to deposit in John Twohig's bank and your plan to purchase land through him will make the man a very close friend, you don't need to worry 'bout that. Just remember, he must remain the servant in this relationship, he's here to render you a service, you don't let him get the upper hand."

"I suppose you're right Noah," Callie smiled, "Men do seem to want to always lead."

Noah thought about that comment in silence. Beau was smiling at the glint of mischief in Callie's eye when he saw her mouth gape and her eyes widen. Her eyebrows lifted in a question as she stared at the door behind Beau's shoulders. Everyone's eyes at the table followed hers and focused on a tiny black woman who had entered the restaurant, a very young and pretty woman whose full lips were stretched in a heartfelt smile as she gazed silently at Beau.

Beau turned and saw her. He slowly raised himself to his feet, his eyes wide and unblinking pinned on the vision before him. He stumbled toward the little woman who stood there and she held her thin arms out to him.

"Beau," she whispered.

"Ruby," Beau managed as he floated across the floor to her. They kissed and held each other almost violently. Her tiny boots left the floor and as she was lifted a tiny baby boy tottered from behind her long skirts and she broke the kiss. Beau followed her eyes to see his son for the first time staring wonderingly up at him.

"What's that?" Beau asked

"What? That 'what' is your son, Little Beau!"

Everyone laughed.

Beau went down on one knee before the knee-high child.

"You my Dada?"

Beau hugged him, lifted him, kissed his wife and said "Shore am. I shore am son."

Everyone clapped and hollered, whistled and laughed.

"How'd you find me Ruby? How'd you know I was here?"

"I came here with my boss to sell some horses and he told me he'd seen a handsome little black man and an older, dignified black man that rode thoroughbred horses." she smiled at Micah and walked into his arms. "And who else could it be but you two? I thought I'd better come over here and catch you before you got away."

"Oh, I wouldn't want to get away Ruby. Not ever. I's just fixin' to come to Gonzales to look for you."

"Yep that's where I was. Work for a family that has a horse ranch there, the Cuellers, really fine folks."

"We're going to need some horses, maybe you could help us get some decent prices. My name is Callie, by the way."

"Pleased to meet you Ma'am. I'd be happy to take you to the Cuellers. They are very fair horse traders. Are these young ladies your daughters?"

"Yes," Callie introduced everyone all around, then added, "Waiter, would you bring two more chairs for our new friends here and please take their order?"

The smiles of Beau and Ruby were infectious and they all had questions for Ruby, but Callie asked the most pointed one.

"When do you two want to be married?"

Beau answered, "Miss Callie, the Freedman's Bureau says that two former slaves who've lived together as man an' wife whilst they was in bonds is married already now that they is free."

"Oh pooh! Beau we know what the government says, but I'm sure that Ruby wants a wedding. All women do. Am I right?"

"Yes Ma'am," Ruby replied, "That would be nice, but not necessary. 'Sides, a wedding costs lots o' money an' we gonna' need our money."

Beau agreed by nodding his head.

"Well, I'll put it this way. There ain't nobody living on my ranch as man and wife without getting married, so you two will have a wedding if you work for me. Boys and girls finish your eating and come with me. We need to give these two sometime together. And Ruby, you start thinking about a wedding dress. I'll pay for it and for a suit for you Beau. Little Beau too. So just be ready to do some shopping tomorrow. Oh! And we'll have to find a ring. Girls, we're gonna' have ourselves a wedding!"

The group snatched last bites off of their plates and followed the chattering MacGillicuddy girls out of the restaurant. Ezekial settled the bill and smiled at the exuberant couple who could see nothing but each other.

Beau put his arms around Ruby and Little Beau and kissed them tenderly. Beau and Ruby were both so happy the tears ran down their cheeks.

"Why you cryin' Momma?" Little Beau asked.

"Because I'm happy baby."

"You come all this way by yourself?" Beau asked.

"No, I rode in from the ranch where I work with the Cuellar family. They had to deliver more horses to the army."

"Think they'd like to come to the weddin'?"

"Why shore they would. They's good friends. But Beau, can we let Miss Callie pay for this weddin'? Th's a lot o' money."

"I 'spect we could pay her back. I'll be workin' for her and Ezekial on the ranch they's gonna buy. I'll be in charge of the hosses. I expect we'll have our own house there too."

"Oh Beau, I'm so glad you came for me. I've been so lonesome for you. I prayed for so long."

"Ruby, I tol' you I'd come for you. I love you. And now we have a son to love. Won't be long we'll have other children."

"We gotta' wait to start that 'til after the weddin' Beau. Miss Callie wouldn't approve."

"Miss Callie ain't our master. We's free Ruby."

"Yes, but woulden it be right and woulden even Micah like it if we's to be married by a preacher an' all?"

"Yes Sweetie," Beau chuckled, "We'll wait. I'm just kinda' in a hurry after all this time."

"You think I'm not?"

The waiter had to set the hot plates down and pardoned himself but the hugging and kissing went on undisturbed. Little Beau stood up in a chair and began the meal alone. He already knew better than to eat the chilies.

The gentle old army captain had escorted the red-haired girl all the way from the panhandle. They had traveled by wagon and coach and finally by train and had arrived in San Antonio this morning. She was exhausted. The good captain had delivered her to her father's banker as had been arranged by telegraph and Mister Twohig had taken her to the Menger Hotel where he had reserved a room for her. He had arranged to have a trio of clerks meet her at the hotel and provide her with decent clothes more suitable than the hand-me-downs she'd been given at the Indian fort after their rescue by the hunter. After the clerk had left she had bathed, ate some of a meal brought to the room and was nearly asleep on the high and soft bed.

The clean smell of the sheets brought her mother and home to mind, both gone forever. The pillow soaked up her tears.

There was little money left in her father's bank account, enough to keep her in San Antonio for a month, maybe, and she had nothing but the three dresses and the slippers that the clerks had brought her. The Indians had burned everything else or stolen it. Except the land. She had that. For what it was worth. To her it was priceless. Her parents had worked so long and hard to make it a successful ranch, and a home. She was hesitant to sell it as Mister Twohig had suggested. She had such sweet memories of the only home she'd ever known. The lace curtains her mother had stitched by hand and the quilts they'd made together. The rugs they had woven of rags, the meals they had cooked and shared. The furniture her daddy had made, and the tree house, her own tree house her sweet daddy had made her. All gone. All except the sweet old horse that had brought her away from the red murderers. The army colonel had promised he would have her Betty shipped to her in San Antonio. Sweet, brave Betty, all she had left of the love she had known.

She hated the thought of selling the ranch, but she knew she must. What choice did she have? She couldn't run a ranch by herself. She had no money to hire hands and there was no longer any place with a roof over it there. And the Comanches. She trembled when she thought of them. She whispered, "Thank the Lord" as she recalled her providential escape from an unimaginable hellish future. She had nightmares filled with the cruel face of the Indian who those at the fort had told her was called Bloody Roe. Several times she had awoke with a start, screaming, sweating, shaking, knowing he was coming for her. She feared him. But she hated him more. He had murdered and raped and mutilated her precious family and left her here to suffer the sorrow. She fought the fear and nourished the hate. She wished she were a man. Then she would find this Bloody Roe, no matter what it took, and he would definitely be bloody when she finished with him.

She pushed her thick red hair back from her face and lay still and quiet. Despite the fear and the hate, despite the memories and the pressures of the present, her exhaustion took her down in the peaceful oblivion of sleep.

Chapter Nine

"Don't be misled by history, or any other unreliable source."
---Will Rogers

"Smooth seas do not make skillful sailors"
---African Proverb

NOAH AND EZEKIAL had purchased some new shirts and bathed at the hotel. They visited the barber shop for a hot shave and looked uncharacteristically domestic and civilized as they strode to John Twohig's bank. They spoke to the young, thin teller telling him of their desire of an audience with the old man. Mister Twohig came barreling out of a nearby office heartily welcoming Noah.

"Mister Noah Lister. I am honored to again meet the hero of Texas. Come in, come into my office. Please have a seat. Would you like coffee? Perhaps a taste of brandy?"

Ezekial inspected Noah to see if he had transformed from the reformed drunken hobo they had found unconscious and filthy in the road. He did seem to appear a different creature.

"No sir Mister Twohig, thank you. We won't take up much of your time this morning. Let me introduce Mister Ezekial Robertson, one of my two employers."

As they shook hands Twohig said, "I must say Mister Robertson, you are quite a physical speciman, as I am sure you're aware. Are you new to the area?"

"Yessir. Jes' came from North Carolina."

"Mister Robertson's business partner is Misses Callie MacGillicuddy whose banker in Virginia has written you about her relocation and her wish to acquire ranch land here."

"Yes Noah, I have that letter from my dear friend in a file here somewhere,….let me see if I….."

"No need to be in any hurry, there's no rush. Misses MacGillicuddy must rest from the long, arduous journey from Virginia. Although I will assist her and represent her and Mister Robertson, she will want to attend all negotiations.

"That's fine. I completely understand."

"Could you meet with us sometime this week at the Menger?"

Mister Twohig readily agreed and an appointment was set. Noah arranged for a meeting room to be reserved at the hotel and coached Ezekial and Callie not to seem anxious to acquire land, but to appear bored with Twohig's offerings. A trip to actually view the properties would likely be necessary to see improvements in the form of houses, barns, and other construction such as fences and wells. Access to sure water, grass and richness of soil need also be checked.

Sam accompanied Ezekial throughout San Antonio and found ample opportunity to roll in the dusty streets despite Ezekial's efforts to dissuade him. Consequently, a bath was required for Sam each evening and a fresh one was needed directly after for Ezekial. Neither had ever bathed so much in their lives.

The second night in the hotel, Sam was pawing the covers back right at sunset. He crawled beneath the sheets, turned around and stuck his head out from under the covers onto a pillow.

Noah laughed and said, "Would you look at that mutt, hope there's room for you in that bed Zeke."

"C'mon Sam, scoot over."

Noah laughed more at the impatient look on Sam's face.

"I know one thing Sam," Ezekial complained, "I'm shore tired of bathing us both ever' night. I'm thinkin' 'bout jes' leavin' you in this room all day so you won't roll in the dirt."

Sam yawned in reply.

Noah asked, "You think he'd use the facilities down the hall? You'd have to let him out to do his business."

"Yea, I'd have to let him out an' when I did he'd roll in the dirt. He does that so he can get another bath. He's grown to like 'em. Maybe I can l'arn him to bathe hisself."

"Heh-heh," Noah chuckled, "Not likely. Sam's no dummy. He ain't givin' up the good thing he's got goin'! You'd better get used to it Zeke."

Ezekial appeared thoughtful, then said, "You know them, gals bathe most ever' day here in town, maybe they'd spell me some days."

"Good idee. They'd likely get a giggle out of it."

Ezekial turned his big head quizzically and asked, "Noah, how come yer talkin' normal-like now, but when you talked to John Twohig you talked different? Using big words and such?"

"Well, Zeke when you meet a Comanche, you have to speak Comanche or use sign language. When yer in Mexico you can't expect to speak American. An' when you have a conversation with a banker you have to speak banker, otherwise they'll think they have the advantage of you. Bankers are like Comanche in that regard, they'll do their dead-level best to sneak up on you. An Indian'll use animal and bird calls to signal the other warriors, bankers will use big ol' words no normal fella' knows and even put 'em on paper an' get you to sign 'em. Thoses papers they'll get ya' to sign are worse than a bear trap."

"Well. I'm glad yer he'ping us deal with that banker Noah."

"Um huh."

Promptly at ten on the designated morning, Mister Twohig introduced himself and his skinny clerk to Callie. They all sat down at a polished oak table and the clerk began spreading neat files over its surface.

"Misses MacGillicuddy, Mister Robertson, Mister Lister, I have several properties that are currently available for purchase that I believe will be of interest to you and I'd like to discuss them with you...."

"Excuse me Mister Twohig..."

"Please call me John."

"John. And please call me Callie. It won't be necessary to review any properties as yet, though we may decide to consider other ranches at a later date. You see, I have met young Misses Curtsinger whom you are representing and whom is also staying here in the hotel. She has told me of the land she has inherited and I feel it would be in all our best interests to view her property first."

"Yes, Misses Curtsinger's property is one I'm trying to sell and the first one I intended to present to you here this morning. I believe it will meet your qualifications perfectly. The girl is almost destitute. She told you about her family?"

"Such a tragedy."

"It is located on the very border of civilization, but, given time, the white population will increase and the area will be divested of the savages which raid there. Besides, with Mister Noah Lister as your foreman, the Indians will stay away."

"We'll travel with Mabel to see the place, whatever is left of it. She wants to see it again before it's sold but doesn't want to go alone. She emphasized that you have been very kind and considerate of her and that if we agree to purchase you should receive your full percentage."

"Certainly I will forego any profit whatsoever in the transaction. My hope is that the sale of the land will provide sufficient funds for the lady to sustain her until other prospects appear in her life. When do you plan to go to the ranch?"

"In a few days. We must have a wedding first."

"Who?"

"My employee, freedman Beau Johnson and his beautiful bride Ruby. It will be held down by the river next to the bridge. It will be Sunday morning at eleven."

"Thank you. I will ask my wife if we have prior commitments and if not we will surely attend. Noah I was under the impression that you would be representing Ezekial and Callie in this land purchase."

"So did I. But, she's the boss."

Twohig chuckled and appeared pleased.

"I don't believe Misses MacGillicuddy, er, Callie, has need of other representation."

"She knows her mind. A man has to respect that."

"Amen to that. Does your decisiveness extend to the shopping for and selection of clothes Ma'am?"

"Certainly not. It's a woman's natural inclination to be careful in her selection of adornment. Women must be particular, men certainly aren't. But, to get back to business, here's a draft from my bank in Virginia and Ezekial has a cash deposit he would like to make in your bank. For the present, please hold these funds for us to draw against."

"It will be done. Martin, please take these deposits and see to it," Twohig addressed his clerk.

"May we have receipts please?" Callie asked.

Twohig chuckled merrily.

"See to it Martin."

After the meeting with the banker was concluded, Callie collected Ruby, Mabel and her daughters who had waited under a mote of cottonwoods close by the river. Beau was there as well.

"Beau, you're going to have Ruby for a lifetime so you can let me borrow her for a few hours today. Ladies, come with me."

The women and girls sashayed down to the nearest mercantile chattering like happy birds. They invaded nearly every shop in town, inventorying what was available and procuring what they deemed essential for the ceremony. There was some initial opposition to Ruby entering a few of the shops but after Callie fired the opening salvo, Mabel quickly conquered all opposition with her loud, indignant and overwhelming argument and threats invoking the continued patronage of the Cuellars, the Twohigs and most importantly, the MacGillicuddys. Mabel's tongue lashings quickly cowed and quailed those who resisted the integration of their customers. At first it embarrassed Ruby and the girls, but after watching and hearing a couple of Mabel's attacks they enjoyed the show.

Callie was accustomed to leading the fray in such instances of opposition, but with the young vociferous vixen that was Mabel along, she was able only to follow the charge. Not only was the reluctance of the shopkeeper's service for Ruby quieted and overcome, their enthusiasm was actually inspired by Mabel's persuasive discourse.

SEPARATE REALITIES

The prices were even reduced significantly in some cases. Mabel's pretty face and big blue eyes induced surrender in most cases of the male clerks. Callie thought this girl's a pistol!

After directing the delivery of her purchases to the hotel, Callie rounded up Beau, Little Beau, Ezekial and Chas and shooed them into a haberdashery. With Ezekial looming menacingly over the tailor and Mabel bargaining for quicker completion times and lower prices, split-tail tuxedoes would be ready for them all in three days time, just when the ladies dresses would be ready.

Callie then asked Ezekial to pick up the pretty gold band that Ruby had picked out and was being sized at the jeweler's shop. All the purchases were to be wedding gifts from Callie and Ezekial they'd decided, there was to be no discussion of repayment.

The ladies had planned the entire wedding. It was to be held under the giant pecans along the San Antonio River. Micah would perform the actual wedding, Mabel would be maid of honor, Sallie and Nellie would be flower girls, Ezekial would be best man, Little Beau would be ring bearer and Callie told Chas that the two of them would be proud.

While the clothes and other preparations were being made, Mister Cuellar's son Rueben took Beau, Ezekial and Noah to his ranch to select and buy horses. Noah asked Callie if he could take Chas along, who had aspirations of being a cowboy and rancher. Her motherly, protective instincts had to be overcome to agree, but she allowed him to go. Micah and Luther stayed to tend to the livestock at the livery and keep an eye on the wagons. Strange as it seemed to the others Micah and Luther had become friends, engaging in long conversations which seemed of weighty consequence to the two of them. Perhaps each of them was intrigued by their seemingly irreconcilable perspectives and antithetical experiences. Whatever the cause, the effect was that they each were fascinated and a bit confused by the other.

Micah was so truthful it was often painful to himself and to others. Luther was honest about what he considered important, but he entertained himself and others with stories he deemed more interesting than the truth. Micah believed the Bible was well, gospel; Luther thought it was mostly stories based on fact but mixed with some tantalizing fiction which better illustrated the essential elements. They were both reliable, in each their own way; Micah was faithful and had faith, Luther was faithful but had questions. To each, the other was a puzzle. They were content in one another's company. They became unlikely friends.

Callie herded the two of them into the clothing store and bought them white shirts, collars and ties for the wedding. She found two inexpensive, second-hand suit coats that fitted them well enough. She sent them to separate barbers and was pleased that each of them appeared more dignified and almost refined.

The men, along with the Cuellar family returned the day before the wedding. They had agreed on terms for twelve sturdy cow ponies, none over four years old but broken gently. They had also agreed on four teams of oxen to pull a freight wagon and later to power the plows and logging around the farm. Mister Cuellar would keep the stock for them until they had found their new place.

Callie shooed them into the tailor's to check the fit of their clothes so they knocked the trail dust off washed up as well as they could at the livery and went to try on the swallow-tail suits. They laughed at the sight of one another and of themselves in a long mirror. As they exited the tailor's shop they were instructed by the girls to proceed to the barber shop. They all sighed, and all complied.

In their absence, Luther and Micah had worked with Callie to locate and procure some basic construction tools they would need initially. Mabel itemized some of the tools that had been there and might still be there. Other settlers may have already pilfered the useful items, but may have repaired them and might return them when they learned she had survived. And so, Callie decided to limit her purchases until a later date. They would certainly have to buy foodstuffs and many essentials, but if they decided to purchase the ranch, as Callie was almost certain they would, the town of Uvalde was nearest the ranch and it would be practical to begin trading with the merchants there. The big freight wagon as well as the other wagons would be busy for awhile making trips to sawmills and hardware stores and stone quarries and many other places for weeks.

Callie had hired a photographer and everyone posed for photographs several times, even Sam, who, under protest, wore a starched white collar and bow tie. The ivory shade of the bride's dress and the light pink and pastel shades of the ladies dresses brightened the somber suits and uncomfortable countenances of the long-suffering men.

It seemed half of San Antonio stood on the edges and watched and listened to the romantic melodies played by the Mexican band. Beau and Ezekial and Little Beau walked to the chosen spot amid their friends, and waited impatiently until Ruby stepped down from the hired buggy on the hand of the proud old Mister Cuellar. A collective intake of breath by the onlookers testified to the consensus that here was a beautiful bride, perfect in her physical presence. Seemingly she floated on the bands momentous music to stand beside her Beau. The music slowed and stilled, even the birds were quieted as the betrothed stood under the sturdy pecan trees beneath the bluest cloudless sky.

Micah smiled at everyone and his joy was shared and shone in every eye. There were smiles in every face, in every heart.

"Miss Ruby, Brother Beau, and all the friends who have gathered here to witness this happy occasion,…..this is the day the Lord hath made, let us rejoice and be glad in it."

A few scattered 'amens' echoed the thankfulness in his voice.

"This is your day Ruby and Beau. This is a day that God made 'specially for you. Your love for one another didn't sneak up on the Lord. He knew this day was a'coming, an' He made this day up special. Perfect weather, not a cloud in the sky, joy in every heart and new God-given liberty to express this God-given love. Today is a day dreamed of, wished and prayed for an' the Lord has given you the desires of your heart. The Lord has seen all the way down deep in your heart and He knows the pure love you have for one another. An' He loves you even more than you love one another. He's made this day and given it to you to mark the beginning of a journey that will last your whole life together. You'll keep this day in the treasured box of your heart forever. The memory of the joy, the light of love in your beloved's eyes, the clear blue sky, the warm sun on your cheek, all will be treasured all your days on this earth.

"From this day, you two children will walk together every day, sometimes leading, sometimes following, but always together, heart and mind. You will work together, eat together, play together, together bring new life into this world and raise children together through this love that God has given.

"As in all lives, there will be days of hardship and trials, days of sadness and sorrow, dark days when tears run like this river here beside us. But, 'together' you will withstand the flood. 'Together' you'll be strong enough. 'Together' you'll weather the storm. If one should fall the other will always be there to lend a hand and help you rise again. In the dark days, 'together' you'll find your way.

"Brother Beau, Sister Ruby, we must never forget that just a few years ago the truth of our black lives as slaves was that we didn't even have a hope, we didn't have the faith to even dream of a day like today dawnin'. But, dear children, in God there is always hope. God is ever faithful. Though it may seem that this day, this freedom, this love and joy is merely a dream, Ruby, Beau, it is 'real'. You must take a' hold of this reality an' keep the dream alive. Hand in hand, back to back, side by side you must always stand 'together' and let no thing or no one separate you from reality: this love, this joy, this precious gift of a gracious God.

"The two of you become one flesh on this blessed day. God has joined you together in love. On this wondrous day of celebration two separate paths become one. Two hands become four, two hearts become one on this blessed day. This day will bring forth other glorious days, days of new birth, days of accomplishment, days of pride, days of survival, days of beauty and happiness, days when your love will shine and life will be heaven-sent pleasure.

"Be thankful for each and every day God gives you to share together, no matter what the day may bring. These days you have to share will be the true wealth on this earth, for love is life's richest prize. Cherish each day, ponder them in your heart and wring every drop of joy from each day,.....because my dear children, a day will come that will be the last day.

Micah paused here and the very air around him seemed to darken, his eyes seemed to look far away and long ago, focusing on a terrible loss in his own life.

"Remember always, beloved ones, that a last day will come and it will enrich today and cause you to fully cherish your every day together. May that last day you will spend together be very far away.

"Today, this beautiful happy day is the first shining stone in a long string of jewels God has ordained for you. May the vows you make today ring in your memory always, they are sacred. These words are vessels of promise and love, in these words you will find courage, hope, refuge, faith and comfort. May you find the peace there is in love.

"Remember this day, for 'this is the day the Lord hath made, let us rejoice and be glad in it!"

A chorus of heartfelt amens punctuated this heartening message.

"Ruby, do you take this man Beau to be your husband because you love him above all others on earth, and do you promise before God and this assembly of friends and family to always love him, protect him, obey him, stand with him through dark days and fair and never to desert him?"

"Yes, I do."

"Beau, do you take this woman Ruby to be your wife because you love her above all others on earth, and do you promise before God and this assembly of friends and family to always love her, protect her, consult her advice, stand with her through whatever life brings, fair or foul, and never to leave her?"

"Yes suh. I do."

"And do you Ruby, promise to forgive him when he may stumble or fail, lift him up and encourage him when the dark days come, and nurture him when he is sick and weak, and support him in all his endeavors in life?"

"Yes. I will."

"Beau, will you promise to always defend Ruby and to be always tender, gentle and kind to her, remembering always that she is a lady as well as your wife?"

"I surely will."

"Do you both promise this day that you will forever honor God and His gift of love by your honesty, by being generous with your time and your strength for one another, your children and your neighbors?"

"Yes sir."

"Shore will."

"A man can do no more than what God has ordained. God has graciously given this eternal love in your hearts. So, from this day and always, be ever mindful of Jesus' admonition, love one another my blessed children, love one another.

"Mister Ringbearer, may I have the ring?"

Little Beau had to be gently nudged by Ezekial and he jerked and dropped the ring which had laid on a small pillow. He quickly picked it up and replaced it on the satin, but it again slid off. Exasperated and embarrassed at the tittering crowd, he simply handed the ring to his daddy.

"Thank you son," Beau whispered and smiled.

Little Beau smiled back at the two of them and the vision of those joyous faces smiling down at him, back-lit with the golden morning sun burned itself into his memory. All the days of his life this vision of love and joy warmed his heart!

"Beau, Ruby, the ring is a symbol of the eternal gift of love God has given. This ring binds you together, mind, body and soul. The ring surrounds your body Ruby, protects you with the promise that you will never be alone."

"Place the ring on her finger Beau."

Beau slid the ring over Ruby's offered finger.

"Man, behold your wife. Woman, behold your husband. Seal your promise of love with a kiss."

A cheer that caused the horses to jump went up as the little man and little woman kissed, and the band played a happy melody as cheerful congratulations, hugs, kisses and handshakes surrounded them. Beau reached down and rescued his son from the crowding knees of well-wishers. Little Beau ever after recalled his father's strength and his mother's gentle touch and the comforting love in each.

SEPARATE REALITIES

Mister and Misses Cuellar had set two old doors on sawhorses and placed all manner of food out for everyone. There was beer and wine in iced barrels. Dancing and laughter filled the space beside the river beneath the ancient trees. An hour into the shivaree, only Callie was aware of the newlyweds slipping away to the back room of the hotel, as they entrusted their son to her keeping for awhile. She smiled and reminisced her own marriage day. A single tear was allowed to honor the joyful memory.

"What's w'ong Miss Callie?"

She blinked away the pearly drops and smiled through the love in her aching heart.

"Nothin' Little Beau. Will you dance with me?"

When the band packed their instruments and the Cuellar family put their plates and makeshift tables into the wagon beds and all the people had drifted away and headed home for supper when Callie had gathered her growing brood and sat them in the Mexican restaurant to eat, Noah sat alone and quiet on a great, exposed root of a mighty oak on the riverbank in the twilight. Uncorking a bottle of whiskey, he tilted it and swallowed until it burned.

"Hidy," he greeted the approaching shadow.

"Mind some company, Noah?" Ezekial asked.

"Naw, jes' sittin' here watchin' the river flow. Wanna' snort?" Noah asked, holding the bottle out.

"No sir, don't like the taste."

"I don't drink it for taste. It scratches an itch."

They sat enjoying the song of the river, the music of the dry leaves in the breeze and the singing of the frogs and the turtles.

"That's was the first wedding I've ever seen," Ezekial said. "All the ladies shore looked purdy. Are all weddin's like 'at?"

"Yes, the women were all easy on the eyes today. But, they always look plum beautiful to me. Guess I jes' had'n been 'round females enough in my life to get use' to 'em. Not all weddin's are 'zactly like 'at Zeke, I reckon Micah kinda' made it up best he knew how. He did right well you ass' me. Ever'body was happy. The blacks, the Meskins, gringos, all happy together. War caused so much hate, I'd never thought it could happen."

"Beau and Ruby looked so happy."

"Yep. I 'spect it was the happiest day of their lives."

"Was you ever married Noah?"

"Me? Ha! Naw, naw. Decent women would never have much to do with me. 'Sides, I never was much for civilization. There was some saloon gals a few times I was sweet on. But, soon's there come a chance to fight I was gone. Fighting was always whut I's good at. I did'n pa'ticularly like it, but there was always hate in me. Drove me to keep on killin' those who took my fam'ly an' did them so terribly bad. If all the Comanche died, why, I'd be lost. I didn't really hate Yankees, but they was killin' my friends an' tryin' to kill me, so,... well, you were there, you know. There's still plenty of Comanche left though, an' they'll prob'ly come 'round this ranch you an' Callie 'll have. You'll need somebody who can fight 'em off, an' I'll enjoy it in a way, a sick way. I know it's crazy. I'm loco as a one-eyed skunk, but good, decent people need men like me to protect 'em from their peaceful, trustin' selves."

They sat quietly and viewed the erratic symmetry of the birds searching for their supper in the sky before they slept. The stars began to show in the violet night and the wind gave a warning of the coming chill.

"Don't you ever wanna' wife Noah?"

"Truth is Zeke, it kinda' scares me. I jes' don't know if I could live a married life, settle down an' be a dependable provider, stable and such. There was a girl. I s'pose she woulda' married me. But I 'spect I'da made her miserable after 'while. 'Sides she was a youngster. Ain't no tellin' how long I got left the way I live. I left her behind."

Noah took another pull on the whiskey. He hoped that Brandy didn't cry. He hated the thought that she would hurt and cry. If she did, he hoped she wouldn't cry for long. He missed the girl and his own heart hurt, but he knew that, because he loved her, he had to leave her. He wasn't the man for marriage.

The silver moon soon rose as each of them mused over the joy they'd seen the young lovers blessed with that day and the love each of them had left behind them. Ezekial watched the black water that flowed slowly toward the sea and thought about Cynthia and Gramps and Pop, his brothers, his friends, the future. Noah thought about many years gone by, lost loves, so many mistakes, so much regret. The whiskey and the memories, both bitter and sweet, flowed like the river through his mind.

"'Ever go to church much Noah?" Ezekial asked as he scratched behind Sam's ears as he dozed in the grass beside him.

"Aw, I went once or twice when a friend got married, or buried. I don't have anything 'gainst folks who have the habit of church goin', 'cept some o' them are too trustin'. They think they can pray the devil outa' an Indian an' some keep on prayin' while a redskin is scalpin' their children. Church jes' makes me uncomfortable, to tell the truth."

"I think church is s'posed to make a man uncomfortable, make you think about the wrong way yer livin' and maybe he'p you change. I was goin' to church regular 'fore I left Carolina. Heh-heh. Sam was goin' to church with me too." Ezekial smiled and patted his friends fur. His thoughts inexplicably jumped to Gramps and Sam laying beside him as he sat dying in the rocker on the porch waiting for Ezekial to come home. He was grateful for the darkness that hid his tears.

"Noah, ever wonder what happens when you die?"

"Yep. I 'magine ever'body does. But jes' like ever' body else, I ain't got no answers. I've seen lots of men die Zeke, and that's all I've ever seen, jes' seen 'em die. Nothin' else ever happened. Life jes' stopped. Don't know 'bout no soul nor spirit, an' I don't figger nobody else does neither. If nobody never saw a soul or a spirit, where'd the idea come from?"

"You don't believe in God?"

"Yea Zeke, I guess I do. But I don't feel like He'd be real concerned whether an ol' soldier like me b'lieves in Him or not. He shore 'llows lots of cruelty an' mischief an' sufferin' to go on down here on His earth though. I've witnessed my share of that. Seems like sometimes them that love God the most, He lets suffer the most. I s'pose He has priorities He don' 'llow us to be privy to. There jes' ain't no figgerin' God out."

"That's where faith comes in don't it Noah?"

"Faith? Zeke, I have faith in these Colt pistols of mine. I've relied on these pistols time after time and they do their job near ever' time. Seems to me that faith is an earned thing. Like I have faith in my ol' horse Jughead that he won't buck when I shoot my pistols. I have faith Callie can cook a delicious stew 'cause I've tasted it. But I, nor nobody else I know of has s'perienced death and lived to tell 'bout it. So where the faith that the soul of man lives on past death comes from, well I jes' don't comprende."

"Yea Noah, I know whut you mean. That preacher back in Carolina told it like it was a sin not to have faith, not to believe; made me think I was wrong to wonder, to have doubts. Maybe it's wrong to not just accept what the Good Book teaches.

"An I saw some awful stuff in the war too. Things that made me wonder 'bout God's mercy and love. But, God did'n' start the war. He did'n' make yer pistols Noah, nor the Indian's tomahawks. I guess fear and hate made 'em. But, ever'body dies sooner or later, somehow.

"Nobody can explain it all to ever' body's satisfaction it don't seem like. I guess we'll all find out what's what when we die.

"Well hell Zeke, who'll need answers then? After life's over there'll be no need to know 'bout life, nor death. We need help now, while we're living. My mother needed help when those damned Comanche devils was rapin' her and burnin' her an' cuttin' off her nose and ears and breasts! She needed God's help then! When she was dead it was too late!"

"I'm sorry Noah."

"Sorry? What good is sorry? Sorry has always jes' made me cry inside. A boy shouldn' see his mamma and his daddy done like that! They never did nothin' to deserve what those savages did to them. And I'm supposed to 'pray' for my enemies? That's bullshit! That's what that is. The only way to reform a Comanche is to kill his stinkin' ass! An' I've re-formed a passel of 'em. Ain't through yet."

"I didn' mean to make you mad Noah."

Noah was red in the face and breathing deep. He looked at Ezekial and forcibly calmed himself. He looked up at the cold clear sky and shook his head in reply. Pulling the makings from his shirt pocket, he shakily rolled a cigarette and lit it with a Lucifer match. Uncorking the whiskey he took a long pull.

"Zeke, I wish life was as simple for me as it seems to be for some people. Take Micah, hell, he's been a slave near his whole life, but he don't hold no grudges, ain't no hate inside him. He accepts it as 'God's will', takes the bad with the good. But, I know, if not for men like me, the Indians would massacre the whole white population."

"Maybe yer doin' God's work too Noah."

"Naw, I'm jes' getting' revenge."

"Reckon Injuns' ll bother us at our new place?"

"I'd be very su'prised if they didn' Zeke."

"Will it be safe for Callie and the girls?"

"Not perfectly safe. Not at first. But, if ever' one' ll listen to me it should be safe enough. I've found four men here who have 'sperience fightin' Indians and as cowboys. They need work, an' we'll need 'em if we wanna' discourage the redskins. I'm hopin' you an' Callie will lemme hire 'em right off."

"Go 'head an' hire 'em Noah, in the mornin. Who knows, we may run into Injuns when we visit Mabel's ranch. But Noah far as possible, we'll be wantin' to live peaceably with ever'one. Injuns, Germans, Mexicans an' ever'body else. We don't wanna' start no trouble with anyone.

"Germans will be peaceful enough and good neighbors. Most Mexicans 'll be friendly too. But Comanche hate you right now, 'fore they even see ya simply because you ain't Comanche."

"An' I unnerstan' how you might think I'd start trouble with the Comanche, but I won't. I'll run their feather-sproutin', naked asses off if they come 'round an' may 'accidently' murder a few, but I promise they won't bother the females."

"What 'll these men work for?"

"Zeke, seein' as how some of 'em are shovin' horse patties in the livery an' another is swampin' out a hoodalum saloon an' one jes' lost his last dollar at a faro table, I 'spect they'd welcome whatever they get."

"Tell 'em if they make us good hands we'll pay 'em a good wage. If they're caught loafin' or drinkin' on the job, no chance, they can draw their wages an' move on."

"I'll make sure that's clear, but they're mostly ol' rangers and discipline themselves. I truly think they'll be fine or I wouldn' want 'em."

"I trust your judgment Noah. Completely. An' don't never think Callie an' I don't appreciate you. We know we need you."

"I wouldn' want anything to happen to those children, or Callie. Or you. You ain't too big to take an arrow."

"I'm an easy target ain't I?"

Noah laughed, corked his jug and said, "Let's get some shut-eye."

Early next morning Noah walked down the dusty road before the hotel then took an intersecting wide path a hundred yards, there finding a ramshackle structure that a hand-painted sign deemed the Quatro Caminos Cantina. He ducked beneath the small door and let his eyes adjust to the dark interior. One of the men he was looking for was emptying spittoons into a larger bucket.

"Chuy, can you be ready to ride this morning? Cowboy work later on but we may have to rebuild a ranch that the Comanche burnt down first. Out other side a' Uvalde. Ten dollars a month and found to start. But we gotta' leave San Antone this mornin'"

Chuy dropped the nasty bucket and spittoon where he stood. He smiled, wiped his hands on his pants and said, "Jes' lemme' saddle my horse. Les' go."

"Know where Shorty, Billy Hell and Cacahuete are?"

"Si Noe, you wan' them too?"

"Yep. Gather 'em up, git yer horses an' meet me at the wagon yard by the livery. Pronto."

"Ho-kay. I go."

Chuy was a small man, a Mexican vaquero approaching middle age. Cacahuete was also a small Mexican cowboy and he'd fought Indians with both of them. They were good hands with a job of work and with firearms. Dependable. Shorty was dependable too, just not much of a horseman or fighter. He was adept at building though, with wood or stone, and there may be much construction to be done. Billy Hell, whose real name was Billy Hill, was a long-haired, thirty-something, wild, long, tall drink of water who was good on a horse and deadly with any kind of firearm. Noah had fought and chased Indians and outlaws with all these men and herded stolen horses and cattle back to civilization from the wilderness. He knew they'd all not shirk from labor nor run from a fight.

Money and work were rare in these early days of Reconstruction. These men were thankful and eager as they gathered at the wagons. He explained briefly what would be required of them. He assigned Chuy, Billy Hell and Cacauete to drive the small horse herd. He told Shorty he'd be in charge of the two wagons of construction supplies along with Micah. He told them Beau was in charge of the horses, that he was foreman of the ranch and who the big bosses were. He impressed upon them that as far as defense against Indians and bandits went, he was the boss and not to let the lady nor Ezekial countermand his orders.

Beau had taken their horses and fed each one of the skinny cayuses a healthy bait of oats. Callie looked over their meager possessions and escorted them to a general store where she bought the two of them that didn't have them ground tarps and blankets to sleep on. She bought three of them coats, all of them gloves, rainproof dusters and gave each one five dollars as a draw against wages for personal items.

The newly formed company set out southwest smartly, to the Nueces River, the Frio River and the remnants of the Curtsinger ranch.

She had felt terribly nauseated this morning. She had vomited into the chamber pot. Was it just the mystery meat she'd eaten at the tiny cafe last night? The wet, muggy Georgia weather reflected her feelings exactly. She hoped it was simply a passing infirmity, but she had seen these same symptoms in the whores she had worked with before, symptoms that foretold pregnancy. She was too young for that, she had no time for a baby. She had a life to live, a life that could not be restrained by a baby.

But, she admitted to herself that if her luck ran true to the past, then she was certainly pregnant. That bastard. That dirty bastard! This is what falling in love got her? Now she was pregnant, alone and near broke in a strange town decimated by war and still filled with hate and distrust. To Noah she'd been just a slave, something to be used and thrown aside. She should hate him. But she couldn't. She was determined to find the low-down, old bastard and she was nearly of a mind to put another bullet in his skinny ass. But she wouldn't. She couldn't. If she ever found him she would cry and beg him to stay with her. She loved him, needed him. Life could be so wonderful. If only.

Montgomery was a war-torn symbol of the South. There was hunger, poverty, brutality and crime everywhere. There was no refuge to be found in the South. Humiliation, degradation, sickness, suffering and sorrow were fixed in so many faces. Smiles were rare and usually seen above blue coats which inhabited every corner. These Yankee soldiers would be her salvation though, only they had money and they would spend it for a few minutes to relieve themselves in her. She knew Cecil would loan her money, even give it to her, but she didn't want to put herself in an obligatory position or be beholding to any man. Strangely, she wanted to save herself for Noah, though she had never restrained herself before. How could she? And why should she? She had to utilize what she had to sustain herself. And she was all she had.

She had sold her mules and wagon to Cecil who had given her more than they were worth, but she must make that money last as long as possible and supplement it with what earnings she could get from whoring. It may be a long winter. She had gone into a clothing store to buy an alluring dress. Just one. Then she would troll the streets and saloons for prospective customers. The rooming house she had found had an understanding owner and a room with a private entrance. The owner would be rewarded with a small stipend for his understanding and for his apparent protection. Once she had purchased a seductive garment she would go to work this very day.

The dry goods store's inventory was not impressive, but it was the largest in town. Fashion in the post-war South was principally the same as it was prior to the War of Northern Aggression. The old man was eager to make a sale and advised her that alterations could be made to any selection she chose and a fitting could be done quickly due to his recent purchase of the new invention, the sewing machine. Her choice of a dress was a matter of eliminating the bland grandmother's dresses. She was escorted into a fitting room by a matron who made disapproving faces at Brandy's insistence that the waist be tightened and the neckline be lowered significantly. Brandy suppressed her giggles at the perch-like lips and raised eyebrows and chin of the old lady.

The process of alteration to the garment was begun by removing certain stitching, then the proprietor's wife made marks and pinned the cloth. Brandy was much affected by the impressive machine the old woman sat before, working the treadle. Impressed by the magic of the machine, Brandy asked so many question that the lady finally located an instruction manual and pushed it into Brandy's questioning face. Soon, Brandy was telling the woman how to do her own work and happily took the exasperated lady's seat before the machine when invited to do so. When Brandy slipped the dress on again it fit perfectly, and though the good wife sniffed her disapprobation, she went out into the store and spoke with her husband about offering the young lady the alteration work that she detested herself.

When she came out of the dressing room wearing the fitted dress, the owner stared, suffered the sharp elbow of his wife, then cleared his throat and offered Brandy employment making alterations for the store. When told it would pay a percentage and told she could set her own time to work as long as alterations were ready within a reasonable time, she accepted. The crafty wife detested the sewing with the newfangled machine and though she knew her husband would look and lust at Brandy, she also knew his days (or nights), of being capable of doing anything about it were over. Brandy took the offer of work not for the pay or the convenience of the hours, but because she was fascinated by the machine and it's endless possibilities. The remuneration for what was so easy and fun seemed a double blessing to her, and she could use the machine to make her own garments. The money would be a supplement to her primary occupation.

As she was leaving the store she met Cecil on the street. He invited her to a noon-time meal and she, of course, had been preconditioned to never turn down a free meal. Over the food she effusively displayed her enthusiasm over the sewing machine and told him of her natural aptitude and enjoyment of the craft. Cecil asked incisive questions about her agreement with the old proprietor and the capabilities of the amazing new machine. Assessing the situation with his business acumen and considering her new and enticing dress and his suspicions of her further plans to make money, Cecil asked her to excuse him for a few minutes. He returned only when she was ordering pie to delay having to pay the waiter's bill herself.

He sat down with a smug smile on his face and began eating the cold chicken remaining on his plate and ordered a piece of pie for himself.

"Why are you smiling like a possum eating persimmons Cecil?"

"I'm a businessman my dear partner. I always enjoy exercising my foresight in establishing a new business to serve the public."

"Cecil,..." Brandy accentuated the last syllable, "What do you mean 'partner'?"

"We are in business together Brandy, business partners, fifty-fifty. You supply the labor, I supply the capital. Of course, business will be slow at first, until a clientele is established, but I have such faith in your enthusiasm and energy, that I will pay you a decent wage against the time when our venture becomes profitable. You'll need to move, of course, to a more reputable dwelling. I'll send a man and conveyance to accomplish your move this afternoon, so please pack your things quickly. I have a small house which hasn't been leased which will suit you and we can settle on payments later when the money starts rolling in."

"Cecil! I won't be a kept woman, nor will I work for you in any cathouse. So just stop your planning mister!" Brandy spouted with indignation.

SEPARATE REALITIES

"Brandy, please give me some credit for possessing a semblance of decency. Besides, it seems to me by the appearance of this, this...'garment' you have designed and created that your intent was to attract bees to your honey and my intent is to keep you a respectable lady. This is a new place for you, a new time, so please seize this new opportunity to change your life.

"I own a small shop which is currently vacant adjacent to the haberdashery which offered you employment. I have already purchased the sewing machine which you are so taken with and have sent a man out to purchase all available fabric in the city. By tomorrow the machine and fabric will be moved to our alteration and tailor shop. I have also taken the liberty of retaining the services of a needy grandmother who has made many children and others clothes for more years than I've lived. I'm sure her expertise will benefit our business. You must learn to use the machine quickly and well because you'll soon have more work than you can manage, believe me."

"Oh Cecil," Brandy breathed,... "I don't know..."

"I'll see if the sign-painter can be there tomorrow. What shall we name this enterprise? Brandy's Dandies? What do you think?"

"I don't know."

"Well, think girl. A manager must often make quick decisions. Oh yes, I almost forget. Here." He handed Brandy a small golden ring.

"What is this?"

"It's a wedding band. You must wear it so the customers will believe you're married. It will limit the number of young men flocking to the shop in pursuit of you and satisfy the gossipy females populace when your pregnancy becomes more evident."

"Cecil! How could you possibly know..."

"Dear child, I am the father of a houseful of children. There are physical signs that can't be hidden from an old dad."

"But...Cecil, I was thinking of seeing someone to end the pregnancy..."

"Ridiculous! Too dangerous. And what would the man you were chasing think? It is his child isn't it?"

"Yes, but he,..."

"No argument Brandy. You must have the child. You will always regret it if you do not. God and love produced the life within you. Would you murder the innocent babe?"

Tears of confusion, fear, loneliness, and guilt ran across her cheeks. Cecil reached for her, held her as a father would and quietly assured her that all would turn out well. She trembled in his arms and felt not lust, but a protective love, a love she'd never experienced before. A tiny seed of trust was sown deep within her heart.

Peta Nacona had died the previous winter of an infection in a wound while the Kwahadi Comanche camped on the Canadian River. His son, Quanah, was now looked to by most of the Antelope Eaters sect as inheriting the leadership role that Peta Nacona had established. Quanah was the son of Cynthia Parker, a woman who had been taken captive while a child at the place the whites called Parker's Fort. Cynthia had become a Comanche and a respected member of the tribe as wife of the war chief Peta Nacona. Rutting Roe hated Cynthia Parker and Quanah because of their white blood and hated all those who recognized Quanah as their leader. Roe had his own followers who were more fierce and bloodthirsty than the other Kwahadi warriors. His troop was richer too, taking hundreds of horses, many guns and other valuables from the weak, the few and the isolated.

Though Rutting Roe's followers were fewer among the Comanche than Quanah Parker's, there were also Kiowa, Tonkawa, Kickapoo and even some Mexican renegades who rode with him. Roe knew there was little loyalty or respect in his followers, but they feared him and followed him because they were greedy, lustful, addicted to alcohol and were filled with hate as he was. Roe's cowardly tactics earned them great wealth among their people and the admiring girls saw them as brave warriors when they returned with much plunder and many presents. Bloody red scalps always adorned their trappings and weapons when they rode into the camp, the hair of babies, women, the old and the weak. But these trophies revealed no evidence of how or from whom they were obtained. The stories of their heroic deeds grew greater with every telling. And the grateful young squaws welcomed them beneath their blankets.

Roe laid on the thick pile of buffalo robes in the sumptuous teepee his wives had made for him and watched the yellow-haired girl as she carried the wood inside and fed the warming fire. She had cried for many days even though he had beat her until she bled and her pale skin turned black, she refused to stop her crying. He had cut off her ears, slit her nose and lips, bit deep into her breast and removed most of the fingers on one hand. Finally, the stupid white girl stopped crying. Now she trembled and shook all the time, even in her sleep. Roe hated her even more now that she was so repulsive. He had bedded her repeatedly at first, before he mutilated her face and body, and now she was with child. He had beaten her swollen belly trying to kill the life within her, but the living demon-child within her seemed to mock him. His hate kept him from killing her and releasing her from suffering, but he feared and hated the growing and living evil within her. It must never see the light of day. It would die on the day of its birth.

He yelled at her and made her look at him. As her eyes never quite met his, still she understood the motions that he made with his hands. He wanted her to bring him food. As she approached with the meat of a mule that she had butchered and cooked, her trembling increased and she dropped the hot meat from the skewer onto the buffalo furs. He cuffed her on the head and screamed insults at her retreating back.

The other white girl, the red-haired one that had escaped, haunted his thoughts and the anger and hate ate at his spirit. It was an affront to his manhood that a mere girl had escaped him. The loss of her burned within him, souring his favorite meat in his belly. He yearned to find the red-haired girl. He must find her. It was bad medicine to allow a captive to escape, it had never happened before. He must redeem himself in the eyes of the spirits and his people, if not, then bad things would find him, evil spirits would trick him, lead him astray and overcome him. He could not rest, could find no peace until she was again his prisoner. And then she would surely suffer as he had never caused another to suffer before. She would beg for the death he would not give her.

The Mexican girl had also escaped him in her own way with the big knife a squaw had given her to butcher a buffalo. She had cut deep into her own thin neck and smiled in triumph as the streaming red blood had poured down her body. When she fell and died, the smile remained. When the fat squaw took the knife to scalp the girl, Roe knocked her away. The girl had shown her bravery and he would reward her courage by letting the wolves and the buzzards have her. But first he had tasted her heart, stole her bravery for himself.

He was anxious to raid and murder and steal and burn. He wanted to gather his ponies and his killers and go to rape and pillage and kill now. But the cold winds were beginning to blow. He must rest, heal, plan and dream. He imagined the capture and the delicious torments he would bring to the red-haired girl.

He lifted the stolen jug of rye whiskey from the robes beneath him and drank deeply, letting the fiery liquid burn his mouth and throat, relishing the sweetness in the pain. Soon the spirit of the whiskey soothed the burning hate in his belly and he slept. The women were thankful that he slept. They quietly relaxed and spoke softly of the concerns that women of such men have. Rutting Roe's women wanted warm weather to come quickly too, so he would leave them in peace for awhile.

As she had done for quite awhile now she huddled in the alley, shivering in the freezing cold and wet, waiting for the saloon and cafes to close. The cafes sometimes threw out food she could swallow and hold down, though often her stomach rejected it and she vomited. She could never refrain from eating even when it smelled bad, her hunger made her eat despite the rotting stench. She waited until the quiet told her that the saloons had closed because she feared the violence of drunken men who stumbled their way to their dark houses.

She was alone. A drunken soldier had shot her mother when the air was still warm. Now, when the cold wind made her shiver, she trembled at the memory of the loud noise, her mother's scream, the smell of hot blood and gunpowder. She had remained with her mother as she lay still and silent in the alley. Her sickly brother had cried and cried until he had grown too weak to cry and laid still and become cold and stiff like their mother.

After some days a man had come and she had hidden herself beneath the building, which cramped darkness had become her home. The man had cursed as he had thrown her stinking, maggot-covered mother and brother in the bed of a wagon filled with other rotting refuse and carried her family away. She had been too weak to follow. Since that day, she had been alone.

She was thin and afraid, sick and weak and the shivering wouldn't stop so she could sleep. Loud noises made her panic and recall her mother's screams. She hid most of the time, especially through the light of day. When the darkness came she slipped silently down the deserted alleyways hoping to find food. Sometimes she would find a little.

A day came when she was awakened by a smell, a gentle smell. She didn't know what soap was had never experienced it, but it was a nice smell. It smelled safe somehow, gentle, peaceful and calming. She well knew the smell of fear and hate and violence and it was very different from that.

Peering from under the storehouse in the alley through her jaundiced and seeping eyes, she watched the woman who had come out of another building sit on a straight back chair before a small table. She gathered a wrap around her shoulders against the chill and looked up into the oppressive gray sky. Opening a basket she had placed on the table she removed a wrapped package. The pleasurable savor drew her full attention. It was food. Not the rancid food she found thrown into the barrels in the alleys, but fresh, wholesome food. She watched every move the woman made, her hands taking food from the table and moving it to her mouth. Irresistibly, she was coaxed by her hunger to move toward the food, her hunger overcoming her fear. But even as she crawled forward toward the food her fear made her trembling body shake violently knocking her head against the floorboards.

As her head came into gray light of the winter's day from beneath the floor of the storehouse, the movement caught the woman's eye. The gentle-smelling woman made soothing sounds with her mouth, sounds like her own mouth had made on her mother's teat. Fear fought her hunger, a whine escaped her and she slunk back, then crawled forward, shaking and hesitant. The woman made other sounds, sounds that seemed to beckon her, but her instinctual and learned fear held her like a chain beneath the building.

"Come here puppy. I won't hurt you. You hungry? Oh baby, you're so skinny! Pretty puppy. Come here baby."

The coaxing sounds drew her but she couldn't overcome her fear that held her and shook her frail body. With unblinking eyes she watched the woman place the food on the ground, then gather the basket and go back inside the building. When the door closed and the woman disappeared, she slunk out and snuck up on the food, grabbing a chunk of the meat and running and ducking back into the darkness to devour it. She licked her chops, then scanned the alley to ensure it was safe then warily returned and wolfed down the delicious and juicy treat, retreating quickly to her refuge. The meat, like medicine, allowed her to ward off the cold and to sleep deep and well. She was grateful for the feast, such a blessing as she had never expected or experienced in her short, miserable existence. It was not much of a sacrifice to the woman, but it had been the best day of the dog's life, since her family was no more.

That was a beginning. Every day after that first glorious day the woman had brought her food, hearty, delicious food. Twice daily she waited for the woman who was angel-like in her canine perspective and never failing, the woman brought her food twice daily. The woman's gentle persuasion and soft, safe smell had drawn her out to eat. These minutes given and shared with the woman were the very best times of her life. The woman even placed a pail of clear water by the door which she knew was placed there especially for her.

A morning dawned when the puppy looked out from her den beneath the floor and the ground was white. She sniffed at the snow and withdrew to the dry safety of her lair. Earlier than usual, the woman came out of the door and called to her. Surmounting her fears, she walked gingerly out onto the snow to get to the offered meat. As soon as she had come out from under the building the woman snatched her up and carried her small, struggling body into the warmth of the other building. Though she trembled at the woman's touch at first, she welcomed it. She had been shivering in the cold air outside, but even in the heat inside the building she shook in fear as the other women there made sounds with their mouths while the tables before them hummed a busy buzzing like the bees that had bitten her long before.

They made her a bed in a small storeroom, putting soft and nice-smelling cloth in a basket and that was where she slept at night. But, during the workday she dozed near the soap-smelling woman's feet, close to the warming stove. The woman gave her milk in a platter and soon the new and frightening captivity became comforting and her evident gratitude and happiness caused her tail to wag and her friendliness to shine in her big brown eyes. At the woman's side a sure friendship grew. Each of them relished the love and companionship.

After two weeks she followed the woman to her home and slept on a rug beside her bed. She grew anxious and worried when separated from her for even a short while. She liked the other women in the shop and tolerated others who came around, but she knew the woman loved her best, she knew she would be always devoted to the woman, always loyal and protective until death. It was in her very nature, her blood and bones.

Brandy woke most mornings to see the mongrel bitch she had named Shoestring sitting on her skinny haunches staring at her. The adoration in the dog's eyes was a welcome waking. She spoke to the dog always as she would to a friend and realized only infrequently that the beloved beast may not understand her every word. But Shoestring understood a lot and sensed much more than even Brandy imagined. People in Montgomery grew accustomed to seeing the two of them walking side by side, jauntily and happily, on the streets of the city.

Shoestring grew into a muscular but still thin physique. The coat that had been filthy and matted now shone with flourishing health and smelled of the gentle soap that Brandy used. She no longer trembled in fear and cowered from people. At times her hackles rose when she sensed evil or ill intent in men. She would protect Brandy, warn her of the dangers only she could sense. It was a comfort to each of them to have such a God-given friend.

The entire winter was a flurry of activity for Brandy. Cecil was a great help, teaching her the basics, then the intricacies of running a business. He also sent his friends, family and business associates to Brandy for their clothing work. The soldiers came in squads for tailoring to their uniforms and to see the pretty, young proprietor. Suits and dresses and children's clothes were altered and when she started designing and making ladies gowns the women vied for her time. Brandy soon had to hire clerks to take orders and measurements so she could sew and soon after had to order two additional sewing machines and train operators. The long hours of the days of winter flew by as her business, and her belly, grew.

Chapter Ten

A friend is long sought, hardly found, and with difficulty kept.
---Jerome, Letter to Rufinus

For the thing which I greatly feared is come upon me,
and that which I was afraid of is come unto me.
---Job 3:25 (KJV)

One of these days I'm gonna' climb that mountain. Walk up there among them clouds, Where the cotton's high and the corn's a 'growin' And there ain't no field to plow.
---Walter Brennen

THE CLOSER THE growing assembly of souls got to Mabel's home the more often the familiar landscape brought smiles and unrestrained tears. Both sweet and horrible memories assailed her. The twisting trail round and over the evergreen hills and through the clear, spring-fed streams that sang over the stone beds caused her to want to run away from this beloved country and to embrace it as an old friend at the same time.

Callie noticed the heart-rending emotions that the return to the ranch was causing and offered to turn the buggy around and take her back to Uvalde. But Mabel bravely continued toward the only home she had ever known, wiping her weeping eyes. She heard her sweet mother's voice encouraging her, whispering in her mind. "Hush baby, crying will only make it hurt worse." That's just what Momma had always told her when she scraped her knee or was stung by a wasp. She missed her Momma so. Daddy too. And her brothers and uncle, but she missed Momma most of all. That thought caused her to feel a tinge of guilt.

The light, two-seated buggy they had rented pulled by the livery's team stepped lively through the last oak mote and the burned ruins of her once happy home presented itself starkly to the bunch of them. Unconsciously, everyone came to a halt, beholding the spectacle of destruction. Everyone sat quietly, respectively, allowing Mabel to gather her resolve. The men sat on their mounts surrounding the buggy, glancing at one another and commenting by their silence the effect the all too familiar scene still had on them. The only sound was the horse's tack as it rang in the stillness of the noonday as they blew and fidgeted in their impatience to continue on.

Callie, feeling stress building, spoke, hoping to ease the tension.

"Seems like only the roof burned and fell in on the barn. The outer walls of the house are still standing too."

"The Germans helped Daddy and Granddaddy build the house and barn. Built both with thick stone. He wanted the animals to be warm in the winter," Mabel's voice was deep and controlled.

"That's a big barn," Ezekial observed.

"The fences of the corrals are all in good repair, looks like," Noah stated.

"And the only thing left of the house are the walls, chimneys, and the fence around the yard," Mabel whispered as if to herself.

"Well, let's get down and rest a bit. Then we'll set up camp and eat a bite," Callie directed.

The men unsaddled their mounts in the corral beside the burned barn. The women spread a blanket over the knee high grass outside the corral and kneeled down to make sandwiches from the meat and bread they had purchased in Uvalde. Everyone sat around eating and expressing admiration of the place. Surprisingly, the Comanche had not fouled the well as they typically did by depositing carcasses in it and the water was cold and crisp.

Callie noticed Mabel looking up the hill and followed her gaze to see the freshly dug graves in the little fenced graveyard. Mabel stood and began walking toward the hill. Ezekial rose, but Callie put her hand on his arm and whispered, "Let me go." Then to her daughter, "stay with Ezekial."

Ezekial's heart dropped in his chest as he watched the young girl walk to the graves of her family. His empathy nearly overwhelmed him, it was only through a great effort of will that he was able to withhold a groan of grief and a stream of tears. He realized the pain and sorrow Mabel was dealing with and the love of a brother grew in him. Amazing courage and moral strength in one so young, so tender. As he watched her climb the hill alone he admired her, and he prayed for her.

Callie stopped at the base of the hill and let Mabel climb to the graves alone. Her cheeks trembled as she restrained her emotions. The young lady was just too young, too innocent, to have this horror to deal with. Callie had lost her family members too, but not all at once and she had not witnessed their violent deaths, the mutilation and desecration of those she held most dear. The poor girl was all alone in the world now. Callie wanted to reach out and help her. Somehow.

Mabel was shaking all over by the time she reached the crest of the hill, but she took control of herself and stopped her trembling. She inhaled deeply, exhaled slowly, then walked forward into the low-fenced enclosure. Here they were, what remained of their earthly bodies, just beneath the soil and caliche. Reading what was carved into the cedar post crosses, she wondered who had given them such respect. There lay her two little brothers who had struggled so bravely and futilely for their mother's life and had been slaughtered with no thought of mercy. She recalled how she had scolded them for dallying at their chores that final morning. She thought of how beautiful they had looked when they were all cleaned up and dressed for Sunday meeting in town whenever they got to go. And the vision of the knife in one's thin neck and a steel hatchet splitting the other's skull, the thick, hot blood covering his red hair.

And Daddy. Daddy had died in the field where he was chopping down the cotton stalks. The family had watched from the window while the Comanche rode their ponies around him and shot him with bullets and arrows, screeching like crazy birds. They cut the hair from his head, removed his clothes and dressed in them and when he was naked they sliced his body and stabbed it and drug it behind a horse with a rope tied around a foot until her crazed mother ran out of the house with the rifle cursing the devils and was shot and raped and cut and raped and kicked and beat and raped until she died and then the Comanche had desecrated her body without restraint of conscience.

As they raped her mother Mabel had frozen in fear. She had watched her brothers run out into the yard with Daddy's turkey gun and the big shotgun and be slaughtered in their courageous attempt to defend their mother. Mabel hadn't been able to remember anything more until she seemed to awaken tied to Betty, a red sun setting to her left.

She felt regret, shame and guilt that she hadn't died in defense of her family and her home. Would she feel better if buried here by those she loved, would she feel anything at all? Was her family even aware that she was here? Were they aware of anything at all?

Her brothers lay next to her mother who lay next to her father who lay next to her uncle who lay next to her grandmother and grandfather. All her family was here. And not here. All she loved was here. All gone. All her life was here. And over.

"Why?" she said aloud to the heavens, just as untold millions before her had asked.

"Why didn't you let me go with my family? What am I supposed to do? How can I carry on alone, without them? Why couldn't you leave me one of them? Why?"

And she cried. And cried.

When she had no more tears she spoke to each of them, saying her goodbyes, making promises that would never be broken.

After a lengthy hour, Callie watched her begin to step determinedly back down the hill. Callie held her hand out to her as she approached. Their eyes met and Callie somehow knew then that Mabel would get through even this unimaginably terrible catastrophe. She was of good stock, mentally, emotionally and spiritually strong. Callie somehow was certain that Providence would provide for and protect this survivor. Through such terrible sorrow would strength emerge. It must, and it would.

The men, along with Sallie and Nellie wandered over and through the fallen roof timbers of the barn and house sifting for tools, tack and any other salvageable items. As Mabel and Callie joined the others, a hush fell over the searchers. Mabel's eyes moved to the slope of a small hill behind the house and she walked to it, apart from the others. Bending down, she took hold of the handle of the angled door of the storm cellar which her mother had also used as root cellar and storage. Struggling with the heavy door she let it fall heavily back against the hillock and looked down into the musty darkness. Callie and the others watched her disappear down the shaped earthen steps.

Although Mabel's eyes were not adjusted to the little light in the cellar, her hand found the box of long Lucifer matches Momma kept on the nearest shelf next to the kerosene lamp. Just the smell of the kerosene and the sight of the cellars contents by the lamp's yellow, dim glow made her heart lurch. From training and habit she searched the floor and shelves for snakes, mice and other varmints. Placing the hissing lamp on the small worktable she sat in the much-repaired chair beside it. Still and quiet she sat, allowing memories to wash over her, immersing her in days gone by when she was so much younger, times on the very edge of memory. Those were happy times when she was ever safe in the fold of her family, eternal days that would surely never end. Oh! How short that hour was!

The preserves in their jars shone dully and dusty on the sturdy shelves. Tomatoes, okra, peaches, pickled cucumbers, chili peppers and chow-chow relish that Momma learned to make from Granny who learned it at her mother's side and so on and on back into the forgotten past. Where had they gone? Were they here? Were they here inside her, living still and ever being reborn in each successive generation? She didn't and couldn't know this in any reasoning or logical sense, but she felt that it was true nonetheless.

Her eyes surveyed the figs, the berry jelly, the sacks of seed potatoes and pecans, the crocks of homemade wine. A thought rose and surfaced into her conscious and she stepped up on the chair, its broken and tied joints groaning their protest, then stepped lightly up onto the worktable. Reaching back over the sealed jugs and jars against the dark earthen wall, her fingers searching, then stopping, grasping the small tin box and lifting it over the preserves. Sitting back down in the rickety chair she placed the dented box on the table beside the lamp and let her eyes and hands help remind her of a moment long past.

Momma and her had carried jars of peach preserves to the shelf when Momma had shown her the old tin box. "If anything ever happens to me and your Daddy, you remember to come get this box Mabel. Inside here is the deed to this land, the family birth and death records in this old Bible wrapped in this canvas, and...." here her mother's lip had trembled and she shook her head as a tear trailed down her cheek.

"Momma?"

"It's okay baby. It's just,...this was your Granny's wedding ring. It will be yours someday. Granny wore it for over fifty years, wore it proud and true. Through happy times and terrible times. I hope and pray you'll find a man like mine is and have a full life together like they did. Like me and your daddy have. You wear this ring proud girl. And you give me some grandbabies to spoil like Granny spoiled you."

"Oh Momma," Mabel blushed.

The memory brought a smile and a tear.

Mabel fingered the golden ring with the small diamond mounted in it. She held it in her palm and in her mind's eye she saw her Granny twisting the ring on her finger as she sat on the porch in her final days smoking the briar pipe that also lay in the box alongside Grampa's spectacles.

"Mabel?" Callie's voice intruded on her reminiscence. "You alright?"

"Yes'm. I'm fine. Come on down."

Callie tiptoed down the chipped earth stairs.

"My goodness! There's enough preserves down here to feed an army. And what's all this other stuff?"

"Momma was always industrious. Never wasted much. She gave lots away to neighbors and hungry travelers. And the fat Baptist preacher in Uvalde, Brother Beal, he got his share too," Mabel smiled.

"What's in the box?"

"Lots of stuff. Granny's wedding ring and pipe. Grampa's spectacles. These locks of us kid's hair when Momma cut it. A real old, family Bible with the family tree written in it. Some photographs of the family back in the olden days. This is the deed to this land. And there's some other deeds here for some other places."

"Well Lordy be. Your mother was a prudent woman to think to put her valuables down here. I wonder why the Indians didn't take all this?"

"May not have noticed the old door, laying on the little hill like it does."

"Maybe not. Is that gunpowder? And whiskey?"

"Yes'm. That's gunpowder. Lead over there with the other bullet-making things. Daddy made his own bullets. And that's wild grape wine that Granny made, years ago. Momma didn't allow no whiskey drinkin' on the place. But Daddy drank a little whiskey in town sometimes, or at a neighbors place."

"Well. All this will have to be added to the price of the ranch. We'll have to list it all and figure it into the cost of the whole ranch, because, Mabel, Ezekial and I have decided we want to buy the place."

The expression on Mabel's face as she held the wedding ring and the land deed silenced Callie.

"Mabel?"

"It's just that,...well, I know I have to sell the place,...but I just, it just don't feel right. This is my home. I was born in that burned down house. My Gramps and Granny are buried up on the hill and my Momma and Daddy and,...well,..." tears drown out the rest of her words and Callie kneeled down and took her in her arms.

"Callie, my folks have fought Indians and Mexicans and Yankees,...oh excuse me,...but they've fought and worked for this place for so many years and it just don't seem right for me to give it up now."

Tears washed Mabel's face. Callie kneeled down and took her in her arms.

"You all alright down 'air?" Ezekial called down.

Callie answered, "We're fine Ezekial. Just give us some time alone."

Ezekial went back to the girls who were covered with smut and ashes, sifting through the burned, fallen timbers of the house.

"What are they doing down in that hole?"

"It's a storm cellar. They're jes' talkin'. Give 'em a little while."

"There don't seem to be anything here Ezekial. All we've found is just a couple of bed frames, two spoons and a knife."

"Well, I 'spect somebody has already picked through the ashes. Somebody had to come and bury,...," he cut his words off.

"Ezekial, we know Mabel's family is buried up on the hill. We've seen graves b'fore," Sallie said.

"Yes, I 'spect everyone has these days."

Micah's pan-fried hash was served to four of the hungry at a time as it came out of the pan. Callie and Mabel shared the final pan with Micah and Sam was rewarded with what remained. After they finished Micah poured them each a cup of hot coffee. Callie and Mabel were both smiling a little and Ezekial was puzzled at their peaceful, content composure. He sat on a lower rail in the corral fence and studied them as the girls chattered, showing the trinkets they had found in the ashes. It seemed to Ezekial that Callie and Mabel shared a secret, but maybe their closeness was simply female friendship.

The sun was setting on the horizon, a big yellow-orange ball casting long blue shadows. Everyone had washed the soot from their feet, hands and faces and the tents and bedrolls were ready. The men had found hardly anything serviceable in the ruins of the barn, but had made a huge burn pile of the burned remains of the roof timbers and cleared the ground inside the high stone walls. There was little conversation as each made covert glances at Mabel periodically, looking for some indication of pending loss of control. But, she quietly went about her business, strangely tranquil, helping the girls washing the tin plates in a big bucket they had found in the barn.

Sam sniffed the breeze and chuffed, glancing at Ezekial to ensure he was paying attention, then stood facing the dying light and growled. Noah finished the rolling of the cigarette he was building, then licked and sealed it and placed it behind his ear. He stood, picked up his rifle, placed his hand on the butt of the Colt holstered on his hip. He walked apart from the others and peered into the western distance, legs apart, eyes squinting.

"Riders coming," he said into the questioning silence. Ezekial and all the men went quickly for their rifles and joined him to watch the indistinct, approaching riders who came on at a brisk trot.

Four men on horseback rode before a wagon and came to a stop ten yards from Noah's assembled crew.

"Evenin'. Can I he'p you boys?" Noah asked.

"Well sir, I expect you can if you have a cupa' hot coffee and extend an invite."

"Stranger, I'm a careful man and I like to know who I'm sharing coffee with 'for I..."

Mabel interrupted Noah's investigation with her friendly greeting.

"Welcome Mister Black. Please, get down and visit."

She turned and asked Micah if he could prepare a supper for the five visitors. Mabel then introduced Mister Black to everyone, explaining that he was a neighbor and a best friend of the family. She and Callie poured coffee for the visitors, while Micah peeled a few more potatoes with Nellie and Sallie's help. Mister Black began to explain his mission.

"Miss Mabel, foremost, I want to extend my family's heartfelt sympathy for your great loss. My heart goes out to you. Your family was some of the best people I've ever been privileged to know. I also want you to know that all our prayers were answered when word came through the army that you had escaped those Comanche devils without harm. We organized a troop to chase the low-down murderers, but we were too late. We had to take the time to honorably bury your folks before,...well, before we chased the bastards. I want you to know we prayed over your family proper and buried them deep."

"Thank you Mister Black."

"You're just like fam'ly Miss Mabel, your momma and daddy were good and decent people, good neighbors and Christians. Anything we can do for you Mabel, you just ask. Fact is, Misses Black wanted me to bring you back home with me to stay with us for awhile, 'til things get settled."

"Thank you, but I'll be fine with these good folks."

"We took the liberty to salvage the tools and some supplies from the barn and what we could find in the remains of the house. I have it there in the wagon."

"Did you find Mother's ring? Or the necklace she always wore?"

"No Mabel. There was no jewelry on your mother's body. And I didn't find the pocket watch your daddy always carried. The thieving, murdering scoundrels took all they could carry and burned the rest."

"Did they burn my family?"

"Yes Mabel. They did."

Mabel's jaw clinched along with her fists and she shut her eyes tightly. When she opened her eyes they were filled with hate, hard, cold and focused on the distance.

Mister Reading Wood Black was the founder of the town of Uvalde. Since he'd purchased his over four thousand acres for fifty cents per back in 'fifty three', he had fought Indians and drought, rustlers and Mexican banditos, both Yankee and Confederate Army provisioners who had "acquisitioned" his beeves. He had been a true friend to all the courageous settlers who braved all the dangers and hardships of this frontier to build homes and a life here. Mabel thought of Mister Black as a wise and protective uncle.

"Mabel, I wanted to catch you while you were in town yesterday, but I missed you. Just as well though, as I intend to help you rebuild your place and then leave some hands here with you to help out 'til you get on your feet and hire your own men."

"Ezekial and Callie have hired some men and have some more hands in San Antone. You see, I'm discussing a partnership with them."

SEPARATE REALITIES

Ezekial gave Mabel, then Callie a questioning glance.

"Um huh. Well. If there's any way I can help ya'll, jes' holler. There's some supplies in the wagon too, some food, some coffee, blankets and a few things my misses packed for you Mabel."

"Thank you both for your thoughtfulness Mister Black."

"You'd do the same for me, now, I'm right pleased to have all of you as neighbors, and all the folks hereabouts will be happy to hear that Ranger Captain Noah Lister and these other brave Rangers and Indians fighters will be here."

"You know Mister Black, these Comanche pups may just come here to make coup because I'm here. I hope not, but I've seen 'em do it a 'fore. Course, none of 'em survived their bravery."

"That's what I'm bankin' on. Jes' be sure to have a fast horse and rider at hand to send to town or to my ranch an' we'll all come in a hurry to he'p ya'll with any trouble. Indians, rustlers, banditos and wild white robbers too, lots o' worries 'round here. Jes' get us word, we'll come a' runnin'."

"Now, if you don' mind, I'll pay my respect to this fine supper Mister Micah and these ladies have prepared and then find a soft spot in the grass nearby and get some sleep. Us ol' folks ain't accustomed to these late hours," he smiled.

Mister Black and his cowboys ate quickly and before heading to his bedroll he tipped his hat and said, "Nice meeting all of ya'll. Good night neighbors."

Everyone was tired. Noah set a schedule for night owl guards. Just in case. It was a full moon, a Comanche moon.

Death would be preferable to his present existence. Pain overcame his every thought and fogged his vision. He lived in a darkened world of suffering. He had managed to strip the bark off a willow tree that grew by a muddy stream. Using his incisors and canines, he chewed the inner tissue until his jaws became exhausted and the salicylic acid thus ingested took the edge off the incapacitating pain.

He had almost caught up with the red-haired girl on the tired horse, she had been almost within his grasp when he had been knocked from the running pony's back. He heard the deafening boom after he had hit the hard ground and before he lost consciousness. He awoke momentarily with the impression he had no arm, then darkness swallowed him again.

It was night when the excruciating pain woke him, and freezing cold. Shivering, he gathered himself into a ball trying to keep the biting wind away. A dusting of stars lit the night and he began to act instinctively, then consciously, of survival. He crawled, though suffering electrifying jolts of pain, to a group of large rocks which would block the wind. Once there the smell of blood and exposed meat nauseated him. Surveying his body in starlight, it appeared he was painted in black.

One arm would not move at all. With the other he discovered a tear in his ribs and felt the small pieces of gristle and bone stuck inside the wound. It seemed the bullet had not entered his trunk but had tore across his ribs and through his arm above the elbow, breaking the bone there which was protruding from the flesh, visible even in the night.

The pain was unbearable and rendered him unconscious twice, but when he awakened the second time he found that he had managed to push the bone back in line with the bone that had remained in place. He had grown weaker at every waking but now the pieces of bone below his shoulder were approximately lined up. He used the blood and dirt to make a muddy plaster to fill the torn flesh after he had tied them together as best he could using the leather fringe of his buckskin britches.

He crawled toward the smell of burnt flesh in the hour darkness returned, his vision blurred by weakness and pain, fainting, then waking to crawl some more. He wasn't aware that it was the wagon of the hunters they had killed and the roasted and charred buffalo meat that he spent his miserable life crawling toward. Holding his body off the ground with his good arm and pushing with his legs, he finally covered the hundred yards to the meat.

Eventually he grabbed a spoke of the wagon wheel to pull himself up and burned his hand with the exposed glowing coal of the wood. As he fell against the burnt wheel, sparks flew and the last wheel holding the burned-out wagon up and the hot carcass of a buffalo cow fell on and against him, shocking him with pain.

In spite of the physical suffering, hunger for survival drove him to push his face into the hot meat and tear it with his teeth like a wolf. Pausing only to breath and again diving into the hot flesh. When he was sated and exhausted by his efforts, he slept, enveloped and warmed by the hot dead flesh of the hunter's take.

Some hours later he awoke. Strengthened by the nourishing meat and driven by thirst, he found water and his pony a little over a mile distant. He managed to mount the horse and ride back to the meat wagon where he clumsily tied big chunks of the buffalo flesh to his horse. Keeping the sturdy mustang at a walk he directed it with his knees to walk south, away from his people, away from the vengeful Rutting Roe.

Dark Cloud knew if he returned to his people without the red-haired girl, he would have to fight Rutting Roe. He was too injured, too weak to fight. Rutting Roe would dishonor him, possibly cast him out or even kill him. He must bring the girl to Roe, or bring him her hair. Thus, he must return to the burned ranch where the girl was taken, hoping she would return there.

The journey took many days. From near the Red River to the Frio River there was only empty land for the most part. A little over halfway there along the branches of the Concho Rivers, there was some white settlement. He crept into a farmhouse at night and managed to steal a pie and a holstered pistol with two dozen bullets in the belt before the ancient hound awoke and alerted the house with his hoarse baying. Dark Cloud jumped back through the open window rolling and hurting his arm, but outrunning the old dog to his pony, losing neither the pie nor the pistol.

Two days further on he stole up on a hen-house at a tiny sod farmhouse and choked a chicken so it could not cluck. Miles away south, he built a fire and restrained his hunger long enough to somewhat heat the pink meat before devouring it.

The pistol came in handy the next evening just before dark when he rode up on a fat skunk and shot it four times before it died. His hunger overcame his olfactory aversion and with much cooking he was thankful to the skunk for a full belly. A cold stream and it's sandy bottom dispelled most of the polecats perfume and washed the grease of the buffalo meat he had slept in away from his skin, allowing the chill of the air down into his very bones it seemed. He built a roaring fire and warmed himself, then slept.

Creeping into a house on the edge of a small town he didn't know was Uvalde he was able to steal a whole pot of red beans spiced with peppers and onions. The pot was heavy and he couldn't carry it far from the house with his crippled arm, so he sat a hundred yards away and, using his hands, ate the entire pot.

He was very adept and much practiced at creeping and burglarizing in the dark of night as this had been Rutting Roe's modus operandi in his war against the frontier settlers. Leftover food, pies, day old biscuits and cornbread, whiskey, a coat, a hat, and even one little pig were stolen by the one-armed outcast in the area in and around Uvalde. The citizens were alarmed and began locking their doors and discussing who might be pilfering their belongings.

When he finally arrived at the burned-out ranch he found a well-camouflaged spot behind an outcrop of rock and a line of juniper on a hill a half mile from the place. He observed the freshly dug graves and watched a crew of cowboys as they finished searching the ruins for what could be saved. The crew loaded a wagon with charred black utensils, tools, pots, pans, dishes and other things Dark Cloud could not identify. Even after the cowboys left with the loaded wagon he remained away from the burned buildings leaving his hideout only to satisfy his thirst or at night to hunt for food.

After a week or more a buggy with women and girls arrived escorted by a contingent of what appeared to be rangers. Dark Cloud fought down the fear that rose in his chest. The appearance of the much-armed men alarmed Dark Cloud. He thought the rangers were a thing of the past, dissolved by the great war between the blue coats and the gray. Knowing the rangers would extend no mercy if he was sighted, he muzzled his pony so it could not neigh to the other arriving beasts. He also checked to ensure the juniper branches concealed him perfectly. He sat silently, perfectly still, watching.

When she took off the bonnet and shook out her long mane, the red-haired girl was easily identified. Dark Cloud watched her every move. She visited the graves alone, kneeling, standing, walking, sitting. After a time she came down from the hill to be held by the other woman there, obviously a kinswoman, or so it seemed to him. He had thought of taking the red-haired girl at the graves, but the older woman at the base of the hill would raise an alarm and the graves were too close to the rangers.

The women returned to the others but the red-haired girl soon separated herself again from the group. Dark Cloud saw her open the ground and walk down inside the earth. Now it was becoming clear to him how she had escaped from them. She was clearly what the Mexicans called a bruja, one who consorted with evil spirits. He surely would not follow her down into the underworld where evil dwelt.

In awhile, the older woman approached the hole and also stepped down into the ground. He wondered what they did there, but his curiosity could not overcome his fear. The two women stepped back onto the skin of the earth mother carrying a box and jars, surely containing powerful talismans, demons, or potions of wicked purpose.

How could he hope to catch such a one? He was sick, weak, one arm almost useless. Still, it would be a memorable deed to capture the red-haired sorceress. His own medicine would become great, the children would be told of the legend of Dark Cloud. Such a coup would ensure his acceptance with Rutting Roe and he would be welcomed home with great ceremony. He must find a way to capture her and not kill her. The tribal shaman had taught that the spirits of evil ones could enter your body at death and your spirit would be cast out of its fleshly home to wander forever alone in the cold winds. Somehow, he must capture the red-haired bruja.

Noah woke to a welcome breath of bacon, persuading him to stretch and smile on his bedroll. It was a good life he thought. He shook a tarantula out of his boot which leveled his exuberance. He told the tarantula after whisking it away backhanded, "These are my boots podnuh, they won't fit you. 'Sides there's only two of 'em."

The delicious fragrance of the pan bread and strong coffee brought him stumbling to the fire. Micah handed him a hot tin cup of coffee.

"'Mornin' Noah, bacon'll be ready in two shakes of a lamb's tail. They's sugar an' cream fo' yo' coffee if'n yo' wan' it."

"Naw, sugar and cream's fer the babies."

"Heh-heh. Well, I s'pose I'm a ol' baby then, cuz' I sho have a taste fo' it."

"Yore up mighty early."

"Yes suh. I wanted to be sho' that Mista' Black an' his men eat sumpin' 'fore they lef' this mawnin'. I 'spect they'll be awake early."

"That's mighty decent of you Micah."

"Jes' obeying the Lawd, Noah, treatin' folks like I'd like to be treated. It's plum selfish behavior if you truly b'lieve that you get back mo' n you give, like the good book says."

"Kinda' early for preachin', Micah."

"Jes' an observation Noah, don't mean no harm. Mawnin' Mista Black. Gots a bite of breakfast ready heah fo' you and yo' men."

"Why thank you Micah. Mighty thoughtful."

"That's what I tol' 'em Reading, but he "observed" that such kindness is actually sinful behavior for a true believer, since it's like loaning money at usury."

"Mmmm. Deep thought for so early in the day."

"Umhuh. My thoughts exactly."

"They's suga' and cream fo' yo' coffee if'n yo care fo' it Mista' Black."

"Yes sir, shore do. I'll take all the sweetness life offers."

A glance occurred between Noah and Micah. Noah shook his head and Micah smiled.

"Here's you some bacon an' bread Mista Black. They ain't no molasses though."

"Why Micah, you must have read my mind. Molasses or honey shore makes bacon an' bread slide down nice."

Noah sniffed and shook his head.

SEPARATE REALITIES

Mister Black ate and drank as he strolled over and kicked his men's feet to wake them for the repast. As they assembled uncombed and unwashed before the fire, Micah greeted each hand with a smoking plate, a steaming cup and a big wrinkled smile.

Sam trotted to the circle of light by the fire, seemingly indignant that others were eating bacon without him. Micah chuckled.

"I ain't forgot you Sambo. Heah you go boy," Micah said as he laid down some thick bacon on a flat rock.

"Noah, I'd be obliged if you'd pass along word that I've got some of Mabel's cows and calves at the ranch. I've also got as many chickens as we could catch when we got here. Would you tell her to let me know what I should do with them?"

"I'll sure tell her."

"And Noah, I'm plum tickled you and your men are here with these folks. I don't need to tell you how dangerous it can be around here when the Comanche are on the prowl. Just your presence will cut down on some of the mischief and murder around these parts. If there's anything I can do,..."

"Thank you kindly Mister Black. You holler if we can he'p you with anything."

All that day the men raked and toted and burned and the women scrubbed the soot from the stone walls. That evening Callie, Mabel and Ezekial discussed their partnership. Mabel hadn't been able to sell her home and leave. Callie had invited her to join her and Ezekial in ownership of the ranch. It could be their business and it could be home for all of them. The young Mabel and Ezekial were enthusiastic about establishing their own ranch, the future seemed bright. Callie was caught up in their excitement as well as the infectious wonder of her two energetic daughters. The commercial enterprise would be an equally shared ownership, one third each. Ezekial and Callie would pay Mabel two-thirds of the worth of the ranch, the worth to be determined by Mister Twohig, then they would all invest equally in the rebuilding and costs of the business. Initially, Mabel would reside with Callie and her daughters. A separate nearby house would house Ezekial, Noah and Chas. Beau, Ruby and Little Beau would also have their own house. A bunkhouse would be constructed for the hands with attached rooms for Luther and Micah. The bunkhouse would also contain a kitchen and dining room. The barn would be rebuilt in the same location, utilizing the high stone walls the wise German masons had built. The women's house would also employ the stonework which had survived the fire. The locations and arrangement of the structures had been discussed with Noah with defense against Comanche raids in mind.

Noah wanted to clear the brush and tree line back from the proposed structures another two hundred yards as well as arrange the buildings so that there were no blind spots or places close by where Indians could lurk or gather in a battle. The three partners advised Noah as to what they wanted and left it to him to devise a layout of the settlement while they went back into San Antonio to establish the partnership with Mister Twohig's help.

Micah allowed Chas to ride his thoroughbred for an hour or more on the way back to Uvalde. Along a stretch of land he knew to be level he allowed Chas to let the long-limbed horse to run. Not having run in awhile and feeling his oats in the cool air, he enjoyed stretching out and doing what he was born and bred to do, what he did best. Both horse and rider were exhilarated and soon winded.

Directing the tall horse up beside Micah and Ezekial, Chas gushed, "This boy can fly! I nearly blew off of his back! It seemed like he was jumpin' twenty feet a stride. What's his name Micah?"

"You know Chas, I ain't give that hoss no name, had'n' rightly thought 'bout it. You think of a name?"

"Yep. I think you should call him Bolt, you know, like a lightning bolt."

"Heh-heh. Dats' a likely name Chas, an' dats what we'll call him, Ol' Bolt."

A great smile broke out across Chas' freckled face and he patted the great muscled neck before him.

"Ol' Bolt's thirsty after that run. I'm gonna' ride up here an' let 'im drink."

"Don' let 'im drink too much Chas."

"No sir, I won't," Chas yelled back over his shoulder as he galloped toward the stream.

"That's a good boy."

"And a prize horse."

"Yes suh. Kentucky born and bred. All ol' Masta's studs were the best, jes' like Kentucky whiskey."

"He'll start a good breed here in Texas, him an' his cousin that Beau rides."

"Sho' will. They is money-makers I expect."

"We'll need to find some good mares an' let nature take its course, as Gramps use' to say. Next spring we'll have some fine colts," Ezekial added.

Sam had been running beside Ezekial's and Micah's horses and he stopped, sniffed the air and growled, gazing at the mesquite brush alongside the trail.

Staying beside and behind the buggy of the women and children and the three riders, Dark Cloud stayed well away as he realized the dog was very aware of him. He knew that his position on the hill behind the juniper had kept the air from carrying his scent to the dog, but now the wind, despite his efforts to dodge it, was carrying his scent to the dog's sensitive nose. Only the giant man on the great horse noticed the suspicions of the dog, and he alone kept his eyes alert and moving over the landscape where the dogs eyes directed.

The group moved steadily toward the settlement Dark Cloud had stolen from, stopping only twice to attend to natures call and rest the horses. Dark Cloud was forced to find spots on the hills to watch for the movements of the red-haired girl. He only hoped she didn't leave during the blindness of the night as he could not see well into the buildings of the town. Awake before dawn, Dark Cloud saw with the first light the gathering of the travelers at the livery. Two of the rangers must have come to join them in the night. Dark Cloud had thought of giving up his quest, but he had no choice. He must take the girl back to Rutting Roe, alive.

Noah had felt it was safe enough for the women to ride the relatively short distance back into Uvalde with Micah, Ezekial and Chas. And the road from Uvalde into San Antonio was well-traveled enough to make it reasonably safe also. The twelve to fifteen miles into Uvalde, taking only three hours or so, should present no problem, yet Noah was nevertheless uncomfortable not going along himself. It was a feeling, a premonition, and he had experienced such inexplicable sense of foreboding before.

It was late November and beginning to be chilly in the evening and early mornings. The Comanche typically wouldn't wander far from home during the winter. Sometimes they would make one final foray of the year when and if the weather warmed for a few days before the cold wind from the north blew down and dissuaded all peoples from unnecessary rambling far from fire and kin.

Noah and his first four hands had gone to work restoring the ranch, preparing level land for the erection of the planned structures and cleaning, clearing and burning the wreckage wrought by the Comanche. Everyone had been included in the planning and Noah's suggestions had been heeded, causing the lay-out to resemble a frontier fort. There would be no outer wall surrounding the compound of structures, but the houses and buildings would be situated in such a manner as to provide maximum protection for one another. Noah had added a few further precautions and protections in the plans.

After spending the day of his employers departure laying out and preparing the areas for the new buildings and while the hands finished their supper, Noah's thoughts kept returning to the uninitiated pilgrims traveling without his protection. Wasn't that his primary function as an employee, to protect them? What was he thinking letting them travel without him? This was still wild and wooly country, dangerous even for old soldiers like him.

Restless he paced and, from old habit, began to walk the perimeter beyond the tree line, viewing the place as an enemy would. As the sun sat on the horizon, big and red, Noah climbed the hill opposite the hill where the graveyard was. After all the years of fighting and chasing Comanche, he had learned some things and although it had been a few years, he had not forgotten their ways.

His eyes flitted over the rocky ground as he climbed at zigzagging angles up the hill in long, sure strides. His nose gave the first clue, he smelled something human. He stopped and surveyed the area, selecting a likely spot to spy on the people below. Parting the heavy lower limbs of the juniper he saw the still discolored soil that was darker than the surrounding dirt. Crawling to the darker patch of earth beneath the umbrella of the juniper limbs and leaves, he pinched some of the damp dirt and sniffed it. It was the smell of urine, human urine. They had been watched by Indians, there was no doubt, probably Comanche. They had been here yesterday or the soil would be drier. Where had they gone and why? The answer came instantly to mind and he hurried down the hill, skipping and slipping and sliding.

He spoke to his men as he caught up his horse and slipped the bridle and saddle on. He told Billy Hell to get ready to go with him and instructed the remaining three to continue the work they'd laid out and keep their eyes open for Comanche raiders.

Noah wanted to get to Uvalde before dawn which wouldn't be a problem, but he wanted to scout the road along the way in the dark and see if there was any sign of anyone trailing them. He also wanted to snatch a few hours sleep if possible, before escorting the group to San Antonio. There was no certainty that Comanches had followed them, but indications suggested the watcher or watchers had left off their observation about the time the others had left the ranch. He could only hope they had made it to Uvalde without tragic incident.

After a short night's sleep outside the livery stable in Uvalde, Noah and Billy joined the others for a hearty breakfast at the small cafe across from the hotel. The beasts were eager to exercise and they traveled a good distance through that day. Noah noticed Sam sniffing the wind and watched him growl low in his throat twice along the road to San Antonio. Ezekial also was aware of the uneasiness of his friend and mentioned it to Noah the first night east of Uvalde.

"Noah, Sam smells somethin' out there follerin' us."

"Yea, I know. I'm watchin' for 'em. I think it's a Comanche or two. Somebody watched us while we were at the ranch too. Keep it to yourself though Zeke, we don't want to alarm the ladies, nor do we want to let the Injun know we know he's out there."

"You gonna' catch 'em?"

"Maybe. Maybe not. We'll see."

Noah had advised Billy Hell that he did not intend to make the others aware that they were observed by at least one Indian, likely

Comanche. He wanted them to act naturally so as to increase his chances of catching the scout. He was curious why the observer was going to all the trouble to watch their every move. Whatever the watcher's purpose, it was his intention, and his job, to protect them, and he intended to be with them all the way.

The rest of the journey into San Antonio was uneventful and John Twohig took quick care of the legal particulars that established the three-way partnership. Mister Twohig also took the initiative to have Mabel's horse, who had finally arrived in San Antonio through the efforts of the U.S. Army, delivered to her as she left the bank. The reunion of Betty to Mabel was heartwarming for the partners to witness.

Noah found three more hungry ex-rangers and he hired them, fed them, and bought them a few drinks to seal the deal.

The partners made arrangements for building materials to be transported to the ranch and they bought two wagon-loads of food and other essentials. Noah stressed the prudence of sufficient ammunition. Noah also located some army 'surplus' for sale on the cheap and bought tents, lanterns, saddles and tack, as well as some rifles and sundry other handy items. On the fifth day after arriving in San Antonio, a caravan of seven wagons loaded with building materials, tools, supplies and settlers left for the Frio River country. Following the overloaded wagons was a herd of horses and mules driven by Beau, Ezekial, Chas and Noah. Billy Hell and the new hands rode point, flanks and drag.

Along the way Noah took time to reconnoiter their backtrail and wide out from their flanks. He felt in his gut they were being followed but was frustrated in every attempt to find the watcher. A few miles east of Uvalde Noah asked Ezekial to bring along Sam and slip away with him from following the herd. Once out of sight of the others Noah dismounted and took a tobacco bag out of his saddle bag in which he had placed some of the urine damp soil he had taken from under the juniper at the ranch. He let Sam get a good whiff of it, then stuck it back in his saddle bags.

"What's that?" Ezekial asked.

"Comanche piss," Noah answered shortly. "Let's go," he said as Sam had already begun trotting and sniffing.

They followed Sam as he moved faster and faster through the brush, and Ezekial and the big Percheron soon came to a place too narrow for them to pass and backing away and going around, he could only guess where the others went by the sound of Jughead's hooves.

Sam began moving faster and faster through the trees and Noah noticed the unshod hoof-prints and spurred Jughead past the running Sam until he caught a glimpse of a lone Comanche riding his pony hard away. He gave chase and slipped his Colt from its holster, but couldn't catch the slippery savage who lost him in the mesquite and juniper and oak. The pony's tracks vanished on a large slab of solid rock and he was forced to ride the edges of the rock in search of a track.

Even before Noah and Billy Hell had caught up with them in Uvalde, Mabel had known someone was following, watching. She knew. How she knew she could never have explained, but she knew. And when she noticed Noah and Ezekial slip away with Sam into brush her curiosity was whetted.

She had watched Noah from beneath her bonnet and knew he was also aware of a watchful presence nearby. She admitted to herself she was apprehensive, even fearful at times, but she felt the fear of another too. Her skin tingled at times under the intensity of the watcher's gaze. She felt hunted, like game must feel. She saw Noah scour around searching the ground just inside the tree line, it was obvious he believed they were followed also. Through the trees she saw Sam begin to run, then saw Noah and Ezekial spur their horses to follow Sam, she knew they were on the watcher's trail.

She faked a yawn and turning to Callie on the wagon seat beside her she said, "I think I'll ride Betty awhile."

"Alright Mabel. But please stay close to the wagons. You know I'll worry."

"I'll be careful."

Callie reined the mules to a halt and Mabel hopped down and untied a bridle from the side of the wagon. She loosed Betty from where she was tied to the wagon's tailgate and talked lovingly to the old horse as she slipped the bridle on.

"Go on ahead Callie. You're holding the others up. I'll be along."

"See that you do. Don't be long."

Mabel rode along beside the trailing wagons on Betty's wide sloping back for a short ways, then turned into the trees following the general direction Sam, Ezekial and Noah had taken, urging the horse into a lope.

The ranger followed the dog. Dark Cloud saw them closing the distance from less than a quarter mile away. He heeled his pony down the small hill he had stopped on and rode in and out of the small trees until he came upon a swath of solid rock. He turned his pony almost one hundred eighty degrees and returned almost the way he had come directly to the stream he had drank from earlier. He hoped the water would wash away his scent and he could escape the dog. He walked the pony knee deep down the stream back to the southeast. The sight of the red-haired girl mounted on the same old mare she had escaped on and riding toward him brought him to a standstill midstream, his mouth open in shock.

Fear of this mysterious woman caused his weakened body to tremble yet he fought back his terror and slowly led his pony up onto the sloping gravel bank, tying him to the brush beside the shallow stream, hiding him from the approaching woman's vision.

Knowing he must capture the woman and take her away alive, he quickly moved to intercept the path the red-haired girl was taking. He stood tight to the trunk of a great oak, his heart pounding in his ears. Listening to the trotting horse approaching, he gripped the barrel of his rifle with his one functioning and sweating palm. When she passed he took two running strides and swung the rifle with all his strength at the red hair.

His swing was a bit low and the heavy rifle butt struck her spine in the middle of her back, knocking her from Betty who jumped away instinctively and ran. Mabel struggled for breath as she lay in the grass, momentarily paralyzed by the force of the blow. She fought to regain use of her limbs.

Dark Cloud rolled her onto her back and the wide green eyes alight with shock burned into him and his own black eyes reflected them as evil and threatening. He clubbed at the frightening eyes with the rifle and they closed in unconsciousness.

Leading his pony beside her, he tied a rawhide rope around her neck and threw it over the horses neck. He rolled her back on her stomach and tied her hands together behind her. He tore a piece of cloth from the sleeve of her dress and tied it around her mouth, then mounted his pony and drug her through the grass to the edge of the stream. Dismounting, he splashed the cold water over her face awakening her and causing her to choke and cough up water around the gag.

Again his eyes covered the area searching for her horse but it was nowhere to be seen.

Sam had run so far ahead so fast that only Noah was able to keep him in sight. On the bank of the shallow stream the scent and trail had ended. As Sam stood catching his breath Noah rode up beside him, understood what had occurred and started Jughead upstream. Sam watched him go, his ribs heaving. After a half a minute, he caught a familiar feminine fragrance from the bareback of the slowing horse. He recognized the horse as one that had begun traveling with them and noticed the reins were hanging from the bridle and dragging. Sam made no logical determination from these impressions and clues, but his instincts, courageous and loyal, determined his reaction. He looked upstream where Noah had disappeared, barked loudly, then began to run in the lingering scent the horse had left in her wake in the air and on the ground as it escaped whatever had frightened her.

Topping a mound, Sam saw Dark Cloud jerk the rope around Mabel's neck, pulling her across the shallow stream. He barked, growled and ran into the water causing the Indian pony to rear, slip and fall into the cold, rushing water. Dark Cloud's shoulder was driven into the stone bottom of the stream and his breath was taken by the shocking pain. Before he could recover, the dog had his privates between his sharp canines and this elicited a fearful, uncontrollable scream. His penetrating cry was silenced as Mabel, balancing on her tied hands behind her, wrapped her legs around his head pulling him under the surface of the clear water.

Dark Cloud fought with his one good arm against the dog, then against the strong, young legs of Mabel. The twisting attack of the dogs teeth between his legs and the strength and weight of Mabel around his neck did not allow him to get his legs under him and save his life. He saw, through the cold, clear water, the brilliant blue sky and the white light of the sun as he died in the grip of the red-haired woman's legs and the dogs jaws.

When Mabel felt the man's struggles cease she continued to hold him under the frigid water until she was certain he was dead. Sam was on the bank barking and shaking his coat free of the soaking water as Noah pulled Jughead to a sliding halt beside him. Jumping into the stream he waded to Mabel and carried her to the bank. He cut the gag tied around her mouth and she coughed and spit as she tried to speak. He cut the ties that bound her hands, removed his coat and placed it over her shuddering shoulders.

Striding back through the stream, he pulled the floating corpse to the bank and out of the water.

"No sense fouling the stream with a rotting carcass," Noah said as Mabel stared wide-eyed at the still, drenched body of Dark Cloud and tried to catch her breath as she shivered wildly.

This was the scene that Ezekial rode his Percheron upon.

"What in the world,...?" he managed as he beheld the drenched and the drowned.

Between shaking breaths Mabel explained briefly some of what happened. As she finished her tale Betty came walking up and put her nose on Mabel's head, nudging and nuzzling. It was Betty's return that finally brought the tears to Mabel's green eyes. Mabel stood and hugged the horses neck, then suddenly moved and knelt to hug Sam as she silently cried and shook from the cold and shock.

"Go on Zeke, get her back to the wagons and get a fire started to warm her up. Tell 'em to circle the wagons. I'm gonna' make certain this is the only Comanche around. Go on."

Ezekial lifted Mabel up onto Betty's back. Mabel took Betty's reins from Ezekial hands with a meaningful glance. Noah watched the youngsters head out for the wagons accompanied by the shivering Sam. He surveyed the dead man's wounds and shook his head. Pulling the corpse further away from the stream, he then sat and removed his boots, dumping the water out. His eyes searched the surroundings and he spotted the Indian pony two hundred yards away rolling in the yellow grass, then standing and shaking water from his coat. He would circle, watch the pony and return to the Indian's dead body, knowing if another Comanche were around he would try to recover the horse and the body. He mounted and rode a wide circuit around the wagons and only went into the welcoming fire when he was relatively sure they were safe from attack. He had found no sign of any other Indians.

Sam and Betty had been brushed and dried by the girls and they continued to make a fuss over them as they lingered by the fire. Mabel sat close by in dry clothes with her head covered in a fresh bonnet. She had told Callie and the others that the Comanche she had killed was the same one who had tried to rape her and been knocked away by Bloody Roe. She believed he was also the one who had chased her and been shot by the meat hunter from the fort.

"Hmmmp. Guess he wanted you bad Mabel. He's been following you ever since you escaped. He must have believed you were big medicine. Prob'ly amazed by your hair. Prob'ly never seen red hair before."

"Well," Ezekial chuckled, "He won't never see it again neither."

He looked at Mabel and the smile melted from his face. He saw the effect of his words and regretted speaking. Mabel was looking inside herself, pensive, obviously fully realizing she had killed a man for the first time. She was emotionally shaken and retreated inside a wagon, Callie following her beneath the canopy.

"I shouldn'a said that."

"You didn' mean no harm, she'll get over it in a day or two. Killin' a man for the first time is,…well, I 'spect you know 'bout that Zeke."

"Shore do. Shoulda' known better."

"Let's load up and get on into Uvalde."

The fire was covered with dirt, cinches were tightened and everything and everybody was again loaded. In two hours they were getting down at the livery in town. Ezekial caught up with Mabel.

"Mabel, I'm sorry. I shouldna' said nothing…"

"It's okay Ezekial," she patted his arm, smiled and added, "I'm okay. Just cold. And hungry."

"Me too."

Together they dried and curried their beasts, feeding and watering them and getting them settled amidst all the busyness around them. As they left the livery together Mabel stopped, looked up at Ezekial and softly said, "I'm glad he's dead Ezekial. He deserved to die. He would have done worse things to me than killing me. And he's one less devil to contend with for our land. That's our ranch now partner an' I'll be damned if any Comanche runs me off! We'll fight for that land, just like all my family did."

"An' we'll whup 'em too Mabel, jes' like you did."

She squeezed his giant arm and grinned, nodding.

Chapter Eleven

"Accept whatever comes to you woven in the pattern of your destiny, for what could more aptly fit your needs?"
---Marcus Aurelius

"Each generation imagines itself to be more intelligent than the one that went before it, and wiser than the one that came after it."
---George Orwell

"Be joyful always; pray continually; give thanks in all circumstances,....."
---I Thessalonians 5:13 (KJV)

"You girls get out of that water, you'll catch pneumonia! And get your stockings and boots back on. Land's sakes! And Sallie, you quit that infernal whistling, you'll spook the stock. Where did you learn to whistle like that, girl?"

"Ezekial taught me Momma. He said that way I can call my horse and he'll come to me."

"A horse would be more likely to run from that loud whistling. But everybody around for miles could hear you whistle. Besides, you don't have a horse."

"I mean, when I get one."

"And who said you'd get one?"

"Callie, you oughta' let these girls learn to ride," Noah started.

"We know how to ride," they said in unison.

"Yes, they've been riding since they were little, thanks to their daddy who tried to make them into boys, bless his soul, but I don't want them riding out here where it may not be safe. I want them close to me with all the Indians and bandits and varmints around here."

"Callie, it may come a time when they could outrun trouble on a horse, they couldn't outrun banditos or Comanches in that buggy."

"You may be right, but a heathen would have a very bad day should he try to take my babies from me."

"Ma'am, ain't no outlaw nor redskin gonna' harm none of you ladies. The Lord and these men won't 'llow it." Micah assured her.

"I have faith in the Lord and in all you men, but me and my girls will put our hands in if it comes to a fight. They've both been taught to load and shoot back in Virginny, the Unionists weren't well liked by the Secessionists. We had to be prepared."

"If any of them boogers see Ezekial they'll be too scared to bother us," Nellie added somberly as she slid into her boots.

Everyone chuckled at Nellie's serious proclamation.

The group had allowed Mabel to show them some of the ranch that the river ran through and a cave that Indians had used long ago in which several primitive paintings of a hunt had survived. It was a Sunday break from the work of the building that had consumed their every day for the past month.

The Texas hill country wasn't as beautiful in winter as it would be in springtime with the blossoming bluebonnets, Indian paintbrushes and blankets, wine cups, Mexican hats, yucca and prickly pear. But even now, at the beginning of winter, the juniper, cedar and oak forested hills gave the fragrance of life. The hardwoods grew in the river bottom, giant pecan and oaks, cottonwoods and graceful willows. From limestone caverns gushed crystal springs that had run under the endless Edwards Plateau to surface all along the Balcones Escarpment. German settlers made efficient use of the clear rushing water, establishing mills and breweries and adding a natural charm with strong stone houses and fences that meandered over the hills, all built to last for many generations.

Mixed amidst the stoic stone structures of the German settlers were the Mexican's adobe houses, and there were a few long, low log houses. In the town of Uvalde there were beginning to be more and more milled lumber houses and businesses and a few of brick. But here, west of Uvalde, farms and ranches were far between. It was the very edge of European settlement and none too civilized.

The urge to ride out further into the wild west welled up in Noah's chest. It was there he was revitalized, felt younger, stronger, more energetic. There was a shining in his eyes as he looked westward to the plains. The closer he was to the Comanche, Apache, Kickapoo, Mescaleros and the other wild tribes the more alive he became. The urging inside him was for war, an attacking war. This defensive employment was necessary, but he yearned to take the fight to the enemy.

Like many who had witnessed the atrocities of the plains tribes, he considered them less than human. There were many who viewed the Indians as demons along the line of the frontier. The two sides of the struggle were trapped in hate, fear, sorrow and death. And through all the blood and horror, the mutilation and rape, the cruelty and death, the spark of life burned bright and intense, though only for a moment for many young warriors and women, wasting away in war. Selfishness, greed, exploitation, theft, destruction and murder became normal and justified behavior. White men were perceived by the red men as all the same; dishonorable, liars, thieves and killing devils. The Indians were viewed with the same prejudiced opinion. There could be no trust, no peace.

The Mexicans they had hired as well as Billy Hell and the recently hired ex-rangers were well-versed in the ways of the Comanche and were ever vigilant in their protection of their employers and one another and their religious watchfulness infected the others. All those who had been born and raised in the peaceful east began to acquire the habitual careful behavior of those raised on the frontier.

The group at the river made a picnic and fished, enjoying the leisure of the Sunday afternoon. Mabel had rode her old horse with the men while Callie and the girls had come in the wagon on the trek. In mid-afternoon they started back to the ranch and Mabel, being recruited by the daughters, wheedled Callie into letting Nellie and Sallie ride Betty back to the ranch. They were ordered to stay near the wagon and to ride beside Micah, whom Callie trusted implicitly. The girls loved old Micah and loved to listen to his stories.

"Micah, what is that bird?"

"Well child, I can't rightly answer that. What, 'xactly do you mean?"

"I mean what's the name of that bird?"

"I kin tell you a name Nellie, but just 'cause you know a name don't mean you know what sumpin' is."

"When Ezekial told me you were Micah, I knew then who you were."

"No child, you only knew a name. You didn' know nuttin' 'bout me, only what you could see. You didn' know I was a Christian, you didn' know I could read, you didn' know I could play harmonica. The quicker we put a name to sumpin', the quicker we stop considerin' what a miracle this thing, this animal, this person God has created really is. That ol' bird would somehow lose its myst'ry and lose your int'rest if I tol' you it was a scissor tail. And the next time you saw one you'd likely think, 'Oh thas' jes' a scissor tail, I know what that is'. But you see, you'd be foolin' yerself, you really wouldn' know nuttin' 'bout it 'cept a name somebody done named it. You have to look deep and study things 'fore you kin know what they really is."

The scissor tail swooped down and bit at Sam's fur as he was jogging along in front of them, then circled quickly and swooped down on him again.

"Ha! You see that?"

Then the bird rose in the sky and dived at Sallie who sat behind Nellie and pecked at her hair. Both girls screamed.

"Whoa! Did you see that? Get him away from me!"

Micah chuckled and waved his arms at the bird as it circled and dived at them again. They screamed, waved their arms and Betty broke into a trot, startled by their behavior. Micah rode close and settled Betty speaking soothing sounds.

"Why'd that bird attack us Micah? We wasn't bothering him."

"How you know it was a him. May ah been a hen jes' protecting her nest, or meybe jes' wanted some of your pretty soft hair for a nest. Like I said, you jes' don' know about nothin' nor no one jes' cause you know a name. We can't ask ol' Misses Scissortail why she pecked ya'll an' ol' Sam, we kin only watch, an' learn. Some things you'll never know, even if you study them all yer life. But, they's a kind of beauty in the myst'ry, don' you think?"

"Yes."

Sallie grew thoughtful as she watched the circling bird with the long tail feathers. The bird was a mystery. How did it glide so gracefully and fast? Where and who was the wisdom that designed the bird? And the world? And all that's in the world? And the sun and the stars and so much it made her dizzy to think of all that was. There was much mystery in it all as Micah said. And Majesty.

She was silent and smiled sweetly as she looked up at Micah's hoary head.

Sam enjoyed the getaway as much as anyone, even enjoyed the play with the feathered friend. He wasn't mad at the bird, the bird was just doing what the bird did. Sam grinned up at Ezekial on his high horse and grinned on one side and winked. Ezekial laughed in response, as he always did.

Along the way back home Sam would veer away from the other's direct path and explore the new land, running sniffing, looking and listening. He had discovered that this new place was filled with scents and sights that were the same, yet unique. With the approach of winter the wildlife was dormant. There was olfactory evidence that spring would bring an abundance of creatures forth from their holes and dens, but now the land was graying and silent.

Ezekial surveyed this country that was now his home and felt the subtle size and quiet dignity of the rolling hills and canyons. He knew the trees called post oak to be well suited for pens, fences and corral posts. They had come upon many various numbered groups of the wild, long-horned cattle and watched them graze on the high, yellowed grass as well as deep-green winter grass. He even noticed purple grass in places. It was wonderful ranch land; usually mild weather, abundant natural feed and plenty of good water.

The sky seemed bigger here to Ezekial, but then so did the land. He realized how stupid it would sound to say so. Eagles and hawks hung miles up in the white clouds, mere specks that floated on the clear air. The cold night sky held so many stars they reminded him of white flour dusted across Gramps dough board and the sunsets were daily paintings of ever original, glorious shades of color only God could produce on His palette. Every evening the painting in the sky was different evoking a different mood and seemingly more beautiful for its ephemeral nature. It was a time natural to a man to reflect on the wonders of creation. A time to let all troubles, all thinking subside in the presence of such a display of power and of wisdom and of beauty, and be absorbed into the spirit of the eternal moment.

Chas was of the age or the temperament to ask many questions and as he considered Noah the ultimate authority regarding many matters, Noah was pestered with regularity with Chas' inquisitiveness. There were times when Noah enjoyed talking with Chas, as now when they had enjoyed a relaxing time away from the work of building the ranch. Chas listened intently and learned through other's experience. He was one of the rare people whose learning did not require personal miscues. Much of Noah's learning had come through mistakes and suffering, he'd been alone in the world from an early age, and headstrong. Chas learned from just watching Noah at times, Noah habitually repeating behavior that had become almost instinctual through the years of surviving in the wild, unsettled lands, behaviors that might make the difference between prospering or perishing.

He was enjoying Chas' respectful listening now, he often spoke things he didn't know he knew and surprised himself. No one had ever listened to him with the avid interest that Chas displayed. The pair honed their abilities, intelligence and knowledge of one another, and they became closer.

Noah knew there was much of life on the land that could not be taught, that must be absorbed. Some survived the experiences and learned. Some neither learned nor survived. Though he struggled to explain some things that must be sensed, he knew that many lessons cannot be contained in the simple sounds men make with their mouths. Words, Noah knew, were often inadequate tools, messengers which try to place perception of reality from inside one skull to another. The whole of reality could not be fathomed or reduced to be contained in a cranial box, so Noah showed Chas as much as he told him.

Noah showed him the prairie dog's holes that were so dangerous. He demonstrated how to ease up onto the ridgeline and the summits of hills and to put a rock or tree behind him so as not to be an obvious silhouette against a background of sky. He showed him that most game could only see you when you moved and how to rope a longhorn steer. Chas watched Noah and everyone and everything else and learned quickly through his innate and curious intelligence.

Chas already knew to be alert to the nuances of his horse's ears for foreknowledge of something his own ears could not hear. To watch the horses nostrils, his eyes, his head, the way he shied, trembled, turned or slowed his pace. The horse conveyed information in other ways than words, as did the other animals. The manner and direction the birds flew at certain times told tales as did their songs of silence. The ways the cows grazed, the lounging of lizards on hot rocks, and the sawing sound of the cicadas or their sudden hush spoke to those who would hear and understand.

Noah taught Chas to listen for water and watch for certain signs of a stream or spring. He taught him to always approach water with caution as water drew others, both beneficial game and dangerous foe. He taught him to build small cook fires and fires for warmth, how and where to lay his bedroll and how to place his head to sleep so he could hear and smell as he slept and see quickly upon awakening. He taught him to ride with his rifle ready and his pistol close to hand. Chas soaked the teachings up eagerly. Noah was impressed with both his aptitude and attitude.

And Beau learned just as fast. He was small but athletically built, all lean and hard muscle and gristle. His hands were hard and rough with work yet still dexterous. He was fast of hand and foot which enhanced his chances for survival and success in this wild country. He weighed a circumstance before riding into it and took good advice and put it to use. Noah had decided he would do to ride the river with, at least when he could keep his mind on his business and off of Ruby.

That he loved Ruby there was no doubt. His every gesture in her presence communicated how he cherished her. Everything he did and all he hoped to be related to his love for her. And he saw Little Beau as a miracle, a magical creation of their love. If life continued to smile on them and didn't bring them sorrows, they had a chance to live a life of wonder, joy and fullness.

Beau realized that he needed to accept guidance from those he trusted, by Micah, Callie and in some instances by Noah. Noah taught him about the land, about cows and the native people. He taught him how to shoot and how to scout for Indian signs, but he couldn't accept Noah's hating all red men before he even knew them. He understood why Noah hated them, he knew Noah's heart had been busted to pieces when he was a boy and his young heart had never healed. Everyone Noah loved had been murdered, mutilated and desecrated and the horror was more than a boy could bear. Noah's mind and heart still dwelt on that past and defining horror and he believed he was doing good work, being loyal and devoted to his parents by slaying the red man. Beau believed Noah didn't realize or care that he was creating young red and white killers in his own image by his playing God in his attitude and actions, perpetuating the horrors of hate.

Beau's big thoroughbred pranced through the warm air beside the wagon which held the happy, tittering ladies. Beau's eyes were full of Ruby and her gaze across the valley and her changing facial expression drew his eyes to the distant figures of Chas and Noah who were sitting motionless peering up on the crest of a low hill where an Indian mounted on a paint horse was looking down at their party. Beau rode beside the halted wagon and lifted Little Beau from the saddle before him, handing him to his mother in the wagon. He loosed the rifle hanging under the cantle and let the long-legged horse gallop to where Noah and Chas sat astride their mounts, still and silent.

As Beau rode up beside Noah and pulled his reins, a dozen more Indians rode up around the Indian on the hill and they all began walking their horses down, approaching the three of them. Noah heard Callie holler at the hands to arm themselves. He stood in the stirrups, turned and held up his hand, stopping them. Billy Hell trotted his horse up beside Chas. The wagons and all the horses came to a halt and a seemingly long silence ensued as each group examined the other.

Among the Indians were blacks, either freed slaves, runaways or free-born. There were also three Mexicans among them. The Indians were dressed mostly in white men's clothes, pants, shirts, boots, hats, coats, but the hats were adorned with long feathers and the clothes with beads, conchos and tooth and bone adornments.

A squat Indian with a wrinkled, leather face spoke into the quiet.

"Got tobacco?"

Noah looked over at Beau and asked him, "Got a cigar with you?"

Beau felt his shirt pocket and answered, "Got two."

"Let 'm have 'em."

Beau pulled the cigars out and sidled his horse closer to the Indian. The Indian took the cigars with a nod of his head and put one in his pocket, cutting the other into three pieces. He lit one of the short stoogies with a Lucifer match, then handed a section to each of the men beside him. The Mexican lit his piece with the lit end of the other's cigar, but the black man bit off half of his piece and chewed it, putting the other piece in a pocket.

Blowing out smoke luxuriously, the old Indian asked, "You now live at Curtsinger ranch?"

"Yes."

"Is good. Curtsinger was good man. Brave, but a fool. Think Comanche come no more. Comanche kill all."

"Not all. Curtsinger's daughter still lives." Noah motioned down the hill to the wagon of women.

The Indians murmured among themselves in other tongues and the old Indian said, "Yes, see red Curtsinger hair. Girl has strong medicine. Hair should be on Comanche lance."

"Well, it's not. Her hair's still on her head and it'll stay there. Any Comanche that comes 'round here anymore will lose his own hair. Where do all ya'll come from?"

"Live in Mexico, across Rio Bravo, near town Piedras Negras. We are Seminoles, Cherokee, Creek, Kickapoo, Mexicans and Negroes. We live there fifteen,...no, sixteen years."

"You followed Wildcat there?"

"I am Wildcat. You are Noah Lister, Texas Ranger."

"I'm not a ranger anymore. I'm foreman of this ranch we're building here on the Frio. What are you doing on our ranch Wildcat, here in Texas?"

"We hunt and trade."

"Looks like you haven't had much luck."

"Many deer here. We send men back with deer meat to our women and children. We go farther north and west, to the Concho Rivers to find buffalo."

"Hmph. If you go too far you'll find Comanche." Noah made a backwards weaving motion with his hand, denoting the 'snake you do not see' which the Indians called Comanche.

"Comanche no bother us."

"If you're friend to the Comanche, you're no friend of mine."

"No friend of Comanche. They hunt in Mexico, we not fight. We hunt in Texas, they not fight."

"Well, if we see Comanche, there'll be a fight, that's sure."

"You have bullets, tobacco, sugar to trade?"

"No. Not now. We may have more supplies later to trade, but only with our friends. If you won't help us fight Comanche, are you our friends?"

Wildcat turned his yellowed old eyes on Beau and said, "We are many like you in Piedras Negras. You come. Bring bullets, horses, tobacco, whiskey. We trade with you. Find fine woman for you, fat and black."

"I've got a woman."

"Maybe want two, three woman," Wildcat smiled.

"One's plenty."

"One's plenty if right one," Wildcat chuckled.

"We may need help in spring herding longhorns." Noah said, "We'll pay trade goods for a few good men."

"Maybe so," Wildcat answered, then turned his horse and rode away, the others following.

Beau, Chas and Billy Hell watched Noah as he sat and watched the band of survivors, refugees and misfits ride away. After a couple of minutes Noah turned Jughead and rode down to the others. As he rode up to the wagons Callie spoke.

"Ain't them Indians Noah?"

"Some. But they won't bother us. Not today. They see that they don't outnumber us and see we have 'em outgunned. They say they're huntin' buff, but I expect they'll steal cattle and horses given an opportunity. That's some of ol' Wildcat's bunch. Around eighteen forty-nine or fifty he gathered Seminoles, Caddos, Wacos, Creeks, Cherokee, Kickapoo, runaway slaves, Mexican outcasts and some white trash and settled across the Rio Grande from Eagle Pass near Piedras Negras, Mexico. Coacoochie, that's the Injun name for Wildcat, he left Florida because the gov'ment promised land west of the Mississippi, but they sat his people down among the Creek who gave them no voice in affairs. The Mexicans welcomed him and his refugees, thinking they'd protect them against other Injuns. But the Kiowa, Comanche, Wichita, Apache and others still raid and Coacoochie's people don't take sides. So, seems to me, he can't be trusted."

Those who listened to Noah withheld their judgment. It seemed, by the little they had been told and the little they had seen, that those who followed Wildcat trusted him and respected his judgment. He had taken a ragtag, diverse group and found them the home they didn't have, gave them the self-respect they may have lost, some measure of hope and confidence in a future. Though none of these who listened to Noah spoke of it just then, to varying degrees they all understood that Noah's own distrust and hate of Indians clouded his judgment and he painted them all with the same brush.

"Will they bother us?"

"No, I reckon not, not now. They may steal from us later, or come to beg and trade. We'll have to be prepared. They ain't that far away. They ain't mean like Comanches but I expect they'll steal. Let's go ahead home. I think we're safe, but stay close and keep your firearms handy."

Noah rode to the front and everyone followed his pace, and his lead.

Wildcats bunch had stopped atop a nearby hill and watched the new settlers pass by. As Billy Hell who was bringing up the rear passed the still watchers, he swung a leg over the saddle and rode sideways. Farther on, he swung one leg over the horse's rump and rode backwards, smiling, waving, and keeping an eye on the hunters. As he passed out of their sight beyond the hill he stood, waved once more, turned and dropped into the saddle. Yelling, "Ahhh-ha!" Chuy and Caballo, the Mexican hands, yipped the high pitched Mexican wail, a cry sounding of both pride and pain, and pranced their ponies in a circle.

"Why are those men acting like that Momma?"

"Honey, they're men and hard to understand sometimes. I expect it's bravado, showing they're not afraid and that they're ready to fight. Maybe it's hope and relief that they didn't have to fight, kinda releasing the tension that built up when they thought they might have to fight, I don't know. Baby, they're men. They do silly things."

That evening, back at the ranch houses, as the girls washed the supper dishes, Callie gathered Mabel and Ezekial and strode to where Noah was sipping a steaming cup of coffee beneath a cottonwood.

"Noah, I want to speak with you about the way you think of those people we met today and the manner in which the hands you've hired acted."

"Yes ma'am?"

"Well, it seemed more than a bit provocative. I intend to live in peace here with my neighbors whoever they may be if I possibly can and I will not abide you men pawing the earth like wild bulls and daring these people to be our enemies. I've been told the word Texas comes from an Indian word or tribe meaning friendly, and that's what I'll expect from those in my hire, to be friendly and promote friendship and be neighborly unless and until forced to be otherwise."

"Ma'am, with respect, I wasn't tryin' to stir up that bunch today. I was demonstrating strength and courage so as they understand it. An' I's friendly. I gave 'em tobacco and tol' 'em we might need hands to round up cattle in the spring. But these people often mistake kindness for weakness. If we was to give 'em a cow today, the day would soon come when they'd take whatever they wanted. Injuns are better understood as beasts, wild beasts mostly, than as human. Christian kindness is as foreign to their nature as to a snake."

"The antics of Billy Hell and the Mexican hands were uncalled for. They seemed to be trying to start trouble and I never want to see that behavior again, especially when my children are present and may be endangered."

"Miss Callie, you hired me to be foreman of this ranch ya'll intend to establish. Being foreman means protecting your property as well as yourselves. I have spent my life holding the line in Texas against redskins and bandits and, with respect, I won't be told how to do that by a greenhorn Eastern woman who has never dealt with these animals before. With all respect ma'am, ask Mabel what good neighbors redskins can be.

"Right now, these pa'ticular renegades may be friendly, but let 'em tie up with a few Comanche bucks an' they'll kill us all at the first chance, scalp us, burn us an' do worse to you females they 'llow to live. You've hired me to do a job of work an' I'll lay my life on the line for you and yours, but I will not allow you or anyone else to persuade me into befriending snakes or allowing murdering scum to approach you or your babies."

"But, surely we could catch more flies with honey..."

"Catch more arrers in the back too. Now ma'am, we may's well get this straightened out now. I'll do my job, earn my wages, but I'll do it the way I know to do it or you can hire another man."

"Callie," Mabel spoke softly, "I'm young, but I've lived my whole life here. An' I know you can't let these people get too close.

They don't like us, an' they don't think like us. It may seem cruel or un-Christian, but it's the way most ever'one b'lieves 'round here."

"Can't you see Noah, how I feel your men's behavior endangered my daughters?"

"Callie, I kin see how you might see it that way, but that behavior protects 'em more 'n it endangers 'em. When you decided to buy a ranch in west Texas, you endangered your daughters. You didn't know it, but you did. Trust me to protect all of you the way I know or turn 'round and head back to San Antone and civilization."

Ezekial spoke.

"Noah, you have experience dealing with these people, we don't. You've fought Indians and Mexicans for a lot of years. Maybe you see 'em all as enemies now. Now I know I'm just a big ol' kid and I don't know much, but it seems Injuns are just people like us, just like Micah and Beau and the Mexican hands. Why can't we jes' try to get along?"

"Zeke, Micah and Beau and the Mexican hands have been around civilized people long enough to know how to act. Y' know, those ol' milk cows Callie bought in San Antone are cattle same as one of these wild, mossy-horned, brush-popping, snot snortin' long horned bulls, but you can't treat 'em the same jes' 'cause their both bovine. The milk cow will welcome the hay and give you milk, but that wild-assed bull will graze where he wants and put a horn through your gullet and not lose any sleep over it."

"I see your point. But can't we be Christian-like?"

"Zeke, you kin be a rancher, or you kin be a missionary, but you can't try to be both or you won't succeed at either."

"Noah, don't be angry at us for our ignorance," Callie interjected, "We're creatures of our Christian upbringing."

"I understand that. But this ain't a New Testament country. This is the land of the Old Testament. We're uprooting tribes who've lived here for generations. An' they'll fight, tooth and bone."

"Well, I suppose we need time to learn Noah. Thank you for protecting us as you know how. Have patience with us."

"Yes ma'am. An' please have patience with me. I know I'm an ornery ol' cuss, but I mean well."

Noah placed a roving picket out that night and every night thereafter, three men per night in three shifts of two to three hours each. When one got sleepy he was to awake the next. Every man took his turn except Micah the cook and his helper. He showed the inexperienced ones where and what to look for. Sam, the horses and cattle were good at watching too. The horses didn't sleep as much as people.

Several trips had been made to the mill run by the Mormons a few miles from Smithwick on the Colorado River. The mill was located on a waterfall down a steep grade of rock on a stream that fed into the Colorado between Burnet and Smithwick. It was a long haul, but the good Mormons did good work at a fair price. Wagons of heavy lumber, small lumber, shingles and even some sturdy furniture was transported to the building site.

The barn was finished first, with a large room at each end which would serve as a tack room and a supply room later on, but in which they would live, separated by sex, until the housing was complete. The work crew grew as friendly neighbors arrived with many skilled hands to contribute and the buildings were completed quickly. The freight wagons were always busy coming and going pulled by the long mule teams. They arrived, unloaded their lumber and stone, ate and rested the night, then left early next morning for other loads.

The roof of the barn was completed a half hour before a freezing rain began and, as the stone walls still stood and the barn doors had been rebuilt, everyone gathered around the two cook stoves that Callie had bought in San Antonio and that Callie had the men fit with flue pipe to remove the smoke. The warm air was scented with the resin of the recently cut wood and the animals in their stalls. All the residents and helping neighbors were grateful on that windy, wet and freezing night for the shelter of the new-old barn.

The construction was slowed for three days of ice and wind. Finally the sun broke through the clouds and the ice melted in the puddles on the ground. Flocks of geese were heard and sighted high overhead heading south.

A couple of years before, in 1863, President Lincoln had established the fourth Thursday in November as a national holiday, a day of thanksgiving to Providence for the abundance of blessings given. Most of the native Texas weren't aware of the holiday until informed by the federal troops, but Callie, being a Union sympathizer and wife of a U.S. officer, was aware of the holiday and began baking cakes and pies and other dishes in preparation. She sent out three hunting parties of the men until they came back with enough turkey to feed everyone. She had a calf butchered, bought a pig from a neighbor and had venison too. She opened tin fruit she'd purchased and cooked potatoes and stuffing. It was a feast they had rarely seen.

The main house had been finished just two days before the fourth Thursday, so Callie had the men set up plank tables on saw horses inside, employing barrels and boxes and whatever would serve as chairs. The dining room, the parlor, the kitchen and what they would later call the office were filled with makeshift tables and chairs. A few of the neighbors celebrated the holiday with them.

After all had gathered around and found places at the tables stacked with food, Callie asked Ezekial to pray a prayer of thanksgiving. Ezekial was surprised and unprepared. It was usually Micah who did the praying, but feeling his face heat and redden, he bowed his head and waited for the words to come, praying a silent prayer for fitting words.

"Lord,.....you've brought us safely a long distance to this beautiful land You have given us,...and we thank You. There is a growing love here amongst us,...and its love that'll make this a home. And we thank You for the love. Thank You for the care and concern of good neighbors who have lent their hands to build this ranch with us. We ask You to bless them with abundant reward for their brotherly love.....We thank You for one another...for the friendships and the joy we share,...We thank You for the strength and the opportunity to build a life here on this fine land You have given. Please bless our efforts and keep us safe from those who would harm us.......We thank You for this fine day and this fine meal You have given us,.... and thank You for the bountiful game and rich earth to grow the seed You have provided. Father, bless our efforts here. Give us prosperity, health, joy and peace with all people. Thank You for bringing us all together in this time we will always remember, this wonderful beginning of a wonder-filled life You have prepared for us…..May we care for one another as a family, because Lord,…You know all of us here has lost precious members of our families. They are sorely missed, every day. No one can ever take the place of these dear loved ones who we pray are now with You,…but bring these broken pieces of families together into a,…a special family,…and let us grow close together and strong so that nothing but You calling us home will ever separate us. Remind us You are always with us, beside us,…blessing our efforts to build a life, a ranch,…a home. Let us never fail to love one another as You love us. We thank You for your love….Amen."

"Amen."

"Amen."

"Amen."

Sam barked, smiled and winked one eye, licking his chops looking at the steaming turkey. Everyone laughed.

"Can I fix Sam a plate Momma?" Nellie asked.

"You sure can baby, and give him plenty," Callie answered.

"Give him whatever he wants, he's earned it," Mabel added as she ruffled his fur. "I thank God for Sam, he sure saved my bacon. Give him some of that ham too, come to think of it."

Everyone smiled. Even Sam.

On one of Noah's scouting excursions Tom was led by a honeybee to their hive in a standing, hollow pecan tree. Soon thereafter Noah shot a white-tail deer and after cleaning it, he cut through the skin around the neck just above the shoulders and stripped the hide down to the heels and cut it from the legs. He sewed up the rips and the bullet hole with buckskin strings, utilizing mesquite thorns as pegs to keep the strings taut. Turning the hide inside out with much patience and strength and ensuring all the holes were closed tightly, he blew it up and tied it closed, laying it in the sun to dry.

A fortnight later he returned and scraped the deer hide again making the bag more supple. He built a small fire close to the base of the honeybee tree then began adding green mesquite so as to smoke and calm the bees. With cheese cloth over his hat and tucked down into his leather coat he was protected from bee stings and could see just well enough to guide his gloved hands in gently sawing a section out of the hollow trunk. Slowly, he scooped up honey and filled the deerskin with fifteen or twenty gallons of rich, golden nectar. With Micah's help, he loaded the honey in a wagon and brought it back to the settlement.

They hung the case by the neck to a rafter in the tack room in the barn so that a leg could be untied and honey would flow out in a slow, sweet stream. Everyone was delighted with the honey. It became a regular part of their early breakfast.

The wagons made three more round trips to the mills near San Antonio, Burnet and Smithwick, the huge freight wagons carrying the heavy milled lumber for the building. The wagons would be unloaded and the wagoneers would rest the night and leave the following morning for another load. By Christmas, most of the rough building was completed.

Callie convinced herself it would be best to ensure that her girls could ride as well as anyone and asked Beau to accompany the freight wagon to San Antonio and, with Ruby's influence in securing a good price from her ex-employer in Gonzales, buy the girls well-broken and gentle horses as Christmas gifts. She allowed Chas to go along and pick his own horse after securing his promise to keep secret the girl's gifts.

Callie also wanted a piano so she could continue to teach the girls, but decided to wait until a herd could be gathered and sold. She gave Ruby money for presents for Beau and her son as well as to buy treats for everyone for Christmas, especially the children and the poor, deprived cowboys. Such little thoughtful blessings bought an inordinate amount of loyalty, though Callie's intent was simply to share God's goodness and grace.

The first Christmas together at the old Curtsinger ranch was a joyous gathering, well-remembered by all. The fare, the fellowship, the laughter and love began to further bond these who had worked so hard side by side to re-establish the ranch. These first holidays together were part of the foundation that knit the group into a family. Work, struggle, hardship and celebration, these are some of the cornerstones of a heartfelt community.

SEPARATE REALITIES

As the new year of 1866 dawned, a freezing rain had covered their world with ice and days were spent gathered round the fires in the new, separate dwellings. The women's house, as it was called, was finished first and was directly across from the big stone barn at a distance of around seventy or eighty yards and faced north. A smaller house was built behind and above the women's house on a rising knoll which was where Ezekial, Noah and Chas now dwelt. This is where Ezekial carefully put Gramps old rocking chair he had brought from Carolina. Thirty yards beside Ezekial's house on the rise a slightly larger house was built for Beau and Ruby. Ruby had a room built for a kitchen, but no cook stove had yet been secured.

The two cook stoves had gone into Callie's kitchen and into Micah's kitchen in the bunkhouse. Callie had ordered another cook stove through the hardware store in San Antonio but it hadn't arrived by the new year. The shiny new cook stoves were a source of pride and wonder and were kept sparkling clean and in almost constant use.

At a neighboring ranchers suggestion, the bunkhouse had been built with sixteen wooden bunks, eight on a side, with a warming stove and long worktables down the center. At the end of the bunkhouse, farthest from the barn was Micah's kitchen and a bedroom attached to it where he slept. Both these rooms were off-limits to the other hands and Micah possessively enforced the boundaries. Between the kitchen and the bunkhouse was a dining room with its own stove, table and chairs. The bunkhouse was located between the women's house and the barn, the three buildings forming a three-sided plaza, all on the same level. Other out-buildings and smaller houses for married hands were being built around in studied and mutually protective locations, each house protected by others.

Every house had native stone fireplaces and chimneys well built into framed, planked and expertly adobed walls which Chuy and Shorty took pride in. Tall narrow windows with glass panes were installed with shutters on the inside in case of Indian attack and with transoms over the doors to help dispel the summer heat.

The corrals beside the barn could be seen from all the other structures as horses were a primary target of Indians and banditos. At one end of the barn was a tack room and an area for a blacksmith's chores. Between and above Ezekial's and Beau's houses was a rock smokehouse. Another storm cellar was dug into the side of the small hill beside the one Mabel's grandfather dug so everyone had room to hide from the tornadoes which often threatened. There were many short gray days too cold to venture far from fire and everyone did inside chores repairing tack and mending boots and coats, cleaning guns and playing dominoes and cards. After the ice was gone the men went out to hunt and brought in deer, turkey and quail. And then the winter came again bringing freezing rain and cold, cutting wind. It was a time to stay close to the fire.

In the bunkhouse many tales were told over the whistling wind in the eaves. The hands wore all the clothes they owned through the day and kept most of their clothes on through the night. Hot coffee and tobacco were constantly consumed.

Billy Hell came in from seeing about the horses in the barn and squeezed into the only open space round the stove.

"Move over and make room Luther, it's freezing out there."

"Heck, this really ain't bad weather. Back in the mountains in western Virginia it got cold. Why, it got so cold one February night I stood up in the campfire to melt the ice off'n me and the ice that melted froze in drops 'fore it hit the ground. Looked like pearls or ice marbles layin' all 'round the fire."

"Aw, Luther, quit that lyin'"

"Ain't no lie. The icicles from off'n the roof at the home place was two foot thick and reached to the ground. Had ta' take an axe an' cut our way out. The snow covered up the whole house, we couldn't get no air. Had ta' dig a tunnel up to daylight 'fore we plum suffocated."

"C'mon man."

"You don't know what cold is. We had ta' dig a path through the snow to the stream to get water an' take an axe to chop blocks of ice to melt in a big pot. The water in the stream had froze so fast we found fish froze solid inside the ice. We had water and supper in the same pot."

"Yer fulla' beans Luther."

"You jes' don't know. They was buzzards froze on the glide, jes' floatin' frozen through the sky. The doggone clouds froze and stuck to the sides of the mountains. A man could walk right off the side of the mountain and onto a cloud."

"If it was that cold, how'd you keep from freezing?"

"Mountain moonshine o'course. Keeps the heat in a man's skin. But there's danger if you open your mouth to talk. The cold would freeze all your spit and your tongue would need several applications of that moonshine to thaw out."

"Luther, your lying makes me wish your old tongue would freeze."

"Now that ain't no way to be. Jes' cause you ain't 'spearienced real cold like I have ain't no reason to wish me harm. A frozen tongue is a painful thing."

"Your unfrozen tongue is painful to me."

The door opened and frozen rain and air accompanied Ezekial into the bunkhouse. He shook the ice off his coat and hat by the door, then moved closer to the stove as Noah hurried through the door behind him.

"Ya'll ain't playin' cards nor dominoes?" Noah asked.

"Naw, Billy Hell done won all our wages 'til Spring," Chuy answered.

"Chuy, me and Ezekial been talkin' an' we decided we'll need some more hands when the weather clears. Ezekial needs some men to help him clear land, plow and plant. He wants to grow some corn and oats, feed and truck. And we'll need some hands to round up what cows we can drive outa' the brush and get branded. We need to drive some of these wild longhorns to market and get money for 'em while they're still worth somethen'."

"Noah, they ain't many men way out here who ain't already hired, 'cept fer bandits. We may have to go to San Antone to find any hands willin' to fight cows and Injuns," Billy Hell pointed out.

"I was thinking of going over there to Wildcat's place in Mexico and picking out some of the good 'uns there. Family men who'd stick when things got tough. Think we could find any?"

"Meybe, wouldn't hurt to go see," Chuy replied.

"Thought we could ride over there when the weather turns more favorable."

"Awright."

"Ezekial here wants to ride south and west out to a ranch his ol' army friend's family has. The Chavez family. You heard of them?"

"Yep. It's a good ways out there. More'n a hunerd miles I'd say. Take the best part of three days on good stock. Shouldn't be no Comanche or Kiowa out prowling this early though."

"You know where the Chavez ranch is?"

"About. Chinati has been there."

"Yes, I know Chavez rancho," Chinati said.

"Would you guide Ezekial there Chinati? And help him talk to the Mexicans?"

"Chure."

"An' while they go to the Chavez place, we kin go to Wildcat's settlement Chuy, and see if we kin find some good hands we kin trust."

"Hokay."

There were still frozen-over puddles in the low places when Ezekial and Chinati rode out. Chinati headed due west to the Rio Grande which surprised Ezekial, he thought the way would have led south.

Noah had decided to remain at the ranch. After sleeping on his decision to go with Chuy to Coacoochie's settlement to hire hands, his instinct bade him stay. He felt that the Comanche would come and he might never forgive himself if he were absent when they came. He chose Billy Hell to go with Chuy, he trusted the judgment of each of them.

West of the Nueces the land was flat all the first day, and the horses seemed to enjoy the journey. They were frisky and had to be held back to preserve them for the miles ahead. In the late afternoon they ran into low brush mesquite which was so thick that it barred their passage, and Chinati turned northward to go around it. When questioned why not turn south as Mexico surely lay to the south, Chinati explained that the mesquite had migrated from Mexico by Mexican goats who ate the sweet beans and spread the seeds northward, so usually this particular species of mesquite grew thicker to the south. Sure enough, the mesquite thinned by sunset and the tired pair found a protective copse of oak against the chilling evening breeze to camp in. After settling and feeding the horses and themselves they sat with blankets round their shoulders by the fire admiring the winter array of stars and listening to the ringing silence of the spinning earth. Sleep came soon, and deep.

The air grew colder as the dawn neared and both men stirred and rose to feed the sleeping coals. After quick coffee and a bite they were on their way again.

The third day they rode up on a gushing clear water spring forming a creek which Chinati called the San Felipe. They followed the creek about eight miles down to the Rio Grande, then followed the river north for a mile to a wide, shallow gravel crossing. On the Mexico side of the Rio Grande, Chinati led Ezekial due west away from the river for an hour until they came upon another stream and they followed it southward.

After another hour of following the meandering stream they heard galloping hooves and stopped in the shelter of a large growth of sage as the sound of running horses grew louder and closer. In less than a minute around a dozen ponies were driven by them by four vaqueros who yelled and screamed to keep them bunched and moving. The two trailing drovers noticed the two watchers and broke off from the heard to investigate. Ezekial smiled at the familiar posture and carriage of one of the pair of small riders, it was definitely Samuel, his old army friend. But, it was the other rider who held Ezekial's attention. He was mesmerized.

Long, raven hair trailing and waving behind her under a flat sombrero, the small, thin frame moving in rhythm with the shining stallion, the woman held his gaze even as his old dear friend reined up beside him and stood in his stirrups to reach and embrace him.

"Ezekial! Mi Amigo. You've come so far!" Samuel gushed, "It's so good to see your big face."

"Good to see you too Samuel," Ezekial managed while he could not tear his eyes from the dream of a woman beside him.

"Ezekial. Ezekial! Do not stare. It is impolite. This is my little sister Patricia, this is my army friend Ezekial Robertson."

"Hello Ezekial Robertson."

"Hello. Patricia." Ezekial spluttered.

"Samuel, Patricia, my boss is enchanted. Forgive him, por favor. I am Chinati and et es an honor to meet you."

"Chinati," Samuel grinned and moved to shake his hand.

"A pleasure," Patricia said and touched her hat.

Samuel pushed Ezekial's shoulder and said, "Hey! Amigo! Are you drunk?"

"No. I'm alright," Ezekial smiled and blushed, beginning to regain his composure.

"She is beautiful, no?"

"Your sister?"

"Ha! Who else hermano?"

Red faced, Ezekial answered, "Yes. She is."

"We'll go to the casa, eat, rest, then tonight we'll talk. Come my friend, it's not far."

It was good to be with his true friend Samuel, but Ezekial was constantly distracted by the proximity of Patricia. She was captivating. Graceful, unpretentious and natural, not pretty actually, but handsome like a well-formed deer. Intelligent, inquisitive, aware, with an easy smile and a charming laugh. Strong, energetic, full of life, engaged and interested in Ezekial as if he were as intriguing as she. Friendly, as her brother was friendly. And both Samuel and Patricia were immediate friends with Sam.

The second day Ezekial and Chinati spent with Samuel riding over the ranch and being taught practical applications of ranching. Sam spent the day with Patricia, enjoying a bath and the luxury of her company and her undiluted attention. The third day Patricia kept Ezekial at the hacienda with the legitimate explanation that he needed to learn the economics of the ranch and farm business. As she taught him from the balance books receipts and inventory list, her mother Consuelo was their constant escort, but not knowing English, she was only eyes and not ears. And the young pair spoke of much the mother may not have approved of.

Ezekial was surprised that Sam would stay with Patricia all day while he rode away with Samuel. Sam typically wanted to stay with him every minute. There was something soothing, assuring, and worthy of trust that was instinctively conveyed from Patricia's good and true heart. Ezekial didn't want to leave, but Chinati reminded him of their responsibilities back home and he was torn from his old and his new friends.

They woke on the second morn on the trail to find ice covering the hard packed ground reflecting the weak white light filtering through thick, low clouds. Ezekial carried Sam across his saddle and sharing his coat, only his head appearing betwixt the buttons from time to time. Not stopping to eat they pressed on until mid-afternoon, then found a steaming spring to let the animals drink. There, by the vaporous stream, they put feed bags on the horses and shared the delicious mixture of meat and chilies wrapped in thick flour tortillas that Consuela and Patricia had prepared for their journey. The chilies added a welcome warmth inside them. There was an abundance of the burritos as the Chavez family had become familiar with Ezekial's appetite.

The wind came with the night, blowing stinging needles of ice against them. On the south side of a hill they found a few fully-leafed spruce to block most of the winter's breath. Sam snuggled close to Ezekial's chest beneath the heavy hide coat and they fought the cold for what little sleep they got. Chinati somehow managed a fire just before the dawn and the whistling wind stopped suddenly, eerily. The quiet bringing a foreboding feeling of closeness. And then the snow began to fall, slowly, softly, falling like feathers on their shoulders slumped toward the fire. They slugged coffee down, chomped some chow and hurriedly headed home, knowing it was near.

The girls met them at the barn and had a hundred questions. Luther tended to their shivering beasts and they headed to the warm women's house to eat a noonday meal of chicken and dumplings, fried potatoes and cornbread. It was good to feel the comfort and care of home.

But, the following day as he was about the work of helping complete the interior of one of the small houses built for the married hands, Ezekial grew quiet and distant. His heart ached as he found he missed Patricia, and it was a good ache, not like the lonesome ache he had in missing Gramps. Through the following days he envisioned her lithe form as she moved around him and heard the joy of life in her voice. He longed to be with her and soon found reason to ride to the Rio Grande once again.

Arriving at the ranch, Ezekial explained to Samuel that he wanted him to teach him more about the diseases these wild cows had, how to treat them and how to put weight on them for the trail. He needed to make a drive the next spring and wanted Samuel's advice. Samuel agreed to teach him what he knew and did his best, but it was quite a chore for Ezekial to keep his mind on steers and ticks when Patricia was so near. Samuel's wife, Rosita, had died of pneumonia while he'd been away at war and Samuel understood the manners and ways of love. It was fortunate, in God's often mysterious methods, that the government in Texas had taken the portion of their rancho in the United States, because the move back to his parents place across the river occupied his otherwise grieving mind.

At the first Ezekial had felt dizzy when he looked into the depths of the dark pools of her laughing eyes. He could hardly utter a complete sentence without stumbling over his words. But her friendliness and earthy personality soon put him at ease. It seemed they'd been friends and more forever.

Ezekial had taken Chuy with him on this second trip and he learned from working with the Mexican hands while Ezekial endeavored to justify his presence there as a student of the ranching business also. Too quickly Ezekial began being truant in Samuel's school and attended Patricia's classes exclusively. But, between Consuela and Samuel, the pair were not alone often. Still, all they saw was one another.

Patricia wasn't a tiny girl, but neither was she big. She was thin, long limbed. Certainly she felt small when with Ezekial, yet she discovered and relished the new-found power she had over such a man. A fast learner, she quickly knew how to wrap him around her finger. Her mother smiled at the child's behavior and shook her head.

The pair had long conversations through the short winter days, mostly of their dreams and aspirations. Patricia told him how she loved to read, learn new things, see different places. The location of her home limited her desires. Books were rarities in the Coahuila state of Mexico, hundreds and thousands of miles from any meaningful civilization. She loved to pick the brain of any stranger, anyone who had been anywhere other than northern Mexico and Southern Texas, she questioned Ezekial thoroughly about the places he had been. She dreamed of going to school, traveling to distant shores, meeting interesting people.

Her excited, exuberant nature inspired Ezekial. He imagined how wonderful life would be traveling the world with Patricia, sharing the wonders and pleasures with her. He was pragmatic enough to realize he had struck a bargain with Callie and Mabel to build a successful ranch, so his next few years were promised. He believed he could make a good return on his investment of the money he had been paid for Gramps' farm, but there was much work ahead of him. There were thousands of cattle for the taking on their many miles of ranch and even more on the unclaimed land surrounding them. And the level land could be irrigated to produce cash crops. Unlimited land to grow crops and cows and cash and when he had accumulated enough money, then he could take the two of them anywhere. This dream and ambition inspired him and motivated him. His only reluctant restraint was that he must leave Patricia to accomplish his goals. He never voiced his ultimate intention to her, nor his deep feelings for her, he felt sure she was aware of his plans and his infatuation. He was sure everyone must know how he felt about her. And they did.

Their mother, Consuela, took Samuel aside and told him it was improper for Ezekial to be spending so much time with Patricia, she was too young for so much manly attention. Besides, she told Samuel with emphasis, "El es muey grande." So, Samuel spoke to Ezekial, advised him that their mother felt Patricia was too young for so much male company. Ezekial assured Samuel that he meant no discourtesy and would not do anything to hurt Patricia. Samuel replied that he certainly knew that Ezekial meant no harm nor disrespect, but for proprieties sake, he must refrain from spending so much time with his baby sister.

As was his bent, Ezekial apologized to both Consuela and Patricia, expressing that his intentions were honorable and would henceforth limit his visitation with Patricia to less frequent chaperoned meetings approved by her mother. Patricia made protest, but yielded obediently to her mother's glare and quietly stared at Ezekial under long dark eyelashes as he made his retreat.

When he left the Chavez ranch the second time Samuel and several of his chosen hands rode with him and Chuy. Upon arriving home, Callie, Mabel, Ruby and the girls came to the barn with steaming cups of coffee, sugar and cream, as well as freshly baked pie for all of them, serving them with welcoming words and pretty smiles. This prompted one of Samuel's men to pronounce, "Este es un campo de los angeles." Samuel told Ezekial that their ranch had been christened "Angel Camp" in honor of these beautiful ladies. And so it was.

The hands at Angel's Camp had begun finding the wild cattle which were thick between the Nueces and Frio rivers and driving them to catch pens they had built at four different locations on the ranch, several miles apart.

A branding iron was fashioned with a halo over an A for Angel's Camp, and they struggled to brand as many as they could find. There were many wild and dangerous bulls, young and old, that had to be roped, heeled, hog-tied and castrated as well as branded. Some of the well-formed and large young bulls they didn't castrate, but released them to stud.

One misty morning in mid-March, the men left early for the northern reaches of the ranch in search of cattle, leaving only Micah and Luther to shoe horses and cook for their return in the evening. Ezekial and Sallie persuaded Sam to stay at the ranch on days like this when Ezekial would range far from home and Sam would be wearied trying to keep up with the horses all day. Sam had quickly become a fair cow dog, instinctively doing what was required of him, but the hands would be riding far and hard this day catching crazy cows and risking injury. Sam wasn't really needed and the girls loved having

Sam with them. Callie was comforted by his constant presence with the girls also. Beginning in the days of riding with Sam and tending his wounds after he had fought for them at the river ford, Sallie, Sam, Chas and Nellie had become real and lasting friends.

The hands of Angel's Camp pushed found cattle to a catch pen they had constructed about ten miles from the ranch houses. Ezekial and Shorty made a good team in the pen, Shorty roping and tying and Ezekial wrestling the cattle down. Chuy and Chinati found one gathering of cattle that numbered over sixty filling the pen with wild, bawling bovine. Shorty and Ezekial were bumped and ducking horns for hours getting these beasts branded. They required other hands aid in managing to castrate the furious mossy horned bulls.

Billy Hell's hand got caught between his rope and saddle horn, luckily it was his right hand as he was left handed. And the horse Beau was riding got a blunt horn in the shoulder and again it was lucky that he was riding a cow pony and not his thoroughbred. By mid-afternoon Shorty and Ezekial were all in from handling the wild beeves, as were all those in the saddle and their horses, so they decided to head back to the ranch and prepare for an early start in the morning.

By Ezekial's tally they had branded one hundred three cows and castrated nine bulls. They had even found a cow with Samuel's brand on her and were amazed. They discussed how this cow could have made it across the river and the long way north and east. Their neighbor's brands were also among the gathered cattle and Shorty advised Ezekial that this was the beef that Texas ranchers typically ate. Ezekial laughed but Shorty was serious.

When the other men had rode out this morning Micah had helped the women haul water in buckets from the well to fill the big cast iron pots they heated in the fireplace and on the cook stove in the women's house to use in washing clothes. He also filled the washtubs for them. There wasn't a lot of clothes really for the number of people, they didn't own a lot of clothes and it wouldn't take very long.

An hour after eating dinner at noon Micah and Luther led all the mules into the barn and placed them in stalls, then began a fire to work with the bellows. The mules had all been down many a long road and had loose shoes and hooves that needed trimming. Luther pulled all the shoes and, using the old ones for patterns, fashioned new ones with the hammer and anvil after heating them red hot.

After more than two hours Micah drove the last nail to hold the shoe on an impatient, rabbit-eared mule when he and Luther heard the first whoop and the sound of horses running. Moving quickly to the barn door they saw Sallie and Nellie beside the house staring transfixed at the corrals by the barns. They had been gathering clothes previously hung on lines stretched between poles beside the house. The horses and a few mules were being driven out of the pens and northwest toward the Nueces River by half a dozen almost naked and painted Indians. They screamed like wounded cats astride sprinting ponies, waving lances, bows, and rifles.

Another half dozen had ridden to the house and the sound of Sam barking, the wild screams and the beating hooves of running horses alerted Callie, Ruby and Mabel and they dropped their washboards in the washtubs and all ran in different directions. Mabel yelled, "Indians!" and ran with wet hands to the gun rack. Ruby jumped to where Little Beau stood with wide eyes in his little round face and snatched him up into her arms, quickly placing him down into an almost empty flour barrel. As she lowered him down into the barrel she admonished him, "Sssss! Hide and seek," and smiled at him in reassurance. "Stay here!"

Callie started to the nearest window to call for her daughters when a shot from Luther's rifle in the barn dropped a painted Indian as he tried to come in the open window. Another red monster tried to squeeze through the narrow opening and Callie grabbed a bucket of boiling water from the cook stove by the bail and threw it into the screaming maniac's red face which was suddenly much redder and screaming even louder after his unexpected baptism of fire. As he writhed, half in and half out the window, Mabel dispensed a double dose of lead to remedy his pain effectively putting him out of his extreme misery. She then pushed his body out the window with her boot.

Micah was putting away the tools when an arrow pierced his shoulder. He looked down at the quivering fletches just below his eyes, then heard the scream and looked up to see the grimacing, painted warrior running at him with a long knife in his hand. Without conscious thought, he threw the heavy hammer into the Indian's chest, which drove him back. As he gathered himself to attack Micah again, Luther put two shots into him in as many seconds and he fell onto the dirt and straw on the barn floor.

Micah ran to his room at the end of the bunkhouse to grab his loaded rifle, not feeling any discomfort from the shaft piercing him. Luther had worked with a rifle beside him through the morning and was shooting steadily at the red-skinned hellions from the barn door. Micah had been repeatedly told to keep a firearm near him, but had not admitted the necessity until this mad moment. Running back out of the door of the bunkhouse, he saw the Indians around the women's house, brandishing their weapons which were draped with bloody scalps and dancing feathers and ribbons.

Callie screamed at the girls to get inside and they had already pulled up their long skirts and ran for the house. Mabel and Ruby had already moved to the windows firing at the painted naked devils. Luther and Micah were doing their best to move to the house too but the galloping Indians ponies with the arrow and bullet shooting Comanche hindered their efforts. Callie grabbed a rifle and ran out on the porch just as one of the cruel fiends rode beside the running Sallie and butted down on her head with his rifle. Turning and sliding his horse to a stop he swiftly dismounted. The men coming from the barn and all the women were afraid to shoot at the Indian attacking Sallie fearing they may hit one of the children.

Nellie screamed as the wiry redman bent over her sister and Sam exploded upon him, ripping and tearing his arm. The savage managed to club the fierce dog several times with his rifle and finally Sam fell lifeless beside the sprawled Sallie. Nellie picked up the rifle that had fallen from the demon's hands and pulled at the trigger as she pointed the barrel at his chest. Uncocked, the rifle didn't fire. The small man tore the gun from the child's hands and swung it against her little head, knocking her several feet to the ground.

Callie had witnessed all this and screamed like a banshee as she ran to protect her daughters. An arrow turned her back the way she had come and put her on the ground. The Indian started for the fallen Callie but Luther and Micah, shooting as they came, changed his mind and he replaced his scalping knife, lifted unconscious Sallie and threw her over his horse's withers. Riding low over the back of his horse he stole the helpless child away as everyone was afraid to shoot and possibly hit Sallie.

An arrow protruding from her side, Callie cried and crawled to the small body that was Nellie, her hair matted in blood. She screamed at the fleeing Comanche who had taken her sweet, innocent Sallie.

Mabel's eyes locked with the crazed, obsessed eyes of one of the rushing red men and a paralyzing fear stopped her heart as she breathed the name of the attacking Comanche.

"Bloody Roe."

Rutting Roe saw the fear in the red-haired girls eyes as he charged. He raised a coup club and screamed his victory as he neared the porch, his dark, crazed eyes burning into her frozen blue eyes. He turned his horse to leap onto the porch or swing the club and take her again, but her fear gave birth to courage and she raised the rifle and fired directly at his vicious face.

Noah thought he heard gunfire as he rode toward the ranch. He rode faster toward the source of the gunshots, but his cow pony was exhausted after chasing cows all day. With about a mile to go, he saw the herd of horse's being driven by Comanche along the river northward. He knew his horse wasn't capable of giving chase and also knew that no horse would be left in the corral.

The horses and thieves were perhaps a quarter mile eastward and drawing closer. He reined in the cow pony and pulled his rifle from the saddle holster, letting the animal blow and walk away, reins trailing the ground. He kneeled on the hard packed ground and cocked the lever action. As the horse herd passed as near as they were going to get he began firing as fast as possible into the air and waving his arms and yelling. A few other of the hands were quickly beside him doing the same thing. He heard firing to his right and saw Ezekial yelling and firing his rifle directly in front of the stolen herd, causing the leading horse, one of the Kentucky thoroughbreds to veer away from the river toward him. Four or five of the horses behind followed the stallion's lead.

The Comanche in the rear closest to the breakaways kicked their ponies to head off the bunch quitters and when they came in range, riding directly at him, Noah started picking them off. His first shot knocked a Comanche off his pony, the second shot wounded another who turned away back to the herd. He shot a horse out from under another and the de-horsed Comanche waved his arms while running back to the others. One of his kith turned his horse to pick him up, but turned back when Shorty found the proper elevation and hit the fleeing redskin in the spine.

Noah hollered at Beau, "Catch me that thoroughbred!"

And Beau loosed his catch rope as he whistled at his horse. Billy Hell, Chuy and Chinati joined him and quickly turned the quitters and stopped them. Noah loosed the girth and slid his saddle off the winded cow pony, then took the bridle from his mouth. He had the wild-eyed thoroughbred saddled, bridled and mounted before the others had stripped their tired mounts of gear. All he said as he rode away was, "Come along soon as you can."

The Kentucky bred stallion ate up the distance between him and the retreating herd. He looked back and saw four hands whipping their horses, doing their best to come along. He fleetingly wondered where Ezekial went, then immediately knew that he would hurry home to check on the women and children. A pang of conscience shamed him, but he had little hope Ezekial would find anyone alive. He hoped Zeke would not have to find their mutilated corpses in a burning wreckage as he and many other survivors had. Centering on the hate burning in his heart, he focused on the thieving and murdering Comanche ahead of him, fully intending to catch and kill them all.

Chapter Twelve

"Greater love hath no man than this, that a
man lay down his life for his friends."
---Jesus, John 15:13 (KJV)

"Blessed be the Lord my strength, which teacheth
my hands to war, and my fingers
to fight:"
--King David, Psalm 144:1 (KJV)

"Before you embark on a journey of revenge, dig two graves."
---Confucius

Brandy was miserable. She was fat and tired and lazy and ugly and depressed. Shoestring was confused, nervous, apprehensive, wary and wondering in her non-logical mind what she had done or not done to cause Brandy to hate her and ignore her. Hunger drove her to bring her food dish to Brandy to remind her she had not been fed, then silently suffered the groaning, complaining, whining verbal abuse that had become normal behavior for the goddess of her life.

Brandy was so incredibly fat. Shoestring's inherited sense made her aware that her friend was in a family way and she wished Brandy would hurry and have her puppies. Then maybe they could move from the current misery to another.

All the women at her shop were sugar sweet to Brandy and wanted to do everything for her. She hated it. And so she stayed away as much as she could. She was sick of being at home all day and night too, but everywhere she went people stared and whispered behind their hands. But, she didn't care what they said. And she wondered what they said behind her back.

She couldn't get comfortable. Walking, sitting, lying down, standing, it was all a misery. She couldn't sleep and her thoughts were stuck on that bastard Noah Lister. She hated the dirty, low-down, old son of a bitch and oh how she missed him. Wanted him. Needed him. She dreamed in her waking imaginings that he would come to her. But, her intuition and experience of reality advised her that it would not happen. She would have to find him, somehow convince him that he loved her and needed her, that they were meant for each other. But his damned baby would not allow her to go anywhere. It was a chain, a trap, a prison.

Truly, she loved the baby inside her so much. After all, it was created in a moment of their pure love, a sharing of their souls. It was a tender portion of each of them, a melding of their love.

She hated the living, swelling, embryonic weight inside her. It reminded her of her foolishness, her naiveté, to let herself yield to the ludicrous emotion of love. So many men had told her that they loved her, typically just after copulation, and they were all so full of bull. And now, she must admit, she was just as full of it. The baby was the issue of that sneaky, untrustworthy, broken-down, ungrateful, cowardly, Texas-raised beast and she wanted no part of it.

But, another part of the maturing miracle within her was the wonderful, vulnerable, innocent and precious part of her that had been lost so long ago. The part that laughed and smiled and yearned for fullness of joy in life and love. And a part of it was the funny, gentle, thoughtful, strong, pensive and wise man who had given her a reason to hope for a better life,……the sorry son of a bitch.

****

Rutting Roe's horse ran with the other fleeing Comanche who had not expected such fierce resistance from women and two old men. Somehow he managed to stay atop the panicked pony. These brothers who rode with him who were last to retreat seemed fearful of him. He was a fearsome specter, a bleeding half-a-face. Blood blurred his vision and ran in thick rivulets down his throat, chest and arm, carrying fragments of tooth and bone. There was yet no pain, only surprise, shock and survival instinct giving him strength to remain conscious and hold onto the horse. The horse would be his salvation, or his demise.

He had not believed the red-haired girl would shoot, he had clearly seen the great fear in her eyes. He had been sure that his medicine was invincible. Had his strong medicine deserted him? He had never doubted he would take her as his prisoner and impose his wicked will on her until he tired of her. He had never experienced defeat and he was stunned, perplexed, disoriented.

Many miles away from the red-haired girl's ranch the others became aware of pursuit and hurried on without him. He found a deep bank beside the river and here he fell from his horse. He crawled to the river and washed his terrible wound. His fingers told him that the bullet had hit the bottom of his cheekbone and somehow had deflected down and through his mouth to exit through the back of his neck. He had spit out much blood and many pieces of tooth. Now he washed bone and blood from his torn and tender flesh.

As his exhausted horse stood in the shallows and drank he untied and pulled loose a blanket from his bundle and wrapped it around his weak, shivering body. The pain overwhelmed him and he lost consciousness, falling onto the gravel and sand riverbank.

He was awakened by the terrible pain and the cold of the night. He managed to eventually build a small fire against the steep bank and he huddled close to the flame wrapped in the old trade blanket. Hate grew inside him fed by the pain and the sting of defeat at the hands of a woman. The hot hate warmed him and gave him strength and resolve. At the first violet hint of dawn in the eastern sky he mounted his horse despite the tremendous pain and headed him north. His kinsman had left him to die so great was their fear, but the pony knew the long way home and plodded slowly on.

Roe had become overconfident as he had observed all the men ride away from the ranch on the morning before. He had a warrior follow the men and knew they were too far away to help. With the number of warriors with him he was sure he could take all the horses and all the women. He never imagined that two old men and three women could defend themselves from his brave, experienced men.

He had abandoned his usual practice of creeping in and quietly killing the men before taking the women and children and this terrible wound was the result. He vowed to return and take the red-haired sorceress who had surprised him by daring to fight him. Yes, he would surely return, but not for many days. He must go to his women and make them tend him and feed him until his strength and strong medicine returned to him. A time would come, a night, and he would take the bruja and she would see and feel the strong medicine of Rutting Roe. For each day he waited and suffered his wound, she would suffer two. Thus he vowed to his spirit.

Ezekial had dismounted directly before the charging herd of horses, holding his own horse with difficulty in the path of the stampede, yelling and waving his arms. He managed only to split the driven herd and dropped to one knee adding his rifle to his comrades firing from a distance away. The Comanche rode through the withering fire hanging by their heels on the away-side of their ponies. One fired his rifle at Ezekial as he galloped by behind the herd and missed, as did Ezekial, but a brother warrior hard on his heels put an arrow in Ezekial's horses neck.

It took all of Ezekial's great strength to hold the wounded and panicked horse, but he managed. He broke the arrow's shaft before the fletching and remounted. He must get to the women and children and this horse must carry him.

Even in his own extreme anxiety Ezekial felt sorry for the horse. This may be his last run, he might fall dead anytime. But the great heart of the Percheron carried him steady and sure toward home.

Ezekial became aware he was trembling, so great was his fear for his friends, his family. There was only Luther and Micah there to protect them. Did any still live? He took notice of the empty corral as he rode past right up to the porch where he jumped from the exhausted horse.

On the porch lay dear Sam on his side, his head bleeding above his half-closed eyes. He whimpered at the sight of Ezekial and tried to rise. Ezekial knelt and spoke softly as he examined the wound and knot on his head. He patted Sam tenderly and lovingly.

Nellie came running out onto the porch, her own hair and face streaked with blood, screaming, "Ezekial, the Indians got Sallie!"

"We'll get her back Nellie. Don't you fret," he assured her and laid Sam gently down and ordering him "Stay."

Walking into the house he saw Callie struggling with Luther and Ruby, trying to get up from the floor where they had held her to remove an arrow and tie a tourniquet around her and over the wound which was gushing blood with her exertions.

"I've got to get Sallie! Let me up!"

"We'll get her Callie. You're too weak right now, you'd never get to her. Lay still! Luther is there any horses left? Where's Mabel? And Micah? Ruby?"

"We're here Ezekial," Ruby said from in the dining room where Micah laid on the table with the shaft of an arrow protruding from his shoulder.

"You allright Micah?"

"I'll live."

"Ain't no hosses left, jes' the mules we was shoeing," Luther answered.

"I'll ride a mule. The others are chasing Indians. They've prob'ly got Sallie an' the horses back by now. Let Ruby put some stitches in you Callie. I'll go get Sallie, don' you worry none."

"Please get my baby Ezekial. Please!" Callie cried and trembled.

"I'll get her. I'm on my way. Nellie, would you look after Sam? Get 'im some water?"

"Oh! Poor Sam. I sure will."

Ezekial trotted with his horse to the barn and transferred the rigging. Mounting the tall, white mule, he fought the braying rascal until he started off at a bone jarring trot following the path of the stolen remuda. After following the fresh tracks for a good distance he noticed one set of unshod hoof tracks angle off from the others toward the river. He knew Noah and the hands were after the herd and would get Sallie if she were with them, so he turned the stubborn mule to follow the single set of tracks.

At the river his young eyes saw the wet ground and crumbled bank where the Indian pony left the river on the other side. He was into the river on the recalcitrant mule despite the hybrid's hesitancy. The mule was stubborn and strong, but Ezekial was determined and stronger. Somehow he knew this was the right course. And then he heard the whistle.

Sallie slowly became aware of what was happening in jerky insights as she bounced, sprawled atop the galloping horse before the Comanche who had taken her. As her wits began to return and she felt his hands upon her she reacted instinctively, kicking her legs and straightening her back and fell from the horse knocking the wind out of her.

The wicked child-thief turned his horse, dismounted and bent over Sallie as she lay momentarily paralyzed, trying to regain her breath. He spat some language of invectives by which she realized he was not pleased with her. He slugged her with his fist and she came near losing consciousness again. She was only vaguely aware of being slung over the horses withers and back and saw the ground move as the horse began a trot.

She began to bounce and to slip and the foul-smelling Indian again put his hands on her, grasping her dress to pull her back on. Her thin cotton dress tore and she jumped backwards off the horse. The Comanche stopped and turned his horse again. She jumped up from the ground and ran. The savage rode his horse beside her and kicked her down, jumping from his horse onto her, continuing to kick her and slap her. She tried to defend herself and this made the bully even madder, he hit her with the back of his elbow, bloodying and breaking her nose. She could hardly see.

The brute went to his horse and returned with rawhide strips with which he tied her hands. He drug her to the horse by her hair and lifted her onto its back sitting up, her legs astride. He began to tie her feet beneath the horses belly. Sallie realized she'd never get away if he tied her to the horse and she fought him as best she could. Then she heard the bray of a mule.

What made her do it she didn't know, but she folded her tongue and whistled, loud and clear, like Ezekial taught her, and kicked the

Indian pony with her one free foot as hard as she could. She leaned forward and grabbed the horses long mane to keep from falling as the horse bolted beneath her. The surprised Comanche lost his grip on her boot, gave chase and dove for the reins and missed. She continued to kick the horse and whistle as well as she was able aboard the jumping, jouncing horse.

Ezekial turned the complaining mule toward the shrill whistle. He rode through the thin line of mesquite bushes and saw sweet Sallie atop the horse riding away from a chasing Indian. Sallie's face was hurt. Ezekial stopped between the Comanche and Sallie, jerking and tying the obstinate mule securely to a tree. The Indian stared at Ezekial with fear in his eyes, but did not run. He unsheathed the only weapon left to him, a long metal knife and stood his ground, chanting or singing some primitive repetitive tone. Maybe some of the sounds were words, Ezekial didn't know. He looked and saw the Indian pony standing and Sallie running back to him, stumbling, bleeding, crying, and he ran at the Comanche.

He didn't recall the fight, if there was one, he didn't know what had happened until he realized that he was on his knees hugging Sallie and trying to hush her crying. Looking over her shoulder he saw the Indian on his back. What once was a face was no longer recognizable as such. It was just a red, caved-in hole, like a busted, rotten tomato. And the neck looked too long, and crooked.

Sallie said, "You're bleeding."

He then noticed a long, fairly deep gash across his ribs. It bled slowly, so he wasn't much concerned with it. He was concerned only with Sallie, her humped and bloody nose, her scrapes and torn dress. He calmed her, kissed her wild blonde hair and put her on the mule. He walked back to the ranch, leading the hammer-head, loudly braying mule.

Noah got close enough behind the Comanche to see that there were only four of them behind the herd. He pulled his revolver and spurred the long, limbed racer toward them. As he drew closer they made a fatal mistake. They turned and charged the single pursuer. He shot the nearest one in the middle of his chest, then shot another in the forehead on the first pass. And, as he passed, an arrow was stopped by his shoulder blade, nearly dislodging him from the saddle.

The shock of the flint against bone caused him to fumble the Colt, but he managed to get a grip and to turn the wild-eyed stallion to meet the remaining two warriors. But, the warriors were in full retreat fifty yards away and headed west, away from the seven cowboys riding hard after them and putting lots of lead in the air around them. Noah thought the hands would stop when they saw the murdering thieves had forsaken the stolen herd and were running for their lives, but the cowboys had their blood up and continued the chase to dispense with the cowardly pair.

The arrow in Noah's back was so painful that he almost passed out. He let the winded racehorse walk at his own pace toward the ranch. In half an hour the hands caught up with him and Billy Hell made the astute statement.

"You got a arror' in yer back Cap."

Noah looked at him seriously and answered, "Glory be. I didn't realize that. Thought I's sproutin' feathers."

Billy chuckled.

"Don't look ta' be va'ry deep. Can ya' make it on in ta' home?"

"I reckon so. Catch them Comanche?"

"Not 'til lead did. Won't be none ah that bunch doin' no more stealin'."

"Did we lose any stock?"

"Nary a one that I kin tell. There's some other brands amongst 'em too."

"Texas brands?"

"Nope. Meskin."

Callie's arm was stitched and bandaged and she and Mabel were fussing over the long cut along Ezekial's ribs and Sallie's busted nose. Ezekial was concerned about the cut and swelling on Sam's head, but was reassured when Sam winked and grinned his lop-sided smile. Billy Hell pulled the wood and flint out of Noah's back after getting Chuy to bring him the bottle of mescal he'd hid under his bunk. Noah took a healthy slug of the almost clear liquid and looked up to see Callie staring at him.

"Medicinal purposes, ma'am."

"Yep. Bring me some. You alright Noah?"

"Gettin' too old for this."

"Well, lay down on that table and let Ruby clean that, an' sew it up. She's had her practice on me and Ezekial."

Noah lay on the table and Ruby took the mescal and poured it into the wound. Noah winced, rolled onto his side and snatched the bottle back.

"This medication works best when taken by mouth," and he turned the bottle up and chugged a couple of big swallows, grimaced and blew. "Whew! Tastes like kerosene!"

"You don' like my drink, give it back," Chuy said.

"Didn' say I didn' like it, jes' that the taste takes some getting' used to. Ouch! Doggone it Ruby, be easy."

"You stay still Mista' Lista' an' it won't hurt so much."

Callie said, "Pass that bottle Noah, 'fore you drink it all."

Micah had began peeling potatoes and was humming a hymn.

"You want some of this medication Micah?" Callie asked.

"No ma'am. Ruby done sewed me up so good I don' feel no pain. 'Sides, I got my own med'cine," he smiled and showed her a half full bottle of the wine that had been in the storm cellar.

"Granny's wine," Mabel explained.

"Forgot about that," Callie said.

"There's a time for every season, so the good book says," Micah quoted, "And this is sho' a season for the fruit of the vine."

Billy Hell reached for the bottle Callie held, she pulled it back.

"Nope. Only for the wounded, Billy. Besides, there may still be Indians about. Somebody has to be alert and watching."

Billy smiled, "So a man has to be nearly killed to get a drink?"

"Yep, a woman too."

"What about a girl?" Sallie asked.

"Oh baby. Are you hurting? Come here. Micah pour her some of the wine."

"Ain't this a fine howdy-do?" Luther said "It takes a Comanche attack and near killin's to have a party round here, and the healthy are excluded. What about ol' Sam? He's wounded too."

Sam turned his head away from the offered alcohol and chuffed.

"Only one of us with any sense," Noah observed.

Everyone smiled. The victory felt good despite the injuries. No one had died, everyone had shown courage. The battle had bonded them even closer. And, they had learned, and re-learned.

The following mid-morning Callie was alerted by Sam's weakened woofing from the porch. Mabel and Ruby followed Sallie and Nellie to the door and Callie sat up from her place on the couch and shuffled out behind them. Ezekial stood beside Sam twenty yards out from the house watching a small herd of cattle and half a dozen horses being driven into the ranch compound by three vaqueros and a tall white man shaded by a huge sombrero.

"Those are our cattle, ones we've branded," Ezekial spoke over his shoulder to the ladies.

"Who are these men?" asked Callie.

Nellie and Sallie held Little Beau on the porch as he called out to Chas who had walked out of the blacksmith shop with Luther, rifle in hand.

The white man pushed the sombrero off his head and it hung by a cord down his back. He put his hand up in a friendly wave and spoke "Howdy" with a deep baritone voice.

"My, my, it's plain to see why the Mexicans call this place Angel's Camp. May I say you ladies are cool water to thirsty eyes. It's reassuring to see that there are still white folks in this world. Ha! It's been a while, yes, quite awhile.

"I am Milton Faver, I have the Cibola Springs Ranch out by the big bend in the Rio Bravo,...well, the Rio Grande to you. I'm on my way to San Antonio de Bexar and I ran into this livestock. Is it yours?"

"Yes. They are Mister Faver. Thank you."

"Mister Faver, I am Callie MacGillicuddy. The big man before you is one of my partners, Ezekial Robertson, and this lady beside me," here she put her arm on Mabel, "Is my other partner, Mabel Curtsinger."

"A pleasure to make your acquaintance," Faver dipped his head.

"Please. Won't you step down and rest awhile sir? We so seldom have visitors, please forgive our staring."

"I'm afraid it is we whose eyes may be rude madam. But, yes, it would be a pleasure to visit with you all for awhile." He gave some instructions in Spanish to the vaqueros, then asked, "Where would you like to put this prodigal beef sir?" to Ezekial.

"Jes' drive 'em behind the hill there. That'd be fine."

Faver gave them further instructions and they quickly rode away to push the beef to the designated place.

"Come in Mister Faver and have some coffee and pie."

"That does sound delicious."

"Luther, take care of these men's mounts. Make them fresh coffee and feed them well. It's the least we can do. Come in Mister Faver, come in."

Faver dusted himself off with his wide-brimmed Mexican hat and stomped his worn boots to remove the trail dirt and stepped up on the porch, followed the ladies inside as Ezekial held the door for him. After the ladies served him a hearty breakfast of griddle cakes, butter, syrup and honey, bacon, eggs, medium rare steak and sour dough biscuits, Mister Faver waved off the pie.

"Too full ladies. Goodness! That was enjoyable. My good wife is quite a cook, but she's Mexican, so it's rare I eat a meal like this. Puts me in mind of times when I was a wee lad. At my place it's mostly tortillas and enchiladas and tamales and tacos and,...well you get the idea. Been a long while since I've had griddle cake and sour dough biscuits. I am much obliged to you for such a fine repast."

"Well, you're welcome Mister Faver. How else can we repay you for coming such a distance to return our property?"

Chuckling, Mister Faver explained.

"Ma'am, the facts are that some half-tame Indians and poor Mexicans rustled that stock I've returned to you. You see, during the war the Comanche ran off all my cattle except the near two dozen heifers and calves I had inside my walls. I've been paying Indians and Mexican to round up wild cattle and mustangs to restock my ranch. I've known they sometimes took cattle from ranchos in Mexico and

I wasn't adverse to that because those same ranchos likely have lots of my cattle.

"But, these cattle were on their way to me driven west and I met them on my way. I didn't recognize the haloed A, but seeing it was a fresh brand and being driven from the east, I suspected they came from a Texican ranch. With a little whiskey and some tricky questions, they admitted the beeves may have come from America and with some very real threats and a bit more whiskey, the thieves allowed us to return your property.

"On my way to San Antonio de Bexar I learned from a lonely sojourner of the re-establishment of this, the old Curtsinger place, and, long story short, I felt it would be neighborly to take these weary beasts home."

"Neighborly?" asked Ezekial, "Mister Faver, it's two, three hunert miles to the Big Bend ain't it?"

"It's a far piece Ezekial, but truth is you are likely my closest neighbor! For certain you're my closest white neighbors."

"We can't thank you enough for your courtesy Mister Faver," said Mabel.

"You are most welcome young lady. I would have driven these cattle another thousand miles to view the beauty God has gathered here."

"So, old man, you can understand why I've started kickin' cows fer a livin'." Noah said from the door, "Lookin' at these ladies ever' day is easier on the eyes than rough rangers and nasty Comanche."

"Why, Noah Lister. You old devil! I thought the war had probably taken you," Faver said heartily as he stood and shook the offered hand.

"Oww! Easy Milton. They just cut Comanche flint outa my ol' hide yestiddy."

"Oh? Did you all have a visitation from Quanah's delegation?"

"No sir, they wasn't Democrats, they was some O' Bloody Roe's bunch. Jes' a few. An' they took a good whippin'."

"I had questions about the injuries on these children and your arm Callie. Seem's you're a bit stiff there also Ezekial."

"Yes sir, we took a few arrers an' bullets, but nobody killed," Ezekial answered.

"Thank God," Callie added.

"Amen," echoed Ruby.

"You know, I saw a flock of buzzards circling south of here,...?" Faver began.

"Yep, we had Comanche carcasses carted away and buried under some rocks down that-a-way," Noah explained.

"Is Bloody Roe among the resting?"

"He may be, but we didn' find 'im. Mabel here put a rifle bullet into his face," Noah answered.

"Well, bless you Misses Curtsinger. And may I say I was sorry to hear about your family, they were good Christian folks. I came by here when you were just a tiny lass and your parents made me welcome."

"Thank you, sir. Mister Faver, we get so few visitors, in fact, I should say you are our first visitor besides Samuel, Ezekial's Mexican friend. We'd be pleased and honored if you would stay with us until tomorrow. We would make all of you welcome and comfortable."

"Thank you Miss Curtsinger,..."

"Mabel."

"Mabel, I'd be pleased to delay my journey and rest with you until the morrow. And I'm sure my men would enjoy the respite."

Throughout the day and evening Faver spoke of his experiences with the Comanche, with the wild longhorns, sheep and goats, vaqueros and Mexican farm hands. He spoke of the fort he had built with a twenty-eight foot walls, portholes and even a cannon donated by the commandant of nearby Ft. Davis. He taught them much in the day he spent with them and enjoyed the cooking, the friendship and the hospitality. Callie and Ezekial persuaded him to promise to return and visit on his way home from San Antonio.

Faver offered to bring them any provisions and tools or other items they might need from his visit to civilization. Both Callie and Ezekial handed him separate lists of essentials as well as a letter to John Twohig at his bank to release necessary funds to Mister Faver for the needed items. Noah sent three hands along and the big freight wagon to effect the transport of the goods.

Noah and Billy found a pair of hours early next morning before Milton Faver left for San Antonio to share a few swigs from a bottle of peach brandy Faver had brewed and to converse about the Comanche problems they faced. Faver suggested a few improvements on both the fortification and the preparation for the sneaking attacks they were noted for.

The two old rangers envied Faver his happy attitude which bubbled through his old hide despite the privations and sorrows of his life. He was a very knowledgeable man whose alert intelligence observed pragmatic systems in nature and behaviors in men and found ways to incorporate these beneficial devices into his life. He lived in the midst of many enemies and found ways to not only survive, but thrive. He had gathered allies among the Mexicans, the Apache, Kiowa, Kickapoo, Navajo, and even some Comanche and melded them into a force effective enough to discourage and withstand the often marauding Comanche and Kiowa.

Faver asked the pair about several battles with the native tribes and Mexican banditos they had survived. He had a good belly laugh at Billy Hell's interpretation of the grouping of citizens, rangers, and confederate soldiers who attacked and immediately retreated from an angry thousand Kickapoo south of the confluence of the Conchos at a place called Dove Creek. It seems ignorant pilgrims had misidentified the friendly Kickapoo who were traveling south to Mexico to relocate under the invitation of the Mexican government as belligerent hostile Comanche on the warpath. Faver said the battle was so short it could not be called a battle. The two hundred citizens armed with old muskets and single shot pistols and shotguns were routed after their initial volley and, if they'd been timed with a pocket watch, would have beat all records for the marathon on their hurried way home, the Kickapoo nipping at their heels.

After the departure of Mister Faver, everyone returned to work. Always leaving men around the ranch houses and rotating several out riders who would serve as early warning of any war party in the vicinity, the remaining hands continued the branding, castrating, herding and penning. Ezekial, Luther and Micah had managed to plow and plant a good-sized truck garden as well as some hay and oats. It was well into May, eighteen sixty-six, and the rains seemed to fall by punctual appointment once a week or ten days, nourishing the crops as well as the wild grasses, shrub, herbs, trees and blankets of colorful wildflowers.

Faver brought all the supplies and tools Ezekial and Callie ordered. Ruby was happy to get her own cook stove, Callie was happy to get the schoolbooks she'd ordered for the children. The children were not. Ezekial was pleased with the tools, Noah satisfied with the ammunition. Mister Faver added a bitch hound dog with a passel of pups. These along with a mated two pair of peacocks would be the early warning for any visitors, welcome or unwelcome. The female hound was not pleased to meet Sam, being still protective of the puppies. The hounds were situated in their own area of the barn and soon had all been named by the girls and Chas. Sam had healed well from the blow to his head and, since the puppies got most of the attention from Sallie and Nellie, he began going with Ezekial and Chas to work the cows.

All through the late spring and into July, the hands improved their dwellings. The herds increased and there was discussion of a drive somewhere to sell some beef. As soon as he had been able Ezekial rode with Chuy to visit the Chavez's. He had been worried that Comanche may have attacked them also and he had been right. It was another, larger war party who had assaulted the Chavez rancho, and they had lost a large caballada. Several outbuildings had been burned to the ground and the main house had suffered damage. Several men had been killed and three children had been stolen. Samuel's mother and Patricia had been sent further south to stay with kin in a more populous area until it was deemed safer. There had not been enough men and horses to chase the Comanche and try to retrieve the children and horse herd. A few families had left the rancho in fear of another attack. Samuel had heard from a traveler that Milton Faver's place had also been attacked, without much success.

With the help of Chinati and Chuy, Ezekial hired some Mexican peon families to relocate to Angel's Camp. The Mexican had brought a small herd of goats with them and Callie had purchased a few sheep and pigs. A big chicken house was built a ways from the main house and two Mexicans put in charge of them. The Mexicans were excellent farm hands and even better vaqueros. They were treated well and became very loyal and trustworthy employees. In just three-quarters of a year, the enterprise had made great strides despite the threat of Indian attacks.

Ezekial yearned for Patricia. For her laughter, her touch, her fragrance when she was near. Memories of moments shared, golden, cherished memories beset him. There was an emptiness within him that only she could fill. Samuel couldn't tell him when she might return and, when he thought about it, he felt guilty that he would have her in danger to fill his lonely need. His friend advised him that he also missed his beautiful sister and mother, but he dealt with the sadness by staying busy, preparing for their return. Ezekial determined he must do the same.

Ezekial began attacking his work, no one could keep up with him. Whether it was diggin postholes, branding, or building, his strength and energy was prolific. His enthusiasm inspired those who worked with him and much was accomplished. They had established a five and a half day work week for all hands, but Ezekial and Noah typically worked at least six days. All hands were off on Sundays.

Of course there was a small amount of necessary work which must be done on Sunday as well. There was milking, gathering eggs, feeding the animals and cooking as well as any preparations for the planned work for the next week. For the most part though, everyone slept a little later on a Sunday morning.

It was on such a lazy summer Sunday morning that the peacock's screams woke those who had slept past the dawn and then Micah's dinner bell ringing loudly and incessantly drove the alarm through to their brains. Some trumpet-mouthed hand from the bunkhouse hollered, "Injuns!" and then the shooting began.

Rutting Roe's horse had been seen by the Kiowa hunting party and Lone Wolf found Roe covered in flies and red ants beneath a young mesquite. Water on his face and lips woke him and he groaned as he asked to drink. The Kiowa mounted him on his tired horse and led him to their camp two days away to the west. Once there, Lone Wolf's squaws washed his wounds and a Comanche trader picked the particles of tooth and bone from the wound, washed it with whiskey over the protest of the weakened warrior and, with strips of buffalo intestine, sewed first the muscle and then the skin.

The squaws fed him softened soups of boiled buffalo and deer and turkey, rich gravies and broths and soon Roe could sit up without help. Another few days he gained the strength to stand and walk a short distance. When he pushed back the flap of the small shelter that the squaws had made for him, the children screamed and ran, some of the younger ones cried. Though one side of his face was a cruelly handsome as always, the wounded, stitched and swollen side was a grotesque mask of a demon, grimacing hate, the sharp remains of teeth exposed within the drooping lips, the eye almost slipping from its socket.

Returning to the shelter after defecating, he urged an attending woman to bring him a looking glass. Only Lone Wolf's sits-by-wife had such a luxury and she came with the fragile glass to protect it from the monster, and it was only by Lone Wolf's cuffing her that she overcame her reluctance to let the one who nearly died peer into the mirror. It seemed bad medicine to let the eye of the glass view such an ugly one.

One long look at his reflection was all that was necessary to bring Roe's hate again to a boil. The hate would heal him, strengthen him, restore him so he could continue his quest. He would crush the people of the red-haired woman, burn what they had built and take her, break her with ceaseless torture and pain. His every thought built on this goal.

Where were his Comanche brothers? They had deserted him. In their fear they had left him to the white eyes. Why should he return to them? He could not lead cowards to destroy the red-haired woman. The spirits had led the Kiowa to him. It was they who would reap the bounty of the battle. He would teach them and lead them. There were many brave men here in this camp and there were other camps of Kiowa not far away. He would recruit them into his hate-filled scheme of cruel retaliation.

The notoriety of the Comanche criminal who had lost half his face in his war against the whites grew and drew many of the fiery Kiowa youth anxious to prove their manhood. The great hate of Rutting Roe seemed to accelerate his healing and quickly restored his vigorous strength. He was seen by many as a warrior of great bravery, no fear and strong medicine.

Roe chose a few of his followers to reconnoiter the ranch of the red-haired bruja. They returned to report that there were only fifteen men there, though many more women and children. Roe wanted to catch them all together, to kill them all in a show of strength. Kill them all except the red-haired girl, she would die slowly. She would beg for death. He wanted to hear her screams and cries as he cut her, burned and disfigured her. Her pain would bring him peace, prestige and joy. These were the dreams that hurried his healing and increased his infectious enthusiasm. He held no doubt that the day of his desire would dawn.

The scouts reported that there were watchmen day and night, on horseback around the ranch and one atop the animal house in a little structure that gave a view of the surroundings. The plans for the attack would have to include dispensing with these who would give warning. This time Roe would follow his old way, tried and true, men first to die, then toy with the women and children.

Just before the dawn that Roe had dreamed of and planned for. Micah woke and made a big pot of coffee. Grabbing a pair of buckets he carried them to a stall in the barn and sat on the milking stool. He began singing an old gospel song to soothe the milk cow as he massaged her swollen udders in the near dark. He called out to the lookout in the crow's nest atop the barn that had been added at Milton Faver's suggestion. There was no answer and he finished milking the first cow. Believing the watchman had fallen asleep, he climbed the ladder to the barn roof.

"Hey! Lookout! Ready for some coffee?"

As Micah's head cleared the shingles, the body of the man appeared, throat cut and head scalped. An arrow thudded into a rafter, just missing his face and he saw an almost naked Indian running across the roof toward him.

Micah missed a step on the ladder in his hurry down and fell part way, stunning him and twisting his ankle. As he rose he reached for the pitchfork and as the Kiowa jumped from the ladder toward him he held the fork before him in defense and the naked Indian impaled himself on the tines.

Limping to the dinner bell Micah began ringing it as loudly as he could. He didn't feel the bullet that knocked him off his feet. Struggling to rise, a painted Kiowa grabbed his wooly hair and pulled his head back. Micah heard two shots and then Noah was standing over him, half dressed, a smoking pistol in his grip.

"Can you stand?"

"Help me."

Together they stumbled toward Micah's room at the end of the bunkhouse, Micah's arm over Noah's shoulder. Micah felt he was moving through molasses and he couldn't move any faster. Men were shooting out the bunkhouse windows by now at the screaming, naked demons riding painted ponies in the first light of dawn. Indians were charging them on horseback shooting all around them. Micah heard a bullet hit then another. He didn't know which of them had been hit until Noah stumbled, then they fell together.

There was a fusillade from the bunkhouse and then a half-dozen hands surrounded them, shooting, lifting and pulling them through the bunkhouse doors.

"Put them on these corner bunks away from the windows," Billy Hell yelled.

After they were situated Billy cut their shirts searching for the wounds. Micah was hit in the lower back, a hole punched all the way through to his belly. It wasn't bleeding much, at least on the outside. Noah was hit twice, high in the back and in the back of the thigh. Both bullets were still inside him.

"How you feelin' Noah?" Billy asked.

"Like I'm gonna' die purty quick."

"Aw, yule be awite, jest gotta' get them bullets out."

"Naw, I'm gone this time Billy. Don't waste time messin' with me. You go look out fer them women an' kids."

Chinati brought blankets to cover them. The attack was continuing, the Kiowa trying to set the bunkhouse on fire and concentrating their efforts on killing the men there. The cowboys killed all the Indians with torches and several Indian ponies riderless, the Kiowa trying to lift their fallen comrades onto their horses shoulders, removing them from the battleground.

At Milton Faver's suggestion, thick stone exterior wainscot had been laid from the ground halfway to the roof line and this kept the Indian's lead from penetrating the milled lumber below a height of four feet of the bunkhouse. The tall thin windows allowed the defenders to shoot out along all four walls, but few bullets made it into the bunkhouse.

Chuy directed three of the cowboys to make for the barn and corral and protect the horses. Billy Hell grabbed two other half-dressed hands and told them to follow him as he broke out shooting and running for the women's house.

Ezekial had jumped into his pants and pulled the suspenders over his shoulders, hollered at Chas to get dressed, grabbed his pistol and a shotgun and followed Chas out the door running barefoot to the women's back door. Chas stopped along the way and shot an Indian who was climbing onto the women's roof. Pounding on the barred back door, he yelled, "It's Ezekial, let me in!"

Callie opened the door and Ezekial let Chas and Sam slip in before him. Sallie and Nellie, dressed in their nightshirts were shooting rifles out the windows at the front of the house.

Callie yelled, "You girls get away from those windows!"

The pair quickly obeyed, putting their backs against the stone walls, but Mabel, little more than a girl herself, continued to cock, aim and fire a Winchester. Callie and Ezekial took the girls place at the front window.

"There must be a hunnerd of 'em out there."

"Naw, jes' seems that way. But there's shore a passel of dead injun's awready."

"Where's Noah?"

"He went to help Micah. Micah was shot."

"Shot bad?"

"Don't know."

"How 'bout Ruby an' Beau?"

"They're both shootin' out the winda's."

"Here comes Billy an' some hands. Shoot fast and straight. Sallie! Open the door for 'em."

Kiowa's tried to ride down the running ranch hands, but the concentrated rifle fire made them turn their horses away. Sallie and Chas slammed the heavy door behind them and Nellie helped them with the crossbar.

Ezekial looked out the window at the back of the house and hurriedly opened it and took dead aim at one of the copper-skinned, wildly painted savages who were lurking beside Beau and Ruby's house. He pulled the trigger, cocked, moved the barrel slightly and shot again, hitting both Indians. One of them fell like he was dead, the other was struggling to get back to his horse. Chuy knelt beside Ezekial and shot, hitting the young Kiowa and driving him against the wall of the house, then dropping dead to the ground.

The barrel of Ezekial's rifle was jerked outward and Ezekial, holding on tight, was jerked head and shoulders out the window. As one Kiowa pulled on the rifle, another beside him shot his rifle at the huge man emerging from the window and, in his excitement, missed. Almost immediately another shot knocked the Indian who had missed to the ground, and Ezekial, yelling in his fighting frenzy, pulled the over matched Kiowa who had pulled his rifle half inside the window. Another shot punctured the warrior's head. Turning to see the shooter beside him and expecting Chuy, he was surprised to see Chas standing grim-faced with a smoking pistol held in his two steady hands. Beyond him, Sallie and Nellie were loading rifles, Callie, Mabel, Canejo and Chuy were shooting with deadly purpose through the windows.

Turning back, Ezekial saw the attacking devils throwing torches on Beau and Ruby's roof. Ezekial brought one of the mounted warriors down and the other two turned their horses and rode to the other side of the house. Ezekial slammed the window and locked it, then ran to the door. Sam followed on his heels.

"Stay Sam! Sallie! Keep Sam here. Close and bar the door behind me," Ezekial yelled, then bolted toward Beau and Ruby's house. A screeching Kiowa tried to ride his horse over him as he crossed the open ground. Ezekial took a step back and pushed as the horse ran past, toppling horse and rider. He clubbed the stunned rider with the stock of the shotgun, busting his head like an over-ripe Presidio cantaloupe.

Another screaming rider approached him and a shot from the window he had left removed the Indian from the wild-eyed pony. Ezekial looked back to see Sallie and Chas at the window, both with smoking rifles.

"Get away from that window!" screamed Callie as she replaced them at the post. She watched Ezekial climb from Beau and Ruby's porch onto the roof scramble across the shingles at the edge and began kicking the burning shingles off. As warrior rode toward him, Callie, along with Beau and Ruby, made the warriors avoid and back away from their protecting volley. Ezekial kicked the remaining fire and embers from the roof, Beau looked at Ruby holding Little Beau and gave God a silent thanks. He looked up through the smoking hole in the roof and hollered, "Drop down here, Zeke."

Before he could drop through the rafters, a bullet pierced his shoulder. He hit the floor hard, knocking the breath from him. Beau had returned to a window, pouring fire at the wild, murderous attackers. He had also been hit, flesh torn from his face by a ricochet and his ribs skint by a hot bullet. But, his jaw was clamped against the pain and he continued to cock, aim and fire, fiercely defending his family and home.

Chinati threw open the door at the bunkhouse and yelled to the hands behind him, "Vamos a agarrarlos muchachos!" A group of five screaming and shooting cowboys ran at the remaining Kiowa who had been gathering their dead and wounded. Blood covered the hard, baked earth and the conquered received no mercy. The Indians were in full retreat and everyone in all the separate houses came outside to shoot at the fleeing survivors, hastening their exit from the ranch. Almost half of the warriors had been killed or wounded. The air itself held the brassy smell of spilled, hot blood, even over the smell of gunpowder and the burning houses. Everyone on the ranch was hooting and shooting, dancing and celebrating the clear cut victory. Everyone but the wounded, and the dead.

"Shouldn't we chase them Ezekial?" Beau said.

"What does Noah say? Where's Noah?" Ezekial asked

Chinati replied softly, "Noah's dead. Micah may not make it."

The celebration ceased. They looked at one another in silence. Their general had died. Ezekial looked at Billy Hell and simply said, "Billy?"

Billy peered at Ezekial, then at the crowd of eyes that looked to him. His thoughts were with Noah as he looked at the ground.

"They're whupped today. They ain't coming back today, maybe never. They still outnumber us and we need to save what ammunition we have left. Just in case."

"Anyone else die?" asked Callie, as Ezekial strode with Beau to the bunkhouse to see about Micah.

"Ol' Toby and his wife Tabitha. Dead and scalped."

"Espuelo, Manuel's son caught a bullet in the head."

"Some of you come with me and help put these fires out. Some of you help with the dead and the wounded," Billy directed. They hurriedly broke into groups.

"Don't get too far from your rifles!" Billy added.

The Kiowa had effectively removed all their dead except half a dozen who had been shot too close to the houses and the enemies guns. These remaining corpses were loaded into a wagon-bed, carried to an area known for the many surface rocks and interred there beneath a pile of stones. They all knew this was a much more decent deposition of the dead than their dead would have received at the hands of West Texas Indians. They left nothing to mark the spot of the burial, no words were said over dead flesh or of departed spirits, but neither were the remains desecrated.

Deep graves were dug on the low, sloping hill where the Curtsinger dead had been laid, beneath a sheltering coppice of young oak. Crosses were fashioned and carved for each of the beloved and successive funerals were held for each. Words were spoken by those survivors who loved them. Heartfelt songs were sung, simple, but fervent prayers were offered aloud and silently for each departed friend.

By the second day after the attack, Micah was able to be helped to the graveside and he spoke short sermons over each grave. Looking down upon the simple pine box in which Noah's body lay he spoke softly in his weakness.

"Here lies the earthly remains of Mister Noah Bradley Lister. This man was a brave man, a man of courage, a man skilled in the art of war. The wise and holy Word of the Lord says that a man who lives by the sword will die by the sword. Our friend Noah's life and demise is evidence of the truth of God's Word.

"From an early age, in his boyhood, Noah was alone in life. His family was massacred by savages for no other reason than they had claimed and farmed a small plot of God's great earth, scraping a living in the dirt by the sweat of their brow. Noah never forgave the Indians. He nurtured hate in his heart and took Old Testament vengeance on the Indians his whole life. 'An eye for an eye and a tooth for a tooth.'

"Jesus taught us to forgive our enemies. When our enemy attacks us without cause or warning, rapes and kills our daughters, wives and sisters, kills our brothers, fathers and sons and mutilates their defenseless bodies and take our children as slaves to abuse and torture,...well, the Lord knows it's hard for us to forgive. Without God's help, hate will rule us as it has ruled the life of this brave friend of ours."

"Noah saved my life. He stood over me, protected me, gave his life for me. The Bible says there is no greater love than this, that a man would give his life for a friend. So, though hate surely lived in Noah, in the end, love overcame the hate. Let's remember Noah for the love he had for all of us, not for the hate.

"Noah was a young Texas Ranger, he grew to manhood protecting settlers from Indians and outlaws. He was a soldier in the recent war. He fought because it was all he knew. When he had no one to fight, when the war was over, he began to fight the war within him. He tried to drown the demons in alcohol, tried to quiet the spirits of all those who had perished by his hands and to erase the memory of the terrible murder of his family that had always haunted him.

"Then we came along the trail. God, in his wisdom, united us. God knew that we ignorant pilgrims needed protection and knew Noah needed someone to protect. We became his family, he loved and we loved him.

"Lord God, we pray you have forgiven Noah of all his sins and have given him the peace he never had here on earth. Thank you for sending him to us to protect us for a time. And please give him my personal thanks for saving my ol' hide. Allow him to rest in peace. We will all miss him. Amen."

A sad old hymn was sung over his grave as tears fell on the freshly turned earth which covered his grave.

> The marker read: Noah B. Lister
> Died July 30, 1866
> Indian Fighter, Soldier,
> Friend.

And so a part of Noah Lister passed from this earth, and a part continued to live, a tiny part he never knew.

Brandy's mood was ebullient since the birth of the boy. She felt freed, unchained, with a new chance at life. Having suffered and survived many pains in her short existence she had managed the birth itself bravely with the wise attendance of a negro midwife whom Cecil brought. Cecil had also necessarily located a nanny to feed and tend the baby as Brandy was too busy catching up with life and getting all in order so she could leave for Texas. She had made plans for months now, made lists of things to do, things to buy, things to take on her quest to find Noah.

Cecil and the women who worked for her as well as the friends she had made over the months badgered her to name the baby, but she wouldn't.

"His last name is Lister, his daddy will give him his Christian name. When I find him."

"But Brandy, the child is too small, too fragile to survive such an arduous voyage. Wait a year or two, maybe your husband will find you."

"Ha! No Cecil, there's small chance of that happening. No. I'll leave the baby with the nanny. The boy will be well cared for, you'll see to that, and the nanny desperately needs the money. I'll return with Noah for the boy and he can name him then."

So everyone called the boy simply 'Boy'. Little Boy, Big Boy, Sweet Boy, Pretty Boy, Hungry Boy, but always Boy.

And then, one day in July, Brandy was gone. She left a letter for Cecil behind her, and with the letter, keys to her house, their business and a legal power of attorney so he could manage her affairs. She left the boy. She took her dog.

She had purchased a ticket to the coast in a coach and spent two days there in a hotel awaiting the departure of the ship that would take her to Corpus Christi. While waiting, she whiled away the time shopping for gifts, not for her newborn son, but for Noah. Shirts, socks, an ivory-handled Colt revolver, a beaver hat. She smiled at the imagined vision of surprise on his face when he saw her. He would certainly be surprised, he would be pleased as well, though he'd never admit it, not at first sight. Her intuition assured her that he loved her. It was only his damnable notion of nobility, sacrifice and unworthiness, as well as his fear of domestication that had led him to flee from her. Well, she would change his mind, no doubt about that. They had many happy years to be together.

No one on the ship knew where Noah Lister might be, although she did find two men who had heard of the famous ranger. Shoestring shivered and shook throughout the sea voyage, refusing to eat, and could barely walk when her feet again found solid ground.

Once in Corpus she spent an unproductive three days inquiring in places she deemed appropriate, the Sheriff's office, saloons, bawdy houses and with every ex-confederate soldier she came across. The best advice she got was to go to Austin and check with the new state police, though some doubted that a man of Noah Lister's character would be associated with that disreputable gang.

A rough two days coach ride brought Brandy and Shoestring to San Antonio and she immediately began getting information about Noah. First a stage driver, then a bartender, then a horse trader and finally a freight wagon driver gave her Noah's exact location on a ranch west of a small town named Uvalde. These men all helped her not only rent a buggy and team to get her there but recommended an unemployed ex-soldier to travel with her to dissuade the sundry miscreants who frequented Southwest Texas and the wagon track that would take her to this frontier settlement and to her love.

Her driver found them a place to stay after a long drive the first day and pulled the buggy into the livery in Uvalde towards the end of a second long day. While Brandy and Shoestring stretched their legs and visited the outhouse, the driver helped the livery man water, feed and put the horses to rest. Brandy wanted to rest from the tiring trip and bathe so she would look her best when she surprised Noah. They entered a small cafe in the late afternoon and ordered food for the two of them as well as some meat for Shoestring. While they waited on the food the driver told Brandy that the liveryman had asked him if they had seen any sign of Indians along the way and told of a ranch west of Uvalde that had been attacked by a large war party of Kiowas two days before. Brandy asked the waitress if she had any information about it.

"Oh yes! Terrible thing. Kiowa Indians, it's said, not Comanche for once. Burned some buildings and killed several people out there at Angel's Camp, the old Curtsinger place. There was a hun'erd or more of 'em it's said, not usually that many. Good thing that ol' ranger Noah Lister had 'em ready for Indians, plenty of experienced soldiers and ol' rangers, plenty of rifles and ammunition too. Drove those Indians off in about fifteen minutes, killed a bunch of 'em too. Too bad about Mister Lister though."

"What,...what happened to Lister?" Brandy managed.

"Oh, he was shot and killed while rescuing the cowboy cook. Fought Indians all his life and they finally killed him. Ma'am, are you awright ma'am?"

"He's dead?"

"Noah Lister? Yes ma'am. Dead and buried as of today. Mister Black said he was given a fine Christian burial right out there at the ranch along with the others who were killed."

Brandy struggled to rise to her feet despite the dizziness that overtook her. She stumbled and her driver caught her.

"C'mon," she ordered, "Let's go."

The driver followed close behind her, giving the waitress a message as he passed in a whisper, "Her husband."

"Noah Lister?"

The driver nodded his head.

"Oh! I'm so sorry. I didn't know. Oh my. I'm sorry Misses Lister..."

Brandy trotted down the rough, dusty road back to the livery. Shoestring ran playfully beside her jumping and barking. Brandy swung her bag at the dog and hollered, "Git!"

Shoestring shied away, confused.

She yelled at the livery man, "Hitch that team up. Now! We're going out there. Now, I said!"

"Ma'am," the driver tried, "Maybe we should..."

"Now! Go on! Hitch 'em up! Let's go!"

The tired horses were back in the traces headed into the sinking sun in just a few minutes, a crying, cursing, crazy woman scaring the driver and the horses. Shoestring, forgotten, tried to keep up with the buggy, squinting her eyes in the dust.

Chapter Thirteen

"I've come a long, long way to learn that which
I've sought lies in what I've left behind."
---anon

"Freedom's just another word for nothing left to lose." from
'Me and Bobby Magee' by Kris Kristofferson and Fred Foster

AFTER THE FLEEING felons had winded their mounts with a good long gallop, Hoss held up his hand.

"Hold up. Ya'll g'down and untie that roll behind your saddles, there's free world clothes there. Strip off those stripes. We'll hide the prison clothes a ways down the trail."

The night seemed to echo with quiet. The only sound that interrupted the silence was the blowing of the horses. Listening intently and peering back toward Huntsville, Hoss could sense no alarm. He estimated a half hour or more had passed.

"Yea!" Jack said as he stomped back into his brogans, "Feels good to have on real clothes."

"There's a place we can get to 'fore the sun comes up to hole up. We can't go down the road or cross country in daylight with big 'un here with us. Ever' body for miles around Huntsville will be told about us 'fore dawn. There's an abandoned place back in the woods I found and we'll wait until dark again and make a run to where I have an automobile waitin'. If we make twenty-five miles tonight, rest these horses all day, then twenty more tomorrow night, we should be okay once we get to the automobile and then big 'un can lay down in the back."

"What 'bout the hounds Hoss?"

"With all the other convicts who escaped runnin' ever which a' way, they'll have their hands full catchin' all the ones on foot an' makin' tracks. Least for a day or two. We're gonna' cut south up a creek here in a mile or two, the hounds will lose the scent in the water. An' I've got some tender bites of steak here in my saddle bags which we'll spread here and there on each bank to get them dogs to put their noses to sniffin' for a snack 'stead of for convicts. An' these are peppered steaks, get their nose to running so they can't smell so good. Just in case. We should be okay once we make the abandoned cabin I found. Let's go."

In the violet dawn they walked the horses into a hidden little shack back in the woods. Edward had been here and stored food and water for them and the horses. They unsaddled the tired horses, rubbed them down good and gave them some hay, oats and water. Then Hoss spread out the canned meat and bread he had placed there for them. Jack had brought as much laudanum as he could get, knowing it would be awhile before he might procure any while on the dodge. He took a healthy swig after he had eaten some food and was soon asleep. Ezekial and Edward tried to wind down, Edward rolling cigarettes and smoking, Ezekial petting Sam and looking out the window.

"Don't be scared Ezekial, ain't nobody gonna' find us here. Not unless they see you peepin' out that window."

"Sorry. But naw, I ain't scared much. All they can do if they catch me is put me back in prison or kill me. Ain't much loss either way. I jes' enjoy lookin' at the trees, the grass, the birds. It's been a long, long time."

"Yea. I guess it has. Wake us up if you see any law. Maybe we can outrun 'em."

"I will."

Jack slept under the calming influence of the narcotic. Hoss slept in the secure knowledge of a well planned getaway. But, Ezekial had woken from a long nightmare into a dreamlike freedom, wonder and beauty. The feeling of liberation, the absence of restraint, the sights, sound, smells of normal human experience thrilled him and flooded his mind with memories. He had forgotten the magic, the beauty and charm of God's creation. The day was half spent before exhaustion and sleep overcame Ezekial and a smile remained on his old face in his slumber.

The day passed without incident or even any interruption of their rest. They ate again and found a likely place to bury the prison clothes. With a mallet and wedge they had removed the clasps of the shackles and that hated metal was hidden in the hole with the filthy, torn clothes. At full dark they started down the trail that Hoss had mapped and planned. A few barbed wire fences were necessarily cut, but they took time to repair them so that their passage would not be soon recognized. The path that Hoss had laid out made it easy to traverse the distance away from the prison center of Huntsville. There seemed to be no pursuit, and the seeming was so, though they did not know it.

Two dozen men and more had seized the opportunity to escape the Walls and led the servants of the state down many separate trails. Most of those who had escaped were recaptured by the end of the second day, but reports of sightings of running and hiding men were being received by all the police agencies in the state. Hoss had even hired a few good people to call in false sightings from different places for three days. That should give them time to clear the immediate search area.

Typically, many of the escapees were "found drowned" or were "shot in self-defense." As was usually reported some were found "expired from exposure" or from "over exertion." Of the deaths of the escaped prisoners so labeled, most were actually tortured and drowned, beaten to death, killed by the dogs or simply shot like deer. Operating procedure of the prison administration was to release no information at all regarding escapes or any other trouble within the prison, but in this instant case, it was imperative that the media and populace be forewarned. The escape of so many prisoners cast the keepers of men in a bad light, but safety of the citizenry had to be considered primarily.

The second day was spent by the three in the barn of a trusted confederate, where Ezekial studied the contraption he had seen only at a distance when the prison truck delivered new prisoners to the back gate. This automobile the confederate showed him had a backseat instead of a wagon bed behind the driver's seat. Up close, this horseless carriage was a wonderment to him. The man explained the working of the engine and worked the crank to start it and show him how it ran. Ezekial shook his big, gray head and felt his age. The world had passed him by.

Later, as the others slept, Ezekial walked with Sam out behind the barn, across plowed furrows to the windbreak of a line of trees beside a sparkling stream. Sitting back against the thick trunk of a towering pecan, he listened to the water sing with the birds, felt the gentle spirit of the breeze touch his withered cheek and cherished the moment. The rainbows in the water transformed the time and place to a day long past and he saw the perfectly beautiful children wading and playing in the stream and in their innocence. Sallie, Nellie, Chas and Boy, where were they now? He heard their voices ring in his memory, the simple natural joy of life in the music of their laughter. Such hope, promise and wonder bloomed in all their hearts then. His old heart swelled in the recalled delight of those golden days, but he wondered if he realized then how precious those moments were, and how fleeting.

His mind's eye saw another stream, far away, where he had fished and swam with his brothers and his Gramps. They had never given a single thought that those priceless days would pass. Death was a devil they had never expected. Life was surely everlasting.

He was again blessed with the vision of the perfect beauty of Cynthia. In his mind, she was forever young, ethereal, too beautiful for this world. Unassuming, just a farm girl, she didn't realize then how her God-given beauty could render a man breathless and speechless.

Ezekial was even then a bear of a man who had found little in life to fear, but such a woman, a girl really, evoked a fear that froze him, the pumping of his great heart was a bass drum beating in his ears along with a ringing dizziness. But the girl was blameless and unaware, confused by the manner of men.

Angelic she seemed, feet barely touching the ground in the graceful dance that was her natural movement. Every part of her was perfect, hand-crafted by the Almighty Artist of the Ages. Her face was without blemish, flawless, enchanting. Her beauty was a power that was fearful to a man. In a wondrous paradox, it was hard for a man to look on her, and once he did, it was a great effort of will to look away. He had been blessed to share even a moment in time with her.

The vision of her then faded into the more earthly loveliness of Patricia riding the powerful stallion, the wind in her straight, raven hair, the shine of brilliant teeth, the gleam of pleasure and intelligence in her deep, dark eyes. Such a vital, exciting, inspiring creature she was, life and laughter in her voice. He could hear her laughter even now, cutting cleanly through the zephyr. Simple times they had shared, pulled apart finally by the demons of those days, but oh how often had he relived those happy younger days when it seemed they could take the world by the tail and shake loose the life they wanted.

Patricia was a thin girl, a fawn. Every facet of life excited her. A fashionable woman, the very first to conform to the latest style but able, in her intelligence, to make the new-custom or dress her own. She flourished and loved each day and could hardly wait for tomorrow. Sadly for Ezekial, a tomorrow came that snatched her away. The wound to his heart had never healed.

The fast friendships of Callie, Noah, Beau, Micah, Samuel, Chuy, Luther and so many others were brought to memory, triggered by this re-immersion into the natural world, the real world, the world that God made and continued to make each succeeding day. It was such a blessed gift to finally be separated from the punishing sorrows and horrors of the man-made world of prison. Tears flowed down the wrinkled skin of the cheeks that dimpled in a smile of joy and gratitude. The long drought from the love and wonder of God's world whetted his appreciation and he whispered a simple prayer of thankfulness up through the dancing leaves and the lazy white clouds to the Spirit that dwelt everywhere, and surely in his heart.

Sam, seated on the ground beside him sensed his mood and whined. Ezekial hugged the dog to him and smiled. He was especially thankful for Sam. This non-existent vision or apparition, as others would define him, had loyally stayed with him through all the intervening years, through all the endless, dreary days and hardships, and made the loneliness less so. Sam had kept him sane, though Ezekial knew few would assess him of possessing a sound mind. Normal, as he understood it, was the middle of the road. He realized his reality was on the edge, but wasn't it still the same road? Where the road led was a mystery. He could only hope that he was headed in the right direction.

Laying down in the shinning green grass beside the susurrus stream, he lowered his great head and submerged his face, experiencing the refreshing clearing of mind and wakening power of the clear, cool water. Deep he drank relishing the chill passage of life's liquidity. Then he breathed life's gas deep inside his chest, cherishing the vital pleasures so often undervalued. God was so good, so wise. He memorized the moment, for he realized now more than ever before that the present moment was all he had, all that he'd ever had or would ever have. This moment only was real.

Weary, Ezekial returned to the barn. Even the hay was appreciated as he lay his body down. The soft fragrance of the hay enveloped Sam and him as they curled together, sharing dreams of yesteryears and hopes of tomorrows, but treasuring the present moments.

When he awoke, last minute preparations were in progress and a homemade map was being studied and discussed. In the royal blue twilight Ezekial walked and viewed the uninterrupted panoply of heaven's arch and the first penetrating twinkling of the early stars. The still, silent symphony of the evening enveloped him in a private soliloquy of praise to be blessed once again with such a sight. His murmured dialogue was disturbed by the unnatural growl of the automobiles crank and engine.

"C'mon Zeke, le's go," Jack urged. "Get in the back. An' lay down an' look smaller if we see anyone, hear?"

"Awright."

With a grinding of metal gears and a lurch another nights travel was begun. Ezekial and Sam had to share the cramped rear space with a box of food, cans of gasoline and oil and water and...?

"What's this?" Ezekial asked, holding up the light-weight object to be identified.

"Toilet paper. You never seen toilet paper before?"

"Nope. Heard about it. But no, this is sumpin' new since they locked me up. You know we didn't have it in prison."

Hoss and Jack looked at one another and chuckled.

"Well, you'll soon grow accustomed to the luxuries of the twentieth century. Never rode in an automobile 'fore now either didja' Zeke?"

"Course not."

"It won't take you long and you'll be all knowed up on all the new fangled stuff."

"Yep. I reckon."

Ezekial looked at the toilet paper and seemed doubtful.

The automobile rolled along on it's tall, skinny wheels at a breathtaking speed. The curves in the road threw Ezekial against the metal sidewalls. The holes in the road jarred his old spine mercilessly. Sam jumped from one side to the other, sniffing the rushing night air and letting it have its way with his ears and lolling tongue. It seemed to be great fun to Sam.

"Can't you slow this thing down some Hoss?"

"I could, but we want to put some miles behind us. I was thinking of going faster."

"Faster? This thang'll go faster?"

"Oh yea. We only going twelve, maybe fifteen miles in an hour. This baby'll top twenty five miles in an hour. Ya wanna' see?"

"No! I believe ya! It's fast enough Hoss. Any faster an' I may get sick. Anyways, I think I gotta pee."

"Aw heck Zeke, ain't there an empty jug back 'ere?"

"C'mon Hoss. I couldn' hit no jug with all this swayin' an' bouncin'. I'd likely get more on us than in the jug. 'Sides, I wanna' try out this here toilet paper."

"Man, we shore don't need to witness that! I'm pulling over and stopping right now."

Hoss pulled off the narrow dirt road at the bottom of a short rise and left the engine running. Ezekial struggled out of the back and headed into the trees. The constant shaking and shuddering had loosened things up inside him and he was relieved in no time. He quickly learned that toilet paper had to be folded over several times before it was safe to use. It was a learning experience. Sam had stuck close by him until he had seen him pull his britches down and squat, then his best friend had deserted him.

As Ezekial was readjusting his pants Sam returned and seemed to be trying to tell him something. Hoss and Jack had used the stop-over time to put water in the radiator to cool the little engine, finishing up as Ezekial and Sam walked up. They watched the big, crazy man trying to get his invisible dog to get in the car. Sam wouldn't load up and Ezekial wouldn't leave without him.

"Get in Zeke, le's go."

"Not 'til Sam gets in. Get in Sam!"

The dim yellow lights of an automobile topped the low hill and the driver stopped beside them and hollered over the clacking engines.

"Ya'll awright?"

"Yea, jes' answering natures call," Hoss answered.

Jack motioned for Ezekial to stoop down.

"They' got the road blocked up ahead jes' over the hill a'ways. Police say they lookin' fer escaped convicts from Huntsville. Them laws looked all in my automobile and made me prove who I was. They held me up fer fifteen minutes. Hell, I thought they's takin' me to the hoosegow."

"Oh yea? Well, that's good to know. We ain't got the time to mess with them po'lice though, is there a way 'round 'em?"

"You know, they shore is. Ya'll turn around and foller me. I'll show ya ol' Charlie's ranch road. You jes' turn around and foller me."

After Hoss got turned around, Sam, then Ezekial loaded up and they followed the farmer back the way they had come for perhaps a mile. The friendly farmer stopped just past a barbed wire and cedar post gate and got out of his car and opened it for them.

"Ya'll jes' foller this ol' road right past ol' Charlie's house, he won't mind. He'll likely be asleep fer hours by now. Jes' stay on the road and it'll come back out on this same road 'bout three miles the other side a' them laws. It'll wind around quite a bit an' you may have to push a cow outa' the way, but jes' stay on the road and it'll take you around them nosy sons of bitches."

"Thank you mister. We appreciate ya'. Yer a good man."

"Heh-heh. I wish them convicts'd come by here, I'd send them around them smart alec police too."

"Night."

"G'night. Drive careful."

Driving without the lamps Hoss drove slow and careful along the winding farm road. Despite his care however one of the rubber tires picked up a mesquite thorn and they were delayed changing the wheel and tire. Once back on the main road and with the police roadblock behind them, Hoss picked up the speed again trying to make up for the lost time. Ezekial was relieved when Hoss steered the automobile onto a long farm driveway and into an old barn. Hoss turned around in his seat and grinned at Ezekial.

"Uh. Zeke."

"Um huh?"

"Uh. Tell Sam thanks for giving us the warning 'bout them laws. If we'd of topped that hill and run into them police why, chances are we'd all been shot."

"Prob'ly so. But he knows that Hoss."

"Well, thank you Sam," Jack said.

"Yea. Uh. Thank you Sam," Hoss managed.

They got out and stretched and took turns in the outhouse, then shared a cool dipper of water from the bucket at the well.

"You boys want breakfast you'd better come on 'fore I throw it out," hollered a tiny old woman from the door of the farmhouse over the hoarse barking of an old dog. "You hush Happy! Ya'll come on in here. Wipe your feet."

"C'mon, le's see what the ol' widow's cooked up for us I'm hungry as a winter wolf."

There wasn't much talking over a fine country breakfast of fresh milk and buttermilk and coffee, hash brown potatoes and biscuits and gravy, bacon and sausage and ham and eggs fried to their preference. There wasn't much conversation after eating either as the unaccustomed richness and quantity of food lulled the men into slumber. The widow had soft feather beds for each of them, with clean tight sheets and warm soft quilts. Jack thought that there wasn't a hotel in Texas that could beat this hearty welcome. Whatever Hoss was paying her, it wasn't enough.

Awakened at noon by the tiny widow beating on a pan with a big serving spoon and hollering, "Come and get it boys 'fore I feed it to the hogs! It's getting' cold. Hurry up."

The enticing aroma of fresh baked bread and with a thick Irish stew hurried the hungry to the widows board. All the men had two helpings which made the widow smile.

When the table was cleared, Hoss asked for some playing cards to while away the afternoon. He loaned both Ezekial and Jack some money and he had already paid the widow so they all anted up for a game of poker.

Before the wall clock struck three, Ezekial had lost his money and refused another loan. By dark, Hoss had lost enough to be disgusted, if not busted, and quit. It took Jack another hour to win the widow's money. She looked so defeated then, he gave her all the money she had lost plus some of Hoss's money as well.

"Why give her money back and not give mine back?" Hoss asked in agitation.

"Hoss my friend, let me explain. First off, she plays cards better'n you. Plus I'm mindful that she's the one who's gonna' be doin' the cookin' for the next few days. But, most of all, she's got the purtiest smile I've seen in many years."

Jack was treated like the widow's prodigal son and enjoyed the sight of her smile for all the days they spent beneath her roof.

Hoss counted his remaining money added to that of Jack's and he figured it really wasn't enough. Jack and Hoss had planned to leave the country, to cut through Mexico to a small country in the Yucatan peninsula, British Honduras. They knew a man there from prison and were confident he could set them up with new identities. The government officials there were amenable to palm greasing, but to get there with sufficient money to apply the grease and set up a life for themselves was the controlling factor to their continued liberty. They discussed banks, trains and other places they might rob. Ezekial counseled against any law-breaking as it could only serve to put the law back on their trail.

When it became apparent that Jack and Hoss were determined to risk their lives to get the money they felt was needed, Ezekial told them about the gold. Hoss was skeptical at first, after all, this man who claimed to have stashed a treasure of gold also had an invisible dog as his friend. Jack however, listened to the tale from so long ago and believed. Ezekial had surprised him before. He had only one question to ask to determine his course of action.

"Zeke, after all this time, you think that gold is where you left it?"

"It's still there."

"Well, le's go find it," Jack said and looked at Hoss.

"We won't have to look for it, I've been back there a thousand times in my mind."

"How much gold is it Zeke?"

"Well, I needed two mules to carry the gold. I'd say it's four hunnerd pounds or so. I'll want to give some to the survivors of my partners in the ranch and ya'll can have a share. I'd planned fer that."

"What about you? Ain't you comin' with us to Honduras?"

"Don't know. Maybe. Maybe not. And ma'am?" Ezekial spoke to the eavesdropping widow, "I'll send you some gold too."

Though it was Hoss's money that had paid the widow to hide them and feed them until the heat from the escape had died down some, after Ezekial's promise of gold, Hoss's was the third plate served at mealtime after that.

The fugitives laid low at the widow's house for a week, until most of the excitement of the escape had diminished. Other news pushed the search for them off the front page of the newspapers and the lawmen were forced to pursue other pressing issues. Jack and Edward did not have to be convinced that Ezekial was a liability to their continued freedom due simply to his size. He would be noticed, remarked upon and reported to officials. The early reports in the newspaper had portrayed them all as desperate killers and Ezekial as the most dangerous monster of them all. There were not many men approaching seven feet and it would be a big feather in any man's hat to bring him in. Ezekial knew the attention he generated better than anyone, the thousands of stares and wide eyes as they focused on him through his life assured him that he was noticed.

Ezekial did not want anyone to get hurt in order to retain his recently removed restraint. He didn't want to use the rifle Edward had given him, neither did he want to be shot. He knew that people were fearful of him at first sighting because of his size and he knew fear had caused a multitude of murders.

He convinced Jack and Hoss that they must separate for awhile, though they now wanted him close by so they could ensure getting the gold. They agreed they would drive him to the old ranch, then they would go on to the little Mexican border village of Villa Acuna. The village was across the Rio Grande from the small town of Del Rio. He would manage to meet them there in three or four days and then they would travel up the river to the gold.

Ezekial wondered if Callie still lived. He wondered about Sallie, Nellie, Chas, Beau, Ruby and Little Beau. Then wondered what became of Boy. Luther and Micah had surely passed on. He wondered if they were buried in the hillside graveyard behind the ranch where the oak shaded the rest of those who had died for their family and friends. Were there many more buried there? And what of Mabel? Surely she still survived.

Ezekial thought about Samuel and Patricia too, but decided he would not go there along the way to the gold, though their rancho was only a few miles south of Villa Acuna. Samuel may still be there, but he was sure that Patricia had almost certainly remained in the big city of Mexico, for she had aspirations and ambitions and a strong character that, joined with her beauty and exuberant personality, would certainly open the door to her desires. No, it would be too painful to go there.

Through all the intervening years none of his old partners and friends had known where he had gone. He had managed to keep his long stay in prison from all of them. He was certain they had made inquiries in the gold fields, but they would have never imagined that he would murder anyone or be in prison. They would never look there.

Ezekial knew that if the corrupt officials in Mexico and in El Paso were to connect him to Angel's Camp it could only bring danger and hardship to his friends. The soldiers, banditos, and lawmen believed him to have hidden gold somewhere. He had only ever told them that he was from Carolina and they had never questioned that assertion. There had been two men he had met in prison who had known him from Uvalde, but he had paid one to keep his secret and the thief turned out to be honorable. The other man who had known him in Uvalde had died in an accident in a prison granite quarry in Burnet. His secret had been safe through all the years.

In the beginning Ezekial was stunned, not quiet believing he was going to be in prison for long. He thought that if he did his work and kept out of trouble that they would release him in a few years. Then he broke another man's back and then a guard's skull, or vice versa, he really couldn't remember. After that it seemed he had never been considered for release. Confused, depressed and not able to think clearly after the many beatings the guards gave him, he resigned himself to his fate. He thought he would someday die inside that Texas prison and then he and Sam could move on and see Gramps and the family once again. And then he awoke one night to see Jack sprawled bloody and beaten on the floor of that dark, tiny cell where so many years had passed. With Jack had come a friend, and hope.

He was persuaded in his thought that all his old friends at Angel's Camp would believe him dead, probably somewhere in the mountains in his quest for gold. He would make no claim to own any portion of the ranch now, he had abandoned them all those many years ago. Without him they had worked to build the ranch. Were they still there, had they moved on or died? If there were anyone of his friends left on the ranch he would take great pleasure in simply seeing them and hearing all their stories. He knew he could not stay long nor chance bringing trouble or danger there.

With Ezekial scrunched down in the rear seat Hoss stopped in a small town along the way to the ranch and bought, among other things, a paper from Houston that was several days old. There was an article about the escape at the bottom of the front page. The paper was dated three days after the escape and reported twenty seven prisoners had escaped. Fourteen had been recaptured the following day or found dead, leaving thirteen still being sought. The article quoted the superintendent of prisons as reporting that guards had been drugged and rendered unconscious. All the guards had since recovered from the near overdose of unknown drugs. Changes had been instituted in prison procedures to prevent any such reoccurrence and there was an ongoing investigation to discover the source of the drugs. All police officials in Texas and surrounding states had been notified and given descriptions of the escapees. Texas Rangers and units of the U.S. Army were assisting in the search. Five hundred dollars reward were being offered by the state for information leading to the apprehension of each fugitive. The names of all the prisoners who had escaped were listed and those who were still at large were described. When Hoss read the description of Ezekial as being six feet nine inches in height and convicted in El Paso County as well as other murders while in prison, Ezekial managed to get even lower in the back seat. They would all breathe easier when they were separated and off the Texas roads.

It was further agreed that Jack and Hoss would wait just outside Acuna until Ezekial came or until they were forced to leave by the law's pursuit. In that case, they would move to a tiny, mostly Indian settlement named Ojinaga. Ezekial would go there if they were not at the appointed spot outside Acuna, or if he were delayed.

"I won't be long at the ranch, no more than two days. I'll borry a horse and it shouldn't take more'n three days to get to Del Rio an' I'll swim the river,…"

"Naw, that ain't gonna work. To hell with that plan. We'll jes' find a place 'round here somewhere to hide out 'till you get finished visitin'. There's just too much could go wrong and we ain't got the time nor the liberty to go scoutin' around tryin' to find one another," Jack said.

"Well, I'd jes' like to know ya'll are safe over thar in Mexico."

"We won't be safe in Mexico. Them bandito army officers over there will want to collect that reward same as anybody else. An' the damned rangers don't let no international border stop 'em no way. Never has. We won't be safe 'till we get plum to Honduras and we'll only be partly safe then. We'll get as much safety as we can buy. Freedom's jes' like justice, you get about as much as you can pay for."

"Where will you hide out?"

"We'll find a place. You jes' tell us where to pick you up and when. And you be there ready to go."

"Awright. Ya'll jes' pick me up at midnight two days from now right where you drop me off. I don't want to bring trouble to my partners at the ranch. I may bring someone with me from the ranch so's I kin send some gold back to he'p them that's kept the ranch all these years. They'll be plenty of gold to go 'round. Ya'll will have enough to go wherever you want and do whatever you want. Jes' don't go to robbin' places, you'll have more money than you know what to do with directly."

"Ol' Ezekial. Ain't you a prize? Why didn't you say anything before about your ranch or the gold?"

"Yea, I wouldn't have had to rob them places to get seed money if you'd have told us 'bout the gold. An' we coulda' jes' beat it for the ranch and hid out there 'stead of payin' the widow," Hoss added his two cents.

"I wuden gonna' bring trouble to the folks at the ranch. I'll run if theys trouble at the ranch, I ain't gonna shoot nobody. You two would shoot it out if push comes to shove an' I don't wanna' hurt nobody at the ranch or no place else."

"Well, we 'preciate yore he'p Zeke, jes' remember we're countin' on ya'. "Sides, it'll be the first night we've spent away from each other in a long time, Ezekial," Jack joked.

"Yep, won't that be a blessin'," Ezekial sighed.

The road that ran west out of Uvalde to the ranch was wider and obviously much more traveled now. There was even a lumber bridge built over one of the more constant streams. There were a few farms and houses along the way too. Ezekial and Sam climbed out a quarter mile past the road that wandered off the main road down to Angel's Camp. Ezekial shook hands with his cohorts and promised to meet them two nights hence.

At past one in the morning the silvery rustler's moon lit his path cross country around mesquite, sage and prickly pear. The brush ended abruptly at long rows of furrows ready for planting. He walked quite a way to find the turn row and he was impressed by the neat working of so many acres. Gramps would have been amazed. In fact, Ezekial was amazed. Tilling the earth had come to a future that he had never imagined.

He could see the small hill behind the ranch houses as a dark shape rising into the bright night sky. He rounded far out from the buildings so as not to alert the dogs or anyone who might be awake at this hour. The thought came to him that everyone he knew may be long gone, the place sold to new owners who read the newspaper and would gladly try to collect the five hundred dollars reward. And what would he do if all those he knew were gone? Nothing for it, he thought. He would cross that bridge when he got to it.

He climbed the hill on the side of the hill away from the house and was winded with aching thighs by the time he reached the summit. He found a thick patch of purple fountain grass and laid down in it, utilizing a smooth stone for a pillow. A smile formed from his wrinkled face as he peered down on the ranch. The old rock barn that Mabel's daddy and the Germans built still stood, beside it a bigger barn with lots of pens behind it, full of cattle and horses. The women's house was still there and had grown wings. The house he and Noah and Chas had lived in had not changed at all that he could see, it had been kept up and tended well over the years. Beau and Ruby's place had doubled in size as had the old bunkhouse. There were several additional family houses spaced out down a long ranch road and good sized trees now stood where none had lived before.

There were three automobiles with wagon beds attached and one of them had another rubber-wheeled wagon hitched behind it. It seemed a prosperous enterprise.

He wondered who slept beneath those low pitched roofs now. He patted Sam's head as he lay beside him. Sam looked up at him and grinned his crooked grin, the stars twinkling in his eyes.

"Yep, you know where we're at don' cha' boy? We're home Sam. Never thought I'd see the day,…"

The sun woke Ezekial an hour after dawn, warming his face and coloring the clear sky a promising, happy shade of yellow. He blinked up and through the lacy lime green leaves of a crazy limbed mesquite and breathed in the remembered sweet fragrance of the tree's budding beans. Listening to the cicadas' lazy morning song, he felt the wonder of simply being alive and free. He had not understood, or admitted until now, how much he had missed a normal day on God's good earth.

Old and cold bones popping, he struggled to his big feet and walked stiff-legged into the surrounding brush. He unbuttoned his fly and relieved himself onto a thankful prickly pear. He moaned in the pleasurable relief to his bladder as he surveyed his surroundings. The sound of a motor drifted up to him and he watched a smoking contraption something like a tall automobile with big rear wheels dragging a plow and turning the soil like a knife through butter.

He heard a familiar distant ringing and knew there was someone doing blacksmith work in the barn. Two cowboys were catching horses in a corral, smoke was rising from most of the chimneys. Sam whined and couldn't keep his paws still. He wanted to run down the hill into the yard and be hugged by those he had loved there. Those loving friends may be long gone Ezekial thought.

And then the pair of friends watched a woman in a long dress and apron come out of the old ranch house carrying a basket and begin hanging wet clothes out to dry on a wire strung between poles beside the house. The long blonde hair was streaked with white and tied into a pony tail. The woman's gait and movement caused Ezekial to think of Callie, but this woman was not old enough he figured. Sam barked and smiled and, of course, no one heard him but Ezekial.

Sam wanted to run down the hill and looked to Ezekial expectantly. Could this be Sallie? Nellie?

"Stay Sam. Wait," Ezekial said and hugged his oldest friend.

They waited and watched several cowboys ride out, then saw one of the automobiles with a wagon bed load up with ten or twelve children of various ages. A man and woman cranked the engine started and headed out down the road. The children all held books and pinched bites of food out of sacks and boxes they carried. Ezekial figured they were being taken to school. The children were both Mexican and white, there were no black. Little Beau and his brothers and sisters came to Ezekial's mind. Where were Beau and Ruby?

Walking a wide circle in descending the hill he passed the graveyard, keeping the woman's house between him and the working hands. He climbed over the high banister at the side of the house and walked lightly over the porch floor boards to the open door of the house. Sam paced beside him. Peering into the relative darkness inside he bumped his knuckles against the door frame in a quietly respectful manner.

The blonde petite lady who had hung the wet laundry out to dry came walking from darkness into shaded light as she approached the screened door, her eyes staring and growing wide. Putting a trembling hand to her heart, she breathed, "Oh my Lord. Ezekial?"

It was Sallie. No doubt. Sam jumped and spun and barked and whined, and Ezekial wished all of Sam could be there. Despite the years of separation, Ezekial could see by what light filtered into the parlor that this was the girl he had taught to whistle. Her long, snooty nose with the acquired hump gave her away, despite the changes the years had wrought.

The crazy woman had descended on them as they were preparing for bed, beating on the door and demanding to know where Noah Lister was. Standing in their nightdresses and robes, Callie, Mabel and the girls had tried to explain the attack of the Kiowa, then tried to calm the stranger to no avail. The wild, crying and screaming woman continued to demand to know where Noah was. Exasperated, Callie blurted, "He's up there, buried in the graveyard."

The emotionally distraught woman had snatched the coal oil lamp from Mabel's hands, exclaimed, "We'll see about that!" and stomped away up the hill to the graveyard.

Billy Hell had heard the commotion of the buggy and horses arriving and had put on his boots and walked out to meet the driver, who had volunteered what information he had. The woman had hired him in San Antonio to drive her here to find her husband, Noah Lister. She had told him that she had just had Noah's son and that he had deserted her last year. She had called herself Misses Brandy Lister. He apologized for bringing them this crazy woman, but he hadn't heard about the Kiowa attack and Lister's death.

The woman was cursing up on the hill.

"You dirty old son of a bitch. You found a way to desert me too, didn't you? What am I supposed to do now, you no good bastard? It's a good thing for you that you're dead 'cause I'd kill you myself you rotten, no good, low down coward!"

She had torn the marker from his grave and was beating the ground with it when Mabel started up the hill.

"Let me Mabel," persuaded Callie. She quickly climbed the hill to grasp the exhausted, emotionally wrecked woman and let her cry uncontrollably as she led her back down the hill. Watching the pair stumble down the hill, Mabel empathized and forgave the woman as she remembered Callie holding her in much the same way not so long ago as she too had walked from her family's grave.

The women took the stranger inside. Luther came out and directed the buggy driver to the barn to loose, water and feed the exhausted team. Billy Hell washed and curried the sweat-foamed horses as Micah put a meal together for the driver. After conferring with Ezekial, Micah gave him blankets and a place in the bunkhouse.

After an hour the crazy woman wound down and Callie and Mabel put her to bed. The woman had told them how she had come to know Noah and of her experiences and her hopes since. Once in bed she slept as though she were drugged and did not wake until near noon the following day.

The woman who they had learned was named Brandy quietly accepted some simple fare at the table. Without a word she again climbed the hill and stood beside the fresh grave. In half an hour she returned and walked to where the buggy driver sat on the fence by the barn. She told him to hitch the team, she would return to Uvalde today and continue on back to San Antonio tomorrow.

Mabel walked out and invited her to stay awhile and rest, but she refused, saying she must get on with her life. The buggy driver stood listening to the women's conversation. Brandy glared at him and screamed at him to hitch the horses.

"Now! Damn it! Right now!"

"Yes ma'am."

The woman's behavior scared the driver, and surprised the others standing near. The driver hurried to comply and Luther helped him.

During the night sometime, Shoestring had drug herself down the long road to the ranch and to the buggy which was parked beside the barn. She had been exhausted, famished. Chas had fed and watered the stray dog and she had slept under the buggy. The noise awakened her and she stood wearily on weak wobbly legs and whined as Brandy approached. The loyal, loving dog looked up at her beseechingly, but Brandy angrily pushed her aside. Sam growled and Chas knelt and held Shoestring protectively.

"Boy, you want a dog? This is Shoestring. You can have her. I'm starting all over and I don't want nothing to remind me of my misery. There'll be no place for a dog where I'll be. Tie the bitch to a post for a couple of days, 'till I'm long gone. Feed her and you won't be able to get rid of her. You want her boy?"

Chas looked at Callie who nodded her head.

"Yes ma'am."

"Okay. She's yours."

The buggy driver helped her to her seat, then quickly swung up to his seat.

"Lets go!" she ordered the driver who popped the reins over the horses' backs.

Shoestring whined and struggled to follow, but Chas hugged her close and held her. Shoestring cried. Sallie and Nellie ran to join Chas in consoling her.

Cecil quickly investigated and found out where Brandy had gone and made ready to follow her. He was almost certain that she had determined to chase the father of the baby. He felt a responsibility toward her. There was a nagging belief in his heart that their paths had merged for the purpose that he should shepherd her and eventually lead her into a productive Christian life.

He could not allow her to abandon this child. The baby needed his mother, but the mother needed the baby almost as much. If Brandy was to be shaped and trained into a person of character, of self-respect, then she must accept and fulfill her responsibilities.

There was little chance she could find the father. And even if she should find him, why would such a man who had deserted her before accept her now with the added burden of a child to provide for? He believed if he let her go now, she was lost, she would revert to the sad and hopeless life she had lived before.

Cecil didn't see himself as any saint or savior, he humbly helped those who came into his life and believed that to be his duty, his stewardship. His wife and children thought of him as a good Christian man and had no doubt of his motivations. They were not surprised that he intended to chase Brandy down, they had come to expect such drastic measures to save or help others. His wife knew him to be an excellent provider, always making time and expending thought and energy for those he cared for. His friends and employees were the same as family to him and he helped them in ways they would never ask or expect. He inspired loyalty in most all of his relationships and so he was surprised and unprepared for Brandy's departure and struggled to understand and love her through this crisis. He had always gone the extra mile to assist the downtrodden, it gave him joy to be an instrument of God's grace. He had invested much into Brandy, he had come to feel like a father to her. He didn't want to lose her now.

And what of the baby boy? What chance of life was there for him without a loving mother? It was the same malady Brandy herself had suffered repeating itself in successive generations. The cruel chain must be broken and the child set free from the heartless cycle. Brandy must be convinced that she was strong enough, capable enough, if she could be taught to love enough. Sadly, Brandy had been taught nothing of real love.

Efficiently, Cecil prepared a team to pursue Brandy. He made necessary purchases for the baby's needs and for Beulah the child's wet nurse. He prepared a maid from his house to help Beaulah manage the baby and brought along Otho, a trusted man he often employed for jobs and situations no one else was suited for. Otho was an agent who accomplished the job, whatever it took. He was a quick thinker and as tough as he needed to be. Otho dressed like a gentleman and acted as civil as the circumstances allowed, but in most every case, he accomplished his purpose. As was Cecil himself, Otho was a reliable man.

By the time the group had prepared, tracked Brandy, and boarded their passage to Corpus Christi, they were three days behind her. And upon arriving in Corpus Otho found they were only hours behind her. Unfortunately, the voyage across the Gulf had made the baby slightly ill. The doctor Cecil located suggested only rest, diagnosing near exhaustion by the interruption of the newborn's sleep cycle. Otho went on ahead after Brandy to San Antonio so she would not be lost, while the others stayed and rested with the baby in a seaport hotel.

In two days the child had rallied and was restored to health. Cecil was making arrangements to travel to San Antonio when a clerk from the telegraph office brought him a message from Otho advising him that Brandy had hired a buggy and driver in San Antonio to take her to a ranch outside a small settlement on the western frontier where the father of the baby had been employed. Otho had followed Brandy as far as the settlement named Uvalde and had learned Noah Lister, the father, had been killed several days earlier in an Indian raid. Brandy had stayed at a boarding house overnight in Uvalde after returning from the ranch and was currently returning to San Antonio with the same buggy and driver. Otho would follow them back to San Antonio and continue to monitor Brandy's whereabouts.

Three days later, after Cecil had transported the women and the baby to San Antonio, Otho took him to the crib Brandy now inhabited behind a rundown cantina. There was no one other than a bartender in the saloon as Cecil and Otho walked through it toward the back door.

"Ese!--jew can't go back there, Meester."

"Sure I can. My friend is back here," Cecil said.

Otho stepped between them and put his hand on the fat Mexican's thick chest, pushing him back behind the makeshift bar.

'Sides amigo, I need a drink this fine morning while my friend visits his friend."

"No! You must pay me to go back there."

"You misunderstand. It's not that kind of visit."

The bartender began to reach under the bar but his hand stopped when Otho pulled a revolver from a shoulder holster beneath his coat and laid it heavily atop the counter.

"You know, this ol' pistol gets heavy lugging it around all day. You mind if I lay it here on the bar? "Sides, I like to keep it close to hand in case there's unexpected trouble. Comprende? Give me a beer and whiskey. In separate glasses, por favor."

Cecil found the rickety door that Otho had learned Brandy now lived and worked behind and tapped on it. There was no response so he knocked on the door harder. When there again was no reply he pushed the door inward and entered a tiny, shabby room that was almost filled by a ragged, filthy bed. Daylight filtered through cracks in the wood and adobe walls and the remaining panes of glass in the single window were frosted with dust and grime.

Brandy lay naked on a narrow, lumpy mat, a moth-eaten blanket covering only her legs. A foul odor of sweat and worse was trapped in the small enclosure and Cecil propped the door open to air it out. Whiskey bottles sat and lay on the uneven caliche floor. Cecil saw a robe thrown over a broken and wired together chair in a corner and threw it at Brandy angrily.

"Brandy! Put that on. Wake up!"

She woke and slung the robe away.

He shook her leg and said "Get up! Now!"

"Get out of here!" she screamed and glared at him. As it penetrated her fogged brain who was waking her, she slurred, "Sheshul?"

"Yes, it's Cecil. I've chased you halfway across the continent, now get up! Get dressed. I'm taking you home."

"You ain't taking me nowhere. Get out of here!"

"Brandy, please. Think about what you're doing. You have a fine baby boy, a business, a home. And friends who care for you."

"No! No! I don't want any of that! I don't want no baby. Leave me be!"

"I won't. You have a child who needs his mother. You have escaped this sorry life and made a place for yourself and your baby. Why would you give up all you have worked for to live like this? Now come on Brandy. Please. Get dressed. Come home."

"No! Leave me alone! Get out of here! I don't want none of it. That life ain't my life. You can have it, you can have it all. The business, the home, the baby, I don't want any of it! Get out! Get out! Get out of here!"

In the cantina Brandy's screams were plainly heard. The fat Mexican bartender again moved his arm to reach under the bar.

"No, no Sancho. Leave the gun there. My friend is just having a friendly discussion with the lady back there. So just draw me another beer and relax."

Brandy frantically jumped up off the bed and slung the robe on. She pushed by Cecil and he grabbed at her shoulder. Knocking his hand off she screamed, "Get your hands off of me! Get away from me! Leave me the hell alone!"

She strode into the bar and told the bartender to give her a drink. He poured her three fingers of whiskey which she threw back in one swallow. She coughed and said, "More."

The Mexican poured more and Cecil put his hand on her shoulder.

"No, Brandy,..."

She turned and threw the whiskey in Cecil's face screaming, "Leave me alone! Go away!"

The bartender managed to get his hand on a short, double-barreled shotgun and began to raise it when Otho grasped the heavy pistol on the bar top and hit him in the face, grabbing the shotgun and wrenching it from the fat Mexican, who fell back into the whiskey bottles on a shelf behind him.

"Stop! Go! Leave! Get your hands off me!"

A big shadow fell across them and a voice said, "Hold it stranger."

In the door stood a man with a badge pinned to his vest aiming a hog-leg pistol at Otho.

"Throw that shotgun and the pistol over here by my feet mister, and do it slow and gentle. We don't want no accidents and I ain't shot nobody yet this mornin', so lets be reasonable and talk about this problem before it gets complicated. Le's don't have no long conversation though 'cause I ain't had breakfast an' I get ornery when I let hunger gnaw on me too long. So jes' kinda' slide them firearms over this a'way."

Otho complied and immediately the bartender began to snitch on him, pointing out his bloody, separated eyebrow, demanding the deputy arrest both Otho and Cecil. The deputy questioned each of them and when he heard that the woman had abandoned her baby to return to a life of prostitution and drunkenness, it seemed that he'd heard enough. He held up his hand to signal an end to the conversation, bent down and unloaded the shotgun and laid it on the bar and stuck Otho's pistol in his gun belt. He told the barkeep to go get his eye stitched, told Brandy to go get some clothes on and ordered Otho and Cecil to come with him.

Walking away from the cantina, the deputy pushed back his hat, took a deep breath and blew his cheeks out as he looked the pair over.

"You two fellers have come a long way to try and redeem a whore. Can't be done."

"She's a friend," Cecil stated.

"Yea. I'll bet," the deputy snickered.

"It's not like that, I..."

"Mister! It don't matter how you think it is. What does matter is what that woman thinks an' she don't want to go with you. So, leave her where she wants to be, go back where you come from, find another friend."

"Just let me talk to her, show her the baby, maybe..."

"Listen! I'm not gonna' repeat myself all the mornin'. I'm going to get some flapjacks and bacon. You can't make a silk purse out of a sow's ear and you can't make a whore be a lady. Nor a fit mother. So just go on home an' find someone nice to raise that baby."

"But,..."

"I've done with talkin'. If I hear of you goin' back to that cantina or botherin' that woman again, you may not get a chance to go home again fer quite awhile. Here's your pistol. Get your things together and get on outa' San Antone."

The big deputy turned and entered a cafe as Cecil and Otho reluctantly walked back to the hotel. Cecil and Otho both kept an eye on the cantina for two days but Brandy never left. Many men came in the night and her laughter could be heard with the drunken, raucous voices of the barrachos. Food was delivered several times a day to the patrons from an eatery across the way.

Cecil wrote a letter to Brandy in an effort to bring her to her senses. He hired a Mexican lad to take her the writing. Less than half a minute after the lad entered the cantina he was chased out by the fat bartender brandishing his shotgun. Looking up to where they watched and waited he thumbed back the hammer on the shotgun.

"Acercate mas, pendejos."

Brandy came out half dressed, pale and drunken.

"Leave! Go back home! Take the damned baby and go! Leave me alone!"

It seemed hopeless that she would return to a semblance of sanity. He had never imagined things would come to this. Had he so misjudged the girl? Cecil decided that his next course of action should be to travel to the ranch and see if the man Noah Lister had family there or anywhere. He had come this far, he may as well leave no stone unturned.

In a rented two-seated buggy they traveled west, stopping frequently to rest the baby. It was further to the ranch than he had thought and an arduous journey over rough country, sparsely settled. With the baby and ladies it was a three day effort to arrive, but they were all welcomed and made comfortable at the ranch. There was quite a fuss over the baby, after all, it was Noah's son.

There was discussion and confusion about Brandy's behavior, and several silent prayers. Cecil recognized these folks to be good, responsible and a loving family. He was surprised that Noah had no blood kin. In two days of almost continuous conversation and deliberation, and after invitation from the women of Angel's Camp, Cecil agreed it was best all around to leave the boy with them. These people would provide all the love and all else the child would require. If Brandy came to her senses, the boy would be relatively near to her. He would make Brandy aware of the baby's location by sending word through the deputy he had met, she may not read a letter.

Beulah had no kin anywhere that she knew of. She had given birth to two babies but they both had died. Being welcomed and wanted by the women at Angel's Camp, she was happy to stay. Callie promised she would be paid as a valued employee and she would have a room built just for her and the boy. She also promised that if she should decide to go elsewhere that arrangement would be made and her passage paid. Ruby would be having another child in a few months and it would be a great help to have someone specifically for that purpose.

Cecil promised to write, as did Callie, and he reluctantly, yet confidently left the healthy, promising baby in the care of these warm, good people. He had been attracted to Callie, she was an intelligent, loving, handsome woman of strong character. In the short time they spent together they had become good friends, each feeling that they had known the other for a much longer time. Each of them promised to write occasionally. The boy had tied them together.

Billy Hell had listened without comment and mulled over the circumstance of the abandonment of his longtime friends son. Noah never knew he had fathered a son. If he had known, Billy was sure the boy would be his highest valued treasure. Noah Lister deserved better. So did this innocent boy. He vowed to find a way.

Roe was anathema to the Comanche and Kiowa. Even the accursed Tonkawa and Kickapoo south of the long river had driven him away. He had wandered alone, his only companion his pain, for a handful of moons. He spoke only to the spirits and to himself.

None knew the vision that had been given him, he was sure he was the one chosen to drive the pale eyes back to the rising sun.

He had all he needed. He had his rifle, his bow, his knife and well-learned stealth. He could go alone where many together could not go. Sleepy villages he plundered for only his needs, he took nothing highly valued by the whites, he had no use for jewelry or money. He took only food, ammunition, a chicken or a pig. He left them their lives. For now.

He had waited until it was time. He had watched and learned all that he must know to succeed. No one at the ranch of the red-haired bruja knew of his presence. He would capture the red-haired sorceress and he would conquer her with long-imagined torments. Finally, she would cry out to him as her god, begging him for the release of death.

She had turned half his face into a death mask. She had great power, strong medicine that had tested his spirit and strengthened his resolve. What he had been unable to do with his own people or with many warriors of the Kiowa he would do alone as he had done at the first when he was little more than a child.

Tonight, if the winds and the spirits agreed, he would take her. All through the day he had kept a distance away and downwind from the houses. He knew the dogs had sensed him and he would not tempt the spirits. He was aware he smelled like a human being, much different from the white beasts. The dogs knew him to be an enemy. When he began his attacks for vigil there was only one dog, now there were several along with peacocks and they sometimes ranged together without the white eyes. Sooner or later, the dogs would give warning of his presence. He knew he must take the red-haired one quickly and silently.

Before he discovered the place where the red-hair slept, a girl child had seen him peering in the window one morning long before the dawn. She had screamed and he had run like the wind, his chosen path of retreat hidden from the man who watched through the night atop the house of the animals. The dogs barked until the big man awoke and opened the door and by then Roe had been to his pony and he put distance between them quickly. As no one gave chase, he thought the mother may have dismissed the girl's vision as only a bad dream.

Roe believed he had found a way into the women's house, the safest, most direct way. He had little fear of being caught inside as his watching had convinced him that there were no men in the big house in the night. Why the men did not pleasure and warm themselves with the women during the night he did not understand. Strange were the ways of the white people. The days and nights were still hot and the high place in which the red-hair slept above the others had two windows, one window was on the side of the house where it could be reached from the roof and out of the sight of the watchman atop the animal's house. The red-hair opened the windows to let the breeze cool her, he had seen the cloths in the window move with the air. If he could get onto the roof he could lower himself with a rope into the window. Once in the room, he would hit her hard in the head to put her into a deep sleep, then tie her and muzzle her and lower her by rope to the ground below. The ponies would be only a short distance away.

He must choose a hot night. He must not let the dogs smell him. There were peacocks there also that could give warning of him, but he had seen the giant oak tree where the peacocks roosted and he could avoid them.

This would be a coup to be heralded in song and stories around the campfires of his people for generations. He would return to his people and be welcome. No longer would he be an evil omen of ill fortune, he would again have status, his face would be his pride, not his shame. A great leader he would be whose medicine and methods would conquer all enemies, a hero, a legend.

The late summer night he chose to steal the red-haired girl, the moon was dark and a wind blew hot whistling gusts which stole the breath and disguised the sounds of his climbing and walking across the roof. The darkness was deep beneath thick clouds and the dawn was closer than the last sunset when he tied the rope around the chimney stone and quietly lowered it down the side of the house. Peering over the peak of the roof he noted the watchman was smoking a cigarette and looking away from him over the fields. Backing off the roof, rope in hand, feet backing down the side of the house, he gained a spot beside the window. Leaning to the side he peered over the window seal into the dark interior but could see nothing but the fluttering cloth that hung there. Lifting a foot to the window ledge he swung his other leg up and silently slid his lower body through the open window.

Mabel couldn't sleep. Again. Night after night there had been a trembling trepidation in her stomach as darkness came. Somehow she knew that Bloody Roe still lived and that he would come for her again and again until he got her. Again. Callie had tried to calm her, tried to convince her that he was dead, that he could not survive the shot to the face she had delivered to him, but her fear did not agree. Mabel believed he was the cause of the Kiowa attack, that he had waited and watched the battle, hoping for an opportunity to swoop down and take her when most of the danger was past. She knew him to be a coward, but a dangerous and vicious coward.

She believed that Nellie had not simply had a bad dream a fortnight ago, she knew it was him at the window looking for her. She worried that Bloody Roe would take or hurt one of the children or Callie, that was her greatest fear. She could fight the fear that she might be captured or killed by the murderous savage but the thought of those innocents suffering the tortures of that devil haunted her unbearably.

It was hot. Even the gusts of the night breeze were not refreshing but stifling. Her hair and nightdress stuck to her sweating skin. She threw the covers back, swung her legs to the oaken floor, stood and walked to the window. Standing beside it she looked at the trees bending and swaying in the wind.

A joist groaned under the weight of the wind. There was no light to be seen in the bunkhouse or elsewhere. She began to turn to the pitcher for a drink of water when a thump drew her attention to the window sill. There was a flexing human foot clad in a moccasin. Mabel froze in shock momentarily, then extreme rage was born of great fear and as the legs swung and slid under the raised sash she reached up and slammed the window frame down on the stomach of the monster who had terrorized her and so many others. She screamed her hate in a primitive cry that sounded like a panther or an eagle and pushed the window down on the heartless monster with all her strength and wrath.

Sam's angry barking woke Ezekial and Shoestring joined in when she saw the man would join them in the fray. Grabbing only the loaded shotgun he ran dressed only in his union suit to the door. The dogs sprang off the small porch and sprinted toward the women's house and stopped beneath Mabel's window, jumping, growling and barking at the strange apparition of half a man twisting and writhing there.

Callie had jerked awake, shaken by the piercing screams. Grabbing the big Colt revolver that she kept on her bedside table, she ran to her daughter's room. They were awake too, sitting up in their beds.

"Momma?" Sallie asked as Callie lit the coal oil lamp that she took from the table there.

"Are ya'll alright?"

"Yes."

"Um huh."

There was a crash of broken glass upstairs and Callie pushed her daughters out of bed.

"Get up! Come with me. Now!"

The girls stumbled up the stairs behind her as there was another shattering of wood and glass from Mabel's room.

"Mabel!" Callie hollered above the din.

Roe had managed to pull the heavy club from his waistband and swung it against the windowpane. The fragments of glass and mullions rained down over his naked torso as he continued to beat the window which held him fast. Through the wreckage a pair of hate-filled murderous eyes gleamed into another pair that reflected every bit as much insane and deadly loathing. Lifting his upper body as he swung the rock-headed club, he saw the red-haired one holding the remaining frame of the window against his stomach and saw by the light of the lantern the pistol the other woman aimed at him.

Callie yelled, "Get out of the way Mabel!"

Mabel looked behind her, saw Callie and the pistol and moved aside, releasing the window frame. The laws of gravity and karma took over. Before he began to fall Callie put two hot hunks of lead into his flexing chest. Ezekial dodged back out of the way beneath the window and fired both barrels of the twelve gauge into the wriggling body as it hit the ground head first and was attacked by the dogs.

Ezekial pulled and pushed Sam and Shoestring and the other hounds away from the corpse whose head and neck were bent and broken by the fall. He looked up at Callie and Mabel leaning out the window, Callie pointing the Colt down at what had been a man seconds before.

Seconds later Billy Hell and all the cowboys were there asking questions, spreading out in search of any other hostiles. Beau and Micah and the men from the family houses gathered and discussed the madman's attack. When the body was examined the result of Mabel's shot into Roe's face were evident. They were amazed a man could survive such a maiming and desecration of a human face. Teeth and bone were exposed to suggest a demonic smile and snarl, the eye almost rolling from its socket. There were two holes in the skinny chest and two in the upper back where Callie had shot him and the shotgun had gutted the body. The neck was grotesquely broken and the arms were torn of muscle where the dogs had ripped it.

Callie and Mabel looked into one another over the lamp lit body. Unspoken was the shared knowledge that if not for Mabel's fear and resulting insomnia, she would now be Bloody Roe's captive once again. Fear and intuition had warned her. Love had saved her. Roe's hatred and pride had finally brought him to suffering, banishment and death.

In the first light of dawn Billy Hell drug the carcass miles from the ranch houses, poured kerosene over it and burned all but the blackened bones of Bloody Roe.

Chapter Fourteen

"Can a woman forget her sucking child, that she
should not have compassion on the son of her womb?
yea, they may forget, yet I will not forget thee."
Isaiah 49:15 (KJV)

"What a strange illusion it is to suppose that beauty is goodness."
---Leo Tolstoy

IT WAS REALLY a three day trip from Angel's Camp west to the Chavez Ranch, especially for a horse to carry Ezekial's weight. As he was always in a hurry to get there though, he took three horses, his Percheron and two other big strong horses and he switched them often. That way he managed the distance in two long days. Sometimes when Sam got weary, Ezekial would put him on one of the extra horses. The horses he took were all accustomed to Sam sometimes riding with Ezekial and accepted Sam riding them without much fuss. Folks got a chuckle out of Sam lounging on a horses' back and, as always, Sam would grin his lop-sided smile back at them.

Patricia was still far away and Ezekial missed her more than he would admit, even to himself. He enjoyed spending a few days with his friend Samuel, but he yearned to be with Patricia. He had even thought of riding all the way down to Mexico City just to visit with her for awhile, but was afraid that her mother would be offended by his effrontery. She never said anything that justified his opinion, but in Consuela's facial expressions and behavior it was obvious to Ezekial that she neither liked nor trusted gringos. He had hoped that he could change her mind in time. But, without warning to him, Consuela had taken her daughter a thousand miles away with no assurance they would ever return.

He and Samuel talked of the cattle drive that their hands would make the next year along the path that Charles Goodnight and Oliver Loving had used earlier in the year. Neither of them would be making the trip, they would each stay at home and guard the ranch. Though the Yankee army had established and re-established forts all along the line of western settlements in Texas, no one who knew the Comanche or Kiowa thought they would be impressed or intimidated. Close by Uvalde and Angel's Camp was Fort Inge which had been again populated with blue-coats. Just how effective these troops would be against perhaps the world's best cavalry and guerrilla fighters was debatable.

Samuel was relieved that his mother and Patricia were safe from Indian attacks and the many banditos on the border, but he was also lonely for those he loved, just as Ezekial was. Neither was good company for the other because they reminded one another of the joys and comforts the simple presence of the women bestowed. There were long and frequent silences between the friends and Ezekial soon made his excuses and headed his horses home.

Sam hung his head all the way home. He missed Patricia too, because without her Ezekial wasn't there, a piece of him was missing. Sam wanted the happiness of their youthful lives to return. Life wasn't whole without laughter.

The sound of building, saws and hammers, filtered through the scrub oak and prickly pear before they came in sight of the ranch. Sam saw the children, barked, and bee-lined to their happy playful laughter. It was just the balm they both needed, Ezekial chuckled at their antics, and his smile soothed his sore soul.

A room was being built for Beulah and a small nursery adjoining were being added to the side of the women's house. A wooden frame and roof had been almost completed and thick blocks of native stone was being mortared and stacked outside the frame. When Ezekial stepped down from the saddle Chas was there to hug his leg. He reached down and lifted him and threw him in the air.

"Hey pardner!"

"Hey Zeke. Next time you go see Samuel, can I go?"

"Well, we'll see. It may be awhile 'fore I go back over there though."

"How come?"

"Cause, well, we'll be busy around here getting' ready for the cattle drive in the spring and those Comanche have to be kept away from here. Me and you, why, we gotta' protect the womenfolk."

"Heck! Them Comanche are the ones who need protection from the womenfolk."

"Ha! Yea, I know. But don't tell them that, they might figger out how useless we are and quit feeding us."

"Zeke! Zeke!" the girls screamed as they ran to him and hugged him.

"Come see Beulah and Boy's room."

"I seen it, it's almost finished, ain't it? Say, I'm sure hungry, yore mother got any goose bumps cookin'?"

"You're always hungry. Come on. Let's go see."

The simple welcome and love of these little ones was sweet and soothing medicine for his melancholy mind. The children made this particular place on the planet feel like home. They were unrestrained in their love and they got as much as they gave.

As Callie and Mabel sat at the hand hewn cedar table watching their big friend eat, the children ran outside to feed Sam some big bites of beef. Between bites Ezekial answered their question. They had, of course, discussed Ezekial's feelings for Patricia and agreed not to mention her to him. It was obvious that she had not returned from Mexico City, otherwise Ezekial would be full of news concerning her. He told them that Samuel would have a herd of about three hundred to add to the cattle drive, it was all he expected to retain from the reduction of his herd by the Mexican army, the bandits on both sides of the Bravo and the Indians. Billy came in and heard the news about Samuel's three hundred and told them that Angel's Camp would have five to seven hundred head, according to the size of the herd they wanted to retain. They had branded over a thousand cows.

Billy also said that Reading Black had told him that Charlie Goodnight was in San Antonio for business reasons and planned to be there for another week. Mr. Black had suggested that Billy travel there and speak with him about the trail he had taken last year to market cattle in New Mexico at Fort Sumner and in Denver. Mr. Black was not in the best of health, had been advised to rest, so he was asking Billy to go as he had served with Goodnight in ranger service and they were friends. He had offered to pay half the costs of the trip.

The three owners agreed that it would be beneficial to speak with Goodnight and since Billy was his friend it was decided that he should go and meet with him as soon as practicable before he left San Antonio to return to his CV ranch in Rock Springs near Weatherford. With Ezekial's return to supervise the ranch work, there was no reason Billy couldn't leave in the morning.

Two days later Billy stabled his two horses and found Goodnight at the Menger Hotel. They just had time for a late night cap before going to bed and they set a time to talk after breakfast in the morning. Billy had paid a clerk when he checked in to have a bath drawn in his room and he soaked the trail grime off while he shaved. The whiskey, water and weariness of the journey brought him a deep healthy slumber between the clean, crisp sheets.

Dressed in his other clothes from the saddle roll and eating the perfect medium-rare steak with eggs, gravy and biscuits at the hotel restaurant in the good company of his friend Charlie put Billy in a fine and rare humor. Re-living and embellishing experiences from their adventures as rangers, they lied and laughed through coffee and cigars on the veranda. Charlie reminded and regaled him of the crazy days they had shared.

Charlie's black friend and favored employee Bose Ikard who Goodnight said was his top night herder, best roper, bronc-buster, cook and Indian fighter was sitting, smiling and listening to the tales. He had been born a slave in Mississippi and brought to Weatherford at five years of age in eighteen fifty two. He was about twenty now and still not completely comfortable sitting on the porch of the best hotel in San Antonio with two white men. He had noticed the scowls of several patrons and passersby, but was tickled to see their expressions change drastically when Charlie or Billy looked up. The citizens and guests who did not actually know who these men were recognized the type. High heel boots and Spanish spurs, hard muscled, tanned and fit, wide-brim hats, low-slung Colts and confident demeanor, relaxed and sure.

"Bose, did I ever tell you 'bout the time ol' Billy complemented a young vaquero and then took offense when the cowboy expressed his gratitude?"

"No suh."

"Come on now Charlie, it was a simple misunderstanding and,... hell, I could still get arrested if you continue to testify to everyone about my criminal past."

"Aw Billy, nobody who's running the gov'ment in Texas cares 'bout any Meskin cattle thief getting wounded years ago."

"You don't know he was a thief."

"Why, he was a Meskin wuden he? That's a good start at being a thief ain't it? Ha-ha," Charlie winked at Bose. He went on in his unhurried drawl to tell of the pair of them drinking away an infrequent payday on a freezing cold winter's day at a saloon in Waco. Rain and sleet made their breath fog their vision even worse than the rot-gut rye whiskey. There was a pot-bellied stove in the middle of the small barroom, but it did little good against the wet wind blowing through the cracks in the clapboard walls.

Billy had held his bladder as long as he could, not relishing braving the weather to the ditch out back that was what was left of the out-house that had blown down. It was use the ditch as a urinal or walk a quarter mile to the livery and use the outhouse there. He staggered to the edge of odorous ditch and squinted through his frosty breath to see where his smoking line of piss was falling. Small particles of ice fell on his shoulders and hat, some finding a way down his collar.

He noticed the skinny, big-hatted Mexican standing there beside him also draining his tank, and, being happily inebriated and trying to be friendly he had said, "Purty chilly."

SEPARATE REALITIES

The little Mexican looked at him quizzically, then his eyes lowered to his anatomy his hand was holding, smiled proudly and replied, "Gracias."

The Mexican had been unable to replace his dangling appendage before Billy had drawn his Colt, cocked it, and threatened, "Why, you li'l smartalec, bean-eatin', taco bending, chihuahua-looking som' bitch,...don' you run!"

Billy was only prevented from murder by the alcohol he had consumed, drunkenly putting one chunk of lead in the Mexicans small behind and another through his big hat. Charlie had been there in a tick, pistol in hand, and, seeing the limping cabellero trying to run through the frozen mud, he managed to convince Billy to holster his pistol and head for the livery to get their horses and get out of town before the town marshal arrested him. They hightailed it to the ranger camp and soon as the weather broke they headed out to their new assignment close by Weatherford at Fort Belknap.

"If not fer me Bose, Billy Hell would be a convict with striped clothes on 'til this day. Heh-heh."

"Yea, I still owe you on that deal, I guess."

"You shore do. An' I intend to collect on it too."

They talked of the trails and the lessons learned by Goodnight on his trail drives the first year and the potential hazards he would avoid in the future. They talked of horses best suited to raise for the conditions in Texas. They spoke of Indians and weather and water holes. Over cheesy enchiladas and frosty beer Charlie told him of the new army posts the army was building and the ignorance of assigning infantry troops there to chase Comanche and Kiowa. A fort would be built at the juncture of the Concho river and Middle Concho next year and Charlie wanted to merge herds there then follow the narrow stream west as far as it went before the long dry journey over the plain to the Pecos river. After a rest at the Pecos they would drive the herd along it northward. A long way northward.

Billy kept quiet about Mabel's plan. Maybe she'd change her mind. Mabel had plainly stated her decision to drive her own cattle to market. To those who knew Mabel well, it was no surprise. But, it may be a deal-breaker with Charlie. A trail drive wasn't the kind of trip to have a female along on. She said she was aware of the hardships she would be required to endure as well as the allowances the men would believe would have to be made for her, but they would learn that no exceptional concessions would be necessary. Some allowance would be required, but those allowances would entail no inconvenience for the men. She was an owner and she would make the decisions about her herd. And she made it clear, her plans were not up for discussion. Ezekial was needed at the ranch to supervise the remaining hands and fend with Indians, bandits, and whatever miseries might present themselves as Billy would be away on the drive. Callie had children to mind and was not as young as Mabel. An owner needed to go with the herd and it was up to her. Besides, Mabel wanted to go. She was going. Billy had no doubt of that.

Billy had tried to make her understand how the men would feel. Men had always known that women were bad luck on such a venture. A woman on the battlefield, a woman aboard a ship at sea, such places were not for women. The men would be looking to her too often and not at the cattle or their surroundings. She would not only be a distraction but would undermine his authority. If she disagreed about a decision he made on the drive, would she yield to his experience and judgment? She was a headstrong woman, she had demonstrated that. But, she was young, inexperienced, and just too damned pretty to take on a long trail drive.

Her presence would be a constant reminder of his feelings for her. He was afraid he would be so mindful of her that he would make a costly blunder in his management of the herd. She was a full-grown woman, ripe for the picking, and he was too much aware of it when she was close by. Then again, he hated to leave her as well as the other women and children at the ranch. Noah was dead and if the Indians came back around he was worried about being away driving a herd.

Truth was, he had a hard time keeping his eyes off her, her every movement seemed a dance, every word a song. She was so young, was she too young? Oh, she was mature in every way, no doubt about that, but he was an older man. She was his boss and he felt uncomfortable when he imagined that she might think he was a gold digger. He didn't care what others thought. Not much.

He believed what he felt for her was the right kind of love, but he wasn't purely sure. He wanted to protect her like a father or a brother. He admired her character. He saw her as the most beautiful woman he had ever laid eyes on, but was that love? He had not been around women much, not good women. He had spent most of his adult life out in the wild, trailing and fighting Indians and bad men. When he had been in the towns, he had done what all the other rangers had done, got drunk, gambled, maybe paid a whore to relieve the pressure. He had never had opportunity to speak to the good girls, the girls who went to church and stayed at home at night. Even now, he wasn't real easy when he had to have a conversation with Mabel or Callie or Ruby or any other decent woman. There were words and ways he had acquired that he knew were not suitable for polite company, he was rough as a cob. He had looked forward to the trail drive as a time to get away for awhile, get some distance and perspective and maybe figure things out some. As things were, he was uneasy when he thought of her.

And the fact that he believed Mabel knew how he felt about her made him all the more uneasy. He wasn't really around her much at the ranch, she was in the house a lot. Tending to those things women tended to and when she came out and saddled Betty to ride alone or with the girls, she stayed apart from him or the hands. He didn't like her and the girls riding too far from the ranch house without an escort, so he had kept them in sight as he tried to keep out of their sight. He felt like a sneak following her and having to hide, but he knew that he would feel worse if something were to happen to her or the girls. Besides, it was his job to look out for them. And despite some people's opinions, there were still bad men all around them, red, brown and white. Maybe a few black ones out there too, so he was going to do his duty.

He was almost certain she had seen him following her despite his efforts to hide. She always had a knowing look in her eyes when they met at the ranch, and a secret smile that was clear as Indian sign language telling him she knew how he felt about her. And, if he wasn't mistaken, she seemed real pleased about his interest. But, he wasn't sure how she might feel about his intentions.

There wasn't anyone around the ranch he felt he could talk to about the situation to ease his mind. Except her. And when he thought about talking to her about his feelings for her his heart just about jumped out of his chest. He had no experience to guide him in dealing with these feelings and it confused and frustrated him. He could wrestle a brand-dodging steer, ride a mean and wild bronc or fight a whole passel of Indians, he had learned how to do these things, but this hundred pound female was a fearful foe. And he didn't want to feel like she was a foe or that there was any competition. She just seemed to be on top in their relationship. She had all the confidence. That dog-gone smile!

When Charlie went up to his room in the hotel, Billy went for a walk down by the river to think about things. He sat on a big rock and rolled a cigarette. He let the smoke calm his thoughts as he watched the huge white clouds and the slow-rolling river.

The abandonment of little Boy was a situation he had not been able to stop trying to solve. He couldn't help but feel that, as Noah's friend, he should put his hand into solving the dilemma. Any child should have a father and a mother. Noah had lost his parents in a terrible way when he was just old enough to suffer the worst. He knew Noah would want his son to have parents. If he were alive, he would give Boy a good life. He'd watched Noah around Chas and saw how much he enjoyed giving of his time, his experience, his heart. He had loved the boy. How much more would he love his own son?

He had also observed Mabel around Boy and knew that she loved him. It just seemed fit that she and he could be the child's parents. He just couldn't see how to get there from where things were and he couldn't shake his troubled mind.

And what if this prostitute decided that she wanted her son in a year or in a few years? Could she just come and rip him away from those who had loved and cared for him? He would have to find out about that.

Walking back to the hotel he came upon a sign on a shingle hanging above his head that had the words Attorney at Law freshly painted in gold leaf. A very interested, energetic young man extracted the whole story from him with cutting, precise questions and then presented what seemed at the moment a perfect solution. He explained that since the only married people at Angel's Camp were either Mexican or Negro, and since it was Billy's plan to wed Mabel soon, he would prepare adoption papers so that the dates could be filled in after the actual matrimony. This all cost the princely sum of ten dollars, five for the attorney and five for the drunken judge who would approve the irregular document. Billy thought five dollars was robbery, but he paid the lawyer and gave him five for the judge. Ten dollars was two weeks wages for Billy and this greenhorn had made five dollars in an hour.

The attorney, his clerk and Billy then walked the quarter mile to the cantina where Boy's mother lived and earned her wages, which also impressed Billy. The fat Mexican bartender acted ignorant, like he didn't savvy English, and charged them two dollars each to go back to Brandy's shack.

After enduring her cursing and screaming and waiting until she medicated herself with a quarter of a bottle of mescal, the papers were eventually signed, duly witnessed and sworn to. The clerk put a seal on the papers and they proceeded to a red-nosed judge's office who cut the attorney's long-winded tale short, snatched the half sawbuck and signed the papers with a flourish and a smile.

With a farewell and a handshake the smooth young lawyer left him on the sidewalk, the expensive piece of long paper in his hand. He sat on a porch step and tried to read the words he guessed were English. The attorney had explained that Billy and whoever's name filled in the blank space that had been provided were 'henceforth' the legal guardians of the male child, Boy Lister. Durn, Billy thought, being a father was an expensive position. In the last hour it had already cost him sixteen dollars. He thought he had better buy himself some tobacco before this fatherhood bankrupted him.

That same night at the supper table he told Charlie all about it. He listened politely without comment as he devoured a huge beefsteak. After ordering apple pie and coffee, which he drank straight down despite it still being almost boiling, Charlie asked who it was that he planned to marry.

Billy blushed and stuttered, "Well, I...I hope, maybe, I mean, if things go right and she can see her way, why, I'm thinking that maybe..."

"C'mon Billy, spit it out. Who'll be the mamma?"

"Well, Charlie, I'm hoping that, if things go..."

"Who? Who, Billy?"

"Mabel. Mabel Curtsinger."

"Little Mabel? Why, is she full growed yet?"

"Yep. She's seventeen Charlie."

"Damn. I'm getting' old. Seems jes' yesterday when I saw her there in Uvalde while visiting Reading Black. She was a purty lil thing."

"Still is, 'cept she ain't so little anymore."

"Seventeen! She's nearly an ol' maid. And, if memory serves, you're my age. Thirty."

"Yep."

"Well, she may think thirty to be old as saltwater boy. Do you think she has a shine for ya' then?"

"She smiles at me Charlie. Sometimes."

Charlie rocked back on the hind legs of his chair and laughed so loud everyone at the other tables looked and had to chuckle at a man who laughed like that. Between struggling breaths he managed to encourage Billy, whose ears were red as roses, "That's a good start Billy-Boy. Yes sir. You're half way home."

"Charlie, now this ain't no laughing matter."

"Shore ain't. Oh Lordy. Let me breath a minute. Whew! Don't you think she'll see it as a bit presumptuous, you adopting children into the family when you ain't even asked her if she'd marry you and without her knowledge or consent? Women usually like to be consulted about such things as marriage and children. I mean, hell Billy, you ain't got no experience with womenfolk do you?"

"What's that mean? That word, pre...presu..."

"Presumptuous. Means you're so sure she's gonna want to marry you that you done adopted this child of Noah's without even askin' her nothin'."

"Maybe I better ask her."

"Ask her what?"

"You know. Ask her if she'd want to adopt Boy when we get married. Oh. An' ask her if she could see her way to marry me."

"Ha! What you gonna ask her first?"

"I see what you mean."

"Let me give you an idea about how you go about this, charmin' Billy. Soon as you get back you give the girl a pretty present you bought her here."

"But I ain't got no money left."

"I'll loan you the money. With interest of course."

"What do I get her Charlie?"

"Sumpen purty. A necklace or a comb for her hair."

"Okay."

"Then, you get somebody that plays the guitar or the fiddle to play something romantic the first evenin' you get back and you take that girl for a walk."

"Uh huh."

"You give her your present, kiss her, tell her how beautiful she is and how much you love her. Then you take her hand, bend down on one knee and ask her if she'll marry you."

"On my knees?"

"On one knee son, one knee. That's how it's done."

"That's all there are to it?"

Charlie's smile split his face. "No. No, that's not 'all there are to it,' but it's a start. She'll either say yes or no. Maybe. If she's like most females she'll say that she'll think on it. Women just naturally like fer a man to wait on 'em. They figger the more you wait on 'em, the more you love 'em. So be prepared to do some waitin'. And get used to it. A married man does lots of waitin'.

"An' boy, don't say nothin' 'bout this here adoption paper until you're hitched. Wives like to think they have some say in what a man decides to do. Unnerstand?"

"Yea Charlie. Say, you asked a girl to marry you awready?"

"Naw. Not yet. But I've been studying on it for quite awhile now, lucky for you. My girl Molly won't be able to tell me she won't marry me. I'll have all the angles figgered."

"Seems like."

"But Billy, don't put it off, do it soons you get back or you'll chicken out."

"No. I won't."

"Billy, you better ask her before somebody else does."

"Who'd do that? Why, they'd better not, I'd whup their ass!"

"Wuden do no good. Not if she's awready spoken for."

"That Ezekial. He might ask her. He'd own two out of three parts of the ranch then."

"Would he now?"

"Yep. I'd better get on back to the ranch."

"Better hurry."

"I'll leave in the mornin'. Early."

"Hello Sallie," Ezekial smiled, feeling the old, familiar warmth of tender love as she came into his arms.

"I can't believe my eyes. Mother! Come look at this!"

"What is it honey?" came the same voice from the back of the house, followed by the smiling form of an old woman with a roll of gray pinned up and wiping her hands on a towel. Callie just stopped at the door to the parlor. The smile slowly dissolved into the soft wrinkled folds of her face and she began to shake and tremble as tears began to fill the faded blue eyes. Gathering her emotion, she lifted her arms and smiled so sweetly that a flood of love rushed into Ezekial's deep old chest.

"All these years," Callie whispered, then louder, "All these years." She walked to him, never taking her eyes from his and put her arms around him as far as they would reach, her head against his belly. She just held him, trembled, cried in silence. Sallie hugged them both.

Ezekial smiled and almost spoke to Sam who only he saw bouncing around them and barking so joyfully. The softness of these long-loved ladies, their firm hold on him, the clean, gentle smell of them, it was a golden moment, an eternal moment, forever cherished. Ezekial felt the rich flow of love and life inflate his withered heart. He could not speak or move. Was this a dream?

Callie stepped back and held him at arm's length staring at him intently and echoed his thoughts in her words.

"Is this a dream? Praise the Lord. God has answered our prayers Sallie. Oh! We've missed you! All these years. Thank God, He's brought you home."

They all stood silently for a long moment, absorbing the reality they shared.

"Where have you been? No, don't tell me. Not yet. Wait 'til we get everybody here and you can tell us all at once. What a story it must be! Do you know we hired detectives all the way from Chicago to look for you? And they couldn't find hide nor hair of you. They looked in California, Nevada, Oregon, New Mexico, Arizona, Colorado, I don't remember where-all they looked. For years! Oh Ezekial. You look so skinny! Are you hungry? Of course you are. Come on in the kitchen where I can keep an eye on you while we fix you up something to eat."

Callie on one hand and Sallie on the other pulled him into the kitchen and sat him down at the table. Their voices and the sight of the huge, hulking form that had entered the house brought a tall, raw boned, middle-aged man into the house and then the kitchen. He was burnt-red from the sun except where his hat kept the top of his forehead a paler hue. His dark brown curly hair was beginning to gray and he and Ezekial stared at one another as he stood silently in the kitchen doorway. When Sallie looked up from her preparations to feed Ezekial she noticed the man standing quietly and she ran and grabbed his hand, pulling him over in front of Ezekial.

"Abraham, this," (she emphasized 'this' with a flourish of both hands) "is Ezekial, our friend and partner, come home at last. Ezekial, this is Abraham, my husband," Sallie said.

Each of them just stared.

"Well, go on. Shake hands."

Shaken from their respective trances, each of them extended a hand and exchanged howdy dos.

"Goooolly," Abraham drawled. "Ain't this something like a miracle?" He inspected the faces of his wife and mother-in-law.

"A miracle it is. A pure miracle. Now I know how the old prodigal son's daddy felt. Have we got a fatted calf handy?" Callie asked.

"We got a whole bunch of em Momma, and this good man seated at our table can eat all of em he wants."

"And he can sure eat a bunch!" Callie laughed and skipped over to hug his big head. Oh Ezekial it's good to have you home," she rocked back and forth as she smiled and wiped her tears with her apron.

"I've heard lots of stories about you Ezekial, and up to now, I've been skeptical. But now, looking at you and all, I'm more inclined to believe the stories I've often heard."

"Abraham, you should have learned by now that none of us MacGillicuddys lie. Mother, should we call Nellie?"

"Yes! Call her and tell her we have an emergency and need her and all her family out here in time for supper. Call Beau too. Don't tell them nothing about Ezekial, let them be just as surprised as we were."

Sallie clapped her hands and ran to the telephone and began turning the ringer.

"Ya'll have your own tellyphone?"

"Why, 'course. Most everybody does." Callie looked at Ezekial with a question in her eyes. "Where have you been Ezekial? No. Don't answer. Wait and tell us all after supper tonight. Oh, what a tale will be told, I'm sure."

Sallie joined Callie in heating roast beef and gravy, and then fried potatoes and okra, and cooked sweet corn and big buttered biscuits. Sallie laughed as she told them how many questions Nellie and Ruby had asked and how she'd dodged giving away the surprise. They'd all be here for supper.

Ezekial wolfed down his first plate and Sallie whisked it away and refilled it with even more food the second time. After a third plate, he sighed and pushed away from the table.

"Ladies, that was the best meal I've had to eat in many, many years. Thank you. I couldn't eat another bite."

"Some pie and sweet milk?"

"No room."

"Ezekial, you look exhausted. Would you like to lay down?"

"Well, yes, I wouldn't want to impose, but I am awful tired. I've come a fair distance in the past few days and I'm not as young as I was when we last saw one another."

"Come with me. You can take a nap."

"Do me a favor Callie, Sallie, Abraham."

"Sure will. What do you need?"

"Don't let anyone know I'm here except family, and tell everyone to keep it quiet. I'm wanted by the law."

"Pshaw! Ezekial, I can't believe that. You'd never break the law."

"Well, I did. And I'll explain it all to you tonight."

"We'll fix things Ezekial, don't you worry none. Now, we'll fix you a pallet by the parlor windows where it's cool. You're still too big for a bed," Callie chuckled.

Ezekial took off his brogans and laid back on the spread quilts, his head on a soap-smelling pillow case and quickly fell into a deep peaceful slumber listening to the whispers of the women he loved. Close by his side lay Sam.

He was awakened by a woman's body against his, hugging him and a voice from long ago cut through his lethargy.

"Ezekial! Oh Ezekial, where have you been? Wake up! You've slept all day. Come on, we're anxious to visit with you. Oh Ezekial, I love you. We thought you had died! I've missed you terribly," she managed through her tears.

"Hello Nellie."

"Oh hello Ezekial. Hello, hello, hello. Don't you ever leave here again, you hear?"

Nellie pulled one hand, Sallie the other. He blinked his eyes as Sallie combed his tousled white hair.

"Get up and come to the table Ezekial. Momma's cooked your favorite just like you like it. Steak, medium-rare, fried potatoes, flour gravy, biscuits and butter. Come on."

"Girls, let Abraham take Ezekial to the outhouse and to wash up and wake up," Callie managed to get in, "He's not gonna' run off again."

"He'd better not."

Abraham led him out a back door to the outhouse and then to a wash bowl on a stand behind the house. He washed his hands and face and Abraham handed him a towel. He looked at the little house he had lived in with Noah and Chas, then Billy Hell and Chas. It was well-maintained, freshly painted and what looked to be new shingles.

"Callie insisted on keeping that place up all these years, nobody has lived there in years, not since Chas left. She's kept it up because she knew you'd be back someday. I've heard her say that a dozen times or more. She knew, somehow."

"Well, she had more faith than me then."

"You boys get in here, supper's getting' cold," Callie ordered with a smile from the back door. "I got holt of Ruby. Beau and Lil Beau were away deliverin' horses, but they'll be back tonight. Prob'ly late tonight. But they'll be here first thing in the mornin', soons they kin get here," reported Sallie.

Seated around the table were Sallie and her husband Abraham, Nellie and her husband whom she introduced as Ronald Lee, and Callie. A wide place filled with plates, bowls, saucers and glasses was provided for Ezekial at the opposite end of the table from Callie. All the eyes and all the smiles brought a nervous welcome feeling to his great chest. Callie bowed her head and everyone followed her lead. As she began to pray, Ezekial remembered and realized and also bowed his head. He was no longer properly socialized for Christian company.

"Lord, You are ever faithful in providing us with a bounty of food and for keeping us all safe and in good health. We thank You for your forgiveness in our failings, for Your perfect love and grace. Today You have blessed us greatly, fulfilling our hopes and answering our prayers. We can't thank You enough for restoring to us the one who was lost, our beloved brother, son and friend. With our whole hearts we thank You and praise You. And Father, I'm sure that you know we'll have more prayers concerning Ezekial soon. In Jesus name we thank You. Amen."

Everyone at the table added their amen, Ezekial last of all.

SEPARATE REALITIES

Nellie and Sallie began loading Ezekial plates with lovingly home-cooked food and he felt Sam lean against his leg. Furtively, he put a bite of beef and a small chunk of cheese on the floor beside his foot so Sam could experience the pleasure of eating without eating by whatever sense was available to him, but as all eyes were on him, Callie and Nellie noticed the strange action. Nellie opened her mouth to comment, but Callie shook her head and held her finger to her lips.

When everyone had ate their fill and Ezekial had eaten enough for a family of four, the girls who were far from being girls began to clear the dishes and Callie led Ezekial and the husbands into the parlor where a fire burned low in the old fireplace. Abraham stoked the fire with dry mesquite limbs and Callie explained that Abraham was now the ranch overseer and Ronald was the owner of the only automobile sales company in Uvalde. Callie recited the names of all her grandchildren and great-grandchildren and most of their locations and avocations before the old girls joined them.

As Ezekial listened to names to which he had no faces of the still extending family, his eye was drawn to the tall narrow window beside him. The sun was a half hour from setting and the sky and land were awash with brilliant warm hues. Flocks of birds hurried homeward overhead. He knew the chickens had already found their roosts and the milk cows were surely settling into their stalls. How he wished he had his own happy home, a restful refuge.

Ezekial observed that of the three dogs at the ranch, two favored old Shoestring and one favored Sam somewhat. He'd been told these dogs were the 7th or 8th or 9th generation of Sam and Shoestring's progeny, no one could remember exactly how many generations of the dogs had lived on the ranch. The dogs were shy of Ezekial.

Sallie had noticed the ranch dogs didn't bark at Ezekial when he walked up to the ranch house that first morning. And none of them would look Ezekial in the eye, but directed their gazes fearfully at a spot around his knees at the spot where Ezekial moved his hand in a seemingly palsied manner through the air. There was something strange in the behavior of the dogs and of Ezekial. But, of course, she had no inkling that the cause of their behavior was Sam.

He heard the sound of conversation of the family that surrounded him but Ezekial felt apart, the words had no meaning as his thoughts turned to Sam who moved beneath his hand while lying here beside him on the soft rag rug. Sam was filled with joy to see the girls that he had romped with over these fondly held hills when they were all young and sure. Ezekial knew that Sam understood that his presence and continued existence must be hidden from those they both loved.

They must not question his sanity as others did if he were to gain their trust and their aid. And so, the hand that had been poised to pet his oldest friend was stilled, withdrawn to the chair's armrest.

"Ezekial?' he finally heard Sallie say.

"Sorry. What did you say?"

"We were telling you about Beau and Ruby, Ezekial," said Nellie. "They have a horse ranch about fifty miles from here toward San Angelo,… you know, where Fort Concho used to be? Little Beau and his family live there too, but Ruby's girls have all flown the nest. One lives in Dallas, one in San Antonio. And of course there are a bunch of grandchildren."

"Mabel married a railroad man who worked for Santa Fe Railroad and finally became the Railroad Commissioner for the entire state. He's retired now, of course, but they still live in Austin. Mabel went to school and became a nurse. She still does a bit of nursing."

"I wondered if Mabel would marry after Billy died."

"Yes, she went to college some years later and met Walter, her husband, there. They had three sons, but the oldest was killed. The second son was adopted and the youngest, William, is a pugilist of some renown."

"And Chas?"

"Chas is still a cowboy. He drives a truck, hauling livestock usually, and he stops by from time to time. He has the sweetest wife. They raised four boys and all of them take after their daddy. Cowboys. They have a place in Alpine."

"Alpine?"

"Yep. Right next to the livestock sale barn, of course. Chas gets lots of his work from there."

"I guess old Micah passed away."

"Yes. He had a good long life though. Lived to be ninety-five. They made a preacher out of him up there at Beau and Ruby's. He had a little church and little flock he looked after there. You know Ezekial, most churches are either white, Mexican or black. Not his. People came from miles around and stayed all day on Sundays, whites, blacks and browns. Was even a red one or two in there. We made it to his church several times before he passed. And oh! Ezekial his preaching was just so sweet and good. They buried him right there in the churchyard, started a graveyard and he was the first one buried there."

"He was a wonderful man."

"Yes, he was."

"Ezekial, we're all anxious to hear how you come to leave us all who love you for so many years without a word or a letter. We've wondered and worried for so long."

"Well," Ezekial started, then shook his head and looked down at Sam. "It's a long story. I want you to understand that I didn't desert you 'cause I didn't love you. I was gone all these years because I did love you and because I didn't want to bring you trouble. And that's the reason I'll have to leave here tomorrow night, 'cause I love you with all my heart, an' I won't bring you trouble."

"Ezekial, that's what families are for, to help one another in time of trouble," Callie said.

"There just wasn't anything you could do for me at the time."

"Would you please tell us what happened?" said an exasperated Nellie, "We've been waiting for over forty years Ezekial."

Ezekial smiled and shook his head.

"Yes. It seems like another lifetime to me sometimes. Well. Let me start at the beginning. I'd been heartbroken for a few years because of Patricia leaving an' never comin back. Then Samuel tol' me she'd married some powerful fella' down in Mexico city an' it jes' busted up all my dreams an' hopes an' plans.

"We'd had a hard time making ends meet for a coupla' years, 'member? An' then the Panic of '73 came along an' cows weren't worth a dime Mexican money. I was shore discouraged an' figgered that Patricia, my sweet Patti, had been the smart one. She'd known there wuden no future in the ranchin' bidness, an' she caught her a rich man to make her life easy.

"By then, I guess I'd about worried Micah to death 'bout findin' gold. 'Member he'd studied all 'about geology as well as the Bible and I expect I ast 'im 'bout a million questions. I figgered I knew all 'bout finding gold an' thought I'd go get a passel of it an' we'd all be set fer life. Ya'll member that don't ya?"

"Yes I do Ezekial Robertson. I tried ever' way I knew to convince you that you wouldn't find any gold, but you were bound and determined."

"Yep, all ya'll thought I was crazy. But sometimes a thought takes root and keeps on growing like a weed and chokes out all the common sense, takes over a person's mind. It was all I could think about. An' I jes' had to go an' do it and get it behind me. The prospectors have a name for it, call it 'Gold Fever'. Well, I had it. Had it bad.

"The Indian trouble was mostly over with an' Chas was 'bout grown an' there were plenty of good hands in the bunkhouse workin' for grub an' a promise of wages later on when times got better. An' so, me an ol' Sam left here and headed west for the Pecos."

Ezekial looked down at Sam and had to stop his hand from reaching down to touch him.

"I had in mind to hit the Pecos and travel up that stream through New Mexico like Charlie Goodnight used to go. Maybe up to Colorado, then on to California.

"When I made it to the Pecos, I came to a camp with two old gentlemen who'd been prospectin' round about the big bend of the Rio Grande. They hadn't come up with much, a little silver is all, so they was headed fer Arizona to prospect some. Well, they was down on their luck, didn even have coffee nor tobacco. I had plenty so I kept 'em drinkin' an a' smokin' and they kept tellin' me of their experience in searchin' fer gold. They had me near burnin' up with the 'gold fever'. They invited me to go to Arizona with them, equal podnuhs in all we found. They'd provide the know-how if I bankrolled the expedition. I tol' 'em I'd sleep on it.

"Next morning, I headed west with them for El Paso. I figgered I could learn from them and increase my chances at finding gold with three of us lookin'. They had two horses and two pack mules who weren't packing much more than couple of picks, some pans and shovels. It was a weary way up the river to El Paso and when we got there, I bought us all a bath, a shave, some clean clothes and a room at a boarding house. We had our animals fed and put up at a livery an' we put on a feed bag at a local cafe. That first night we were bone-tired and went to bed early.

"After breakfast next mornin' we went down to check on our animals an' after discussion, we decided the animals needed to rest and eat some grain a couple of days before we headed out to Arizona. At the store we'd bought clothes at the day before we'd met an ex-miner. I thought maybe he'd heard something of news about prospecting out there, so we spent the mornin' listenin' to his tales.

"Well, Abe and Stepper, those were the prospectors I'd teamed up with, we hung around El Paso for two days jes' watching the people comin' and goin'. We had decided to get up early the next mornin' an' get the animals ready an' head out."

Here Ezekial's voice began to break and tremble as he recalled and told of the events of so many years ago. Those who loved him learned of the mean drunk who had stumbled into the livery that morning long ago as the prospectors completed their preparations to leave. The drunk had cursed at Sam to get out of his way and when old Sam hadn't moved fast enough the belligerent drunk pulled his pistol and shot Ezekial's oldest and dearest friend in the head and in the back and in the side. Ezekial was unsure about the next sequence of events. His new partners told him later he had run to Sam and held him close, but Sam was gone. Then he had turned to the killer who was saddling his horse and despite all efforts of everyone there to intervene, he had beaten the drunk to death.

Abe and Stepper had made him mount his horse, Sam in his arms, and get out of town. There was no doubt that Ezekial would go to jail and be convicted of murder if he stayed and went to trial. The livery owner, his worker as well as another few early morning travelers had been witness to the furious and bloody beating. Even though the killing was justified in Ezekial's mind, a court of law would not condone the savage murder of a man because of the death of a dog.

They crossed the Rio Grande and continued all day and all night, stopping only to rest the horses and mules. The two grizzled old prospectors pulled Ezekial's big horses behind them with the pack animals as Ezekial sat in the saddle holding the bloody dog's carcass and crying silently.

At dawn the following day they came upon a narrow beck below a low hill where a copse of old oak had gathered long ago. As his horse drank deeply from the stream, Ezekial carried Sam up the hill and laid the body down in the fresh new grass beside the canopy of oak. He walked back to the pack mules for a shovel and silently dug Sam's grave back from the stream on a gentle slope of hill beneath the stately oak.

When he had a deep hole dug he looked about him and walked away around the hill. Abe and Stepper looked at one another and wondered. When Stepper had rose from the ground to see what Ezekial was about, he came back around the hill carrying a huge white rock bigger than two or three normal men could lift and sat it beside the hole. He sat in the tall swaying grass, lifted Sam's body into his lap and quietly cried. And cried.

Stepper made a move to go to him, but Abe bade him to leave him alone to mourn.

Ezekial spoke his prayers not with spoken words, but with the language of his soul, in wails, in pain and sorrow, in tears of loss. No comfort came. No word of commiseration. Just the sound of the wind in the leaves and the stream over the stones.

He took off his shirt and tenderly wrapped his friend's corpse and gently laid him in the hole. The tears washed down his cheeks, his neck, his chest, as he sprinkled the soil softly over the beloved body that seemed to have been the best of his life, now forever gone. Tears sprinkled the soil in the hated hole and when the grave was filled he tamped the soil, lifted the big white stone and sat it atop the mound.

He stood, rolled his stooped shoulders back and looked to the clear morning sky. He whispered a long fervent prayer, then slowly climbed to the top of the hill and sat. Silently he watched the sun lift into the heavens, listened to the lonely wind, and grieved.

Memories came to his mind seemingly of their own volition. Remembrances of the playful pup. Memories of Sam's courage. Visions of his loyalty and devotion, of his noble character, of his exuberance and joy of life. His humor. Bright, shining days of exploration and discovery when they both were young. Memories of journeys traveled together, of rest and sleep shared side by side. His sometimes sad, one-sided smile, his deep soulful, understanding eyes. Theirs had been a brotherhood that would ever be revered, a melding of spirits, a life shared and this final separation was a deep rending that could never heal.

As he sat, the sympathy of sleep overcame him and he awoke with a start after a short hour. Realization of his loss washed over him and he held his big head in his hands and wept once more. And then, steeling himself, he took a deep breath and rose. He walked to his horse and saddled him. He loaded the packs on his mules and mounted. Abe and Stepper did the same. Not a word passed between them. Ezekial looked long at the place where his dearest friend lay, then turned and rode away.

Just before sunset Ezekial stopped at another stream and let the animals water. He fed them all some oats, stripped their saddles and packs and brushed them down as they rested. Abe and Stepper ate a bit. Ezekial just drank coffee and wandered off alone.

In two hours he returned and re-saddled and packed. His partners made no comment except to follow his lead. They realized it was best to put as much distance as possible between them and the sheriff of El Paso. They were close to the border. There was no way to determine exactly what country they were in out here, there was no river or any other visible boundary. Any posse that might be in pursuit would give no thought to jurisdiction and any reward would likely be dead or alive.

The desert land they crossed was desolate, dry and flat. Distant violet mountains to the west drew them on. There seemed to be an unnatural amount of light in the night, a clear blue light from the countless stars in the endless heavens that made the sand, the cactus and the sage glow with the reflected light. When the huge silver moon rose it became even brighter.

In the golden dawn Ezekial wanted to push on toward the hazy mountains, but his concern for his struggling horse and stumbling mules caused him to realize that they must stop. Abe rode up beside him and peered at his stony face.

"Brother, they's a spring 'bout a half mile south. See it? They's a stand a'trees there. Good place to rest fer awhile. We need to eat too. Le's stop fer a few hours."

Ezekial nodded his head and turned the animals to the left. He went through the motions of making camp, first tending to his animals. He made coffee and drank while the two other men cooked food and ate. Ezekial bade them sleep while he watched.

Mid-afternoon, Abe awoke and made them both coffee wrapped a tortilla round some soft jerky and gave it to Ezekial.

"Eat this and lay down awhile."

"I can't sleep."

"Don't matter. Jes' lay down and rest. We'll take off again at dark."

Ezekial consumed the food and drink perfunctorily, then spread his ground cloth beneath a stunted mesquite tree. As soon as his head hit the folded blanket, he was asleep. With his boots on.

At twilight, as they finished the pot of coffee and covered the coals with the sandy soil in preparation to continue their journey, Ezekial spoke.

"Ya'll can separate from me anytime you want, no hard feelings. I'm wanted for murder in Texas, I 'magine. An' some lawmen or bounty hunters may shoot first an' not ask questions. I'll understand if you want to go your own way."

Abe looked over at Stepper and then answered for both of them.

"We signed on to be partners. We'll take the bitter with the sweet. I don't expect anyone 'll try too awful hard to find you. That ol' sorry drunk needed killing as far as I seen. Let's ride."

They continued westward and passed through a Mexican settlement, just two or three families living in jacales with a few goats and sheep, some chickens, a burro and a small garden. Why they suffered and stayed in this stingy land Ezekial couldn't understand. Perhaps they saw it with different eyes.

After four days travel, long days, they struck northward. When they had gone a full day without water and when they were ready to stop and make dry camp, the animals nostrils flared and they began to pick up their pace and veer west.

Stepper said, "Believe they smell water, let 'em go."

The horses and mules found new energy and within ten or fifteen minutes they were pushing around each other at a natural tank fed by a spring. The bottom of the pool was rock and the water was clear as air and cool as autumn.

Ezekial silently gave thanks for good water. He thought of Sam in the water and chuckled aloud as tears burned his eyes. He had been such a lonely man all his life despite being surrounded by loving others. He felt even more alone and lost without Sam in his life.

"I b'lieve we're in Arizona now boys," Stepper gauged, "Though we could be in Mexico. It all looks 'bout the same out this 'away. We can start lookin' fer gold anytime now. Ever step you take keep yer eyes peeled fer a sparkle."

"Yea," joined in Abe, "Or an Apache."

They both laughed at what must have been an old joke between them. Abraham and Stepper had been together so long that they were like an old married couple, knowing what the other would do before he did it. Next morning they split the ground before them and surveyed the rocks with yellowed but practiced eyes. The pair realized that their big partner wasn't looking now with his eyes for gold, but was looking back with his heart at a treasure forever lost. Sorrow and tears blurred his present and he could see no future. He was not good company.

At the end of the day all they had found was a place to camp. There was a seep of alkaline water that was drinkable. They cooked beans and bacon with their coffee and sat in silence. The old pair of prospectors watched Ezekial as he sat apart and muttered to himself and gazed into the horizon. After an hour he came to the fire, poured a fresh cup of the thick brew into his tin cup and sipped it as he peered at the pair. He seemed to gather his words, then he spoke.

"Fellers, I kin see yur worried 'bout me, but there ain't nothin' fer it. It don't make sense fer ya'll to stay with me. Someone, sooner or later, is gonna see my big self an' know I'm the one who killed that man in El Paso. That's gonna' bring trouble down on us all, trouble that ya'll don't deserve. I can't let that happen. T'morra' at first light, I'll be going on alone."

Both his partners started to say something. Ezekial held his hands up and said, "That's not up fer discussion.

"I figger ya'll kin find a town somewhere in this wilderness where you kin buy some supplies. I'm gonna' give ya'll money to get yerselves whatever you need 'cause I'm taking most of the grub we got since I need to avoid towns and the law fer awhile. I won't be responsible fer bringing trouble to you who don't deserve it. I have enough regret."

"Well durn it Zeke, we sure hate it that things turned out this a'way. We'd go on with you, whatever may come, if you'd allow it," said Abe.

"I know you would, but I need to go it alone fer awhile."

Ezekial handed them most all his money.

"Thank you fer this partner," said Abe.

"Shore do thank ya," repeated Stepper.

"You shore don't owe us this," Abe admitted.

"Way I see it, I owe you fer stickin' by me this far. I thank ya. And I wish you the best in yer enterprise."

"We'll be thinkin' 'bout you Zeke," was all Stepper could manage.

"Where will you go Ezekial? No, don't answer. I don't wanna' know. Jes' take care of yerself. Yor a good man."

"Ya'll are good folks too," Ezekial said as he dished out another plate of beans. "I'll miss yer cookin'."

"Ha!"

"I bet."

Conversation waned that night and goodbyes were terse the next morning. Ezekial pointed the horse north and west as the terrain dictated, alternately riding and walking, steadily putting miles behind him. The April sun friendly warmed him and the desert zephyr cooled his face. He wondered as he walked how long would it take for his mind and heart to adjust to Sam not being beside him. How many years had he woke with Sam at his side and shared every minute of every day with him? And at the end of every day, when Ezekial lay his head down on a pillow or on the ground, Sam lay there beside him. Sam spoke to Ezekial in his barks, whuffs, growls and whines. His eyes spoke volumes as did his lopsided grin and his movements. Sam had understood Ezekial's words, moods and even his thoughts as no one else ever had. They were as close as beasts could be.

The days turned into weeks as Ezekial traveled. Alone. He had never felt so alone. Everyone was gone. The urge to leave those he loved back in Texas to search for gold had overcome him. He could feel nothing of that urge now. Now, the realization of the true riches of life had dispelled the mistaken notion that precious metal weighed more than love. He now knew that there was nothing so precious as love.

He consoled himself with the sure fact that love, or the seeming need of those he loved and the survival of the ranch had motivated his quest. But he was also haunted by the indisputable fact that he had left and gambled the love he had been given for love he had hoped to gain. Oh! How he wished he could turn back the clock, do it all again.

Sam had been perfectly loyal, loyal and loving, wanting no more in life than to be with Ezekial. And now he had lost him. Leaving his home in Carolina had brought death and loss, and now leaving his home in Texas had again brought death and sorrow. And for what? To chase honor and glory in the war? That decision had cost him the one man he loved the most. And now his seeking riches had cost him the true riches God had blessed him with. His best friend was dead, never to return. And he could not return to the home he had built with those he had come to love and who he knew loved him. If he returned to Texas, he would eventually be arrested and tried for murder.

Not that he really cared. He didn't really care about living now. His world was a memory now a sorrow that couldn't be soothed. He felt old. Racked with guilt. He had only hurt those who loved him.

The years behind and ahead weighed heavily on his soul. Oh! If he could only return to the golden yesterdays. If he had only made other decisions, understood the cost of what might be lost, realized the riches of life and love that surrounded him. His life had been full, joyful, wonder-filled and blessed, why had he wanted more?

He could never cry enough tears, could never suffer enough guilt, shame and regret. He could never forgive himself. Forgiveness would be dishonor, disgrace and a cheapening of the love and character of those who deserved so much more from him. He owed so much that he could never repay. He must always shoulder the guilt and the remorse and suffer for his sin of self centeredness. He had failed an ultimate test, committed an unpardonable sin. There was no home for him now, not ever again. Home would haunt him, always. Love would ever be a memory, closely held. The sweetest prize of life unreachable, unattainable, evermore.

He sat, his big head in his hands. Tears from his busted heart bleeding over his face and arms. No hope lived in him, no desire for survival. Death would be a welcome respite.

Day after day Ezekial trudged from place to place, picking at the rocks, searching the stone for a shining. He ate without taste, looked without seeing, walked mile after mile without getting anywhere. Absent in the now, present only in the past, he was lost in thoughts of yesterdays.

A day came when Ezekial awoke to another day of life, another lonely, painful day. He filled his canteen and his coffeepot at the tiny spring he had chanced upon the previous eve. He started a fire utilizing the dead branches of the striving bushes close by and poured ground coffee in his pot, setting it on the side of the fire. He took his short handled shovel and dug the sides of the spring to widen the pool so the animals could drink. Then he sat back by the fire and waited for the coffee to brew.

He noticed the horse and mules looking at the cool clear stream of sparkling water fall from the rock into the full pool. The beasts were all looking at the water but weren't approaching it. Was something wrong with the water? He took the cork out of his canteen and sniffed the water, then took a sip. Seemed fine to him.

He looked back at the spring and the sound of the stream brought to mind the sound of a thirsty Sam slurping water noisily. He smiled at a vision of old Sam's flews dripping water. From habit, he asked, "Thirsty Ol' Sam?"

The vision looked at him, smiled on the near side of his face and lowered his head to drink more.

Ezekial laughed at the memory and rose and pulled the halter of one of the mules toward the water. The mule jerked his head away and stepped a few feet away, eyes rolling toward the water hole. He knew the mule had to want water, they hadn't been watered all night, yet none of the animals would approach the spring. Ezekial looked back at the small pool and saw Sam still standing by the water, grinning at him. Ezekial squeezed his eyes shut and shook his head. When he opened his eyes, Sam was right in front of him. Those soulful eyes looked up at him, then Sam stood up on his hind legs and put his paws on Ezekial's legs and smiled as he panted. Automatically, from long repetition, Ezekial's hand went to Sam's head to pet him. When his hand actually felt the furry skull, warm and alive, his big heart skipped a beat. He kneeled and Sam whined and licked his face, then barked happily.

"Sam?" he whispered. He couldn't catch his breath.

"Sam?"

He hugged the vision to him and felt the lively dog wiggle and jump in his arms.

"Oh Sam!"

He lifted Sam up and spun around laughing. Sam barked and licked his laughing face. He was dizzy, breathless, incapable of thought as emotion flooded his every fiber. The ground seemed to tilt as they fell together laughing and barking, each absorbing and reflecting the other's joy. They rolled over the cracked dry ground and Ezekial kissed Sam's head and muzzle and looked into his big golden eyes. Then a strange tingling washed over Ezekial's skin and he shivered. As he held Sam, as he heard Sam and felt his breath on his face, he realized that Sam was dead. He heard the gunshots, saw and smelled the blood, held the dead body of Sam. Yet Sam was here in his arms alive, as he had always been, whining and whuffing his love for Ezekial.

Was he crazy? He had to be. Yes, that was it, he had gone insane. So this was how it felt to be completely insane, deranged. It felt wonderful! He closed his eyes hard, took a deep breath, opened his eyes. Yep, Sam was still there. Oh! It was so good to have his friend back. He thanked God, over and over and begged 'Please God', don't take him away again. He prayed that he would not return to sanity, crazy felt so glorious! He stood and danced with Sam jumping and laughing. He was afraid to let him go. The horse and mules shied away and watched them wild-eyed. Ezekial laughed and cried, praised God and disbelieved and held Sam close.

After a long while Ezekial slowly released Sam and when his friend didn't disappear, Ezekial walked to the pack, pulled out a pan and bacon.

"Hungry, boy?"

"Woof."

"Ha! Me too! Let me cook you some bacon. Your favorite meal, huh? Ol' Sam, I missed you so much. I'm sorry that drunk shot you."

As those words passed his lips, Ezekial sat the pan and bacon down.

"Come here boy. Let me see,…" Ezekial looked through his fur for the scars, but there were no scars, no evidence of the terrible bullet wounds that Ezekial had seen with his own eyes.

Standing back and trying to be objective, Ezekial studied the dog. Head to tail, it was Sam. Couldn't be another dog. Not possible. Yet, how could it possibly be Sam?

Sam shadowed his every move as he gathered sticks and brush to build up the fire. He fried bacon as Sam danced by his side, panting happily and licking his chops. Ezekial burned his fingers on the pan as he couldn't take his eyes off of Sam, afraid he would vanish.

When the bacon was crisply done he offered Sam some. Sam had always loved bacon since he was a pup. Sam ate at it, licked it, chewed it, swallowed it, but the bacon remained where he had placed it. Ezekial picked it up and held it out to Sam and Sam made all the motions as if he were eating, but he didn't. Abruptly, it dawned on Ezekial that Sam was a spirit. As this truth took root in his consciousness, he could now see the slight transparency of Sam's body.

He reached out to touch Sam and his hand felt the solid body, yet he could see, faintly, the ground on the other side of Sam. He lowered his head and kissed Sam's head and felt Sam's rough tongue on his cheek. How could this be?

Eventually, through the next weeks, Ezekial came to understand that Sam enjoyed the 'act' of eating and drinking, but didn't actually partake. Ezekial had tried Sam's capabilities in various ways. He found Sam still could see, hear and smell and even seemed to understand Ezekial's words as well as some of his thoughts. He had picked up a stick, shook it back and forth and threw it a dozen feet away, Sam had ran to it, as he always had before, tried to pick it up in his mouth but couldn't. Still, he ran back to Ezekial like he had picked it up and acted as if he had dropped it at his feet.

Ezekial thought that Sam didn't fully understand that he was a spirit, maybe it would take him awhile to learn about his new existence, just as Ezekial was learning. It was sad that Sam wasn't able to be the Sam that he had always been. But even as he was, Ezekial was grateful for Sam's presence any way he could get it. Sam seemed satisfied too. Mostly.

The entire episode and phenomenon of Sam's return was purposely skipped over in Ezekial's tale to his old friends. Still, when he had spoken of the murder of Sam in El Paso he had unconsciously kneaded Sam's head which laid against his knee. This ghostly petting was witnessed by the others present and though the husbands did not place any relevance on the rather strange mannerism, the ladies of Angel's Camp had seen Ezekial touch Sam in just that way many times long ago.

Ezekial remembered, but didn't relate how he had been fearful to take his eyes or hands off of Sam that first day and night. That first night, when coals had covered themselves with a gray blanket of ash and Sam had crawled beneath Ezekial's blanket as was his habit of old, Ezekial kept his hand on his friend and kept his eyes on the dusting of stars in the desert sky as his mind still struggled with the miraculous happenstance. Was this real or insanity? And if it were insanity, was it any the less real? A dream, he thought, it must be a dream. Despite the feel of the cool air, the pain in his hand from the earlier burn as he cooked, the touch of Sam's body against him, how could it be a dream? He began a prayer of thanks for the joy, for the respite from loneliness and pain, for the miracle, but finally, weary muscles and overloaded synapses shut down. The two old friends slept side by side as they had for so many years.

Sam had woke Ezekial at dawn by nudging and licking his face. Ezekial reached out and hugged the dear animal to him. A peace and quiet joy of thankfulness filled his chest. Ezekial didn't understand this continuing manifestation of his old friend, but his presence comforted his young, torn heart. It would definitely take awhile to accept and to live harmoniously in this unique kinship of such divergent forms of life.

As he built a fire and started coffee, each of the pair kept their eyes on the other. Sam seemed to be comfortable in his new skin, if skin it was. He also seemed confused by some facts of this new life, like the freedom from the need to eat and drink, but he enjoyed going through the motions.

It was evident that the horses and mules were aware of him by the wild rolling of their eyes, their nervous prancing hooves and their switching, alert ears. It seemed that they could not actually see Sam as Ezekial did or hear him, but by some sense they knew he was there. Maybe Ezekial could see him because he'd known him longer and better, or maybe it was because he wanted Sam more. Maybe it was great love, or need.

Ezekial felt no urgency to continue to travel, he realized he had found his riches with the return of his friend. He would really enjoy just returning to Angel's Camp, returning to the life he'd had before. That wasn't an alternative now though, the law would eventually find him there. Wherever he went the law would eventually find him, but maybe he could extend the time he would be free.

After drinking a pot of coffee, he picked up his shotgun and walked out across a wide level terrace through the cool morning air, Sam trotting along before him. In some unknown manner,

Sam flushed out a covey of quail and then another covey and then another. Ezekial managed to bag quite a few. After cleaning the birds and building up the fire, Ezekial pierced a number of birds with spits and placed them carefully over the fire to cook. The fragrance of the meat was delicious and was enhanced by the open air. Ezekial thought how little he had appreciated such rich blessings as the clear air that touched his face, that carried the huge, fluffy clouds so easily across the sky. All the 'simple' experience of life now seemed so exquisitely beautiful, magical and eternal. Soon he knew these sights and experiences would be taken from him with his freedom. He must absorb all he could of God's creation before he was arrested and forced to exist in a dark, ugly cell.

Filling his canteen at the bubbling spring, he noticed a wet, shining rock a few feet from the pool he had dug before. He wondered how the rock had managed to stay wet and stepped over and picked it up. His hands and eyes revealed that the rock wasn't shining because it was wet, it was gold. Gold! A thumbnail sized nugget of gold! He turned the gold over and over in his hand, inspecting it. It was gold through and through. By its color, by its weight alone it had to be gold. Gold! How had he missed it before?

Putting the heavy rock in his pocket, he began to look for others and soon found three more crawling round the spring on his hands and knees. How he had missed them before he couldn't understand. He must have dug them loose when he widened the small pool for the animals to drink.

Presently Sam's incessant barking drew Ezekial's attention. Sam was dancing around the fire where the smoked meat was charred and beginning to burn. Ezekial ran to the fire laughing and thoughtlessly grabbed the hot spits bare-handed, immediately dropping spits and meat beside the fire.

"Doggone! That burns! Well, you saved the bird-meat boy so that's all yours. Watch out it's hot."

Sam was wolfing at the smoking meat, but it remained lying on the ground.

"Gold Sam! Gold. It was there all the time. Heaven is smiling on me for certain. Gold Sam! Gold!"

Ezekial excitement incited Sam and they jumped and danced together. Ezekial held out the few nuggets to Sam who sniffed them and ran to the cliff wall from which the spring issued. He stood on his hind legs and dug with his front paws beside the water's flow. Several more nuggets of almost pure gold fell from the wall into the clear shallow pool. Ezekial removed them from the water examined them and stuck them down in his pockets. Utilizing his small pick Ezekial dug into the wall alongside Sam, laughing and whooping as Sam barked and danced. After a dozen or more golden stones had been dislodged the two collapsed together, rolling on the wet ground, laughing and hugging.

In late afternoon Ezekial paused in digging into the wall. He stood and stretched. Noticing his sweating canteen, he lifted and drank deeply from it. He hadn't eaten all day. He was tired and hungry. Sam lay in the shade of the cliff watching him. Using his shovel he carried the nuggets over by his still spread bed roll. It took quite a few trips to transfer the pile of gold. He estimated there was three or four hundred pounds of surprisingly sheer gold. He didn't know how much it was worth, but it was enough. There was more gold there, he could see it, but he had as much as the mules could carry all the way back to Angel's Camp.

Starting the fire again and looking at Sam, looking at the pile of gold, he shook his head as if to clear it, then chuckled.

"Maybe I've gone insane Sam. Sam, maybe I'm just crazy. What do you think?"

Putting his blanket aside he ran his big palms over the canvas ground cloth, stretching it out flat against the ground. Unsheathing his knife he cut the cloth lengthwise into three strips, than cut the strips into two foot squares. Emptying his saddlebags, he first filled them with nuggets, and tied them tightly shut. He cut lengths of the rawhide laces he'd removed from the saddlebags and used them to tie the bags he fashioned from the ground cloth after he'd filled them with gold.

Piling the bags on the blanket, he separated them into two equal portions, one to be carried by each mule. It was a long way back to Angel's Camp. He'd have to go easy on the beasts.

SEPARATE REALITIES

Returning to the spring he worked with the shovel and his hands in the dirt and rocks trying to disguise the digging he had done in the cliff's face. When he was satisfied he had done all he could to make the cliff wall and the ground look natural, he sat down, with Sam by his side, and discussed what his next move should be.

"Well. My friend, it's been a right smart of a journey. I've seen you die and I've seen you come back to me. I've killed a man. I've found more gold than I could imagine. It's all been easy, and so hard. It's like it was meant to be. I've done what I set out to do. God has blessed me. Now, I guess I should finish what I set out to do. Go back to the ranch and give 'em this gold.

"I don't expect I'll have much use fer it where I'll be going. Theys gonna' hang me. Meybe. I'll turn myself in to the marshal there in El Paso an' go to court to be tried. I know it was wrong to kill that man, I shouldn'a killed him. I jes' lost my head when I seen 'im shoot you, an' kill you like it wuden nothin'.

"We'll leave here in the mornin', head on back, slow an' easy. The girls will shore be glad to see ya'. Well. Meybe they'll be able to see ya', don't think the horse or the mules can.

"Meybe I'm insane," he petted Sam's head. "But, I'm happy."

"But, you never made it back here Zeke, what happened to you?" Sallie asked.

Ezekial jerked back into the present, taking a moment to regain his composure. He quickly took his hand from Sam's crest and withers, still hiding the fact of his presence. He didn't want them to think, or know, he was crazy.

"Well. I'll tell ya'. We started back, follerin' the trail that took us there. When we got close to El Paso we were on the Mexico side of the border an' we skirted Juarez. 'Bout fifteen miles outa' there my horse came up with a slit hoof. He'd need a few months rest fer it to heal proper. Couldn' be rode. I led him down to a small rancho and bought the strongest horse the man had fer a gold nugget. Left that ranch and made ten er fifteen miles fare I camped. Next mornin', early, I'd jes' started out when I seen a cloud of dust a few miles back. So, I climbed a hill soons I could an' saw 'bout eight men follerin' my trail.

"At the bottom of that hill I unloaded the gold from the mules and hid it all under a big ol' rock I could barely move. I put that rock back on top o' that gold an' wiped out my tracks back a' ways, so's my trail diden go by where the gold was hid, then I hurried east and north toward the Rio Grande.

"When I seen the bunch was gainin' ground on me, I let a mule's lead rope go, lettin' 'im go his own way. Then, 'nother hunerd yards, I let the other'n go. Two of the bunch that was a' chasin' me broke away to chase each mule so I had less of 'em to deal with. When they started chasing the mules, I figgered the man I'd bought the big horse from had told 'em where he got the gold. Banditos or Federales or whoever they was, I figgered they was after that gold and meant to have it.

"The place I hit the river was shallow, but I had to dismount halfway 'cross 'cuz the winded horse was having trouble keeping his head up with me on 'im. The four Mexicans caught up to me whilst I was still in the water and they's doin' their best to put lead in me. I managed to make the bank with jes one slug in my back. I held on to my horse and got behind some big river rocks. Two of them tried to cross after me but I made it too hot fer 'em and they turned back. They got smart and split up, two goin' each way up and down river to cross.

"My horse had caught his breath a little by now so I skedaddled and headed north at a pretty good clip. It'd been cloudin' up all day and the smell of rain was in the air. I was two-three miles away from the river when I heard a deafening sound of thunder, and I was falling from the horse, sliding across the muddy ground. That's the last I remember."

Chapter Fifteen

"Study me then, you who would lovers be At the next world, that is, at the next spring; For I am every dead thing, In whom Love brought new alchemy. For his art did express A quintessence even from nothingness, From dull privations, and lean emptiness; He ruin'd me, and I am re-begot Of absence, darkness, death – things which are not."
---John Donne, 1627

Ezekial drank from the glass of water that Nellie had brought him and took a deep breath before he continued.

"When I awoke, I could see only dark figgers all around me. I couldn't make them out, they were all blurry, kinda' foggy. The rain was stinging my face an' I shook it off and tried to sit up. A pain like fire hit me in the shoulder an' my leg was busted. Right then I thought I'd been hit by lightnin'. Later I learned I'd been hit in the leg with a fifty caliber bullet from a Sharps rifle. I knew how the buffalo felt then.

"I kept trying to clear my vision to see the banditos an' when I could finally see a little bit better I didn' see Mexicans a'tall but a doggone marshal with a posse. The news of that nugget and that a big feller had it had shore traveled fast. They'd caught my horse and found the saddlebags full of nuggets. I'd forgot to hide the gold in them saddlebags. The Marshal, he said he'd keep the gold 'til a 'formal 'vestigation could be abducted! That's what he said, but no 'vestigation was ever abducted at all, that Marshal jes' took that gold fer hisself.

"They herded me back to El Paso in a steady rain an' found a drunken ol' sawbones to dig the lead out o' me. I believe he took more flesh an' bone than lead. Them wounds never did heal in El Paso 'cause that ol' mean marshal kept me shackled an' tied and beat me up most ever day tryin' to get me to tell 'im where the rest of the gold was. That calaboose didn' feed much either, jes' beans and water once in awhile.

"Every day the marshal would come in that little cell an' ast me where the gold was. I'm fair certain that ol' Mexican rancher I got the horse from not only tol' the banditos 'bout the gold, but tol' the marshal 'bout the grande gringo to try an' get the reward on me. The marshal was nice some days, telling me he could put a word in the judge's ear if we could work sumpen out 'bout the gold. But I knew he was not to be trusted.

"I'd given him a statement about what had happened at the livery when Sam got killed, an' that drunk got killed too. It musta' matched what others had told 'cause the grand jury out there charged me with murder. The man I'd killed was the son of a rich merchant-man an' a known belligerent drunk who'd been in jail for all sorts of mischief for years. Nobody but his daddy was too upset with him dying, but his daddy was a big wheel out there an' elections were comin' up an' the marshal wanted to make a good showin' of law an' order or get the gold from me.

"I never tol' that marshal no lie. I tol' 'im I did have a little gold, but it came off them mules somewhere in the chase by the Mexican banditos, an' who knew what ever come of them mules. That was the truth an' I stuck to it. I'm sure there were quite a few searches fer that gold. But, they ain't nobody can lift that rock I hid it under. Nobody but me. 'Sides, nobody knows to look under that rock. It's still there, a' waitin'.

"It was over a year 'fore they held a trial. I guess they thought I'd break down and make a deal fer the gold but Gramps never raised no foolish children. Well, 'cept me. I've been foolish at times, but not that time.

"After waitin' over a year fer the trial, it was over in a' hour. I tol' 'em it was a' accident, that I jes' got mad an' lost my head. The livery man an' the marshal tol' what they knew an' the judge found me guilty. They was some talk of hangin' me, but the judge didn' go along with that. He gave me life in prison.

"An' my friends, that's where I been."

The silence in the room contained an assortment of emotions.

****

All their separate chores done, the ladies sat around the table having coffee and conversation.

"Mabel, you may want to try and give it some more thought, it's plain as day that Billy's head over heels in love with you," Callie advised.

"He sho' is," Ruby piped in and giggled.

"I woulden know, all de men in my life was sent to me from de massah to make babies. Ain't none of 'em loved me. Well, not 'til after," Beulah smiled.

"Well, that's over with Beulah, you need to find you one good man to marry too," Callie replied.

"Where? All we do is work an' sit 'round this house and mind the chillen."

"Sho do," Ruby agreed.

"Maybe we oughta' have a shindig an' invite all the folks hereabouts. It'd give us a chance to meet somebody."

"We could roast a side of beef. Get a pig and cook it in a pit. Drink some of Granny's old wine."

"Micah could play. An' they's some a' them Mexican hands play guitar. One a'them's even got one a'them squeeze-boxes."

"We could dress up, and dance."

"When could we do that?"

"I don't know. Soon. Let's think about it. But Mabel, are you still planning on going on that trail drive?"

"Sure am. Why not?"

"Well, there are considerations. You'd be the only female for hundreds of miles."

"Um huh."

"Well. You are young. And pretty. The men will be distracted and won't be able to keep their minds on their work."

"Ha! They'd better work. Or they'll draw wages and find another job. Callie, come on. They'll get used to it."

"I'm sure Billy is not happy about the prospect."

"Billy Hell works fer us. He don't give no orders 'round here. 'Sides, you jes' got done sayin' he loved me."

"I did. An' that's just why it might be best if you didn't go. It'll be tough on him."

"An owner from every other ranch plans on going. Ezekial is needed here. He'd be 'bout useless anyhow up on a little cowpony. It'd be all the horse could do to carry him. An' you have the girls. Billy is a good hand and I trust him, but I want to be there to make any decisions about our cattle. An' I want to see some other places, get outa' here fer awhile. But, if you and Zeke don't want me to go,..."

"No, Mabel, it's your decision. We jes' feel it will be a hardship."

"I'm young. Strong and eager. An' I want to go. Let me stretch my wings while I'm able."

"Okay Mabel. I'll be worried to death. But okay. What will you do about Mister Billy Hill?"

"Why, I'll keep him in line doing his job, that's what. He won't have time to think about nothin' else."

"Ha!" Ruby said, "Men are 'always' thinkin' 'bout sumpin' else!"

"Um huh," said Beulah.

They laughed and started planning the shindig.

The children were playing catch with the baseball and gloves Billy had brought from San Antonio. They had quickly grown more adept at catching and Nellie was better at throwing with the older children's instructions. Sallie was almost as good a thrower as Chas already, but Nellie didn't seem very inspired to learn to throw a ball. Chas thought Sallie was okay to play catch with, but he wished Billy or Ezekial would play catch instead of work all the time. Maybe after supper tonight, they would.

"Momma tole me that Mabel was going on the cattle drive. Ain't that sump'n?" Sallie said.

"I wish I could go," Chas replied.

"Me too," Sallie said.

"You couldn't go. Yer a girl," Chas judged.

"So? Mabel's a girl an' she's goin'. 'Sides yer jes' a boy."

"Am not. I'm near twelve, most grown. I kin ride a horse gooder'n most a' these cowboys round here."

"So kin I," replied Sallie, her chin sticking out.

"Well. Yea. Guess you can. But girls ain't s'posed to wanna' go on trail drives and such. They's s'posed to wanna' wear dresses an' not get dirty. Like Nellie. She's a 'real' girl."

Nellie beamed. And preened. She loved Chas.

"I'm a real girl too, l'il boy. An' I kin beat you doin' most anything. Runnin', jumpin', ridin',…"

"Cannot."

"Can too."

"Yer older'n me."

"So what? I'm better'n you too."

"Well. You can't whup me."

"Can too."

Luther, at work on the harness in the barn, had been listenin' to the children and deemed it was time to head them in a different direction.

"Hey! Chas, Sallie, Nellie! C'mere an' gimme a hand."

Nellie came happily, skipping and tattling.

"Sallie an Chas was gonna' fight."

The belligerent pair walked warily apart into the barn.

"Here Sallie, hold this end a' these reins. An' Chas hold this end an' stretch 'em out so I kin see if they're tore anywhar. You he'p me look for tears with yer young eyes Nellie."

"Here's a tore place Luther."

"Shore is. Ya'll hold it while I patch it up."

A little bantam hen pecked at Nellies bare feet. She jumped and hollered, "Quit that!" She kicked softly at the hen. "Get outa' here ol' chicken!"

Chas and Sallie laughed.

"Guess that l'il hen's needs some spectacles," Luther said.

"Chickens don't wear spectacles," Nellie said.

"Well, they oughta'. That li'l hen thought yer toes was kernels o' corn."

"My toes ain't no corn!"

"Well, they might look like kernels to a 'bout blind hen."

"Hens ain't blind."

"Why, I expect some are. Chicken are jes' like anybody else. Some are smart, some are mean, some are nice, some are purty,… and some,… need spectacles."

"Hmmph."

"I remember a neighbor back in Virginny who was partial to drumsticks. His wife liked drumsticks too and so did their only boy. When they'd kill a chicken to fry only two of the three of them could have a drumstick. So, the old farmer bred a chicken with a centipede and got chicks with three or four legs."

"Chickens with four legs?"

"Yep."

"An' so they could all have a drumstick?"

"Well, yea. That was the idee."

"How did they taste?"

"We never found out. Nobody never could catch one. Ya' see, they's twicet as fast as two-legged chickens."

"Luther, is that a true story?"

"Why shore it is. You think I'd tell a windy?"

The kids looked at one another and didn't say a word.

"Hey ever'body. Glad to see ya'll fixin' that tack. We're gonna' shore need some extry on the drive," Billy came in and commented.

"We'll have it all fixed up fer ya' Billy," Luther replied.

"An' Chas, I'm gonna need yer hep tomorrow. We got some cows with unbranded calves penned up in the river pens an' some a'the calves got to be branded fore somebody claims they's Samuel Maverick's cows."

Chas caught Sallie's eye, smiled and said, "I'm yer man."

"What's these gloves an' ball doin' jes' layin' around? They need some work. You 'bout through with these rascals Luther? I need someone to play catch with."

"Yea, I s'pose I can manage now without 'em. 'Cept fer Sallie. She's my best hand." He'd seen the competitive look between Sallie and Chas after Billy's roping invitation. "Could you he'p me fer a few more minutes Sallie?"

"Yessir."

Nellie ran for the house, throwing an "I don't wanna play" over her shoulder. Sam and Shoestring ran to her and escorted her to the house, trotting along beside. Billy and Chas beat the gloves into shape with their fists and put the proper distance between themselves to play catch as Ezekial came walking up. Billy threw Ezekial a glove and Chas a skinner which he fielded handily, whizzing the ball side-armed to Ezekial who caught it in self-defense.

"Say Billy, can I go on the trail drive with you? If Mabel's goin', then I should be able to go too."

"Well Chas, Mabel's part owner of this ranch, can't hardly tell her she can't go. But, it's no secret, I'd rather she didn't go. I'm 'fraid I'll spend half my time lookin' after her."

"You wuden have to look after me. You tole me I was a good all-'round hand."

"Yep. You are a good hand Chas. An' you're gonna' be a really good hand when you've growed some more. But it ain't up to me. I'm jes' the foreman 'round here." He looked at Ezekial accusingly.

"Well, if Mabel and Ezekial say I kin go, can I?"

Ezekial interjected, "Whoa Chas. It ain't up to me and Mabel, it's up to Callie."

"Why? She ain't my real mother."

"No, she ain't," Billy agreed. "But, she loves you an' she feels like she's your mother. God musta' put ya'll together. She diden have no boy an' you diden have no mother. You orter treat her like she's yer mother, she's as close as you're ever gonna' have to one."

"I know. I love her too. But,...well, she oughta' see that I'm near full-growed and need to see somethin' besides this ranch. Being a kid ain't much."

Billy chuckled and said, "Being grown ain't all that great sometimes either Chas. Enjoy what ya' got while ya' got it."

Chas had lost his enthusiasm for playing catch.

"Le's go see what Micah's cookin'," Billy said and pulled Chas along.

Ezekial stood alone watching them walk away together. The phrase strangely echoed in his mind, "Enjoy what ya' got while ya' got it." He looked all around at the ranch and the hills and sky surrounding him. No one was around. Just Sam, standing on the porch in the shade, watching him and twisting his head in question.

In the barn Luther asked Sallie, "You diden really wanna' play catch anymore didja'?"

"Not really."

"We're 'bout through here. I jes' wanted to talk to ya a minute Sallie 'bout, well about boys an' men an' how to handle 'em."

"Momma already talked to me about the birds an' the bees Luther. 'Sides, I live on a ranch, don't you think I see what's goin' on?"

Luther's ears turned red.

"No! No, Sallie. I don't mean like that. I mean like Chas. He's yer friend. More like yer brother ain't he?"

"Yessir."

"Well, I heard ya'll talkin', or arguin', 'bout who could run faster, jump higher an' ever'thang earlier. An' heck, ever'body who knows ya'll knows you kin beat Chas at near ever'thang right now. Even Chas knows, but his man-pride won't let him admit it. But, ya' know, in a few years, when ya'll are all grown up, Chas'll catch up with you an' pass you ever' kinda' way. He'll be bigger an' stronger an' faster'n you 'cause he's a man. That's jes' the way things are.

"Right now you need to realize the one important thang to a woman. An' that one thang is that even though someone is bigger 'n stronger than you, he'll never be smarter. Yer the smart one. Always will be. Jes' don't never let a man know yer smarter, let 'im think he's the smart one, that ever good idee was his idee. Long as he believes he's the one runnin' the show, he'll be happy. And you'll be happy an' havin' things yer way. Unnerstan'?"

"I think I do."

"I think so. Jes' keep thinkin'. That's what you do best of all. A quick mind is like a steel trap. Jes' never let 'em see the trap."

Luther winked. Sallie winked back at him and laughed.

****

Callie's soft old voice interrupted Ezekial, "Life? But Ezekial,... did you spend all those years down there without telling us? Why?"

"What could you have done Callie? I killed a man. I was guilty. And if I'd ever wrote you or sent you word, I's afraid I'd bring you trouble from all those bad men lookin' fer the gold. The way it was, they thought I's from Carolina. I didn't want to put you out."

Callie's voice turned strong in reply, "Put us out? Ezekial Robertson, you are family!"

"Well,...what's done is done. I didn't want to endanger you. I couldn't stand the thought that you all might be hurt 'cause of me. And, by then, I'd learned that ya'll still had true riches in yer life an' diden need no gold."

"Over forty years we've worried Ezekial. And now? You've escaped?"

"Yes ma'am."

What will you do Ezekial?" asked Sallie.

"I'm goin' to get that gold I gave up so much for an' I'm gonna' give it to ya'll and a few others who'll put it to good use. My life is about over. I'll divide the gold to the deservin', then I'll turn myself back in to the prison."

"Back to die in prison? No Ezekial. We'll help you. We'll hide you out,...we'll..."

"No. I won't have it. I won't bring trouble to those I love. Not anymore. I s'pose I belong in prison, I've killed two more men there."

"If you did, then they deserved it. You're a good man Ezekial and you don't deserve to die in prison," said Nellie.

"It ain't so bad in prison. I'm most used to it. Truth is, I'm scared outside of prison. The world's changed, passed me by. I been gone too long. I don't fit in out here."

"Aw, you'll get over all that. It'll just take awhile," assured Sallie.

"Ezekial Robertson, you always were a stubborn man once you set your mind to do somethin'. What're your plans? How kin we help?"

"Like I said, I'm goin' to get the gold. It's way out by El Paso, 'cross the river. I jes' wanted to see ya'll, see the people I love once more 'fore I go, an'…"

"Oh Ezekial, please don't go!" Sallie fell on his neck, her arms around him.

"Let us help you stay out of prison," said Nellie. "We don't want no gold."

"Let him be daughters, his mind's set."

The girls cried and held him. Ezekial blinked back his tears and his old heart swelled within him. After a few minutes the two women left the parlor to wash their faces.

Callie and her two son-in-laws drew Ezekial's plans out of him and found ways they could help him. Jack and Hoss had planned to cross over into Mexico and then follow the river west and north to the place that Ezekial had hid the gold. But Ronald and Abraham advised against that since, as usual, there was a lot of political upheaval and mischief going on in Mexico. Ronald could provide a Model T truck that was enclosed in the bed and would hide the extra large escapee from sight. And he had another truck that could pull a trailer that had been especially made to pull horses and Beau had several of those trailers and trucks. Plans were made to give him a call and ask for the loan of a trailer to haul horses to cross the river at the closest point to the buried gold. Ezekial had re-lived the chase across the river thousands of times over the past forty-plus years and he believed he could get fairly close to the spot he had crossed the Rio Grande and then back-trail to the gold from there. Hopefully the river hadn't changed its course in that particular area as it was wont to do.

Without Ezekial asking or inviting, the mission had become a family affair. Ezekial's attempts at dissuading his friends were pointedly ignored, his arguments and objections had no effect. Details that he had never even considered in his decades of planning were lovingly attended to.

SEPARATE REALITIES

Beau was called on the telephone and asked to bring four good horses, at least one of them big and strong. Food and essentials were packed through the next day and by the time Beau and family arrived in two vehicles, most everything was prepared.

Beau, Ruby and Little Beau jumped and laughed and danced and were delighted to see their old friend. Each of the three were dismayed at the aging of Ezekial and he was surprised that they had aged so well. Beau shook his head in wonder and Ruby looked through her tear-misted eyes at the sky and said a silent thank you. Little Beau just kept on hugging Ezekial and smiling his big bright smile.

The last hours of the day were spent sweetly, but too swiftly slipped away. The time quickly came when those who would go on the quest loaded in the trucks. Ezekial would ride in the truck with the enclosed bed and the food and essentials were packed in boxes which could hide him somewhat from casual glances should the need arise. Little Beau would drive this truck and would pull a trailer hauling three horses, while the trailer hauling four horses would be pulled by Nellie's husband, Ronald Lee. Along the way, they would meet Jack and Hoss and the caravan would follow the ragged roads westward.

As the truck and trailers pulled away from Angel's Camp, Ezekial still felt the love in the hugs and tears from the ones he loved who had been left behind. Shouts of love and luck had followed the trucks away from the ranch and when Ezekial thought he had left it all behind once more, Sallie's shrill whistle split the air. Memories flooded his soul at the sound and he ordered Little Beau to stop.

Sallie ran to the idling truck and, with tears streaming down her softly wrinkled cheeks reached out and held Ezekial's head, kissed his forehead and whispered, "Ezekial, please, please come back."

"I'll do all I can Sallie."

"We love you so much."

"Well. I love ya'll too. Always have."

"Come back."

"I'll try."

Ezekial motioned for Little Beau to drive on as Sallie stepped away from the truck, waving as it pulled away.

A few minutes short of midnight Ezekial had little Beau drop him off along the designated assignation and drive on ahead. He walked along the dark dirt track and was lost in the thick sweet smell of mesquite and the sight of an uncountable number of stars that shone so bright that he was walking on his shadow. The simple pleasure of walking under the stars alone with his thoughts was interrupted by the ticking rumble and popping of an automobile approaching from behind. Yellow light from the headlamps washed over him and a familiar voice rang in his ears.

"Aw shucks, Ezekial. I was hopin you'd have a basket of home-cooked food for us to eat. I know you been feastin' like a king." Jack's voice rose over the syncopated rhythm of the tired little engine.

Before he could answer and assure them that good food was waiting not far down the road, Hoss hollered at him.

"Get yer big ol' ass in this backseat quick Zeke, 'fore this dad-blamed engine quits again. We gotta' get someplace where we kin get another automobile, this'n ain't gonna' get us much further."

Ezekial stepped up over the automobile sidewalls and the overloaded springs caused the carriage to lean hard right.

"Well. Hidy. Thanks to the good Lord and good friends they's he'p jes' up the road a'piece."

"Whatcha' mean?"

Ezekial explained what his old partners and friends were doing for them and the pair were both amazed and suspicious. Ezekial's assurances and confidence eased their fears.

They were greeted warmly by Little Beau and Ronald and the delicious cold meal that had been laid out for them allayed any remaining apprehensions about the new plans. In the starlight beside the road, with the help of Ronald holding a succession of matches Hoss penned a note and attached it to the steering wheel of the tired automobile that had brought the felons that far.

"If you want this trublesum bunch of roiling scrap iron, you are wellcum to it. Singed, the x-owner."

The automobile was left right there beside the road, the still hot motor ticking and sizzling.

Ronald asked Hoss innocently, "That automobile give you some trouble?"

"Man, nothin' but trouble. Tires went flat 'bout ever' mile, needs water, needs gas, needs all, needs a'justin' here or there, it's worser than a baby. An' then the pile of bolts has no 'preciation. That starter crank slapped me up 'side my head, like to have knocked a back tooth out. I'm glad to be shut of it."

Ronald tried to calm and console Hoss as they rode down the bumpy, twisting trail.

"I sell automobiles Hoss, that's how I make my living. So, I've learned a thing or two about 'em. Ya see, they're just like horses or dogs or people for that matter. There are stubborn ones an' patient ones, strong ones and weak ones, good ones and bad ones. An' I know we shouldn't have much trouble outa' these trucks 'cause I sold this one to my friend Beau and the one Little Beau's driving come from my store too and I know them to be good natured, hard workin' trucks. Me and Beau know how to take care of our machinery, just like taking good care of our animals. Those are Beau's horses in the trailer we're hauling, good strong, dependable horses with a deep bottom. Yep, we'll get there an' back without too much trouble I 'magine." Ronald's prediction was accurate. The miles slid under and behind them steadily, if not smoothly, and in two long days they were about fifty miles short of El Paso. They slipped south of the beaten path and made a meandering way to the river and followed it northwest as Ezekial studied the landscape and tried his best to recall to mind a chase of long ago. Not recognizing any landmarks, Ezekial suggested they make camp at sunset beside the river.

They leaned back against their saddles and bedrolls as they drank cool water and ate steak and biscuit sandwiches along with the last of the potato patties the ladies had packed for them. There was even a small sliver of pecan pie left for each of them.

After eating, they shared a pot of coffee and the conversation turned to the new developments of this modern year of nineteen fourteen. A war had started in Europe, as it usually had through the past. There was now a zoo in San Antonio that Ronald had seen. And a canal had been cut through the isthmus of Panama connecting the Pacific with the Atlantic. This was of particular interest to Jack and Hoss, as they had discussed locating in the English speaking country called British Honduras which was not too awfully far from Panama. Jack and Hoss walked apart from the others and debated the merits of the possibly safer route west to a port on the Pacific and securing passage through Panama. Going south back through Texas or Mexico would be perilous for the pair, so they were encouraged by the news of the canal.

Jack and Hoss returned to the fire and the others just as Ronald was telling Ezekial that the legislature had passed a bill that outlawed all the dangerous and addictive derivatives of opium from over-the-counter sales except a new, non-addictive compound developed by the Bayer Corporation which they had named Heroin. Jack touched the bottle of laudanum in his coat pocket and felt the eyes of Hoss and Ezekial on him.

Ezekial felt a need to talk to Sam. He'd been around those who didn't understand, those who may be uneasy or frightened by his relationship with Sam. He walked up the river and found a place on a bar of sand to sit and talk to his friend and watch the river flow, together.

The refreshing dry air of the next morning and the great yellow sun greeted the anxious seekers. The trucks were quickly loaded with the camp gear and the trailers with the horses. They continued upstream a ways back from the river until late afternoon when Ezekial called a halt. The distant shapes of the purple mountains, the rock formations, the very color of the ground seemed to speak to his memory. He knew it wasn't far from here where his freedom had been taken from him by the law from El Paso. It had been four long decades ago, the land here was much all the same, yet Ezekial and Sam sensed this to be near the place they sought.

"We'll camp here. In the morning we can cross the river. It shouldn't be far from here."

The camp was quieter that night. The men's thoughts were consumed with gold, the dangers of crossing the river, what their plans should be upon retrieving their share. They all went to their bedrolls early, but sleep was long in coming, and dawn seemed to be delayed.

Four horses were saddled by first light, Ronald would stay with the trucks and trailers. Two horses were fitted with packsaddles. The big beast that had been provided to carry Ezekial seemed relieved to be freed from the confines of the trailer for a day and friskily skipped through the border water. The horse found an animal track on the other side that wound away from the river up to the plain. Little Beau, Jack and Hoss followed through the shallow stream and fell in line behind Ezekial up the winding, narrow way. Cresting a ridge a mile from the river, Ezekial pulled rein and sat staring at the horizon.

"We don't want to be long south of the border Zeke, either federales or revolutionaries would likely take us prisoners, or worse, if we're discovered. Fact, Pancho Villa would probably execute us, so we need to be as quick and quiet,..." Little Beau was advising when Ezekial interrupted.

"There it is."

"What?"

"The gold. It's right over there under that slab of rock," Ezekial pointed.

"You sure?"

"Yep. I'm sure."

"Lead the way big man. Let's get it and go," Hoss encouraged.

Ezekial grinned back at them and walked his horse down the switchback ridge and over the dry, hard pan to the rock formation that still stood as he recalled it. He stopped and sat astride the tall horse when he neared the rocks, surveying the perimeter of the wagon-sized slab of rock at the base of the pile.

"What you lookin' at Ezekial?"

"Somebody done dug up some of the gold."

"What?"

"Who?"

"No!"

"What do you mean?"

"Look. See the hole under the side of that rock? Animals done dug their home where I hid the gold. See? See those nuggets shining there beside the hole?"

Hoss started forward.

"Le's get 'em."

"Hold up. Could be a skunk up in there," warned Little Beau.

"Shoot. Skunk'll just have to spray me," Hoss said as he knelt, laughed and began inspecting the stones, putting what was obviously gold in his coat pockets. The others soon joined him and the ground beside the hole beneath the big rock was hastily cleared.

"Watch yerselves," Ezekial said. He had positioned himself at the point of the huge stone. He ran huge hands over and under the great slab of rock until he could manage the cumbersome weight. Setting his feet and bending his big legs, with his bare hands and back and arms and legs he lifted the ton of rock and then walked in short sidewise steps, moving the stone from its ancient bed. The others watched in awe as the old man pitched the great weight aside.

"What a man he musta' been at twenty-five," Jack said.

"He's still strong as a horse."

"Ha! A team of horses."

A fat armadillo lay undisturbed in his comfortable lounge by the removal of the roof of his palace. The unexpected light and breeze as well as the spiritual prodding of Sam's nose moved him from his comfortable, familiar depression and he lumbered stiffly away from the crazy creatures who were noisily destroying what had been his golden home.

The canvas Ezekial had used to bag the gold had rotted and turned to dust, but the piles of nuggets lined the small cave in which the burrowing native had dwelt.

"Get the gold packed up the best you can, and quick. We need to get back on the safer side of the river."

The ground was cleared, dug and cleared again. Ezekial smiled as the thought occurred to him that chances were, not a single nugget had gone unfound. In less than an hour they were retracing their path northwards and by noon they had reloaded the horses and driven the trucks to a spot away from the river, a small oasis surrounding a desert spring.

As Ronald finished cooking a bait of beans and bacon, Ezekial spread his ground cloth and remembered doing this once before. He asked the men to pile all the gold on the canvas. Jack had to remind Hoss to empty his coat pockets and Hoss expressed his innocence as if five pounds in each pocket could escape his notice.

He began dividing the treasure into eleven separate piles. Jack and Hoss each had a pile, the Chavez's had their pile, one for Beau, one for Little Beau, one for Ruby, one for Callie, one for Sallie, one for Nellie, one for Chas and one for Boy. When he judged the eleven piles were as nearly equal as he could make them, and as the men watched and wondered what his method and plan was, a thought occurred to him and he began taking a nugget from each pile in turn and making a separate, though smaller pile. He looked up into Jack and Hoss's questioning eyes and answered them.

"The widow."

Jack smiled at Ezekial's thoughtfulness. Hoss frowned.

He handed Jack and Hoss their gold and, as earlier agreed, they packed it on two of the unbranded Angel's Camp horses with the grub and essentials and saddled the other unbranded horse they had been gifted and prepared to leave Texas forthwith, heading west to a port on the Pacific to find passage down to Central America. They decided to travel a fair distance back from the border on the American side to avoid the bandits, but close enough to the border that they could make a run for it if they were chased by the law.

Before they left Ezekial walked a ways apart from the others and said his goodbyes. He handed Jack a roll of small bills that Callie had given him.

"Here. I won't be needing this money. Ya'll may need it, may not want to flash any gold along the way."

"Zeke, I don't know how to thank you. You're the best friend I've ever had. You've given me a chance at a life. A good chance," Jack said, a soft and serious look in his eyes.

"Yea, thank you Zeke. I gotta' admit I doubted this gold was even real. I thought it was prob'ly jest yer imagination, like yer dog.

I'm sorry. I apologize fer thinkin',...well fer believin' you's crazy. Now I gotta do some thinkin' 'bout Sam too, he might be as real as this gold. I know you wouldn' lie," Hoss stammered.

"Well. Yer welcome. Both of ya. You'll always be my friends an' it'll do me good to think 'bout ya down there somewhere eatin' bananas and fishin' an' laughin'. Jes' knowing yer free and happy, that's all the thanks I'll be needin'. Jes' get on outa' the country an' settle down and fly right, ya' hear?"

"So long Ezekial."

"So long Jack. Hoss."

"So long."

They shook hands and the pair rode away leading the pack horses. Jack kept looking back. He felt like there was more he should say, something he should do. At the last little rise he looked back one final time and Ezekial still stood, like a statue, watching them. He waved. Jack waved back, then rode on, his eyes burning with emotions he couldn't name, a gratitude he couldn't give words to. He would forever remain amazed that a man would give so much to his friends. The fact that someone thought that much of him began to change his thoughts of his own self-worth. Life seemed more meaningful, more valuable. Jack found his thoughts on Ezekial more and more. Hoss did a lot of thinking about Ezekial too through the quiet times ahead.

Ezekial smiled and felt a bone deep joy as he watched the pair disappear over the horizon. It felt so good to be able to do something that could be life-changing for someone. He would miss Jack. Hoss too. But he knew there would have been no chance for the pair to stay free were he to tag along. He was too easy to identify, too hard to hide. Still, it would have been a great adventure to have been able to experience the journey with them.

Ronald and Little Beau were ready to break camp and head home. They had packed up all the gold in separate bags and even labeled them in their effort to be honest stewards. Ezekial appreciated and chuckled at their truthfulness and loyalty. It had been a lifetime since he had been blessed to be around such plain good folks who didn't think of their good behavior as being exceptional.

It was after midnight by the time they had made it to a place where gasoline could be purchased. It was a small hut with a big tank beside it and a sign as big as the tank advertising the sale of gasoline and beer and emphasizing the fact by underlining, 'last gasoline, food or beer for a hundred and fifty miles', all lights were out, but Ronald beat on the door until an old bear of a man opened up, cursing and growling and pulling suspenders over his long underwear.

"What the sam hill are ya' wakin' a man up fer in the damn middle of the night? I don't open 'til eight in the moanin!"

"Hold up Mister," Ronald stuck his foot in the door to prevent its closing. "We wanna' buy a lot of gas an' a lot of food. We'll pay extry."

"Well,… meybe I kin make allowances, seein' as how you'll pay extry,…"

"We will Mister. An' we'll buy a lot."

"Lemme get my shoes on. Hold on."

The old proprietor lit a cigar with a big kitchen match as he came out of the shack. The stoogie was short and he almost burned his long nose with the tall flame. He lit two kerosene lamps.

"You got an outhouse I could use?" Little Beau asked.

"Nope. Jes' got one out house an it ain't fer colored."

Little Beau gritted his teeth and glanced at Ronald. There wasn't much they could say or do in response to the man's rudeness and racism. They needed the gasoline and water and there wasn't another place to get either for a hundred miles. A hundred-'fifty' miles the sign warned.

"Both these engines need water…"

They's a pump and a water hose, water's free. But gas and all ain't free. How much ya' need?"

"Fill up both gas tanks and all the gas cans in the back of the truck here," said Ronald indicating the second truck bed. He and Beau walked to the first truck and lifted the engine cover. The engines weren't too hot, it was a cool night, but it was best to always check the water they knew, and carry extra in case it was needed.

As the pair of them were checking the engines, the old reprobate began pumping gas into the trucks and then into the cans in back of the second truck. The bags of gold were stacked up in the front of the bed next to the cab and they piqued the old man's curiosity. He stole a glance to the front truck to ensure the two customers were out of sight, then flipped the latch on one of the bags and peered inside. An exclamation escaped him, "Lordy, lordy, lookee here."

He opened another bag and saw the gold nuggets inside it also, then began filling his pockets as he leaned close to the truck to hide his movements.

"Put that back mister, it don't belong to you."

The body less voice from out of the night scared him so bad his heart hiccupped. He couldn't see anyone around and wondered if he had imagined the voice.

"Put it back."

"Where you at?"

"I'm right here in this horse trailer watching you. You put them nuggets right back where you got 'em."

Beside a stack of saddles and under a tarp the old man saw a pair of eyes focused on him.

"Are you callin' me a thief? Why, you come on out from under that canvas boy. I've a mind to whup yer ass, callin' a man a thief. How big a boy are you anyhow?"

"I ain't no boy. I'm full growed."

The grizzly old man quickly tried to fasten the buckles on the bags, but by this time Little Beau and Ronald had walked up on either side of him and caught him fingering the straps of the bags.

"What you doin' man?"

"Oh! These straps seem to of worked their way a'loose. I's jes' closin' em up when whoever the boy is in the trailer 'ccused me a' stealin'."

Ezekial had worked his way out from under the tarp and stepped down from the trailer. In three long steps he moved to tower over the lying thief.

"Lordy be! You ain't no boy, that's fer sure."

"Put the gold back."

"I ain't took nothin'..."

That was as far as the gas store owner got with his denial. Ezekial reached down and grabbed the cuffs of the man's dirty dungarees and snatched the man heels over head and shook him. The nuggets fell to the ground around him and Ronald and Little Beau picked them up and replaced them in the bags, buckling the loose straps. The old codger yelled until Ezekial tossed him aside. He began cussing Ezekial.

"Ya big rough sonuvabitch, I's only takin' a souvenir, jes' a little samplin'. I thought it'd pay fer the gas and all. Whatchu doin' hidin' under that tarp anyhow? I'm a' thinkin I recall a lawman passin' through here a' tellin' me 'bout some 'scaped convicts from Huntsville. He said one of 'em was a giant. Yea. I b'lieve that must be you. Prob'ly stole that gold. Might be a reward fer yer big ol' ass."

The old man was edging toward the door of his tiny house. Ezekial reached out and snatched him by his long, thin, gray hair and said, "C'mere."

"What we gone do now Zeke?" Little Beau asked.

"First off, get that scatter gun I'm thinkin' this ol' thief has by the door in 'ere, then finish getting fuel an' water an' whatever else you need. An' go on and use that outhouse, Little Beau, if you ain't afraid you'll be inflicted by cooties. I think we'll have to take this un with us fer a'ways."

"Why, you can't do that. That's kidnappin'. I own this place an' I say you can't use that privy, nigger!"

"Niggers are people from Nigeria mister. I'm from Texas, born and raised. An' I don't care to use yer outhouse, think I'll jes' use this house," and Little Beau squatted down in the door of the old man's shack with a roll of toilet paper pulling his pants down over his boots.

Ezekial shook his head and chuckled. "Like father like son," he muttered to himself.

"Why you dirty little sonuvabitch! Don't you dare do that. I'll kill you, you..."

"Shut up! 'Fore I wring yer neck like a chicken."

The man quieted down post-haste.

"Now get in that trailer an' sit real still. If you give us any trouble I'll hog-tie and muzzle you. Or worse if you make me mad. I was in prison fer killin' an' I'm tryin' my best to let you live. I'd 'preciate it if you didn't aggravate me."

"Yessir."

Ezekial put him in the trailer and slid the bolt barring the gate. He got a drink of water out of the hose and watched the other two finish preparations for the road.

"We're gonna' have to carry him out to where he can't get to no lawmen 'fore we clear outa this part of the country. When we get twenty, thirty miles down the road, stop an' we'll let him go."

He walked back to the trailer and asked the old man, "How much we owe you fer the gas and all?"

"Four dollars oughta' do it."

"That's double what it's worth," Ronald said.

"Pay him what he wants, we don't wanna steal nothin,'" Ezekial said.

Ezekial walked into the shack and found a gallon of wine, half full, and a full quart of tequila. He stepped around Little Beau's fragrant gift and carried the alcohol back to the trailer and got in with the old man. When the trucks pulled out, Ezekial spoke to the frightened old bigot.

"Now you sit still. If you behave I'll let you go after while an' you can walk back home. If you give me any trouble,...well, you won't be doin' any more walkin' an' the buzzards'll have breakfast waitin' on 'em."

After they'd traveled about twenty miles toward the dawn, Ezekial opened the bottle of tequila and handed it to the old man.

"Drink it."

"But,...I,..."

"You wanna' walk back to yer place? Drink it!"

The man took a small taste.

"I didn't say sip it. I said drink it. I ain't gonna' tell you no more."

The old man turned it up and swallowed four times before he turned the bottle down and blew out his scalded breath.

"You got ten minutes to drink that bottle, then I'll have 'em stop an' I'll turn you loose. But, you better get it drunk or I'm a' gonna' break yer legs an' throw you outa' this trailer while we're rollin'. Now drink."

After the man had drank half the bottle, Ezekial yelled at Little Beau to stop. He drug the half drunk man out of the trailer and gave him the gallon of wine.

"Ain't no water 'til you get back home so you better take this wine. You'll get thirsty. If you walk steady you might make it home for dinner. Or supper. Maybe you'll get lucky an' somebody comin' this way from Presidio will give you a ride. Luck to ya. Don't be diggin' in people's bags no more. So long. Oh! Here, may as well take this with you too."

And Ezekial baptized him with what remained of the tequila.

Along the way, all through the day traveling south along the river, Ronald and Little Beau did their best to persuade Ezekial to promise to return to his friends and family after he went to Samuel's ranch over the border, but he made no promises. He just continued to remind them that it was a serious felony charge to help or harbor a fugitive from justice. He wouldn't bring trouble or more heartache and sorrow to those he loved most in life.

Just after sundown they stopped on the river road just a few miles from Del Rio. It had been an endless, exhausting ride all the way from the Big Bend. They unloaded the big Percheron-Morgan mix gelding, saddled and loaded him with the last share of the gold, then had a quiet bite to eat together. As they finished the small meal and as Ezekial prepared to mount up and head for the river, Little Beau spoke.

"Any words for the folks back home Ezekial?"

"Well,…I ain't never been much at goodbyes. Jes' tell 'em, each and ever' one of 'em that I love 'em. Always have, always will. I don't intend to hurt 'em, jes' like I have ever' day fer all these years. A lifetime. Now that it's about over with. I wish I could do it all over agin, but….. I hope the gold does 'em more good than it done me, it shore weren't worth the misery it's caused.

"My time's 'bout over with, Little Beau. I'm ready to go on over that Jordan River that Micah used to tell us 'bout. I had my chance. Shoulda' done better.

"Jes' tell 'em all I love 'em Little Beau, each and ever' one. That's all that's important. Jes' tell 'em I love 'em."

"Okay. Ezekial."

Ezekial stepped into the stirrup and swung up into the saddle. He looked down at Little Beau and smiled. "I 'member the first time I seen you Little Beau, you was jes a little-bitty boy, jes' barely walkin' good. You was hidin' behind yer momma's skirts there in that cafe in San Antone. An' now, well, you been a man all these long years I been gone. You've had the good sense to stay close to home, been blessed with the wisdom to know that the important things in life are always close to home. Close to love. Fam'ly. Those that love ya, that's the real riches in life. I learned that a little too late.

"You jes' tell 'em I love 'em Little Beau. So long. So long Ronald. Ya'll have a good life."

Ezekial pushed his heels into the big horse and rode toward the river. He didn't look back.

Jack and Hoss traveled fast and made a good distance the first two days and had left Texas far behind them by the third day. They hadn't spoken much on the trail, their thoughts were unsettled, confused. Not sure of what lay ahead of them, feeling chased by what lay behind, excited by the possession of so much gold and bound to keep it a secret. Neither of them understood Ezekial's sacrifice, his freely given gift. Ezekial had to be insane, but what kind of man could be so good at heart? Hoss knew that he would never even think about traveling halfway across the continent to dig for gold, then risk his life escaping prison so he could give it away and go back to prison to die. Insane. Hoss wasn't that crazy but he was sure glad Ezekial was. Still, he had come to begrudgingly like this crazy old man and he now felt uncomfortable, unfamiliarly guilty. He felt like he was abandoning a friend, a very good friend.

Jack knew that Ezekial was right. If he had stayed with them, eventually word would get back to the authorities of the really big man and they would all have to run again and again. Ezekial habitually thought of others first. That noble peculiarity caused Jack's valuation of Ezekial to continue to grow in his estimation even bigger than his physical stature. He already missed him. They had lived close together and been close friends for years through hard and hostile times. There should be something he could do for Ezekial. The man was near a saint, he deserved something more of life than a return to that hate-filled prison. Jack's mind turned and worried the circumstance as a dog does a bone.

That night, somewhere in New Mexico, Jack sat awake by their small fire staring into the flames. The gold just didn't mean as much now. He couldn't get a grip on how he could help his true friend, Ezekial. He felt he had used him, abandoned him. He loved him like a brother, even closer, life just wasn't as rich without him. Sure, Hoss was an exceptional friend. He had chanced his own freedom, worked, saved, stole, connived and plotted to free him. And he had done it all without him even asking with no hope of reward. A man couldn't ask for two better friends. But, he had lost one of his dear friends and he felt torn, unwhole.

He had refrained from taking any laudanum, he had wanted a clear head to examine the possibilities, to try and find some way for Ezekial to find some joy in the life that remained to him. Frustrated in his efforts, his body was beginning to remind him of its need, of its addiction. Without the laudanum there would be no sleep. What there would be is pain, severe cramps, diarrhea, fever, chills, delirium. Maybe if he medicated himself, maybe then his raddled brain could devise a solution to help Ezekial.

He chuckled as he witnessed his body and his mind coercing him for the potion to induce forgetfulness and relieve his guilt, his grief. He pulled the saddle bags from blankets and reached inside a pocket taking out the small bottle of laudanum. He held the bottle before the firelight and spun the thick, dark liquid inside. He uncorked the precious bottle and brought it to his face. He sniffed it and the welcoming, pungent redolence caused chills to cover his body. He held it over the fire and, with trembling hand, poured it into the coals. With all his strength, he hurled the enslaving dregs into the dark brush as far as he could.

"That's for you Zeke. That's the best I can do for you. Thank you my friend," he spoke to the sky.

He laid back against his saddle, closed his eyes and waited for his punishment, the pain.

Ezekial crossed the Rio Grande at first light, swimming beside his horse the thirty yards to Mexico. He let the horse graze as he stripped and laid out his clothes on the rocks to dry. He situated himself on the high ground because he knew the river was patrolled by the Mexican Army and the rebels associated with Panco Villa terrorized the border regions. When his clothes were mostly dry he dressed, saddled up and rode southwest until he began to recognize the low hills which directed him to Samuel's rancho.

Farther along than he recalled he found the singing stream that led the way. He and the horse drank deeply of the cool liquid of life. Sam stood beside Ezekial and watched them drink their fill and then the three of them followed the meandering water south.

Ezekial relished the fragrances carried on the gentle wind and enjoyed the loving warmth and ancient beauty of the sun and it's light in which life dwelt. Ezekial knew his return to close gray walls of stone and iron bars was eminent and realized his remaining days of freedom were few and so he cherished these sacred, perfect days, each hour a precious gem he would lock safely in his memory to be revisited and relived through the empty dark days until death came to his cell and released him. These memories would strengthen and sustain him.

When the trio of mammals reached a meadow rich with blossoming bluebonnets, Indian paintbrushes and Mexican hats, Ezekial dismounted and enjoyed the beauty of their blooming while the horse sampled the various clumps of grasses. Sam cheerfully chased a big yellow butterfly and a mockingbird sang an endless repertoire of chords that may or may not have impressed the females of his species that he courted, but amazed Ezekial. He thought of the infinite intelligence that had crafted such a creature as this and a million others just as intricately designed, a world of wonder in a universe that had no beginning nor end. Ezekial's mind and senses had been dormant for decades and he was now intensely conscious of the grace of God and His loving hand in the ever-continuing creation.

He realized that his moments under the sun were diminishing and he valued this freedom much more than the gold he had given away.

He didn't feel that life had treated him unfairly, he had killed a man, a grievous sin, and had received the prescribed punishment of the law. Now that he had helped his friends in the ways that he could, he knew he must return to the penalty and penance of prison. He determined to treasure these last days as he traveled to give the remaining gold to his friend. The beauty surrounding him on the earth, in the wind, the light, the sky filled his soul. He realized that through his suffering he was blessed beyond those who were forever free because he greatly valued each day; days that others considered common, ordinary days he knew to be filled with awe and wonder. Every majestic cloud, each colorful petal of the flowers so vigorously living their lives as their creator designed, every fragrant breath of the atmosphere further instilled in this old prisoner the love and power of the Creator. Life truly is love he thought, he laughed with delight at the profundity of the deep realization. How was it possible that one could live surrounded by such delicate beauty and charming love and deny its Creator?

Ezekial had heard others deny that there was a God, heard them promulgate chance, coincidence and accidental fortune as creating the intricate, infinite universe. Surrounded by evidence of a Creator, how could they deny Him? God is no man-made explanation, no fairy tale handed down through generations: Ezekial knew that chance and coincidence were the man-made fairy tales.

With a smile felt from his face to his feet he rose and grabbing the reins led the horse across the meadow. He felt the years peel away, feeling youth return to him. Hope, dreams, enthusiasm, energy, anticipation of blessings to come infused him. He felt the faith that God's favor was on him, and though it didn't make sense to him, wasn't logical, still the sure truth of this knowledge lightened his step and strengthened his heart. Even knowing he would certainly soon surrender himself and return behind the dismal walls of prison, still his spirit soared in the grace of love and the beauty that love had created. In his depth of impending suffering and sorrow, he found faith, favor, joy, beauty and grace-filled love embracing him. He felt life as God intended it to be.

The strength of the big Percheron breed moved Ezekial much too swiftly toward his penultimate destination. He wondered how Samuel was doing, what he looked like after all these years, what the old rancho looked like. He would be continually reminded of Patricia, still his cherished love. His youthful, foolish, idealistic perfect love he had invested on her and his big heart had swollen to fill his whole world with the adoration of her. He cherished her still, through all the years he had loved her and longed for her. When she left his world his heart was shattered with his dreams. She had taken much of his life with her when she went away. His soul had never healed. An ever-echoing emptiness within him, a dream that wouldn't die, memories cherished and a still struggling love was all that remained to him of his youthful paramour and though it was painful he held it close and dear. Sorrowful smiles moved over his face daily as memories of her came to haunt and delight him in the endless eons inside the tiny cell. The love of her had branded him, heart, body and soul, she had owned him from his first sight of her. And now, returning to this land in which that love was born and grew, that yearning for her which had lived in him through those lonely years burst from his heart as he groaned and called her name to the wind.

Often he had endeavored to convince himself that the past was indeed passed and should not be allowed to hold such power over him. He could not understand why, how he had lost her. She must have wanted more from a man than he could provide. Maybe she wanted riches, prestige, power. Surely she must have known no man could love her more. In some way, he didn't measure up to her dreams.

Ezekial knew that was the reason that he had left his home at Angel's Camp to seek gold and riches, hoping that money would cause her to see him in a different light and bring her back to him. Now that his life was waning, he still loved her but fully realized his mistake. He had lost his dearest love, true, but he should have mustered the character to value the love of his friends. God had given him a good life, he should have been satisfied with it. Yet he had thrown it all away.

He couldn't blame Patricia for the wreck his life had become. He had made wrong choices because his values, his priorities, his loyalties became confused. Wallowing in self-pity, drowning in despair, he had not thought to reach for the lifeline of the love that surrounded him. He had a family, friends whom he deserted in his selfishness and foolishness.

He looked down at Sam, still trotting beside him and he smiled at the reality of love. He knew now that love was eternal, that even death cannot defeat love. Love truly conquers all. The love of God through the fidelity of Sam had saved him from utter despair and sustained him through desolate years. He had been given insight and a peculiar vision of eternal reality that few others had been allowed. He could never imagine why he, of all people, had been chosen, but he was so very grateful. Death held little fear for him now, it was just a passage into another sort of life. There was certainly much that he didn't know of that continuing life, but there was no fear of it. Love had conquered fear as light destroys darkness.

The golden warmth of the sun blessed all living on the earth throughout the morning as the strong horse carried Ezekial south with Sam as escort and scout. The variety of God's creation presented itself to Ezekial's ready mind. Hawks soaring on the thermals, lizards zipping across their path. Lanky and playful jackrabbits, curious coyotes, graceful deer and ground squirrels. Butterflies of many colors and sizes, busy bees and wandering yellow jackets. Noisy locusts, red-legged grasshoppers, a sidewinder snake. Sparrows, grackles, doves, quail, wrens, cranes, mockingbirds, robins, bluebirds and eagles looking lordly from nests as large as wagons high up in the towering oaks. In the stream silver flashes jumped into the air and dove gracefully back into their water world as minnows darted in the shallows and frogs voices spoke their repetitive basso refrain and dragonflies patrolled the surface of the stream. Ducks and geese sounded their grievances at his intrusion and his horse shied at the suddenness of an egret taking flight, his wings sounding like slapping hands. Some long-legged creation of insect ran across the water and sunlight danced and sparkled in every ripple and the river mirrored the sky and sighed it's contentment.

A distance down the stream in the umber beneath the low, spreading limbs of the wise trees that lived by the water, Ezekial saw a small group of cattle standing and drinking and laying in the cool shadows along the bank. Rather than disturb them, he pulled the reins and turned the big horse away from the water, and into the lea where the long-bladed grasses sent up thick plumes of seeds to be borne by the wind to settle the earth in a farther frontier.

Something triggered a memory deep in his mind and a magical melody rang in his ears. The musical note reverberated, a sound from the distant past, a joyous tone, a sweet sensation, sweeter than the song of birds.

"Ezekial! Ezekial!"

Once again, as if in a recurring trance, feeling as if he were reliving a day long past, he turned the horse as Sam barked happily, jumping and running. Surely all who had deemed him irredeemably insane were right. He closed his eyes hard, shook his big, hoary head to clear it of the vision riding toward him. His eyes grew wide, his mouth fell agape, he was paralyzed as in a dream.

The fine female figure rode easy and erect atop the black stallion, black hair streaked with white blown in her wake as she flew toward him. She seemed mythical, beyond beautiful, the vision filled him with wonder and awe. His mouth wouldn't shut, his eyes couldn't blink.

She galloped the horse up beside him, reached up to him and he lifted her onto the Percheron's withers. She threw her arms around him and kissed him. Time was suspended, the world stopped its spinning, nothing existed except the two of them. Possessively, he pulled her against his swelling heart and so tenderly returned her kiss, lovingly, longingly. Neither was aware of ending the kiss and they peered into one another's eyes to see the truth, the reality of their reunion. And then Ezekial kissed her again, crushing the tender petals of her lips, hungrily, desperately.

Regretfully, he pulled himself away, lowered her to the meadow and stepped down beside her. Breathlessly, he managed to whisper.

"Patricia. I'm sorry."

"Sorry?" She laughed, "Why are you sorry?"

"Your husband..."

"...Is dead. Many years ago. Oh Ezekial!" She hugged him to her as he bent over her and put his face in her hair.

"I believed you were dead! Surely never to return. God has answered my prayers, my dearest, fondest wish! My mother,...my sense of adventure,...my youthful folly,...Ezekial, please forgive me. So many times I wanted to return to you. But then came the children and...oh Ezekial. Just hold me."

She cried. He cried. Tears of love, sweet dew of life.

He held her, drank in the fragrance of her and was transported to another golden day and time. Trembling, afraid he would lose her once again, he fought the fear and held on tight. It was all a dream, a passing symptom and delusion of his insanity. A cruel, teasing hallucination. He held her too tight and she groaned.

"Ohhh. Too tight. Loosen up Ezekial, I'm not going anywhere."

"I'm sorry."

"Quit saying you're sorry!" she smiled.

"I'm sorry."

They both laughed and she pulled him down to kiss him. They hugged and kissed and he held her and swung around, dancing with joy, love and abandon. They fell into the grass and just lay there in one another's arms and looked at one another. Into one another. Remembering. Soaking languorously in this long-awaited, impossible, gracious and pleasurable gift of Providence. Silently and simply trying to believe this belated, unbelievable second chance. All they had yearned for and dreamed of had been given them.

These heavenly moments were a time they would cherish forever. Rising, they walked hand in hand through the green sea of grass and wildflowers under the bright blue dome of the firmament. Blissfully, they were together at last, hearts melded, united into the coupling they had longed for through the lonely, separating years.

Each thirstily absorbed the words of the other, soaking in the stories of the intervening time. Through these first hours their revival of love welded them together, nothing could separate or would interrupt their reunion. Their conversation fed their mutual need to understand, to know how the other had changed and how they remained the same.

Returning to the rancho, Ezekial was surprised at what was new construction to him. There seemed to be a stability and a serenity about the place, a peaceful assurance. They turned their horses over to curious cowboys to curry, comb and feed. Ezekial slung his heavy saddlebags over his shoulder and they walked arm in arm into the old ranch house that had been expanded and redesigned but still exuded the warmth of the home he remembered. Resting in the coolness of a trellised patio with cold drinks while the cook prepared a meal, Ezekial learned of Samuel's demise at the hands of marauding banditos. Consuelo had passed away at a good age as had many of the men Ezekial had known who had worked for and with Samuel. He learned of Patricia's grown children who remained in Mexico City and whom she missed terribly. Her daughter was wed to a government official and had several children. Her eldest son was also a government official as his father had been and had grown children who were married and parents. Her youngest son, Miguel, had come with her when she had returned to the rancho and was still here managing the business and doing it well.

Her husband had died of pneumonia after a long illness that the doctors could not identify or successfully treat. He had been a good man, an educated and refined man of undefiled Spanish ancestry. She had loved him. Through those years in the capitol city she had missed her brother, her land and home. She had thought often of Ezekial and imagined that he too had found another, married and built a family and life.

She had enjoyed the culture, the social events and festivities in the hub of Mexican civilization, but when her husband died, she felt the need to return to her roots so far away. She'd been blessed to have time with her mother and her brother before they had died. Now her youngest son ran the big rancho and she enjoyed the isolation, peace and quiet.

Ezekial told her of his life since she had gone away to attend the school for young ladies. He told her of his mistake of leaving his home to search for riches because he had erroneously believed he could bring her home to him if he were rich and powerful and how his mistake had cost him the riches he already possessed. At the end of his sorrowful tale he informed her of his purpose in coming to the rancho, to give her family his share of the gold to ensure the continuance of the wonderful institution. He placed the heavy saddlebags before her on a table and opened them to reveal the gold nuggets, uncovered from the earth so long ago.

"Ezekial, sweet Ezekial. I can't accept this."

"You gotta' accept it Patti. I have to go back to prison 'fore long, it won't do me any good there. Fact is, they'd jes' take it, believing I'd stole it."

"No! No, no, no. I've just got you back. You must stay with me."

She came into his arms.

"Sweetness, if I stay, the law will come and cause you a lot'a trouble, or worse. Word'll get out 'bout a big ol' man livin' here an' they'll come fer the reward. We'll have a few days together dear lady. Don't let sorrow mar the short time we have."

She argued that with the gold they could travel far away and make a life in some hide-away, but he refused to take the chance that she would come to harm. She plead with him to reconsider but when she was convinced he would not waver, she cried in his arms.

The days passed beautifully and lovingly and much too swiftly. The physical passion of youth was not missed as the purer passion of the soul caused their cup to run over. Laughter lifted their spirits every hour until heaven seemed within reach. Her eyes were on him most every minute willing him not to leave and, being observed so closely, he had to tell her about the phenomenon of Sam. She accepted his perception, understanding the power of and the need for love and he was gratified. She didn't pretend to understand, but she didn't deny or judge. Some people believed in guardian angels, some believed in witches, Ezekial had his Sam, who was she to deem anyone wrong? His need, her love, God's grace allowed her to accept Sam's presence and even to rejoice in it and find humor in the absurdity of it. The three of them were comfortable together.

And since Patricia accepted Ezekial's belief in Sam's presence, he cared less whether her son and the hands saw him interact with the dog. The hands already feared the giant for his size and his antics with his invisible dog increased their unease. Consequently, the country all around had heard of the crazy giant in residence at the rancho. The day quickly came when Ezekial knew he must leave before he brought trouble to the love of his life.

"Patti, you know I love you. You know I always have. I've missed you fer most'a my life and I'm bound to miss you awhile longer. It cuts me through the heart to leave you, but I'm honor-bound to return to prison to keep you and my friends from more pain. Very soon they'll come for me. An' they'll kill me or catch me an' take me back to prison anyhow. I don't wanna' hurt you by leaving you, but you'll be hurt worse if I stay. I've had the time of my life these past days with you, I've never been so happy. I'll re-live these moments and keep them in my heart all my days. But, 'cause I love you. I must go."

She had determined to cry no more, still, she had to blink her burning eyes and force herself to smile. She took a deep breath and held him. What he said was sadly true. What sustained her was the idea, the plan that she was devising. She had hope that she could recruit others who would gladly help her.

She told Ezekial that she had changed her mind, that she would accept the gold he had offered. She didn't tell him why she'd changed her mind, it would be a cruelty to give him what might be false hope. She wouldn't chance breaking his big, noble heart more than it would be torn.

She had the cook come in and take a few photos of the two of them. Hopefully, one of the shots could be developed and she would always have it to remember this wonderful season of joy they'd been given together. She'd try to get a copy of the photo to him in prison. The cook had prepared his favorite meal of enchiladas, guacamole, tamales, posole and rice with jalapenos and tortillas. He enjoyed all he could of the hot, delicious repast.

Afterwards, they sat on the porch hand in hand and watched as God painted another of His endless and glorious sunsets. They viewed the violet gloaming as it faded into indigo and a million stars twinkled across the canopy of infinite space. As they held one another and absorbed the love a huge silver moon rose and bathed it's cool blue light across the verdant earth especially for them.

Young love was not forgotten, but this love, this mature, boundless love could not be contained or adequately expressed by any number of words or acts. This love was fully fermented, perfectly rich, delicious and intoxicating.

They built a small fire in the old fireplace, not because it was cold, but simply because they felt they should. They sat close on the rug before the fire, listening to the crackling embers against the quiet of the night. Gently they kissed, touched one another's faces, looked deeply into the other, memorizing the moment. They didn't make love. It was made long ago. They had found the perfect pleasure inherent in God's greatest gift, their pleasure was simply the presence of their precious love.

Chapter Sixteen

"The sacrifices of God are a broken spirit: a broken and contrite heart, O God, thou wilt not despise."
---David, Psalm 51:17 (KJV)

"The owl of Minerva spreads its wings and takes flight only when the shades of night are falling."
---Georg Wilhelm Friedrich Hegel

"As for man, his days are like grass, he flourishes like a flower of the field, the wind blows over it and it is gone, and its place remembers it no more."
---Psalm 103: 15,16 (KJV)

BILLY HAD BEEN doing his best to follow Charlie's wise advice, but couldn't seem to find an opportunity to ask Mabel to walk with him. She was hardly ever alone and he was uncomfortable with the idea of asking her in front of someone else. What if she asked him why he wanted her to walk with him? Or what if she just turned him down flat? He sure didn't want any witnesses.

He and Charlie had found a tiny gold cross and chain for Billy to give her. Charlie said it would send a message of the right kind of love, a love of respect and decency and maturity. The cross and chain was so tiny that Billy thought it didn't amount to much. Charlie assured him that women set store by little things, the smaller it was the better they liked it. He qualified that general statement somewhat in a longer conversation, but convinced Billy that in the matter of the little golden cross, Mabel would adore it.

On the third day back at the ranch he was still carrying the fancy little box with the necklace in it. He was fiddling around in the barn with Luther trying to work up the courage to walk up to the house and ask her to take a walk with him when he saw her walking toward the barn from the women's house. His heart lurched in his chest and he looked for a nook to hide in or some busywork to occupy him. His love and resolve overcame his fears and he managed to take control of himself and stand his ground. This love thing had a lot of fear mixed in it. He was acting like a coward, like a nervous boy and she certainly wouldn't consider marrying a nervous boy.

He squared his shoulders and faced the barn door. He greeted her as she entered.

"Mornin'."

"Good mornin' Billy. You still here? I thought you'd be out with the hands by now."

"Mornin' Mabel."

"Mornin' Luther."

"Uh, Luther, ain't you got sumpen to do?"

"Umhuh. Shore do. An' I'm a' doin' it. Forkin' hay fer these hungry hosses."

Mabel assessed the situation and glanced at Billy who seemed flustered. She instinctively acted to help the socially inept suitor.

"You got time to ride out to the herd and show me the gather for the trail drive?" she asked Billy.

"Oh. Uh. Well, yea, s'pose I kin make time."

Luther and Mabel exchanged grins.

Mabel saddled up old Betty who was livelier and seemed younger at the sight of her friend Mabel and the pair rode out of the barnyard with curious eyes from many windows and doors watching them. Billy pulled his hat down tight and put on his 'all bidness' face.

They rode the two miles out to the gathered herd close by the river in silence. Billy led her up a small knoll which gave a further view of the hundreds of grazing longhorns.

"Well, whad' ya think?"

"That's a bunch of beeves Billy. I didn't realize how much space seven hundred cows take up. How many hands you think it'll take to drive 'em?"

"Well, we'll bunch 'em with Samuel's and Mister Black's herds to the Concho River, then we'll join up with the Goodnight and Loving herds. We might have five, six thousand head all together. Six or seven men from each ranch 'll be plenty. Maybe twenty-five men to drive that big a herd, then a few for the remuda, cooks, scouts."

"But how many hands from here?"

"I figger to take Chinati, Chuy, Cabio, Beau and Wayne Robbins for the herd an' Squirrel Boy to scout. Then I'll be there to help out. So, what? Seven of us?"

"Make that eight Billy. I'm goin'."

"Wish you wuden. I mean, yore the boss an' it'll be fine to have you along fer comp'ny, but, well, Charlie Goodnight, he won't like it. It may cause trouble."

"If Charlie Goodnight don't like it, then we'll take our herd out and drive 'em to market ourselves. I'm an owner. I've fought Indians, worked cattle and can out ride most of the cowhands around here. I can likely keep up with Mister Goodnight at any job he can name. He ain't the king of Texas anyhow. He don't make no rules 'bout my cows."

"Yes ma'am."

"When we gonna' leave?"

"Samuel 'll send a rider any day now to tell us his herd's crossed the river. Soon's we hear from him we'll send a rider to Mister Black an' meet up with him up by Fort Inge. Then we'll all head fer the Middle Concho River south a'that new fort an' meet up with Charlie an' Mister Lovin'."

"Any idea when that'll be?"

"I figger Samuel'll be ready in two week er so."

"Guess I'd better get my things ready. We gonna' take a wagon?"

"You gonna' drive the wagon?"

"Nope, I'm gonna' ride herd, earn my way."

"You wanna' take a wagon we'll need to take another hand. Mister Black's sending Big Bud to cook so he'll have a grub wagon, an' Samuel's sendin' ol' Gravy to cook with a wagon."

"Don'tcha' think we oughta' contribute to the feedin'? We oughta' take some other things too, extra tack an' feed for the horses an' lanterns an' coal oil an' medicine. Haden you thought about that Billy?"

"Well yea. But I jest figgered Mister Black an' Charlie'd have enough to take care of us."

"Nope. No way will I depend on anyone else to take care of my hands or my stock. We'll pay our own way. Luther's been spoilin' to go. Tell him to get a wagon ready."

"Awite."

Mabel's heels touched Betty's ribs to head home but Billy reached out and pulled her reins.

"Hold up fer a minute Miss Mabel. I, uh, I got sumpen I need t' give ya."

"What's that Billy?"

Billy got down from his horse and stood lookin' up at her.

"Well?" Mabel asked.

"I need fer you to gi'down Mabel."

"What for?"

"I wanna' do this the right way an' I can't do it with you up thar on Betty."

"What in the world are..." escaped Mabel's mouth and her words added to Billy's discomfiture. When she had dismounted and stood before him he dug in his pocket and retrieved the pretty little box and pushed it out to her.

"What's this?"

"It's fer you."

"What...? Oh Billy! It's beautiful. But,...why?"

Her beautiful eyes beneath those long pale lashes cut into him and the near trembling bronc busting, bull-wrestling, Indian fighter and Confederate cavalryman managed to drop to only one shaky knee and look up into beautiful, young, freckled face and say the words he had rehearsed a hundred times.

"May,...Mabel," he had to swallow so he could speak the rest, "Will you marry me?"

The suddenness, the surprise made a tinkle of laughter escape her and she shook her head in silence.

He misinterpreted her reaction and he said, "Well, Mabel, I love you an' if yore answer is no, why then,..."

"No! I mean,...I don't mean no! An' I don't mean yes neither! But I might. Billy stand up! I'll just have to have some time to think about,..."

The rest of her words were cut off by Billy's kiss. He only meant to give her a gentlemanly peck on the lips as Charlie had directed but her lips were so soft and so warm and welcoming. Both of them lost themselves in the moment of that first kiss. It was so delicious, so exciting, somehow comforting and promising and it went on and on and ended much too quickly when they both had to pull away and breathe. Breathless, dizzy, blood rushing, hormones gushing, they leaned into one another and held on tightly. Mabel's head was pressed against Billy's chest and she couldn't decide whether it was her heartbeat or his that beat so loudly and rapidly in her ear.

"Oh Billy!"

"Mabel."

"Billy. Hold me Billy."

He held her closer than close until she raised her head to look at him and then his lips were somehow on hers once more. The kiss was so tender and conveyed a love Mabel could feel everywhere their bodies touched. She giggled with the pure joy of it and the alluring magic of her laughter filled Billy with such a whole happiness as he had never known.

"Will you marry me Mabel?"

"Hmmm...maybe."

He kissed her again, pulling her even closer.

"Oh, marry me Mabel."

"Maybe I will."

He began to kiss her perfect, pale ears, her graceful neck. His hands moved on her back.

She pushed herself away, reluctantly.

"I can't think like this. Give me some room Billy. I need some time."

Billy took a deep breath. Mabel handed him the necklace. "Put this on me." she said and turned her back.

Billy put the cross and chain around her neck as she held her hair up out of the way. He fumbled and struggled until his calloused fingers finally found purchase on the tiny clasp and secured it. Mabel turned to him and straightened it with her hand.

"Thank you Billy Hill. I'll cherish it forever. No man ever gave me anything like this before."

"It's 'cause I love you. Mabel Curtsinger."

Now that he'd told her he loved her he couldn't seem to stop telling her.

"Well,… thank you. I might love you too. Jes' give me some time."

"I hope you'll hurry up and decide. I love you."

She giggled.

He smiled.

It was a near perfect world.

Any and all were invited to the get-together at Angel's Camp. It was an opportunity for all the region's neighbors to get to know one another better and was a send-off to endow favor and friendship upon all parties attached to the trail drive. Those who would push the herds to market as well as those who would wait, wonder and pray all enjoyed this happy time together. Some neighbors came from as far as forty miles and many came from town. Happy times and holidays were rare out on the edge of nowhere and everybody was glad for the invitation and relished the chance to socialize and enjoy a respite from their endless labor. They came and camped on the grounds, some arrived two days before the shindig to prepare, and they brought sundry sweet and savory sustenance to share under the brilliant spring sky.

They had mostly all arrived and settled in by sundown on Friday, though some tardy riders and wagons of families rumbled in through the night. Buggies and riders from town arrived through the morning too. The ladies took advantage of the occasion to dress in what fancy finery they possessed, in bustles and bonnets, straw boaters and fine feathered hats. Even the poorest cowboys had washed and shaved and cleaned their boots.

There were games and contests of all sorts throughout the Sabbath. Luther was proud to be champion horseshoe pitcher, (he had practiced every spare minute for a fortnight), as well as undeclared but undenied prince of prevarication. Callie was the surprise winner of the checker tournament, defeating Reading Black in the final, decisive game. Chas' boys baseball team lost their game against the boys from town, but he and Beau finished in a dead heat in the mile long horse race around the cleared perimeter of the ranch headquarters. Both were delighted at the result, and of course, both rode the thoroughbreds Beau and Micah had rode to Texas. Big Bud Phillips won the wrestling contest and Angel Camp's Kickapoo cowboy Squirrel Boy won the footrace. Chinati won the roping contest after a long, closely contested competition between the cowboys. Mister Black had brought a croquet set, wooden balls and mallets and iron wickets. The ladies and children played joyfully and fiercely all through the perfect weather of the afternoon. Towards evening the men played a baseball game and the lack of skills caused a hilarity of merriment which, with the other pleasures of the day, served to join the neighbors into an even closer fraternity.

The evening repast outshined even the noonday meal and everyone enjoyed more than they should. The children had taken pleasure in helping to create the many gallons of ice cream and took particular satisfaction in destroying most of it with the many different pies. At dusk the lanterns were lit and the music and dancing began. Though at first lethargic from the rich and rare meal, the party grew and soon the fat May moon reflected it's silver light on the crowns of heads that would ever contain the affectionate memory of that blessed evening of congenial companionship and old-time merry-making.

Coyotes on near hills quieted their howling to hear the music, the song and the laughter from the happy gathering in the lantern's light. Children skipped and danced in the circle surrounding the square dancing couples. Pain, sadness sorrow, worry and despair were driven out and could not enter here.

Mister Black had several black employees and two of the cowboys from his ranch vied all throughout the day and night of the party for the attentions of Beulah who was flattered, flustered and pleased by their competition. Big Mo was a forty year old runaway slave from Mississippi who had joined up with Wildcat and his band of misfits in Mexico for awhile, then came north after the war to find work and then a wife. Mister Black had allowed him to work and now that he had seen Beulah he decided he would take her as a wife. He was not going to allow the young buck who made Beulah laugh as they danced to steal his future bride's affection. Big Mo had learned his manners as a boy and Beulah was impressed by the strong and courtly older gentleman whose deep slow voice was so comforting and gentle. But the exciting, demonstrative and good-looking young Shadrack was so compelling. Beulah felt so alive and new and pretty, so excited with the moment and with her prospects. And her joy was shining through her eyes and making her pretty smile irrepressible. Her blossoming fullness of life was revealed in her dancing and her happy eyes.

Mabel also had her suitors, but they tended to be older, more successful men. None of them interested her as a prospective husband but each of them was of interest in other ways. She was friendly to all and took pains to nourish their hopes, as she delighted in the reactions of Mister Billy 'Hell' Hill with every touch of a man's hand during a dance, every smile, every spoken word he couldn't hear, every laugh. His jealousy was evident and she allowed him to stew in it awhile before she cooled him off with assurances at intervals during the evening. Billy truly wanted her to give him all her time and attention, but she wouldn't think of allowing that.

Callie's contained and controlled custom in dealing with men sent the message clearly that she was interested in being a good, reliable friend to her neighbors but not interested in any romantic relation-ship. Still, she also appreciated and enjoyed the flattering efforts of the interested and seemingly enchanted men.

Sallie and Nellie danced together, danced with many of their new found friends and Nellie was in heaven when Sallie bribed Chas to dance with her. Beau and Ruby danced nearly every dance together wearing their love on their faces. And several ladies persuaded Ezekial to dance, but he was so careful not to put his big foot on their delicate feet that it wasn't really dancing at all.

The Mexican ladies and their men taught the others some Mexican dances and there were sad Mexican ballads sung by various good, and not so good, Mexican singers.

With the help of the children and Micah playing his harmonica, Luther had written a song for the party. They had practiced it together in the barn so no one could see them and so it would be a surprise to all. With the girls and Luther touching and indicating those body attributes mentioned in the song in a rough but funny choreograph as they sung, they soon had their audience laughing at their antics. Luther started the song with a chorus singing alone, then the girls joined in the verses. Sam lined up between the girls with Chas and sang along, unfortunately.

"Oh I love you baby, from the crown to the ground.
You're a ton of fun and I love every pound.
"Ya got lips like a llama, momma,
Eyes like a frog,
"Ya got hips like a brahma, momma,
Breath like a dog!
"And yes I love you baby, bottom to the top,
Oh I love you baby like a hog loves slop.
"Ya got ears like a bunny, honey,
Ya sleep like a log,
Smart as a dummy, honey,
Nose like a hog,
"And yes I love you baby, bottom to the top,
Couldn 't run me off my baby, with an outhouse mop.
"Ya got stinkie on your feetie, sweetie
Warts on your nose,
Got all your teeth nearly, dearly,
Corns on your toes,

"An I couldn't leave you baby, I ain't never lied
I'll stay close by you baby, till I'm sure you died."

Everyone was delighted, especially with the little dancing antics of the children and the people asked them to sing it again. Later in the evening a third performance was called for. At the third rendering some of the other children knew every word and sang and danced along with merry enthusiasm.

It was much later than anyone there had stayed awake in a coon's age when Callie, Mabel and the girls retired and the others gratefully, yet reluctantly found their way to their beds, cots and bedrolls. Billy, ever vigilant, took the watch from Chinati who had foregone the last two hours of the party to relieve another watchman. Noah and Billy and the other rangers had learned long ago that Comanches loved to crash a party or spoil a holiday.

After climbing the gentle hill above the ranch graveyard, Billy sat on the crest under the starlight and let the refreshing breeze carry his thoughts far ahead to hopeful, imagined days, wedded days and nights that seemed to be promised. He thought of children born, raised and taught, beginning with little Boy. He saw the work ahead, the growth of the ranch and maybe an influx of settlers wherein there would be safety from the wild Indians and outlaws. He thought of how he wanted to provide for, protect and please Mabel, Boy and the family they would become. There was a promise abiding in him, a sacred promise and presence of love. And in that love was such joy and peace and hope as he had never known. Billy didn't often pray, but tonight he looked up into the infinite and said simply, "Thank You." And he truly meant it.

The first day of the cattle drive the Angel's Camp crew managed maybe five or six miles. It had been an exhausting day. Quitters and fighters in the driven herd were abundant and horses had been chasing and dodging longhorns all day. Billy was impressed that Mabel still had the energy to prepare a hot meal for the tired hands with Luther's help.

Reading Black's herd waited at his ranch a mile north of Fort Inge and Billy had sent Chinati to let Mister Black know where they were and that they'd try to have their herd there within two more days. The plan was to merge the herds and head north together. He had also sent Squirrel Boy, the Kickapoo Cowboy, to Samuel a week ago and expected the Mexican herd to overtake them within five or six days. Besides Chinati and Squirrel Boy, Chuy, Cabio, Beau, Wayne Robbins and Luther were on the drive with Mabel and himself. They had left enough men with Callie and Ezekial to protect the ranch and handle the crops and other work.

Mabel had proven to be a proficient cow chouser and handled the cow pony with a natural bent, but, being born and raised to the saddle he should have not been surprised. The cow ponies were quick and with so little weight to carry could stop and change direction so fast that a less skilled rider would have been unseated. Mabel had a light hand on the reins and signaled and guided a horse as much with her legs as her hands. She was a joy to behold astride a cow pony. Of course Billy had a hard time keeping his eyes off of her at anytime.

Beau, Cabio and Squirrel Boy were excellent riders too, all of them small men. Chuy, Chinati, Wayne and Billy could out ride most men, but their expertise was really riding to fight. They had outfought the Comanche many times and it was generally acknowledged that the Comanche were likely the world's best cavalry, especially guerrilla tactics cavalry. Billy believed that the eight of them could manage to drive seven hundred cattle up the long trail, but if every day turned out to be the constant battle this first day had been it would be far from easy.

Billy assigned himself the first night watch on the herd along with Wayne and put Beau and Cabio on the second watch, Chuy and Squirrel Boy the third. Mabel overruled him out of his hearing, telling Squirrel Boy she would take his place. She wanted Billy to be the boss, but she intended on doing her part without any special consideration or favor. She had established parameters on the first morning of the drive by calling the men together at the ranch as she spoke of her expectations and demands.

"Fellers, it's gonna' be a long drive and it's just natural that we're gonna' irritate one another some. But, until we get these cows to market, I'm not gonna' tolerate no fightin'. Once we get these cattle where they need to be, why, then you can fight, get drunk, gamble, whatever you've a mind to do. You will have earned that. But, while we're herding our livelihood to market, no fightin' an' no drinkin'.

"Mister Billy Hill is the boss of this drive, not me. What he says, goes. An' that includes me. I won't ask for no special favors, except those of normal social convention and consideration. For instance:

"I shouldn't have to say it, but I will. I don't want any misunderstandings. When I head out away from the herd to answer nature's call…"

Wayne Robbins snickered and elbowed Chuy standing beside him, then, when he saw Mabel's burning stare aimed at him, he reddened and looked down like he found something interesting on the bare ground before him.

"…or when we camp by water where I can find a private place to bathe, any cowboy I see in the general vicinity will draw wages and get somewhere if he's lucky enough to dodge the lead I'll be sending his way. Some of you already know, but for those of you who don't know, this Colt revolver on my hip isn't for show. I've been using it since I was knee high to a short horse and I'll have no compunction nor hesitation in justly rewarding any two-legged varmint who chances a peep. We all got that straight?"

"Yes ma'ams" were unanimous.

Conversation was minimal at dusk that first day, everyone was just too tired. After eating, sleep couldn't come soon enough and the soreness and stiffness set in both people and cows. There was little unnecessary movement. Dawn came too early, but Luther lured the hands from their blankets with fragrant bacon and biscuits. Lots of coffee was swallowed as saddles were strapped down tight on fresh horses. Nobody noticed or appreciated the beauty of the pink and yellow spring dawning, their minds were filled with the dread of another long day kicking these crazy cows down the trail.

"Don't get used to me doin' the cookin' boys. I know yer glad of that. Mister Black is sendin his cowboy cook an' a wagon fulla' grub to go 'long with us. 'Course we'll have beef on the hoof an' you may get a gullet fulla' cow meat by the time we sell 'em all. And Senor Samuel Chavez is sending his good Mexican cook, ol' Gravy, an' let me tell ya whatever he cooks'll be plenty hot enough. But, Mister Black's cook, whom I'm sure you've heard of, Big Bud Phillips will do most of the cookin' an he is one fine cook, lemma tell ya. Jes' don't get on his wrong side though, when he gets his hackles up, he's plenty rough."

"When's Mister Black's herd gonna' meet up with us?" Wayne asked Billy.

"Soon's we get this ornery bunch o' devils up to Fort Inge. I figger day after tomorrow by noon if this herd 'll break into the trail. Ya'll rotate like a clock after noon, jes' like we did yestiddy, left flank point, point to right flank, right flank to drag, drag to left flank. Aw 'ite? We'll do it that way 'til these herds come together, then we'll see what Frank Callender says. We'll have to work with his hands and Samuel's too 'til we get to the Concho River, then we'll havta' see how Charlie Goodnight wants ta do it. Le's head 'em north boys. And girl." He smiled at pretty Miss Mabel.

Once the stiffness loosened in the muscles of her legs and butt Mabel began to focus on other things and appreciated the fine May morn. The temperature was perfect, the sky perfectly clear of clouds and the sea of wildflowers and tall grasses waved in the breeze and softened their passage. Some of the unruly steers of yesterday were in a more cooperative mood today and the few that fought for their freedom seemed only playful in their intent, returning to the trotting herd as if they had been only testing and teasing.

She rode drag this morning and was grateful the path lay over the thick vegetation, the thick, endless expanse of blooming bluebonnets sparing her the typical cloud of dust drag riders had to breathe. Still, there was enough dust to merit wearing a bandanna over her nose and mouth. White cowbirds found the herd mid-morning and alighted in the herd's wake as it passed. Billy had told the drovers to allow the herd to graze as they walked and let them trot if they wanted, but not to push them, let them set their own pace.

By Billy's reckoning they made between twelve and fifteen miles that second day. The herd seemed to get the idea of the drive, most of them, and though there were several jousts at the point to establish a leader, one rust and white brindle steer with one down-turned horn seemed to make his point that he wouldn't be led.

Mid-morning of the third day Squirrel Boy climbed a tree as was his wont and with his keen black eyes had seen Mister Black's herd maybe two miles ahead. The word was passed back to Mabel and Wayne at the point to just walk the cows fast enough to keep them reasonably bunched. It took over two hours to travel those two miles to where Mister Black's eight hundred head grazed in tall spring grasses. As they passed half a mile out from Fort Inge they could see soldiers clearing brush and the axes of those chopping firewood echoed across the distance.

Over a long, lazy lunch the principles discussed the logistics of the joining of the herds and hands and found that they were in accord that no binding decisions should be made until Samuel's group joined them and until the ranches united and they met and had a discussion with everyone in attendance.

Bud Phillips, the Black ranch crew's cook, was a popular fellow with the cowboys the night of the herds coming together as he served up heaping plates of a thick, rich beef stew with fat and flaky sour dough biscuits slathered in butter. When everyone was served and the savory juices brightening everyone's mood he lifted his robust voice to give a little speech.

"Some of you fellers know me and you can ignore me cause you already know, but this is fer you fellers who don't know me. I'm a friendly man an' easy to get along with. I don't bother nobody an' I mostly do a good job of minding my own business. You can count on me to do the best I can cooking whatever food I have to work with. 'Member, I'm eatin' the same chow you are, so don't make the mistake of figgerin' yer getting' the raw end of the shank. I'll trade plates with any one of ya, anytime long as you ain't put yer nasty hands in it.

"One thing I can't abide though is a whiner. If yer ever thinkin' 'bout complaining about the cookin', jes' keep it in mind that I'm sensitive 'bout my work an' I get so mad I'm most delirious and wanna' fight.

"Now, I ain't sayin' its right an' I ain't proud ah my temper, I'm jes' advising ya how I am. Some say it's a sym-tum of my im-mature-ity. Some say I'm a bit in-sane. But, it's a sad fact I ain't never learned to control my mad. So, if yer hankerin' fer a fight boys I'm tellin' ya how to get one. Jes' complain 'bout the cookin' an' yule prob'ly be a' fightin' me affore y'can put the plate down. An fellers, ya may not survive it. I'm a big ol' boy an' when I get mad I'm mad all over and all the way through.

"Other'n that, I'm real easy ta get 'long with. These fellers here 'at know me, they'll tell ya. I'm mostly friendly as a box a' puppies.

"They's fried apple fold overs fer desert after ya'll fill up on that stew and biscuits."

Those fried apple fold overs with cinnamon sealed the deal with those cowboys after the mouth-watering stew. Also contributing to their unsigned contract with Big Bud the cook was the fact that he was a big ol' boy. There would be no complaining about the food.

A buffalo soldier from the new fort on the Concho River rode in and asked for Billy Hell specifically, said he had a message from Charlie Goodnight. When Billy identified himself the long-winded soldier explained that he had been in a saloon over-the-river from the fort and Mister Goodnight had overheard him telling a friend that he was going to San Antonio at first light in the morning on leave to visit his wife there. Goodnight had hired him to find these herds coming up from Uvalde and deliver this message. The note inside the envelope advised that he had discussed the combining of the herds with his partner Oliver Loving, and he had been dead set against it for the reason that it would be more cattle than could be grazed, watered and protected from Indians and bandits on the route they'd planned on taking. There hadn't been much rain out west and grazing would be slim for their own herds. Goodnight apologized and suggested they take their herds to Sedalia, Missouri as there would be a good market there at the rail head.

"Charlie didn't say anything about a woman on our drive?" Mabel asked the soldier.

"Well, no, not to me ma'am. But I did overhear some talk 'tween him an' Mister Lovin' that it'd be bad luck an' a hardship an' askin' fer trouble to take a woman on a trail drive. But ma'am, my hearin' jes' ain't right sometimes, so I wouldn't swear they's talkin' 'bout this drive or you."

"I suspect you heard perfectly well sir, and your truthfulness will be discreetly held between us. I've asked Bud to feed you some of his good cookin' 'fore you continue your journey. Thank you."

As the soldier ate. Frank told Billy and Mabel that he'd been up the Sedalia Trail years ago and thought he could find the way fairly well. He believed it would be a good market, maybe even better than what they would have found with Goodnight and Loving. They were well west of the trail, but if they struck northeast across the Colorado River they could be on the old trail by the time they forded the Brazos.

"I'll send word back to Mister Black that we're heading the herds to Sedalia if ya'll are agreed," Frank said.

"Whaddaya think Billy?"

"It's a long trail. More settlements and farms to go 'round. But, may be easier traveling, more water, better grazing, more weight on the cattle when we get there. I'm told there are always buyers there bidding against each other."

"Let's send riders down to Samuel's herd to lead his crew here, then, if they agree, we'll head to Missouri. We don't need Charlie Goodnight to tell us how to herd cows, or how to sell 'em."

And so the trail drive took another direction. It was four days before Samuel's herd caught up with them and they let his herd rest a day before pushing on to the northeast along the winding clear waters of the Llano River. The Llano was long and often wild, but usually very shallow. The clear spring waters that filtered underground in the Edwards Plateau had cut through granite many thousands of years and even the heavy cattle and horses trailing in and out of the river didn't muddy it unless an earthen bank caved in and even then the swift current cleared the cool waters rushing over the speckled pink stone.

A few miles before the Llano fed into the wide and deep Colorado Mabel took advantage of the crystal clean water to take her first bath since leaving Angel's Camp. The ever vigilant Billy knew she was slipping away even before she did it, as he saw her surreptitiously slip another set of clothes, soap and a towel from the bed of Luther's wagon after she ate her supper. He stayed within a short distance from the river, far enough to give her privacy but close enough to hear her if she ran into trouble.

She slipped up on him as she walked away from the river, punched him in the ribs playfully and said, "Standing guard soldier?"

"Well, yes'm," he smiled.

She leaned into him and quickly kissed him. As she skipped away she pitched the towel and soap to him.

"You could use a bath too Mister Hill. You're beginning to smell like livestock."

Billy grinned as he watched her sashay back to the camp. He put his nose to his arm pit and grimaced. Then he put the towel to his face, inhaled, and the grin returned to his sunburned cheeks which he ran his calloused hand over feeling the stubble he had ignored too long. He went to the camp and collected his kit. He found a likely spot and stripped down to his union suit, figuring he could wash it the same time he washed himself. He sat down on the stone bottom of one of the many narrow channels cut into the solid rock and balanced the surviving triangle of mirror on a limb of juniper which grew close by the stream. The cool water dividing around his stomach carried the scraping from his face and the soap off his straight razor and down the fast flowing cut. In a few minutes he could see most of his face again as he had shaved around his thick mustache. The pulsing flow felt so relaxing it was a balm to aching muscles and stiff joints. He came near to sleeping and forced himself to awaken when he realized the sun was casting its final orange light through the tall oak canopy. He stripped off his underwear and gave it a hard scrubbing with soap and sand over the rock beside him, then washed himself head to foot. The air was cool and invigorating as he stood and dried himself on the stone bank with the soft towel that had touched his love. He just couldn't wipe the foolish grin off of his face.

When he walked into camp Big Bud handed him a tin cup of boiling hot coffee.

"What's that ear-to-ear smile about Billy?"

"Bud, you know, life sometimes has a shine on it."

"Um huh. An' usually it's a woman does the polishin'."

Billy just kept smiling.

The Chavez herd finally caught up to them and they explained the situation. All together, plans were solidified to head to Sedalia. The Chavez ranch trail boss was Arthur Gonzales whom everyone called 'Pancake' and he introduced his cook Roy Garivay called 'Gravy' to Big Bud. They agreed to work together on the drive and seemed to like one another right off. Luther would help them out as he was able. The other crew members were Old Tonk, Anthony Ball, Espuelo Hernandez and Tony Reyes. Old Tonk was their scout, over six foot, in his fifties probably and he answered to 'Tonk', since he was a Tonkawa Indian so that's what everyone called him. He spoke several Indian languages and dialects as well as good Spanish and passable English. Anthony Ball was a stocky white man who had survived being a gringo on the border for a lengthy life and was a good all-around hand as was Espuelo Hernandez. Tony Reyes had been a sergeant in the American army before the Civil War and had returned to Mexico when war broke out so as not to have to fight his friends. This crew had brought four hundred wild Mexican cattle to join the drive.

Billy said, "I halfway expected Charlie to pull out early if he heard about Mabel comin' along, but I tol' Mabel that 'fore we left. Don't know how he found out, might have a spy here amongst us."

The cowhands all looked sideways at one another, wondering who it might be.

"But, it don't matter. What matters now is that we all work together to get this bunch of beef to market. Frank's been down the trail before, so he'll be the trail boss. Any objections?"

Pancake spoke up, "It's a good ways longer up to Sedalia an' Senor Chavez, he'll wonder what is taking us so long, but, it can't be helped. I guess we'll just have to hurry every chance we get. Hokay?"

"Okay Pancake," Frank replied, "Let's get some rest so's we kin start 'em early an' make some miles tomorra'."

As the herds merged into one and the lead steers were accepted, the cattle fell into the daily patterns and practice of traveling. The hands became familiar with one another and became a more effective team as the days and the miles began to pile up behind them. It wasn't all an easy journey though, there were rivers to ford and detours around various obstacles such as hills and farmer's spring crops and the small settlements that seemed to be springing up every few miles. The trail boss, Frank Callender, was an older man and gruff in his speech, appearance and carriage, a man to get things done, but not one adept at conciliation and manipulation. And neither Billy nor the other trail boss, Pancake, could deal with the ranchers and farmers whose land they must cross as effectively as Mabel, and she quickly became their arbitrator and primary spokesperson. She exuded just the right combination of tender and tough. The hard-bitten, leather-faced country boys were charmed by her speech and demeanor and vanquished by her smile.

The days begat weeks and eventually they found and fell into the old track that had become the Sedalia Trail since back in the forties. The drag riders reported to Frank at supper that first day on the trail that there was a big herd not far behind them. As they were discussing this development over coffee after enjoying Bud's good cooking a trio of riders hailed the camp and then rode in. When asked politely to 'gi-down' and drink a cup of coffee they rudely refused the hospitality.

"We got our own coffee when we want it, an' we got a five-thousand head herd bedded down just behind you. We don't 'preciate ya'll cuttin' in front of us on the trail and hoggin' up all the grass. We don't aim on eating yer dust all the way to Missoura. We was on this trail first. Been on it since way south uhtha Nueces. So, you jes' move yer herd east or west off the trail in the mornin' an' let us pass our herd. You don't want no trouble with us."

Frank looked at Billy and Pancake and Mabel and then shook his head and chuckled.

"Mister, don't know who you are since you ain't been civil nuff to introduce yerself, but, fact is, you don't look so scary to me that I'd let you buffalo us off this trail. We've drove these beeves from south uh-tha Nueces too, hell, some from even south un-tha Rio Grande, fer some weeks now, an' we ain't about to allow some Johnny-come-lately blow-hard push us to the side."

"You been warned ol' timer. Tomorra' we'll drive our herd through yours if it ain't outa' our way. An' if you lose some cattle, well, we'll jes' let 'em trail along with mine to the rail head. I got twicet the cows and twicet the cowboys you got so if it comes to a fight you got a losing hand."

Billy Hell's temper flared at the threat and he bowed out his chest like a game rooster.

"Pilgrim, it ain't always the amount of dogs in the fight, it's usually the amount of fight in the dogs. This bunch uh-men you judge you kin whup has fought more bandits and Indians than you got cows an' they still got all their hair. They was raised on bear milk an' cactus cookies an' most has rode with rangers since they was pups an' all of 'em are full-growed bulldogs by now. So if yer' thinkin' you kin talk us off this trail or kin ride through us like a shalla' stream then you need to get yer thinker adjusted. jes' take a holiday fer a day or two an' let us get up the trail a' ways an' you kin avoid the spankin' you'll get if you try ta ride rough through this troop."

"Ha! Ya'll don't look so tough ta me. 'A broke-down ol' saddle tramp trail boss, a buncha' yeller whupped rebs, some taco-bendin Meskin goat herders, an' I'm damned if'n you tin horns ain't got a woman along. Son, don't you know that a whore's bad luck on a job of work like a trail drive?"

"Whore? Why you..." Mabel started.

Billy put his arm out restraining her and said low in his throat, "Cowboy, yer alligator mouth jes' overloaded yer hummin-bird ass. Gi-down off 'at hoss an' le'see how tough you are."

"Heh-heh. Naw, you jes' be shore..." was all he got out of his foul mouth before Chuy's lariat loop squeezed around him and he was jerked to the ground like a yearling bull, one that would become a steer shortly.

The two riders who'd come with the would-be bully reached for their heavy pistols hanging on their hips but Luther and Big Bud hollered at them and they kept still when they saw the two double-barreled shotguns leveled at their bellies.

Billy bent over and loosened the rope and slung it back toward Chuy with a grim grin.

"Thankee Chuy."

The man who had been so ingloriously dismounted kicked and his boot caught Billy in the chest knocking him back against a wagon. As the man gained his feet Billy was on him like a wildcat. In the next minute the loudmouth was split and bleeding at every point fist met face. It took Big Bud, Wayne Robbins and Beau pulling and persuading to get Billy off the beaten and prostrate man.

As the severely beaten man was lifted into his saddle and Billy struggled to regain his breath, Frank instructed the two cowboys who held their boss in the saddle.

"Like my friend said, ya'll would be wise to rest yer herd a day er so an' let us get ahead an' outa' yer way. We don't want no trouble, but if'n you bring it we'll deal with it. Now go doctor yer' boss up an' try'n talk some sense to 'im. Git!"

As the trio rode away, everyone around the camp was silent looking at one another, wondering what now lay ahead. Frank Callender didn't allow them to wonder for long.

"Fellers, looks like we done run into a passel of worriment. That ol' boy was a'lookin fer a fight when he rode up here an' damned if he diden' find one. Now, I expect, his bruised pride'll lead him to try an' run us off the trail. Since I'm not lookin' to go to war an' since we need to get to the railroad afore this bunch behind us so's we kin sell our cows, we're gonna' race that big herd behind us. Ya'll ready fer that?"

Enthusiastic affirmations were spoken by most of the hands despite their weariness from the day in the saddle.

"If's that's the plan boss, how early we gone start out?"

"Not how early, how late. We gonna' start right now. We got a little starlight and these beasts can see a whole lot better'n us anyhow. By daylight I hope to be ten or more miles ahead of that big mouth's herd an' we'll drive all day tomorrow 'til we tire these cattle out, then we'll rest a few hours and hit the trail again. It's a race now boys, so find a fresh horse an' cinch 'em up tight, slide them spurs back on, get another cup a Joe while you can an' le's get 'em moving."

All hands lined up for a refill from the several coffee pots.

"Bud, Luther, Gravy, ya'll try an' stay up front with the scouts close as you can. Tonk, Squirrel Boy, ya'll pick an easy trail, it may be hard to see the old trail in the dark, jes' find us the fastest way. Sid, I want you to trail back behind the drag and watch them that's behind us, see what they're gone do. Don't let 'em see ya' or catch ya', an' lemme know if they're doin' sumpin that might cause us concern.

"Let's get 'em movin' at a trot fellers an' don't let none of 'em quit the herd an' get lost and left behind. Keep 'em tight in a bunch. Let's move on out. An' don't let any of these leather-skinned, razor-footed, long-horned devils hurt you or your hosses. They're tired an' won't be happy to be bothered."

They started the reluctant herd quicker than they wanted, the few that got spooked at the unexpected interruption of their bedding seemed to infect the others and they all began an angry, rolling run. Several steers had to be fought back into the herd.

"Let 'em run a'ways. They'll slow down in a mile or so," Billy hollered back at the flankers, "Jes' keep 'em together."

It was mostly level ground with a few settlements of the scrub oak family here and there and the cattle naturally ran wide of the bunches of brush and trees. Billy kept one eye peeled for Mabel as usual, because he felt like she wanted to head back and shoot the rude oaf who had insulted her without provocation. She was spoiling for a fight and not happy with Frank's decision to run. She realized he was right to get ahead and get their cattle to market first, but it went against her grain to let this blustering mean-mouthed fool even imagine they might be afraid of him. Mabel's cow pony stumbled as he ran in the darkness beside the herd and she had to grab the horn to keep her seat. This near catastrophe forced her to focus on what she was doing instead of what she would like to do.

The herd ran, as Billy predicted, around a mile before they slowed to a bawling trot. In another half-mile they slackened their speed to a fast walk.

"Keep 'em steppin' lively and steady," the word was passed back to each hand down the line and around the herd and they kept the cattle at a fast walk all night with pops of their lariats, sharp yells and quick horses. Just before dawn the point men turned the lead steers back into the herd which began to bunch up, mill and widen as the long herd came tiredly to a halt. Billy met Mabel and Frank at the front of the herd and they were discussing the obstruction.

Billy questioned, "What's the hold-up?"

"Farmer's got long rows of corn across our way."

"Well? Le's go 'round."

"You don't understand Billy," Mabel explained. "These are mile-long rows with a deep feeder stream of the Brazos River on one end and the river itself on the other end. To go around we're gonna' have to swim the herd across and as tired as the cows and the horses are, we may lose quite a few."

"Where's Bud, Luther and Gravy and the wagon?"

"They made camp up against the corn crop. They've got breakfast cooked and lots of coffee on."

"I'll go an' start the hands in a few at a time to get a bite an' a cup, awright?"

"Yea, go 'head Billy," Frank answered, "An' hurry back yerself so we kin talk this over."

The tired hands began coming in four to six at a time for chow and coffee. The herd was mostly all laid down and resting, ignoring the lush growth of tall grass they were laying in. Billy took note of the exhausted state of the cattle and the cowboys and wondered if there were a wise solution to the problems besetting them.

Frank set a watch of half a dozen men and let the rest eat and get some sleep while they mulled the problems. After two hours, he sent six of those who had slept to relieve those who hadn't. Mabel had slept in the first group and Frank and Billy laid down after she and Pancake were awake to stand guard and ponder the situation.

Around eight o'clock a short, bearded farmer and three stair-stepped boys rode up in a farm wagon pulled by two big white mules. Mabel and Pancake employed smiles, hospitality and Bud's pecan fried pies to woo and win the farmer's good will. Mabel used her wiles in explaining their dilemma, bringing out the paternal instincts in the man. She readily and quickly became the daughter his good wife had never given him. When Mabel had completed her tale of their hurry to get their herd to market and the bully behind them, the farmer patted her on the shoulder and assured her "Now darlin', don't you worry that perdy li'l head, ever thang'll be alright. Now listen here,…"

Mister Andrew Royal Junior had been unconscious until around three o'clock in the morning. He awoke to the realization that he was missing three front teeth, two got completely knocked out and one was broken off at the gum. Throughout much cussing, threatening, yelling and whining, the cook managed to extract the partial root with a pair of horseshoe pliers and a butcher knife employed as a fulcrum that the foreman held up against Mister Royal's chin.

At first light of day he looked in the small mirror and he saw through the one eye that wasn't completely swollen shut that his nose was severely bent, jaw swollen, knots on his cheekbones and forehead and cuts over and under each eye. His mouth was still oozing thick blood from cuts inside and outside his mouth and a ripped and torn lip and cheek. One ear was puffed up to the size of a coffee cup saucer and exhibited every color of the rainbow. Every breath and movement emphasized his bruises, if not busted ribs. The longer he stared at his ruined visage and he began to accept the conception that his face was irredeemable, the anger and hate began to roil and boil.

He saw in the looking glass the reflection of his foreman who had sat idly by on his horse and watched that wild man assault him. The foreman and cook were whispering to one another and grinning. He whipped around and cuffed the cowardly curs and cussed them until the pain in his ribs and a wave of dizziness almost rendered him unconscious once again. He squatted on the ground to keep from falling.

"You a'wite boss man?"

"Hell no, I'm not alright. Do I look alright to you, you ign'ant coward?"

"Boss, they was ten guns aimed at us. Wuden nuttin' we could do."

"Humph! There's damn sure sumpen you kin do now. You get this herd movin' an' you keep 'em movin' 'til you run slap over those graze stealin', trail jumpin', suckerpunchin' jaspers, an' if any of 'em give fight I want 'em surrounded an' shot. If you can't shoot the men, shoot the hosses an' if you can't shoot hosses, shoot cattle. Do whatever you gotta' do but you put this herd out in front."

"Yessir." You comin' along?"

"....Naw, I'm headed back to Austin fer a square-dance. Hell yea I'm comin' meat head! I'll be along with the cook in the wagon 'til I heal up some. You send riders back to let me know what's goin' on up the trail. You hear?"

"Yessir."

"Get movin'!"

Andrew Royal Junior was a man accustomed to having his way. He was a hard man, a man who got things done. Without empathy, unforgiving and ruthless, he had expanded his father's south Texas holdings and his wealth. He mostly had things his way because he just wouldn't have things any other way. He had been whipped before, lost some battles, but had never lost a war. In his mind this was war and there was no way he would allow this rag tag outfit ahead of him to remain out front and get their beef to market before his.

"You want some breakfast boss?" the cook asked.

"Dumbass, how you think I'd eat with my teeth knocked out an' my mouf cut to smithereens? No, what I do want is fer you to get that dadblamed wagon loaded, the mules in harness an' get up beside the herd. An' hand me another bottle of whiskey."

The cook handed him the bottle warily and hurriedly threw unwashed plates, pots, pans and cups into the wagon bed, yelling at his helper to hitch up the team. He kicked dirt on the fire and jumped up on the wagon seat hollering at his helper to get on the wagon too. He released the brake and popped the leads and the mules jerked in their traces.

"Hold up! You woofless, birdbwained idjit. What? You think I'm gonna walk?" He slapped the cook's helper with his hat as he gingerly climbed up into the wagon seat.

"Get in the back boy! Was you jes gonna leave me here a' sittin on the prairie? I musta' been dwunk when I hired you. Now move this wagon down the trail, keep up beside the herd. Slowly! An' don't hit no holes er bumps."

He looked through the slit he could see through at the side of the cook's trembling and sweating jowls and tried to recall what advanced state of inebriation must have dissolved his discretion when he decided to employ this mentally deficient, dippy ding-dong.

When the good husbandman heard of the disrespect paid to this decent rancher's daughter and opened his heart and mind to the artful and natural people skills Mabel had been blessed with, the farmer was determined to help in any way he could. After Frank and Billy had rested for a couple of hours they all stood around drinking coffee and enjoying Big Bud's corn meal fritters with syrup. The farmer spoke to Billy and Frank and presented the idea that he and Mabel had devised.

"I tell ya' mister, ya' did the right thing a' whippin' that rascalion fer insultin' this fine young lady. I'd a'done the same. I won't abide rude speech or ill-behavior in the presence of womenfolk, no time, no how, no way.

"But, concernin' yer present problem, ya'll got off the Sedalia Trail sometime in the night. The crossing of the Brazos that's been used fer twenty years or more is eight-ten miles downriver on the trail. I never expected a herd to end up here when I planted this crop. I planted it here 'tween the river an' this feeder stream so's I could irrigate from both ends.

"Now, ya' can't see it from here, but about a hunnerd yards that a'way there's a mounded up turn-row road about ten or twelve rows back. Ya see, these good sons o' mine started the plowin' last winter when I was down with the flumonia or some such plague and they plowed the first dozen rows from water to water, stream ta river, without giving thought to the distance they'd have ta tote them corn sacks come time ta pull the ears. When I see'd what they'd done, why, we built us up a sorta' turn-row dam in the middle there and jes planted these outside rows all the way a'crost so's it looks like there ain't no break in the corn stalks, but they is. Bout a hunnerd yards that 'away they's a thirty-forty foot wide turn-row. Step up on the wagon an' you kin see what I mean."

Frank, Billy and Pancake climbed up on the wagon and viewed the road in the midst of the corn.

Having been apprised of this information earlier along with Sid's report that the herd behind them was definitely following their herds tracks and not the old Sedalia Trail which lay several miles southeast, devised a way to defeat the depraved old dastard chasing them. Questioning the farmer regarding the surrounding geography and the way the river ran she suggested her subterfuge to the men. They laughed in delight at her deceitful design of action and hurriedly began setting men to work to accomplish her scheme.

The rider ran his horse up to the cook's wagon and let the lathered beast blow. Andrew Royal Junior was drunker than he had been in years, medicating his injuries and pain with whiskey.

"Well? Have ya'll caught that other herd yet?"

"No sir, we ain't. There's sign that they drove their herd all night an' the foreman says they've run up against a crop of corn that runs clear acros't the trail. The other herd turned northwest and forded a stream that runs into the Brazos. They'll have to cross the river where its deep the foreman says and go several miles out of the way. The other end of the corn crop is up agin' the Brazos. We could ford there, but it's deep and fast and we've run the cattle hard an' fast. Foreman's a'feared we'd lose lotsa cows by drownin' them. He sent me back t'ask whatchu want us t'do?"

"The trail leads right into that corn crop?"

"Yessir."

"Well then, the usual ford must be on the other side 'a that corn. By gawd, drive our herd straight through that damned corn an' get ahead a' that other herd. That stupid farm boy shoulda' known better'n ta plant a crop a'crost a cattle trail. Get goin'. An' tell that fool foreman he better catch that herd an' put my herd out front taday, not tamarra'. Now get!"

The farmer's eldest son had been dispatched to tell the county sheriff that two cattle herds had wandered miles northeast of the Sedalia Trail and the first herd had made arrangements with the farmer to take a path that would not destroy his large corn crop, but the second and much larger herd's drovers seemed to be less cooperative. To avoid trouble, he asked the sheriff to ride out and settle the dispute.

Mabel's scheme had been to drive a portion of the herd down to the stream northeast of the crop and push the cattle across and then turn them back upstream on the other side. After driving them a quarter mile or so back the way they had come, they drove the cattle back across the stream to join the herd. The first ten or twelve rows of corn would be pulled up by the roots, allowing access to the turn-row road that led through the corn. Their herd would be driven on the turn-row to the other side, then the corn stalks would be replaced and replanted in their original spots, disguising the route they had actually taken their herd.

Everyone believed the second herd would continue to follow their trail until they discovered it went in a circle over the stream and back. They would lose time and eventually would have to either drive their herd south and find the Sedalia Trail or go around the crop to the north and go quite a distance farther to find a ford. Just beyond the corn crop there was a shallow crossing, but it couldn't be reached beyond the stream to the north because of a rocky hill and neither could it be reached by going around the corn crop to the south because of a fifteen foot steep bank. Any way the big herd was driven would lose them more time to the joined three smaller herds. No one imagined the angry, foolish Mister Royal would take the route he took.

The county sheriff and his single deputy,(who happened to be the county judge's grandson), arrived in time to witness the stampeded herd gain speed and explode into and through the tall, budding corn stalks, totally destroying the half of the corn crop east of the turn-row. The sheriff's screams to stop were not understood by the wild-eyed, driven herd and he was pulled to safety out of the path of the five thousand longhorns by his deputy. Sheriff, deputy, farmer and sons then rode the short distance to town and raised a posse mostly comprised of other farmers and friends. They overtook the exhausted herd within six or seven miles from the scene of the wanton and willful destruction of private property and the attempted assault on a peace officer. The foreman was identified and handcuffed.

"You thank you kin jes' ride roughshod over people's prop'ty?"

"That corn was planted in the middle of the ol' Sedalia Trail sheriff, ain't there no law of right-a-way?"

"The Sedalia Cattletrail has run quite a'ways southeast ah here fer over twenty years boy. That dog won't hunt."

"Sheriff, we was follerin' another herd."

"That was yer first mistake. Where's yer boss, the owner of this herd?"

"He's comin' up this same trail in a wagon. Ya' see, he was beat up in a fight yestiddy an' can't ride yet, so he's comin' with the cook."

"Who's fool idea was it to trample this man's corn crop with this multitude of beefsteaks?"

"Well,...sheriff, I can't really say. I might lose my job."

"Son, you wanna' go to prison fer the next ten years? This farmer's good friend and neighbor is the county judge," the sheriff warned, indicting the victim.

"You put it like that, I guess I hafta tell the truth. My boss, Andrew Royal Junior, ordered me to drive that herd through that corn field."

The sheriff grunted and motioned for a big farmer to come up and take the foreman.

"Elton, take 'iss cowboy to the judge's house an' chain him to that big tree beside the porch. Make shore them coon hounds can't get to 'im. Tell the judge we're goin' after the owner of these cows and soon's we round 'im up we'll be there di-rectly with the witnesses to give their statements."

The sheriff hollered at the cowboys who had watched the arrest from a distance.

"You cowboys who work for Mister Royal, you drive these cows back just this side a'that corn field you destroyed an' you bed 'em down there. I'll do my best to see that none of ya'll are charged with any felony offense in 'iss mess, you have my word on that. You was jes' follerin' a fool boss's orders. Ya'll round 'em up an' head 'em back.

"Come on fellers, le's go arrest this fat-cat rancher who thinks he kin do what he pleases 'round here."

"Yea!"

"We'll l'arn 'im!"

"This ain't gonna' be no lynchin' now, neighbors. We jes' gonna arrest 'im an' tak 'im to the judge. He'll do what's legal an' proper to the dirty, sorry,… to the defendant."

Mid- afternoon the stone drunk rancher came in sight of the posse. Mister Royal sat on the wagon seat cussing the cook who was trying to keep his employer from falling off the wagon.

"You drove over ever' hole an' bump 'tween the Nueces and the Brazos, you stoopid escuse fer a goose. Heh-heh! Thas a good un. Was you hatched from a goose egg boy? Ha! What's 'at? What chu doin'? Who in hell er you?"

The sheriff had grabbed the lead horses and halted the team of mules.

"Are you Andrew Royal Junior?"

"Who's askin'?"

"The sheriff of this here county of the sovereign nation of Texas is askin', thas who's askin'. Now, are you Mister Royal?"

"Maybe I am, maybe I ain't."

The sheriff looked to the cook and asked, "This Andy Royal?"

The cook looked sidewise at his boss and cautiously nodded his head.

The sheriff walked back to the wagon seat, reached up and grabbed Andrew Royal Junior by his belt and pulled. Andy's breath was lost by the excruciating impact of the simultaneous shock of the pain from damaged nerve endings all over his head and trunk as he hit the ground.

"Thow 'im up 'air on 'at hoss," the sheriff indicated the horse tied to the tailgate of the wagon. He reached down and picked up the pistol that fell from Andrew's holster and stuck it in his belt.

"Le's go see the judge."

The county attorney, having been apprised of the events that had led to the arrests of Andrew Royal Junior and his foreman, had written an instrument called an information which was a detailed account of the incident in question. It would typically be taken before a grand jury chosen from the citizens of the county, but the judge, being a man who both liked to get things done expeditiously and liked to be a good neighbor, thought he should be able to accomplish his purposes in this circumstance by circumventing some court protocols. After reading the report of the offense, he peered over his spectacles at the defendant and his employee who had been chained to his porch. The foreman looked as he should under the circumstances, remorseful and afraid. Mister Royal however, besides appearing to have experienced a severe beating and still suffering from the injuries as well as from the effects of an over abundant consumption of alcohol, was exhibiting impatience, anger, frustration and insolence.

The particulars in the case all stood around the judge's wide porch which served as a courtroom until sufficient taxes could be collected to rebuild the old courthouse which had been burned down by parties unknown. Since the county had no jailhouse either, defendants were chained to a post or a pillar here and there throughout the settlement until the matter was resolved, usually by reparation or a fine but sometimes by a sentence to the prison in Huntsville.

"Mister.....Royal, is it? You have been charged with serious felonious offenses and a motion has been duly entered into the record that you be held without bail until a trial on these charges can be held. Have you anything to say to these charges?"

"This ain't no courtroom. An' you don't look like no judge I ever seen."

"Be that as it may, good sir, I am the duly elected official who has the power to grant you bail or refuse you liberty until trial can be had on these felony offenses. If you have nothing more to say, then..."

"Judge! Some ign'ant farmer done planted a corn crop slap-dab in the middle of the Sedalia Trail an' I's jes' tryin' ta get my beef to market. Far as bond's concerned, they shuden be no bond cuz they shuden be no charges. They's a right-a-way on these roads an' a farmer who blocks a road with a crop oughta be charged with..... with sumpen!"

"Mister Royal, your herd of cattle was and still is several miles north of the Sedalia Trail. Mister Trojcak is my close-by neighbor and your herd was intentionally and knowingly driven directly through his corn crop, destroying it," the judge looked down at the charging instrument again, "En toto'. And, you are charged with attempted assault on a peace officer with a deadly weapon, to wit: a herd of cattle," the judge read.

"Well judge, my men were follerin' another herd who musta' got off the trail in the night. I expect they went through the corn first."

The prosecutor interjected, "The sheriff reported that there was irrefutable evidence consisting of tracks of a large herd detouring 'around' the corn crop so as not to disturb it. Mister Trojcak also swore to his statement that he gave directions to the first herd that would not harm his corn."

"Well,...judge, I wuden even there when the herd was driven through that corn. My foreman did it."

The foreman, chained to another pillar on the porch squealed, "You gave me the order!"

"Hmmm," the judge sounded, "By their words'...seems you both are clearly, inexcusably guilty as charged. Mister Prosecutor, would you be adverse to settling this issue by Mister Royal paying for the damages?"

"No sir, as long as Mister Trojcak receives a full and fair reimbursement."

"Mister Trojcak, what is your estimate of the value of the destroyed corn crop?"

"Yer Honor, we figgered a edumacated guess at the number of bushels by the crops we grew in past years and my boy, he multimaplied the number of bushels by the expected market price of corn and we rounded off the grantota to be four hunnert dollars."

"Four hunnerd dollars! That whole farm ain't worf no four hunnerd dollars!" Royal squawled.

"Quiet Mister Royal or I will hold you in contempt of this court. Do you have four hundred dollars in gold or U.S. currency Mister Royal?"

"I don't carry that much money around. I guess I could give you a draft on my bank."

The prosecutor replied, "That would not be acceptable your Honor."

"Yes, I wouldn't trust it either. You have a large herd of cattle Mister Royal. Mister Trojcak would you accept cattle in lieu of cash reimbursement?"

"Yessir, yer Honor, if'n that's all I kin get."

"Alright. Mister Royal, if you want to settle this issue, dispense with those chains and take your beef to market, you will agree to give in restitution for the damage you have caused to good Mister Trojcaks corn crop, one hundred choice steers."

"A hundred steers?! Why them steers is worf forty dollars a head in Missoura."

"Likely true Mister Royal. But, sadly, the steers are in Texas and in Texas the value of a longhorn cow is four dollars. Sign and deliver Mister Royal, or be chained from pillar to post without bond until I can manage to schedule trial on our already crowded docket. I estimate six months in chains until a trial can be scheduled and you will almost certainly be found guilty and I promise my sentence will be most severe. And those thousands of head of cattle will not be grazing this county's grass for free. I suggest, strongly suggest that you settle today with Mister Trojcak and go on your way to Missouri."

"This is a damned Kangeroo court!"

"I hold you in contempt of court Mister Royal, and I sentence you to ten days in chains or a fine of,...ten steers."

"Why you..."

The judge waggled his finger at the prisoner and smiled.

"A'wite. Where do I sign?"

"Mister Royal, you are also fined ten steers for the offense of destruction of property, will pay a fee of five steers to reimburse the sheriff and his posse for their time and you will pay five steers in court costs. Court adjourned," the judge ordered.

"Grrrr..." Andrew Royal Junior growled.

CHAPTER SEVENTEEN

"Give strong drink unto him that is ready to perish,
and wine unto those that be of heavy hearts. Let him
drink,...and remember his misery no more."
---Proverbs 3:6,7 (KJV)

"Whose sheddeth man's blood, by man shall his blood be shed...."
---Genesis 9:6(KJV)

"Let the sighing of the prisoner come before thee..."
---Psalm 79:11 (KJV)

AFTER A QUIET and lengthy breakfast, spent not so much in eating food as in consuming the tender, final morsels of the love that would be taken from them once again, the two old lovers stood in one another's arms one more time. Ezekial stood on the ground holding his horses reins, Patricia stood on the porch which equaled-out their altitude. They kissed so softly and held one another gently and long in a screaming silence.

Parting unwillingly, Ezekial whispered, "Goodbye Patti. I've always loved you. Always will. I'll be waitin' on the other side. So long my sweetness."

He stepped and swung up into the ill-fitting saddle and his sad old eyes soaked in her tears, her courageous, beautiful effort at a smile and the radiance of her love. Her lips moved and formed the inaudible words, "I love you." Ezekial touched his chest over his heart with his big hand and his great emotion twisted his effort at a smile into more of a grimace. All the great strength in his arms was required to lift the leather reins, turn the big horse and ride away. His neck and back flexed rigid in his struggle to refrain from looking back. If he looked back at his lifetime love he would be turned from the path he knew was right.

Two of the six caballeros who would escort him spurred their mounts to lead the way, galloping north to the Rio Bravo. Two rode at his side and two rode behind, but Ezekial paid them no mind, his heart was broken and bleeding again. The caballeros had been instructed to take their task seriously. All were well armed with both carbines and handguns. Dark, grim faces beneath the sombreros were shaded from the searing sunlight and the dark eyes somberly searched their surroundings for any indication of trouble. These were men of the land in which they were born and bred to the lean life of the arid plains. They worked and played hard and in a fight they could be fearsome foes.

Each of these border men had various misconceptions as well as accurate insights into the old giant they escorted. They had witnessed him lift an invisible weight onto the saddle before him and some knew that the man's eyes and mind saw a dog where there was nothing. Some had seen him pet and stroke his imperceptible canine companion as he sat with the senora. Among themselves they had discussed the man and deemed him everything from loco to a bruja. Perhaps it was the Indian blood within them that caused these men to see something sacred in Ezekial's spirit, something strange, otherworldly, yet holy in its own peculiar manner, and respected.

Riding downriver at the border they arrived at the ford they had chosen that would allow them to avoid the various officials at the bridge from Villa Acuna, Mexico to Del Rio, Texas. It was the same crossing that Ezekial had used over forty years before when he had been first smitten by the young and radiant Mexican maiden. Once on the bank of the river in the state of Texas, the group rode to the outskirts of the small border town and halted beneath a small steep hill.

"Why're we stoppin?" Ezekial asked.

"The senora tol' me to ride alone to the town and give money and thess letter to a certain man, a man of the law. How do you say? Lawyer? He will go with us as we give you to the sheriff. The senora does not want anyone to say they captured you. She says the truth must be known, that you surrendered."

"Go ahead then. She's a wise lady."

Ezekial separated himself from the others, though their eyes followed him. He walked with Sam to a quiet place beneath a huge pecan tree on the riverbank. He stared at the jewels of light sparkling on the surface of the rippling river. Gazing at the lacy, lazy clouds in the brilliant blue sky, peering at the birds flitting over the reflecting river and listening to the lullaby of nature's song, he tried to absorb and memorize the wonder-filled simplicity of the earth. He petted Sam's shoulders as he breathed in the fragrance of freedom, realizing he would never again experience these pleasures in life that others take for granted. He knew only too well his future, gray stone walls and hard iron bars, the smell of unwashed, dying and defective men in airless confinement, the sound of slammed steel doors and teasing brass keys.

"Ol' friend, you know I'm going back to prison. It jes' ain't right fer you ta have to go back 'ere. I shore wish we could complete my number of days right out here under God's heaven together. But, if I tried ta stay out here at liberty, I'd only bring trouble to others. I don't want that. So, Sam, I have to go back to prison. 'Til I die. Jes' 'til I die. Then I won't have ta be in prison no more. I kin be with you then. An' with Gramps an' Momma an' Poppa an' ever'one else. Won't be long Sam. Lord willin', it won't be long. 'Cause I don' wanna live no more, hurts too much.

"An' so, I want you to leave me Sam. You go stay with Gramps. You know he wants to see ya. He loves you Sam. An' I love you too buddy. Yer the best friend I ever had. I'll be along directly. I jes' have ta go back ta prison 'til I die an' I'm awready diein'. I kin feel the diein' inside me a' growin'. The sad an' the lonely are killin' me, chokin' the life outa' me. So I won't be long. Then I expect we kin be together ferever."

Sam whined and pushed his head against Ezekial's old chest. It tore another piece of flesh from both their hearts.

"Yes, I know. It hurts. Bad. I know you love me Sam. It's been yer love that's held me up all these years in this sad ol' world. I love you too Sam, always will. But you have to leave me an' go to Gramps. If you stay with me, your love'll keep me strong an' I'll live a long time. I don't wanna' live no more Sam. It hurts, it jes hurts too much. So please, please Sam, go to Gramps. Go 'fore I can't bear ta see ya go."

Sam whined and barked and licked Ezekial's wrinkled face as he once did when they were young and he was fully in this world. Ezekial hugged him one last time then pushed him away.

"Go Sam. Go to Gramps."

Sam whined pitifully and ducked his head as he walked away. He turned back to Ezekial and cried in his distress and pain.

"I love you Sam. I'll be seein' ya. Real soon. Now go to Gramps boy."

Sam began to fade away, evaporate like a mist as he walked away and out of Ezekial's life, whining and crying. And then Sam was gone. Truly gone. And Ezekial felt the hollow loneliness. All alone in this world. Ezekial wept.

The lawyer from Del Rio had come out in his buggy and had tried to speak with Ezekial, but he was morose. The attorney had brought the editor and only reporter of the local weekly newspaper along and Ezekial's voluntary surrender would be documented. No one would receive a reward for the capture of Ezekial Robertson. On the third morning in the tiny jail the prison guards arrived to chain him back to the red brick prison where he was tried by an institutional court and sentenced to confinement in the 'hole' for an indeterminate period of time.

Ezekial began to wither and waste away in the hopeless gloom and darkness of the prison dungeon. He embraced the weakness that presaged his demise. His mind dwelt in a world apart, a place without light or hope and where sanity fled from a semi-conscious gray morass where death dwelt and beckoned. He was dying and he welcomed the process. His desire to attain death slowed his breath and weakened his pulse. Deep winter of life had come to him, the cold winds, the short days, the lengthening of shadow. His foggy, dying eyes saw the dark door of death and he yearned for it to swing open and welcome him. Home was just on the other side of that ancient dark door. Home sweet home.

Over the river, around the hills, through the long spring days, the men drove the herds and sometimes the herds seemed to drive them. The cattle acted' anxious to just get there and get it over with' as Wayne Robbins observed. Sid had ridden three horses alternately over three days to get back and forth and learn what the Royal herd was doing and when he made it in to camp the third evening, he had to tell the tale of Royal's woes in between bites of Bud's biscuits, bacon and beans. The boys were delighted at his mimicry of the judge and Mister Andrew Royal Junior's discomfiture.

Frank Callender was adamant about staying in front of Royal's herd but had no cause to worry. Royal's foreman had drawn what little wages he could wheedle from his stingy and betraying boss and then lit out for California. Several of the best hands joined him, without wages, wanting to avoid further verbal abuse and the slave-driving owner who was obsessed with overtaking the herd that he believed was the cause of all his troubles. Every day he lost hands, cattle and more time until finally he was forced to stop between the Red and the Canadian rivers in Indian Territory to lure reluctant Indian drovers with cheap whiskey to finish the drive.

Callender brought the three-herd partnership to the huge stockyards in Sedalia a week ahead of Royal's herd. Buyers were anxious to bid on this first big herd up from Texas and the second day after they arrived the herd was sold. One quarter of the purchase price was paid in United States greenbacks and gold, the rest with a draft drawn on a Chicago bank. The cowboys were called together and paid their wages and each was admonished and persuaded by Mabel to save money and not give it all to the girls and gamblers and on a regrettable drunk. Consequently, quite a few cowboys from each ranch came to her and asked her to hold a portion of their wages for them until they returned to Texas. She complimented each one for their prudence and gave each of them a signed receipt for their money. Luther put all the money in the iron box fashioned under the wagon's seat and put the big brass lock on the thick hasp. Mabel kept the key.

The Missouri-Kansas and Texas Railroad, the KATY, began grazing the herd in a large feedlot in preparation for their shipment to Illinois. The cattle bawled and seemed confused not to be traveling or driven and, seemingly, it took the herd a couple of days to get the idea that their walking days were finished.

The cowboys weren't confused at all. They knew the hard work was finished for awhile and the jingle in their pockets seemed to inspire a skipping stride that rang their spurs into the stores for tobacco and sundry 'pretties', as well as liquid celebration and, for some, female companionship. Old Tonk followed those of the most thirsty souls into a saloon from which a lively tune from a piano promised a good time. These eager and parched cowhands had done little to groom themselves for civilization other than beat some of the dust from their faded and patched clothes. These few had dreamed of cold, golden beer and hot, soothing whiskey through a thousand miles and more and now there was no reason to delay.

Their raggedy old high-heeled boots clumped over the thick plank floor to the polished oak bar and their happy voices echoed in the cavernous dark room. The mustached bartender sized them up and began filling their orders with a wide smile that bristled the stiff hair on his lip. When he got to Old Tonk he pulled the foamy mug back and pointed to a hand-lettered sign nailed behind the bar. Old Tonk's perfect illiteracy was easy to read on his face that formed a silent question.

"We don't serve Indians in here."

Old Tonk frowned, looked down the bar at his friends, then turned an abashed and offended visage to the bartender and spoke his indignation.

"Hmph! Me no Indian. Me Meskin!"

His friends and the bartender broke up in laughter. The cowboys then agreed, testifying as false witnesses that he was indeed Mexican.

"Say sumpin' in Meskin fer 'im Tonk," Wayne prompted.

Old Tonk's big head twisted, his eyes peered upward in thought then returned to gaze at the foaming, frosty mug of golden ambrosia and he promptly demonstrated his Spanish ancestry by uttering an array of words in his native tongue.

"Um. Enchelotties. Tortilos. Wayvos."

The bartender's stern visage broke and he laughed with the celebrating cowboys. He pushed the golden mug into Old Tonks welcoming hands. The toothless ex-Indian consumed half the mug and deemed it, "Mooey Booano!" to the laughter of the crowd.

Most of the cowboys celebrants, being unaccustomed and intolerant to alcohol, were drunk by the end of the day and a few were sick. But, they kept one another out of trouble and they all made it back to camp. Eventually.

Mabel had located a suitable boarding house on Smith Street and treated herself to a hot bath and a bed with crisp, clean sheets and a roof over it. It was so close to paradise that it made her wonder why she had ever even gave thought to the torturous trek of the drive. She knew that she would never voluntarily come along on a cattle drive again, she had experienced enough of it to know that it was not a woman's work. Women were much too smart generally, and it had taken only one trip for her to learn. It was enough to have done it and know she could. She intended to give each of the Angel's Camp cowboys a bonus when they came to collect their saved wages back at home. They deserved it.

Frank, Bud and a few others who had driven herds out of Texas before assured her that the drive they had just completed, though long in distance, was unusually uneventful and an easy journey. She had heard the stories of stampedes and swollen streams and terrible storms, bandits, rustlers, trail-blocking ranchers, Indians and wickedly hot and dry weather, when the cattle died like flies. She was happy to have no stories of major hardship to tell of the drive, she would never again voluntarily desert her bath and bed, civilized meals and creature comforts again. She had come to appreciate even simple things like chairs and outhouses. Ezekial could accompany the drive the next year.

The cowboys mostly recovered by sundown the next day from their inebriation and resultant maladies. They left camp in small groups of from two to five to seek cafe-cooked meals and see something besides dust and the ugly end of a bovine. Luther, Bud and Pancake stayed in camp with the wagons and the remuda and nursed a bottle together accented by fresher tobacco than they had enjoyed in quite awhile. The store at the rail head had much more merchandise, newer and greater selections than could be found south of the Nueces where the rails were years away. Each of the boys had found some item of interest and novelty they couldn't do without and the merchants did a brisk business for the first days after the herd's arrival.

Mabel and Billy spent their last day together shopping for gifts for those who had stayed at home. Mid-afternoon Billy rode out to camp to get Luther and the wagon which they almost filled with the things they had bought as gifts for everyone back home. Mabel had purchased all sorts of items for the ladies and the children and was surprised to see Billy Hell buying several items that she surmised were for Chas.

"I've bought some things for Chas, you're buying him more than the girls will get."

"Not for Chas. This stuff's fer Boy."

"Billy. He's not old enough or big enough for those things."

Billy smiled and said, "He will be. Soon enough."

They sent Luther and the wagon back to camp and the two of them went for a walk to see the train engine move the cattle cars into position to load the cattle at the chutes. Mabel was impressed by the smoothness of the operation and the number of loaded cars the engine could pull. They continued their walk, hand in hand, along a little stream that led lazily out of town beneath towering oaks. Billy felt like he was walking on a cloud.

"Miss Mabel, why don't we get married right here in Sedalia tomorrow? Then we could ride the train to the Mississippi and take a fancy steamboat to New Orleans and then on to Galveston or Corpus Christi. It would be easy on both of us. It could be our honeymoon."

"Mister Hill. I have never said I was going to marry you," Mabel smiled, "Now did I?"

"Well, I thought…"

"I'm the one doin' the thinkin' Mister Hill. 'Bout whether I'll be your wife or not. And I surely won't marry you here. I would want my friends around and have a preacher do the deed. I'd want a fancy dress and a suit for you. These things can't be rushed."

Billy grinned and lifted his eyebrows, encouraged by her words and demeanor.

"So, yer thinkin' an' plannin' the weddin' huh? Sounds like to ol' Billy Hell that you've decided to be my wife awready."

Mabel shook her red head and smiled as she looked up at him under her thick golden eyelashes.

"Billy, women begin plannin' their weddings when they're still girls. Yes, I'm plannin' my wedding, jes' ain't decided on a groom yet."

"That right?" Billy grinned.

She continued teasing him through what remained of the fine, new born summer afternoon and basked under the warmth of his adoration.

That evening they enjoyed a meal together at a tiny cafe, grateful for the opportunity to sit in a chair at a table, use normal dining utensils, and drink cool sweet tea while they ate something other than a trail meal. It was a long road home and neither looked forward to the journey though both relished the thought of arriving there and beginning a new life together.

Billy held her hand as he walked her back to the rooming house. An orange sun seemed to swell as it sunk below the western horizon. The light seemed to form an aura around their heads as they gently kissed and bid their adieus until the morrow. Life was sweet and promising. Their young hearts were filled with God's blessing of budding love.

As she put the key to the keyhole and opened the door of her rented room she was startled by the shocking sound of gunshots very close by. She ran to the upstairs window and looked down to the street to see Billy lying bloody on the ground. She screamed and the man standing over Billy's body looked up at the window, his face revealed under the brim of his hat. It was that man! Andrew Royal Junior! She ran and grabbed the pistol that hung on the bedpost and hurried back to the window. The coward was riding away into the gloaming and her shots went over his head as he spurred the black horse into the dusk.

She flew down the stairs and by the time she knelt beside poor dying Billy others were hurrying to the scene. As she held his head and his near closed eyelids lifted, his clear blue eyes focused on hers looked into her soul for a fleeting, eternal moment. His brown, leathery cheeks dimpled as he smiled, and he died. She cried and held his face to her heart, his warm, spilled blood soaking her new dress.

Eventually she was persuaded to lift her head and tell the gathered group, "It was Andrew Royal. Andrew Royal shot him. I saw from the window. He rode off that a way on a black horse."

The men quickly began to form a posse, but the sheriff arrived and vetoed that intention. He said there was little chance they could find tracks or catch up to the murderer in the dark and any posse of mounted men would destroy any tracks. He convinced them they should wait until first light and try to find the man then. Besides, he reasoned, the man has a valuable herd headed here which he would not abandon.

Mabel was separated from Billy's body long enough for the men to take it to the backroom of the tonsorial parlor where the barber utilized his undertaking skills. The landlady of the rooming house took Mabel in hand and took her inside to calm her. A young doctor came to the barber shop's back room to examine the body and pronounce it dead. As he removed the clothes from the corpse to examine the several gunshot wounds, he found a few items in the pockets which he placed in a small cloth sack. After completing his task, he left the body to the barber/undertaker/notary public to prepare it for burial and he walked down to Smith Street and the boarding house.

The old widow who owned the house had heated Mabel a bath and a two-jigger hot toddy to help her relax. The warm elixir had helped Mabel lose her misery in sleep.

The young doctor gave the landlady a powder to calm Mabel if she needed it upon awakening. He also entrusted the small bag containing Billy's possessions with the widow to give to Mabel at the proper time.

The hands who had been in town when the murder had occurred discussed the killing over another round, then headed back to camp to sleep so they would be fresh to join the posse at dawn. Billy Hell had been a friend to all these men, some were old and dear friends, friends he had rode the river with. It was unspoken knowledge among them that there would come retribution.

At the end of a long and thirsty day, the posse returned the next evening having lost the trail of the bushwhacking coward who shot Billy Hell Hill. Sid had been dispatched to locate the Royal herd and find out if he was there. He returned and met the boys from the posse at a saloon on Main Street and reported that Royal was there at the herd riding in a wagon, still bandaged, and the tall, black horse was tied to the wagon bed.

The following day, after being ordered by the county attorney, the Pettis County Sheriff rode out to the approaching herd and arrested Royal for the murder of Billy Hill on the testimony of an eyewitness who saw him standing over the body and who further witnessed him fleeing the scene of the murder, which flight was indicative of guilt. Royal protested that he had a dozen witnesses who would testify that he had been right here with the herd and had not left it. Unheeding, the Sheriff advised him to tell it to the judge and served the duly issued warrant by taking Royal to the small, newly constructed jail to await a hearing.

Upon arrival of the prisoner, buyers flocked to the jail trying to purchase the herd and the sheriff allowed them to speak with Royal one at a time. Royal had made up his mind to accept bids from the prospective buyers. The buyers went to the herd, made a count and appraised the value and came to the jail next day to make bids. Royal accepted the offer of the third buyer that he spoke with and asked the jailer to tell the others clambering to see him that he had made a deal and would not speak with other buyers.

The third bidder had considered the circumstances and advised Royal that he was not only a beef buyer but an accomplished defense lawyer from St. Louis and had investigated the evidence in the accusation of murder and was confident he could manage to have all charges dismissed forthwith at a hearing on an application for writ of habeas corpus. The lawyer offered a fair price for the cattle and Royal agreed to deduct a healthy sum for attorney fees. Royal didn't savvy the legalese, but he thought he was a good judge of character or, in this case, lack of character, and he hung his hat on the ability of this shyster to free him from this predicament.

The lawyer filed the paperwork with the court for a probable cause hearing and a time was set on the court docket for the following morning. All the cowboys from each herd as well as many concerned townsfolk tried to crowd into the courtroom and there just wasn't space for them all. The red-nosed judge asked the prosecutor if he intended to institute 'the rule' and he replied in the affirmative. 'The rule' was a legal device whereby any witness who might be called to testify in the proceeding before the court could not be in attendance to hear the testimony of any other witness in the matter. By this legality all the cowboys were cleared from the courtroom.

The hearing was being held to determine if there was sufficient evidence to charge Royal with an offense. The first witness called by the prosecutor was Frank Callender who laid the groundwork to establish the motive of Royal to murder Billy Hill. He testified as to Royal's visit to their camp, his threats, rude speech and resultant beating at the hands of the deceased. Big Bud Phillips and Wayne Robbins were also called to buttress the motive testimony. Finally, the prosecutor called Mabel who also gave her sworn testimony as to Royal's threats and ill-mannered labeling of her as a loose woman and his deserved beating.

The attorney for the state led her slowly and kindly through the details of the murder and her voice broke in sorrow, revealing the condition of her heart as she told of Billy's murder at the hands of a cowardly killer. She was definite in her identification of both Andrew Royal Junior as the man holding the smoking gun standing over Billy as well as positive in identifying his tall, dark horse.

On cross examination, the pettifogging St. Louis attorney immediately angered Mabel and the judge by his first question in which he queried whether Mister Royal had not correctly deemed her a soiled dove. Mabel came off the witness stand and the bailiff barely intercepted and restrained her before she reached the defense attorney. The judge first asked Mabel to answer the question yes or no and when she had emphatically answered in the negative, the judge directed a warning at the nattily dressed lawyer.

"Mister Malarkey, your questions has been asked and answered. You will ask no more inflammatory question nor pursue any further attack on Miss Curtsinger's character. I have never been hesitant to charge attorneys with contempt in my court and mete stiff punishment. Continue your examination of this witness carefully."

"Miss Curtsinger, at what time did you hear the shots and rush to the window as your sworn statement reads?"

"Mister Malarkey, I must first state that you are aptly named..."

"Misses Curtsinger," the judge leaned down from the bench and directed over the tittering courtroom, "just answer the question."

"Yes sir. I don't know what time it was. It was at sunset."

"Near dark then."

"Not dark yet. Enough light to see that murderer's face," she pointed at Royal.

"There were long shadows on the ground there at dusk, were there not?"

"I really didn't take note of the shadows Malarkey, but I expect there were long shadows at sundown. There usually are."

"It's 'Mister' Malarkey, Miss Curtsinger."

"I'm skeptical about the Mister part, but I'm sure about the Malarkey."

The judge banged his wooden mallet and again told Mabel to answer the questions without comment.

"And, 'Miss' Curtsinger, you have sworn that from a second story window, a good distance from the house at the edge of the street where Mister Hill laid, you could distinctly see Mister Royal's face despite the distance, the shadows and the failing light?"

"Yes, I certainly could."

"Mister Royal had nothing covering his face?"

"Why, no."

"Wouldn't you think that a man who planned to kill someone in the middle of town might consider covering his face so as not to be identified?"

"I have no idea how such a man thinks."

"Well, Miss Curtsinger, if you were planning to kill someone in the middle of town wouldn't you cover your face?"

"I would never plan to kill anyone."

"Yet you had to be physically restrained from attacking me just minutes ago."

"I didn't plan that confrontation Malarkey, you did. And I didn't plan on killing you. I intended to slap your rude and vulgar mouth shut."

The judge quieted the snickering of the townsfolk behind the balustrade.

"Is that a threat Miss Curtsinger? I should advise you that you can be prosecuted for threatening a person in this state."

"Sir, outside this courtroom it would not be a threat, but a result. And then I might be charged with justifiable pesticide."

The red-nosed judge joined in the general laughter, then managed to straighten his face, bang his gavel and again warn the gallery and Mabel.

"Let's move on from this provocative line of questioning," the judge added.

"Alright. Miss Curtsinger, you have given testimony that there was no covering on the face of the man who was standing over the body of Billy Hill. Isn't that so?"

"Yes."

"So you could clearly see his face?"

"I sure could."

"Could you describe the injuries to that naked face as you saw them that night?"

"Why, I suppose there were minor cuts and bruises, but I wasn't trying to diagnose his injuries. It was him, that man," she pointed, "Andrew Royal."

"Mister Royal," Mister Malarkey asked, "Would you please remove the bandage on your face?"

Royal gingerly removed the winding cloth covering his cheek and mouth, revealing a ripped rending which had been stitched together on his newly shaven face from the side of his mouth almost to his ear. His rictus revealed the broken and missing teeth and Mabel hoped he was in pain.

"Would the court please take notice of the very severe slash on Mister Royal's cheek which would certainly not go unnoticed as clearly as Misses Curtsinger said she saw the man standing over the victim's body, especially in light of the fact that this vicious tearing of the flesh was untreated, unstitched and gaping wide and bloody until the local doctor, who will directly so swear, stitched it and closed the horrendous wound."

"So noted," spoke the judge as he looked askance at Mabel.

"That wasn't there before," Mabel told the judge.

"There will be several witnesses to swear the wound was suffered in the attack of Mister Royal by the deceased, Billy Hill. And, if it wasn't there on the face of the man you saw so clearly with smoking gun in hand standing over the body of the victim, then it couldn't have been Mister Royal, could it?"

"I,...," Mabel stammered.

"You did not see the clearly visible and undeniably severe wound on the face of the man standing over the body of the victim, did you Misses Curtsinger?"

"No. But it was him. He had a beard then!"

"A beard would not hold such a wound together nor would it hide it. His face was uncovered without any bandages is that right?"

"...Yes."

"I have no further questions of this,...'only' witness your Honor."

"Wait just a minute...," Mabel began only to be interrupted by the judge.

"You may step down Miss Curtsinger. Bailiff, please escort this witness from the courtroom."

The prosecutor informed the judge he had no more witnesses nor evidence and the St. Louis lawyer and cattle buyer made a motion to dismiss all charges against the accused for lack of evidence. The defense attorney offered to call a dozen alibi witnesses who waited just outside the courtroom to testify that Mister Royal never left his herd until the sheriff came to arrest him. Testimony could also be presented that the accused had suffered the severe facial wound during the beating he took from the deceased and the doctor here in Sedalia could be called to testify of his treatment of the severe facial wound. The prosecutor conceded to those facts and stipulated that such testimony could be presented.

The judge spoke his ruling.

"There has been no physical evidence presented by the prosecution that in any manner implicates the defendant. The testimony of these several witnesses has clearly shown only that Mister Royal suffered a malicious, though likely judicious beating at the hands of Mister Billy Hell Hill for his despicable language and vulgar accusations against a fine young lady.

"The only evidence that purports to show that Mister Royal was even present at the scene of Mister Hill's demise is the testimony of Miss Curtsinger, which does claims that she saw a man which she believed to be Mister Royal standing by the body after she heard gunshots.

"She gave further testimony that she ran to get her pistol, returned to the upstairs window and began shooting at the person she saw standing over Mister Hill's body. Any sensible person would flee when being shot at, so I do not agree that flight from the scene indicates any guilt whatsoever, indeed, such flight is a reasonable response when under attack.

"There are other possibilities as to why a person could have been standing over Mister Hill's body with a smoking gun which was Miss Curtsinger's only relevant testimony. This person could have defended Mister Hill from whomever shot and killed him for all we know. Miss Curtsinger, asking no questions, began shooting at a person whose only transgression was in standing over a man who had been shot. Just moments later another person could have seen Miss Curtsinger also standing over the body with a smoking gun.

Should they have also mistakenly presumed that she had murdered Mister Hill?

"Miss Curtsinger vehemently testified that she saw the face of Mister Royal clearly, yet she failed to see the horrific wound to his face which at that time was untreated and gaping, a wound which is even now, after medical attention, the outstanding feature of the defendant's face. Does this not suggest to a person of reason that Miss Curtsinger is mistaken in her identification of Mister Royal as the person at the scene of the murder? I have serious doubt about Miss Curtsinger's vision.

"No one saw Mister Royal shoot the deceased, or at least no one can so testify. There has been absolutely no physical evidence linking Mister Royal to the murder scene or to the murder. Therefore, I believe the proper course is to dismiss all charges against Mister Royal. Bailiff, please release the prisoner. This court stands adjourned. Mister Malarkey, I will see you in my chambers."

Mabel was standing outside the courthouse with Frank and Luther and all the hands when she heard a whoop from the Royal cowboys who had gathered in the halls of the courthouse. They were shaking Royal's hand, pounding him on the back in congratulations as they exited the courthouse. The cowboys weren't happy because Royal was their friend, but because they stood a better chance of getting paid if he were out of jail.

Royal saw Mabel standing with her mouth agape, surprise and mounting anger evident in her face. He stopped, pulled the bandage down off his face and smiled, exhibiting his missing and broken teeth. He spoke audaciously.

"My sympathies to you madam on the death of yer boyfriend," and broke out laughing as he was almost carried away by his thirsty cowhands to a nearby saloon.

The prosecuting attorney stepped before her and said simply, "The judge dismissed the charges. He ruled there was no evidence that Royal shot Mister Hill."

"But,...I saw him."

"No, Miss Curtsinger, you said you saw Royal standing over the body of Mister Hill with a gun, just as you were standing over him a few minutes later. And the judge was not convinced you saw Mister Royal's face clearly as you did not notice the prominent wound on his cheek."

"The beard must have hidden it. Who else would have had any call to shoot him?"

"I'm sorry Miss Curtsinger, I did my best."

The St. Louis lawyer turned at the door of the judge's chamber as he replaced his wallet in his coat. He smiled, slightly bowed and said, "It was a pleasure doing business with you Judge. I've found that there often are additional costs in the business of purchasing beef. Perhaps another occasion will arise in the future when we can help one another."

The judge smiled as he counted the greenbacks.

"I'm sure another circumstance will eventually arise in which we can serve one another and expedite our purposes. Have a good day sir."

"And you," replied Mister Malarkey as he lit a crooked cigar and stepped out of the room.

Andrew Royal Junior went directly to the jail after his release to retrieve his money and pistol from the safe there. His hearty crew followed him like the hounds they were, hoping he would pay them and further hoping he might pay them a bonus for their readiness to falsely testify regarding his constant attendance at the herd. The raggedy bunch followed Royal to the largest saloon in Sedalia and he ordered drinks for all his hands. After the fourth or fifth round of whiskey one of the recently hired herders from Indian Territory asked for his wages so he could head home. This angered the belligerent fool.

"You want yer money? Awright. I got 'cher money," he growled, pulling out a thick money bag from his coat. "All you saddle bums line up an' I'll pay ya yer nickels and dimes. Thas' all yer worth."

He took a small notebook from an inner pocket of his coat and matched names, dates hired and sums, doling out each man's due. His cursing and belittling them as was his habit should have been restrained, he could have used the protection that they may have offered. As each of them received their begrudged wage, they exited the saloon, happy to separate themselves from his disparagement.

Luther, Chuy, Squirrel Boy, Chinati, Cabio, Wayne, Sid and Beau, all the Angel Camp hands made their way into the saloon singly and in pairs, Chuy coming in alone last of all. His shirt was tucked into his trousers, sans a coat, it was obvious he was unarmed.

"Barteender, you are making the mistake of serving a zorillo,…a skunk, who pretends he is a man.

Thes trash drinking at chor bar es a back-chooting coward. He choulden be 'llowed to drink with decent men. Chu wan' me to put hem out?" Chuy asked, pointing and indicating Royal.

"Who you talkin to bean-eater?"

"I'm talking to the barteender, skunk, an' the peece of trash I'm talking about pooting out of here es you."

"An' how you plan on doin' that meskin? You ain't even got a gun."

"I done need a gun for dirt like you, I only need a broom," and Chuy began walking down the bar toward Royal.

"You better watcher mouth taco-bender…" Royal began as he pulled the long barreled revolver out of his holster.

As Royal's gun cleared leather Sid's double-barreled shotgun spoke deafeningly and splattered portions of Andrew Royal Junior all over the bar, the mirror and the floor. The rest of the crew had leveled their pistols at Royal, but their bullets were unneeded. The power of the shotgun loads cause Royal's entire body to lift and jerk his thumb releasing the hammer of the single-action Colt he had cocked and putting a bullet into the planks at his feet. He was dead before he began to fall.

Chuy looked at the other patrons as he spoke to Sid.

"I chore tank you Meester Patton. I do believe thees man, he was going to keel me."

SEPARATE REALITIES

"Shore was about to shoot ya," spoke Wayne, "Don't you think so?" he asked the bartender.

"Why....yes sir, shore looked tha-a-way ta me."

"He even fired a shot diden he?" Beau asked another customer sitting at a table.

"Yes. Yes he did."

About five minutes elapsed before the sheriff and a deputy made their appearance. The sheriff wanted to let things settle some and be sure all the shooting was over before he poked his nose in.

"What happened here?"

The sheriff was acquainted with the facts by a dozen eyewitnesses and determined there was no crime committed by any of the survivors of Mister Royal's attempted deadly assault. He sent for the barber/undertaker/notary, etc to bring his wagon and remove the carcass while he took charge of the deceased's personal belongings including the fat moneybag. He advised the saloon's clientele that inquiries would be made by Pettis County officials via telegraph to authorities in Texas regarding the disposal of Mister Royal's possessions.

The saloon's clientele, to a man, doubted that.

The way homeward was somber and tedious. Mabel's days were joyless, her only respite from sorrow were her thoughts of the child, their child, now her child alone. No longer was his name only Boy, she had altered the name on the adoption papers to Boy Lister Hill. He would grow up proud of his two brave, heroic fathers. And he would be surrounded by those who loved him and had loved and respected his fathers.

She was already thinking of herself as a widow, as she had long accepted Billy as her husband in all the important ways. At times she imagined Billy with her, inside her spirit, in her mind and heart. She heard his encouraging words as she walked apart from the camp in the evenings, and she began to believe he was still somehow, somewhere, still loving her. It was a comfort to her to visualize his laughing eyes and let his love envelop and warm her, cheer and assure her of another place when time was over and done and life was lived forever.

She knew her dreams of a life as Billy's wife must be put aside, that path had ended and she must find another path for Lister Hill and herself. She had many years still appointed to live and Billy would not want her to pine and make others miserable along the way. He wanted her to find wonder and laughter along her way and build a full life for herself, for her son and her friends. It was likely that she would meet another man she would love. She would marry and have other children and a life she could not now even dimly envision. But, she would carry Billy and their love all her days.

They buried Billy's body in Sedalia. She had paid to have a tombstone fashioned marking the spot. She'd had the words carved on the stone that she felt appropriate. The stone could not contain what she held in her heart.

> Here Lies
> Billy 'Hell' Hill
> 1836-1867
> Ranger, Soldier,
> Dear Husband,
> Father, Friend.

Mabel had been unaware of the violent execution of Andrew Royal Junior until her gentle land lady relayed the news to her over her coffee, eggs and biscuits the morning after. The fact of his death brought neither happiness nor sorrow, she felt empty inside. Later that day she took Chuy aside at the camp and asked him if he felt any better that Royal was dead. She told him it was the same as murder.

"Yes ma'am. We keel him. He keel our freen. We keel him. As it should be."

She wondered about that.

Mabel altered their course from the Sedalia Trail on their return and went again to the Trojcak farm. She was welcomed effusively and the family made it an occasion of celebration for the whole crew, grilling thick steaks out in the farmyard and drinking gallons of sweet tea. Mister Trojcak refused her offer to repay the financial loss and make amends for the trouble they had caused. The good and honest farmer did ask that if they brought another herd for market in Missouri the next year or two, she would send a telegraph and make arrangement to include his few cows with her herd. His guileless trust delighted her and she felt honor-bound to do the favor he asked. She was gratified that this was one calamity that had turned out well for the well-deserving, except for dear Billy.

At every river, every campsite, every landmark she recalled from those few days ago where Billy had been beside her on the trail northward, with every sight a memory came. She only allowed herself to smile at treasured moments she held in the vault of her heart. She smiled and often a chuckle escaped her, but she withheld the tears with a clenched jaw as she knew Billy wanted her to be happy when she thought of him. She smiled at the thought of how Billy must have been before she met him, wild and free, when his companions dubbed him Billy 'Hell'. The thought came that she'd like to raise Billy Hell and she smiled, then blinked back the hot tears that blinded her.

And when she finally made it home to Angel's Camp and told the tale of the loss of her husband, she cried in the arms of those who loved her for the last time for Billy. As she cried, her self-appointed brother Ezekial held her in his huge, gentle arms and cried with her, and for her. And now, after the near half-century had passed, she fondly recalled that moment and his tender affections. She determined as only the fiery and stubborn Mabel of all those many years ago could determine, to get her friend, her brother, freed.

Callie, Sallie, Nellie, Mabel, Ruby and Patti Chavez ran up large telephone bills in the first weeks after Ezekial's arrest. Of the group of Ezekial's surviving friends, only Patti and Mabel really believed that Ezekial's freedom could be purchased. The others thought that Patti's beliefs were tainted by her experiences of the corruption of Mexican officials, and believed government bureaucrats and political figures of the state of Texas were almost totally beyond reproach. Conversely, Mabel knew better. She lived in the capitol and was aware of the major larceny in the souls of the power brokers, having socialized with them in Austin for most of her adult life. She had made a telephone call to the governor's mansion and eventually spoke with her new friend Ma Ferguson. An appointment was made to meet and discuss a family matter she needed advice with.

Since his release from the hole, Ezekial had lost weight. His eyes were ringed with dark blue tones and sunken into his great skull. He never spoke to anyone, just sat in his cell staring at the wall two feet away, waiting for the freedom that he knew death would bring. It was an effort for him to sit up now. His strength had left him. Food did not interest him at all and he rarely trudged to the chow hall, and only nibbling in his infrequent visits. His lips were dry, cracked and bloody because he forgot to drink. There was running water, a sink and toilet which had been installed in the cell in his absence, but he rarely used them. Through the gray days and long nights he sat and stared at the stone wall and the peeling paint until, in exhaustion, he fell over onto the bunk, passed out into sleep filled with dreams of long ago and with strange, distorted visions and beckoning from loved ones who dwelt in everlasting ether.

The assistant supervisor, Mister Peterson, stood before his cell on the catwalk looking in on the man who had spent nearly half a century in such confinement. He watched the man's trunk and head weave weakly, as if he were about to fall. The eyelids were mostly closed and fluttered. He wondered where such a prisoner's thoughts took him.

"Zeke! Ezekial Robertson! Look at me."

The wizened old head slowly turned toward the incongruous suit with a head atop that floated before his cell.

"Ezekial, I have sent to the kitchen for some soup and milk. I'm going to stand here and watch you eat and drink. You must begin to eat or you are going to die. Do you understand me? Answer me Ezekial."

Ezekial stared at the floating suit which talked but he could make no sense of the words. He knew that the sounds were auditory symbols for the transmission of ideas, he knew he once spoke and understood such words, but no more. He had forgotten so much, dispensed with the baggage and utensils of life on earth, that even the English language was only confusing noise. Shadows of white appeared and the steel bars parted and metal rang in his ears.

"Feed him the soup. Ezekial, open your mouth."

The prisoner in dirty coveralls put a spoon of a warm broth to Ezekial's bloody lips and he jerked away from the pain.

"Gently. Ezekial, open your mouth. Open up,...there."

The spoon slid over his swollen tongue and the soup ran out of his mouth and dripped off his chin. Ezekial smacked his lips and he opened his eyes wider and stared at the bowl.

"Ezekial, you must eat. Keep trying to feed him. Give him a drink of milk."

The struggle to feed the dying man continued for half an hour and a few spoonfuls of soup and milk were swallowed and caused a gurgling in Ezekial's empty esophagus before he began to refuse any more by turning his head away, lying down with his face to the wall.

"We'll try again later," said Mister Peterson and continued standing and staring at Ezekial as the guard and the kitchen inmate walked away down the narrow, plank catwalk.

A miasma of impending death surrounded the long and skeletal old man who lay in the dark, airless and tiny man-cage. His breathing was shallow and sporadic, a pulse in his temple barely discernible in a thin blue vein under pale, papery flesh. Ezekial dwelt in a purgatory, not truly alive in any dimension, nor quite dead as some understand the term. His mind rarely realized a conscious thought, there was no self-conception. When consciousness fought to the surface and for a fleeting moment he remembered who, what and where he was he was confused, then depression engulfed him and sucked him back down under the dark, liquid embryonic creation of his approaching corpse. Soon, very soon, his great wounded heart would pump a final time, then come to rest, forever. He then would be free. Free to go. No longer in danger of the dungeon, unchained forevermore.

Assistant Superintendent Peterson stood just inside the door of the doctor's office in the Walls infirmary. Doctor Lewis spoke.

"Yes Mister Peterson, I have completed my examination of Ezekial Robertson. I ran laboratory tests, took X-rays and did a blood test as well. I discovered no physical disease, injury or malfunction which could be causative of his worsening and critical condition. I have seen this malady before however in prisoners who had made the choice to die, simply giving up on life, wanting to die in order to escape the endless misery and suffering in their lives and mind."

"So your diagnosis is that Ezekial has given up?"

"In a sense, it seems so Mister Peterson. But, the phrase 'given-up' suggests simply going with the flow of life, accepting whatever comes, no longer fighting, surrendering to life. Robertson is actively seeking death, struggling to escape life itself."

"Is there any treatment you might recommend?"

"Love. Hope. Freedom. An infusion of faith. If there were some way to surgically eliminate loneliness, despair, sorrow, guilt, regret. Can you provide any of these medicaments?"

"It has always seemed to me that these are gifts of Providence. Do you believe in prayer Doctor?"

"Yes. Without doubt. I have witnessed many benefits from prayer when all else failed. One must secure some small seed of hope however, before his knee can bend or his head bow. Probably faith isn't required initially, it may develop later, but hope must be born to open the doors of heaven."

"Well," said Doctor Lewis, "And where can hope be found for Ezekial Robertson?"

"Does he have relatives?"

"None listed in the records."

"Friends?"

"If there are friends, they have never wrote or visited him in all the years he's been in prison. He made a friend in his old cell partner, Jack Williams, who escaped with him, but it seems he had the good sense to separate from all the others who escaped to keep from returning to prison. Maybe if he returned..."

"No Mister Peterson, I recall Jack Williams. I don't believe he'll be returning. He's a smarter man than most prisoners."

"You know Doctor, Ezekial had an imaginary friend, an invisible dog he used to talk to and pet, remember? And I've not heard of him interacting with his ghostly pet since his return."

"I do remember Ezekial's dog, or at least the dog he conjured. Perhaps something that happened during his escape has, in his mind, separated him from his dog. Rumor has it that Robertson turned himself in at a border town. Why would a prisoner go to all the trouble and risk to escape and then give himself up? I'm sure something happened out there that devastated him."

"I'm certain you're aware Doctor that often, all too often, we keep men locked up so long that they lose their ability or desire to be successful or even to survive in a free society. Freedom frightens them, it's new and unknown. They have learned to be comfortable, even successful within a prison. Here they have friends, out there people mistrust them, look askance at them, distance themselves from them, fear them, belittle them, hate them. Here they are not so lonely nor despised. Here they are trusted, respected, accepted, even held in esteem as 'stand-up' men. Prison is preferable to the alien, excommunicated, exiled existence a 'free' society subjects them to. Once free, after far too long separated from the real world, citizens and criminal justice officials expect them to return to crime and these attitudes are absorbed and accepted by ex-convicts when they are hedged-in by corrals, barricades and endless obstacles and restrictions created by legislatures board members, unions and associations which dishearten, discourage and depress the released prisoner into the funnel which drops them back into their prison home."

"Yes, it is a revolving door Mister Peterson. I've seen it time and time again. I've seen the smiles and happy greetings of those who have been released from prison and return. They seem happy to be here, even proud to have lived up to everyone's expectations. Everyone is rewarded by their return. Everyone benefits. The law enforcement community from the policeman to the lawyer, the judge and the jailer all justify their wages, expand their ranks, move up the ladder and increase their influence by this continual re-creation of the criminal class. Politicians employ this socially-created phenomena to secure perennial re-election on a law and order platform. No mercy wins by a land-side over understanding, treatment, forgiveness and support. Mistrust, hate, disdain and disrespect await every man who has supposedly paid for his crime, who has completed his suffering and punishment, served his sentence, when truly the sentence and the punishment never end in this life."

"That's true Doctor. And the fact is that the average citizen, be they prospective employer, landlord, government or law enforcement official have a state of mind that is very resistant to change because they regard ex-prisoners as things less than human, their own self-worth is falsely exaggerated and makes them feel good about themselves when actually they should be ashamed. Christianity, indeed all religion teaches us to forgive, not to condemn, not to exclude, but to include, to trust, to share, to love, to help.

"There is approaching a time when there will no longer be institutions for the insane, nor treatment for alcoholics or drug addicts, all these illnesses will be punishable by sentence to prison.

"The penitentiary becomes part of a prisoner's personality when they are too severely punished by too many years apart from freedom. Free society needs to admit that their own negative attitudes, prejudices, and self-righteousness, their own created bureaucracies and legal systems and their own churches are major contributors in the equation of habitual criminality."

"Yes Doctor, we are able to see it because of our perspective, because our station in life gives us a clear view. We see the hate, the retribution, the fear, the cruelty, the ignorance, the careless and self-sustaining failing attitudes of the majority. But, they are an uncaring majority. They will continue to reap what they sow, endlessly, just as the Good Book promises. They plant hate, disrespect, violence, suffering and sorrow and seemed surprised and disgusted when that which they have sown and nourished comes to fruition."

"And, Mister Peterson, this 'system' as we often deem it, sometimes overcomes men like Ezekial Robertson. There is no escape from the revolving system except through the door of death. Only then will he be discharged from his life sentence, nothing he can do, except to die, will rectify his dilemma, fully restore his liberty and relieve his suffering."

"I wish it were not so. Is there any hope to be found Doctor?"

"There is always hope in prayer Mister Peterson. We must believe that, and pray."

Mabel had made arrangements to house her friends at the Driskill Hotel on Brazos Street. The group included Abraham and Sallie, Callie and Nellie. Also Beau and Ruby came, leaving Little Beau and the rest of the family to handle the ranch. Patricia came alone, struggling with the weight of Ezekial's gift of gold in a valise, not trusting the hotel porter.

The evening of their arrival Mabel told them of her meeting with Ma Ferguson. The governor's wife had told her that her husband was angered by conditions at the prisons and was amenable to consider clemency for those prisoners who he believed were no longer a serious threat to society. Pa Ferguson had weighed Ezekial's prison record, which wasn't bad for the last twenty years, excluding the escape, and he deemed that the great number of years he had already served and his age should merit his release. But, there were costs that could not be paid by the state and if an adequate 'campaign contribution' could be given by Ezekial's patrons, then the required bureaucratic red tape could be expedited and Ezekial's release would not be further delayed. Pa Ferguson was particular however, as to how the 'campaign funds' were donated.

A man must meet him at their farm and discuss the purchase of an old prized bull. Ma intimated that Pa found it difficult to discuss business matters with ladies, as his conversation often became quite colorful, for lack of a better adjective, when he bargained. Ma further explained that the discussion regarding the sale of the bull would actually concern the price of the release of her friend. Pa also required that the man who came to deal for the bull not be an attorney or work for the government in any capacity. And it just happened that Ma and Pa would be journeying from Austin to their farm for the coming weekend.

After further discussion among the committee of friends, Mabel made a telephone call and, after a half-hour delay, a call was returned from the governor's wife. Mabel advised the others after the conversation that the governor preferred to speak with Beau regarding the purchase of the breeder bull rather than Abraham as he was very interested in securing support from the negro electorate. The group all held the unspoken surmisal that Pa Ferguson believed he could milk more from a black country boy than from citified car dealer. They all smiled at the thought that the calculated choice of the governor was about the horse tradingest bargainer in Texas.

The group met with a buyer at a downtown bank who weighed and purchased their collective gifts of gold for cash. The money barely fit in Patricia's chunky valise which accompanied Beau in his rusty old ranch truck down the dusty road to the Ferguson farm. The governor sat on his wide porch at the appointed time, welcomed Beau and invited him to sit with him.

"So, you are Mister Beau Johnson? A pleasure to meet you sir."

"Thank you suh. It's an honor ta make yo acquaintance."

A matronly black servant in a starched white apron brought an iced pitcher of lemonade and tall monogrammed glasses on a tray and set them down on a small table between them. The servant smiled at Beau with a curious glint in her auburn eye. She poured each glass full with a strong and practiced hand, setting them within reach of each man on the small table between them.

"Thank you Matilda."

"Yo welcome Govna'. Jes' holla' if'n yo need anythin' else suh."

"Mister Johnson, have you examined the bull? I assure you he is a fine specimen."

"I saw the bull in the pasture as I drove in suh. I'm sho' that bull is all you say he is. Jes' wanna get 'im on back home."

"Umhuh. You realize of course that pa'ticuler bull is expensive, it'll take quite a bit to get him to your pasture."

"Yessuh. How much a bull like 'at sell fo' Govna'?"

"Well," the governor chuckled, "I'm not sure you have enough money to buy that ol' breeder bull. But, I'm feeling generous today. I b'lieve I could see my way to give you ol' Ezekial,...that's what I call that ornery ol' bull,... I'd sell 'im for, oh, say ten thousand."

"Dolla's?"

"Yes. Ten thousand dollars. Worth every penny."

"Yessuh, I b'lieve it's woof whatevah you say it is. Yessuh. Woof evah penny. But, all us frien's, we put in all we's could affode togetha an' we's only got us fo' thousan' fer that bull."

"You are talkin' 'bout that 'white' bull out yonder aren't you Mister Johnson?"

"Uh, yessuh, he's white."

"Why you want a 'white' bull Mister Johnson?"

Beau leaned close over the table and whispered into Governor Ferguson's ear, "Used ta be my boss suh. He a good man. Owe that man a lot."

"I see. You sure you can't pay five thousand?"

"Wellsuh, I b'lieve I could meybe round-up and borry 'nother five hunnerd taday."

"Mister Johnson, suppose you could talk me up with your black friends, get 'em to vote for me on the strength of my giving you a deal on that ol' bull? If you could, why then, I suppose I'd take four thousand now and another five hunnerd 'fore sundown."

"Yessuh! I sho' could get you all the votes 'round home. Yessuh!"

"And you have four thousand now?"

"Yessuh. Right out dare in tha truck. Cash money."

"Well, you give me the four thousand now and get me five hundred more out here, let's say by tomorrow, and we got ourselves a deal."

The governor held his hand out and Beau shook his hand to seal the deal.

"Done," Beau said, "Lemme go get yo money."

At the truck Beau opened the valise packed with bundles of hundred dollar bills in stacks of fifty and removed five bills from one of the bundled stacks and pitched the loose bills back in the suitcase and secured it. He carried the money back to the porch and bowed as he handed Pa Ferguson the stack of bills.

"They's forty-five hunnerd dolla' bills tha' Govna' as we agreed."

"Why,... I thought you said you'd have to borrow the five hundred."

"Yessuh. I jes' bawed it 'head a time," Beau answered with a grin.

The governor's scowl slowly turned into a smile. He said, "You rascal. You skinned me you crafty ol' coon. But, a deal's a deal. I do admire a good bargaining man. I'll be letting ya'll know when you can pick up that ol' bull."

"Yessuh. Thank ya' suh. Sho' will be a pleasure to see that ol' Bull ta home."

"See that you keep him outa' trouble."

"Yessuh, won't be no trouble. Good evenin' suh," Beau said over his shoulder. He waved and smiled as he pulled the door shut on his old truck.

"And get me some votes Mister Johnson. Don't forget."

"No suh, I won't forget. I won't never forget. Thank ya suh."

Chapter Eighteen

"Was my arm too short to ransom you?
Do I lack the strength to rescue you?
---Isaiah 50:2 (KJV)

He was standing in the water and pointed at the flow. He said, "Once this water hits the ocean, the sun lifts it up and collects it in the clouds until they get full enough, the wind blows, nudges them back over the land, where they empty themselves across the continent."
"Meaning?"
"The river never ends."
---Charles Martin
Where the River Ends

"But about the resurrection of the dead-have you not read what God said to you, 'I am the God of Abraham, the God of Isaac, and the God of Jacob'? He is not the God of the dead, but of the living." ---Jesus
Matthew 22:32 (KJV)

MABEL RECEIVED A telephone call the following week from Ma Ferguson advising her that she should let her friend know that the bull he had purchased could be picked up on the next Monday morning at around nine in the morning. Mabel thanked her effusively and sent her gratitude to the governor along with a promise of political support.

After hurriedly dressing, she drove her Hupmobile to the Driskill and broke the news to her old dear friends who were loitering in the Romanesque Revival lobby reading newspapers. They broke out in cheers, hugging and talking, all except Patricia. She sat in silence paralyzed by the instant, staring at the future, and the past.

Assistant Superintendent Peterson received the telegraph and later a telephone call from the governor's office informing prison officials that the governor had issued a declaration of clemency and had commuted Ezekial Robertson's sentence of life to time-served. Mister Peterson's first thought upon learning of the governor's action was that Ezekial must have a wealthy friend out there somewhere, or a politically well-connected friend at least, because he had previously witnessed the type of prisoners that were granted clemency and he had seen the men in new suits and fur-adorned women bedecked in fine jewelry arriving in shiny new automobiles to collect their wayward sons, crazy brothers or wealthy husbands who could pay the price of freedom. It was the pervasive expression of capitalism whose roots and vines penetrated every portion of a society. Money is power and those bereft of lucre are powerless against the added punishment for their poverty.

Mister Peterson knew, or had previously believed wholeheartedly, that Ezekial was a long-standing member of the lowest class of this capital-structured nation. He was pleasantly surprised that some wealthy good Samaritan had extended the Lord's grace and charity to such a one in such a dire need of hope. He thought a prayer of thanks for his answered prayer and his spirit basked in the warmth of rewarded faith. He walked briskly to the prison hospital to ensure Doctor Lewis could prepare Ezekial for release.

The group left Austin in their automobiles and truck in a convoy headed for Huntsville to pick up their ransomed friend. They joked and spoke of the Ezekial they had known in another time, when the world seemed young and fresh. The roads were rough and dusty and the rattling metal and clacking motors necessitated maximum vocal volume to carry on conversation so that when they pulled under a copse of cottonwoods beside the road to rest their bruised bones, the quiet rang in their ears. Abraham and Beau let the red hot engines cool in popping increments before they dared give the thirsty radiators a filling drink.

Callie had tired quickly of the jarring ride over the rugged road and the respite was welcome. She was too old for such fast transport she thought, and promised herself she would stick to the railroad if she had to travel far and fast again. She lay back on a thick, homemade quilt of rags laid over the long-bladed, late winter grass and relaxed her sore muscles, letting her mind meander back into past years.

"Sallie, Nellie, do you remember the first time we saw Ezekial?"

"Yes, I do."

"Of course Momma. It was rainin' an' our wheel fell off the wagon."

"Luther couldn't get it back on an' Ezekial stopped to help."

"And Beau, you were there too. Lots younger and thinner."

Beau chuckled, "Yes Callie, I 'member. Long years ago. We thought we could whup the world."

"Ezekial was always a good friend. Reliable. One to lend a helpin' hand, an encouragement. Gentle and thoughtful. I can't imagine that he spent so many years in prison."

"He doesn't seem to have been changed much by prison, seems the same ol' Ezekial. Jes' older."

"He'd keep it inside if he was hurtin'. He always kept his pain to his self."

"Still, we must all keep in mind that being in prison for so very long may have changed him, he may not be the Ezekial we knew all that time ago. I pray that he is, but let's be careful. For his sake as much as ours. For all those we love, including him, let's be careful. We need to get to know Ezekial all over again."

It took a long two days from Austin to Huntsville as they stopped halfway to allow themselves time to recuperate. The overnight intervals relieved them somewhat, but they were all mindful of the long road home. They found suitable lodging and lounged around the little prison town over the weekend. Beau and Abraham took an evening walk around the high red-brick walls of the prison under the watchful eyes of the guards in the watchtowers. They could feel the paranoid distrust, the hate and fear emanating from the prison guards, or perhaps the prison itself.

On Monday morning they drove directly to the Walls and inquired regarding Ezekial's release. A guard escorted the group into a foyer where a lean, tall man with a wry grin dressed in a loose, working suit met them and introduced himself.

"I am Assistant Superintendent Gerald Peterson. We have received the official clemency papers which effectively pardon Ezekial Robertson. There are, however, certain requirements and paperwork which must be completed here before Mister Robertson can be released. These technicalities will be completed by ten o'clock this morning and he will be released to you at that time.

"It is good that you are here for him. I regret to inform you that he is not in the best of health. He has not eaten much at all since his return despite our efforts to feed him. He has fallen into a semi-conscious condition, well, mostly unconscious, but he does awaken at times, for a few seconds at a time, but seems disoriented, confused when he wakens. The doctor here believes Ezekial has simply given up hope on life and that only love might restore his will to live. He believes Ezekial's infirmity to be a sickness of the spirit and untreatable with normal remedies. Hopefully, the company of his friends will restore hope and vitality to Ezekial."

"He was fine not so long ago."

"Yes. He walked into this prison. But his health soon deteriorated."

"Will he be able to ride home in an automobile sir?"

"He hasn't the strength to sit up. Considering his size, he might be more comfortable in the bed of a truck."

"I have my truck heah."

"Get him to a doctor when you get him home. And give him love folks, he's been a long time without it. It may be the best medicine."

They bought a mattress at a local store along with blankets and a pillow and made Ezekial a comfortable bed in the back of Beau's old truck. Four trusty inmates carried Ezekial's desiccated body on a stretcher out of the Walls and gingerly placed him on the prepared bed. Together with Beau and Abraham they rolled him off the stretcher and settled him on the mattress. The women tucked him in and saw by the golden morning light Ezekial's blue-white and shrunken skin that seemed so thin and fragile. His eyes never opened, he uttered not a sound.

Patricia climbed into the bed of the truck and sat with her back to the cab and here she remained throughout the slow journey to Angel's Camp. The three younger women of Mabel, Sallie and Nellie took turns riding in the back with Ezekial and Patricia as Beau and Ruby took turns driving the truck. Callie rode in the trailing vehicle driven in turn by one of the younger women, her eyes and her prayers focused on the dying man she looked on as a son as the miles meandered over the long road home.

The family doctor was summoned when the caravan arrived in Uvalde and he examined Ezekial as he lay motionless in the truck. It was hard for the doctor to believe that this body was the same man he had known near a half century before. But, he admitted to himself, the same could be said of yourself. This world of woes and time's erosion must be suffered by us all.

"Has he eaten anything? Or drank?"

"A little soup. Some milk. Water a few times."

"And has he voided?"

"Once. Not solid stool."

"Mmm. Has he spoken?"

"No. He hasn't opened his eyes."

"Umhuh. I'll be out to see him in a day or so. Until then try to get as much food into him as possible. Be careful he doesn't choke. Try to have him drink as often as he seems willing. Move him from side to side so he doesn't get sores, that will aid his circulation also. And talk to him. Tell him who you are and where he is. Tell him that you love him and miss him and want him to be well. The brain is a very mysterious and marvelous creature, you never know when he may be receptive to you or aware of his environment. Try to have someone with him through the night.

"And Patricia, you look almost as bad as Ezekial. You let Ezekial's friends help you look after him and you get some rest, you hear?"

Patricia nodded her head.

"Thank you Doctor Landy," Callie spoke wearily.

"You too Callie, you get some rest. We're not as young as we used to be. Let these youngsters pull the plow awhile," the doctor grinned.

Callie smiled weakly and nodded.

They stopped at Mister Carter's store and bought a few things. Mister Carter was surprised at the appearance of Ezekial and at his condition. Callie signed the credit receipt and thanked the sturdy old grocer for his concern. While they were in the store others had gathered around the truck viewing what remained of Ezekial. A few had known him when he was young and were shocked how the years had weathered and eroded even this Herculean man. The younger people had heard the legends told which were initially disbelieved, but now, with the sight of the long body in the truck bed, their disbelief wavered.

At Angel's Camp, Ezekial was carried by the hard, callused hands of the cowboys into the little house he had helped build for Noah, Chas and himself long ago. The ancient, much repaired rocking chair that Gramps had died in began slowly rocking as they carried Ezekial past it over the porch. Only Callie and Patricia noticed the capricious movement and they held one another's eyes as the rocker squeaked and groaned.

Patricia had Noah's old bed moved close to Ezekial's big bed and Callie shooed the hands out after a few minutes.

"Open the windows Nellie, it's musty in here." Callie directed, "And Sallie, see about getting some good beef soup brewing for Ezekial. Patti, help me put some fresh sheets on these beds and then you lay yourself down and take a nap. I'll take care of our big ol' boy for awhile. You can spell me after you rest."

Callie turned to see where Patricia's eyes were fixed and saw Mabel standing on the porch beside the rocking chair watching it move steadily back and forth seemingly on its own volition, the cracked, curved rockers singing their old repetitive rhythm. After another half a minute, the chair slowly ceased its motion.

Mabel looked at Callie and Patricia as she came to stand in the door with a look of wonder.

"There was no breeze. That's Ezekial's grandfather's chair brought all the way from Carolina."

"Maybe it was a welcome home from Grampa," Callie said.

"He knows his grandson is near, I think." Patti added.

"Maybe so," Mabel said, then spoke over her shoulder, "I'll get some sheets."

Day after dreary day, Ezekial lay still and silent and his sitters sat and spoke to him, telling him of their love and beseeching him to return to them. They spoke of days they had shared, sweet days held dear to their hearts. They told him of times he had missed and had been missed. Silently they cried and held their sorrow inside as they watched him waste away. Dark day followed dark night and he slept and his sleep carried him ever nearer to his death.

In his subconsciousness Ezekial searched for Sam who had gone this way, but he could not be found. He called to him and the calling echoed in the empty gloom. He spoke into the emptiness for Gramps, for each of his family and his friends who had passed this way before him, but none answered. The dismal depths that led to death were desolate and lonely. He had thought he would meet his loved ones here, but the void was devoid of any comfort, hope or joy. The endless, vacuous space and perfect darkness terrified him and his spirit fought for the surface, for the light, for life. In the sucking morass of his condition he could not determine the direction in which salvation shone. He fought against the current of the cold, murky stream, hoping he could find a stable shore, a glimmer of hope. He almost yielded to the unceasing draw of death, was near to surrender to the unceasing sorrow that pulled him to a place where hope had never dwelt.

Faintly, very far away, from an undetermined direction, he heard a revered voice that called to him, calling him back home. The voice was musical, the song of an angel and with what remained to him of his will he grasped onto this tenuous hope and held on, for life. Such a sweet sound strengthened his shriveled spirit and aroused emotions that had long lain dormant. He began to feel the warmth of love as a faint light glimmered far away and overcame the dark despair that drew him to death. Hope stirred in his soul and he sought the light, the love, the life as it also sought him.

And then, in the dark waters of his mind, Ezekial was again swept by riptides of despair into depths further from the surface and light of consciousness. The incapacitating cold there froze his emotions and vitality, preparing him for eternal sleep. At times, some distant tolling would fall through the inky morass to interrupt the tranquility of his expiring and lift him unwillingly toward the light. A part of him fought against the buoyant, lifting lilt of life and struggled to dive deeper into drowning destruction and the promised comfort of extinction.

Once again came a disturbance into the dismal depths of his sinking soul, bright light dimmed by the distance from life and cheerful, hopeful voices he once had known pulled him in warming currents back up to the pleasures and pains of living and in turns he both fought and sought the promising, saving flow. Memories of life in the light assailed him with visions of faces and echoes of voices he had once cherished, so long ago. The upward current pulled against the draw of death, and he was too weak to choose between them. The light of love grew brighter and shined through the barrier of his long closed eyelids. The door to his heart was opened despite his efforts to bar the pain and promise of love and his mind was returning him to the impossible past and to the place he had loved and left so very long ago.

Briefly, his consciousness had broken the surface and perceived faces, nurturing, hopeful, dear, that yearned to welcome him back to the land of the living, but his long-held despair would not allow him to believe the promise and with waning strength he dove down into the dark cold womb where hope and love did not dare, where the light of life did not penetrate.

Patricia sat with Ezekial through the dark, quiet night when the only sound came from the fireplace where the mesquite logs popped and moaned in their cremation. She sat in the straight-backed chair, hopefully knitting Ezekial warm, thick socks. Her hands moved autonomously as her mind was mulling the oft-reviewed regrets of her life. Ezekial was a major mistake. Certainly she loved her children that her husband from Mexico City had given her and she had mostly enjoyed her life of comfort and ease that his wealth had afforded, but she had never been in love with him. She often even disliked him for his expected entitlements and his aristocratic airs. She had missed Ezekial and his honest, loving affection that he had displayed unashamedly. Through those years living in palatial estates she had sometimes imagined Ezekial's sorrow and misery, she knew she had torn his heart by leaving. It did not excuse her that she had wanted to see more of the world than the barren expanse of the isolated ranches of the frontier in northern Mexico. She should have let love lead her, not wanderlust, envy, greed, curiosity and the aspirant desires of youth to experience, to see, to acquire. All those years guilt had weighed her spirit. She had abandoned his love. For through those years she had come to realize that she loved Ezekial just as he so openly loved her.

And now, as she stared at the noble old visage that lay so pale and withered upon the pillow, the white hair accenting the fading red, she considered the wear, worry and woe written in the wrinkles and wondered how many of those lines she had caused. Oh! To be able to somehow, some way make it up to him. To be given a chance to live it all over again.

"God, give me some time with him, some years to give him joy and comfort for the despair and pain I have caused. I will cherish every day, every hour."

She lay down her knitting, picked up her rosary and prayed as her mother had taught her, "Santa Maria, Madre de Dios, Ruega por nosotros los pecadores…"

And she cried.

Callie lay her tiny failing body down on the bed she had shared with her husband so long ago and had brought from western Virginia what seemed a hundred years ago. She had missed him every day since he had last gone to war, but she had missed Ezekial, her son, her friend, almost as long. And it was heart-wrenching to have him back yet not have him wholly home.

Callie had apologized to the younger women and had asked for their forgiveness for shirking her share of the responsibility of sitting with Ezekial and taking care of his needs, but she could not bear to sit and watch the man she had held in her heart as a hero so diminished by despair and impending death. She knew he had given up, surrendered. For all his strength and courage, life had overcome him. She was so disheartened that such a man as he had been, could be so utterly defeated.

She had rose in the hours after midnight one night, put on her robe and walked out to Ezekial's house where he lay. She had felt a need to look upon him, to speak to him, to encourage him, to tell him she loved him. As she stepped up onto the porch of the little house, she saw through the window, in the lamplight, the trembling form of Patricia, as she sat beside Ezekial's still body and wept. Watching and feeling Patricia's sadness and regret, the tears flowed over her own weathered cheeks and she quietly withdrew.

Back beneath her bed-covers she recalled the obvious heartbreak Ezekial suffered when Patricia had gone away. They all had tried to cheer him to love him through his grief, but they had failed. Her long life and her own sorrows had shown her that some wounds just never heal. Ezekial's pain had driven him to seek a solution in riches, mistakenly believing he could provide the more important necessities of life through wealth, seemingly having been shown that true love was just not enough. Callie knew Patricia wanted that love once again, more than all the world's wealth, and her tears would never cease unless Ezekial awoke.

Callie lay awake trying to imagine the circumstance that led him to murder and how prison had caused him to change. She knew he had loved Sam, he thought of Sam as the last of his old family, all that remained to him of the hope and happiness he had at home in Carolina. Sure, they had done all they knew to become his new family and provide a new home for him, but she felt that they must have failed him. She loved Ezekial like a young brother, a son, a dear friend, and she could not endure seeing him dying, decaying day by day. She felt so helpless, so worthless and so angry. She wanted to take him by his broad shoulders and shake him, scream at him that he must fight against the darkness of death that drew him away from them. There were too many here who loved him too much for him to go away again, and forever.

Visions of their first meeting came into her mind's eye, she saw the robust boy-man and felt the gentle ease with which he lifted her heavy wagon. He had taken Beau and Micah under his young and sturdy wing and they had loved him and taught him what they knew. Beau still pined away in his sorrow, struggling in his spirit to accept the loss of his friend, his brother, once again. And Micah, long gone from their sight but remaining in them in his faith, what would Micah do? Certainly he would pray, and she did. The prayer comforted her, she sensed empathetic ears and a comforting, bleeding hand that dried her tears, allowing her blessed assurance, rest, and sleep.

Sallie and Nellie spent their energy supporting their friend Patti and helping her in a hundred ways with their brother Ezekial. Each of them cherished the broken man who lay helpless and hopeless, lost to them once again. In many ways it was worse having him here like this than when he was wherever he had been for much of their lives. Each of them could still see vestiges of the man he had been, he had been their unappreciated, noble and humble hero. They had re-lived their many experiences with Ezekial, both mundane times and life-changing moments, a thousand times in their minds and shared their feelings for him with one another in words, tears and hugs. Each of them had determined that there would be no dignity in the death of such a one as he had been and they did all they could to actively demonstrate their love and respect. Ezekial lay unknowing, dying, in their constant care.

Beau had visited a few times, hat in hand as he frowned at his old friend and benefactor. He too felt helpless in the presence of such hopelessness. What could he say? Or do? The women provided for Ezekial's every physical need, there was nothing he could do. He was unaccustomed to feeling useless, sadness assailed him. His visits grew more infrequent, then stopped. His smile deserted him, his laughter was no longer heard. Rarely he spoke and he seemed irreversibly disheartened.

The days of their youth, their strength, their dreams, seemed to be another life, another age, an ethereal imagining that passed too swiftly, and each of them yearned to find that place once more and find the joy and confidence they'd had. Yesterday seemed so glorious, so golden, so full. Today was a sorry existence, regretful, doubtful, depressing and sad. And tomorrow? Where could hope be found?

Beau spent his days atop a horse where he had spent much of his life, away from people, looking at the land, the beasts, the clouds. When darkness drove him homeward, he wasn't the happy, teasing daddy and husband he'd always been, he was quiet, pensive, staring into the fire until sleep assuaged his disenchantment and sorrow.

Then the rueful day came when Little Beau rode out and found him sitting on a hillside, chewing a stem of grass, watching the cows graze.

"Daddy, Nellie called on the telephone. Said if we wanna' see Ezekial 'fore he dies, we better come. Doctor said he only has a day or two."

Beau didn't move Just kept staring at the cows.

"Daddy? You hear me?"

"I hear ya' boy. Reckon we better go pay our respects."

"I'm sorry Daddy."

Beau rose and patted his son's shoulder.

"Life is as full of sorry days as happy days son. It's day like this that make the happy days shine, he'ps us 'ppreciate the good. Le's go cry our friend on his way and 'member the sweet times we shared."

On the ride back to the house they rode in silence and when they got to the barn and dismounted Little Beau spoke.

"I'll mind the hosses Daddy."

"Thank ya son," Beau answered. "Ya know, some old day it'll be me tha's diein', and you'll be sad. I want you to 'member this L'il Beau,... We all gone live forevah, we jes' gone be sommers else. An' after I die, a part o'me gonna still be here, a part in yore heart an' head. That's the way God made us. Ever' one of us lives forevah. 'Member that."

"I'll remember Daddy."

"An' evah time you laugh or cry, I'll be there, inside you, a part a' me, laughing an' cryin' wit you. An' if you try, you'll feel me there, inside you. So don't be too sad when I'm gone, cuz' I won't be all gone. A piece a'me will be in all ya'll I love. An' ya'll will be wit' me. Forevah."

Doctor Landy had examined and re-examined Ezekial, then he had managed to get a tube down his big throat. And pump some liquid nourishment into the long trunk. While he had the tube into the esophagus Ezekial began to vomit. The good doctor struggled to roll the big man onto his side and remove the tube to stop the choking. After getting Ezekial to clear his throat by swallowing a few ounces of water, he tried to get some more of the nourishing liquid down his throat but, again, Ezekial threw it up.

The doctor gave Ezekial a shot trying to strengthen his heart beat which was faint and tried propping him in different positions to help his shallow breathing, but nothing seemed to help. He shook his head and stood beside the bed looking down at his old friend.

"Doctor?" Mabel asked.

Doctor Landy shook his head and pointed outside. Mabel and the others followed him onto the porch where Beau, Little Beau and Abraham leaned on the rail smoking. The doctor looked at them all, swallowed, grit his teeth and shook his hoary head.

"Nothing more I can do. I don't think he'll last long, maybe a day or two. Seems like he has set his heart on dieing."

"Should we get him to the hospital in San Antone?"

"He'd never survive the trip Mabel. I believe you all should prepare for his funeral."

Patricia collapsed into the old rocker and Sallie and Nellie fell to their knees to hug her and cry in chorus.

"I'm sorry. But all I would suggest now is more prayer. Nothing a man can do for him, he's in God's hands."

"Thanks for coming, and trying Doctor."

The old doctor nodded and wearily carried his bag of equipment to his awaiting Studebaker automobile. As he drove back to Uvalde, he passed a truck driven by Chas and his wife. Both drivers stopped and circled back.

"Howdy Doc."

"Hello Chas. Ma'am," Doctor Landy tipped his bowler.

"How are you sir?"

"Physically I'm as well as can be expected Chas. Tired, but that's normal for an old country doctor. I'm sorrowful Chas, disheartened. I want to help Ezekial, but there's nothing I can do. He's in God's hands. You need to hurry on home if you want to see him before he dies Chas. A day or two and he'll be gone."

Chas was speechless. He stood staring down the lonely, dusty road as the shadows of the mesquites along the path lengthened. He felt the doctors hand patting his shoulder, then his wife's voice interrupted his trance. He stepped up and into his truck and hurried it down the familiar road to his old home with an emptiness in his chest.

Ezekial's exit was disturbed by the ministrations of the good doctor, but he didn't know the cause. The continuous cold flow of the passage enfolded him in black folds of wings and the life that had gone before was hidden from his subconscious mind. Though he was unaware, his determined destination of death was ever nearer and the dark stream rose around him as he was swept by the sweet seduction of death into the infinite ocean of eternity.

The boy who had become quite a man, Lister Hill, had come from Austin to be with the family as they endeavored to restore Ezekial to life. He didn't know Ezekial as the others had known him, he had been a small lad of only five or six when Ezekial had gone away. A soft-spoken man of stature and strength was a foggy memory, a big man who had carried him high on his shoulders and taught him to whistle was a recollection that caused a heartfelt smile. He sat in the parlor of the women's house and listened to the tales of the man who lay dying in his small house close by.

"One time ol' Luther was telling one of his tall tales 'bout out runnin' a rabbit when he was jes' a boy an' how his ol' pappy would bet on him in races 'gainst horses over a course of a hunnerd yards. Well, Ol' Micah kept a donkey's tail he'd cut off a dead donkey that he used to swat flies an' Ezekial, he snuck up behind Luther who was a' leanin' on the porch rail and tied that tail on the back of Luther's britches. He bore that tail fer near an hour 'fore the girls gigglin' and pointin' finally caused him to discover the tail. I'm sure he felt like a jackass," Beau finished with a chortle.

"I remember that like it was yesterday," Nellie chuckled. "And I remember a time Luther was havin' trouble shoein' a nervous horse. Horse kept tryin' ta' run an' was a'kickin'. Well, Ezekial had enough of it and he ducked down in the well that horse and jes' lifted him up in the air an' held 'im 'til he calmed down and Luther got 'im shoed."

"C'mon Nellie, nobody's that strong," Lister grinned.

"Ezekial was."

"Shore was."

"You diden' know Ezekial."

"And gentle and good. Good as gold."

"How come ya'll never got married Patti?"

An uncomfortable quiet descended over the group.

"Lister, my mother took me away from the rancho to Mexico City. She was afraid of Ezekial, I suppose, and she wanted nice things for me, away from the lonely life she had led. And I, I was too young to know my own way. I was excited by the adventure and if,… I wish I had my life to live over again…"

"We all have regrets Patricia," Callie spoke, "We live and sometimes we learn, and we all wish we'd done things different. Yer' a good woman, and Ezekial will come around soon—I don't care what the doctor said. Doc Landy's smart, but I,…we just have to believe God will give 'im back to us. You two'll have wonderful years to share. He loves you so much."

"Mother, don't get her hopes up, the doctor…"

"And I… I broke his heart," Patricia said softly.

"Life broke his heart Patti," Sallie spoke, "And soon, in life or in death, his heart will be mended."

"Oh I hope,… I wish…" Patricia tried.

"And pray," Callie continued, "Pray."

That evening, Sallie and Nellie were helping Patricia change Ezekial's soiled sheets. They rolled the long, unconscious man one way and then the other, gently and lovingly, then tucked and tied the clean sheets in place as a team. Nellie gathered up the soiled sheets and walked out toward the mud room of the women's house to put them with the other clothes in need of washing. Patricia looked at Ezekial's face and combed his long hair back onto his head with her fingers and noticed the pillowcase. She said, "Oh, we forgot to change the pillowcase."

"Let me catch Nellie," Sallie said over her shoulder as she hurried to the open door where she whistled loudly and hollered at Nellie, "Bring a pillowcase."

She walked back to the bedside where Patricia stood silent and still, mouth open and staring.

"What's wrong Patti?"

"His eyes."

"What?"

"His eyes, look at his eyes," Patricia whispered.

Ezekial's eyes fluttered and rolled beneath the thin membrane of skin, pulling against the gluey mucous which held them closed.

Patricia moved the damp cloth over his eyes that they had used to wash him, and his eyes opened to their amazement, blinking in the dim light.

"Ezekial?" Patricia managed to speak as his eyes, unfocused, slowly closed again.

Sallie had a memory come to her, a possibility, a realization struck her and she whistled, long and loud.

Again Ezekial's eyes opened and his lips moved without sound. He reached up and touched Patricia's face with a trembling hand and nearly smiled. Then his eyes focused on Sallie and he tried to whistle weakly, but failed. He tried again, failed, then pulled a long draught of air into his atrophied lungs. His eyes moved to focus once again on Patricia's wide eyes and then they slowly closed once again, a slight smile still splitting his frozen face.

"Did you see that?"

"It was your whistling..."

"He remembered!"

Nellie stood behind them, pillowcase in hand. She said, "Oh Patti, Sallie, he's coming back to us."

They hugged, smiled and tucked the crisp pillowcase beneath Ezekial's freshly shaven face, which still seemed to slightly smile.

Chas had made arrangements for his home and business in Alpine to be looked after while he and his wife made the trip to Angel's Camp to see Ezekial. It had taken three days to make those arrangements and the better part of two days to make the trip despite his urgent, determined driving. Now, after speaking with Doctor Landy, he wished he'd been able to get away quicker.

Nellie had called on the telephone and had told him that Ezekial was not making any progress toward health and that he may die soon. Chas wanted to see the hero of his childhood once more in this life. It was a long and desolate road but Chas had driven a million miles it seemed over such country delivering livestock over his life and he drove without conscious thought to the driving, his shifting and turning as automatic as his heartbeat. His thoughts and hopes were with old Ezekial as the barren landscape fell away behind him.

His good wife Sloan had heard him speak of the gentle giant a thousand times, and how he had gone away so long ago and never returned. She knew that Ezekial had been a major influence in the forming of the character of Chas the man. It was obvious Chas loved the man who now had returned only to lay dying, so she understood Chas' non-stop effort to get there in time to see him. She was exhausted and knew he was tired when finally and gratefully they arrived at Angel's Camp.

Callie had been told of Ezekial's momentary awakening as had all the others and they gathered in the little house to whisper their hopes and stare at the quiescent giant. They spoke and listened to their hopes and fears. The fleeting consciousness encouraged them all, even though it didn't last or occur again. He continued to sleep deeply as if in a hibernating state, his pulse, breathing and all bodily functions slowed markedly.

Abraham heard the sound of an engine and wondered who would be coming home so late. He glanced out the curtain and was initially confused until he recognized the truck.

"Chas jes' drove up ya'll."

"Good."

"Let's go see him and tell him 'bout Ezekial waking up."

"Don't get his hopes up, still a chance he…"

"Is Sloan with him? And the kids?"

The room emptied to greet their beloved Chas, all but Patricia. She stayed with Ezekial and shut the door behind them to keep the cold air out. She petted Ezekial's brow.

"Can you hear me Ezekial? It's Patti. I love you and miss you so much. Everyone you love is here, the whole family, all your friends. You need to wake up, wake up please."

Upon their arrival in the violet light of early evening Chas and Sloan were met by all the family as they came to a stop in the well-maintained truck. Chas had brought a puppy from Alpine, a direct descendant of dear old Sam and sweet Shoestring. The puppy was a dead ringer for Sam, from his coloring and personality even to the seeming affliction of grinning on one side of his face while his eyes winked and blinked. This atavism was eerie to anyone who had known Sam so many canine generations ago. Chas had named this puppy Sam's Son, or Samson and Chas had hoped that the sight of Samson would please Ezekial, remind him of a happy time years ago, lift his spirits and help restore his health. He intended Samson as a gift to Ezekial, if he lived.

With all the hugs and greetings it was a few minutes before Chas noticed that Samson wasn't in the truck. Samson had jumped down from the truck and rolled across the roadway until clumsily gaining his big feet. He sniffed the air and headed directly to Ezekial's house. Climbing the steps and running across the porch he began scratching at the door and whined frantically until Patricia left Ezekial's side and opened the door. The puppy barked up at her joyfully and grinned his half-smile.

"Where'd you come from?"

She was moved by fascination and friendly surprise to pick the puppy up. Samson kissed her laughing face with his rough tongue, then yipped and wriggled in her arms, struggling to be released, so she sat him down on the wooden floor. He ran to the big, high bed and tried his best to jump or climb up on it, barking and whining.

"No puppy, he is sick," Patricia reached down and picked the jumping dog up in her arms. The puppy barked and struggled, then continued to bark and whine as he looked at Ezekial. Ezekial's head bobbed and his eyes fluttered open. The pup escaped Patricia's enclosing arms and leaped onto Ezekial, hurrying to his face, licking and whining.

Ezekial's big chest rumbled and emitted a chuckling laugh, his face split into a perceptible smile, eyes sparkling with tears, and his great hand lifted to cover the small dog. He spoke a word.

"Sam."

The family had come in and surrounded the bed by then and Chas responded to Ezekial's word.

"No. Ezekial, that's Samson. He's a great, great, great descendant of ol' Sam and Shoestring."

Everyone else watching Ezekial's awakening seemed to be in shock, frozen, speechless, mouth agape.

"Not Sam's... son. This... Sam. My Sam. Oh Sam," Ezekial's rusty voice crackled.

Sam barked, danced on Ezekial's wide chest and smiled and winked, deliriously happy, licking Ezekial through his weak laughter.

Everyone laughed at the antics and the awakening and hugged and kissed Ezekial, the dog, one another. Tears of joy were happily, unashamedly displayed.

Ezekial's eyes were drawn and captured by his old love's crying eyes. He stared as silence fell around him and the puppy laid down across his chest and neck, trembling with joy and excitement.

Ezekial managed to mumble, "Patti?" and reached out for her. She flew into his arms, kissed him, and they held one another as close as possible as Sam wriggled between them until he was free. They all laughed as he danced and barked, turned in circles on Ezekial's chest and licked both their faces in a frenzy of joy. Both Patricia and Ezekial were confused, almost numb by the flooding rush of emotion, unsure if this were only a dream. Could life really be so sweet?

Each of his friends, his family, came to him and he named each one, though it took a few moments for his rheumy eyes to focus on each individual face.

"Callie,…"

"Mabel,…"

"Beau,…"

"Ruby,…"

"Sallie,…"

"Nellie,…"

"Chas,…"

"Boy,…"

"Sam,… oh Sam," he spoke and thought, "My best friend Sam, my Sam came back to me."

Ezekial looked at Patricia and said with a weakening voice, "Patti, and you,… you came back to me too."

"With all my heart Ezekial. I love you so much."

He smiled and fell asleep once again. And Sam curled up next to him on the pillow and would not be moved.

The good doctor came as he was called the following day and attributed Ezekial's continuing restoration to health to a miracle. Medical science could not have managed it he judged, and he ascribed Ezekial's renewal to lots of love, prayer and the grace of God. He was still shaking his old bald head and chuckling as he got in his stately Rio automobile and headed back to Uvalde. As he returned to town he mused how joie de vivre was blessedly contagious.

It took awhile for Ezekial to stay awake for any length of time, even though he desperately desired to and struggled against the somnolence. He cherished the hours shared with his Patti, with Sam and with his other dearest friends. Still, he was weak. Slowly, their loving nourishment strengthened him physically and his resolve was unyielding. It was not soon enough for him but wasn't many days until he stood, and walked. A few steps at first, but in a few days he walked unaided and moved over the beautiful fields under infinite skies with his Patti and his Sam. Smiles were always on all their faces and life was a new and shining promise, faithful and full.

SEPARATE REALITIES

There was talk of Ezekial, Patricia and Sam returning to her ranch in Mexico, at least for awhile, and one evening while they were all gathered on the porch after supper sharing the light of a majestic sunset and enjoying one another's company, Callie broached a subject that others had whispered about.

"Ezekial, Patricia, you know I love you and there's nothing you do that bothers me, but some may have been talking about the two of you living together without being married."

"Yep," Ezekial smiled, "We know."

"Talk doesn't bother us," Patricia added.

"We're all good friends, that's all that matters."

"Well, Ezekial, Patti, don't you two want to be more than just good friends?"

Ezekial continued to grin, reached down and patted faithful Sam, put his long arm around his Patti and reached out to take Callie's withered old hand. He spoke as he looked steadily into her honest and dear old eyes. "Callie, they 'ain't' nothin' more 'n good friends."

Epilogue

And the years sweetly and swiftly passed Ezekial, Patti and Sam celebrated and cherished their love through thick and thin, until the end. Except, there was no end. Patti passed from this world first, then Sam left this world once again. Ezekial suffered in the separation, alone for a few more years. But his suffering was assuaged by God-given assurance and when his great strength waned and he was called from this location of life into another, he found the mysterious and separate reality, our eternal home.

ABOUT THE AUTHOR

W.W. WORLEY WAS born and raised in west Texas where Texas heroes and Confederate generals are revered even to the naming of streets and schools. From an early age he wondered about these names, like Beauregard and Twohig, Crockett and Lee, Travis and Lone Wolf. 200 years ago it was a wild and woolly land. Worley's imagination dwelled there in his formative years. Perhaps this yearning toward wild and uncivilized contributed to his own untamed nature, but whatever the cause, his life in prison has largely been spent in the study of those yesteryears, those seemingly simpler times that truly were not so simple at all. He blends history with imaginings to recreate a world long past, a world of our beginnings. Worley is a prodigal son, a struggling Christian who reads his Bible daily and like the good thief, Dismas, he asks for grace and mercy, not justice. Using the means available to him, often meager in prison, he earned four college degrees. He enjoys painting in oils and drawing. He is an avid reader and still, in his aged years, a curious student of life. He hopes to climb the mesquite covered hills and walk over the wind-blown west Texas plains again someday. In his mind and writing, he walks there every day.

www.ingramcontent.com/pod-product-compliance
Lightning Source LLC
Chambersburg PA
CBHW030314100526
44592CB00010B/427